FOR YOUR FREEDOM
THROUGH OURS:
Polish American Efforts
On Poland's Behalf,
1863-1991

Donald E. Pienkos

EAST EUROPEAN MONOGRAPHS, BOULDER
DISTRIBUTED BY COLUMBIA UNIVERSITY PRESS,
NEW YORK, 1991

EAST EUROPEAN MONOGRAPHS, NO. CCCXI

© Copyright 1991 by Donald E. Pienkos
ISBN 0-88033-208-5
Library of Congress Catalog Card Number 91-73671

Printed in the United States of America

To Stella and Edward, Angela and Joseph

Table of Contents

FOR YOUR FREEDOM THROUGH OURS:
Polish American Efforts on Poland's Behalf, 1863-1991

Forward

On behalf of the officers and members of the Polish American Congress, I welcome the appearance of Donald Pienkos' new book, FOR YOUR FREEDOM THROUGH OURS: POLISH AMERICAN EFFORTS ON POLAND'S BEHALF, 1863-1991. Our organization has proudly supported this publication out of a firm belief that it has been needed for quite some time. With its publication, interested readers -- Polish and non-Polish alike -- can gain their first opportunity to learn of our ethnic community's many and significant actions to assist the people of Poland over the past six generations. Dr. Pienkos' work is comprehensive, well-documented and engaging. What is more, the story of American Polonia's political and humanitarian services is both interesting and significant. It certainly deserves to be better understood.

As Pienkos demonstrates, these essentially volunteer activities have not only been considerable, they have frequently been pursued in the face of real logistical and political obstacles. By persevering in their efforts, however, Polonia's representatives have accomplished much -- both for Poland's freedom and its people's material betterment. Along the way, Polish American efforts to defend Poland's right to true independence have helped reshape American public opinion in increasingly favoring not only Poland's aspirations, but those of all the nations of Eastern Europe. Without these constant and concerted efforts, especially those directed by the Polish American Congress since the Second World War, America's interest in the fate of Eastern Europe would surely have been much reduced, thus adversely affecting the lives of the inhabitants of the entire region.

Clearly, Polonia's efforts are by no means completed, even as we celebrate Poland's restoration to independence and its people's reassertion of their age-old ties with the culture and traditions of Western Europe, Canada and the United States of America. Great things have been achieved since the revolutionary year of 1989 -- yet much still remains to be done. For my part

I pledge, in the name of the Polish American Congress and our many member organizations, to continue our efforts on Poland's behalf. In so doing, we are operating in the spirit of our predecessors, both in the Congress and in the Polonia federations that came before it. All in their time labored honorably for the Polish cause in the belief that by working for a Poland "whole and free" they were indeed acting in the very best interests of their fellow Americans.

This book is the third in a series of works by Professor Pienkos that deal with the evolution and development of organized Polonia. The first covered the history of the Polish National Alliance fraternal insurance society and appeared in 1984. The second told the story of the Polish Falcons of America and came out on the occasion of its centennial in 1987. Together, all three books constitute a kind of "trilogy" and contain a number of common themes, one of which I'd like to note here. Simply put, it is that the memory of our ancestral roots in Poland remains a central element that accounts for the maintenance of our people's self-awareness as Polish Americans. But this tie with our ancestral homeland is not simply a matter of nostalgia. Rather, it provides a vital link that can bring us together -- both in solidarity with one another here and with the people who remain across the ocean in Poland. This tie can also provide us with a sense of what we ought to be doing, both in preserving our heritage and in working with our fellow citizens of other ethnic origins to advance the ideals that America and Poland have always stood for.

Speaking to his emigrant colleagues in the United States more than a century ago, the first leader of Polonia, Henryk Kalussowski, asserted that "Constancy is our duty -- devoting ourselves to the homeland and its people is a precept that must govern the Polish heart." It would be well indeed if we might keep these words in our own hearts as we go about our daily business -- as Americans mindful of and inspired by all that is good in our Polish heritage.

Edward J. Moskal
President, Polish American Congress
and Polish National Alliance

Introduction

This work deals with the efforts of Americans of Polish origin and ancestral heritage to work in an organized fashion on behalf of the Polish nation. As such it is the history of one aspect of the experience of the millions of Poles who migrated to the United States during the past 150 years and who, together with their children and descendants have retained a concern for the homeland they had left behind and their families and friends who remained there.

This work is not intended as a general history of the Polish immigrant and ethnic experience in the United States. That is a broader subject, one extensively studied by a number of competent American and Polish scholars in recent years. These provide us with an understanding of the motives which led the Poles to leave their homeland, the size and social composition of the emigrations, the conditions of the immigrants in America, the institutions they formed to meet their varied needs, and the experiences that led most to enter the mainstreams of American cultural and economic life.[1]

Yet, for the most part, the published histories of the Polish American experience give but fleeting attention to the immigrants' perspectives toward Poland and their considerable attempts over the years to work on its behalf. Several specialized studies have been written on this topic, but their findings have seldom been integrated into broader works focusing either upon Poland's history or that of the Polish ethnic community in America.[2]

Moreover, this work is confined in its purposes to the study of the efforts by the members of the organized Polish ethnic community in America, or "Polonia," on Poland's behalf. It is thus beyond its scope to more than mention the activities of individuals acting on a private basis for Poland, although these have on occasion been considerable. The same is true for the work performed by Polonia communities located outside the

United States over the years. They too have often been substantial. Rather, this book deals with the efforts by Poles in the United States to act through their own voluntary associations in support of their old homeland's political independence and its people's material needs. The beginnings of this work date back to the year 1863, when a committee was formed in the city of New York to generate support for an uprising which had recently broken out in the territories of partitioned Poland under imperial Russian control. Ever since that time, organized activity on Poland's behalf has figured in the pattern of Polonia's affairs, sometimes quite prominently.

That this concern would persist for so long a time is partly explained by the character of the Polish emigration itself and partly by Poland's political fate since the end of the 18th century. Once a large state in East Central Europe, Poland's decline was so precipitous and complete that by 1795 it had lost its independence. Over the next 123 years Poland would be subjected to foreign partition at the hands of Russia, Prussia and Austria.

Throughout the 19th century, the Polish lands remained economically backward and impoverished under their foreign overlords, even as the population doubled in size. As a result, living conditions deteriorated and as many as 3.6 million people found it necessary to emigrate to find work, most of them poor or landless peasants from the increasingly overcrowded countryside. The greatest number settled in the United States, which became the home of the largest of the Polonia communities.[3]

Poland's plight also led a succession of patriotically minded activists to organize national insurrections to win back the country's independence. The first of these efforts was launched in 1794 under Tadeusz Kosciuszko in order to save what still remained of Poland from final destruction at the hands of its enemies. A second occurred at the time of the Napoleonic Wars and witnessed the temporary creation of a tiny "Duchy of Warsaw" dependent upon the fortunes of the French emperor. Less than two decades after its demise in 1813, the Poles organized a massive uprising against the Tsar, the tragic "November" insurrection of 1830-1831. Following a short-lived rebellion in 1848 in the Prussian zone, yet another great revolt against

Russian rule broke out in January 1863. From 1900 on, general unrest again prevailed over most of the country for several years, first in response to the repressive policies adopted by the German empire in its Polish provinces, later in Russian-ruled Poland in connection with the revolution of 1905 against the Tsar.

Each insurrection, though brutally suppressed, had its impact upon the national consciousness in keeping alive into the next generation the dream of a Poland restored to independence. The revolts also had their effects upon the burgeoning emigration in America since their failures forced some who had taken part in the struggles to flee abroad. There they did enjoy the opportunities to organize anew to perpetuate the memory of the fight for independence and to work on Poland's behalf from across the Atlantic.

In the meantime, the largely peasant immigrant population in the U.S. continued to mushroom, from an estimated 30,000 souls in 1860 to 500,000 in 1880 and 2,000,000 by 1900. In America for ostensibly economic motives, the members of this "for bread" emigration were understandably absorbed with work and family responsibilities and had little time for political matters. What energies they could devote to community concerns were focused upon building their Roman Catholic parishes, the early mainstays of immigrant social, cultural and spiritual life in the new homeland.[4]

Indeed, the first enduring federation of immigrant societies was church-based, the Polish Roman Catholic Union in America, created in 1873 in Detroit and Chicago. Its founders sought to unite the immigrants in their efforts to preserve their religious heritage in Protestant America and at first had little to do with the fate of the partitioned homeland. In 1880, however, several of the existing patriotic societies succeeded in organizing a "Polish National Alliance" to represent the nationalist aims of the emigration. From the start this Alliance had a following from around the country and could claim supporters in Illinois, Wisconsin, Michigan, Minnesota, New York and Pennsylvania.[5]

Formed to mobilize the immigrants in support of Poland's independence less than two decades after the suppression of the "January insurrection," the Alliance also included among its objectives the gathering of funds for its members' countrymen who were then suffering through a famine back home in Silesia. To broaden its appeal the leaders of the new organization also offered a simple form of life insurance protection to those who joined in their cause. The strategy provided the Alliance's intended members with a sound practical reason to enter its ranks to go along with its patriotic idealism; in any event the Polish Roman Catholic Union soon adopted an insurance plan of its own to match the one proposed by the Alliance.[6]

After the clergy-dominated Roman Catholic Union and the secular (but not anti-Catholic) Alliance would arise a number of other voluntary associations over the next two decades. Among these were the Polish Singers Alliance, formed in 1889, the Polish Falcons Alliance (1894), the Polish Young People's Alliance (1895) and the Polish Women's Alliance (1898-1899), all of which adopted patriotic programs having much in common with the Polish National Alliance. Together they would have an influence in deepening immigrant community interest in the cause of an independent Poland.

Yet another organization wielding its influence in Polonia was the Polish Socialist Alliance, which was founded in 1900. Much smaller in membership and more radical than the patriotic societies, the PSA nonetheless shared with them a powerful commitment to the independence cause. Together, the various Alliances, with the support of the many Polish language newspapers and periodicals already in operation in America by the early 1900s, imbued the immigrant community with their ideological perspective. Indeed, by the outbreak of the First World War in 1914, even the Polish Roman Catholic Union and the many other clergy-led societies in Polonia had also come to identify with the independence cause, if in their own somewhat more conservative fashion.

The World War years proved to be momentous for both Poland and Polonia. On November 11, 1918, the final day of a conflict fought extensively on Polish soil, the country's independence was proclaimed, although it would require more that two more years of fighting before its borders could be secured. For the nearly four million people of Polish origin in America, the war years witnessed the consolidation of most of Polonia's organizations into a largely unified structure for the very first time. This was a considerable achievement given the many prewar divisions which had typified the community. Working for the many Polish victims of the War was the Polish Central Relief Committee; raising the banner of the homeland's right to national independence was the Polish National Department. Together, the two federations achieved much in infusing a large portion of the Polish population in America with fervor on behalf of their objectives. An army of more than 20,000 American Poles was even mustered and dispatched to the European front in support of the cause of Poland's restoration.[7]

Politically, Polonia's efforts prior to and throughout World War I had centered upon realizing the dream of Polish independence. With that aim seemingly achieved after 1918, Polonia's interest in the fate of the homeland dimmed in the 1920s and 1930s, with the federations that had been so prominent in the war years quickly fading into oblivion. The interwar period also witnessed efforts by the Polish government to draw the emigrant communities together into an agency, the World Union of Poles Living Abroad (popularly known as *Swiatpol*), for the purpose of advancing the homeland's interests internationally. But that effort too largely failed when most of the leadership of American Polonia declined to participate in its activities.

Still, Poland's rebirth could hardly help but raise the prestige of Polonia's organizations. After all, they had contributed substantially to the independence cause in the war years. And if the complex character of postwar Poland's political, social and economic problems was a source of great frustration to most Polish Americans, they could at least feel a certain pride that Polonia had done its bit on the homeland's behalf.

In turn, Poland's tragic fate during and after World War II (1939-1945) served to reinvigorate Polonia's identification with the homeland and its suffering people. Indeed the ethnic community's successful mobilization on both the humanitarian and the political levels demonstrated that concern for Poland retained its hold upon thousands of activists; what is more Polonia's efforts during and after World War II showed that ethnic commitment on behalf of the homeland could be successfully transmitted from the "first generation" veterans of the World War I period to their "second generation" offspring.

On the humanitarian side of the ledger, the Polish American Council *(Rada Polonii Amerykanskiej)* played a notable role in Polonia's relief efforts both during and after the war. The Council collected thousands of tons of clothing, food and medical supplies valued in the millions of dollars on behalf of people in need wherever they could be helped.

In 1944, political activities on Poland's behalf commenced with the formation of the Polish American Congress. Through the PAC, Polonia pressed its concerns for a free and independent postwar Poland liberated from all foreign occupation. Following the war's end, the Congress vigorously repudiated the Soviet Union's domination over Poland and its creation of a communist dictatorship against the wishes of its population. Through the next forty-five years and more the Polish American Congress held to its founding objectives, even in times when they were less than universally supported in Polonia.*

After the war, the PAC's founders were joined in their activities by new emigres, many of whom had come to the United States out of opposition to Soviet-dictated communist rule in Poland. Many of the newcomers in the late 1940s and early 1950s were "displaced persons" who entered this country after surviving years of mistreatment as prisoners of war or slave laborers in Nazi Germany. Others had fought on different fronts for the Allied cause and refused to return to a Poland

---

* During the war, Polonia identified with Poland's government, which eventually set up its headquarters in London following the Nazi and Soviet conquest of the country in 1939. This government lost its status as the recognized representative of the Polish nation in 1945; still it continued to retain the respect of the Polonia communities in the West. For its part, the Polish communist regime sought to gain a measure of recognition from the emigration for its rule by establishing, in 1955, its own "Society linking Polonia with the Homeland," the "Polonia Society." The Society's efforts to generate political support for the regime through its cultural projects were sometimes controversial and generally failed. Early in 1990, the Society was reorganized as an independent and apolitical agency by order of the newly established Solidarity-led Polish government. It took for itself a new name, *Wspolnota Polska* (the "Polish Community") and stressed the ideal of partnership and cooperation between the Polish nation and the emigration.

whose postwar independence had been forfeited at the Great Powers' conferences at Teheran and Yalta. In time, their ranks would be complemented by later waves of emigrants along with the American-born descendants of the pre-World War I and post World War II immigrants.

Indeed, by the 1980s Polonia had swelled to include as many as 10-12 million individuals. Within its ranks one could identify a great diversity of people - the foreign born, their children and descendants, both those who were completely Polish in family heritage and others having only one parent or even one grandparent of Polish origin.[8]

Polonia's political and lobbying activities on behalf of Poland's independence continued in Washington under the auspices of the Polish American Congress after World War II. The PAC's persistence was in contrast to the fate of its World War I era predecessor, the Polish National Department, which disappeared in the early 1920s. The Polish American Council would also persist for some time, although its organizers did act to dissolve it in the 1970s.

In its place the PAC established a charitable foundation under its own direction, an agency that became extraordinarily active in generating material aid to Poland during the 1980s. Indeed in late 1990 the Polish American Congress Charitable Foundation had delivered nearly $170 million in goods to the ancestral homeland, an amount roughly comparable to that collected by the Polish American Council in the Second World War.*

---

* Measured only in dollars, the charitable help from Polonia to Poland in the two World Wars and in the years since 1945 has been enormous, exceeding $400 million in today's currency. What is much more difficult to calculate is the dollar value of all the volunteered hours of labor connected with gathering, packaging and shipping the goods so needed by the Polish people. Just as difficult to estimate have been the effects of Polonia's humanitarian aid to its recipients, whether they happened to be refugees, orphans, the destitute, prisoners of war, or those who had been hospitalized.

Because this work focuses on the efforts on Poland's behalf by Polish Americans operating through the organizations of Polonia, it must of necessity leave out the systematic study of Americans of Polish origin who have participated in non-Polish organizations to further the legitimate aspirations of the Polish nation, as well as individuals who have done what they could for their countrymen on a private basis. Thus, with regard to the cause of the homeland's independence, Polish Americans have involved themselves in political party activities, as elected and as appointed government officials, as academic specialists and as members of interested social organizations, such as the labor movement, the Church and business. The same can be said for the actions of many Polish Americans working through non-Polish charitable associations.

Private assistance efforts benefiting the Polish people is a second area of involvement, which while extraordinary in its size and significance over the years, is a subject that is beyond this study's scope. Nonetheless, it should be noted that from the earliest days of immigrant settlement to the present time a continuing stream of money and material has found its way to loved ones who remained in the "old country." It is known, for example, that already in the years before World War I, immigrants originating from the Austrian zone of partitioned Poland were transferring some $4 million annually to the homeland under the auspices of the imperial bank, with comparable sums flowing to Poles in the territories of the country under Russian and German rule. Assistance of this sort continued, on a more modest scale, in the interwar years and commenced once again in greater amounts after World War II. Indeed, one estimate of private and largely familial assistance activity placed its total value in the mid 1980s at approximately $600 million annually, a sum then equal to one-tenth of Poland's entire foreign export earnings.[9]

Polonia's Concern for Poland: A Neglected Subject

Given the substantial nature of Polonia's historic and ongoing concern for Poland, it is ironic that so little attention has focused upon telling the story of organized Polish American efforts on behalf of the ancestral homeland, either by students

of Polish or Polish American history. A look at the scholarship
on Poland, for example, reveals that the story of the emigrations
receives little attention, even in works running into the hundreds of pages. For example, in the one volume history of
Poland compiled in the late 1960s by a team of respected senior
Polish scholars, less than one page out of 716 in all dealt with
the mass migrations, with no mention at all of the role of
Polonia's service on the homeland's behalf. A more recent
general study of Polish history published in the West similarly
covered the mass migrations to America in less than a single
page. Such works are by no means exceptional, but follow the
pattern set in earlier serious works whose authors wrote next to
nothing on the subject.[10]

Fortunately, a few contemporary writers providing an overview of Polish history have done better in at least characterizing
the emigrations, if not in giving a detailed analysis of their
importance to the homeland. Here the words of the British
scholar Norman Davies merit extended quotation in providing
some insight into Polonia's place in Polish life, at least in the
pre-World War I era:

> The mere existence of a numerous Polish emigration
> outweighed all the shortcomings, or achievements, of its
> individual members... With a solid base abroad, immune
> from the pressures of the political authorities in Poland, the
> emigration could play a role in Polish life of incalculable
> importance. In the political sphere, it provided the only
> forum for free debate and critical analysis of all Poland's
> problems. With the perpetuation in Poland of alien, imperial
> regimes with little provision for democracy, it fulfilled the
> function of the principal, if absent, opposition. In the eco-
> nomic sphere, it provided a much needed source of foreign
> income and eventually, trade and enterprise. In the cultural
> sphere, it insured that free expression could be given to the
> full variety of ideas, arts and genres on which a living culture
> depends. In the period of Partitions, a large part of the
> classics of Polish literature could only be published in emi-
> gration. Lastly, in the moral sphere, the emigration be-
> stowed a measure of prestige and respectability on Polish
> nationality which was officially forbidden in Poland.
>   Nineteenth century Poland produced a great number of
> talented artists, musicians and scientists, who if they had

only performed at home, would only have been known to the world as talented figures in the life of Russia, Germany or Austria. As it was, because they made their reputations abroad and could freely advertise their Polish connections, they were widely known as 'Poles'... A nation which continued to produce people of the caliber of the composer Chopin, the explorer Strzelecki, the Architect Gzowski, the actress Modjeska, the novelist Conrad, the pianist Paderewski, the physicist Sklodowska-Curie, the anthropologist Malinowski, among many others could hardly be said to have disappeared. Poles abroad no doubt made a worthy contribution to their host countries. Yet their contribution to the survival of their own nationality...was even greater. However strong, however tenuous the link, they continued to be part of Poland.[11]

Other scholars have also given favorable mention to the emigration's role in Poland's history, among them Piotr Wandycz and M.K. Dziewanowski.[12] Still, seldom if ever have the organizations of Polonia received the attention due them, given their actual involvement in Polish affairs. A similar fate has befallen the leaders of the Polish American community whose many activities on the homeland's behalf have been very little noticed.

One hypothesis to be offered in explaining this minimization of Polonia's place in modern Poland's history is offered by Benjamin Murdzek, the author of *Emigration in Polish Social and Political Thought: 1870-1914.* Murdzek concludes that the mass migrations from the countryside and towns of partitioned Poland were viewed unfavorably by the educated and influential Poles of the day, as actions taken by people who lacked a patriotic devotion to remain in the homeland to work for its betterment there. In turn, the difficult economic conditions the emigrants experienced abroad were generally underscored in Poland, while their advances were accorded little recognition.[13]

Indeed, because the Poles from the end of the 18th century looked to Western Europe for inspiration in defining their ideas about national independence one might readily understand why they paid so little attention to their own emigrant communities as possible contributors to the nation's eventual rebirth.

After all, the masses of people who departed England, France, the German lands and Scandinavia for America had made little if any impact upon their old homelands; why should the impoverished and frequently unskilled populations from Poland's towns and villages be any different? Whatever its roots, the neglect of Polonia's contributions to Poland must be regarded as a serious flaw in the study of the country's history over the past two centuries. Works which fail to consider the linkages between Poland and its huge diaspora can at best be judged incomplete in depicting the country's modern experience, especially to Polish Americans who must ask why their role in the ancestral homeland's evolution is either left out or treated in only cursory fashion.[14]

Similarly, little attention has been paid by students of American Polonia to the emigration's continuing concern for the homeland over the past 125-130 years. Indeed, a look at two recent bibliographies of published research on Polonia indicates that only a couple of dozen works have dealt extensively with the emigration's ties to Poland, out of more than 1,100 scholarly articles and books on Polish ethnic topics which appeared in print during the past two decades.[15]

In one sense, one should not be too surprised by this finding. Scholarly interest in the Polish immigrant and ethnic experience is itself a phenomenon of recent vintage. Indeed, the entire field of research on "white ethnicity" of which "Polonia Studies" is a part dates back only to the early 1960s. It was only then that sociologists and historians began to analyze Polish Americans and other nationality-based populations from a new perspective, as persisting and dynamic elements contributing to the country's pluralistic culture, rather than as mere survivals of foreign folkways doomed to disintegrate soon within the vast American melting pot.[16]

Consequently, "Polonia Studies," particularly as practiced by a number of younger Americans of Polish heritage schooled in the academic study of the American experience, has understandably stressed the interactions of the Polish immigrants and their descendants with the American social and economic systems with which they came into contact over several generations' time.

Research on Polish ethnicity published over the past twenty-five years has indeed provided a wealth of information about the actual number of immigrants who came to, and remained in, America, their motives for leaving their homeland, the work they performed and the community life they established in the United States.[17] While we know relatively little about the experiences of the immigrants' children, the "second generation" of Polish Americans, and less still about the fates of their descendants, research findings indicate that Polish Americans have generally succeeded in moving into the economic and cultural mainstreams of the nation's life.[18]

Nevertheless, in their efforts to describe the life experiences of the Polish immigrants, their offspring and later generations of Polish Americans, students of the subject have rarely focused upon the Poles' relationship toward the ancestral homeland. This is especially surprising because at first glance one would imagine this connection to be very significant in providing some understanding of their identification with their heritage and interest in participating in the activities of the ethnic community.

Indeed, it would appear that a person's ethnic identification must be rooted in some fashion to one's personal or ancestral ties to the homeland, as perpetuated and even rejuvenated in some way through involvement in ethnic community life. And while ethnic feeling can take many forms, ranging from one's interest in maintaining family or folk traditions in the home to a preference for certain foods and specific forms of entertainment, a person's ethnic consciousness would still appear to be fundamentally rooted in one's own past participation in the life of the Polish national cultural community in Europe and/or the memory of one's familial or ancestral roots in the old homeland. Such experiences can take many diverse forms, of course, but without some personal linkages to the heritage of the homeland, it would seem to be very difficult to understand just what it would mean for one to be a "Polish American."*

---

* Clearly, knowledge of the Polish language, involvement in ethnic associations and subscribing to Polonia publications, whether they

This work, in addressing itself directly to the subject of organized ethnic involvement on Poland's behalf, aims at realizing two interrelated objectives. Not only do I seek to take up a topic that has received little general attention in research on the Polish ethnic community; what is more it is my hope that this effort will stimulate greater concern among students of nationality-based groups as to the reasons for their continued existence in American society. Indeed, while I would be the first to agree that the phenomenon of organized Polonia involvement on Poland's behalf has seldom been the only significant form of ethnic activity in the Polish American community, it has been the kind most explicitly dedicated to the maintenance of nationality consciousness and mobilization of group solidarity through the past one hundred and twenty-five years. Indeed, without organized ethnic appeals on behalf of the homeland's humanitarian and political concerns one might well doubt whether a Polonia having any semblance of mass support would have persisted in America to the present time.

Acknowledgements

This work is the product of more than four years of research and comes in response to an invitation from the Polish American Congress to write a comprehensive study of Polonia's services to Poland. Through this period I have benefited from the help and advice of many; each in some fashion has enriched my appreciation of the Polish ethnic community's enduring concern for Poland. Hopefully, through the appearance of this book, others may at last learn of the scope and significance of this concern.

---

appear in Polish or English, all represent forms of ethnic participation that define membership in the Polish American community. Travel to Poland and correspondence with individuals living there, together with study of its history and culture, also count as measures of psychological involvement in the ethnic community. On the other hand, one's enjoyment of polka music, in itself, would appear to be a far weaker indicator of one's identification with the concerns of the ethnic community.

Among the many individuals with whom I have spoken, some on numerous occasions, I would like to single out several who have been particularly helpful in contributing to this work. Foremost was Aloysius A. Mazewski, the late President of the Polish American Congress and the Polish National Alliance, who spent many hours with me discussing the activities of both organizations on Poland's behalf. As President of the PAC, Mr. Mazewski dedicated himself for nearly twenty years to the cause of Poland's political freedom. And it was he who took a leading role in organizing the Polish American Congress Charitable Foundation to manifest anew Polonia's humanitarian concern for Poland's people. As he mentioned more than once, "the story of Polonia's service to Poland needs to be told - it is too important to go neglected as it has for so long."

Among other Polonia leaders with whom I have spoken on topics pertaining to this work, several merit a special mention here. They include the late Francis X. Swietlik of Milwaukee, Chairman of the Polish American Council; Wanda Rozmarek, widow of Charles Rozmarek, the President of the Polish American Congress from its founding in 1944 until 1968; their daughter, Cook County Judge Marilyn Rozmarek Komosa; Kazimierz Lukomski, Vice President of the Polish American Congress; Adele Lagodzinska, former Vice President of the Polish American Congress and the long time national secretary of the Polish American Council; former Chicago Alderman and U.S. Congressman Roman Pucinski; Adam Tomaszkiewicz of Cicero, Illinois; Col. Casimir Lenard and his wife Myra, each the National Director of the Polish American Congress in Washington, D.C.; Attorney Leonard Walentynowicz of Buffalo, past National Director of the PAC; Eugene Rosypal, Director of the PAC Charitable Foundation in its work for Poland from the early 1980s; veteran PAC activist Jerzy Przyluski of Chicago; Helen Wojcik, Vice President of the Polish American Congress and President of the Polish Women's Alliance; Edward Dykla, Treasurer of the PAC and President of the Polish Roman Catholic Union of America fraternal; Ewa Betka, Executive Secretary of the Illinois Division of the Polish American Congress; Bonaventure Migala of Chicago; journalists Wojciech Wierzewski, Jan Krawiec, Anna Rychlinska, and the late Joseph Bialasiewicz, all of Chicago; and Edward J. Moskal,

President of the Polish American Congress and the Polish National Alliance following Mr. Mazewski's death.

A number of PAC leaders at the state level of that organization have also deepened my understanding of Polonia's activities and its problems over the years. They include: Edmund Banasikowski, Thomas Czerwinski, Eugene Kaluzny, Edward Tomasik and Edward Wojtkowski, each in turn a President of the Wisconsin division of the PAC since the 1970s; Michigan PAC leaders Paul Odrobina, Casimir Olejarczyk, and Wilhelm Wolf; and Pennsylvania PAC activists Hilary Czaplicki, Michael Blichasz and Joseph Dolegowski. Helpful and informative on various matters pertaining to this work have been the officers and directors of the Polish National Alliance fraternal with whom I have been pleased to serve since my election to its Board of Directors in 1987.

My earlier published histories of the Polish National Alliance (1984) and the Polish Falcons of America (1987) proved to be of help in providing me with a better grasp of the character and dynamics of the organized Polish ethnic community in the United States. Of all the individuals whom I have previously thanked in those volumes I would like to single out several persons whose assistance was especially beneficial in research on this book. These include Bernard Rogalski, past President of the Polish Falcons of America and a past national secretary of the Polish American Congress; Edward Rozanski and the late Joseph Wiewiora, Editors of the Polish National Alliance publication, *Zgoda*; and Helen Szymanowicz, Vice President of the PNA.

In this research project I also benefited from the opportunity to look over the holdings of several archives and libraries around the country. These include the archives of the Polish American Congress and the Polish National Alliance, both located in Chicago; the library of the Polish Museum of America, in Chicago, where a mass of material on the Polish American Council is stored; the library and archives of the Polish Falcons of America in Pittsburgh; and the libraries of the Alliance College in Cambridge Springs, Pennsylvania and St. Mary's College, in Orchard Lake, Michigan. In August 1987, I also visited the Immigration History Research Center of the University of Minnesota where I examined the voluminous records of both the Polish American Congress and its special Committee for the Resettlement of Polish Displaced Persons. My visit was partly funded by a grant from the Center, for which I am grateful. Individuals at each of these facilities were very helpful in facilitating my work and all merit my thanks. They include Jean Dybal, Wanda Dziob, Ludwika Rozwadowska, Blanche Malinowicz, and the late Josephine Rzewska of the PNA; Tadeusz Nowakowski of the Polish Museum; Wladyslawa Koziol of the PRCUA; Eugenia Bar of the Polish American Council; Timothy Kuzma, Editor of *Sokol Polski,* the publication of the Polish Falcons of America; Maria Lorys, Editor of *Glos Polek,* the organ of the Polish Women's Alliance; and Dr. Rudolph Vecoli and Anna Jaroszynska of the Immigration History Research Center. Visits paid to the Franklin D. Roosevelt, Herbert Hoover and John F. Kennedy Presidential Libraries in 1987 and 1988 also proved to be enlightening.

Further, I have benefited from my associations and conversations with scholarly colleagues who share with me an interest in the study of Poland and Polonia, whatever their particular disciplinary focus. Especially helpful have been Professor Stanislaus Blejwas of Central Connecticut State University, who made many excellent comments in reading through an earlier draft of this work; Dr. Frank Renkiewicz, past Editor of *Polish American Studies,* the journal of the Polish American Historical Association; and Professors Thad Radzilowski, Joseph Hapak, Thaddeus Gromada and William Galush.

I am grateful to Witold Plonski, Director of the Polish American Ethnic Committee of New York, for his help in sponsoring a series of lectures I delivered around the country in 1986 under the auspices of the National Endowment for the Humanities and the PNA. These talks afforded me an excellent opportunity to develop several of the themes which were later incorporated into this work. Similarly, I have benefited from my conversations with colleagues at my own university, both within the Department of Political Science and in our institution's interdisciplinary Polish Studies Committee. This group includes Professors M.K. Dziewanowski, Neal Pease, Victor Greene, Barbara Borowiecka and Michael Mikos; each has encouraged my work on this project in various ways.

A special word of thanks is due Chester Sawko and Walter Koziol of Chicago for their generous financial support of this project. Over the years Polonia has been very fortunate to have benefactors such as Chester and Walter. Professor Stephen Fischer-Galati, Editor of East European Monographs merits "prolonged and stormy applause" for his encouragement throughout the publication process. More generally, he has made an inestimable contribution to scholarly knowledge of the history, culture and political dynamics of the peoples of East Central Europe and the Balkans over the years, both in their homelands and in emigration, by publishing more than three hundred books in this broad and many-faceted realm. Nearly last but by no means least is my appreciation of the help I have received from our Department secretary, Lois Kohlmetz, for doing her usually solid work in typing the successive drafts of this work.

Finally my thanks go to my wife Angela and to our sons, John, Thomas, Paul and Mark for their support of this project. Each represents what is great and good about our heritage, from their love of Chopin's music and Sienkiewicz's novels to their interest in and solidarity with their relatives in America and Poland, from their enjoyment of our ethnic customs as we continue to practice them to their hope that Poland will some day again be Poland.*

---

* "For your freedom through ours" - about the title. These words derive from the motto, "For your freedom and ours," first heard during the "November" insurrection of 1830-1831. From that time on, Poles have given their lives in the thousands - both for their own country, and when that was impossible, for the cause of other nations. This out of their conviction that liberty is a good to be experienced by all. Thus, over the past 160 years Poles have been found in the front ranks in the struggle wherever freedom was at stake, whether the cause took them to other European lands, to the Western Hemisphere, or even to the Third World. In America of course, the immigrants found a country where liberty already existed and with it the freedom to organize publicly on behalf of Poland's betterment and independence. What then could be more appropriate than to gather together to take full advantage of the conditions of liberty which they as immigrants had encountered in the United States and to unite as Polish Americans, to help bring about Poland's own rebirth through the freedom they already enjoyed?

1. Total Number of Polish Immigrants to the United States, 1820-1990[19]

Time Period	Characterization of Immigrants	Total Number
1820-1885	Persons identifying themselves as Polish	33,489
1885-1898	Persons identifying Poland as their native land	131,694
1889-1919	Persons identified as Poles by "race" or "people"	1,352,658
1920-1932	Persons identified as Poles by "race" or "people"	90,815
1933-1946	Persons identifying Poland as the Country of their Birth	46,573
1947-1972	Persons identifying Poland as the Country of their Birth and entering as immigrants	301,709
	Persons entering during the same period as Displaced persons and as ex-combatants	164,292
1973-1980	Persons admitted into the United States from Poland	33,603
Since 1980	Persons entering the United States from Poland	200,000 minimum

Total Minimum Estimated Number of Polish Immigrants   2,354,833

Figure 1. Relations between Poland and the Polish American Population.

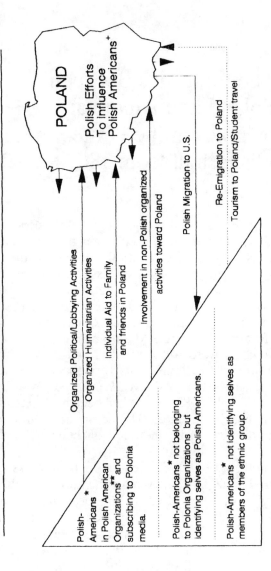

POLAND

Polish Efforts
To Influence
Polish Americans[+]

Organized Political/Lobbying Activities

Organized Humanitarian Activities

Individual Aid to Family
and friends in Poland

Involvement in non-Polish organized
activities toward Poland

Polish Migration to U.S.

Re-Emigration to Poland

Tourism to Poland/Student travel

Polish-
Americans [*]
in Polish American
Organizations[**] and
subscribing to Polonia
media.

Polish-Americans [*] not belonging
to Polonia Organizations but
identifying selves as Polish Americans.

Polish-Americans [*] not identifying selves as
members of the ethnic group.

Graphic by
Victor Modinski

* Polish-Americans:
(a) Persons of Polish national origin.
(b) Persons of Polish-born parent(s).
(c) Persons having Polish-born grandparents and ancestors.

** Fraternal, political, educational, community associations and
churches.

+ Government-sponsored efforts: Polonia-oriented publications; cultural
influences (films, dance and theatrical programming); church influences.

I. The First Ties Between Poland and America: Efforts by Poles in the United States on Poland's Behalf from 1863 to 1900

This story focuses upon the organized Polish efforts in America on Poland's behalf, one whose formal beginnings can be traced to March 1863. In that month the first committee of Poles in the city of New York was established to inform the general public of the uprising in the homeland against tsarist Russian rule which had broken out in January of that year, and to mobilize popular support for the Polish cause. Though the committee's effort came at a time when the Polish immigrant community's numbers were still very small and its members were scattered around the country, its very appearance was significant. Indeed, at the time of the Polish insurrection against Russian rule of November 1830, there had been no substantial Polish immigrant community in the United States upon which any organized effort could be mounted on behalf of independence.

While the Polish committee's creation in 1863 marks the birth of organized immigrant activism for the homeland, there is a "pre-history" to the story of Polish American involvement on behalf of Poland's cause. It can be found in the memory of the exploits of such patriotic adventurers as Tadeusz Kosciuszko and Kazimierz Pulaski, the most renowned of the Polish participants in the American revolutionary war of independence which was fought between 1776 and 1781. As significant is the fact that both men were also leaders in their time in Poland's struggles to preserve its national independence during the last decades of the eighteenth century. Those efforts would fail with Poland suffering military intervention and eventual political extinction at the hands of Russia, Prussia and Austria in the partitions of 1772, 1793 and 1795.[1] This pre-history also involves the experiences of political emigres arriving onto America's shores following a series of unsuccessful uprisings to regain Poland's independence during the Napoleonic wars up to 1814, the "November" revolution of 1830-1831, the revolts in 1846 (against the Austrians) and 1848 (against the Prussian partitioners), and the "January" uprising of 1863-1864 against Russia.[2]

While the number of emigres coming to America following these events was small, especially in comparison with the masses of largely peasant migrants who flooded into this country in an almost ever rising tide after 1854, they contributed much to the future shape of Polish ethnic interests towards the homeland and frequently provided leadership for the immigrants as well. Moreover, the earliest emigre activists, from Kosciuszko and Pulaski onward, provided attractive models for Polish immigrants and their children to cherish later on in their own ethnic community involvements. Thus Pulaski was a revered martyr for the causes of Poland and America. In turn, Kosciuszko served as the personification of ethical commitment to human rights and social equality, both in his exhortations to the serfs to fight for Poland in 1794 in return for full freedom and later in his famous American will where he called upon Thomas Jefferson as executor and friend to use his estate to free and educate Negro slaves.

> The legacies (of Kosciuszko and Pulaski) were to be effective in two ways: they engendered pro-Polish sympathies in the American public through the nineteenth century and afterwards. They gave newcomers from Poland--first political exiles, later peasants coming 'after bread'--surrogate roots in the American past which psychologically lessened their feelings of being 'strangers' to America.[3]

The first Polish political emigration was composed of refugees from Napoleon's "Duchy of Warsaw" (a small territory carved out of Prussian and Austrian portions of the partitioned land and in existence as an autonomous state from 1807 to 1814) was in America in 1818 and many of its members eventually wound up in Alabama. In 1834, a shipload of some 234 political emigres arrived in New York harbor, having been permitted by Austria to leave its territory following the collapse of the November insurrection and their subsequent interment in 1831 in the Hapsburg-run Polish partition known as Galicia. While these political emigres endured many hardships and failed in their attempts to establish a colony, "New Poland," in Illinois, members of the group did succeed in organizing the very first Polish societies in this country, the Polish Committee (1834, later the Polish National Committee) and the Society of Poles in America (in 1842).[4] These groups, especially the Society of Poles, had close ties with political emigres operating in France, their aim that of keeping alive the idea of independence. Leading the Society was Henry Kalussowski (1806-1894), who was to play a pivotal role in Polish emigre affairs in this country from the time of his arrival in the United States in 1842 until his death.[5]

The Society of Poles, however, disappeared not long after holding commemorative programs in 1844 on the anniversary of the November insurrection. So did the very first periodical issued by the emigres. Edited by Paul Sobolewski and Eustace Wyszynski and appearing in English under the grand title, *Poland, Historical, Literary, Monumental and Picturesque,* it lasted less than a year.[6]

In 1852, another organization, the Democratic Society of Polish Refugees in America, was formed. Its members were veterans of the 1830 uprising and more recent emigres who had participated in the 1848 revolutionary "Springtime of the Nations." Inspired by Kalussowski, this group adopted a liberal program based upon the precepts of Poland's May Third, 1791 Constitution; membership was open to all regardless of their religious affiliation. The Society was opposed to slavery and eventually became identified with the new Republican party, founded in 1854.

With the outbreak of the American Civil War in 1861, Poles from the political emigration actively sought out command positions in both the Union and the Confederate armies. Among those who won appointments in the Union forces, thanks to help from Kalussowski (by then a Federal Treasury Department employee), were Wlodzimierz (or Wladimir

Krzyzanowski), Joseph Karge and Albin Schoepf. In the South, Caspar Tochman of Virginia and Valerian Sulewski held military rank at different times during the war. The most famous of the Civil War Polish military officers was Krzyzanowski, who rose to the rank of Brigadier General and took part in the battles of Chancellorsville and Gettysburg.[7] In all, estimates of Poles fighting in the Union forces range from 1,000 to 4,000, with at least several hundred in the ranks of the Confederacy.

Coinciding with the American Civil War of 1861 to 1865 was a major event in the Russian-ruled zone of partitioned Poland. This was the "January" insurrection of 1863-1864, which in turn gave rise to the very first organized action on Poland's behalf in America. In response to news of the uprising's outbreak in Warsaw, a Polish Central Committee formed in the city of New York in March 1863 under Kalussowski's chairmanship. The Committee's purposes were to rally American public opinion in favor of the Polish independence cause and to raise funds for the revolutionaries. Not long afterward, in June, a patriotic Polish language newspaper, *Echo z Polski,* also made its appearance, the first of many such publications in the years to come.

The Committee had expected a favorable American response to its appeals, given its reliance upon traditional and often-expressed sympathies for the Polish cause which dated back to the exploits of Kosciuszko and Pulaski and the failed uprising of 1830-1831. In this it was seriously disappointed. For one thing, public attention focused upon the Civil War rather than events in East Central Europe. Moreover, alone among the European powers (which generally favored the Confederates) Tsarist Russia stood firmly on the side of the Union. In this light some Americans went so far as to portray the Polish insurrection as but another secessionist uprising against a friendly government. The crushing of the January insurrection in 1864 eventually brought an end to the Polish Central Committee in America as well. All told, it raised about $16,000 for the cause throughout the country; what little money still remained in its treasury following the uprising was then distributed to the first new exiles from Poland. In early 1865, the Polish migration's first newspaper also disbanded. Efforts to form other patriotic groups in New York after the war came to nothing. The time was simply not ripe for further political activities within the still tiny Polish immigrant community. It would not be until the late 1870s that the veterans of this first organized effort would succeed in working with the growing number of new arrivals to the United States in forming an enduring mass-oriented movement committed to Poland's independence.

Nevertheless, the first efforts to establish associations in America of emigres on Poland's behalf were not without impact. In the judgment of one student of early Polish settlement in America:

> With the last years of the 1860s and the first years of the next decade the first era of Polish immigration came to an end. The end was not an abrupt termination. It was, instead, a fusion. The exiles--one might even term them 'proto-ethnics'-- fused with the 'real ethnics' - the immigrants 'after bread.' They made their influence felt for several decades to come as they became moving spirits behind American Polish organizations, the strongest of which was the Polish National Alliance founded in 1880. Thus, on one hand, they were instrumental in fostering 'Polskosc' (Polishness) in the new arrivals; on the other, they were also often instrumental in encouraging the new arrivals to take part in American life.[8]

Mass Migration to America: The Beginnings of a Polish Immigrant Ethnic Community

The traditionally recognized beginnings of Polish mass migration to the United States date back to 1854; it was in that year that the earliest groups of immigrants established settlements in this country. The first of these was in Texas, where the Panna Maria colony was formed by Silesian Poles led by Father Leopold Moczygemba. Another was created in Parisville, Michigan near Detroit, not long after. Already in 1858, a parish had been established by immigrants to Polonia, Wisconsin, the third community of Poles in America. They had arrived there in 1855, coming like the others, from the German-ruled zone of partitioned Poland. Indeed, by 1870, there were approximately seventy Polish settlements in America and some 30-40,000 Poles in this country.[9] By that time, perhaps seventeen parishes, the earliest community-directed societies of the emigration (or *wychodztwo*), were already in existence. In time the numbers of Polish Roman Catholic parishes would mushroom along with the population of immigrants, to 75 in 1880, 170 in 1890, 330-390 in 1900, 500 or more by 1910, 760 by 1920 and as many as 830 in the 1930s.[10]

This mass migration of Poles to America has been called the economically-motivated migration of landless or nearly landless peasants, the emigration 'after bread' - *za chlebem*, or *emigracja zarobkowa* (the migration seeking employment).[11] This generalization about these immigrants, who together with their American-born children and descendants came to compose the overwhelming majority of the Polish population in America after 1850, is in the main accurate. Poland during the partitions period between 1795 and 1918 remained a country whose rural population, though freed from serfdom under the Germans and Austrians during the Napoleonic era and the Russians at the time of the January uprising of 1863-1864, suffered a dramatic decline in its economic conditions. Land itself, the basis of economic and social position in the village community, was in short supply and land ownership was increasingly beyond the means of even the most hard working and ambitious peasants. The country itself underwent a population explosion, with Poland's numbers doubling from 12.8 million to 25.6 million inhabitants between 1850 and 1910 - despite the outflux of more than 3.5 million people during this period.

Under foreign rulers both unable and unwilling to promote the industrialization of the lands under their sway, Poland's towns remained relatively small and incapable of absorbing the growing number of landless and pauperized peasants who sought work wherever they could find it. Not surprisingly, peasants turned to labor opportunities outside the country, initially as seasonal workers on the great agricultural estates of Germany and Austria, later to seek employment in the mines and factories of the Ruhr and Rhine River valleys and in the Western Hemisphere. Enticed by promises of work and land in the New World, Poles travelled mainly to the United States, but also to Brazil, Argentina and to Canada, countries which possessed wide open spaces and an interest in attracting immigrants willing to work them.[12]

Of the more than three and one-half million people who emigrated out of Poland, perhaps 2.5 million came to the United States between 1850 and 1914, when mass migration was halted due to the outbreak of the First World War. Of this number, perhaps one-third of the migration was composed of non-Poles, mainly Jews and Ukrainians hailing from the old Polish territories. Not all remained; perhaps 20 percent eventually returned to Poland after several years in the United States having achieved their aims of finding work abroad and saving enough money to return home to establish themselves as landed farmers. Some also came home disillusioned by their experiences in the new land.[13]

The massive "after bread" migration entered this country in wave-like fashion, with peasants and townspeople from the Prussian or German territories of Slask, Poznan and Pomorze (in German -- Silesia, Posen and Pomerania) leading the way. During the 1870s about 150,000 Poles entered the United States, with 400,000 more coming during the 1880s. By the mid 1890s immigration into the U.S. from "German" Poland was tapering off rapidly and between 1895 and 1913 only about 50,000 people entered from that region, a total comprising less than four percent of the Polish migration in those years. Beginning in the 1880s, Poles from the western part of Austrian-ruled Galicia began increasingly to enter the United States. In the 1880s approximately 60-80,000 people came, during the 1890s approximately 330-350,000, with approximately 500,000 more between 1901 and 1913. The Poles from the Russian-ruled lands came last, 40,000 during the 1880s, about 150,000 in the next decade, followed by about 700,000 in the twentieth century period ending with the outbreak of the war.[14]

Accordingly, the Polish ethnic population in America grew rapidly in the decades after the Civil War. In 1870 the Polish immigration and its offspring could be estimated at 40,000 persons. Ten years later the figure was 500,000 and by 1890 it reached some 1,000,000 individuals. In 1900 a reliable estimate of 2,000,000 Poles in America could be reported and by 1910 the total reached 3,000,000. By 1914-1918, one could speak of a "Polonia"--the community of Poles in America along with their native-born children and descendants--including perhaps four million people, though not all possessed a well-defined ethnic consciousness or strong inclinations to take part in organized ethnic community affairs. Most Poles could be counted as members of the Polish nationality parishes of the time, of course. But fewer belonged to one of the voluntary secular associations of Polonia, such as the fraternals. Indeed those organizations combined claimed fewer than 350,000 members during the First World War year, about 15-20 percent of the adult population.[15] One observer of that time even went so far as to estimate that only about five percent of the Polish American population was fully politically conscious.[16]

Still, it can be argued that even for the so-called "economically motivated" immigrants, there were real and pressing political reasons influencing their decisions to leave Poland in the years between the 1850s and 1914, when the war's outbreak effectively ended further mass movement to America. The absence of political freedom was acute, for example, in the German-ruled provinces, where the Poles felt the effects of Chancellor Otto von Bismarck's *Kulturkampf* against the Roman Catholic Church and his efforts to force the teaching of the German language, in the place of Polish, in their schools. Further difficulties were caused by Berlin's policies designed to force Poles from their own lands by promoting German colonization into their provinces, repressing democratically-minded political parties representing Polish concerns, and silencing the newspapers published in the Polish territories.[17]

In the Russian-dominated zone of partitioned Poland, political repression and Russification had characterized conditions following the crushing of the 1863 insurrection through the next four decades. In 1905, long pent-up economic and political discontent exploded when Poles, many of them partisans of the socialist cause, took part in a general revolution against tsarist rule throughout the empire. Following the restoration of imperial power, thousands of participants in the insurrection joined the ever growing tide of emigrants bound for America. Soon, some rose to leadership in such Polonia organizations as the Falcons and the Polish National Alliance.

Indeed, throughout the entire period of pre-World War I migration, political motives, often unstated but nonetheless real enough, were at the core of many a decision to leave the old homeland for a better economic life in America. One involved the desire on the part of many young men to avoid military conscription in the armies of the partitioners. Clearly, the policies of the partitioners in the countryside, which left Poland in a condition of general backwardness, were an even more universal "political" factor leading hundreds of thousands to go abroad.

Aside from its size and its members' motives for coming to America, what is interesting about the Polish immigration was its success in building an enduring organized system of ethnic life in the new land. Within Polonia, many of the key elements of the society and culture of the old country were indeed preserved. What is more, the very existence of the ethnic community helped greatly in cushioning the shock of adjustment to life in the quite foreign land that was America, while providing many immigrants with opportunities for leadership never available to them in Poland.

Also significant was the gradual development within Polonia of ethnic national feeling. While it is probably the case that many if not most Poles to America arrived without a fully developed sense of national consciousness and identified themselves instead as members of particular villages, regions or religious traditions, in the United States they were viewed as "Poles" by other immigrants as well as by the native "Yankees." National identification was in turn reinforced within Polonia by the community's leaders, whether they were churchmen, journalists or activists associated with the political emigrations from 1830 and 1863. This process of "nationality building" was by no means smooth or complete (after all, most immigrants were poorly educated and little informed about Poland's history); still, by the time of World War I a substantial number of Poles in America thought of themselves along nationality lines.[18]

Already noted in the development of Polonia were the hundreds of Polish ethnic parishes that mushroomed throughout the United States during the years of mass migration. The parishes were significant in a variety of ways which made them central to the newcomers, ways that extended far beyond their conventional functions as centers of worship and made them hubs of the immigrants' social life. The novelist Henryk Sienkiewicz, a visitor to the United States in the 1870s, put this well when he observed:

The Church is the focus they (the immigrants) rally around, a thread linking them to the 'Old Country', something peculiarly their own, something protective. The parish is a unit not only spiritually but also socially... The peasants (that is, the immigrants) are by nature religious and having no knowledge of the country, the language or conditions, see in the clergyman not only a shepherd of souls but also their plenipotentiary, governor and judge.[19]

The Polish Roman Catholic parishes, while not organized to promote the patriotic sentiments of their flock, were not necessarily antagonistic to that cause. After all, the priests and sisters who journeyed to America to staff the churches and schools of Polonia ministered in the Polish language and Polish was taught for decades, if only to help maintain some distance between the immigrants and non-Catholics. By their stress in maintaining the ancestral language and preserving loyalty to the faith, the parishes made a significant contribution of their own to deepening ethnic consciousness throughout the Polish American community.

During Polonia's "first generation," from the 1860s through the turn of the century, the clergy played a preponderant leadership role in the community since priests comprised a large and well organized caste whose members were both well educated and highly motivated to promote their sense of cultural and linguistic solidarity in the new land. By the beginning of the twentieth century, however, there were challenges to priestly leadership, which was itself quite authoritarian in character. From inside the church, pressures built up in favor of greater lay responsibility at the parish level and more recognition of the Polish immigrants by the Irish-dominated Roman Catholic hierarchy.[20] The most notable result of such agitation came in the years after 1897 with the forming of a schismatic independent "Polish National Catholic Church" in the United States headquartered in Scranton, Pennsylvania and led by the Reverend Francis Hodur (after 1907 the consecrated chief bishop of the Church).

Priestly leadership was also challenged by lay persons who argued for the importance of the independence cause as the basis for Polish organizational activity in America. The "nationalist" or "patriotic" Poles were few in number at first, many of them emigres from the failed insurrections of 1830 and 1863; moreover after the crushing defeat in 1864 of the January revolution, the independence cause suffered eclipse as the conquered territory was placed under ruthless martial law and with it, a determined tsarist effort to russify the former Polish "Congress kingdom," now renamed "Vistulaland." For more than twenty years after the uprising, patriotic thought and action was directed away from the idea of winning national independence by force of arms (the perspective of Polish "idealists" or "romantics") and toward a different orientation, that of "realism or "organic work." This realist perspective was rooted in its proponents' effort to preserve the Poles' national identity during its babylonian captivity by working to improve agricultural practices and to promote industrial expansion in each zone of the partitioned country. In the cultural and educational realm, the realists argued that the traditions of learning and respect for the country's history long unique to the upper classes needed to be propagandized to ordinary working people in both the towns and villages. Through such efforts, they believed, it would be possible to resist the Germanization and Russification policies being enforced in more than three-quarters of the ancient Polish lands. (Only in the Austrian-controlled provinces were the cultural policies of the ruling power more moderate.)

The debate between the romantics and realists as to the course patriots should best follow in the partitions period has been well described by scholars of Poland's history.[21] What is most significant here is to recognize that both camps, regardless of their views on specific issues, were committed to the same cause - the restoration of Poland to a place in Europe as an independent, self-governing nation-state. The differences between the two groups, though serious and often a cause of deep animosity, were largely over the methods to be used in regaining independence, with the idealists championing the route of insurrection and the realists favoring non-violent resistance to de-Polonization.

Just as in Poland, where realism held sway in the twenty years after the January Insurrection, so also in the formative years of American Polonia was a similar outlook preeminent. To both the clergy, concerned above all with its parishioners' needs, as well as the largely peasant immigrant community, in the United States to better its lot, a pragmatic perspective prevailed over idealistic sentiments in favor of Poland's restoration. Similarly, within the fraternal movement, after the parishes the most notable mass membership associations to emerge in Polonia, the dominant ideology was initially that of the realists and stressed the theme of social uplift through cooperation. Only later would the patriotic cause win some favor among fraternal activists and bring significant changes within the growing Polonia community.

The fraternal idea was based upon the principle of voluntary participation in a society whose aims combined social interaction with the creation of a simple insurance program that provided a death benefit to families of members. Initially set up as locally-based societies, the early fraternals in Polonia frequently engaged in service activities on behalf of the neighborhood parish to which their members belonged. Some also encouraged involvement in local politics while a few espoused the Polish independence cause. In time individual societies united with like-minded groups elsewhere to form the first national fraternal federations. Such affiliations meant larger memberships, a further expansion of fraternal activities and improvements in their insurance benefits.

The earliest Polish fraternal societies were established at the end of the Civil War. Those in New York city lasted but a short time but two associations formed in Chicago were more enduring. One, the Saint Stanislas Kostka Fraternal Aid Society, was organized to help fund the construction of a first Polish parish in the Windy City, while a second, *Gmina Polska* (Polish Commune), concerned itself with patriotic matters. The rivalry between the two groups was both interesting in itself and significant in a broader sense in helping shape the future development of Polonia, both locally and nationally.[22] Thus, the members of the Saint Stanislas Kostka Society succeeded eventually in building their parish, and in time similar local associations formed to cooperate with parishes in other parts of the country. In 1873, they together with a number of priests and lay activists established the very first nationwide federation of fraternal groups, the Organization of Poles in America (*Organizacja Polska w Ameryce*).

Two men were chiefly responsible for the federation. One, a priest in Detroit named Theodore Gieryk, had issued a call in the Fall of 1873 to bring together Catholic parish societies from around the country. At approximately the same time, a newspaper editor operating in Missouri, John Barzynski, published his own appeal for an organization of Poles in America, to which approximately 360 people responded applying for membership. The two men were soon working together, with Barzynski acceding to Gieryk's view that the new federation would require the support of the Polish Catholic clergy in order to succeed. The founders and their friends held their first meetings in Detroit in July 1874 and there they decided on a new official name for their fledgling federation; instead of "Organization of Poles in America," Gieryk's motion was approved to retitle their group "Polish Roman Catholic Union in America." Barzynski thereupon agreed to transfer the headquarters of his newspaper, renamed *Gazeta Katolicka,* to Detroit where it became the Roman Catholic Union's official voice.

Soon after, the original leadership team heading the society changed hands. Entering the picture was John Barzynski's older brother, Vincent. A priest of the Polish Resurrectionist order, he had served initially in its Texas mission before arriving in Chicago in 1873 to become pastor of Saint Stanislas Kostka parish, the same church originally supported by the Saint Stanislas Kostka fraternal. The Rev. Barzynski shared Gieryk's view that the Union be a strictly Catholic federation but his determined and autocratic style of operation soon caused Gieryk and other clerical members to withdraw, leaving him the unchallenged force dominating the PRCUA for the next quarter of a century, that is, until his death in 1899 at the age of 61.

The stated aims of the PRCUA were ambitious and included the building of schools and hospitals under religious auspices throughout Polonia. Lacking the resources to realize them, the Union gradually became inactive until it revived in the mid 1880s in response to the birth of another federation of Polish societies in America, the patriotic and secular Polish National Alliance. One major achievement was recorded by the PRUCA under the leadership of its President, the Rev.

Leopold Moczygemba. Moczygemba, founder of the Panna Maria colony, was able to secure Papal approval for a Polish theological seminary in the United States. This institution opened its doors in Detroit in 1885 under the direction of the Rev. Joseph Dombrowski and in 1894 relocated to the outlying community of Orchard Lake, Michigan.[23]

Founded in 1880, the Polish National Alliance of the United States of North America was itself the product of a series of efforts by members of the political emigration to unite the local Polish community societies scattered about the country into a durable patriotically-oriented movement. The first such local society had been the *Gmina Polska* group in Chicago. From the start a rival of both the Saint Stanislas Kostka fraternal and the parish headed by the Rev. Barzynski, the *Gmina* promoted the construction of its own church, one built only a few blocks away and named in honor of the Holy Trinity. In the *Gmina's* ranks were Polonia's early nationalist leaders, including Wladyslaw Dyniewicz, publisher of Chicago's first successful Polish newspaper, *Gazeta Polska,* and a number of the founders of the Polish National Alliance, Max Kucera, that organization's first President, Stanislas Kociemski, its first Treasurer and Frank Gryglaszewski, its second Censor.[24]

While the *Gmina's* proposals to form a patriotic federation had come to nothing in the early 1870s, the growth in the number of local Polonia societies having a nationalist orientation, along with the increasing size of the immigrant population, made the idea increasingly practical by the end of the decade. This effort would in fact lead to the founding of the Polish National Alliance.

However, the explanation for the PNA's birth rests not only with the changes going on inside Polonia but with the impact of the continuous interaction between members of the various patriotic societies in America and political exiles in Switzerland, among them Agaton Giller (1831-1887), a leading figure from the 1863 insurrection. Several "American" activists wrote to Giller and his colleagues seeking their advice in proceeding to unite Polonia politically. In 1879 Giller responded to Henry Kalussowski in a thoughtful essay entitled "The Organization of the Poles in America," a work first published in Austrian-ruled Galicia and reprinted thereafter in the United States.

Giller urged the immigrants to unite for reasons having to do with both the cause of Poland's independence and their own individual well-being. Calling upon them to form publicly and to reject conspiratorial activities and violence, Giller linked the immigrants' integration into American society with their enhanced ability to work for Poland. His sensible and moderate counsel was clearly geared to appeal to the immigrants' instincts and indeed it had a salutary impact upon the thinking of the future founders of the Alliance:

> Because the Polish emigration in America constitutes an undeniably great force, it should be the task of those who are motivated by true patriotic feelings to direct this force, so our Fatherland's cause will be presented to its best advantage (in America)...
> In what way can we best direct the realization of Poland's cause? Through organization, we reply, since it is only through organization that our scattered immigrants can be unified. Only organized work will enable us to channel their concerns so that individual efforts (on Poland's behalf) will not be wasted, but rather consolidated for the good of our fatherland...
> Having become morally and patriotically uplifted by the fact that we have unified ourselves, the major task before a Polish organization must be to help our people attain a good standard of living in America. For, when the masses of Poles, simply by their very presence in the country, reflect the good name of Poland to all whom they meet, they will be providing an enormously important service to Poland. In time, this service will be even greater as Poles begin to exert influence upon the political life of the United States.[25]

Not long after the appearance of the essay, several emigre activists in Philadelphia responded to an appeal from one of their number, Julius Andrzejkowicz, a locally prominent chemist and businessman, to found a Polish National Alliance reaching out to Polonia on the basis of Giller's principles. Formed on February 15, 1880 at Andrzejkowicz's office, the Alliance and its aims were favorably received throughout the country over the next few months. In September 1880 the organization held its first national convention in Chicago with fourteen delegates representing seventeen different societies in attendance. There they approved the Alliance's constitution and elected its first officers.

In its constitution, the Alliance set forth its cause, that of leading the immigrant community in working for the homeland's independence "by whatever peaceful means possible." But in its statement of basic aims, the goals of the Alliance were set forth more prosaically, in accord with Giller's advice. Thus, the Alliance promised:

1. to lay the proper foundation for the construction of institutions dedicated to the material and moral advance of the Polish immigration in America, by creating a permanent fund under the Alliance's control. Institutions to be aided by the Alliance include Polish settlement houses, schools, educational training facilities, reading rooms, shelters for the sick, and industrial firms owned by Poles located in areas of Polish immigrant settlement.
2. to care for the needs of the Polish immigration in America;
3. to strengthen the immigrants politically as American citizens by establishing a Polish newspaper and to make contacts with the American press in defense of Polish concerns;
4. to commemorate anniversaries honoring the Polish homeland.[26]

To further broaden the appeal of the new Alliance, its organizers prudently heeded Giller and his fellow exiles' advice to adopt a respectful posture toward the Roman Catholic Clergy, although membership was extended to include non-Catholics. Seizing upon this decision, the Rev. Barzynski and his PRCUA followers moved quickly to brand the Alliance as "irreligious." Indeed, from 1880 through the next two decades, a sometimes bitter fight raged in Polonia between the Polish Roman Catholic Union and the Alliance, a conflict of rhetoric whose greatest apparent consequence was to hold down membership in both organizations at the same time that it deepened militant feelings in each camp.[27]

Branded as anti-Catholic if one joined the Alliance and anti-Polish if he entered the Roman Catholic Union, the ordinary immigrant chose to stay clear of the line of fire. And while each organization set up its own insurance program to bring in new members, such benefits were not in themselves especially attractive in a Polonia whose members were by and large quite young and who in many cases planned to return to Poland after having saved whatever they could in America. Thus, in 1886, six years after the formation of the Alliance, membership was still less than 300; the Polish Roman Catholic Union for its part was hardly much better off, with fewer than 500 individuals in its ranks. This in an immigrant population with perhaps 600-700 thousand members.

By 1895, in a Polish community including some 1.5 million people, the Alliance included only about 7,500 members to some 8,750 in the Union. Only in 1900, with the general cessation of hostilities and after both fraternals had changed their by-laws to admit women to full membership did the two organizations begin to take on the character of mass membership movements. By then, in a Polonia of two million souls, the Alliance could count 28,400 members to approximately 11,000 for the Roman Catholic Union. Even then the two fraternals combined included but two percent of the immigration in their ranks.

During these early years, while the overwhelming majority of Poles directed their energies to the task of establishing themselves in the new land and sending whatever funds they could muster to their families in the old country, Polonia's organizational activists nonetheless continued to devote considerable efforts in realizing their ideological missions. Thus, as early as the year 1886, the founder of the still embryonic Alliance, Andrzejkowicz, journeyed to Switzerland where he established direct ties with the emigre forces there. When he returned home Andrzejkowicz persuaded his colleagues to sponsor fund raising activities to support Polish resistance to foreign rule. Indeed, at the Alliance's 1887 convention, its delegates approved a resolution to transform the fund appeal, named *Skarb Narodowy* (national fund), into an integral part of the fraternal's activities by including it into its constitution. So caught up with enthusiasm for the independence cause was the Alliance that it even renamed its leadership the "central government" *(Rzad Centralny)* of the emigration in its service to the homeland.

While these initiatives met with predictable resistance from Barzynski and his followers in the clerical camp, they did represent a renewed interest in support of the patriotic cause in America, something that had been dormant since the disappearance of Kalussowski's Polish Central Committee during the American Civil War years. Moreover, they coincided with developments in Poland, where interest in the patriotic cause was on the upswing, and in Switzerland.

There, the exiles had established a Polish national museum in the small mountain town of Raperswil in the Canton of St. Gallen around 1870, to preserve the memory of independence following the crushing of the January uprising. Led by Giller, Wladyslaw Plater, and Zygmunt Milkowski, the latter the intellectual force behind the group after Giller's death, the emigres in 1887 organized the *Liga Polska* (Polish League) to promote their cause. (It was indeed the same Milkowski, writing under the pseudonym of T.T. Jez, who in 1886 authored the pamphlet *On Active Resistance and the National Fund*. Though this work was addressed primarily to the homeland, it also served as a blueprint outlining Polonia's future role in the struggle for independence. The plan was the one Andrzejkowicz would carry back with him to America.)

In actuality, the *Liga Polska* would itself serve as but a transitional force. For one thing, the tiny Swiss exile group, composed of the aging veterans of the 1863 insurrection was in no position to lead the struggle in partitioned Poland. Indeed, by the late 1880s activists of the new generation in the homeland were busy formulating new plans of their own and organizing into various formations to promote the independence cause. No fewer than three such movements merit mention here. One was the Polish Socialist Party, formally founded in Paris in 1892 and established the next year in Warsaw but active in various ways from the early 1880s. The socialists, who would later come under the influence of Jozef Pilsudski (1867-1935), combined in their program a commitment to the advancement of the industrial working class with an interest in restoring national independence, by revolution if necessary. As Pilsudski would later put it, "a Polish socialist must strive for the homeland's independence--independence is a condition characteristic of socialism's victory in Poland."[28]

A second force with a mass membership appeal was the Polish peasant movement. Born in Austrian-ruled Galicia in the 1880s, the peasant movement was largely the work of two competing activists, the priest Stanislaw Stojalowski and the journalist Boleslaw Wyslouch. In 1895 a unified peasants party came into existence, committed to the improvement of the material and cultural conditions of the enormous and impoverished rural population. Perhaps the Galician party's main contribution to Poland's national development was in its leaders' insistence that the peasants participate actively in political matters and work for the broad democratization of public life. These themes were to become the foundation of the thinking of Wincenty Witos (1874-1945), one of the movement's early authentic peasant leaders and after the First World War Poland's Prime Minister on three separate occasions.[29]

The third and most important political movement to emerge in the wake of the *Liga Polska* was, however, the National League *(Liga Narodowa)* which formed in partitioned Poland in 1893 under the leadership of Roman Dmowski (1864-1939). Indeed, with the National League, which gradually won supporters in all three zones of partitioned Poland while operating as a secret society, the headquarters of nationalist activities soon shifted from Switzerland, with Raperswil coming to serve as but a point of contact linking the American emigration to the homeland.

Under Dmowski, the National League gave Milkowski's idea of "active resistance" a special twist in meaning. Where the venerable emigre leader had looked upon the need to plan systematically for insurrection against the partitioners, the League stressed the mobilizing of all classes of Poles into determined non-violent resistance against the German and Russian policies of cultural repression. Only by adopting the rigorous "spartan" ways of the Prussians, Dmowski argued, would the Poles preserve their national identity and gradually persuade the partitioners of the futility of occupation. Significantly, the League, in stressing the importance of building national solidarity across class lines and extending patriotic feeling to the peasants and urban working people, rejected the idea of cooperation with the non-Polish ethnic populations which had belonged to the pre-partition Polish state. This view, like the

League's perspective on revolution, placed it in sharp opposition to the socialists, who in fact were in accord with the Swiss-based *Liga Polska* on those concerns. Despite such programmatic departures from the Raperswil-based group however, the *Liga Narodowa* inherited its support thanks to both groups' deep hostility to socialism and Dmowski's nationalism. Indeed, the National League also became the prime beneficiary of the assistance American Polonia could mobilize in support of Poland's independence in the years to come, since groups such as the Polish National Alliance looked to the *Liga Polska* for counsel on Polish matters.

There were several other reasons why Dmowski and his supporters would continue to enjoy support in Polonia after 1893. Aside from his stress upon non-violent resistance as the most promising means of eventually gaining independence, a position which resonated well in America, Dmowski's commitment to social uplift and work with the peasant population and his identification with Catholicism in helping shape Polish culture were greatly appreciated by the emigration in the United States and served to distinguish the National Democrats, the political party that eventually grew out of the conspiratorial and secret *Liga Narodowa,* from the socialists.

Andrzejkowicz, whose thinking on such matters was influential within the Alliance in the 1880s, put the matter quite well. In his observations written during his travels in Europe and published regularly by the Polish National Alliance newspaper, Andrzejkowicz declared:

> A Polish national league is absolutely necessary for the purpose of morally directing and intellectually developing our young generation, to protect it from anarchism and nihilism. ... This league would unite all into a national brotherhood, into one body. ... The systematic and theoretical powers of Polish national identity will thus turn to dust and ashes all the great superstitions of the past, based upon differences in class, caste and religion..."[30]

The Alliance's decision to establish an ongoing national fund drive, *Skarb Narodowy,* in support of the *Liga Polska* also marks an historic moment in the annals of Polonia. From this time, Polonia's commitment to Poland would have a financial character, whether fund raising efforts were directed toward humanitarian or political ends. Over the succeeding 25 years, that is, until the funds in the *Skarb Narodowy* were transferred to Poland in 1913, approximately $60,000 was generated by the Polish National Alliance and its allies in the patriotic camp on behalf of the independence cause.[31]

Predictably, the Alliance's actions met opposition from the Reverend Barzynski and the clerical camp. Best illustrating the problem was his forming in 1894 of a new Polonia organization named, interestingly, the Polish League *(Liga Polska)*. The League, which received its initial backing from the clergy and the Polish Roman Catholic Union, asserted a set of aims that were certainly sound -- uniting Polonia to realize an assortment of objectives to benefit the immigrant community, including the establishment of Polish schools and hospitals. It also included in its program the idea of raising money for the Polish independence cause, thus taking over the operation of the *Skarb Narodowy* from the PNA.

At first, many within the Alliance (including a number of the fraternal's national officers) reacted positively to the declared principles of the Polish League. But fears that the League would be dominated by Barzynski and his followers, along with some ill-chosen words by one of its prime movers, the millionaire philanthropist Erasmus Jerzmanowski, caused the Alliance to reverse its position. (Jerzmanowski was reported to have said that with the Polish League's formation the Polish National Alliance could then concentrate its activities upon the sale of burial insurance, a view that could not help but rankle the officers of an organization which saw itself as first and last patriotic in character.)

Thus, while many PNA members were present at the opening session of the League's first convention in Chicago, most declined to join and thus helped bring about its rapid demise. So ended the first attempt to build a unified Polonia movement committed at least in part to the Polish independence cause -- a casualty of distrust between the leaderships of the two rival fraternal organizations.[32]

There were, nonetheless, other occasions when the organizations of Polonia did succeed in cooperating on Poland's behalf before 1900. One noteworthy example came in 1899 when representatives of nearly every Polonia group gathered in Chicago in response to news that the Tsar of Russia had called an international peace conference to meet in the capital of the Netherlands. There, they drafted a memorial addressed to President William McKinley, urging the United States government to bring up the Polish question at the conference and declaring the issue of the partitioned homeland nothing less than a continuing threat to international peace and stability. The memorial was then personally presented to the President in Washington, D.C. by John Smulski and Peter Rostenkowski. Unfortunately, the effort came to nothing when the Russian representatives refused to include the Polish issue in the agenda. (The memorial itself is included in part in the Appendix of this work.)

Another, earlier, example of cooperation within the early Polonia community came in 1887 when a number of PNA and PRCUA activists helped establish the first Polish Falcons group in America. This society, modelled after an already flourishing movement in the homeland, was dedicated to promoting physical fitness activities and patriotic feeling among young men and women in the immigrant community. In 1894, four such Falcons groups (or "nests" in the terminology still used by the organization) established what they called in English the Alliance of Polish Turners in America. (The term "Falcon" was kept in the Polish language name of the movement, *Zwiazek Sokolow Polskich w Ameryce*). Within a decade the Falcons would embrace nearly 5,000 young men and women members, with more than 25,000 individuals in its ranks by 1914. In addition to continuing its physical exercise, sports and patriotic education activities the Falcons Alliance became the chief sponsor of military preparations for a Polish-American army ready for actual combat in Europe on behalf of Poland's restoration.[33]

The late 1880s and 1890s witnessed the birth and development of a number of other Polish American organizations, a sure sign of the vitality of the rapidly growing immigrant community. In 1889, the Polish Singers' Alliance was established in Chicago. This Alliance, whose organizers sought to elevate choral singing in the community by providing member groups with secular and patriotic music in addition to church song, soon grew into a national movement, contributing much to Polonia's cultural and recreational life. In 1890, a new fraternal association seeking to unite the PNA and the PRCUA came into being, the Polish Union in America *(Unia Polska w Ameryce)*, headquartered at first in Minnesota, later in the East. In 1895, dissatisfied members of the Polish Roman Catholic Union in Milwaukee broke away from the PRCUA to establish the Polish Association in America *(Stowarzyszenie Polakow w Ameryce)*, a fraternal that would grow by 1914 to include more than 10,000 members, most of them in Wisconsin. Another, the Cleveland-based Alliance of Poles also began in 1895, having seceded from the PNA.

Along with the Falcons, the most significant new organization during this early period in Polonia history was the Polish Women's Alliance *(Zwiazek Polek)*, created in Chicago between 1898 and 1899. While women had played a notable role in the early development of both the Polish National Alliance and the PRCUA, they had been thwarted in gaining equal membership status. At last, following the PNA's refusal to grant women equal membership rights *(rownouprawnienie)* at its September 1899 convention, a decision it rescinded in March 1900 at an extraordinary convention called for just that purpose, a number of women activists formally established their new Alliance. Committed to "the preservation of the Polish national identity in America, the upholding of the Polish ideals among the youth through its educational formation in the history and literature of Poland and the maintaining of continued contact with the homeland," the Polish Women's Alliance would include more than 15,000 persons by the First World War. The Women's Alliance experienced continued growth in the next three decades and by the 1950s the organization brought together more than 80,000 members, making it the third largest Polonia federation in the country.[34]

By 1900, in short, Polonia was in a position to play an important role on Poland's behalf, thanks in large measure to the development of its institutional life. By the turn of the century, a number of voluntary associations had formed to complement the activities of the hundreds of Polish parishes operating at the neighborhood and local community level, the scores of Polish language newspapers and periodicals and the uncounted numbers of businesses catering to Polish immigrant clienteles. Four organizations were already, or would soon, be assuming particular significance in focusing Polonia opinion on the key issues of the day, namely the Polish National Alliance, the Polish Roman Catholic Union, the Polish Falcons Alliance and the Polish Women's Alliance--all then headquartered in the "windy city" of Chicago, already the "capital" of the rapidly growing Polish immigration in the United States.

In addition, these four nationally-oriented movements were augmented by a plethora of smaller Polish ethnic organizations of varying sizes, ideological orientations and regional bases. Among these were a large number of smaller and regionally-oriented fraternals, many of which had come about due to dissatisfaction with one of the national organizations.

By 1900 still other organizations were flourishing. These included the Polish Singers' Alliance, the Polish Youth Alliance, the Polish Socialist Alliance in America (the U.S. branch of the movement headed by Pilsudski in Poland), and the Alliance of Polish Armies, an association of local young people's groups whose members enjoyed participating in patriotic commemorations dressed in often lavish military costumes celebrating Poland's past glories and aspirations. Later, another significant movement in this category would be the independent Polish National Catholic Church led by Prime Bishop Francis Hodur and centered in Scranton, Pennsylvania.

Together, all these many and varied voluntary organizations together possessed only modest memberships in 1900, less than 100,000 individuals in all in a Polonia of nearly two million souls. Yet their officers, national and local, together with the clergy and the editors of the Polish language press constituted by then the unchallenged leadership of the immigration. And thanks to Polonia's success in avoiding religious frictions following Barzynski's death (aside from the cases of the Polish National Catholics and the Socialists), the passing of time witnessed not only the establishment of a firmly settled Polish population in America but one whose members were increasingly inclined to participate in Polonia organizational life. By 1914, on the eve of the outbreak of the great war in Europe, total membership in the four leading Polish fraternals alone would surpass 220,000 in a Polonia embracing at least three and one-half million people.

The first six decades of Polish migration to America thus laid the foundations that would define ethnic community life and popular attitudes toward Poland for years to come. Already by the turn of the century, a fair number of immigrants had come to accept the proposition that Polonia had a mission to assist the homeland and a number of voluntary associations had formed to champion this cause to an ever wider audience.

With the outbreak of World War I in 1914, Polonia would be called upon at last to make a first massive contribution to the causes of Poland's independence and the relief of its suffering people. In their responses to these calls, Polonia's members would not be found wanting.

II. Polonia and Poland's Rebirth 1900-1918

The story of the Polish immigration in the United States of America up to the end of the nineteenth century is one of rapid population growth along with the more gradual rise of a national network of local ethnic voluntary associations - including hundreds of parishes, fraternal societies, cultural groups and newspapers. These trends would continue up to the middle of 1914 and the outbreak of the First World War, which, for all practical purposes, would herald the end of unrestricted immigration to the United States from Europe.

But Polonia's political development after 1900 would not continue along the lines characterizing the community's evolution during the previous three decades. This change was due to the incidence of substantial societal unrest in the partitioned homeland, which disrupted the situation prevailing in the Polish territories after the suppression of the great January uprising of 1863-1864.

Beginning in 1900, the German government which ruled the western portions of Poland initiated a new program to denationalize the local population. The region had already weathered nearly thirty years of Germanization during which the Catholic Church had been repressed, German colonization in the territories systematically promoted and severe restrictions imposed upon the Poles in their attempts to purchase land. In addition, the German language had been made the official language of school instruction. Up to 1900 only religion was still permitted to be taught in Polish, a tradition that ended abruptly with the promulgation of new edicts from Berlin.

Student resistance to the ban on religious instruction in Polish (manifested by their refusal to answer questions their teachers put to them in the German language) began in the town of Wrzesnia, east of Poznan. This first students' "strike" was brutally suppressed by local school authorities, an action that brought international attention to the incident. In Polonia, the press gave enormous coverage to the story and many protest meetings were held around the country.

In German-ruled Poland, the authorities' actions to impose the language policy at first appeared to work. But six years later, student opposition surfaced once again but on a massive level and in hundreds of schools in the region. Eventually, more than ninety thousand students in some 1,600 schools participated in the strikes, which reached their peak in 1906 and 1907 in the wake of disturbances occurring in the neighboring Polish provinces under Russian rule. The resistance was finally broken only after the German authorities threatened to withhold their diplomas from the strikers.[1]

In the Polish lands under Russian rule, opposition to the tsar had been led by the socialists from the 1890s on and generally took the form of factory work stoppages in a region undergoing rapid industrialization. Russia's disastrous war against Japan in 1904 deepened popular resentment against the empire, since thousands of Polish soldiers were dispatched to the Far East to fight in what was, for them, a meaningless conflict. On January 22, 1905, "Bloody Sunday," a peaceful workers' manifestation in the imperial capital of Saint Petersburg (later Leningrad) was violently dispersed, an action that threw the entire country into chaos and for a time threatened the very existence of the old regime.

In Poland, a general strike commenced soon after, and even following its settlement an atmosphere of instability punctuated by numerous acts of violence persisted throughout the region. On May 1, 1905 workers' demonstrations in Warsaw led to the deaths of 45 persons; in the weeks that followed life in the city was plagued by guerrilla warfare and strikes. Moreover, the crisis soon extended to the great textile center of Lodz and to other cities and by the end of the year some 1.3 million people had taken part in work stoppages to protest their conditions. In turn, they were backed by strikers who joined with them in both the German and Austrian ruled partitions. School strikes also occurred in "Congress" Poland in opposition to the requiring of Russian as the language of instruction.[2]

These developments in the homeland generated militant feelings inside American Polonia as well. Already, at an extraordinary meeting of the Board of Directors of the Polish National

Alliance in November 1905, a draft resolution was approved calling upon all "in the Polish colonies in America without regard to personal or party views to immediately and wherever possible convene general meetings at which to mark their solidarity" with the motherland.

As the historian Andrzej Brozek, has noted, "the text of the resolution contained a passage interesting from the point of view of the evolution of the ties between Polonia and Polish society..."

> We, Polish men and women, born in the territories of the old Polish republic, Lithuania and Ruthenia, and sons and daughters of immigrants from those territories, born in or naturalized citizens of this country, deeply moved by the news coming from that land of tears and despair, a land with which we are linked by blood, common language, faith, culture and heart, unite spiritually with the fighting and suffering Polish nation in the territories of the Polish Kingdom and pay our highest respects to our compatriots.[3]

By year's end, a Polonia-wide National Committee, headed by President Marian Steczynski of the Polish National Alliance had taken shape in Chicago to raise funds in support of independence activists in Poland, mainly by financing their propaganda efforts. Here, the efforts of the fraternals, whose leaders generally inclined toward Dmowski's National Democrats in Poland, were spurred on by the competing actions of the Polish Socialist Alliance in America, headed by Aleksander Debski. In all, perhaps $40,000 was raised in the drive.

The events inside the German and Russian-ruled partitions between 1900 and 1907 were critical in shaping the direction of patriotic activism in both Poland and in Polonia in the years ahead. In Poland itself, national feeling intensified, as patriotic activists focused upon the defense of the Polish language, religious traditions, and laborers' rights to better wages and working conditions. In the process, both the Socialists and their rivals, the National Democrats grew in stature as genuine proponents of political change. Over the next few years the two political groups, though sharply at odds on many issues and led by men, Pilsudski and Dmowski, who deeply disliked one another, increasingly operated under a new assumption - that independence was a real possibility in the not too distant future. The year 1910 represented an early climax in this movement towards liberation. It marked the five hundredth anniversary of the great Polish and Lithuanian military victory in 1410 at Grunwald over the Teutonic Knights, a particularly significant symbolic event in Poland's history. In Krakow, in the Austrian-ruled zone of Poland, thousands were permitted to gather from all three partitions to commemorate the triumph; there they were joined by representatives of their countrymen living abroad. Indeed, in the ancient capital of independent Poland, a great monument to King Wladyslaw Jagiello, the commander of the victorious forces at Grunwald, was unveiled and dedicated. At the same time, a new national anthem, "Rota" (The Oath), composed especially for the occasion by Feliks Nowowiejski, with verses provided by the poet Maria Konopnicka, was sung. Its words served to underscore the determination to resist Berlin's efforts to eradicate the Polish heritage:

> We'll hold our land our fathers' land, we'll keep alive our language... Our children shall not German be for this is Polish land. We'll keep our precious holy sod, do help us now O God![4]

In Polonia, the crisis in partitioned Poland and the rise in ethnic militancy temporarily benefited the socialists, since they had been the most enthusiastic in actively supporting their comrades in 1905 against Tsarist rule. But even after Russian imperial power in the Congress kingdom was restored, the socialists' position in America continued to improve, thanks to the arrival of several thousand political emigres filled with fire for the independence cause. Many were soon active in Polonia's organizations. Perhaps their most dramatic success occurred within the ranks of the Polish Falcons Alliance, which after 1905 increasingly defined itself as a paramilitary movement preparing for combat in Europe on Poland's behalf. The very motto chosen by the Falcons in these years, *Czyn zbrojny* (direct military action for the homeland), reflected this militancy and represented a notable shift away from the Falcons' traditional program stressing physical fitness activities and sports for young people. Indeed in the First World War, the Falcons' detachments would become the nucleus of a "Polish Army from America" recruited to serve in Europe on the Allied side. Within the Polish National Alliance, by then Polonia's largest fraternal, important changes also occurred. The Alliance had proclaimed itself the leader of the Polish independence cause from its beginnings in the 1880s and early on identified its aims with those of the *Liga Polska* and its successor, the *Liga Narodowa*. In the late 1890s and into the first years of the new century, the Alliance had made other initiatives to lead Polonia, but with mixed results. One involved its attempt to unite Lithuanian and Ruthenian immigrants into a federation backing a restored Polish commonwealth. That effort, however, went nowhere; those immigrant communities were already developing their own sense of organizational and national identity separate from the old pre-partition Polish-Lithuanian state to which their forefathers had been part and they rejected the Alliance's overtures.

Another strategy also seemed promising at first, one aimed at forging a broad front between the Alliance and the various youth-oriented and nationalistic organizations that had come into being in Polonia since the late 1880s. These included the Falcons Alliance, the Alliance of Polish Young People, the Singers Alliance, and the Alliance of Polish Armies. Yet another possible ally was the Polish Women's Alliance, its members for the most part in their twenties and thirties and their ideology very similar to that of the PNA.

In 1900, the PNA succeeded in forging a coalition with three of the youth-oriented Alliances, the Falcons, the Polish Young People, and the Singers. But this effort, the Confederation of Young Poland, proved ephemeral as members in each organization argued that the coalition would soon mean the loss of their separate identities. Still, the Polish National Alliance continued to promote the idea and at last the effort brought some return. In the Summer of 1905, the delegates at the Falcons convention voted to enter the PNA as an autonomous "department" or division *(wydzial)*, in return for substantial financial assistance for their youth activities and a promise from the Alliance of publicity through its extensive system of local lodges and its official weekly publication, *Zgoda*. Within the PNA, the Falcons' action was greeted as a first step in its efforts to unite all the youth groups into a solid all-Polonia federation working under its leadership with the National Democratic movement in Europe.[5] But the Alliance-Falcons merger proved short-lived and with this setback the entire plan eventually collapsed. Within the Falcons' organization, especially among its members in the eastern section of the country, opposition to the 1905 agreement quickly surfaced out of fear of absorption into the much larger Alliance, whose own ranks included members in all age categories. Falcons militants, some of them socialist newcomers, also questioned whether they could long continue their paramilitary training exercises as a PNA affiliate.

In September 1906, the first schism in the movement occurred as a group in Connecticut seceded from the Alliance and set up its own "Union of Polish Falcons." This new organization had a strongly pro-socialist orientation, a factor which may have contributed to its inability to persuade many other disenchanted activists from entering its ranks. Still, criticisms of the merger continued to be heard, despite the benefits the Falcons did realize from the PNA's considerable support. (Indeed, membership in the Falcons Department of the PNA rose from 1,800 to 4,700 between 1905 and 1909. When the organization was at last reunited in December 1912 it could claim between 12,000 and 15,000 members in all, an eightfold rate of expansion in only seven years.)[6]

Dissatisfaction among the Falcons continued to simmer and at the movement's July 1909 convention in Cleveland, misunderstandings between the PNA leaders in attendance and their erstwhile Falcons' partners boiled over into a bitter argument played out before the delegates. As a result, the President of the Falcons walked out of the meeting accompanied by his closest backers and together they set up yet another rival organization, colorfully named the "Free Falcons." While this new splinter movement drew a wider following than the socialist-led Union of Polish Falcons, it too remained far smaller than the PNA-backed Falcons Alliance.

But the events in Cleveland had a greater significance, for they demonstrated that the PNA's dream of uniting the patriotic forces in Polonia was not only unrealistic but counterproductive. In fact, and despite all its entreaties none of the smaller patriotic organizations followed the Falcons into joining the PNA. At last, this connection was itself dissolved in December 1912, as leaders of the two rival Falcons' organizations agreed in Pittsburgh to reunite on an independent basis. Heading the movement was a new President, Dr. Teofil A. Starzynski, a respected spokesman for the dissidents.

New Efforts to Unite Polonia, 1910-1914

While the Polish National Alliance failed to create a broad-based federation of Polonia organizations under its leadership, the giant fraternal remained committed to its goal of leading the community. An opportunity to once again realize this ambition came in 1910, in connection with the dedication of the great monuments in honor of Kosciuszko and Pulaski in Washington, D.C.

The story of the commissioning and construction of the monuments to the two heroes of the American revolutionary war and the eighteenth century efforts to save Poland from foreign domination had its origins in the early 1890s, when observances were proposed to commemorate the centennial anniversary of Tadeusz Kosciuszko's insurrection of 1794. At the same time, a Polonia committee in Chicago initiated fund raising efforts to erect a monument to Kosciuszko in the Windy City.

In 1900, Polish Americans in Ohio uncovered and publicized a long forgotten resolution of the American Continental Congress of 1779 to underwrite the costs of a statue to the father of the American cavalry, General Kazimierz Pulaski. That memorial had been approved only one month after Pulaski's death at the battle of Savannah on October 11, 1779 but never acted upon.

With the help of a U.S. Congressman from Indiana, Abraham Lincoln Brick, the Polish Americans secured Federal approval for a memorial in 1902. That action spurred Polonia activists around the country to discuss a fund drive to make possible a second monument in the nation's capital, this in honor of Kosciuszko, which soon won the support of the government. Following a successful fund raising campaign, sculptors were found to work on both projects.[7] The PNA headed the nationwide campaign to fund the Kosciuszko monument; local Alliance-led committees by this time had funded the statue in Chicago and others in Milwaukee and Cleveland besides.

At the same time, the Alliance leadership saw the benefits in transforming the unveiling ceremonies scheduled for the Spring of 1910 into an event which would be more than commemorative and which would also promote the cause of Polish independence. Thus the PNA decided to call a Polish national congress to bring together representatives of the many Polonia organizations expected for the dedication ceremonies and "a number of prominent representatives residing in the homeland" who were sent invitations to the event. Scheduled for the proposed meeting were discussions on a number of central issues facing partitioned Poland on the political, economic and cultural levels.

On May 11, 1910 thousands of Poles from across the country, their guests from the homeland and many American dignitaries witnessed the unveilings of the Pulaski and Kosciuszko monuments. Following the dedications, at which President William Howard Taft spoke, the congress proceeded as scheduled, without however, the presence of the clergy and the representatives from the Catholic fraternals. They viewed the meeting as but a PNA instrument to reassert its leadership claims in Polonia.

Delegates representing the Falcons, the Polish Women's Alliance, the Singers and a number of other nationalist organizations, along with the leaders of the Polish Socialist Alliance in America, were present and they, together with the many PNA activists in attendance, set out in earnest to discuss the major issues facing Poland.

Among the many thoughtful resolutions that were adopted at the congress was one in the political realm that proved to be quite controversial. Accordingly, the great powers were urged to recognize that "We Poles have the right to existence as an independent nation and we believe it is our sacred duty to strive for the political independence of our fatherland, Poland."[8]*

Soon after the congress, a number of Polonia activists travelled to Poland to participate in the 500th anniversary observances commemorating the victory at Grunwald. Leading the "Americans" were PNA President Steczynski and the past President of the Falcons, Casimir Zychlinski. In attendance were more than 10,000 uniformed Polish Falcons, together with several hundred members of paramilitary units who had organized secretly in Galicia after 1908. (These would become the nucleus of the Polish legions headed by Pilsudski and his associate, Jozef Haller, following the outbreak of the First World War.)

The events of 1910 underscored the rising expectations in both Poland and Polonia that dramatic changes in the country's partitioned status were likely to occur in the near future, at least partly due to the deepening antagonism between Russia and its former partners, Germany and Austria-Hungary. By this time too, a new generation of Poles had arisen for whom the 1863 uprising was literally "ancient history." To many of them, the message of Pilsudski and his commitment to taking direct action to speed the process of Poland's restoration was more appealing than the strategy espoused by Dmowski, who preferred the approach of gaining Russia's confidence and eventually greater freedom from its grasp.

In the Spring of 1912, a number of political groups identified with Pilsudski and the socialists in Galicia formed what they called the Provisional Commission of Confederated Independence Parties, including in their number a few groups with National Democratic leanings. The Commission promptly established contacts with its supporters in America and called upon them to raise money on its behalf. In the view of the Commission's leaders, war among the partitioners was imminent. Consequently the Poles needed to be prepared for the coming crisis.

---

* The resolutions of the congress can be found in full in the Appendix of this work.

The first opportunity for the Commission's American sympathizers to mobilize came in December 1912 in Pittsburgh, in conjunction with the reunification convention of the Falcons Alliance. Invited to the event were leaders from all the major Polonia organizations and representatives from both the Catholic clergy and the press. Immediately after the Falcons' conclave the Polonia representatives convoked a congress of their own, one which achieved what the PNA-sponsored meeting in Washington in 1910 had been unable to do in that practically every wing of the immigrant community was now present to consider how Poland's cause might be supported. Out of the day-long gathering came what was nothing less than the very first all-Polonia federation in the community's history, the Polish National Defense Committee (or *Komitet obrony narodowej--KON*).

The exigencies of time did not permit more than the creation of a steering committee for the new federation, with its top leaders given the responsibility of communicating secretly with the Galician Commission. Nonetheless, *KON's* general aims were made clear from the start. First and most important, the Committee sought to bring together all of organized Polonia, with the formal (though not actual) exception of only one organization, the schismatic Polish National Catholic Church (PNCC). In its ranks, *KON* could claim representatives from the "left" (the Socialists along with supporters of the PNCC), the conservatives (the Catholic clergy and its fraternal friends in the Polish Roman Catholic Union), and the nationalist "center" (the PNA, the Falcons, the Polish Women's Alliance and their allies).

Second, *KON* was decidedly anti-Russian and committed to a "direct action" (or military) resolution to Poland's problems, this in keeping with the thinking of Pilsudski, rather than Dmowski. Third, the Committee viewed Polonia as essentially a "reserve force" in the independence struggle, that is, as a fund raising arm in support of the Polish cause. Significantly, disagreements over all three of these points were soon to figure in *KON's* rapid decline.

At Pittsburgh, the socialists Aleksander Debski and Bronislas Kulakowski were ardent supporters of Pilsudski and enjoyed much influence in arguing for *KON's* creation. In this they

were backed by the militantly nationalistic Thomas Siemiradzki, editor of *Zgoda,* and a force in the Polish National
Alliance.[9] But following the Pittsburgh convention, the headquarters of the Committee were transferred to Chicago; there
under the chairmanship of Zychlinski, the new PNA President,
the moderate and conservative forces in Polonia more sympathetic to Dmowski than Pilsudski gained a dominant position in
KON. Moreover, following the withdrawal of the National
Democratic groups from the Provisional Commission of Confederated Independence Parties in Galicia, the conservatives in
particular became increasingly uncomfortable members within
the Polonia federation.

In June 1913, at *KON's* first plenary meeting in Chicago,
the vexing problem of the Polish National Catholic Church's
membership in the organization surfaced and served as the
justification for a walk-out by the clergy and the conservative
fraternals, leaving the PNA, the Falcons, and the Polish
Women's Alliance within the Committee alongside the socialists and the PNCC. Having withdrawn from *KON,* the Catholic
groups now formed their own patriotic action federation, the
Polish National Council, or *Rada Narodowa.*

In September 1913, the partisans of *KON* achieved their
final major success, at the twentieth *Sejm* (or convention) of the
Polish National Alliance in Detroit. At the convention, the
more than seven hundred delegates not only elected several
KON activists to the fraternal's executive board; they also approved a resolution to turn over the funds in the PNA *Skarb
Narodowy* to the Galician political commission, thus severing
the Alliance's historic tie with the National Democratic movement, a tie that went back to 1887.

KON's victory in Detroit proved ephemeral, however. The
following December, Ignacy Paderewski, in Milwaukee for a
piano recital, gave an interview to the local Polish Catholic daily
in which he questioned the aims of the Galician confederation.
Paderewski's widely distributed criticism had repercussions in
prompting the PNA to reconsider its own participation in the
Polish National Defense Committee. Indeed, after sending two
of its top leaders to Poland in the Spring of 1914 to make their
own on-site review of the situation, the Board of Directors of
the Alliance accepted their recommendation to withdraw from

KON. The Falcons and the Polish Women's Alliance soon also followed suit, the Falcons after a similar visit to Poland by their President.[10] Though unwilling to join the conservative Polish National Council, all three nationalist groups reasserted their commitment to Poland's independence. Thus, the PNA moved immediately to set up its own Independence Department *(Wydzial Niepodleglosciowy)* in support of the homeland, and eventually raised more than $170,000 for the cause. For its part, the Polish Women's Alliance organized a separate War Fund *(Fundusz Bojowy)*, while the Falcons based their political action campaign around their Kosciuszko Fund.

KON, thus shorn of its nationalist allies in Polonia, was left with but two significant member organizations, the Polish Socialist Alliance (that wing of the socialist movement in the Polish American community making the Polish cause rather than explicitly American working people's issues its top priority) and the dissident Polish National Catholic Church. Without a mass membership base any longer, *KON's* influence declined sharply. While it continued to issue several periodicals, most prominent among them *Wici* (The Messenger) edited by Kulakowski and an irregularly published English-language paper, *The Polish Cause,* a *KON* fund drive announced following the outbreak of the war was only modestly successful. Chaired by opera singer Marcelina Sembrich Kochanska, the effort was ignored or opposed by the major Polonia organizations. Most visible in New York, New Jersey and Connecticut, *KON* claimed few adherents elsewhere in Polonia. One estimate placed its size at 176 local committees in 1915, 222 active and 26 "shaky" local groups in 1917 and 186 active committees in 1918, with these circles including approximately 15-20 members each. In 1918, *KON* reported 6,934 members and 9,222 sympathizers nationally, compared to 126,000 PNA members in 1,697 lodges alone.[11] In all, the Polish National Defense Committee raised some $250,000 for its wartime causes, compared to approximately $10,000,000 gathered by the nationalist and conservative Polonia federations and the clergy.

From the outset, the Committee operated with two strikes against it. Thus, it was continually criticized as socialist and anti-Catholic. Furthermore, its support of the "Central Powers"

of Germany and Austria-Hungary against Russia made it sus-
pect to American government officials who, while neutral, favored the cause of Russia's chief allies, Britain and France.
Interestingly, Ignacy Paderewski, the unofficial representative
of the Polish National Committee headquartered in Switzerland, a group which identified with the Western Allies and
sought to be recognized in the West as the representative of
Poland's independence aspirations, experienced few difficulties
in presenting the Polish issue in the United States after 1914. In
sharp contrast, two *KON* emissaries from Europe, Artur Haus-
ner and Feliks Mlynarski were ordered to leave the United
States in 1915 on the grounds that they were foreign agents.

One reason for *KON's* problems was its lack of widely
recognized representatives to promote its aims. Aside from
Debski, who remained the head of the Socialists in America
during the War, the few other fairly well known *KON* partisans
were soon ousted from their posts as leaders in the nationalist
organizations and fell into relative obscurity. Thus, Siemiradzki, the editor-in-chief of the PNA newspapers at the time
of *KON's* founding was effectively "retired" from the Alliance
following his unsuccessful 1913 election bid to become Censor,
one of the two highest offices in the fraternal. Another powerful *KON* partisan, Witold Scibor-Rylski, Chief Physical Instructor of the Falcons, was expelled from that organization in the
Summer of 1914.

The conservative Polish National Council set up its own
headquarters in Chicago under the chairmanship of Auxiliary
Bishop Paul Rhode. The Council included in its ranks the
Polish Roman Catholic Union, the Polish Association of Amer-
ica centered in Milwaukee, the Chicago-based Polish *Alma
Mater* association (a youth-oriented Catholic group), the Polish
Union in America fraternal, the Polish Union of Priests in
North America, and several hundred parishes.

The Council took its name from a federation operating in
Poland aligned with Roman Dmowski's National Democratic
movement. At the same time it also represented the newest
effort by Polonia's clerical wing to unite the immigrant population, something which had been attempted unsuccessfully several times in the past, most notably in 1894 with the creation of
the Polish League.[12]

The Polish National Council also initiated its own campaign to raise funds under the name of the "National Treasury" and later set up its own publication, called *Free Poland* in its English language edition, to propagandize its aims. But the commencement of the World War in the Summer of 1914 temporarily paralyzed the Council, since events in Poland required a profound reassessment of the situation facing Polonia. After all, the conflict pitted the three partitioners of Poland against one another, Germany and Austria-Hungary versus Russia, with the homeland serving as the battlefield in their struggle. In Polonia, a few Falcons' militants urged young men to enlist immediately in Pilsudski's legion which was serving under Austrian command in Galicia, but this option was opposed by U.S. officials concerned that America's neutrality would be compromised by such an action. Although the Falcons and Polish National Alliance set up an officers' training program so that their contemplated Polish army would have its own officer corps, this plan was also short-circuited in Washington. Thus, the prudent course appeared to be one of adopting a "stand ready and wait" posture for the time being.[13]

The war soon saw fierce fighting on Polish territory and with it great havoc unleashed upon the civilian population. In these circumstances, the novelist and Nobel Laureate Henryk Sienkiewicz took the lead in calling for relief efforts for war victims from his residence in Lausanne, Switzerland. On October 2, 1914, fraternal and clergy leaders representing all elements of Polonia outside of *KON* met in Chicago to coordinate humanitarian efforts in America by setting up a new Polonia federation. Named the Polish Central Relief Committee *(Polski Centralny Komitet Ratunkowy, PCKR),* this group allied itself with the Polish general assistance committee in Switzerland. Within a short time, nearly every organization outside of *KON* and most of the parishes in Polonia had affiliated with the *PCKR,* which was chaired by PNA President Zychlinski.

The federation combined appeals for funds with efforts to make and collect clothing for shipment into the war zone. Especially active in the latter work were the women of Polonia, working through the fraternals and the parishes. Facing the *PCKR,* however, was one crucial problem; this involved the belligerents' refusal to permit ships carrying relief aid to reach their destination. Because of this stance, early support for what was widely seen as a seemingly hopeless cause was greatly undermined.

Nonetheless, the Polish Central Relief Committee continued to appeal for support, both from Polonia and the broader American population. A major breakthrough came at the end of 1915 when the Committee succeeded in persuading President Woodrow Wilson to proclaim January 1, 1916 a national Polish relief day around the country. This effort and others like it served not only to publicize the Polish cause but to build contacts between U.S. government authorities and Polonia representatives, of whom the most influential figure to emerge was John Smulski, a Chicago attorney, banker, political leader and an active member of the Relief Committee.

In the face of the United States' continuing neutrality, opinion in Polonia was plagued by division and apathy. *KON,* though weak in numbers, assertively promoted the cause of an independent future Polish state aligned with Hapsburg Austria-Hungary, a position then in accord with Pilsudski's views. But given the mood in America in favor of the Allied cause and against Germany, many Polish Americans had reason to be concerned about this stance. Polish independence would hardly be popularized in America if Polonia was identified with the aims of the Central Powers. In contrast, the *Rada Narodowa,* though linked with the National Democratic movement in Europe and Dmowski (by 1915 in Switzerland to form an erstwhile exile Polish government linked to Britain, France and Russia) was hard pressed to win much sympathy for that cause, given Polonia's traditional hatred of the tsarist regime.

In the Summer of 1916, *PCKR* leaders agreed on the need to go beyond charitable and humanitarian activities and into political and propaganda work. On August 17, a special body subordinate to the Relief Committee was set up, the National Department *(Wydzial Narodowy).* At its first planning meeting, on September 12, 1916, the National Department proclaimed its political position. Declaring that just as the Polish Central Relief Committee had succeeded in fostering solidarity in promoting Polonia's humanitarian work for Poland during its first two years of activity so also the *Wydzial Narodowy* alone possessed the capacity to represent Polonia's concerns on Poland's independence. Smulski was chosen to head the Department, with Casimir Sypniewski of Pittsburgh his deputy.

Through the remaining months of 1916, the National Department worked to make good its claim to speak for Polish Americans on the independence issue. A major opportunity to achieve this objective for the first time came late that Autumn. On November 5, 1916 the Emperors of Germany and Austria-Hungary issued a manifesto declaring their support for the creation of a "free" kingdom of Poland united with them and, presumably, to be carved out of the Russian-ruled partition after the war. The National Department moved quickly to denounce the statement as failing to meet Poland's independence aspirations. Repeating its claim to speak for Polonia, the *Wydzial Narodowy* asserted that Poland's fate was tied to the victory of Britain, France and Russia, the view of Dmowski and his committee. With more than five hundred local organizations throughout the country already in support of its efforts, not to mention the backing it counted on from the Polish fraternals and clergy, the National Department's position already carried considerable weight.

In January 1917, two major developments further raised the prospects of the National Department. Early in the new year, Dmowski proposed that his Polish National Committee be formally recognized by the Western Allies as the provisional government of the future independent Polish state. Ignacy Paderewski was then appointed to represent the Committee officially in the United States, although in fact he had already been busy in this work for some time.

On January 22, 1917 President Wilson explicitly and publicly endorsed Poland's independence for the first time when he declared, "I take it for granted statesmen everywhere are agreed that there shall be a united, independent and autonomous (sic) Poland" (after the war). His statement, coming only a few months after his narrow reelection victory in November 1916, was significant in implying that the United States expected to play an important role in future peace negotiations and at the time underscored his conviction in favor of national self-determination for all peoples under imperial rule. (It is possible that Wilson's meetings with prominent Polish and Polonia advocates of independence for their homeland also had some effect on his thinking.) In any event, Wilson's support for Poland's freedom constituted an extraordinary statement that would greatly advance its cause.[14]

In February 1917, the Tsar of Russia was forced to abdicate his throne in the face of widespread disillusionment over the Empire's failing war effort and its country's economic collapse. Promising the formation of a representative and constitutional system once the war was won, a new provisional government came into power; in March, this nationalistic and conservative regime went so far as to declare itself in favor of some type of independent Polish state, a position also taken by its socialist rivals in the Petrograd Soviet at the same time. Russia's change in policy, coming on the heels of Wilson's declaration and the earlier German and Austrian pronouncements thus set the stage for even more momentous developments in April.

Within Polonia, the atmosphere was electric with anticipation. President Starzynski had called an extraordinary convention of his militant Falcons organization, which was set to begin in Pittsburgh on April 1, 1917. The Falcons had already sent twenty-three men over the Canadian border several months before, there to begin secret officers' training programs in preparation for America's entry into the conflict. Several of these men now appeared, in uniform, at the convention. On April 2, President Wilson delivered his message to Congress calling upon the United States to issue a declaration of war against the Central Powers, a request that was approved four days later. On April 3, Paderewski appeared at the Falcons' conclave and there issued his call for Polonia to raise a force of one hundred thousand men, a "Kosciuszko Army," for service in Europe on the side of the Allied powers and under the authority of Dmowski's Polish National Committee:

> Do you think that I would be hasty to send you to battle, to desire your blood, to assign you the smallest pain, to tear you away from peaceful families? But if you must fight, then fight as befits free Poles -- fight for the recognition, respect and glory of the Polish name. Fight for the benefit of a united Poland, fight for the benefit of all things Polish here.
> If the war spreads then you will all go. If peace comes then no one will go... One should, nonetheless, anticipate events. In case conscription is introduced, at least two hun-

dred thousand American Poles will have to take up arms.
That large number of our youth's flower, separated and
divided throughout many units, will melt in the great American sea. Poles as befits Poles will perform miracles of bravery, but no one will know about it. Foreseeing the problem,
it is proper to do something about it today, at once, which
will help safeguard our identity.

I take the liberty to make a proposal: that the Polish
Falcons Alliance, which is the nucleus of the Polish Army,
send a telegram to President Wilson, offering him a one
hundred thousand man army, requesting that it be named
the "Kosciuszko Army." Whether the offer is accepted or
not, enroll proudly into that army and create a school for
officers... I will be the first to add my contribution to that first
school for Polish officers. Let's establish it on the high level
that it deserves.[15]

Suddenly, after nearly three years of waiting, America and
American Polonia were set to plunge into the conflict, although
Paderewski's Kosciuszko was not to be. The U.S. government
objected to its formation out of a concern that the country's
own recruitment efforts would be adversely affected if large
numbers of young Poles eligible for the U.S. armed forces were
siphoned away, along with individuals joining other nationality-
based armies of liberation then being talked about around the
country. However, on June 4, 1917 the government of France
announced its decision to form a separate Polish army on its soil
and invited Poles living in the United States, Canada and South
America to enlist into this force, along with Polish prisoners of
war captured from the ranks of the German army and Polish
immigrants in France and Belgium.

Already in July 1917, actual recruitment efforts had begun
under the direction of Frank Dziob, Chief Instructor of the
Polish Falcons Alliance and the leader of the group that had
earned officers' status in Canada, and John Zaucha, Chief
Scoutmaster of the Falcons. Dziob concentrated his activities in
the Middle West and Zaucha in the East. On July 25, 1917 the
Falcons formed their own Military Commission to cooperate
with the French government in sending volunteers to the front.
Problems did arise, however, in gaining an agreement from U.S.
authorities as to who in Polonia was eligible to enlist. Thus

while the government, as an ally of France, went along in principle with the decision, it withheld final approval of Polonia's recruitment plan until September 20, 1917. Only then was it announced that a satisfactory understanding had been achieved among all concerned parties.

Under the agreement, only foreign born Poles from the Russian zone who had not yet taken out their final citizenship papers and who had no dependents were permitted to enlist. All other Polish Americans were marked for duty in the American armed forces.

Two days later, the National Department formally recognized Dmowski's National Committee as the representative of the Polish people. It also energetically initiated recruitment efforts in setting up a Polish Military Commission, composed of Theodore Helinski of Chicago, a veteran PNA leader, Alexander Znamiecki of New York, a Paderewski confidante and Falcons President Starzynski. Recruiting stations throughout Polonia were then set up, with recruits scheduled for basic training at Fort Niagara on the Lake, Canada, their expenses and pay provided by the French government. Already, some 389 men had completed an officers' training program sponsored by the Falcons and PNA at the Alliance's School in Pennsylvania. This three month long program was created so that the contemplated Polish army would have its own military leadership in place when the forces were transported to Europe.

Polish Americans constituted a considerable component in the Polish "Blue Army" (from its distinctive uniform) in whose ranks more than 90,000 men eventually served. Initially under French commanders, the Army was placed directly under the authority of Dmowski's national committee in the Fall of 1918.

In all, 38,108 "Americans" actually applied for military service between the Fall of 1917 and January 1919, when recruitment activities ceased. Of these 22,395 were accepted and 20,721 saw duty overseas.[16] Given the extraordinary restrictions imposed by Washington upon Poland's recruitment activities and the fact that in these circumstances the volunteers were under no obligation to risk their lives, the number of Polish Americans who enlisted was impressive. Indeed, both Dmowski and Pilsudski, leader of the new Polish state whose independence he proclaimed in November 1918, were lavish in recognizing the effort's significance.[17] Dmowski, emphasized this in a speech in Detroit in August 1918 where he addressed more than nine hundred delegates representing Polonia at the first Congress of the Emigration, an event sponsored by the National Department. There, he pointed out that a number of Polish Americans had already given their lives for the Allied cause following their arrival in France and that their sacrifice underscored the commitment of Poles everywhere for independence:

> Our Polish Army already has played its part in the conflict and continues to play a part today... And I can tell you with satisfaction that other nations know this--that our forces were in the battle.[18]

By the war's end on the Western Front in November 1918, 206 members of the Polish Army (106 of them Polish Americans) had given their lives in battle for the independence cause. Another 862 men had been wounded, with fifteen individuals suffering permanent disablement. Such casualties may at first glance appear modest in a force counting some 90,000 men in six divisions, yet this was only due to the fact that the Poles happened to enter the war in what proved to be its final six months. Indeed, with the Blue Army now under the command of General Haller, the Poles were included in Marshall Foch's plans for a new offensive just as the general armistice was announced on November 11, 1918. Appropriately, Haller and his men were included with the American, British, French and Italian forces which marched under the Arch of Triumph in the Allied victory celebration.

Following the war and after lengthy Allied discussions over the procedures to be followed in permitting Haller's army to travel to Poland, about sixty thousand troops were transferred overland to the newly independent country, there to begin another chapter of service on the field of battle. Upon the Army's arrival in Warsaw in June 1919, Marshall Pilsudski greeted the men as "members of our soldierly family" who had returned to the homeland as "well-equipped comrades-in-arms, ready to join together in the common struggle." Throughout the rest of 1919 and into 1920, the Blue Army was merged into Poland's forces and its members took part in a number of actions on every one of Poland's fronts. Polish American dedication was especially evident during the Polish-Soviet War which reached its climax in August 1920. In all, some 55 officers and 2,100 soldiers gave their lives in battle during these campaigns, with 90 officers and 1,600 men wounded in the fighting.[19] Fittingly, Pilsudski, in bidding the Polish Americans farewell as they prepared to return home, expressed the nation's regard for their heroic willingness to sacrifice the abundant lives they had enjoyed in the U.S. in exchange for the dangers and discomforts of military service. By their efforts, he concluded, the Americans had renewed in blood the historic ties between Poland and the emigration.[20]

But Polonia's formation of the Polish American army represented only one of its achievements during the World War I period. Ongoing were the lobbying activities in Washington, by the National Department and its two chief spokesmen, Paderewski and Smulski, and their efforts in propagandizing the independence cause. The task was particularly difficult in as much as there was not a single Polish American elected representative to champion Poland's freedom in the nation's capital until March 1919, when John Kleczka, a Republican from Milwaukee entered the House of Representatives.

Throughout the war years, women in Polonia and the organizations they headed played a major, if generally unsung, role in mobilizing the community on the homeland's behalf. Thus, from 1914, for example, the leaders of the Polish Women's Alliance headed by its President, Anna Neumann, along with Emilia Napieralska, Stefania Chmielinska and others promoted fund raising work for both the independence cause and the war victims' needs. In this work, they were joined by women representatives from the other fraternals and the Polish parishes from around the country, including members of religious orders of women.

Women such as Agnes Wisla and Jozefa Rzewska of the Polish National Alliance and Maria Kulesza and Maria Korpanty of the Falcons were among those who served as energetic recruiters on behalf of the Polish American army once it began operations in the Fall of 1917. Polonia's women also responded with vigor to the appeal of Madame Helena Paderewska in February 1918 to form a unit of nurses called the "Polish White Cross" committed to serving on the Western Front along with the Blue Army regiments departing the United States. Following the war, yet another effort on Poland's behalf spearheaded by the young women of Polonia came with the creation of the Polish Grey Samaritans, a force of thirty individuals trained by the YWCA to serve in the hospitals and orphanages of the devastated homeland and to help in the distribution of food, clothing and medical goods being shipped to Poland under the auspices of the American Relief Administration directed by Herbert Hoover. These individuals made an extraordinary contribution to the homeland over nearly three years' time, often risking their lives by working in regions that had become battlefields in the Polish-Soviet War.[21]

In March 1918, the wartime efforts of Polonia underwent a major reorganization when the operations of the Polish Central Relief Committee, up to then the parent of the National Department, were subordinated to the Department for the duration of the conflict. From then onward, the *Wydzial Narodowy* was responsible for directing four distinct areas of Polonia activity -- political work headed by Paderewski and Smulski, military recruitment under the auspices of the Polish Military Commission, the Press Department which among other activities produced and distributed *Free Poland,* and the continuing relief program of the Polish Central Relief Committee, which to that time had collected some $5 million in goods for the homeland. Throughout, the National Department worked hard to maintain close contact with its more than five hundred local affiliates around Polonia.

Of particular significance was the Department's convocation, in August 1918, of what it called the Congress of the Polish Emigration (in Polish, *Sejm wychodztwa*). Organized to demonstrate Polonia's unity under Paderewski and Smulski and its identification with Dmowski's National Committee, the Congress brought together some 946 delegates who heard from both Dmowski and Paderewski and approved the great pianist-patriot's request to initiate a new $10 million fund drive to assist the homeland. This campaign eventually generated about $5.5 million, of which some $4.5 million was collected in its first fifteen months of operation. The Armistice, coming only ten weeks after the Detroit Congress, while a most welcome event, was a major factor behind the dissipation of the drive's momentum.[22]

In retrospect, the emigration congress marked the high water mark in the rising tide of Polonia unity in behalf of the Polish cause in the First World War years. The success in bringing together so many organizations and so diverse a representation of voices (only the Polish Socialist Alliance and *KON* were absent) was largely the work of Smulski, who had thrown himself wholly into the cause. Aside from the Congress' considerable achievements in rallying Polonia behind the National Department, the very effort to determine how to select delegates to the meeting set the pattern for similar federations in future years, in particular the Polish American Congress that formed in 1944. Thus, in 1918 the fraternals were awarded one delegate for every 500 members in their ranks, with each local parish and community entitled to a delegate representing the same number of people. One delegate for every 25,000 Poles estimated to reside in each state was also permitted. Moreover, throughout the Summer of 1918 serious efforts were made to hold elections to the *Sejm*. All these activities helped the National Department to strengthen its claim to be the "central and chief organization of the entire Polish emigration in America for Poland's independence." A resolution to that effect was approved unanimously at the conclave.

The executive leadership chosen at the *Sejm* to join Smulski to head the National Department included the leaders of Polonia's preeminent organizations. Casimir Zychlinski, President of the Polish National Alliance was elected Vice President, and Nikodem Piotrowski, a Chicago attorney and veteran leader in the Polish Roman Catholic Union selected its Treasurer. Another PRCUA leader was the journalist and educator, Stanislas Szwajkart, who became the organization's Secretary. The remaining positions on the Board of Directors were filled by fraternal leaders from the PNA, the PRCUA, the Polish Women's Alliance and the Falcons.

Only ten weeks after the *Sejm* adjourned World War I came to an abrupt halt with the proclaiming of an Armistice on the Western front on November 11, 1918; on that same day Jozef

Pilsudski declared Poland's independence in Warsaw and in so doing made his appeal to head the country while forcing Roman Dmowski, as head of the Paris-based Polish National Committee to yield his group's claims to national leadership. Poland's newly proclaimed independence hardly settled the critical territorial and boundary issues facing the country, of course. But these and many other matters would be left to Pilsudski to deal with, although Dmowski went on to provide substantial diplomatic services to Poland in defending its borders at the Paris Peace Conference.[23]

Paderewski himself left the U.S. for Warsaw in December 1918 declaring that he alone enjoyed the confidence of both President Wilson and Dmowski and thus was the one leader capable of guiding the country. On January 20, 1919 he assumed the posts of Prime Minister and Minister of Foreign Affairs. Pilsudski became Chief of State with responsibility for directing Poland's embattled armed forces. At Versailles, Dmowski struggled to win grudging Allied support for Poland's new borders, including access to the Baltic Sea through the great port of Danzig (after World War II, Gdansk). Back in the United States, Smulski lobbied energetically on behalf of Poland's cause; his efforts in Washington won from the Polish National Committee formal recognition as its U.S. representative until such time as Poland could establish its own diplomatic presence in the American capital.

Smulski also attended sessions of the Versailles Peace Conference by invitation of the Polish National Committee and travelled to Poland in the Summer of 1919 to review conditions there personally. By November of that year he was back in America to chair the second congress of the Polish emigration that was held in Buffalo, New York. There, after reporting on his work for Polonia, he told the delegates that the *Wydzial Narodowy* included more than 800 local citizens' committees; among its activities the organization had shipped some 10,000 packages of clothing valued at $2 million to the homeland along with another $1 million in food.

Already at the Buffalo conclave, however, enthusiasm for the National Department was on the wane. Smulski refused to accept the idea that the purposes of the Department had been realized; instead he argued, with Paderewski's blessing, that the federation should continue on in support of the new Polish state's interests in America. This perspective, reasonable to some, met with opposition from many others.

To Smulski's critics, the presence of official Polish diplomatic representation in America after June 1919 made the National Department a kind of unnecessary "fifth wheel." Pilsudski's prominence in the new Poland also revived the prospects of the Polish National Defense Committee and brought *KON* new prestige while at the same time adversely affecting the status of the National Department. There was also dissatisfaction with Smulski's personal leadership style and this surfaced at the convention of the Polish National Alliance in September 1921. There, the delegates resoundingly voted, 321-106, to withdraw the PNA from future participation in the Department.[24]

Their action was a serious blow to Smulski, who earlier that same year at the third congress of the Polish Emigration in Pittsburgh, had won approval to transform the National Department into a permanent organization in support of the new Polish republic. But fund raising activities continued to diminish, a sure sign that the federation's time had passed. (One noteworthy achievement merits mention here and involved the Department's care of some 370 Polish orphans who had come to this country from Siberia during the war. After the conflict, more than three hundred of these children were returned to Poland.)[25]

Within Polonia, the focus turned to the condition of the Polish American population and its concerns and in defending the community members against the rising activism of anti-immigrant groups throughout the country. These had already succeeded in pushing a severe immigration restriction bill through Congress in 1921. There was also worry about the maintenance of Polish language parishes in the face of policies undertaken by a number of assimilationist Roman Catholic bishops, including Archbishop Francis Mundelein of Chicago. A new slogan summed up the feeling of the early 1920s -- *Wychodztwo dla Wychodztwa*--Let the emigration look after its own concerns.

At the National Department's fourth conclave, in Cleveland in April 1923, 1,600 delegates were present--a great improvement from Pittsburgh, where only 560 representatives had attended sessions graced by Paderewski (by then in Swiss retirement following his brief tenure as Polish Prime Minister in 1919). Surprisingly, not a single Polish government official was in attendance, an amazing development considering the National Department's past record of service to the homeland. Prior to the Cleveland meeting, PNA President Zychlinski had organized a new federation of the leading fraternals, *Rada Polskich Organizacji w Ameryce* (the Council of Polish organizations in America), to coordinate Polonia's actions in dealing with its most pressing domestic concerns. Support for the new *Rada* was so strong that following the adjournment of the Cleveland Congress the National Department itself disbanded. (The next year, the new federation, renamed the Polish Welfare Council in America, *Polska Rada Opieki Spolecznej w Ameryce* was established in Detroit. *PROSA* focused entirely on the issues confronting Polonia in America but accomplished relatively little before also lapsing into inactivity. Without a central unifying mission, concern for Poland, it lacked a real reason for existence).

It has often been noted that following the First World War, Polish American financial support on Poland's behalf dropped precipitously, an indication of the allegedly limited extent of mass support for the homeland's cause. While contributions to the "Ten Million Dollar Fund" promoted by the National Department did decline dramatically in the months following the war's end, it should also be recognized that with Poland's achievement of independence its new government initiated appeals of its own for assistance from the United States. Indeed, only two days after Washington recognized Paderewski's government, the United States Congress passed a $100 million aid bill creating the American Relief Administration under Herbert Hoover for the purpose of assisting the peoples of war-raged Europe, among them, of course, the Poles.

Already on February 17, 1919 the first cargo ships carrying relief supplies to Poland arrived in the Danzig harbor; by August, 80 ships had carried some 300,000 tons of supplies from America to Poland. Over the first three postwar years, approximately $35 million in A.R.A. assistance would go to Poland, in addition to $160 million in low interest loans. Through the auspices of the A.R.A., Poland received approximately 751,000 tons in materials ranging from food, clothing and medications to farm equipment and locomotives. A.R.A. help was heavily focused on feeding the children of the new nation state; at the height of its work, the Hoover-led assistance program was feeding more than 1,300,000 children each day. Indeed, between 1919 and 1922, approximately one-half billion meals were provided to starving children throughout the country. Given the magnitude of such assistance from America, one can well appreciate why privately-based giving from the Polish community organizations lost momentum.[26]

In America, Polonia support for the concerns of the new postwar Polish state continued, but in new form. Thus, Polish language newspapers defended the good name of Poland against exaggerated charges in the American and Jewish press that thousands had died in "pogroms;" in reality there were 280 victims, most of them unfortunates caught in the line of fire in the war that raged in 1919 and 1920 between Pilsudski's forces and those of the new Bolshevik Russian state.[27]

The Polish American organizations also supported the homeland's territorial claims in its political struggle with Germany over the coal-rich region of Silesia, which was located on the border between the two countries. Financial support amounting to several hundred thousand dollars was sent to Poland to enable its government to more effectively propagandize its position in the face of tremendous German efforts to retain the entire region. The issue was eventually settled by means of a plebiscite of the inhabitants, with the disputed territory divided about evenly between the two states.[28]

Finally, following the war there was a rush of Polonia interest in economic investment into the homeland. While much of this money was later lost with the collapse of the Polish economy in the early 1920s, the number of Poles who not only invested abroad but who established direct management of such firms was considerable.[29]

In sum, the years after 1900 mark the first great high water mark of Polonia assistance to Poland on all fronts--political, humanitarian, diplomatic, military and economic. Prior to the formation of the Polish National Defense Committee in December 1912, the organizations of the emigration had been unsuccessful in creating a firm consensus defining how they might best cooperate on Poland's behalf. By 1918, through the National Department, unity had been for all practical purposes achieved--with the exception of a small number of organizations still linked to *KON*.

Through the Polish Central Relief Committee approximately $10 million was contributed by Polonia for Poland's relief between 1914 and 1922, an amount far surpassing anything previously collected on behalf of the homeland. On the diplomatic front, the National Department was successful in establishing productive working relations with Dmowski's National Committee in Switzerland and France with the aim of helping it gain Allied recognition as independent Poland's postwar representative. Paderewski succeeded in promoting Poland's case in America although here the Poles were singularly fortunate in that Woodrow Wilson was both philosophically sympathetic to their aims and able, by virtue of events (mainly the collapse of Tsarist Russia and the defeat of the Central powers), to play a decisive role in their realization in the last stages of the war. Last, but by no means least, the willingness of more than 38,000 young Poles in America to volunteer for military service in a dangerous enterprise underscored their commitment.

Fortunately, all these efforts bore fruit thanks to Pilsudski's establishment of an independent Poland in 1918 and his making the claim good on the field of battle against the Germans, Czechs, Ukrainians, Lithuanians and Bolsheviks. It is no exaggeration to conclude that the restoration of Poland's independence in 1918 after 123 years of foreign rule and partition was the product of extraordinary efforts on the part of many individuals, groups and governments. One element in the struggle was American Polonia; without its considerable efforts the outcome for Poland might have been different and less salutary besides.

III. Polonia's Humanitarian Services to Poland in the World War II Era: The Work of the Polish American Council (Rada Polonii Amerykanskiej)

The story of independent Poland in the years between 1918 and 1939 represent a distinctive era in its modern experience, one that was very different from both its earlier history as a partitioned nation and from what would take place in the years to come. It was on the very last day of the fighting in World War I that Poland's independence was proclaimed, heralding the end of 123 years of foreign rule. Just two decades later, on September 1, 1939, the first day of the Second World War, independent Poland would be marked for extinction.

A new Poland would indeed be reestablished after the war, of course, but this Poland would prove to be radically distinct from its interwar predecessor in a bewildering number of ways. Most significant was the fact that postwar Poland's population had suffered the deaths of some six million of its citizens, victims of six years of conflict and ruthless occupation by the country's enemies.

Poland's borders had also been substantially redrawn with the country physically moved two hundred miles to the West. Moreover, post 1945 Poland was no longer a sovereign state but found itself instead under the domination of Soviet Russia and its agents.

The rulers of this new "Polish People's Republic" would struggle unsuccessfully for the next forty-five years to gain a measure of popular approval of their regime before being ignominiously escorted from power in the Summer of 1989.

Interwar Poland and American Polonia

Significantly, World War I's close was accompanied by a dramatic diminution in Polonia interest in the affairs of the new state. After 1918, the organizations of the Polish community in America increasingly focused their attentions upon their internal concerns, especially those having to do with the preservation of ethnic identification within the younger and American-born portion of Polonia. While there were some attempts to maintain ties with the homeland in the 1920s, exemplified by the forming of the Kosciuszko Foundation in 1925 to foster academic and cultural contacts between scholars in Poland and America and the efforts to promote tourism to Poland, Polonia's emphasis throughout the interwar years tended to be upon the maintenance of ethnic life in the United States.

In the extensive and far-flung system of Polish parishes and parochial schools around the country, Polonia activists concerned themselves with the maintenance of instruction in the Polish language, in the face of actions by diocesan authorities to promote the use of English. In the fraternals, attention was given to working with young people to keep up their interest in their heritage. Great emphasis was placed upon encouraging greater participation in "American" sports activities and in the "Polish" scouting movement or *Harcerstwo,* both of which were sponsored by the fraternals and were quite successful in attracting widespread involvement among young people.

For its part the Polish government did seek to build stronger ties with the emigration. Its efforts, which were promoted in the United States through the Polish embassy and its network of consular agencies led to the creation of an officially-sponsored organization in the late 1920s. This was the World Union of Poles from Abroad, *Swiatowy Zwiazek Polakow z Zagranicy,* popularly known as *Swiatpol.*

However, while *Swiatpol* had its enthusiasts in American Polonia, it also had its detractors who opposed participation on the grounds that Polish Americans were Americans first and foremost and not Polish citizens living in the United States. Significantly, at *Swiatpol's* second international congress which was held in Warsaw in 1934, the members of the large American delegation refused to participate formally in its proceedings. Instead, they supported their chairman, Polish National Alliance Censor Francis X. Swietlik, who asserted that it would be an error for the Polish American community to subordinate itself to any agency of the Polish government. As Swietlik pointed out:

> Polonia in America is neither a Polish colony nor a national minority but a component of the great American nation, proud of its Polish origin and careful to implant in the hearts of the younger generation a love for all that is Polish.[1]

Several Polonia organizations, among them the Polish Falcons of America, disagreed with Swietlik and did become active within *Swiatpol;* indeed they eventually even established a Polish National Defense Fund, or *Fundusz Obrony Narodowej*, to raise money in America for a variety of Polish government needs. The fund's activities came to an abrupt end in early September 1939, following the United States' proclamation of neutrality in the war in Europe, an action strictly prohibiting any American involvement on behalf of any of the belligerents.[2]

This then was the picture of Poland-Polonia relations at the end of the 1930s. On the one hand, Polish Americans remained proud of independent Poland's existence and its accomplishments over the years, although many were critical of the policies of the authoritarian regime headed by Jozef Pilsudski which had come into power in May 1926. On the other hand, the ordinary Polish American's preoccupation was largely with the internal concerns of Polonia, and after the onset of the Great Depression in 1929, with the sometimes dire struggle to keep his job and provide for his family's needs.[3] That very few Poles were permitted to migrate to the United States as a consequence of the restrictive legislation approved in Washington in 1921 and 1924 was yet another factor which affected Polonia's interwar course. In drastically reducing the flow of new immigrants into Polonia, the quotas of the 1920s served to diminish the ethnic community's historically vital sense of identification with the "old country."

Nevertheless, the outbreak of the Second World War signalled the beginnings of new and concerted efforts on Poland's behalf throughout Polonia. Once again, as in 1914, Polish Americans acted first in the humanitarian sphere to aid the victims of the Nazi and Soviet invasions through an all-Polonia federation called the Polish American Council, *Rada Polonii Amerykanskiej* or *RPA*. Only later would Polonia organize politically in support of the homeland's national interests. (That great effort would in 1944 give rise to the Polish American Congress, or PAC, in Polish *Kongres Polonii Amerykanskiej, KPA.*) This chapter then is devoted to Polonia's charitable activities on Poland's behalf and thus focuses upon the work of the *Rada Polonii.*

If Polonia's efforts for Poland in the Second World War in some ways reflected the community's responses in World War I, there were also differences in the ethnic community's reaction to the news of Nazi Germany's attack on the ancestral homeland. Most significantly, by 1939 Polonia was generally peopled by men and women who considered themselves as "Americans of Polish origin" or "extraction," as fiercely loyal to the government of the United States as they were moved by compassion for the Polish victims of the war. Twenty-five years before, the Polish community's relationship to both America and Poland had been far more ambiguous, something reflected even by the word commonly used at the time to characterize the ethnic community, "*wychodztwo*" or the emigration. Happily, the question of national loyalties was not seriously tested during the First World War, since Polonia's work on behalf of an independent Poland never clashed with America's own war aims--indeed, the restoration of a reunified and sovereign Polish state was one of President Woodrow Wilson's celebrated "Fourteen Points" that justified this country's entry into the conflict in April 1917.

A prime example of the differences between Polonia's response to Poland's plight in the two World Wars involved the Polish Americans' interest in creating a special military force to fight in Europe for the homeland's cause. In World War I enthusiasm for a "Polish Army from America" had run high and only Washington's formal declaration of neutrality had deterred the emigrant community from forming a sizable Polish legion at the time of the war's outbreak. With America in the conflict some three years later, more than thirty-eight thousand men did indeed volunteer for the Polish Army that was soon in France in service to the Allied cause, this despite the many obstacles to enlistment placed in their way by the U.S. War Department.

In contrast, when talk of a Polish American legion was first heard in 1939, the response to the idea was exceedingly weak. Indeed, despite the Polish government's hearty endorsement, only 722 men were eventually recruited for military duty during the two year interval between World War II's outbreak and America's entry into the struggle in December 1941 after Pearl Harbor.[4]

Still, most Polish Americans possessed powerful sentimental ties to families and loved ones in the old homeland. Such emotions were coupled with gloom over the Nazi-Soviet partition of Poland and its loss of independence, a cause once so central in past Polonia life. Not surprisingly, the organizations of the ethnic community would soon be propelled into concerted action on behalf of Hitler's and Stalin's victims.

Substantially enhancing the efforts of Polonia from the earliest days of World War II was its close and friendly contact with the representatives of the Polish government-in-exile, which by 1940 was headquartered in London. Journeying to America that year was the eighty year old Ignacy Paderewski, who visited Polonia as the Chairman of the Polish government's reconstituted national parliament. General Wladyslaw Sikorski made three trips to the United States as the London government's Prime Minister and the Commander-in-Chief of its armed forces. Moreover, Poland's cause in World War II was far better represented in Washington, D.C. than it had been a quarter of a century earlier. Thus, in addition to its ambassadorial staff, which enjoyed the United States' full recognition throughout the war, Polonia could also look to no fewer than thirteen congressmen of Polish heritage to speak on behalf of its concerns between 1939 and 1945. By way of comparison there had not been a single Polish American in elective office in the nation's capital during the First World War years.

Moreover, onto the Polonia scene itself had emerged a number of well educated American-born activists who shared a commitment to work on behalf of the homeland's needs. They included the two highest officers of the Polish National Alliance, Censor Swietlik of Milwaukee and President Charles Rozmarek of Wilkes-Barre, Pennsylvania, and the two Presidents of the Polish Roman Catholic Union who served that fraternal during the war years, Joseph Kania of Detroit and John Olejniczak of South Bend, Indiana. Joining them were a number of older Polonia leaders whose careers went back to the First World War era, among them Honorata Wolowska, President of the Polish Women's Alliance and Dr. Teofil Starzynski, President of the Polish Falcons of America.[5]

While Poland had fallen under Nazi and Soviet occupation by the end of September 1939, its government almost immediately reconstituted in Paris and following France's collapse at Germany's hands in the Spring of 1940, was reestablished in London. Recognized by Great Britain, France, the U.S. and many other countries as the legitimate representative of the Polish nation, this "London government" was also fortunate to have General Sikorski, a long time prewar proponent of democratic reform and an advocate of East Central European federalism, as its head. The stature of Sikorski's regime was further enhanced by his success in organizing substantial military forces in the West which were committed to the Allied cause. Moreover, within occupied Poland, the exile government was everywhere recognized from the outset as the voice of the fighting nation. In time, as many as 350,000 men and women would take part in the underground resistance to the country's invaders; overwhelmingly, they affirmed their loyalty to the London government and maintained regular communication with its representatives in spite of the extraordinary difficulties in doing so.[6]*

---

* Confronting World War II Polonia, however, was the extraordinarily complex character of Poland's situation after 1939. In President Franklin Roosevelt, the Polish cause found a champion less committed to Poland's restoration than it had in Woodrow Wilson a generation earlier. Far more ominous, however, was Soviet Russia's role in further complicating matters. In 1917, the Russian revolutions had brought not only Tsarism's downfall but its withdrawal from the World War. Those developments in turn favorably affected Poland's eventual rebirth. Conversely, in World War II, Stalin, after two years as Hitler's partner, became a key ally of Britain and the U.S. following the Nazi invasion of

Organized Polonia's Humanitarian Response
to Poland's Needs

In American Polonia, the initial response to the news of Nazi Germany's aggression was to rally its people throughout the country in demonstrations protesting the attack and to begin collections of funds and material needed in the homeland to continue its resistance efforts. Such manifestations clearly underscored the anger and frustration Polish Americans and their fellow citizens felt about the events in Europe. At the same time, they were not accompanied by calls urging American entry into the war; Polish Americans, like Americans in general, appeared to strongly oppose the nation's immediate engagement in the unfolding European conflict.

Fortunately, Polonia was prepared to plan how it might act to assist the victims of the war. This was thanks to the presence of an already existing nationwide federation of ethnic fraternals, community associations and parishes -- the Polish American Council, or *Rada Polonii Amerykanskiej (RPA)*.

The Council's origins went back to 1935 when it had formed in Chicago as the Polish American Interorganizational Council *(Rada Polonii Miedzyorganizacyjnej)*. Initially created to bring together the leaders of the three large Polish American fraternals based in Chicago, the Polish National Alliance, the Polish Roman Catholic Union and the Polish Women's Alliance -- the Interorganizational Council had as its purpose the directing of charitable activities on behalf of both Polonia and Poland.[6] At the same time, it represented a counter to those in the ethnic

---

the Soviet Union. Most significantly, to the Soviet ruler, control over Poland was from the start a critical and seemingly non-negotiable issue in his ongoing discussions with Roosevelt and British Prime Minister Winston Churchill. In understanding what eventually happened to Poland after the war, it is these considerations that must be given the greatest weight. Certainly, in the face of the Allies' positions, there was very little that either the Polish government in London, its underground forces in the homeland, or organized Polonia could do to affect the nation's postwar destiny.[7]

community who supported Polonia involvement in the Warsaw-directed *Swiatpol* organization.[9]

At first, the Interorganizational Council was headed by Censor Swietlik and PRCUA President Kania, with support from Polish Women's Alliance President Wolowska, Joseph Przydatek, the Editor of the Chicago Polish language daily, *Dziennik Chicagoski,* and Polonia activist Aleksander Hinkelman. But at the Council's third convention, in May 1938, the organization elected a new leadership with PNA President John Romaszkiewicz, an opponent of Swietlik, taking over as Chairman. Kania also retired for the time being and was replaced as Secretary by another PRCUA leader, Joseph Barc, while Wolowska continued on as Vice President. Approved at the meeting was a change of name for the organization, to Polish American Council, along with plans to strengthen fund raising activities on Poland's behalf.

Significantly, the delegates, many of whom represented organizations that were headquartered outside the Chicago area, also approved a proposal to establish a "Polish American Congress" in the near future to unite Polonia behind Poland's national needs. Indeed, the date for such a Congress was actually set to coincide with the celebration of the New York World's Fair in the Autumn of 1939. Poland would be formally taking part in that event and many Polonia organizations were already scheduling their own "Polish Day" gatherings to be held at the Fairgrounds.[10]

These plans were dramatically overturned by the German invasion. A hurriedly called session of the *Rada Polonii* leadership in Chicago on September 4, 1939 found its participants agreed upon the necessity of raising funds and supplies on behalf of the embattled Poles. Put off, however, for the time being were plans for the calling of the Polish American Congress, despite the appeal put forward in favor of the idea by Starzynski. The Council did issue a general call to Polonia to aid the homeland under the slogan, "Five Million Dollars for the Defense of the Polish nation," a proposal that was soon discarded following the United States' neutrality pronouncement. Henceforth, the Council would limit its fund raising activities to the humanitarian sphere.[11]

Another crucial development that would shape the future activities of the Polish American Council for the duration of its existence occurred a few days later, in Detroit, Michigan. There the Polish National Alliance was trying to hold its long-planned quadrennial convention, although the more than 530 delegates in attendance were understandably preoccupied with the breaking events in Europe. At the conclave, Swietlik's opponent, Romaszkiewicz was narrowly defeated in his quest for a fourth term as President of the Alliance. Succeeding him was Charles Rozmarek, a forty-two year old Pennsylvania attorney who had enjoyed Swietlik's support. Swietlik was himself overwhelmingly reelected to a third four year term as Censor and now found himself the unchallenged leader of the *Rada Polonii* as well.[12]

The tasks the organization faced, understandably, were indeed immense and complex in nature. First of all, there was the matter of simply putting together a relief effort that would win wide support from the sprawling Polish American community. Fortunately, one aspect of this problem had already been resolved by September 6, 1939 when the Polish National Defense fund terminated its operations. Its action meant that Polonia would not find itself divided between partisans of military assistance for Poland and supporters of humanitarian aid to the victims of the conflict.[13]

Another potential problem was also resolved fairly easily and concerned the involvement of Polonia in fund raising efforts on behalf of the Polish Red Cross organization. There was some initial interest in such an operation and the appearance of General Aleksander Osinski, head of the Polish organization, in the United States in early September might have prompted a substantial effort in Polonia on behalf of his agency. However, Osinski, in his meetings with leaders of the American Red Cross quickly agreed to suspend fund raising efforts in the United States on the assurance that the American agency would itself direct aid to Poland.[14]

A second and more serious task before the *Rada Polonii* involved its prompt establishment of a national fund raising drive throughout the Polish American community. This was an especially important issue given the fact that scores of local groups throughout the country were sprouting up to take action on Poland's behalf in light of the increasingly distressing news from Europe. Acting quickly following its proclamation of its own relief drive on September 7, the *RPA*'s friend in Washington, U.S. Federal Reserve Board Governor M.S. Szymczak, was able to meet with a representative of the Department of State and gained the Department's backing for the *RPA*'s campaign. As a result, the Department adopted a policy advising all groups applying for permits to assist Poland to either affiliate with the *Rada Polonii* or terminate further activities.[15]

This action considerably strengthened the *Rada Polonii*'s position as the primary relief agency working on behalf of the needs of Polish war victims, although it by no means brought to an end the efforts of well-meaning people in groups around the country to continue their efforts independent of the *RPA*. Thus, at its September 19, 1939 meeting the *RPA* leadership heard that 47 community organizations had already joined its effort. A month later it was also reported that no fewer than 127 organizations, 89 of them led by Polish Americans, had also petitioned to the State Department for permits to collect clothing, foodstuffs, medical supplies and money for Poland.[16]

As the *RPA* began to collect goods for shipment to occupied Poland it faced yet another and yet more perplexing problem. This involved the refusal of both the German and Soviet governments to permit charitable agencies to operate in their zones of occupation. This ruthless policy extended to everyone, whether they were homeless refugees or prisoners of war. It would also include the hundreds of thousands of individuals who were transferred either into Nazi Germany itself as slave laborers or into the far reaches of Soviet Russia.[17]

In trying to deal with this crushing problem, the *Rada Polonii* soon found itself in the middle of a dispute between the two American agencies which were most deeply concerned about providing some aid to Poland, the American Red Cross and the Committee for Polish Relief. The Red Cross, headed in New York by Norman Davies, was already the best known agency organized for the delivery of relief assistance to peoples in need; affiliated with the International Red Cross, it was seemingly in a position to work on Poland's behalf through the German Red Cross, itself also a member of the same international agency. The Committee for Polish Relief was established following the war's outbreak by a number of public-spirited citizens. Former President of the United States Herbert Hoover eventually accepted its chairmanship with Chauncey McCormack the organization's chairman in Chicago.

From the start there were disagreements between the two agencies and Swietlik, an attorney and educator by profession and a courtly, diplomatic person by temperament, required all his skills to maintain good relations with them. In fact, both organizations' concerns on Poland's behalf rested upon solid foundations. Thus, Hoover's Committee had the backing of the Polish government-in-exile in its own efforts to direct relief assistance to the homeland; for its part, the Red Cross was the beneficiary of an Act of Congress which set aside some $50 million in relief assistance to the peoples of war-ravaged Europe.

The American Red Cross, which was able to ship goods to Poland with the Nazis' consent by the Spring of 1940, seemed better prepared to be of real assistance to the victims of the war. But materials sent to Europe under its auspices had to be turned over to the German Red Cross for distribution to the Poles, a practice the Hoover Committee decried on the grounds that it could not be determined whether or not the assistance earmarked for the Poles was actually reaching them.

Insofar as aid to Poles living in the Soviet zone of occupation was concerned, the situation was still more frustrating. From 1939 until July 1941, when the Soviet Union resumed diplomatic relations with Poland's government-in-exile following Hitler's surprise attack on Russia, Moscow strictly prohibited any shipments of relief supplies to meet the desperate needs of the Poles under its rule. Tragically, during the twenty-two month interim, hundreds of thousands of Poles were forcibly resettled to remote areas of Soviet Siberia and Central Asia, where large numbers perished.[17]

As already noted, the war's outbreak prompted numerous manifestations of Polonia solidarity with the homeland. These events, often occurring with little or no advance notice, were good barometers measuring popular concern and some attracted crowds in the thousands. In time, the *RPA* itself succeeded in planning a number of substantial mass rallies in conjunction with fund raising efforts under its sponsorship.

One took place in the Chicago Stadium on February 10, 1940 and brought together some 25,000 people for a patriotic program featuring the well-known tenor, Jan Kiepura. His appearance was followed by speeches from Herbert Hoover, General Jozef Haller, Commander-in-Chief of the Polish Army in the First World War and again in America as the Polish government-in-exile's emissary to the Polonia communities in the West, the Mayor of Chicago, and Swietlik. (Hoover's words at the rally were ominous; decrying Nazi Germany's continuing refusal to permit relief assistance to enter into occupied Poland, the former President called for an international governmental effort amounting to $20 million in food shipments to prevent a massive famine which he foresaw in the coming months.)[18]

Another memorable manifestation organized by the *RPA* came at Chicago's Soldier Field on April 20, 1941. For this occasion the principle speaker before a crowd estimated at 50-60,000 people was Prime Minister Sikorski, making his first visit to the United States and thus becoming the first Polish head of government to appear in this country.

Introduced by Swietlik as "the symbol of the struggle which the human race is making today on many European battlefields to save our Christian civilization from destruction," Sikorski though mindful of America's neutral status, did not limit himself to making an humanitarian appeal on behalf of his countrymen. Instead, he urged Polonia to identify proudly with the Polish nation's struggle and reminded his listeners that his very presence in Polish America was "undeniable proof that Poland still lives."[19]*

---

* Sikorski's extended visit to the United States was significant in several respects. It included meetings with President Roosevelt and the Canadian Prime Minister, with the former leading to Poland's inclusion as a recipient of U.S. lend lease assistance and the latter highlighted by the signing of an agreement to set up military training camps for Polish army volunteers from the two North American democracies. The Polish leader also visited extensively with Polish American community leaders in the United States and Canada. Following America's entry into the conflict, Sikorski would make two more visits to this country; however, they would not include such extended appearances in Polonia.[20]

Despite its many difficulties, the *RPA* worked diligently to establish its presence throughout the United States by building solid relations with the Polish fraternals and by creating its own system of district agencies responsible for fund raising and clothing collection drives. Thirty-six regional district organizations were soon established to promote the work of the *Rada Polonii* at the local parish, fraternal and community level. This organizational work was both time-consuming and difficult, since numerous Polonia activists, especially in the Eastern part of the United States were reluctant at first to subordinate their efforts to the *Rada Polonii*. A similar problem existed with the fraternals and the Catholic hierarchy. Thus, the latter group was interested in channeling its relief efforts through its own Bishops' Charities appeal. Gradually, however, the *Rada Polonii* succeeded in impressing upon the entire ethnic community the value of teamwork under its leadership and already by May 1940, its American operations were running fairly smoothly. By then, when it held a special convention to further outline its aims, the *Rada* was in the position to announce that it had collected $529,053; by the end of the year the *RPA* was receiving approximately $60,000 each month, most of which was spent almost as soon as it was received.[21]

If the *RPA*'s leadership could claim some successes in organizing Polonia's relief efforts and in collecting money and material for the needy in war-torn Poland, the problems concerning the actual delivery of aid remained maddening. Until June 1941, when the Nazi invasion of Soviet Russia transformed Polish-Soviet relations, it had been practically impossible for the *Rada*, working with the Red Cross, to get any supplies into Poland. Instead, relief aid from the Polish American community had to be rerouted to refugees in Romania, Hungary, Lithuania, France, Switzerland, and Britain and to those Polish soldiers interned in German prisoner-of-war camps.

Relief assistance efforts actually improved after the Nazi invasion against its erstwhile Soviet ally. Following the German offensive, Moscow agreed to now permit *Rada Polonii* supplies to reach Polish soldiers and civilians interned in the territories still under its control and following the departure to Iran of the Polish armed forces inside the U.S.S.R. under the command of

General Wladyslaw Anders, *Rada Polonii* assistance was expanded to assist Polish exiles residing in Palestine, Africa and India.

The Japanese attack upon Pearl Harbor on December 7, 1941 brought to an end the neutrality of the United States in both the Pacific and European theaters of the conflict. Not surprisingly, America's entry into the war created new obstacles for the *Rada Polonii*'s activities. It became much more difficult to collect goods for Polish relief once rationing became the official U.S. policy on the home front. Furthermore, the shipment of goods to Europe became infinitely more difficult than ever before. Still, through assistance provided by the Red Cross and the United States Department of State, the *RPA* was eventually allowed to send approximately 12,000 food packages per month to Polish prisoners of war in Germany, an ongoing effort of considerable importance in preserving morale.

This stream of assistance was interrupted at the time of the Allied invasion of Normandy in June 1944. From then to the end of the war in Europe, the *RPA* was required to redirect its activities and to give its primary attentions to the growing numbers of Polish refugees scattered across the globe -- in Egypt, Kenya, Rhodesia, Uganda, Tanganyika, Palestine and Mexico. Already in October 1944, however, Swietlik was in contact with U.S. officials who had been given responsibility to plan the dispensing of relief assistance in Europe following the war. In these talks he expressed the *RPA*'s interest in cooperating with the American government in delivering aid into Poland and to Polish citizens who were found outside its borders, either as inmates of prisoner of war camps or as forced laborers in Germany. Thus, when postwar Allied assistance began in earnest less than a year later under the direction of the United Nations Relief and Rehabilitation Administration (UNRRA), the *RPA* was ready to play a responsible part in that agency's efforts on behalf of the Polish people.[22]

Mention has already been made of the *RPA*'s work in organizing relief activities in Polonia. Here it should be added that the organization also succeeded in integrating its efforts with those of a number of other charitable agencies in the United States, including the Red Cross and the Community Chest programs (today's United Fund Appeal) which operated at the local level across the land. In doing this, the *Rada Polonii* took for itself a new English name, "Polish War Relief," and agreed to participate in general fund raising activities for a variety of worthy purposes in return for an annual monetary allotment from the National War Fund, a privately-run clearing house for all relief assistance efforts under U.S. government direction. In so doing, the *RPA* and its affiliates promised not to organize separate fund raising campaigns of their own, although they were permitted to hold clothing and food drives for Polish relief. (After the war, the official English language name of the organization was changed yet again, to "American Relief for Poland," to denote its new commitment to helping in the home-land's recovery and in the rehabilitation of Polish refugees, exiles and prisoners of war. Throughout the remaining years of its existence, that is into the early 1970s, American Relief for Poland would be its official designation although to many Polish Americans the organization would always remain the *Rada Polonii Amerykanskiej.*)

Its participation in the National War Fund had several consequences for the *RPA*. Thus, for the duration of the con-flict the *Rada Polonii* was singled out as the sole American relief agency working on behalf of the Polish people. This also meant that the funds at the *RPA's* disposal were increased substantially from what would have been available had the organization relied solely upon the Polish American commu-nity for help. Thus, Treasurer John Olejniczak could report that in the two and one-half year period from November 1, 1939 to April 23, 1942 the *RPA* had collected a total of $1,433,703 in the Polish ethnic community. Of this sum $667,140 had originated from campaigns directed by its 36 district affiliates around the country, $548,881 from the hundreds of local organizations, mainly parishes, that recognized its leadership, and $217,681 from Polonia's fraternals. (In addition, the estimated value of goods collected during this period came to $2,294,646.)[23] In comparison, following its entry into the National War Fund Swietlik could announce that the *RPA* would be receiving no less than $2 million for the 1942 fiscal year alone. In April 1943 he declared that the *Rada Polonii's* share of moneys for the coming year would amount to more than $3 million. In all, from mid 1942 until the end of 1946, when the National War Fund was dissolved, the *RPA*'s total allotment came to $6,697,342.[24]

It is no easy task to present a comprehensive picture of the assistant efforts rendered by the *Rada Polonii* during the war years. While facts and figures can be marshalled to summarize what was collected and delivered to meet some of the needs of the Polish people, such data alone do not begin to convey the enormity of the volunteer effort involved in laboriously gathering and delivering goods for overseas shipment and the frustrations encountered by *RPA* activists in overcoming the many obstacles in their way due to the war. Still, perhaps a summary of the data on the various assistance efforts mounted by the organization will provide some appreciation of the magnitude of the *RPA*'s achievement.

In his postwar report on *RPA* activities which he made to the leadership of the organization in December 1948, Swietlik himself tried to do just that. In his presentation he outlined its various areas of wartime endeavor and went on to describe just what the *Rada Polonii* had accomplished in each. He then totalled up the dollar value of the *RPA*'s relief efforts since the start of its activities in October 1939.

In all, between 1939 and 1948 the *RPA* gathered $11,434,958 in financial donations on behalf of its many initiatives. In addition it collected a total of 9,246,555 pounds (or 4,623 tons) in clothing, medical supplies, foodstuffs and reading materials. This aid, Swietlik estimated as having reached more than five million people living inside Poland and several hundred thousand refugees, prisoners of war and soldiers around the world.

All told, the total amount of material shipped abroad by the organization amounted to approximately 18,000 tons, surely the greatest achievement in Polonia's history of service to Poland up to that time.[25]

Over the years the *Rada*'s effort had also taken on a noticeable grass roots character. Thus, as of 1948 no fewer than 615 local organizations of all types in 29 states and the District of Columbia had participated in Polish relief activities under the RPA's leadership. In all they had collected goods amounting to 7,090,473 pounds (3,535 tons) for the cause.[26]

One final point was covered by Swietlik in his report, the cost of the effort. Here he took particular pride in emphasizing that 98 cents out of every dollar collected had gone directly to its intended recipients; total administrative expenses (including shipping bills) had amounted to only $392,682. The *RPA*'s effort had thus been voluntary in the truest sense of the word.[27]

In Swietlik's report, four separate fields of wartime relief activity were identified. These included work (1) on behalf of Polish prisoners of war, (2) for refugees interned in foreign countries, (3) for soldiers serving the Allied cause, and (4) relief assistance to Poles inside the occupied country.

(1) During the war, more than 200,000 Polish prisoners of war were interned by the Nazis; from the outset the *RPA* was on the scene to provide many of them with food, medications and clothing in its cooperative work with the International Red Cross and the YMCA. Faced initially with a host of obstacles to its efforts, the *RPA* was eventually given permission to send out an average of 12,000 aid packages each month. By 1942, the total monthly allotment was raised to 15,000 with each package weighing as much as 20 pounds at the cost of $1 for shipping. Together with some 600,000 other packages put together under the *RPA*'s auspices and another 56,000 packages sent directly by the United States as part of the government's lend-lease program, the *Rada Polonii* succeeded in shipping a total of 1,591,000 packages over the course of the conflict.

(2) *RPA* assistance to refugees outside of Poland was another early priority, if for no other reason than it was not possible to send help directly into the occupied homeland. At first, aid was directed to displaced persons (the "DPs") in Romania and Lithuania; from 1940 help also went out to the more than 50,000 Poles in France and Switzerland who had fled their country after the Nazi-Soviet partition. In addition, the *Rada* also became a continual provider for the more than 10,000 Polish refugees in Iran, Palestine, India and East Africa.

A particular *RPA* concern involved its assistance to more than 1,500 refugees (nearly all of them women and children, 264 of whom were orphans) who were eventually relocated in the town of Santa Rosa, Mexico for future resettlement in the United States. These individuals had arrived from Poland only after having travelled thousands of miles over several years time through Russia and India and they became the objects of considerable interest within the Polish ethnic community from 1943 onward. Through the *RPA*'s efforts, in conjunction with those of the Polish government in London and Polonia's fraternals, most of these "Mexicans" were invited to live permanently in the United States after the war.[28]

In all, *RPA* assistance to Polish refugees during the war amounted to more than 271 tons in food and clothing and another 888 tons in medical supplies, the latter sent under the auspices of the Red Cross. Swietlik estimated the value of the *RPA*'s contribution to these shipments at some $876,000.

(3) A third area of assistance involved work on behalf of Polish military personnel in Great Britain and France under the command of the London-based Polish government in exile. Included here were more than 120,000 packages of food, clothing, medical supplies and reading materials. The *RPA* also supported the establishment of a Polish soldiers' hospital in London. In all, approximately $1.7 million of *RPA* funds was spent on behalf of free Poland's soldiers, sailors and pilots.

(4) Direct relief to Poles in the homeland constituted yet a fourth area of *RPA* activity and remained the most difficult to realize. Early in the conflict, some direct relief aid was permitted into Poland under the *aegis* of Herbert Hoover's Committee for Polish Relief and the *RPA*, which provided $350,000 in supplies. With the United States' entry into the war in 1941 this effort ended, although in 1943 and 1944 the American Red Cross did provide an additional $287,000 in supplies from the *RPA*.

The *Rada Polonii*'s effort to initiate its own assistance program to Poland began at the end of 1941. It was directed to Poles inside the Soviet Union, which was then under fearsome Nazi assault. To achieve its aims, the *RPA* set up a supply base in Lisbon, Portugal headed by Florian Piskorski, a veteran *Rada Polonii* staff member. This base quickly emerged into a quite substantial operation and at the height of its operations employed 24 persons. From neutral Portugal approximately 240 tons of medical goods and clothing were shipped into Poland, along with about 200,000 individual packages that had been delivered to Lisbon from the *Rada*'s affiliates in the United States.

With the war's end in the Summer of 1945, the *RPA*'s activities took on a new character, that of gearing up to deliver relief materials to Poland itself and to the hundreds of thousands of Polish nationals who were to be found in refugee camps in Central Europe. The refugees' plight was horrendous and called for prompt action on the part of the United States to meet a host of problems, ranging from their immediate difficulties connected with housing, sustenance and medical treatment to long term issues having to do with their eventual resettlement, education and employment in the West. That few Polish refugees wished to return to Poland after 1945 was evident: given the war's devastating impact upon their country and its subsequent take-over by the Soviet-controlled Polish Workers (or Communist) Party, the great majority of refugees were not anxious to go home. Thus for them and many other East Central Europeans, the question was one of resettlement and their eventual relocation in the United States, Canada, Western Europe, and Britain and its dependencies.

The actual number of Polish refugees was staggering; just in the Western controlled zones of occupied Germany there were at first more than 850,000 Poles, with smaller numbers of displaced persons to be found in Italy, Switzerland, Britain and France. Not surprisingly, the *RPA* was soon involved in providing whatever counsel and assistance it could in Germany in cooperation with other relief agencies, including UNRRA, Catholic Relief Services and the Red Cross. To help determine the *RPA*'s future role on behalf of the refugees, Swietlik and several of his colleagues were already in Europe by war's end. As a result of their visit, Piskorski, John Czech and several other *RPA* employees were dispatched to Germany to provide whatever help they might in counseling the residents of the refugee camps.

In his first report to Polonia upon his return from Europe, Swietlik offered a graphic depiction of the conditions facing the Poles in Allied-occupied Germany. He noted that more than 140,000 former prisoners of war and nearly 695,000 former slave laborers of the Third Reich had been registered as displaced persons by the authorities but went on to observe that these statistics did not include thousands of other individuals who lived in destitution outside the camps.

I cannot describe the many untold tragedies of life which unfolded before my eyes. It would indeed be difficult to portray the miserable lot of these displaced Poles. The reports (reaching) Americans may make it difficult to understand the depth of savagery of perverted Nazi minds, but I can assure you that these reports were not exaggerated. Unhappy as was the fate of all who fell into the clutches of Hitler's Germany, the Poles were singled out to suffer the utmost...persecution. The specters of what I have witnessed still haunt me... I find in my experience an inspiration to give my utmost aid to those whose spirit no suffering could break, and who have risen from the depths stronger than ever in the resolution that Poland shall never die![29]

In 1946 and 1947 the *RPA* sent nearly $2.5 million in supplies to Germany, aid which helped thousands of refugees to begin their lives anew in the West. Indeed, by the end of 1948 the number of displaced Poles still in the refugee camps had diminished to fewer than 181,000 persons. All through this period the *RPA* provided counseling in assisting people to complete the required paperwork which would enable them to leave the camps or emigrate, although this was formally beyond the *Rada's* area of responsibility.

RPA assistance to Poland itself became the focus of its work following World War II and proved especially significant in the first years of the postwar period, especially in 1946 and 1947. It was during this time that American-sponsored assistance to Poland was especially critical; the country had suffered the loss of more than twenty percent of its citizenry, and destruction to most of its industrial base and transportation system. Politically, the times were characterized by enormous political turmoil, with the Polish Workers' Party struggling to impose its will over a people who overwhelmingly preferred a democratic system with close ties to the West. Indeed, at the very time that American-based relief agencies were doing what they could on behalf of the people's physical needs, the Communists' relentless efforts to crush all who opposed their rule served to alienate Western opinion against Poland, a development which gradually undermined American public support for relief help at the time it was most needed.

In these trying circumstances, the *Rada Polonii* was one of several charitable agencies which nonetheless set to work to provide material assistance to Poland. The prime mover in the immediate postwar aid effort was the United Nations Relief and Rehabilitation Administration, which despite its title was engaged for the most part in distributing American goods. Thus, of the $480 million in relief aid channeled from UNRRA in 1946 and 1947 to Poland, one of the largest of all aid recipients during the period, 75 percent came from the United States.

In addition to UNRRA, there were other privately-organized agencies rendering help to Poland, including the Red Cross, the War Relief Services of the National Catholic Welfare Conference, the American Joint Distribution Committee and American Relief for Poland, the official postwar name for the *RPA*.

The private agencies, in contrast to UNRRA which dealt with official Polish government bodies, carried out their activities in cooperation with the independent Polish welfare association, *Caritas,* the charitable arm of the Polish Roman Catholic Church. They also worked with the Polish Red Cross and the Polish YMCA. In all, they contributed approximately $20 million in clothing, food and hospital supplies during the time of their operation.* However, as the Polish Communist regime established its dictatorship over the country, diplomatic relations between Washington and Warsaw deteriorated severely. In these circumstances, the activities of the private relief agencies became increasingly restricted, despite their real and recognized contributions to the pressing needs of the Polish people.[30] This situation was noted by Honorata Wolowska following her return from a visit in 1949 to Poland where she had reviewed the status of relief activities around the country. In her report to the *RPA* board of directors in August 1949,

---

* Of this sum approximately $2.5 million came from the *RPA,* in the form of donated or purchased goods gathered and shipped to the homeland under the supervision of Dr. Bronislas Smykowski of Bridgeport, Connecticut. Smykowski dedicated many years of service to a variety of Polonia causes and in the World War II era he and the members of his committee shipped some 7,374 tons of goods to Poland.

Wolowska noted that sixteen foreign agencies dispensing assistance inside Poland had already been liquidated, including those of the *Rada Polonii*.[31]

The end of World War II and the onset of the Cold War had thus together served to bring to an end, at least for the foreseeable future, any hopes that the leadership of the *Rada Polonii* might have entertained to carry out its objectives inside Poland. Already in 1946, the National War Fund had ceased its operations, thus eliminating the major source of future revenues for the *RPA*. A new effort to generate funds in the U.S. was tried the following year in the form of a nationwide drive directed by another agency, American Overseas Aid, with which the RPA became affiliated. This drive was ambitious and its organizers hoped to gather as much as $60 million from their effort. In fact, only $5 million was collected and the *Rada Polonii*, which had expected to take in $2.5 million from the $70,000 it had contributed to the campaign, had to be satisfied with a check for only $28,457.

Within Polonia, postwar giving also fell off considerably. A review of the *Rada Polonii*'s 1948 report shows that of the $1.8 million its 36 state and district divisions had contributed to the cause between 1939 and 1948, practically all of that money had been collected before the end of 1946. In the *RPA*'s 1954 assessment of its district affiliates' performance to that time, it was further noted that while total contributions from the districts for the entire period since 1939 amounted to $2,280,000, only $480,000 had been raised during the seven years following the 1948 convention report. Equally telling was Swietlik's statement that as of 1954, only twelve district organizations still remained active. The others had either disbanded or were in the process of liquidating.

Aside from this general decline in interest in giving that pervaded American society in the years after the war, several considerations of particular relevance to Polonia also combined to significantly diminish support for the humanitarian causes the *RPA* espoused. Nearly all were connected with political and ideological issues having to do with the establishment of a Soviet-dominated Poland, a development generating feelings of profound disappointment and betrayal throughout the ethnic community. Had the *Rada Polonii* possessed a political, as well charitable agenda, it might have played a role in shaping Polish American opinion in ways that would help it to attain its aims. But this was simply not possible, since the *RPA* had had to publicly disavow any partisan interest to remain eligible for money coming to it from the National War Fund. While its decision certainly enhanced the *Rada's* standing as a humanitarian agency, it left a political void that would be filled in 1944 with the creation of an entirely new all-Polonia federation, the Polish American Congress (PAC or *Kongres Polonii Amerykanskiej*). Thus, given the preeminence of political concerns over humanitarian ones throughout Polonia after 1945, the *RPA* itself was soon overshadowed by the Congress and its dynamic President, Charles Rozmarek.

Even in the humanitarian field, the *RPA* gradually was eclipsed by the Congress. Thus, it was the PAC which in 1947 took the lead in promoting special legislation in Washington D.C. to allow thousands of Polish displaced persons and political emigres to enter the country outside the usual U.S. quota restrictions, this after Rozmarek's widely publicized and extended visit to the refugee camps in Germany the previous Fall.

The Polish American Congress would also soon take over the responsibility for directing Polonia's efforts to help resettle these people in America following passage of the Displaced Persons Act in 1948. This it accomplished through a special commission that Rozmarek established under PAC auspices, the American Committee for the Resettlement of Polish Displaced Persons. This agency remained active into the mid 1950s.

As the PAC's efforts in the humanitarian area geared up so also did criticism increase over the *Rada Polonii's* continued activity inside Communist-controlled Poland. Indeed, at the *Rada's* 1948 convention Swietlik had to answer some pointed questions over the policy. In doing so, he emphasized his organization's record since 1939 in distributing aid in a prudent and responsible manner. The *RPA's* policy throughout, he asserted, had remained that "a Pole in need was a Pole to be offered assistance, wherever he was to be found, whatever his politics." The *RPA* would continue to adhere to the same principle, in spite of criticisms from within Polonia.

For Swietlik, the attacks on the *RPA* had nonetheless been difficult to bear and underscored the extent of his continuing rift with Rozmarek, his one-time protege, and his followers in the Polish American Congress. Indeed, back in August 1947, Swietlik had announced that he would not seek a fifth four year term as Censor of the Polish National Alliance fraternal, the organization over which Rozmarek presided.[32]

By the end of the decade, the *Rada Polonii*'s actual involvement in dispensing assistance in Poland had come to a close, although it continued to maintain an office in the homeland until early 1951. According to a Polish government announcement of April 20 of that year, economic conditions in the country had so improved that U.S. relief help was no longer needed. By then, the regime had launched a major drive against the Roman Catholic Church and its chief charitable arm, *Caritas,* which had worked closely with the *RPA.*

By this time, the *Rada*'s work among the Polish refugees was also nearly done, since the overwhelming majority of displaced persons had by then chosen citizenship in one of the Western European countries or applied for permits to enter the United States under the 1948 immigration act. (A small number returned to Poland.)

Still, approximately 100,000 Poles in Western Europe retained refugee status, with their needs met in some fashion by a variety of government programs and the International Refugee Organization of the United Nations. Additional assistance continued too from private agencies such as the National Catholic Welfare Council.

It was with the NCWC that the *RPA* increasingly cooperated following its decision to no longer maintain its own personnel in Europe. Instead, the *RPA* continued to ship packages of food and clothing to individual needy families and to orphans, with personnel from the NCWC facilitating their delivery in the remaining camps.

The *RPA* also performed some services in identifying American sponsors for Poles seeking to enter the United States under the provisions of the Displaced Persons Act. This help was critical to persons in the refugee camps who possessed no family or friends in America who could pledge to provide them with food and shelter immediately after the arrival in this country. However, this work also became a special concern of Roz-marek's Polish American Congress with the PAC from 1948 onward declaring that it possessed a responsibility for assisting in the resettlement of the refugees.

Yet another organization, the Polish American Immigration and Relief Committee, Inc., claimed a notable place for itself in the work of resettlement. Established in New York in February 1947, the Committee was initially led by the Rev. Felix Burant and Walter Zahariaszewicz and operated with financial assistance from a number of organizations, including the *Rada Polonii* and the PAC. (The Committee, whose work continues under the leadership of Msgr. John Karpinski, has provided new arrivals into New York with housing, meals and counseling and into the 1980s had helped more than 50,000 persons in their first weeks in the United States. For many years, the Committee also had its own representatives in Germany, Belgium, France, Austria and Italy.)[33]

For its part, the Polish American Congress, though created as a political action federation rather than as a humanitarian agency, had soon become involved in the resettlement of refugees. Thus, at its second national convention in 1948, the Congress approved its own "American Committee for the Resettlement of Polish Displaced Persons" in anticipation of the imminent passage of the U.S. Displaced Persons Act. Nominated to chair the Committee was Judge Blair Gunther of Pittsburgh, who had in 1947 replaced Swietlik as Censor of the PNA.

The Resettlement Committee's sole objective was that of identifying potential sponsors of Polish and non-Polish heritage in the United States who would be willing to help receive Polish refugees under the provisions of the Displaced Persons Act. To help the Committee achieve its goal, the PAC approved a new fund raising campaign on its behalf and committed itself to publicizing the need for sponsors throughout Polonia.

Clearly, the task facing the Polish American community at this point was an enormous one. Thus according to figures presented by Swietlik, by 1948 some 80,000 Poles were already in the United States thanks to a series of government orders. Still remaining in Europe were 170,000 Polish refugees interested in coming to the U.S., of whom only 90,000 at most would be able to enter under the provisions of the 1948 Act. (The legislation permitted a total of 205,000 displaced persons of all European nationalities to enter the country over the next four years--certainly not all could be Polish.) At the same time, if sponsors for Polish "DPs" would not be found for individuals seeking entry, the "Polish quota" would go unfilled and persons of other nationalities would most likely come in their place.

This problem was both serious and complex; it also became a source of tensions between the Polish American Congress and the *Rada Polonii*. Swietlik argued that the *RPA* was best able to handle the processing of Polish refugees, since it already employed personnel in the camps who could handle the assignment, among them Florian Piskorski, John Czech, Eugene Buczkowski and Armela Mix. He also noted the *RPA*'s long and positive relationship with both the U.S. authorities and the National Catholic Welfare Council, the umbrella organization responsible for Catholic refugee resettlement in America.

But here again, Rozmarek as President of the PAC was quick to take issue with Swietlik. Thus, in his remarks to the delegates attending the 1948 *RPA* convention, he contended that few Poles would be likely to come to America under the *Rada Polonii*'s auspices, so long as it depended heavily upon the National Catholic Welfare Council for help. "They bring Catholics to the United States," he declared to a storm of applause. "We want Poles!" To Swietlik's dismay, the *Rada*'s own leadership went along with Rozmarek's proposal to make the PAC's Resettlement Committee responsible for bringing Poles into the country.[34]

In short, by the end of the decade the Polish American Congress had supplanted the *Rada Polonii* as the Polish ethnic community's chief humanitarian agency after a conflict over policy that was accentuated by the personal rivalry between Rozmarek and Swietlik. At the same time, their fight had relatively little impact upon the actual workings of either the PAC, its Resettlement Committee or the *Rada Polonii* in the years to come. Interestingly, a look at the rosters of the leadership bodies of the three organizations indicate that many of the same people served on all three!

Having been forced to retreat from playing a major role in refugee resettlement work in America, the *Rada Polonii* did face a genuine crisis after 1948, whether or not even to continue to operate. Internationally, a tension-filled Cold War had set in between the United States and Soviet Russia and Poland found itself, like the rest of Eastern Europe, under a Stalinist regime that was slavishly subservient to Moscow's every command. In such conditions, *RPA* relief efforts into Poland were doomed with the only task left to the agency the delivery of approximately 12,000 monthly food packages to orphans and the neediest residents of the remaining DP camps.

Over the next few years, contributions to the *RPA* would drop precipitously as well. Indeed, the total collected for the entire five year period between 1950 and 1954 totalled only $78,000. But Swietlik doggedly resisted talk of dissolving the organization and in 1954, a year in which the RPA generated the grand sum of $16,000 for its activities, won his Board's approval to continue in the hope that political conditions inside Poland would eventually improve and with them the *Rada's* opportunity to resume operations there.

In this he was proven correct. In October 1956, following months of steadily growing economic crisis and political unrest throughout Poland and much of the rest of Eastern Europe, the Stalinist regime was replaced and its policies discredited by a new communist leadership committed to bringing some limited, though nonetheless, significant reforms in the system. Returned to office as the Polish United Workers Party's First Secretary was Wladyslaw Gomulka, who had been so unceremoniously removed from that post by the Stalinists. Though no liberal in any sense of that term (he had vigorously led the Communists' campaign of terror against Poland's democratic peasant movement in the struggle for control over the country between 1945 and 1947), Gomulka did order an end to the regime's harassment of the Church and its charitable arm, *Caritas.*

The next year Swietlik initiated contacts with Church and state authorities to learn whether the *RPA* might resume its activities in the ancestral homeland. In 1958, he and Adele Lagodzinska, President of the Polish Women's Alliance and an officer of the *Rada Polonii* (and the Polish American Congress as well) travelled to Poland to formally reestablish the *RPA's* activities there. They returned home with recommendations that the *Rada* focus renewed fund raising and relief efforts on behalf of a number of hospitals and orphanages in special need of equipment available only from the West. A new nationwide appeal was subsequently launched in 1959, on the twentieth anniversary of the beginning of the *Rada*'s work for Poland in World War II. This effort was modestly successful due to the help the *RPA* received from its twenty remaining district affiliates. In all nearly $200,000 was collected during the three year long appeal.

In 1963, the U.S. government inaugurated a program to deliver surplus food products to Poland. At that time it was agreed that persons stationed in Poland in the employ of the *Rada Polonii* could help in distributing these goods to people in genuine need.[35] The program proved to be a real success: during its first year in operation 1.3 million pounds of flour, 533,000 pounds of dried milk, 538,000 pounds of margarine and vegetable oil and 538,000 pounds of cheese were shipped to Poland for a total of 1,450 tons of food. According to Swietlik's report for that year, 51,200 individuals, among them 17,000 children, were recipients of this assistance. The program included some medical supplies as well.

The annual surplus food deliveries from the United States to Poland continued for seven years, through the end of 1969. Altogether, during this period, American food assistance amounted to 14,170,000 pounds or 7,085 tons and had a value conservatively estimated at nearly $3 million. At the same time, while providing its services in the distribution of these foodstuffs, the *RPA* was also engaged in directly assisting a number of hospitals, schools and orphanages in various sections of the country; it also made donations to the Catholic University of Lublin, the only independent institution of higher learning permitted to operate anywhere in the Communist world.

At its January 27, 1970 meeting, Swietlik informed his executive committee of the decision of the U.S. government to terminate its food surplus distribution program. This action, though not unexpected, signalled the final knell to the *Rada Polonii Amerykanskiej,* even though the *RPA* still possessed more than $107,000 in its treasury. Most of those funds were already committed to one of the *Rada*'s varied benevolent projects in Poland, however, and did not require any on-site inspections to be completed. By January 1, 1971, the *RPA*'s treasury had diminished to $74,000 and a year later this figure had been further reduced to $33,000. On November 23, 1974, the last date for which records of the organization are available, only $9,049 remained in its coffers.

The end of the *Rada Polonii* closed a significant chapter in the story of the Polish ethnic community's service to Poland. That the organization disappeared was, however, not so much due to the full realization of its objectives and the end of need in Poland and more the consequence of the structural character of the *Rada* itself. Simply put, the *RPA* remained to its very demise an organization of men and women of one generation, the generation that had initially interested itself in the humanitarian work for Poland at the time of the outbreak of World War II. This cadre included the venerable Swietlik, born in 1890, Wolowska, Lagodzinska, Olejniczak, Casimir Midowicz, Stanley Turkiewicz, Florian Piskorski, Bronislas Smykowski, and Adalbert Soska.[36] With practically no exceptions these individuals and their counterparts in the various local district affiliates of the *RPA* continued in their work either until retirement or death. Few were ever replaced by activists of the next generation. Those, whether American or Polish born, tended to join the Polish American Congress if they were interested in taking part in work on Poland's behalf.

Ironically, the *Rada*'s work would be continued by the Polish American Congress in the next decade and thus serve as the highest act of recognition the PAC leadership could offer its old rival. Already in 1971 the Congress had set up its own charitable foundation as a tax exempt organization to collect funds for humanitarian activities for Poland should they be warranted. This move proved to be far-sighted for the PAC Charitable Foundation would indeed take up the work of the *RPA* after 1980, in response to the Poles' own requests for such assistance.

Yet there was another tie linking the *Rada Polonii* with the PAC Charitable Foundation. In 1970, Aloysius Mazewski, who had only recently succeeded Rozmarek as President of both the Polish National Alliance and the Polish American Congress, was invited to join the Board of Directors of the *Rada Polonii*. In a genuine sense, his participation in the *RPA*'s leadership, as much as the Congress' later action to set up its own Foundation, served to complete a major stage in the process of Polonia's organizational integration, one which had begun nearly a century before but which had never been successfully brought about. Indeed, with the creation of the PAC Charitable Foundation, Polonia was at last united on an enduring basis for the purpose of representing Polish ethnic concerns on both the political and charitable levels. And thanks to the rapprochement between the Congress and the *RPA* that was effected by Mazewski and Swietlik, the Charitable Foundation could indeed later claim to be following in the footsteps of the *Rada*.

At the *RPA*'s January 1970 meeting, Swietlik suggested to Board member Joseph Bialasiewicz that he compose a summary study of the *Rada*'s achievements over the years. In so doing he called upon him to focus upon three matters deserving of specific attention -- the *RPA*'s efforts on behalf of Polish soldiers in Soviet Russia during World War II, the aid it provided to servicemen in Britain, and its activities during and after the war on behalf of the hundreds of refugees, many of them orphans, who had come to Santa Rosa, Mexico from Russia and later would settle permanently in the United States. Clearly, as this review should indicate, that summary merely scratches the surface of the Polish American Council's many contributions during its more than thirty years of voluntary service on Poland's behalf.

Table 1. Total Cash Contributions to American Relief for Poland (Rada Polonii) from its Thirty-Six District Affiliates, 1939-1948 and their Status in 1954

District Number and Locus of Activity	1939-1948 Contributions	Status in 1954+	Total Raised, 1939-1954
1. Western Massachusetts	$90,751	Inactive	$115,558
2. Connecticut	329,468	Reorganizing	369,314
3. Syracuse, New York	24,856	Liquidated	24,859
4. New York, NY	110,772	Reorganizing	116,749
5. New Jersey	127,337	Active	332,228
6. Philadelphia, PA	78,032	Inactive	78,032
7. Wilkes-Barre, PA	24,760	Liquidated	24,760
8. Buffalo, NY	106,900	Active	109,900
9. Indiana	53,783	Liquidated	47,449
10. Minnesota	36,453	Inactive	38,535
11. Omaha, Nebraska	4,990	Liquidated	13,778
12. Pittsburgh, PA	64,846	Inactive	72,056
13. Chicago (disbanded after 1940)	17,267	Liquidated	17,267
14. Baltimore, MD	12,400	Liquidated	13,715
15. Northern Michigan	2,657	Liquidated	4,943
16. Detroit, Michigan	57,905	Active	72,388
17. Cleveland Ohio	149,000	Active	163,500
18. Milwaukee, WI	94,680	Liquidated	82,050
19. St. Louis, MO	29,896	Active	34,784
20. Chicago, Illinois	40,746	Active	46,086
21. Chicago, Illinois	106,630	Active	153,138
22. Chicago, Illinois	40,500	Liquidated	50,100
23. Schuykill & Carbon Counties, PA	12,556	Liquidated	12,721
24. East St. Louis, IL	13,178	Liquidated	14,339
25. Brooklyn, NY	57,550	Liquidated	61,650
26. Polish National Catholic Churches in Scranton, PA	18,184	Liquidated	18,683
27. PNCC in New England, hdqrs, Springfield, MA	10,789	Liquidated	10,802
28. PNCC around Pittsburgh area	2,000	Liquidated	2,000
29. Buffalo-Pittsburgh diocese of PNCC	934	Liquidated	934
30. Rhode Island	17,374	Liquidated	18,896
31. Eastern MA	10,260	Inactive	23,089
32. Chicago, IL ("Little Poland" Clubs)	10,780	Active	22,912
33. Chicago, IL (PNA Members district)	8,842	Active	14,142
34. Detroit, Michigan	11,171	Active	49,473
35. Youngstown, Ohio	11,220	Active	17,486
36. Hamtramck & North Detroit, Michigan	11,500	Active	32,479
Total 36 districts	**$1,800,965**		**$2,280,795**

+12 active, 2 reorganizing and 5 inactive districts as of 1954.

**Table 2. Contributions in Cash to
RADA POLONIA AMERYKANSKIEJ
(American Relief for Poland)
1939-1948, and 1939-1954, by State**

	As of 1948	As of 1954
1. Connecticut	$329,470	$369,310
2. New York	300,550	313,630
3. Illinois	237,950	317,980
4. Pennsylvania	200,850	208,720
5. Ohio	160,220	180,990
6. New Jersey	127,340	332,230
7. Massachusetts	111,800	149,450
8. Wisconsin	94,680	89,050
9. Michigan	83,240	159,280
10. Indiana	53,780	47,450
11. Minnesota	36,450	38,540
12. Missouri	29,990	34,780
13. Rhode Island	17,370	18,900
14. Maryland	12,400	13,720
15. Nebraska	4,990	13,780
	$1,801,080	**$2,280,810**

IV. The Polish American Congress: The Rozmarek Era, 1944-1968

The signing, on August 23, 1939, of a non-aggression pact between the representatives of the governments of Nazi Germany and Soviet Russia was cataclysmic in its impact. Eight days later, German forces launched a surprise attack on Poland by land, sea and air and quickly drove its remaining army units eastward into retreat along the Vistula River. While Poland's allies, Great Britain and France, did honor their mutual security agreement and declared war against Germany on September 3, they made no military moves to come to the aid of the beleaguered nation.

On September 16, the Polish government crossed into Romania, where its members were interned. There, President Ignacy Moscicki resigned after appointing Wladyslaw Raczkiewicz to succeed him. Raczkiewicz, a past chairman of the World Union of Poles from Abroad *(Swiatpol)*, then named General Wladyslaw Sikorski, a democratically minded former prime minister and a respected military man, to head a government in exile headquartered in France. Sikorski had already been recognized by the French authorities as Commander-in-Chief of the Polish Armed forces in the West. A Polish parliament in exile composed of all the major pre-war parties was also constituted, with the venerable pianist-patriot Ignacy Paderewski as its chairman.

The Soviet invasion of Poland from the East, in accord with the secret protocols of the Nazi-Soviet pact, resulted in the fourth partition of Poland.[1] Nonetheless, authority had been transferred to Sikorski, whose position as head of the exile government was reinforced by his command over well-equipped armed forces eventually including nearly 200,000 men. Among them were some 100,000 soldiers and officers under General Wladyslaw Anders, all interned in the Soviet Union after 1939 but permitted to reform and exit the U.S.S.R. through Iran in 1942. In addition, an underground resistance movement soon emerged inside the country, its military wing renamed the "Home Army" *(Armia krajowa* or *AK)* in 1942. By 1944 the Home Army could count on some 350,000 participants; it operated under the authority of Sikorski's government, which reestablished itself in London following the fall of France in April 1940.[2]

In the United States, the spirit of isolationism remained supreme, although President Franklin Delano Roosevelt did what he could to support the Allies' cause. Under such circumstances, there seemed little that Polonia could do on Poland's behalf in the political realm. However, from the start organized efforts were initiated by the Polish American fraternals and parishes to begin collecting money and material on behalf of the victims of the Nazi-Soviet invasion. Most significant, but by no means unique was the response of the largest of Polonia fraternals, the Polish National Alliance, which provided more than one-half million dollars in relief assistance by the end of 1939 alone. As noted previously, the War's outbreak brought about a rejuvenation in the activities of Polonia's chief charitable federation, the Polish American Council *(Rada Polonii Amerykanskiej* or *RPA)*. Indeed, from 1939 into the first months of 1944, Polish Americans concentrated their involvement for Poland by directing their activities on behalf of *Rada Polonii.*

While the *RPA* had to remain apolitical in order to be eligible for formal recognition as a charity it seems doubtful whether its services as a political lobby would have been received favorably by the Sikorski government, at least at first. Indeed, the London Poles were confident of their abilities to represent Poland's concerns to the Great Powers without Polonia's help. Thus, by early October 1939, the Poles had gained diplomatic recognition for their cause from the United States and from the start enjoyed international support.

Given these considerations, the *RPA*'s apolitical character did not appear to pose many immediate problems. Hence, when President Roosevelt and Prime Minister Winston Churchill signed the "Atlantic Charter" in August 1941, the *Rada Polonii* leadership could applaud the statement as expressing its members' hopes, both as Americans and as Polish Americans. Following the United States' entry into the conflict in the aftermath of the Japanese assault on Pearl Harbor in Decem-

ber 1941, the Atlantic Charter would take on a new significance, as America's official rationale for going to war against
both Japan and its Axis allies in Europe, Germany and Italy.
The Atlantic Charter proclaimed the right of all peoples to
choose their own form of government, urged all states to aban-
don force in settling international disputes, and rejected any
territorial changes by one state at the expense of another.[3] The
signing of the Charter occurred at a time when Britain was
already allied with Soviet Russia, itself the target of a massive
German invasion that began on June 22, 1941. Ironically
through Churchill's action, his junior partner Sikorski suddenly
found his government harnessed into a strange alliance with the
same Stalin who with Hitler had participated in destroying
Poland's independence less than two years before. Ominously,
in his subsequent meetings with Stalin, Sikorski failed to win the
Soviet ruler's approval of the postwar return of the Eastern
Polish territories seized in 1939. Sikorski's decision to go ahead
with a Polish-Soviet alliance despite his inability to settle the
border issue not only caused a temporary crisis inside his own
government (three ministers resigned from his cabinet); it set
into motion a determined effort among his critics in America to
begin to politicize Polonia and take the community beyond
humanitarian work.

Almost from the War's beginning, a small number of Polish
Americans scattered around the country had pressed the *Rada
Polonii*, unsuccessfully, to include political action in its program.[4] Most prominent among these early activists were Max
Wegrzynek, editor and publisher of the New York Polish language daily *Nowy Swiat* newspaper, and Frank Januszewski,
who had similar responsibilities with Detroit's *Dziennik Polski.*
By late 1941, they had been joined by several former Polish
government officials closely identified with the person and
policies of the country's prewar leader, Jozef Pilsudski. Among
them were Ignacy Matuszewski, Poland's Treasurer in 1939,
Henryk Rajchman, formerly its Minister of Industry and Trade,
and ex-Minister of Culture Waclaw Jedrzejewicz.[5]

By the Spring of 1942, these individuals had put together a
new political action group centered in the eastern section of the
United States. In May, they issued an appeal addressed to
President Roosevelt outlining their concerns regarding Po-

land's postwar fate. Signed by 130 Polish Americans, the document urged the United States to make the subject of an independent and powerful Poland, with its prewar eastern border intact, an essential element of the peace settlement to be arrived at with Britain and Soviet Russia, all this in accord with the principles of the Atlantic Charter. The statement also included a call for the creation of a nationwide political organization to speak for Polonia on these matters.[6]

On June 21-22, 1942 in New York, the new organization was formally established as the National Committee of Americans of Polish Descent (Komitet Narodowy Amerykanow Polskiego Pochodzenia, or KNAPP). Reaffirming the themes defined in the May Appeal, KNAPP asserted its commitment to the wartime alliance between the United States and Poland and the importance of American postwar assistance to Poland.[7]

In pressing for strong U.S. support for Poland's territorial interests at a time when Nazi Germany's forces had driven deep into Soviet territory, KNAPP immediately found itself subjected to sharp domestic criticism from those who refused to even countenance any comments about the past conduct or future aims of America's embattled Soviet ally. The new organization, in questioning the conciliatory policies followed by the London Polish government toward Moscow, also provoked Prime Minister Sikorski. Thus, in his December 1942 visit to the United States Sikorski declared publicly that "whoever criticizes my understanding with Russia is an agent of (Nazi propaganda chief Josef) Goebbels."[8]

Given Polonia's broad support of Sikorski and his own cordial relationship with the Rada Polonii's chairman, Francis Swietlik, KNAPP's initial pronouncements were received coldly in the Polish American community. Moreover, at its October 1942 convention the RPA approved a resolution to add political work to its activities, a move aimed at undercutting KNAPP. This effort came to nothing; in December 1943 the Rada Polonii was informed by the U.S. Government that its charitable status would be endangered by even the hint of engagement in political activities. Consequently, Swietlik removed the offending paragraph from the RPA's by-laws.[9]

Events in 1943 led to a dramatic change in KNAPP's fortunes. In April the Nazis discovered a mass grave in the Katyn forest in western Russia which contained the corpses of more than four thousand Polish officers captured in 1939 by the Soviet Army. These men were among the 15,000 men, most of them officers, whose whereabouts had been unaccounted for ever since the Soviet Union and the Polish Government in London had resumed diplomatic relations in July 1941. For nearly two years, the matter had been a source of discord between the two allies.[10]

The Nazis declared Katyn a Soviet atrocity, a charge Stalin indignantly denied.* Berlin then proposed that the International Red Cross investigate the allegations independently. When Sikorski and his cabinet supported the idea, fearing that the other missing officers had met the same fate, Stalin abruptly terminated all diplomatic relations with his government. From this point his dealing with Poles would be limited to the leaders of the Soviet-controlled "Union of Polish Patriots" who were living in the U.S.S.R. and its adjunct in the Nazi-occupied homeland, the "Polish Workers" (or Communist) Party, established in January 1942.[11]

Sikorski's tragic death in an airplane accident at Gibraltar in August 1943 was a great blow to the Polish cause, since he had enjoyed broad international recognition and, until the Katyn incident, had maintained good relations with Stalin. His successor, Stanislaw Mikolajczyk, head of the Polish Peasants Party in the London coalition, shared Sikorski's democratic

---

* On April 13, 1990, fifty years after the Massacre, the Soviet TASS news agency issued a statement noting that recently discovered archival documents placed "direct responsibility for the atrocities in the Katyn Forest on (the chief of the Soviet secret police) Lavrentii Beria and (his) henchmen." The statement went on to offer the Soviet government's "profound regret over the tragedy...one of the gravest crimes of Stalinism..." In response, Polish Solidarity leader Lech Walesa very likely spoke for his countrymen when he declared that it was "good that the murderers admit their murder" but at the same time called for compensatory damages from the U.S.S.R. to the families of the victims and the punishment of surviving parties. This view was backed by a resolution of the Polish Parliament on April 28, 1990. *Radio Free Europe: Report on Eastern Europe*, Volume I, Numbers 17 and 18 (April 27 and May 4, 1990).

philosophy and realistic outlook on Soviet-Polish relations; he did not, however, possess either Sikorski's stature or his leadership experience. Significantly, Mikolajczyk was not named Commander-in-Chief of the Polish armed forces, a post Sikorski had held along with that of Prime Minister.

In any event, when Stalin, Roosevelt and Churchill met for their first summit in Teheran, Iran at the end of November 1943, the two Western leaders were willing to concede Poland's eastern territories to the U.S.S.R., although each did so independently and perhaps even without the other's knowledge. In his private meeting with Stalin, Roosevelt made only one request of the Soviet chieftain, that their understanding be kept secret so as not to cause him unnecessary embarrassment in his coming reelection campaign for an unprecedented fourth term. The President expected a close race in 1944 and did not want to risk losing the support of "six million Polish voters" (sic) by advertising his position on Poland's borders. For his part, Churchill told Stalin that the Soviet Union deserved to have secure western borders, a position he took without previously informing Mikolajczyk.[12]

The actions of the two Western leaders at Teheran amounted to conceding to Stalin the final say as to the character of Poland's future government. Less than eight months later, on July 22, 1944, a "Polish Committee of National Liberation" would be proclaimed with Soviet military support in the town of Lublin; leading the Committee were communists whom Stalin would subsequently have installed as heads of the postwar Polish state, despite the fact the they enjoyed little if any popular support.[13]

Also influencing Polonia's mobilization along the lines called for by KNAPP were the activities of several pro-Soviet groups which claimed to represent the millions of Polish Americans and other peoples of Slavic heritage throughout the country. Their assertions were bolstered by the realities of the wartime U.S.-Soviet alliance, which permitted pro-Communist elements to operate publicly as enthusiasts of collaboration between the two countries. The most grandiose of these concoctions was the American Slav Congress, founded in 1942 in Detroit. Headed by Leon Krzycki, a veteran Polish-American socialist and trade unionist who was then a vice president in the

CIO labor federation, the Congress flatly declared itself the spokesman for fifteen million Slavic Americans in proclaiming their allegiance to the United States, the Roosevelt administration, the war effort and America's alliance with Soviet Russia. In turn it sharply criticized the Polish government in London and was especially vitriolic in denouncing Sikorski in connection with the Katyn massacre controversy. In backing the International Red Cross investigation of the atrocity, the Slav Conference's leaders argued that the London Poles had undermined the Allied cause.[14]

Another organization, which took part in the American Slav Congress and was also headed by Krzycki, was the American Polish Labor Council. Calling itself the voice of 600,000 Polish American workers, the Council, like the Congress, was loud in its support of Roosevelt and his 1944 presidential campaign. Not surprisingly, both organizations were accorded substantial recognition in Washington as better representing Polish American opinion than the "anti-Soviet" *KNAPP*.[15]

By late 1943 however, sentiment in Polonia had at long last changed to favor the formation of a nationwide political action movement in support of a truly independent and democratic postwar Poland. By this time too, the tide of the War itself was shifting against the Nazis and in favor of the Soviet forces, which were moving inexorably westward.

Thus, on January 4, 1944 the first Polish territory was occupied by Red Army units. At Teheran, the launching of the long-awaited Allied invasion of western Europe had been set for May 1944; the success of this massive but risky attack at Normandy would be decisive in bringing the War in Europe to a close a year later. In the South, American and British troops were moving slowly in heavy fighting up the Italian peninsula. A major battle in that theater of the conflict would occur on May 18, 1944 at the fortress-monastery of Monte Casino, seized in a bloody struggle by units of General Anders' Second Polish Army.[16]

It was in these decisive weeks that a new truly representative Polish American political action organization was finally born, its name the Polish American Congress *(Kongres Polonii Amerykanskiej,* or *PAC).* The idea for the organization was conceived in January 1944 when Wegrzynek, President of

KNAPP met in Chicago with Charles Rozmarek, President of the Polish National Alliance. Soon afterwards, Rozmarek put together a patriotic manifestation at the Chicago Civic Opera House, an event which brought together a large representation of Polonia activists from the Chicago-based fraternals. There, while still refraining from calling for a new Polonia political federation, Rozmarek sharply criticized Soviet intransigence on the question of Poland's eastern borders. Decrying the flood of propaganda in America hostile to the Polish government in London, he urged Polish Americans to express their support for the London government as the true representative of occupied Poland by deluging the White House with letters and telegrams.[17]

Towards the close of the manifestation, a resolution was approved and forwarded to representatives of the allied powers, underscoring the points Rozmarek had presented, namely Polonia's loyalty to the United States and the war effort, its support for the Polish government in London, and its opposition to American and British approval of Soviet demands for territory at Poland's expense. Only one month later, on March 4, 1944, Rozmarek and the heads of the other fraternals called a second meeting at the headquarters of the Polish Women's Alliance in Chicago, an event attended by fifty leaders. At this gathering, several leaders from *KNAPP* were present, including Wegrzynek and Januszewski.[18]

The main business of the March 4 gathering involved the calling of a congress of representatives from Polish American organizations, parishes and societies to express Polonia's growing political concerns over Poland. An executive committee was established under Rozmarek's chairmanship, with PRCUA President John Olejniczak to serve as Treasurer and Polish Women's Alliance President Honorata Wolowska elected Secretary. Also determined in Chicago were the rules for participation at the planned congress and the various commissions charged with presenting reports at the conclave. The name of the new organization was also approved at the Chicago meeting and some $5,750 pledged to realize its initial plans.

The aims of the new organization as unanimously approved were stated as follows:

We, American citizens of Polish descent, representatives of the Polish organizations from throughout the
country, the clergy and Polish language press, gathered in
conference on March 4, 1944 in Chicago at the headquarters
of the Polish Women's Alliance, keep in mind the need to
strengthen our common efforts to speed the victory of the
Allies over the enemies of democracy, agree with the ideals
expressed in the Atlantic Charter and the statement of the
Four Freedoms strongly stated by President Roosevelt. We
further seek to achieve a just peace, guaranteeing the freedom and independence of the United Nations, large and
small, a peace which will prevent any future aggression; we
wish to come to the assistance of the Polish nation, which
from the beginning of the War has fought on the side of the
Allies on all fronts for the aims that have been previously
stated, and which has suffered the greatest losses. We want
to help a democratic Poland, represented by its one and only
legally constituted government headquartered in London, a
country whose borders are seriously threatened. In closing,
we recognize the necessity of creating a central organization
to defend the interests of American Polonia in all its areas of
concern and thus we proclaim unanimously the calling of a
Polish American Congress in the latter half of the month of
May 1944.[19]

On March 11, the leaders of *KNAPP* called a conference in
New York to approve the plan for a nationwide political action
organization along the lines set forth in Chicago. Playing leading roles at this meeting attended by some 170 activists were
Wegrzynek, Peter Yolles, a journalist with the *Nowy Swiat* paper, Rozmarek, and Starzynski, President of the Falcons, all of
whom had been in Chicago. While those present concurred
with Rozmarek's proposal to call the Polish American Congress, it was also decided that *KNAPP* maintain a separate
organizational existence under the PAC umbrella. The resolution adopted at the meeting, though similar to the one approved in Chicago, also called for cooperation of the entire
Polish American community in defending democracy, Christian
ethics, and the American people from totalitarianism and asserted Polonia's responsibility to defend the interests of a fully
independent and sovereign Poland with its eastern borders
intact and wide access to the sea.[20]

The response to the proposal to hold a Polish American Congress was enthusiastic. In hundreds of parishes and local lodge halls around the country, people met to elect delegates to travel to the Congress, which was scheduled to be held in Buffalo, New York beginning on May 28, 1944. At the same time, the announced Congress was greeted with a measure of concern in Washington, D.C. Well aware of the influential role that members of *KNAPP* were likely to play at the meeting, White House representatives worked to direct its agenda away from criticisms of the American-Soviet alliance and Washington's failure to support the London government on the Polish-Soviet border question. In Charles Rozmarek, they found a leader who would play a moderating role in handling these matters. As a consequence, the Congress did not become a protest over U.S. government policy on the Polish issue, nor did those present take a partisan stance with an eye to the coming November presidential election. While committed to supporting Poland, Rozmarek made sure the Congress was to be equally focused upon asserting Polonia's loyalty to the United States and its war aims.[21]

The first Polish American Congress since the World War I era proved to be the most impressive manifestation of patriotic feeling in the history of Polonia and was recognized as such by observers from Washington who were in attendance. One even wrote back to the White House that the Congress would "go down in history as the most colossal piece of organizational work."[22] In all more than 2,600 delegates from twenty-six states were present, with the fraternals and the parishes together providing most of the participants. What is more, nearly twenty-five thousand people took part in a massive parade before the first session of the Congress and some 16,000 were in the audience at its opening ceremonies where they heard Rozmarek give the reasons for its convocation. Many political officials were also present, including U.S. Senator James Mead of New York and Congressmen John Dingell of Michigan, Boleslas Monkiewicz of Connecticut, Thaddeus Wasielewski of Wisconsin, Thomas D'Alesandro of Maryland and Buffalo's Joseph Mruk. Among the sheaves of telegrams and congratulatory messages read at the ceremonies was one from President

Roosevelt, which the delegates stood for out of loyalty and affection for their Commander in Chief.[23]

In Buffalo, the delegates heard reports from the chairmen of a variety of special commissions focusing upon issues from veterans' concerns to education; the primary purposes of the gathering were, however, approval of the goals of the new organization and the selection of its top leadership. Asserting its patriotic character, the PAC adopted as its two foremost aims its firm support for the American war effort and a just peace based upon the principles of the Atlantic Charter. On the second point, it was understood that the Charter's precepts assured the restoration of an independent and popularly supported post war Poland whose eastern borders would remain unchanged from what they had been before 1939. Winning unanimous approval was a resolution which tied the American war effort to the cause of Mikolajczyk's regime in London, "the only legitimate and constitutional representative government of Poland."[24]

Charles Rozmarek was elected President of the Polish American Congress, with Honorata Wolowska, President of the Polish Women's Alliance, Teofil Starzynski, President of the Falcons, John Mikuta of the Polish National Union (the fraternal arm of the Polish National Catholic Church), and Max Wegrzynek and Frank Januszewski of *KNAPP* chosen to become national vice presidents. President John Olejniczak of the Polish Roman Catholic Union became the Treasurer of the Congress, with Stanislas Gutowski, head of the Pulaski Foundation of New York (and another *KNAPP* leader) elected National Secretary. The new PAC leadership represented a balance between the Eastern and Midwestern branches of Polonia; it also reflected the relative strength of the two main components of the new federation, with three leaders from *KNAPP* and three others from the Chicago-based fraternals. (Starzynski was active in both groupings and Mikuta was included in response to an appeal from the Polish National Catholic Church that it not be ostracized from the new federation).

Approved at the Congress, finally, was a "Memorial" (or Memorandum) addressed to President Roosevelt. This statement, to be found in the appendix of this work, summed up

Polonia's concerns. But Rozmarek's efforts to secure an audience with President Roosevelt to personally hand him the Memorial were rejected repeatedly by the White House, partly on the grounds that its tone guaranteed that such a meeting would only generate anti-Soviet publicity. Indeed, Rozmarek and his colleagues would not be privileged to meet with the President until October 11, more than four months later. That this happened in the last weeks of the Home Army's tragic sixty-three day uprising to liberate Warsaw from the Nazis-and before the Red Army would occupy the capital-made the session all the more poignant. (The uprising had commenced on August 1; its consequences included the deaths of some 200,000 people and the destruction of nearly the entire city. Throughout Stalin refused to provide any assistance to the insurgents while the western allies protested in vain.)[25]

That FDR met with the PAC delegation at all, for what was ostensibly a ceremonial session commemorating the death of Casimir Pulaski, was due to concerns that the President's re-election campaign might be adversely affected by Polish American defections to Roosevelt's Republican opponent, New York Governor Thomas Dewey. Significantly, in the rather informal get-together in the Oval Office, a large map of pre-war Poland hung on the wall behind the President's desk, an unspoken but seemingly significant sign implying where U.S. sympathies lie on the border issue. For his part, Roosevelt made no explicit commitments about Poland's future beyond expressing his hope that the country would be reconstituted after the War as a "strong and independent" state. One alert reporter would observe that the President's formulation was very close to what Stalin had said at the time of the creation of the Communist-led Polish Committee of National Liberation on July 22 in Lublin. At that time, he had declared his support of a "strong, independent and friendly Poland" headed by people who recognized the Soviet incorporation of the disputed territories.[26]

Despite the cordiality of the White House meeting, Roosevelt and his advisers continued, with good reason, to worry about Polish American support in the upcoming elections. Not only was Governor Dewey seeking to persuade Polonia not to take seriously FDR's words on Poland's behalf, an incident in Moscow on October 13, 1944 was cause for new concern. That day, Churchill, accompanied by Polish Prime Minister Mikolajczyk, U.S. Ambassador to the Soviet Union Averill Harriman, and British Foreign Minister Anthony Eden met with Soviet Foreign Minister Vyacheslav Molotov. Mikolajczyk, who had spoken with Roosevelt the previous Spring in Washington, had been led to understand that the border issue between his government and the Soviets could yet be resolved through realistic bargaining. He was thus shocked to hear Molotov declare that, eleven months earlier at Teheran, Roosevelt had agreed to Stalin's demands regarding Poland's eastern borders and that it was his duty to go along with the decision. Moreover, Mikolajczyk was then warned not to relay any word of the disclosure to his government. This instruction was, evidently, followed and no one in Polonia was apprised of the actual U.S. position toward the Polish issue in the crucial weeks leading up to the Presidential election.[27]

One week before the vote, Roosevelt travelled to Chicago for a final campaign swing; receiving Rozmarek in his presidential train car, FDR assured him that the principles of the Atlantic Charter and the Four Freedoms would not be abandoned in Poland's case. In return, Rozmarek gave Roosevelt his personal endorsement; this the Democratic party widely publicized throughout Polonia as the PAC's official position.[28]

In the November election, Roosevelt defeated Dewey by a wide margin in the all-important Electoral College, 432-99. But his popular vote majority of 54 to 46 percent was surprisingly narrow, given Roosevelt's already legendary stature as both the father of the "New Deal" and the Commander-in-Chief of the Allied forces in a war drawing to a victorious close. One salient fact in this election is that the Polish American vote proved indeed to be important in Roosevelt's triumph.

Polish Americans backed Roosevelt by a margin of 9 to 1, and their support was indeed crucial, just as he had told Stalin at Teheran. In the ten states having the largest concentrations of Polish Americans, six were decided by margins of less than one hundred thousand votes. Together, the seven states having large Polish ethnic populations carried by FDR (New York, Michigan, Illinois, Pennsylvania, New Jersey, Massachusetts and Connecticut) provided him with 169 of the 266 electoral votes he needed for reelection. Had Rozmarek known of the President's actual stance on Poland and had he publicly opposed his fourth term candidacy, it is possible that the final election results would have been quite different.[29] Following the election, Mikolajczyk informed his cabinet in London of the Western Allies' true position on the eastern Polish border question and then resigned when he failed to gain an agreement to accept their policy. Mikolajczyk's fall paved the way for British and American actions at the second great "Big Three" summit meeting at Yalta in the Soviet Union in February 1945. There Churchill and Roosevelt formally agreed to Stalin's demand that the Polish-Soviet borders be drawn more than 100 miles to the West of the pre-war boundary. Accordingly, Poland lost a total of 69,000 square miles of territory, two significant and historically Polish cities, Lwow and Wilno, and substantial petroleum resources in the Lwow region. In compensation for these losses in the East, Poland was awarded some 40,000 square miles of German territories in the West, including most of the old East Prussian region north of the pre-war Polish state, the Baltic sea coast province of *Pomorze* (Pomerania), and the coal-rich region of *Slask* (Silesia). After the War, these regions, already depopulated of their German inhabitants who fled west from the approaching Soviet and Polish armies, were resettled by Poles. The new population represented the survivors of the Soviet invasion of Poland's eastern territories in 1939; they had already endured the terror of Stalin's rule and the hardships of forced resettlement in Siberia and Central Asia.[30] In all, the War would result in the deaths of more than six million of the country's citizens (over twenty percent of its population), more than 5.3 million of whom were civilians. No other nation would suffer as huge a proportional loss of population and so high a death rate among its educated and professional classes. Furthermore, extraordinary damage had been done to its cities, transportation system, industry and agriculture, damage that would require years to repair.

Even more significant than the border question was the agreement at Yalta on Poland's postwar government. Already in January 1945 the U.S.S.R. had recognized the Communist-led Polish Committee of National Liberation (the "Lublin Poles") as the government of the new Polish state, despite the absence of any evidence that it indeed possessed substantial popular support. Neither Churchill nor Roosevelt could budge him on this point, although Stalin did agree to the expansion of the Lublin Committee into a "Provisional Government of National Unity" and to include within it "democratic leaders from Poland itself and ... Poles from abroad." This modest concession nevertheless excluded the Polish government in London.[31]

The actual complexion of the Provisional Government of National Unity was left to be settled later in Moscow at a meeting of Polish leaders; at Yalta the Big Three were able only to commit the new government to hold "free and unfettered elections as soon as possible on the basis of universal suffrage and secret ballot," with all "democratic and anti-Nazi parties" invited to put forth candidates for elective office.

To their lasting credit, Charles Rozmarek and the Polish American Congress voiced sharp criticisms of the Yalta agreement as soon as it was made public, this at a time when American opinion was overwhelmingly favorable to Roosevelt's actions at the Conference.[32] Thus, Rozmarek called Yalta a "moral abdication of the Atlantic Charter" and the Big Three's treatment of Poland "a staggering blow to the cause of freedom."[33] Practically alone at first, he called upon the U.S. Congress to repudiate FDR's actions, characterizing what had transpired at Yalta to be a Soviet-American treaty requiring the approval of the Senate. Disseminating its position through its own *Bulletin,* the many Polish language dailies and weeklies then published throughout the country, and in special pamphlets such as *Stany Zjednoczone, Polska i Polonia Amerykanska* (The United States, Poland and Polonia) the Polish American Congress relentlessly condemned Churchill and Roosevelt for having sacrificed the principles embodied in the Atlantic Charter, for which the Western Allied powers had fought and won the war.

In May 1945, Rozmarek headed a PAC delegation to San Francisco, the site of the first meeting of the newly established United Nations. There the group, which included PAC Vice Presidents Frank Januszewski and Ignace Nurkiewicz, Rozmarek's trusted secretary Frank Dziob, Ignacy Matuszewski of

KNAPP, and Historian Oskar Halecki, energetically articulated Poland's case in the absence of representatives from the Lublin Committee and the London-based exile leadership.

In San Francisco, Rozmarek drew attention to the Soviet seizure and imprisonment of sixteen Polish resistance leaders who had been lured to a meeting with Red Army officers, only to be arrested as war criminals. Rozmarek demanded that U.S. Secretary of State Edward Stettinius seek an explanation from Soviet Foreign Minister Molotov as to their whereabouts and fate. The publicity surrounding the matter brought considerable embarrassment to the U.S.S.R.*

At the U.N. conference Rozmarek also repeated the PAC's opposition to the Polish eastern border revisions approved at Yalta. Calling upon the United States and Britain to renounce all agreements pertaining to Poland which had been adopted at that conference, he urged Washington to resume diplomatic relations with the London Polish government. While the PAC effort was unsuccessful in effecting a change in American policy, the noisy and insistent Polonia delegation did make its presence felt. One prominent news commentator of the day, H. V. Kaltenborn, observed that the PAC had engaged in the best lobbying effort he had witnessed in San Francisco.[34]

Following Roosevelt's death and Vice President Harry Truman's accession to the Presidency in April 1945, the PAC was hopeful that the U.S. would take a harder line toward the Soviet Union and strongly support the holding of free elections in Poland. But in June 1945 Washington recognized the new Polish Provisional Government of National Unity, one put together in Moscow and augmented by Mikolajczyk's inclusion as the sole significant figure from the West. Henceforth, the Truman administration did little to influence Communist policy inside Poland other than to consider withholding future economic aid to the war-ravaged country. As Historian Richard Lukas has noted:

---

* On the arrest of the sixteen, see Wandycz, p. 300. Only in the Spring of 1990 did the Soviet government accept responsibility for this injustice.

Rozmarek urged Truman to insist upon guarantees that would enable Allied supervision of the Polish elections. No such guarantees had been provided at Yalta, and Truman did not press the matter at Potsdam (in July and August, 1945). Whatever opportunity may have still been left to alter the conditions that would make Poland more independent was lost at the Potsdam Conference when the United States failed to link its agreement to the Odra-Nysa River line (the new Polish western border) to concessions from the Communist side concerning the political future of Poland.[35]

While continuing its criticism of Yalta, the PAC at first took the position that Mikolajczyk and his supporters in the democratic Polish Peasants Party *(Polskie Stronnictwo Ludowe* or *PSL)* would win handily if free elections were permitted. But Mikolajczyk, though a minister in the provisional government, was ostracized by the Communist members in the cabinet. There were extended delays in holding "free and unfettered" parliamentary elections. Although Molotov had told Roosevelt at Yalta that elections could be held in one month, in fact they were held two years later. During this period Mikolojczyk's Polish Peasants Party was subjected to relentless attacks on all fronts. These developments convinced Rozmarek and his colleagues that Yalta should be repudiated because free elections were not possible.[36]

The United States' reassessment of its policy toward Warsaw in the light of growing evidence that economic levers were not working led to a major change in its position, one having serious implications for Poland and Polonia. On September 6, 1946 Secretary of State James Byrnes, speaking in Stuttgart, Germany, pointed out that the United States had not formally recognized the permanency of Poland's new western borders along the Odra and Nysa Rivers, though both Roosevelt at Yalta and Truman at Potsdam had given their approval to the shifts. The implication of Byrnes' remarks was clear; the U.S. had largely written off Poland to Soviet rule and had determined that its interests lie in building closer ties with the postwar German state.

Rozmarek caustically criticized the speech, declaring that Byrnes' proposal "to dismember allied Poland of territory now occupied by millions of Poles for the benefit of our enemy,

Germany, would be a horrible miscarriage of justice." In condemning the idea, the Polish American Congress found itself in
the extraordinary position of lining up against Washington on
the side of the very Soviet-dominated regime in Warsaw it
found so loathsome. In Poland itself, the Byrnes speech served
to do further damage to American prestige already undermined
by the regime's release of information about the western allies'
behavior at Teheran and Yalta.[37]

Despite U.S. intransigence, Rozmarek and his colleagues
continued to press home their view of the significance of the
Odra-Nysa border to Poland's well-being and America's true
interests in Eastern Europe. Indeed, two veteran Polonia observers of Rozmarek's career would later conclude that one of
the most important contributions during his entire 24 year
presidency of the Polish American Congress involved his constant and principled defense of the Polish western border.[38]
Thus, at the PAC's fifth national convention in Chicago in
October 1960, an event attended by President Dwight Eisenhower and Presidential candidate John Kennedy, one of the
resolutions approved at the gathering stressed the importance
of American recognition of the Odra-Nysa line in "depriving
Russia of powerful psychological weapons she wields over Poland and her neighbors as the 'sole' protector against new
German aggression." Four years later, in a PAC memorandum
addressed to President Lyndon Johnson, Rozmarek wrote:

> No other single act of American diplomacy could
> strengthen the Polish nation more and renew the faith of
> millions of people in East Central Europe in American
> world leadership, than a United States initiative in recogniz-
> ing the Polish-German boundary along the Odra-Nysa Riv-
> ers.[39]

A separate issue following the Second World War involved
the status of the several hundred thousand Polish refugees
confined in camps located in occupied Germany and other
Western European countries. These camps were maintained by
UNRRA, the international relief agency established in 1943
under American auspices. Already in 1946 Rozmarek and his
colleagues were receiving disquieting reports about living con-

ditions in the camps and pressures exerted by UNRRA personnel to persuade the refugees to return to Poland. (*Rada Polonii* Chairman Swietlik had already made his first tour of the refugee camps; at the annual Polish Constitution Day observance in Chicago in May 1946 he appealed for increased Polonia assistance on their behalf. On that occasion he also brought out the plight of thousands of Polish ex-soldiers in Italy and Britain who refused to return to Soviet-dominated Poland. In Swietlik's judgment, it was the moral obligation of the United States and Britain to assist in their resettlement in the West.)[40]

On August 27, 1946 Rozmarek, Januszewski and Nurkiewicz departed for Europe to lobby for free Poland at the coming foreign ministers conference in Paris. Following their arrival the group decided to extend its stay to visit the refugee camps and thus gain a firsthand picture of the situation. All told, Rozmarek and his colleagues travelled to twenty different camps throughout Germany in 83 days and spoke at length with UNRRA officials, camp personnel and the refugees about their plight.

What they saw brought much distress. Material conditions were one significant cause of concern. Many refugees, who had already suffered as forced laborers or prisoners of war during the conflict, complained of poor food allotments and exceedingly bad housing conditions. The psychological climate in the camps also left much to be desired. Not only were the Poles prohibited from setting up their own schools and prevented from bringing in their own priests to serve their spiritual needs, they also were subjected to official propaganda urging their return to Soviet-run Poland. Following their visits, Rozmarek and Nurkiewicz composed a report to Secretary of State Byrnes critical of UNRRA's administration. Their complaints were also presented to the international press in Paris, Brussels and London. (Byrnes, who had already come under the PAC chief's fire for his speech on the Polish-German border issue, may have wished he had never heard Rozmarek's name. In any event he resigned from his post in January 1947).

Upon Rozmarek's return to Chicago in November 1946, he continued his campaign against UNRRA's administration of the camps before a turn-away audience of more than five thousand people. At that meeting Rozmarek called upon President Truman to allow Polish refugees wishing to settle in the United States to enter the country under special legislative action, together with those former Polish soldiers in Western Europe who had refused to return to Poland.

Already in early 1947, a refugee immigration bill had been presented in the U.S. House of Representatives by Illinois Congressman William Stratton. In its original form the legislation permitted 400,000 European refugees, or displaced persons, to enter the United States outside the quota restrictions during the period of the next four years. Despite stiff opposition and many efforts to rewrite the original legislation, a modified measure, the "Displaced Persons Act," was finally approved and signed into law on June 25, 1948. This legislation allowed for a total of 205,000 individuals to enter the country. Proposals to deal with several parts of the original Displaced Persons Act which were seen as discriminatory and unworkable were subsequently approved by President Truman in June 1950. As amended 400,000 applicants were once again permitted to enter the country. The Displaced Persons Act thus indeed achieved its authors' highest hopes in opening America to the victims of the War. As of June 30, 1952 when the Law expired, 393,542 displaced persons and other European refugees had in fact been admitted. Of these 154,556 people listed Poland as their country of origin. Perhaps 120,000 were Polish gentiles, the rest Polish Jews.[41]

For its part, the Polish American Congress took an active part not only in lobbying for passage of the Displaced Persons Act but in the creation of no fewer than three agencies to assist in the admission and resettlement of the newcomers. One was the Rev. Felix Burant's New York-based Polish American Immigration Committee *(Polski Komitet Immigracyny)* which was set up in 1946. A second was the Committee for Refugee Matters *(Komitet dla Spraw Wysiedlencow Polskich)*, chaired by the Brooklyn businessman and PAC activist, Ignace Nurkiewicz. Particularly active between 1944 and 1948, this committee assisted displaced Poles who had been permitted into this country in 1945 by a special order of President Truman. The third and perhaps most significant agency was the American Committee for the Resettlement of Polish Displaced Persons, established by the PAC at its second national convention in 1948. Headed by Blair Gunther, a Pittsburgh Judge and Censor of the Polish National Alliance, the Committee's aims as stated in its by-laws were:

> To help select eligible displaced persons of Polish ethnic origin in the designated D.P. camps in Europe and the members of the former Polish Armed Forces now left in the British Isles, and in accordance with the Federal laws provide them with the necessaries, secure their transportation from their port of entry to their place of residence in the United States, provide them jobs and housing facilities, and to work in cooperation with the State Department, the Federal D.P. Commission, all related Federal and state governmental and civic and private agencies in this regard...(and) to raise funds and borrow money from government and other sources in order to carry out the transportation from port of entry in the U.S.A. to the point of destination and the resettlement program of the D.P.s.[42]

Judge Gunther, in addition to his duties as chairman of the Displaced Persons Committee, was already engaged in resettlement work in his home state of Pennsylvania. In his absence from the Committee's Chicago headquarters, Attorney Edward Plusdrak, its Secretary-Treasurer and later the President of the Illinois PAC's state division, played a leading role in its operations. Working with him were several other Polonia leaders in the Windy City, including Adele Lagodzinska, President of the Polish Women's Alliance, the Reverend Valerian Karcz, past Chaplain of the Polish Roman Catholic Union, President John Stanek of the Polish Alma Mater fraternal, Frances Dymek, Vice President of the Polish National Alliance, Joseph Pawlowski, President of the Association of the Sons of Poland fraternal, Chicago Judge Thaddeus Adesko and Mrs. Kinga Dziubek. Yeoman service to the cause was provided by Mrs. Jean Dybal who acted as Plusdrak's secretary and handled the organization's correspondence throughout. With PAC help the Committee established twenty-six state and local affiliates to coordinate fund raising and the finding of individuals in their communities willing to sponsor the refugees in America.

The task before the Committee was awesome. In 1947 it was estimated that there were still about 233,000 Polish refugees in Western Europe, most of whom were eligible for immigration. By the end of 1948, this number had declined to 181,000, with the others already gone from the camps and in the process of establishing permanent residence in Germany, France, England and elsewhere in the West. Fortunately, it was not necessary for the Committee to be responsible for all Polish refugees wishing to come to the U.S. Many were able to enter under the auspices of agencies such as the National Catholic Welfare Committee, or privately through family members in this country.

The Committee's efforts were hampered by the difficulties it met in raising the funds necessary to accomplish its aims. Initially Gunther had hoped that about one-half million dollars could be gathered for the resettlement cause, not an unreasonable sum at first glance given the importance of the task and the PAC's outreach into Polonia. In fact, the Committee's fund appeal fell far short of its target. In 1952, Gunther reported to the delegates attending the third PAC convention that $77,675 had been collected, an amount supplemented by a $25,000 loan from the Polish National Alliance and another $75,000 from the United States Displaced Persons Commissions. One building in Chicago had been purchased to provide new arrivals there with shelter and food immediately upon their arrival.[43]

Despite its problems in raising funds, the Committee did much to realize its aims during the four years in which the Displaced Persons Act was in effect. Approximately 35,000 refugees entered the country through its efforts and the money raised by the Committee was used very efficiently on behalf of the new arrivals. Thus, new immigrants were given loans upon their arrival on the condition that these be returned promptly so that others could be helped as they entered the country. In Gunther's 1952 report to the Polish American Congress, he noted that some $330,000 in loans had already been made to arrivals in Boston and New York and that approximately $295,000 had already been repaid and since used again.

Practically all of the Committee's work was carried out on a voluntary basis, with very few exceptions. One was Col. Boleslas Wichrowski, who was stationed in Frankfurt, Germany until 1952 and worked with the local authorities and Polish refugee organizations to process immigration applications to the

United States. Assisting Wichrowski and his staff in Germany were several Polonia volunteers, including PNA Vice-President Frances Dymek, who gave six months of her time to the effort.

Aside from its staff in Europe, the only other employees of the Committee during its main period of operations were its representatives in the ports of New York and Boston, along with several office persons in Chicago whose responsibilities included publicizing the Committee's appeals to Polonia. Among the brochures put out by the Committee one might note such titles as "Your Fathers and Ours and Now Our Brethren Too" and "Ten Questions and Answers about Polish D.P.s." Among those who contributed substantially to aiding the Committee in Chicago was PAC President Rozmarek's wife, Wanda. In addition to her activities as a member of the Illinois State Displaced Persons Commission, Mrs. Rozmarek worked hard to find sponsors for new arrivals and opened her own home to hundreds of future Americans. Indeed, for several years the Rozmarek residence was known popularly as the "Hotel Rozmarek."[44]

The Displaced Persons Committee also concerned itself with the admission of former members of the Polish Armed forces in Europe who had refused to return to Poland. Zbigniew Dolega-Jasinski was employed to represent the Committee to both the British and American authorities. The ex-soldiers' problem was complicated, since only some, together with their spouses and children, were eligible to enter the United States in accordance with the Displaced Persons Act. Poles who had already applied for British residency or citizenship status were excluded and still others were informed that their fate would have to be determined by the U.S. State Department on a case by case basis. In 1950, the PAC worked out an agreement with the two governments whereby some 18,000 former Polish soldiers along with their families were permitted entry into the United States within the quota of the Displaced Persons Act. Some 11,500 eventually came, with the remaining 6,500 places later made available to displaced persons still in Germany following the Act's expiration.

In 1953 a new "Refugee Relief Act" was approved in Washington, D.C. and the Displaced Persons' Committee reactivated. This time it did not employ its own European agent but instead relied upon the National Catholic Welfare Conference to identify and process eligible emigrants while restricting its work to assisting Polish refugees upon their arrival. Between 1955 and 1957, the Committee helped resettle some 1,009 refugees.

By 1958, the Committee's work had been largely completed, although it continued to maintain a formal existence under the chairmanship of Rev. Karcz. Until 1963, when the Committee reorganized itself into a charitable trust, its $28,448 in assets were used to provide help on an individual needs basis. This work was completed in 1968 and the Committee ceased operations.

In discussing the work of the Committee, particularly during its most strenuous years, one should not minimize the impact of the general conditions in which it operated. The early 1950s witnessed a rise in anti-Communist feeling throughout American society, an atmosphere promoted in Polonia by the Committee's own parent organization, the Polish American Congress.

Thus in seeking to enlighten the general public about the aims of the Soviet Union and the Communist threat to U.S. interests at home and abroad, the PAC may have helped contribute to a new public mood of fear and distrust of "foreigners," especially those who were refugees from Eastern Europe.

The Displaced Persons Committee's own publicity sometimes reflected its leaders' appreciation of the prevailing atmosphere. One typical piece published in the Chicago *Dziennik Zwiazkowy* in September 1949 warned new arrivals that they would have to "work hard to gain the hearts of Americans" so they in turn would assist more DPs in coming. Further, the new arrivals were told not to expect charity and to begin quickly to master the English language and a trade so they could "fit in." Stress was placed repeatedly on Americanization, rather than upon efforts to enlighten the public about the political reasons behind the refugees' decisions to emigrate, namely their solidarity with the American commitment to freedom and their hatred of the Soviet-imposed communist system set up in Poland.

Conditions for the new arrivals, particularly those with no relatives already in the United States, were often harsh. One family found itself working on a farm in northern Wisconsin and lived in a barn for nearly two years before two of its members could pay what they owed their sponsor and begin life on their own. A man who found himself working on a farm fifty miles from Pittsburgh bluntly declared, "We were treated worse than animals." His wife added, "We got twenty dollars a month and worked like slave labor." Another who was placed in a potato farm near Greenpoint, Long Island recalled that the barracks where he and his friend were housed were "like a concentration camp." After four months he left and moved to New Jersey where he found a job through a friend working in a bakery. For some, the minority, the experience was better. Some remembered the "nice family" which took them in, others the generous sponsor who drove them immediately into town to a store to buy some new clothes.

One Pole who arrived in Chicago in 1948 through the sponsorship of a locally prominent Polonia family remembered little if any significant organized assistance speeding up his establishing of new roots. At the same time, he noted that his initial contacts with people in the Chicago Polonia were almost always friendly and solicitous and from these he quickly got good leads for jobs. Reminiscing some forty years later about the refugees' fate, he observed that the DPs usually found their bearings in their new homeland because "Polish people work things out for themselves, with the quiet help of their neighbors, family, fellow parishioners. One could hardly help becoming absorbed into the community and finding oneself a place in it." Clearly, the newcomers arrived in America highly motivated to start fresh and put their wartime experiences behind them. For most, their stories proved to be tales of success and achievement on the personal and family level coupled with their gradual integration into American society.[45]

Though given very little attention by scholars of Polonia history, the efforts and achievements of the American Committee for the Resettlement of Polish Displaced Persons, like those of the Polish American Council discussed earlier, were considerable.[46] Without the many contributions of the participants in the work of the Committee, far fewer Polish refugees would have been able to enter the United States under the auspices of the Displaced Persons Act. That would have been a loss to both American society and to Polonia.[47]

On the political front, the years between 1944 and 1948 were typified by extraordinary activity throughout the Polish American Congress, much of it made possible by a massive fund raising campaign initiated in 1945. Ultimately, this "One Million Dollar Drive" generated more than $611,000 under the direction of Adam Tomaszkiewicz of Chicago. Some $456,000 of the total went to support the work of the PAC national office, with the remainder going to the state divisions of the Congress throughout the country. (Particularly active in the campaign were the PAC divisions in Illinois, New York, Pennsylvania, Massachusetts and Michigan. Together they collected more than one half million dollars alone.)

The PAC's vitality in these early years could also be measured by participation in the organization. Thus, at its second national convention in Philadelphia, some 1,224 delegates were in attendance. By way of comparison, 794 delegates would take part in the third PAC convention four years later, in Atlantic City, New Jersey, an attendance figure that would be fairly constant for subsequent national gatherings of the organization into the 1960s and 1970s.

In 1948, the PAC published a list of affiliated organizations and individual members around the country, a report with more than 11,220 entries. A look at this inventory, which remains the most complete statement of involvement in the PAC that exists, tells much about the organizational character of American Polonia at the time as well. For the Chicago area alone, one finds the following information: 23 newspapers and periodicals, the central administrations of the PNA, PRCUA, Polish Women's Alliance fraternals, together with their various district units, 20 local PNA councils and 182 lodge units, 14 PRCUA councils and 91 lodges, 74 PWA lodges, the leadership of the Polish Mountaineers association and 6 of its local groups, the Polish Singers Alliance and eight of its affiliates, the Polish *Alma Mater* fraternal and 14 of its local chapters, the United Polish Women fraternal and 34 affiliates, the Union of Clubs of Polish Americans from "Little Poland" (Galicia) and 76 of its units. Also included were the Chicago leaderships of several other fraternals with headquarters elsewhere such as the Polish

National Union, the Polish Falcons of America, the Polish
Union of America, the Polish Legion of American Veterans
and the Polish Army Veterans Association, some fifty parish
societies, the *Liga Morska* society and 22 of its affiliates, approximately 320 locally-owned Polish businesses and Polonia
groups, 1,284 unaffiliated individuals, and 33 Roman Catholic
and 7 Polish National Catholic parishes.[48]

Yet, despite its activities and success in mobilizing Polonia
to its cause, the results of Polish American Congress efforts in
working for Poland's postwar independence and freedom
proved bitterly disappointing. Rozmarek and his colleagues
made valiant efforts toward that end, and were equally vociferous in their defense of Poland's borders, both those to the East,
overrun in 1939 by the Red Army, and those to the West along
the Odra and Nysa Rivers, and provisionally approved in 1945
at the Great Power Summits at Yalta and Potsdam.

On January 19, 1947 general elections were at last held in
Poland, nearly two full years after the Yalta Conference. But
they were hardly the "free and unfettered" contests that had
been promised. According to Stefan Korbonski, a leader in the
Polish Peasants Party who remained particularly active in exile
politics until the late 1980s, 118 local *PSL* activists were murdered by the security police during the prolonged election
campaign; 162 candidates for the Polish Parliament, 1,192 local
leaders and nearly all the Party's observers at the 5,227 boards
of elections around the country were arrested as were about
100,000 of its members.[49]

During the campaign more than three hundred *PSL* offices
were raided by the police. The Party's newspapers were cen-
sored and their distribution restricted. Just before the actual
vote, *PSL* candidates in ten districts were ruled off the ballots,
thereby depriving nearly one-fifth of the electorate of any
choice at the polls. Afterwards, the results of the election were
falsified, with the Communists declaring that their ruling coalition had won 394 of the 444 seats in the Parliament and 80
percent of the popular vote. By their count, the *PSL* received
10.3 percent of the vote and 28 seats. *PSL* leaders in contrast
claimed to have won between 68 and 90 percent of the popular
vote.[50]

Stanislaw Mikolajczyk had returned to Poland as a deputy prime minister in the new provisional government and head of the *PSL* out of a conviction that the Western Allies would insure fair elections-and thus his Party's victory. But despite the energetic support the democratic forces received from the U.S. Ambassador in Warsaw, Arthur Bliss Lane, nothing came of the help Mikolajczyk had hoped for to ensure free elections. By November 1947, out of office and in fear of his imminent arrest, Mikolajczyk fled the country and soon after appeared in America.

Mikolajczyk later met with Rozmarek in Chicago and together they forged an alliance to represent Poland's cause in Polonia and throughout the United States. Given Mikolajczyk's fame as a fighter for democracy, the coalition between the Polish American Congress and the former Prime Minister seemed a sensible way to generate public support for the Polish cause.[51] Subsequently, Rozmarek's action was approved by the Congress' Supreme Council and the delegates at the second PAC convention in Philadelphia. But Mikolajczyk was anathema to the militant *KNAPP* organization, which while relatively small in numbers possessed considerable influence in Polonia. In its judgment, Mikolajczyk, like his predecessor Sikorski, had failed to adequately defend Poland's position on the eastern border question in dealing with Stalin. Moreover, *KNAPP* had opposed his postwar return to Poland as both hopeless and counterproductive. Indeed, it charged that Mikolajczyk's very presence in the Communist-dominated Warsaw government after 1945 had given that regime an unearned aura of legitimacy. Viewing Rozmarek's controversial action to be precipitous and erroneous, *KNAPP* withdrew from the Polish American Congress, to be followed by Polonia's second largest fraternal, the Polish Roman Catholic Union of America.[52]

The Mikolajczyk-PAC tie proved to be a great disappointment; Rozmarek soon recognized this himself and declared in 1952 that the coalition was no longer in force. Still, the initiative signalled the direction in which the PAC was heading, one of militant opposition to the Truman Administration in Washington and to the Democratic party's leadership of the country. Already in 1946, Rozmarek at Stuttgart, had begun to lean toward the Republicans in the Congressional elections held that November. These the G.O.P. went on to sweep, winning majorities in both the Senate and the House of Representatives for the first time since 1930, when Herbert Hoover had occupied the White House. In 1948 Rozmarek would endorse the Republican Presidential candidate, Thomas Dewey. Here too there was disappointment, as Truman unexpectedly was returned to office in an election in which Polish Americans sided with the "Fair Deal" Democrat by a 4-1 margin.

In 1947, Ambassador Lane, who had resigned from his post in Warsaw following the Polish elections, teamed up with Rozmarek to create the "Committee to Stop World Communism," one of the first explicitly anti-Soviet organizations to operate in the U.S. The Committee may have had some impact, since its efforts coincided with the rapid deterioration of postwar Soviet-American relations, a development reflected in the public opinion surveys. Thus, in September 1945 a Gallup Poll had found 54 percent of those surveyed agreeing that the U.S. could cooperate with the Soviet Union in the years to come, with 30 percent disagreeing. By June 1949 only 20 percent of the public agreed with this proposition, to 62 percent who rejected it.[53]

In March 1947 at a joint session of Congress, President Truman proclaimed his new foreign policy "doctrine" to oppose Soviet threats to Greece and Turkey. Several months later Secretary of State George Marshall followed upon the Truman Doctrine of military support for freedom by proposing that the United States contribute substantially to Europe's economic reconstruction. In the ensuing years more than $13 billion in such aid would yield extraordinary benefits in ushering in conditions of economic prosperity throughout Western Europe. (Poland and the rest of Eastern Europe were not permitted by Stalin to accept this offer.) In 1948 the U.S. would sponsor the formation of the North Atlantic Treaty Organization to defend Western Europe militarily from Soviet expansionism. Together, these policies came to serve as the pillars of the postwar foreign strategy known as "containment," an approach that would define U.S. perspectives toward the Communist world for the next three decades.

The Polish American Congress might have taken some credit for having spurred United States' policy in the direction of containment, this country's first systematic response to the global challenges posed by Soviet communism. But containment was never accepted by Rozmarek or his fellow PAC leaders, since the doctrine acknowledged Soviet control over Poland and Eastern Europe. They instead preferred a more confrontational posture towards Moscow, that of "liberation." Indeed, liberation would enjoy some appeal in the late 1940s and early 1950s among political conservatives, among them John Foster Dulles, a key adviser to Thomas Dewey in his 1948 campaign and from 1953 Secretary of State in the Republican Administration of President Dwight Eisenhower.

The Republican Party, ever hopeful of making inroads into the traditionally Democratic-oriented Polish and East European electorate, even included into its 1952 platform a plank advocating the "liberation" of Communist-dominated Eastern Europe. But Eisenhower distanced himself from the idea throughout his campaign and following his victory declared himself in favor of a Republican version of containment, as may be found in the Appendix of this work. (His rejection of liberation became manifestly clear only later, however, in November 1956. Then during the international crisis surrounding the Hungarian Revolution, the United States withheld any military support to the freedom fighters in their struggle against Soviet tanks.)

Thus, already by 1953 the Polish American Congress found itself at a dead end in its efforts to promote Poland's cause with the leaderships of the two major political parties. One, it blamed for having "sold Poland down the river" at Teheran and Yalta, the other it found reluctant to "roll back" the Soviets from their postwar territorial gains in Eastern Europe.[54]

Still, aggressive rhetoric and seemingly endless activity characterized the Polish American Congress in one last area into the early 1950s. This involved its role in generating public awareness of the tragic World War II Katyn massacre of some fifteen thousand Polish military officers through its support of the creation of a select Congressional Committee to investigate and determine responsibility for the wartime atrocity. Chairing this committee which was established in 1951 was U.S. Congressman Ray Madden of Indiana and serving as its chief investigator was Roman Pucinski, then a reporter for the daily Chicago *Sun-Times*.Members included Congressmen Daniel

Flood of Pennsylvania, Foster Furcolo of Massachusetts, Thaddeus Machrowicz and George Dondero of Michigan, Alvin O'Konski of Wisconsin and Timothy Sheehan of Illinois. For more than four decades, the Katyn massacre remained one of the most controversial incidents of the Second World War. At the same time, it is part of a larger story that has become ingrained into the perspective of two generations of Poles and Polish Americans regarding Poland's wartime experience and its relations with the Great Powers. In this context the Katyn massacre continues to have profound symbolic significance more than fifty years after it occurred.[55]

The central facts about the massacre and its impact upon the future course of Soviet-Polish relations have already been summarized. Significantly, at the Nuremberg War Crimes Trials in 1946, the Soviets tried to blame the Polish officers' deaths upon the Nazis but soon dropped their charges when it became clear that their evidence was insufficient to warrant Katyn's inclusion onto the long list of German atrocities. There was, however, no criticism of Soviet responsibility, since this would have damaged the fragile unity of the Big Three alliance. Over the next three years, that unity would evaporate into a Cold War, due to Moscow's imposition of Communist dictatorships upon the nations of Eastern Europe in violation of Stalin's pledge at Yalta, the Berlin Blockade and the U.S.S.R.'s support of the Communists' takeover in China.

In April 1949, the Polish American Congress sent a telegram to the U.S. ambassador to the United Nations urging that he place the Katyn issue before the General Assembly. While nothing came of this request, PAC efforts to publicize the atrocity led a journalist named Julius Epstein to write a series of articles on the massacre for the New York *Herald-Tribune*. Epstein concluded by calling for an objective investigation of Katyn that would determine responsibility in the matter, once and for all.

Finding the U.S. government uninterested in sponsoring an international investigation, Epstein turned to the indefatigable Arthur Bliss Lane, who acted promptly in forming an "American Committee for the Investigation of the Katyn Massacre." Its efforts, along with those of Republican Congressmen critical of American policy toward Stalin, led to adoption of a special resolution of the House of Representatives (eventually approved by a vote of 398-0). Accordingly, a select committee of the House was created to conduct its own investigation. This action went against the wishes of President Truman, who saw the resolution as an assault upon his leadership.

Congressman Madden and his colleagues conducted hearings through most of 1952 and presented their findings to President Eisenhower shortly after he was sworn into office. Eisenhower dutifully complied with the request that the six volumes and 2,363 pages of testimony and findings on Katyn be transferred to the U.N. for its own review. Though nothing came of that effort, the Committee's efforts had their desired effect in providing ample evidence to indicate that the Soviet security police had "committed the massacre of Polish Army officers in the Katyn Forest near Smolensk, Russia not later than the Spring of 1940" and that "there can be no doubt this massacre was a calculated plot to eliminate all Polish leaders who subsequently would have opposed the Soviet's plans for communizing Poland."

More controversial were the Committee's conclusions that while the U.S. government had itself collected an enormous amount of information pointing to Soviet responsibility for the atrocity soon after its discovery in 1943, "these (reports had been) brushed aside, on the theory that pressing the search would irritate Russia and thus hinder the prosecution of the War to a successful conclusion." Blaming the Roosevelt Administration for having kept the facts it possessed from the American people prior to the Teheran and Yalta conferences, the committee asserted that "the Kremlin's hand would not have been so strong at the Yalta Conference and many of the concessions made...would have been obviated."[56]

The Polish American Congress under Rozmarek: 1944-1968

Charles Rozmarek had been elected unanimously to serve as President of the Polish American Congress at its founding convention. Then only 47 years of age, he had already completed more than four and one-half years as President of the Polish National Alliance, having been first elected at its historic September 1939 conclave and reelected overwhelmingly in

1943. The son of an immigrant Pennsylvania coal miner and the holder of a law degree from Harvard University, Rozmarek was an eloquent public speaker in both English and Polish; given his relative youth, training and vigor, he was the ideal individual to articulate Polonia's concerns both in the critical World War II years and those which followed. He would go on to lead the PNA until 1967 and the PAC until 1968, when he stepped down as President of the Congress after twenty-four years in office.[57]

The history of the Polish American Congress under Rozmarek can be well characterized as having two relatively distinct phases. The first extended from 1944 until the early 1950s and was typified, as has been described, by extraordinary activity in a time of momentous and dramatic events. As a leader Rozmarek mobilized Polonia on a number of fronts, even as the PAC was unable to achieve its central objectives, Poland's freedom and sovereignty after the War.

Already noted were the PAC's efforts to represent Poland's cause at such international gatherings as the founding session of the United Nations in 1945 and the Foreign Ministers meeting in Paris in 1946, its lobbying on behalf of Federal legislation on behalf of the admission of thousands of Polish displaced persons in 1948 and Congress' investigation of the Katyn Massacre in 1952. All throughout the early postwar years, the PAC's vigor in taking its stands was matched only by Rozmarek's seemingly relentless activity in criticizing American policy toward the Soviet Union. Indeed, by the late 1940s, such efforts helped recast American public opinion along decidedly Cold War lines. One author, though careful not to exaggerate the PAC's role in this process, has nonetheless observed:

> As a domestic pressure group attempting to influence foreign policy, Polish Americans had several assets: substantial numbers concentrated in politically crucial states; a passionate attachment to the independence of their homeland; numerical influence in several of the groups at the base of the Democratic party coalition, especially the industrial unions, the Catholic Church, and the northern urban political machines; popular support for the principle of small-nation independence; and widespread distrust of the motives and practices of the Soviet Union...[58]

While asserting that the Polish American Congress acting alone could not have changed public opinion toward the Soviet Union, the same writer concluded that "the issue of Poland as a factor in the Cold War crusade cannot be underestimated..."[59] Certainly, Polonia's considerable significance as a potential factor in the presidential elections of 1944, 1948 and 1952 was something that was widely reckoned with. Thus in 1944, Franklin Roosevelt had succeeded in gaining Rozmarek's backing for his reelection on the basis of a set of vague promises on Poland's behalf, promises which could not be kept later on. In 1948 Rozmarek had switched his support to Republican Thomas Dewey against Truman, only to watch Truman win by a narrow margin in a contest in which he was helped considerably by a 4-1 Polish vote in his favor. But while Truman by then had adopted a tough new foreign policy approach toward the Soviet Union, one later termed "Containment," his departure from Roosevelt's wartime accommodations with Stalin went largely unappreciated in the PAC, if not Polonia.

In 1952, Rozmarek and the Polish American Congress strongly supported the Presidential campaign of Republican candidate Dwight Eisenhower and this time were at last rewarded with success as Eisenhower won handily with the help of a substantial Polish American vote on his behalf. Nevertheless, the newly elected President was quick to disassociate himself from his party's campaign pledge to liberate Eastern Europe.

Through the remainder of the 1950s the PAC would be unable to play as influential a role in matters pertaining to Poland as one might have expected, given its salience during the 1940s. Thus, while Rozmarek's rhetoric continued to emphasize "liberation," his "maximalist" approach to overthrowing Communist domination in Poland was simply no longer feasible in Washington.

During the second and longer phase of Rozmarek's presidency, from the early 1950s until 1968, the PAC's mission was transformed into one of reminding Polonia, the American public and U.S. government officials of Poland's plight as "an enslaved nation under communist tyranny." Thus, the Congress supported the formation and activities of the New York-based Assembly of Captive European Nations, an organization of emigre leaders from Soviet-controlled Eastern Europe which remained in operation until the 1970s.[60] The PAC also strongly backed the establishment and activities of Radio Free Europe. This U.S.-sponsored station was set up in 1950 in Munich, Germany for the purpose of transmitting uncensored news and opinion into Poland and the other East European satellites. Rozmarek was a frequent speaker to Poland via RFE, particularly during the 1950s.[61]

Yet another militant stance involved PAC support of "Captive Nations Week," established by resolutions of the U.S. Senate and House of Representatives in 1959. Accordingly, the President of the United States was authorized to declare the third week of July as "Captive Nations Week" throughout the country and to invite the public to plan appropriate ceremonies and activities in support of the aspirations of the peoples living under Soviet Communism. Poland was duly included among the twenty-two captive nations listed in the resolution and the delegates to the fifth convention of the Polish American Congress in 1960 took note of this in approving a proposal of their own calling upon all Americans to put the proclamation into action as a part of the foreign policy of the United States.[62]

Yet while the PAC continued to maintain a militant ideological posture opposed to Soviet rule over Eastern Europe, Rozmarek himself displayed a certain pragmatism on several pertinent questions connected with Poland's situation, especially following events there in 1956.

On June 28 of that year, workers in the city of Poznan demonstrated publicly out of their frustrations with worsening shortages of food and the Stalinist regime's repressive policies. Thousands took to the streets brandishing the slogan of "Bread and Freedom" and their efforts immediately gained them international attention since they occurred as scores of foreign journalists were arriving in the city to cover a trade exposition. Though the demonstrations were soon suppressed at the cost of at least 33 lives-more than three hundred others were injured-the blow to the Polish regime's prestige was a great one. Everywhere, the Stalinist authorities had been required to use force to maintain control over the very workers they claimed to represent.

Rozmarek's public comments immediately following the news of the Poznan demonstrations reflected the PAC's traditional ideological posture. Thus, at a rally in Chicago on July 1 he demanded that the United States publicly identify with the defense of the Polish people and called upon Washington to propose a United Nations resolution calling for truly free elections in Poland and the other Eastern European satellites. If such elections were not scheduled, Rozmarek urged that the U.S. terminate diplomatic relations with the satellite dictatorships.[63]

Soon after, Rozmarek appeared before the Democratic and Republican party platform committees. Speaking on behalf of the 7,215 Polonia organizations belonging to the PAC he once again urged the presidential candidates of both parties to adopt "liberation" positions toward Eastern Europe.

Yet events in Poland seemed to far outrun rhetoric. Thus, when Rozmarek met President Eisenhower in the White House that September, the issue of "liberation" was overshadowed by both men's recognition of the fluid and highly unpredictable situation in Warsaw. On October 19, Wladyslaw Gomulka took over as the new First Secretary of the Polish United Workers Party and *de facto* leader of the country. (Gomulka had served as the Party's chief between 1942 and 1948 but had been removed and arrested for political views which made him unreliable to Stalin.)

On October 21, in a tense confrontation in Warsaw with Soviet chief Nikita Khrushchev who arrived in the company of a delegation of top Communist Party leaders, Gomulka at last persuaded his visitors that he could be trusted to maintain control over the restive satellite. Coinciding with events in Poland was an even more desperate crisis in neighboring Hungary. There the ouster of a brutal Stalinist regime and its replacement by a moderate communist leadership under Imre Nagy would be accompanied by widespread violence, Soviet military intervention and Nagy's own overthrow and execution. It was thus in the atmosphere of the Hungarian Revolution's tragic failure and the final exposure of America's "liberation" rhetoric that Gomulka would labor to establish the new post-Stalinist relationship between Poland and the U.S.S.R.

On October 22, 1956 Rozmarek headed a ten member PAC delegation that met with Secretary of State Dulles in Washington. There he urged the United States to take "concrete acts" to bolster Poland's independence by sending surplus food and technical assistance to help the country in its time of crisis. Identifying Gomulka, who was seen as a "national Communist" in advocating his party's support of a "Polish" (and not Stalinist) "road to socialism," Rozmarek offered the opinion that the new regime in Warsaw merited America's backing as a lesser evil and "the first move toward Polish freedom..." This view was supported by President Eisenhower.[64]

In the following months Rozmarek and the Congress continued in the direction of pragmatism, although PAC rhetoric still rang militant. Thus, a special meeting of the PAC Supreme Council concluded with a resolution urging the United States to provide Poland with $125 million in credits to aid the Poles in their "struggle." On April 11, 1957 when Rozmarek met again with Eisenhower, he urged the President to support the issuing of credits on Poland's behalf so that its government might purchase badly needed agricultural products from the U.S. (Poland itself had requested some $300 million in such assistance.) Following the audience Rozmarek told reporters that Eisenhower had declared himself in favor of the idea.[65]

This new and more pragmatic posture on the part of the Polish American Congress enabled it to identify with the decisions taken by the Eisenhower administration in its later dealings with Gomulka's regime, although the idea of providing economic aid to Warsaw seems to have originated in Washington, rather than with Rozmarek. In fact, American credits to Poland proved to be considerable, amounting to some $95 million in 1957, $98 million in 1956, $103.5 million in 1959, and $130 million in 1960. In all, Poland had received some $588 million in U.S. loans, aid and credits by 1964, when further assistance was cut off by Congress. The PAC did what it could to oppose the move but failed in the face of a growing consensus that the assistance had not achieved its chief aim, that of weaning Gomulka's regime away from the Soviet orbit and transforming Poland into an independent Communist state similar to Yugoslavia.[66]

Indeed, while Poland remained interested in U.S. assistance, Gomulka, a dedicated pro-Soviet Communist, had by the early 1960s reestablished his credentials as one of Moscow's most reliable junior allies in Eastern Europe. This in return for Moscow's acquiescence to his unorthodox handling of several internal matters of peculiar significance to his country. Two of these were particularly sensitive. One dealt with the Roman Catholic Church, which Gomulka permitted greater influence and freedom of action than was possible anywhere else in the entire Communist world. The other concerned Gomulka's decision enabling Poland's peasant farmers to own their own homesteads, a practice which contradicted the Soviet policy calling for the establishment of a state-run, or collectivized agriculture.

The PAC's response to the developments in Poland and widespread awareness that the upcoming presidential election would be hotly contested combined in 1960 to raise the organization's prestige to its all-time high under Rozmarek. That May, Vice President Richard M. Nixon, the Republican Party's future candidate for President addressed a crowd of more than one hundred thousand at the annual Polish Constitution Day ceremonies in Chicago's Humboldt Park. In September, the delegates to the Polish American Congress' fifth national convention assembled in Chicago to review the PAC's activities over the previous four years and to chart its future course. This conclave was especially noteworthy in that the delegates heard from both the Democratic Party's presidential nominee, Senator John F. Kennedy of Massachusetts, and the outgoing President of the United States, Dwight D. Eisenhower. Never before had an American chief of state attended a convention of any Polonia organization.[67]

Given the tightness of the Kennedy-Nixon race, both political parties gave particular attention to the highly visible Polish ethnic vote, which had gone to the Democrats by a 4 to 1 margin in Truman's 1948 victory but had divided about evenly between Eisenhower and his Democratic opponent, Adlai Stevenson of Illinois, in the 1952 and 1956 campaigns. Significantly, Polish Americans returned to the Democratic fold in 1960, giving the youthful, charismatic, Irish-Catholic Cold Warrior Kennedy some 78 percent of their votes. Their potent support was crucial to his narrow victory over Nixon, whose own tough anti-communist views were widely displayed in a vain effort to hold onto a substantial share of the Eastern European ethnic vote.[68]

The Polish issue was not without a certain significance in 1960, due to the changes inside the country under Gomulka after 1956 and the varied U.S. efforts to influence Warsaw toward closer contact with the West. But Rozmarek's own success in moving the PAC somewhat closer to the political center cannot be minimized, since his activities helped enable the Congress to represent Polonia in a fashion permitting both Kennedy and Nixon to aggressively appeal for Polish American votes in politically uncompromising ways.

In the years that followed John Kennedy's election and during the administration of Lyndon B. Johnson, who succeeded to the presidency after Kennedy's assassination in November 1963, Rozmarek and the Polish American Congress continued to maintain a more pragmatic posture toward the White House in its policies toward Poland. Thus the PAC supported economic assistance to Poland as well as U.S. approval of "most favored nation" status to Warsaw in its trade dealings with this country, an action approved in 1960, lost in 1962 and largely restored in 1963. Remaining as a constant theme was the PAC's advocacy of American recognition of Poland's western borders with Germany. To Rozmarek's dismay, Washington refused to consider this advice, asserting that such a decision awaited an international conference bringing together the superpowers and West Germany.

In the Summer of 1964, when Rozmarek once again testified for the PAC to the Republican and Democratic convention committees, he did not even mention the theme of Poland's liberation from Communist rule. Instead both parties were called upon to persuade the Soviet Union of the economic benefits it might derive following its military withdrawal from Poland. Rozmarek further proposed that future U.S. economic assistance to Eastern Europe be undertaken in connection with assurances that the Communist regimes were indeed "liberalizing" their dictatorial systems.

This idea owed much to the analysis of political developments in Eastern Europe provided by Professor Zbigniew Brzezinski of Columbia University. Brzezinski in a 1961 published paper, "Peaceful Engagement in Eastern Europe," had proposed a novel alternative to the West's traditional post War orientations toward the Communist world, "liberation" and "containment." Such thinking, he argued, had not only served to maintain the division of Europe, but also raised enormous obstacles for the Soviet-dominated Polish regime in responding to its own people's aspirations for greater freedom and contacts with the West. Significantly, after 1964, Brzezinski would serve in the Johnson administration and go on to become an architect of the President's "building bridges" policy toward Eastern Europe.[69]

For Brzezinski, America's true interests toward Eastern Europe were better understood as focusing upon the development of trade, humanitarian assistance, economic relations, travel, cultural relations and exchanges of scholars, their aim the expansion of contacts with its peoples in support of their aspirations for greater freedom. Such programs also served, insofar as America's relations with Poland were concerned, to strengthen personal and familial ties between Polish Americans and their ancestral homeland.

One major aspect of this developing relationship involved the financial and material assistance rendered by Polish Americans to their old country cousins, which increased enormously after 1956 and remains to the present time an extraordinary, though seldom explored, aspect of the Polish-American tie. This is simply because such help is private and individual in character and thus very difficult to document, in contrast to the aid rendered through charitable organizations, which is reported periodically. One estimate made in the mid-1980s of the magnitude of this direct help asserted that Polish Americans were sending some $600 million each year in packages and dollars to Poland, a figure then amounting to one-tenth of Poland's total foreign trade activity. It is likely that the size of this individual and unreported aid activity was even greater in the 1950s and 1960s, when a larger number of Polish Americans still possessed parents, brothers and sisters in Poland. By the 1980s, there were fewer such direct family relationships and more situations where Polish Americans could at best identify only more distant relatives in the old country.[70]

Through the renewal of human ties between Poles and Polish Americans in the late 1950s and 1960s, the former not only benefited materially, there have also been more opportunities to travel to the United States and to immigrate permanently to America. Of course, immigration to the United States brought to this country yet another wave of people who could offer their talents and cultural heritage to enrich Polonia. Differing in some respects from the post Second World War immigrants, whose motives for coming were frequently associated with their opposition to the Polish political system, those who arrived from the late 1950s had more in common with the masses who entered this country prior to the First World War in search of economic betterment, the so-called migration "after bread."

At the same time, the increased human contacts made possible by the improvement of U.S.-Polish relations after 1956 also had its political impact in Poland. Whether the Poles' experience was that of welcoming long lost relatives as returning visitors to the old country, their receipt of packages of goods or money gifts from America, or the opportunity to travel or emigrate to the West, growing numbers of people were exposed to the realities of life in free societies outside their homeland. Such contacts could not help but cause ferment within the country in favor of greater intellectual and political freedom.

Aside from the effect upon Poland following from the increase in human contacts from the late 1950s and early 1960s, there were yet other benefits to its people. One came, as noted earlier, with the resumption of shipments of surplus foodstuffs from the United States, under the auspices of CARE and the reactivated *Rada Polonii*, still chaired by Francis Swietlik. During the life span of the *RPA's* program, from 1964 through 1969, some 7,000 tons of powdered milk, soybeans and grains went to Poland. Yet another sign of American concern was the United States' financing of a children's hospital near the city of Krakow, which was heavily backed by Polish Americans in the U.S. Congress. (In 1985, an additional wing of the hospital was constructed, once again with America's financial support, and named in honor of a recently deceased member of the House of Representatives, Clement Zablocki of Wisconsin. Zablocki had been a leading backer of the original children's hospital.)[71]

A retrospective look at United States policy toward Poland after 1956 and through the 1960s is instructive, both in defining the directions of U.S. perspectives toward Poland following the events of 1956 and the obstacles facing Washington in its attempts to influence Gomulka's government. Initially, the emphasis was one of using offers of economic help, including the granting of most favored nation status, as a carrot to encourage greater Polish political autonomy from the Soviet Union. When this stratagem proved unsuccessful due to Gomulka's persistent loyalty to Moscow, Washington adopted a different approach, one of "building bridges" to the people of Poland. This strategy in effect appealed to the pro Western sentiments of the population "over the heads" of the communist regime and became the preferred U.S. policy to the Eastern European nations through the 1980s, that is, so long as they remained under Communist party rule.

To its credit the PAC under Rozmarek played a modest but constructive role in supporting this approach, which represented a realistic and principled alternative to both "liberation" and "containment." The former had been proven bankrupt in the face of the Soviet intervention in Hungary in 1956, the latter consigned the Polish people to the enemy camp. At the same time, the Polish American Congress continued to remind anyone who would listen that Communist rule was morally wrong and that the regimes imposed upon the peoples of Eastern Europe did not have the support of their subjects.

Still, without a credible policy of its own dealing with America' course of action toward Poland, the PAC in Rozmarek's last years in office found itself subject to growing criticism from within its own ranks.[72] Some disenchanted activists complained that the aging leader was deaf to new ideas and that the PAC had become stagnant and increasingly out of touch with the concerns of the Polish American community. There were also growing complaints that the PAC was indifferent to the task of defining Polonia's "domestic agenda" and that it had nothing to say about ways in which Polish Americans might successfully promote ethnic pride and knowledge of their heritage. This issue was especially troubling to those concerned about the maintenance of ethnic consciousness among young people of Polish ancestry. The concern carried some weight, since Rozmarek had focused the PAC's activities almost exclusively upon Poland's liberation from communism.[73]

The foundation of Rozmarek's strength had always been his leadership of the largest component of the PAC, the 340,000 member Polish National Alliance fraternal association. Until the late 1950s, Rozmarek's position in the PNA had been unassailable; however, in 1959 he was challenged seriously for the first time in twenty years. Four years later a Chicago attorney named Aloysius Mazewski made a first, unsuccessful, run against Rozmarek; though defeated in the campaign, he mounted a far more effective drive to unseat Rozmarek in 1967. That September, Mazewski defeated Rozmarek by a margin of 221 delegate votes to 189 at the PNA's thirty-fifth convention; one year later he replaced him as President of the Polish American Congress as well.[74]

With Mazewski's election, an era in the history of Polonia's service to Poland came to a close. The new PAC President seemed quite aware of this himself when he shared his thinking in an address delivered on the occasion of the Congress' 25th anniversary in Washington, D.C. in 1969. In his remarks, Mazewski first summed up the historic aims of the organization, which included the championship of Polish independence and the recognition the Congress had won as Polonia's political representative. The new President went further, however, in listing a series of objectives that were yet to be realized. These included international recognition of Poland's post World War II western borders with Germany and the regaining of its Eastern territories lost in 1939; most favored nation status for Poland in its trade relations with the United States; and increased but "meaningful" cultural exchanges between the two countries. Mazewski then concluded by identifying a set of concerns having to do with the preservation of ethnic life and traditions in the United States, concerns that extended beyond the PAC's historic activities and for the first time reflected the views of younger activists in Polonia.[75]

Yet, if the dynamism that had characterized Charles Rozmarek's leadership of the PAC during the first decade of his tenure had largely disappeared by the late 1960s, the achievements of the Polish American Congress under his stewardship remained considerable. Most important had been his rallying of

Polonia during and immediately after World War II on behalf of Poland's independence, territorial integrity and aspirations toward democracy. In addition, Rozmarek made at least six other specific contributions worthy of note. These included his representation of Poland's cause at the founding session of the United Nations in San Francisco in 1945 and in Paris in 1946; his criticisms of Soviet perfidy over the seizure of Polish underground leaders lured into a meeting with Red Army officers and then illegally imprisoned; his championing of the Polish refugee cause immediately after the War and his successful effort to help in their resettlement in America; his unending defense of Poland's right to its postwar frontiers; and his success in winning a Congressional investigation of the Katyn massacre.

Moreover, as a long time friend, former U.S. Congressman Roman Pucinski of Illinois observed, Rozmarek exhibited great courage in questioning the President of the United States over Poland's postwar fate following the Yalta Conference. In doing this, Rozmarek eventually helped reshape American opinion as to the propriety of FDR's decisions towards Poland and Eastern Europe.[76]

Rozmarek made yet another contribution on Poland's behalf. This came in light of the publication, on October 10, 1962 by the West German weekly magazine, *Der Spiegel,* of top secret N.A.T.O. plans, whereby atomic weapons would be used on Poland in the event of military aggression against the Western Alliance by the Soviet Union and its Warsaw Pact forces. (Publication of the story landed the editors of the magazine in jail and caused a political crisis in West Germany.)[77]

Rozmarek, writing to President Kennedy in January 1963, expressed his dismay at the idea of making Poland, a Soviet-dominated satellite, a possible target for nuclear weapons based in Germany. (On this issue military opinion prevailed--more than a decade later Mazewski would issue a similar complaint to the U.S. Government.)[78]

Rozmarek experienced greater success in questioning U.S. plans to consider granting the West German military an independent say in the use of nuclear rockets located on its territory, a break from the policy of American control over such weapons in Europe. He reiterated this view in a letter to President Johnson on the eve of an official visit to Washington by the

Chancellor of the Federal Republic of Germany in December 1965:

> We (in the Polish American Congress) are deeply concerned with the announced intention of the German Federal Republic to demand co-possession of nuclear weapons within the North Atlantic Treaty Organization. In view of the fact that not only West Germany but all of Western Europe has been, and is, effectively shielded by the paramount deterrent force of the United States, we regard this demand as without...justification... Co-possession of these arms, in effect, allows West Germany to put a finger on (the delivery of) atomic weapons and would be tantamount to proliferation of these weapons.

Emphasizing Europe's continuing distrust of Germany, Rozmarek noted that its partnership in the nuclear weapons field would extinguish whatever hopes existed for the eventual reunification of the country and undermine Johnson's stated policy of "Building Bridges" between America and Eastern Europe. For its part Washington responded promptly to Rozmarek in declaring that this country had no intention of relinquishing its control over all nuclear weapons in Europe.[79]

Interestingly, Rozmarek's concerns placed him in at least partial and implicit agreement with the plan proposed in various forms after 1957 by the Foreign Minister of the People's Republic of Poland, Adam Rapacki. According to the Rapacki Plan, which had been rejected by the United States and its European allies, the deployment of nuclear weapons would have been forbidden in central Europe, that is, in West Germany, East Germany, Poland and Czechoslovakia. Supposedly, these areas would also have been placed "off limits" as targets of nuclear weapons in the event of war.[80]

Rozmarek's concluding comment in his letter to the President was a prescient one. He asserted that West Germany "would facilitate (both) reunification and the normalization of the international situation in East Central Europe... through... sincere attempts at reconciliation with the former victims of Nazi Genocide... Foremost would be Bonn's open acceptance of the irreversible fact of history, which placed Poland's western boundary along the Odra-Nysa rivers." This position was in fact embraced some four years later, in 1970, by Willy Brandt when, as West Germany's newly elected Chancellor, he embarked upon the policy of *Ostpolitik*, visited Poland and formally declared his country's acceptance of the Odra-Nysa border as the permanent boundary between Germany and Poland.[81]*

---

* Rozmarek's successors would continue to make U.S. recognition of Poland's western borders a constant issue in their representations to Washington. Thus, a statement typical of Aloysius Mazewski was one he made in a White House meeting with President Richard Nixon on October 13, 1970 and which read in part: "Recognition of this boundary is of paramount importance not only for the Polish nation, but for peace and stability in...Europe, which in turn would contribute to American security. In the past, our appeals and arguments in this matter received only stock answers from the State Department, that the solution of this problem must await a general peace settlement in some indefinite future. This hiding behind the framework of International Law, however, does not take into account the demographic, economic and historical facts of life which have taken root in the lands east of the Odra-Nysa Rivers since 1945, and which have been growing into irreversible reality since then. ...The time has arrived for the United States to declare that it recognizes the permanence of the Odra-Nysa boundary. Such a declaration...would tell the people of Poland and other subjugated nations in East Central Europe that the U.S. has no intention of abandoning them and forsaking their millennial rights to be returned to the fold of Western civilization and culture... Secondly, it would weaken the Soviet Union's power of blackmailing them, as the sole guarantor of their territorial integrity..." Nearly twenty years later, President Edward Moskal would write to President George Bush in a very similar vein in the aftermath of the

collapse of the East German communist state and rising speculation over its imminent incorporation into the West German Federal Republic: "...We ask you, Mr. President, and your Secretary of State, to reiterate publicly the long-standing American position concerning the safeguarding of the territorial integrity of Poland. A statement by you, Mr. President, reaffirming unequivocally U.S. support for the present Polish-German border will go a long way in alleviating some of the present fears about a strong, reunited Germany. A reunited Germany...could play a very positive role in establishing economic and political stability in East Central Europe. Such a Germany and a democratic, economically sound Poland with inviolable and definitive borders would help strengthen democracy in the area as well. (This letter of February 15, 1990 was followed by many other PAC communications to the White House and Congress; on February 25 President Bush, following talks in Washington with the West German Chancellor, made an historic public statement when he explicitly declared for the first time that "the United States formally recognizes the current German-Polish border."

V. Aloysius Mazewski and the Polish American Congress: Old Challenges and New From the Sixties to Solidarity

On September 27, 1968 some 682 delegates from around the United States met in Cleveland, Ohio to take part in the seventh national convention of the Polish American Congress. The gathering was historic for it witnessed the transfer of leadership in the organization from Charles Rozmarek, who had headed the PAC from its founding in 1944, to Aloysius Mazewski, who now became Polonia's new and all but official spokesman.

This changing of the guard was both inevitable and anticlimactic. The year before, Mazewski had replaced Rozmarek as the President of the Polish National Alliance after a long and bitter struggle. The Alliance, as Polonia's largest mass membership association, was a crucial element in the operations of the PAC. It had also been Rozmarek's power base. Once Mazewski expressed his interest in heading the Congress, his election seemed assured. But Rozmarek, still smarting over his earlier loss, refused to step down from the chairmanship of the PAC and continued on until his term expired at the Cleveland convention.

Mazewski's election to head the Polish American Congress underscored the continued commitment of the Polish National Alliance to the PAC. In practical terms, the Congress was assured the support of the Alliance's two newspapers, its Chicago-oriented Polish language daily *Dziennik Zwiazkowy* and its bilingual fortnightly *Zgoda,* which had a national readership. Both papers' propaganda backing of the Congress was of growing importance by the early 1970s, a time in which many Polish and English language Polonia periodicals had already gone out of business. What is more, Mazewski's presidency of the two organizations meant that PAC concerns would continue to receive the attention of the Alliance's members, who were to be found throughout the country in more than 1,000 local lodges.

But if Mazewski's election meant continuity for the Polish American Congress in its relationship with the PNA, it also signified change in other respects. For one, with Rozmarek's retirement came the departure of a number of persons long associated with his administration. In their place appeared younger activists from among the ranks of the American-born as well as from the post World War II emigration. Too, the years immediately following the 1968 convention witnessed a general increase in overall PAC activity in contrast to the record compiled by the aging Rozmarek during the preceding decade.

Phase One: Renewal

The early years of Mazewski's regime graphically illustrate the dimensions of this stepped-up activism. Thus, in 1968 the Congress voted to schedule its national conventions every second year beginning in 1970, instead of every four years as had traditionally been the practice. This innovative procedure was indeed followed in 1970 and in 1972, its purpose to stimulate broader involvement within the membership in defining and achieving a variety of PAC aims dealing both with Poland and Polonia. Another manifestation of the new spirit of activism was in Mazewski's creation of a set of "commissions" or standing committees to help carry out PAC aims in a variety of areas of concern around the country. In all, some 18 commissions were soon formed, most of them focused upon the "domestic" issues confronting Polonia. One especially active voluntary body was organized to battle the defamation of Polish Americans in the mass media. Known initially as the "Civic Alertness" Commission, this unit has remained to the present time as the "Anti-Bigotry Commission." Other committees devoted themselves to such matters as "Teaching Polish Language," "Fraternal Matters," "Veterans' Affairs," "Polish-Jewish Affairs," and "Education." A "PAC Talent Bank" was created to collect names and resumes of Polish Americans qualified for appointive positions on the local, state and federal levels of government. One committee continued to concern itself with Poland. This body, the

"Polish Affairs Commission," has continued to be one of the most active agencies in the Polish American Congress.[1]

Mazewski's accession represented change in yet another sense in that his election gave expression to a new surge of ethnic pride among Polish Americans, a pride that had first surfaced in the mid 1960s. Dubbed in the popular press as the "new ethnicity," this phenomenon infected substantial numbers of Americans of Eastern, Central and Southern European ancestral origins with a new and assertive commitment to their heritage and a desire that Americans of other ethnic backgrounds give belated recognition to what their communities had contributed to the United States.

The debate over the origins and meaning of the new ethnicity has aroused more than its share of controversy over the years, as any review of the serious literature on the subject will show. In Polonia, it appears that interest in the new ethnicity was genuine and that it served to energize a fair number of Polish Americans into believing that theirs were activities having continued relevance to the larger society and were not simply "survivals" of an old immigrant culture doomed to disappear in the great American "melting pot."[2]

Equally noteworthy, perhaps, the new ethnicity, both for Polish Americans and other "white ethnics," had relatively little to do with their relationship to the ancestral homeland. Rather, it concerned the maintenance of their ethnic heritage in a United States whose society was increasingly becoming defined in terms, not of assimilation, but of "cultural pluralism." Because the "new ethnicity" advocates in Polonia were generally silent about the community's perspective toward Poland, other than in calling for greater cultural contact with the ancestral homeland, their influence in the Polish American Congress proved to be limited, especially after the mid 1970s, when the PAC became increasingly engaged in monitoring the deepening crisis enveloping Polish society. Nevertheless, as a review of the early years of Mazewski's leadership indicates, certain themes of the new ethnicity did affect the cast of his regime.

Already in his first remarks as PAC President in 1968 Mazewski gave expression to Polonia's concerns about its prospects using the tough and colorful language of the new ethnicity:

> Either we follow in the footsteps of our parents and cultivate the cohesive force of our Polish and Polish-American heritage or we allow our children and grandchildren to disappear into the nameless mass of people who lack cultural and spiritual roots and (who are) ignorant of their historic identity.[3]

In later years Mazewski would repeatedly reaffirm the PAC's role in defining Polonia's place in American society. For example, on the occasion of the PAC's thirtieth anniversary in 1974, he declared:

> The first thing to remember is that the Polish American Congress was organized as a significant and articulate part of the American nation...to present to American and to world opinion the case for a free, independent and strong Poland, the historic key to European peace and stability and consequently, an important factor in the security of the United States and the free world. The second, equally important mission of the Congress rested in its anti-communism, an abhorrent concept contrary to the civic and spiritual values that constitute our thousand year old Polish heritage. From these two fundamental concepts, a third simultaneously emerged in our effort to achieve just status as participants in the mainstreams of American life, as Polish Americans.[4]

The first phase of Mazewski's presidency of the Polish American Congress may thus be summarized here as aiming toward rejuvenating the organization and focusing greater attention on the domestic side of its political agenda. The results of this effort were mixed, however, especially in terms of the structural reforms initiated under his leadership. Hence, with regard to the voluntary commissions set up to deal with the major issues confronting Polonia, Mazewski's initiatives met with disappointment. Within a few years time, most of the domestically oriented units were inactive. Indeed, by the late 1970s only two domestic commissions continued in regular operation, those dealing with ethnic bigotry and Polish-Jewish relations.[5] By then, the Congress' attention was focused once again, as it had been before 1968, on Polish affairs.

Similarly, the innovative effort to hold national PAC conventions every other year was discontinued after 1972, with the organization returning to its traditional quadrennial convention in 1976. At that year's gathering, held in Philadelphia in the presence of only 502 delegates, the question of doing away entirely with regular conventions was raised. Following the conclave, a proposal was enacted to suspend the scheduling of future conclaves except for extraordinary reasons and to replace them with regular twice-annual meetings of the PAC national and state leaderships.

In 1976, the idea of discarding the quadrennial convention format seemed to make sense. Mazewski argued that the cost of the events and their unsuitability for serious deliberations outweighed their benefits as gatherings of PAC loyalists. Indeed, in the Congress' early years, there had been ample reason to rally Polonia behind the Polish independence cause. Thus, the very presence of some 2,600 delegates at the PAC's inaugural meeting in 1944 and more than 1,400 activists from around the country at its second convention demonstrated the ethnic community's commitment to policies its representatives hoped would win the support of the U.S. government. These were keyed to the eventual liberation of Eastern Europe from Communist rule.

With the passage of time, it had become clear that Washington had opted instead for a policy of containment and rejected any military challenge to Soviet domination of the region. In these changed conditions, the quadrennial conventions lost much of their early significance. What is more, as gathering bringing together hundreds of individuals for conclaves lasting but two to three days, the convention format had not proven to be conducive to genuine deliberation.

Perhaps the best argument in favor of continuing the conventions involved their timing just prior to the U.S. Presidential elections. The conclaves often attracted the leaders of the two major political parties in search of the always elusive "Polish vote" and thus brought considerable media attention to Polonia and to the PAC's concerns. Hence, in 1960 President Eisenhower and Senator John Kennedy, the Democratic Party's Presidential candidate both spoke to the PAC at its fifth convention. In 1968, Senator Edmund S. Muskie of Maine, the

Democrats' Vice Presidential nominee and the first Polish American to seek that high office addressed the Cleveland conclave. In 1972, both Vice Presidential candidates, Republican Spiro T. Agnew and Democrat R. Sargent Shriver appeared at the ninth PAC convention in Chicago. And in 1976, the two Presidential nominees, Republican Gerald R. Ford and Democrat Jimmy Carter had spoken to the delegates in Philadelphia.*

In place of the quadrennial convention, a different set-up emerged, one featuring semi-annual meetings of a new body called the Polish American Congress National Council of Directors. Belonging to this National Council were the five executive officers of the PAC (the President, two national vice presidents, the secretary and treasurer), representatives from the approximately thirty state divisional units of the organization from around the country, leaders of the various national fraternal, cultural and veterans organizations affiliated with the PAC and a number of activists elected to the Council on an "at large" basis.

In all, the National Council included approximately 120 voting members. True to form, its meetings have indeed been held twice yearly since 1976, generally on an alternating basis between Washington, D.C. and cities having a substantial Polish American population such as Chicago, Buffalo, Milwaukee, Detroit, Philadelphia and New York. Acting for the Council in the periods between its meetings has been its executive committee. Ironically, the creation of the National Council of Directors, though hailed at the time by Mazewski as both a progressive and efficient move for the PAC, in fact represented a return to the Rozmarek years. Between 1944 and 1968, the PAC's organizational structure had provided for an executive committee of seven to nine persons (president, secretary, treasurer and up to six vice presidents) and a board of directors

---

* President Eisenhower's 1960 remarks and the presentation by President Ford are reprinted in the appendix of this work.

including as many as eighteen leaders from around the country. This body met two to three times each year.

Besides the quadrennial convention, the system under Rozmarek had also included another body, the Supreme Council *(Rada naczelna)*, composed of some one hundred activists representing the PAC membership in the *interim* between conventions. But the *Rada Naczelna* was abolished in 1968 after having been called to order only seven times in the twenty-four years of Rozmarek's regime.

Between 1968 and 1976, a new five member executive committee operated between conventions to lead the PAC in concert with a Board of Directors of some thirty individuals, most of them leaders from the state divisional units. After 1976, the executive committee continued on with Mazewski at the helm but without the Board of Directors or the convention. In some respects, the newly created National Council of Directors represented a reversion to the old *Rada naczelna*, although it has met far more frequently. (Following President Mazewski's death in 1988 there were also calls for the restoration of the quadrennial convention as a means to generate broader participation in the Congress.)

A review of the first phase of Mazewski's presidency indicates that it consisted of more than tough rhetoric and the sometimes halting effort toward structural reform, however. There were also some serious attempts to deal with substantial questions facing Polish Americans in their search for "recognition," which itself was an always underlying issue on the new ethnicity agenda.

From the outset Mazewski made the winning of government appointments by qualified Polish Americans his business and indeed did enjoy some success in helping promote the choice of several individuals to responsible posts in Washington, D.C.[6] There was, however, another side to the recognition drive, the PAC's argument against the controversial policy of "affirmative action." This term referred to efforts by government and private institutions to redress the effects of past discrimination in hiring and school admission by giving preferential treatment to some applicants, namely women and individuals belonging to racial minorities, regardless of their actual qualifications. Such preferences were realized through the creation of quotas setting aside a certain share of the available openings for members belonging to disadvantaged groups.

In the early 1960s, Polish Americans, themselves the victims of genuine discrimination in their own efforts to advance themselves over the years, had applauded Federal actions to penalize prejudicial conduct in employment, housing, college admissions and the determining of promotions. At the same time, most objected to affirmative action as an unfair type of "reverse discrimination" which lumped them and other ethnic Americans into an otherwise undifferentiated but somehow privileged category of "Whites." As Mazewski complained when he testified for the PAC before the Democratic Party Platform Committee in 1976, the Civil Rights Act of 1964 had simply been allowed to lapse in the 1970s. That legislation had made sense because it was comprehensive and prohibited all racial, religious, gender and ethnic discrimination. Now, only prejudice of a racial or sexual character seemed to trouble the Government.[7]

But the PAC went beyond rhetoric in denouncing affirmative action. On two separate occasions, Mazewski called upon the Congress' Washington, D.C. Director, Attorney Leonard Walentynowicz, to prepare *amicus curiae* briefs on cases then being considered on constitutional grounds by the U.S. Supreme Court. In the first, Regents of the University of California v. Bakke (1978), the Court was asked to review the University's use of racial quotas in determining who could be admitted into its medical school. In the second, United Steelworkers of America, AFL-CIO v. Weber (1979), the use of racial quotas in determining eligibility for job training programs was the issue. In the Bakke case, the Court eventually ruled against the University's admissions policy, although it did approve its continued use of information on applicants' racial origins as one criterion for eligibility. This narrowly favorable decision on behalf of the opponents of reverse discrimination did not serve as a precedent for the Court's action in the Weber case, however. There, the complainant argued unsuccessfully that his employer violated his civil rights when it used racial quota considerations in deciding eligibility for its job training program.

In its briefs to the Supreme Court in the two cases, the PAC made clear its position regarding the constitutionality of affirmative action.[8] Thus, in the Bakke case, Walentynowicz wrote:

> We ask this Court to intensely scrutinize from a broad perspective what is happening in the United States with respect to 'special admissions' programs in professional schools and other affirmative action programs. Are these programs in reality and practice living up to the majesty of our Constitution, the language of our laws, and the lofty statements of our leaders, or have they become or will they become vehicles by which some disadvantaged and discriminated groups and individuals secure benefits and special privileges while other disadvantaged and discriminated groups and individuals are still denied the promise of America?

In the PAC's brief in Weber, Walentynowicz concluded:

> We are disappointed that the drive for equality and opportunity for everyone that began with the Civil Rights movement of the 1950s and 1960s is turning into a battle for preference and privilege where groups and the individual who are perceived to be politically weaker are disregarded. We believe America can do a better job in securing the benefits of equal opportunity for everyone... The status of any such group and individual in any field of endeavor (regardless of their numbers) should be the result of honest competition and not discrimination, either for or against them.

Given the increasingly conservative cast of the Supreme Court in the 1990s, one might well wonder whether the Bakke and Weber decisions would long be regarded as its final word on affirmative action. A look at the Court's calendar in recent years suggested that this was hardly the case.

Distinct from, but related to, the struggles for recognition exemplified by the winning of political appointment and the argument against affirmative action was Polonia's growing concern over how Polish Americans might better enlighten others about their heritage. This question first arose in response to growing displeasure with the spate of "Polish" jokes which proliferated throughout the country in the 1960s. Polish Americans had traditionally taken themselves and their heritage seriously and had generally assumed that non-Poles in turn respected their culture. They were thus increasingly dismayed to see television programs and joke books poking ridicule at "Polacks."[9]

Coinciding with the rash of ethnic "humor" was a more ominous criticism which also surfaced in the late 1960s, the charge of "Polish anti-semitism." This attack was particularly felt by foreign-born members of the community, since they possessed the most vivid recollections of Nazi rule over occupied Poland in World War II. They had suffered greatly and to be subjected to the charge that Polish gentiles somehow shared in the guilt for the destruction of much of the European Jewish community, simply because so many Jews perished in Nazi death camps established in Poland, was appalling and hurtful. Perhaps as disturbing was the general lack of American comprehension of the actual wartime conditions which Polish Jews and Polish gentiles had been forced to endure. That some three million Polish gentiles had perished in the Holocaust along with three million Polish Jews was a fact almost always ignored in the American media. That thousands of Polish gentiles had risked their lives and those of their families to rescue Jews was also a point that invariably went unmentioned.[10]

General criticisms of "Polish anti-semitism," furthermore, showed America's nearly total ignorance of Poland's history, that Jews had lived in Poland in large numbers for more than seven centuries and in conditions of religious toleration found nowhere else in Europe. Seldom if ever noted was the fact that by the seventeenth century, the largest Jewish community on earth by far was to be found in Poland. So long, rich and complex a history of Jewish life in Poland surely did not lend itself to simplistic and unfair stereotypes.[11]

American-born Poles were also deeply offended by the anti-semitism charge. Indeed, Polish Americans who had been living in the United States at the time of World War II could well wonder why they were being singled out for such hostile characterization. Their annoyance only deepened with the appearance of a series of widely viewed television dramas that picked up the theme of Polish anti-semitism in telling the story of the Jews' wartime fate. Stories dramatizing Polish gentile suffering and heroism throughout the War went untold. These were, apparently, judged as having no audience appeal.[12]

The initial Polish American responses to the "Polack joke" and "Polish anti-semitism" charges came from individuals active at the local community level; these usually involved written complaints directed toward media executives. Increasingly, however, anti-bigotry committees had begun to form by the early 1970s, their purpose to monitor television, motion pictures, magazines, newspapers and even the marketplace (where souvenirs debasing the Poles' good name were sold). One aggressive effort was made by a Chicago-based organization, the Polish American Guardian Society, which brought an ethnic defamation complaint before the U.S. Department of Justice. The organization charged the producers of the Hollywood motion picture, "The End," with besmirching the collective image of Polish Americans. While the Guardian Society's suit was ruled inadmissible on the grounds that a group could not be legally victimized in a libelous manner, the offensive portions of the film were removed when it was shown on television.

Within the Polish American Congress, a number of persons became particularly active in the anti-bigotry campaign, both locally and nationally. These included a Chicago attorney, Thaddeus Kowalski, a Connecticut judge, Thaddeus Maliszewski, and a New York activist, Frank Milewski. The PAC's National Anti-Bigotry Commission remained in operation into the 1990s under Milewski's leadership.

At the same time, it became increasingly apparent that efforts to fight defamation needed to be complemented by focusing greater attention upon presenting the Polish Americans' story to the wider community. Not only was such an effort crucial in the struggle against false and demeaning characterizations of the ethnic group, it was also an activity that served to unite the two major elements comprising the Polish community in America, the American-born descendants of the pre World War II immigrations and the members of the post World War II emigrations, together with their offspring. While these two broad groups had many diverse interests and characteristics, they shared a concern in promoting greater respect for their heritage within the larger American society.

For its part, the Polish American Congress was becoming increasingly sensitized to this same issue, although its success in effectively propagandizing knowledge of heritage through educational efforts has been seriously hampered by a chronic lack of financial resources. One early effort which was seen as having potentially beneficial results involved PAC support of federal legislation to fund, for the very first time, educational and research dealing with the ethnic contributions to America's culturally pluralist heritage. That effort, whose result included passage of the Ethnic Heritage Studies Act in 1972, was sponsored by Senator Richard Schweiker of Pennsylvania and Congressman Roman Pucinski of Illinois. Unfortunately, funding for the program was terminated after two years.[13]

Another action was initiated in 1971 with the forming of the Polish American Congress Charitable Foundation, a tax exempt agency capable of both collecting and disbursing moneys for humanitarian and educational purposes of benefit to Poland and Polonia and under the direction of the PAC. Though the funds available to the Charitable Foundation for educational purposes were very modest, several books and pamphlets dealing with the history and cultural dynamics of the Polish ethnic community and the ancestral homeland have appeared intermittently over the past two decades.[14] More recently, in the early 1980s, the Charitable Foundation joined with the National Endowment for the Humanities of the U.S. Department of Education to contribute funds to create a national "Consortium for Humanities and Arts Programming" under the direction of Mr. Witold Plonski of Brooklyn, New York. Over a period of some five years, this agency sponsored several hundred lectures, conferences and cultural exhibits dealing with a wide variety of topics focusing upon the Polish and Polish ethnic experience. These varied educational programs, directed towards the general public as well as the broad population of Polish Americans both in and outside the organizational structure of Polonia, reached thousands of people and brought them into contact with the ideas of the country's leading scholars in the field of Polish studies.

From 1945 into the 1960s, the Polish American Congress had provided continuing and substantial financial assistance to the country's two main scholarly associations specializing in the study of Poland and Polonia. These societies, the Polish Institute of Arts and Sciences of America, headquartered in the city of New York, and the Polish American Historical Association (PAHA) centered in Chicago, had been formed on the initiative of emigre scholars during World War II, a time of great concern for the preservation of occupied Poland's intellectual heritage. Both have since grown into respected scholarly societies and today each boasts a substantial membership composed of intellectuals from the United States, Canada, Western Europe, Australia and Poland itself. Both associations hold regular conferences and put out their own journals to disseminate research performed in their fields. These are the *Polish Review*, a quarterly established by the Polish Institute in 1956 and the semi-annual *Polish American Studies*, the PAHA journal since 1943.

Early in his administration, Mazewski attempted to establish contacts between the PAC and the intellectual community. This came in June 1969, in the form of a conference at the Polish National Alliance's college in Cambridge Springs, Pennsylvania and brought together professional academics specializing in Polish studies with PAC and fraternal leaders. The meeting concluded with approval of some 32 resolutions aimed at building closer ties between the ethnic and scholarly communities. But, while a few of the resolutions were eventually implemented, the meeting itself did not generate greater cooperation between Polonia and its scholars. Only in June 1986 was another effort of a comparable character again organized, this time between leaders of the PAHA and a PAC delegation headed by Mazewski and occurring in Chicago. Even this meeting produced but one concrete result, the Association's decision to join the Polish American Congress.[15] Again, in June 1988, Mazewski spoke to a scholarly gathering at the annual meeting of the Polish Institute of Arts and Sciences in Washington, D.C., only a few weeks before his death. There, he declared the PAC's support for a substantial proposal addressed to the National Endowment for the Humanities and called upon his audience to give its backing to the effort. (The proposal involved the establishment of a permanent "United Polish American Community Endowment" funded initially at $2 million, with

$500,000 in Federal moneys and $1.5 million to be generated by Polonia.)[16]

Still, these constructive initiatives yielded modest results at best. The PAC's efforts were simply too few and far between to have an impact and, aside from the ventures launched by Plonski in the early and mid-1980s, were too unfocused to generate the cooperation of scholars in Polish studies who remained interested in sharing their knowledge with the public. The Congress' inability, or unwillingness, to systematically work in the educational field for the enlightenment of Polonia proved to be a major negative on the otherwise generally favorable balance sheet summing up Mazewski's twenty year stewardship of the PAC.[17]

Somewhat more positive results were achieved in building dialog between Polonia and the American Jewish community, an activity already underway as early as 1969. At first, meetings were held under the joint sponsorship of the PAC and the B'naih B'rith fraternal and in November 1970 representatives of the two organizations discussed the central issues then confronting the two communities. While sometimes acrimonious, this gathering at the University of Chicago and subsequent meetings both at the national and local levels were helpful in hammering out a general consensus on the agenda for an ongoing Polish American--Jewish American dialog. This agenda included at least four significant elements:

> ---Building better understanding of the actual history of the pre- World War II relationship between Poles and Jews in Poland, one which existed for more than seven hundred years and could scarcely be reduced to a few stereotypes;
> ---Developing broader public appreciation of the destructive impact of World War II upon both the Jewish and gentile populations in Poland;
> ---Fostering greater sensitivity in each community about the damaging effects of anti-semitism and anti-Polish feeling in the United States; and
> ---Cooperating whenever possible on issues, domestic and foreign, in which the two communities were in substantial accord.

Initial attempts to build dialog in the early 1970s, while well-meaning, did not long endure. However, a new beginning was made in 1979, this time with greater success, largely through the efforts of Polish and Jewish activists in the Detroit area. Playing leadership roles in this work were the Rev. Leonard Chrobot, then President of Saint Mary's College in Orchard Lake, Michigan and Mr. Harold Gales, a representative of the American Jewish Committee in Michigan. Joining them were the Rev. Ronald Modras of Detroit (and later a Professor of Theology at Saint Louis University) and Mr. George Shabad, a leading AJC figure in New York. Soon organized formally as the Polish American/Jewish American National Task Force, the group made several noteworthy contributions over the next decade. For one thing, the Task Force eventually became recognized as the official *liaison* between the Polish American Congress and the American Jewish Committee and in this way reconstituted the earlier, but inactive, dialog at the national level. For another, by its practice of holding its meetings in various cities throughout the country, the Task Force, renamed in 1988 the National Polish American/Jewish American Council, helped bring together Poles and Jews wherever it convened. This innovation helped stimulate the rise of local dialogs in a number of communities, including Philadelphia, Washington, D.C., Chicago, Milwaukee, Detroit, St. Louis, Los Angeles and Cleveland; several of these proved to be quite active.[18]

In summing up the first phase of PAC activity under Mazewski's leadership, one might readily note his sense that it was no longer possible to take for granted Polonia's continued existence as a vital and self-contained community, an outlook characteristic of his predecessor, Rozmarek. Put simply, Polish Americans could no longer be categorized as members of an immigrant community, or even as the sons and daughters of immigrants. Nor were they only to be found in the urban working class. Rather, already in the late 1960s and early 1970s it was necessary to recognize that Polish Americans had become a far more diverse people: many were members of the "middle class," they were suburbanites, and they had children in college. Similarly, one could no longer expect that most Polish Americans were fluent in the Polish language, involved in Polonia organizational affairs in their communities, or even especially knowledgeable about their heritage. To his credit, Mazewski appreciated the impact of assimilation upon the Polish American community and made the first, if halting, steps toward making the PAC more responsive to its changing needs.[19]

Phase Two: Charting a Course in the Era of Detente

A second phase of PAC activity under Mazewski involved the Congress' efforts to better establish its presence in Washington, D.C., this in order to more effectively articulate Polonia's views in its unending quest to influence U.S. policy toward Poland. This Mazewski in part did achieve through his assiduous work in developing good personal rapport with each succeeding American President from Richard Nixon to Ronald Reagan, by cultivating regular contacts with officials in the U.S. Department of State, and by lobbying members of Congress having large Polish ethnic constituencies. His accomplishments were all the greater in that the early 1970s proved to be an especially difficult period for any organization critical of Soviet power over Eastern Europe to advance its views in the nation's capital.

A basic problem confronting the PAC in these years came as a consequence of the crisis which then affected American foreign policy in the aftermath of the United States' failure to realize its military and ideological objectives in Southeast Asia. The seemingly endless Vietnam War, which for Americans had begun in 1965, was still going on in the Summer of 1974 when President Nixon was forced to resign over his involvement in the Watergate scandal. By then, public disenchantment over the conflict had grown intense, in spite of Nixon's "Vietnamization" policy which had brought about the withdrawal of some 500,000 U.S. troops from the region and which restricted further American involvement to material aid and advice to its allies. The following Spring, the Congress of the United States voted to terminate even that assistance. Soon afterward, the American-backed regimes in South Vietnam and Cambodia collapsed and they, along with the tiny neutral state of Laos, all fell under Communist control.

With these defeats, public support for "containment," the foundation of U.S. policy toward the communist states since the late 1940s, disintegrated in the midst of bitter recrimination. Neither Presidents Gerald Ford (who had replaced Nixon) nor Jimmy Carter, who defeated Ford in the 1976 elections, succeeded in defining a new American foreign policy perspective which might win general support in justifying the nation's activities as a global power and leader of the free world. In the resulting vacuum a kind of neo-isolationism reigned, its adherents disinterested in, if not opposed to, an assertive American posture in defense of the aspirations of the peoples of Eastern Europe. Not until the accession of Ronald Reagan in 1981 would U.S. foreign policy once again develop a measure of cohesion, purpose and public confidence.

In this difficult environment, the PAC found itself faced with the emergence of a new American approach to the Soviet Union under President Nixon's leadership, one which was especially confounding in character. This approach, called *Detente* by Nixon's chief foreign policy adviser (and later his Secretary of State) Henry Kissinger, provided for the building of normalized diplomatic, military, economic and cultural relationships between the two longtime superpower rivals, with Washington acknowledging Moscow to be its global equal. *Detente* was expected to bring stability to American-Soviet relations and an end to a Cold War rivalry which more than once since 1945 had led them to the brink of nuclear confrontation.[20]

Detente-building efforts reached an early peak in May 1972, when Nixon and Soviet Communist Party General Secretary Leonid Brezhnev agreed in Moscow to freeze their countries' land-based long range nuclear missile arsenals and to downgrade the development of their costly but still embryonic antinuclear defense systems. These agreements, significant enough in themselves, had further implications for both superpowers.

For the U.S., a high priority on the agenda of the *Detente* process focused upon an agreement to reduce both superpowers' conventional military force levels in central Europe along with those of their N.A.T.O. and Warsaw Pact allies. This objective, however, would not be realized for many years. Brezhnev and his colleagues in the *Politburo* had a different goal in mind: winning general approval of Soviet World War II territorial gains in Eastern Europe and legitimation of the communist dictatorships it had established in the region. This second objective was seemingly realized in 1975 through the convocation of an international conference in Helsinki, Finland attended by officials representing thirty-five European states, Canada, the U.S. and the U.S.S.R. At the time, this conclave was viewed as a major triumph by the advocates of *Detente*.

For various reasons, among them President Nixon's career-long record of opposition to Communism and the neo-isolationist malaise then affecting U.S. public opinion, Polish Americans found themselves hard pressed to object strenuously to the President's *Detente* strategy. Still, they could not be comfortable in recognizing that Nixon's emphasis upon stabilizing American-Soviet relations inevitably placed the Polish cause on the "back burner." This was rather glaringly evident in Nixon's remarks to a PAC-dominated audience at the White House in 1972 following his return from the Moscow summit and a brief visit to Warsaw. (A similar statement of the President's thinking appears in the Appendix of this work.)

Given the memories of the Cold War and the continued existence of the American-Soviet rivalry, the character of *Detente* remained fragile and required strong Presidential leadership to remain "on track." Nixon's ignominious fall from power in 1974 thus dealt *Detente*'s prospects a body blow from which it did not recover. Indeed, by the time of the 1976 Presidential elections, Nixon's hand-picked successor, Gerald Ford had opted against even the use of the word "Detente" in characterizing America's stance toward the Soviets, this in the face of rising criticism from the powerful conservative wing of his Republican Party. By then too, *Detente* had become a source of controversy in Washington's relations with the organizations of East European Americans, including the PAC.

One problem involved President Ford's decision to travel to Helsinki to sign the "Final Act" ratifying the international treaty on European Security and Cooperation. After running into sharp criticism of his move from a number of ethnic organizations representing populations whose votes were needed in the upcoming election campaign, the President found himself pressed into calling a hastily scheduled conference with them in the White House just prior to his departure. There, he declared that the government's approval of the Helsinki Treaty in no way lessened America's commitment to the freedom and independence of the peoples of Eastern Europe, including those inside the Soviet Union itself. Mazewski, by this time a trusted Ford ally, was responsible for organizing the conference, which temporarily defused the issue. But America's involvement at Helsinki and the consequences of the increasingly unpopular *Detente* process would continually haunt Ford and help bring down his Presidential election hopes in 1976.

Particularly unsettling was the flap over the so-called "Sonnenfeldt Doctrine." In December 1975, Dr. Helmut Sonnenfeldt, an aide to Secretary of State Kissinger, addressed a confidential meeting of U.S. ambassadors in London where he allegedly argued for a new U.S. *Detente*-based policy toward the Communist Eastern European states. According to his formulation, U.S.-Soviet relations would be significantly stabilized were Washington to accept the evolution of an "organic relationship" between the Eastern European systems and Moscow.

To many Americans of Eastern European heritage, the idea represented a major retreat from the United States' postwar policy in support of the aspirations of their ancestral homelands for political freedom. (One PAC leader bitterly linked Sonnenfeldt's notion to the organic relationship evolving between a MacDonald's patron and his hamburger.) On hearing of Sonnenfeldt's speech, Mazewski hurried to Washington where he blasted the doctrine to a committee of the House of Representatives. Soon after, President Ford categorically denied the very existence of any such "doctrine" and repudiated any interest in the ideas that had allegedly been raised.

Nevertheless, the controversy came to play an important, perhaps even decisive, part in the 1976 Presidential campaign. Concern over Polish American sensibilities certainly affected Ford himself. Thus, on September 28, 1976 in his appearance before the Polish American Congress' national convention in Philadelphia, Ford was at pains to assert that "the so-called Sonnenfeldt Doctrine never did exist and does not exist. The United States is totally opposed to spheres of influence belonging to any power. That policy is fundamental to our relationship with Poland."

Less than two weeks later, Ford and Jimmy Carter of Georgia, the Democratic Party's Presidential nominee engaged in a nationally televised debate focusing upon foreign policy matters. There and with the Sonnenfeldt Doctrine still weighing on his mind, Ford blundered badly in responding to a rather straightforward question dealing with American--Soviet relations:

> There is no Soviet domination of Eastern Europe, and there never will be under a Ford Administration... I don't believe that the Poles consider themselves dominated by the Soviet Union... And the United States does not concede that those countries (Poland, Yugoslavia and Romania--author) are under the domination of the Soviet Union...

Ford's earnest but clumsy effort to once more respond to an issue that had troubled the Polish American Congress but had little meaning to the general public was, ironically, interpreted as demonstrating his lack of understanding of basic geopolitical realities. Indeed, the misstatement, for which he belatedly apologized, may have cost him the election. (Ford's worries over conservative criticisms of the Helsinki agreement also hurt him in the same debate. When the issue came up, the President failed to provide a single substantive justification for the United States' participation in the conference although several plausible ones were readily available.)[21]

Clearly, the collapse of public confidence in containment and the failure of the Nixon and Ford Administrations to persuade Americans of the benefits of *Detente* served to make the early 1970s a time of confusion and bitterness. In such difficult circumstances, the Polish American Congress was hardly alone in finding itself hard pressed to present its concerns in Washington. Yet uncertainty over the future was not only to be found in the U.S. but in Poland as well. Under the leadership of Wladyslaw Gomulka since 1956, Polish conditions had for years been apparently stable. From the late 1960s onward, however, the situation in the country became increasingly turbulent as Poland experienced both a steadily worsening economy and rising political unrest directed against the regime.

In December 1970, general disenchantment with Gomulka and his policies would explode into violence and bring a sudden end to his long rule.[22] By then, Poland's economic stagnation, largely a consequence of Gomulka's dogged commitment to centralized planning and austerity, was evident everywhere. Yet instead of pursuing new initiatives, his regime clung to its old ways. Amazingly, on the very eve of the Christmas holiday season, Gomulka approved a thirty percent increase in the prices of most foods and consumer goods, its purpose to restrict the consumption of the only products Poland could export for the Western currency it needed to deal with its internal economic problems.

But this incredibly ill-timed and politically insensitive move backfired. Along the Baltic seacoast, riots broke out to protest the price hikes. Order was restored by the Army but only after as many as three hundred people lost their lives. In Warsaw, Gomulka was retired from his post as First Secretary of the Polish United Workers Party and succeeded by Edward Gierek, the regional party boss in coal-rich Silesia. Over the years Gierek had achieved a favorable reputation throughout the country by his success in keeping the people in his district satisfied with well-supplied stores. In his new capacity he moved quickly to purge the PUWP of Gomulka's supporters and to meet with workers in the strike-torn regions. His initial words were conciliatory and appeared to provide the regime with an exit out of the crisis. Most significant, Gierek acted to cancel the price hikes that had led to the seacoast riots and he approved substantial imports of Western-made consumer goods and significant across-the-board increases in wages to distance his regime from that of his failed predecessor.

For the longer run, Gierek inaugurated an aggressive modernization program to make Poland a technologically advanced power for the first time and a significant actor in international trade. This he sought to achieve by embracing a policy long avoided by Gomulka, that of borrowing massively from Western and U.S. banks. Through such loans, Poland would at last have the capital it needed to develop into a modern economy, one capable of meeting its subjects' consumer needs. By achieving for itself a spot in the international marketplace, Gierek and his associates trusted that Poland's rising exports to the West would yield profits sufficient to assure repayment of its foreign loans, the seeds of the entire modernization scheme.[23]

Gierek also sought to improve Poland's reputation abroad, this to overcome the negative image left by Gomulka's last years in power. Thus, in his visits to France and to the United States, he underscored Poland's historic ties with the West and downplayed its links with the Soviet Union, a relationship which Gomulka had emphasized. Gierek became the first communist leader to express a serious interest in improving cultural relations between Poland and its massive diaspora. He stressed the benefits of scholarly exchanges, tourism and private investment in his country and extolled the historic ties between Polonia and Poland and the symbolic roles of Kosciuszko and Pulaski in linking the peoples of Poland and the United States.[24] These efforts, however, produced mixed results at best. For example, in 1974 Gierek was President Ford's guest in the White House but his attempts to speak to Polonia representatives were frustrated when the leaderships of the Polish American Congress and the Polish fraternals declined the invitation to meet.[25]

At home, Gierek's economic strategy proved as risky as it had been ambitious. The heavy costs of the wage increases and foreign borrowing could be justified if the resultant efforts to modernize the country's economy were successful. But the plan failed and for two reasons. Gross errors in domestic planning led to the wasting of much of what had been loaned and Poland's problems in this area were compounded by Soviet pressures upon Gierek to make agreements whereby a substantial portion of Poland's production was rerouted to the U.S.S.R. The Soviets in turn paid for their purchases of merchant ships, electronic equipment and locomotives in rubles, which had no internationally recognized value and were thus of no use in Poland's repayment of its foreign debt.

Furthermore, in 1973 the Organization of Petroleum Exporting Countries (OPEC), an international cartel of Arab and Third World oil producing states sharply increased its prices, thus setting off an economic recession throughout oil-poor Europe. The Western democracies promptly closed their trade doors to Polish goods, thus short-circuiting Warsaw's capacity to generate hard currency sales to repay its debts. Even the Soviet Union, which was Poland's chief energy source, gradually raised the prices of the oil and gas it exported to its satellites.

Already by 1976, Poland faced a new crisis due to increasing consumer demand resulting from Gierek's wage hikes, lagging foreign exports and mounting international debt. To deal with this situation, the Polish regime resorted to the very tactic which had brought about Gomulka's political demise; it approved a sharp price increase in food and retail goods. The aim of this measure was to restrict consumption of the only products Poland could still export for hard currency. Ironically, the action was taken at the end of June 1976, almost twenty years to the day of the Poznan demonstrations which had protested the failed policies of an earlier generation of communist autocrats.

Everywhere the hikes met with bitter resentment; at the Ursus Tractor Works outside of Warsaw and the Armaments Plant in Radom massive and violent demonstrations occurred against the decision. While these were suppressed, the regime then caved in and rescinded the price increases. Although Gierek would continue on as First Secretary of the Polish United Workers Party until September 1980, in point of fact his regime had lost whatever credibility it possessed by its confused mishandling of the June crisis.

Indeed, Gierek had already suffered some embarrassment in 1975, when he had failed to effect a change in the wording of the Polish constitution, one aimed at making it more like that of the Soviet Union. Resistance to that move had been surprisingly robust, with intellectuals and Churchmen taking the lead in objecting to the proposals. Eventually some 40,000 citizens petitioned to voice their opposition to the alterations, which were revised or tabled.[26]

Significantly, from the constitutional debates of 1975 there emerged a broadly based human rights movement whose members were willing to express their views publicly in opposition to the communist dictatorship. The opportunity to advance their concerns came soon enough with the regime's suppression of the Radom and Ursus riots. When many of the demonstrators were fired and blacklisted for their part in the riots, members of the nascent opposition formed on their behalf to win their reinstatement. Among the public associations soon in existence were the Workers' Defense Committee (*KOR, Komitet Obrony Robotnikow*), the Movement for the Defense of Human and Civil Rights (*ROPCIO, Ruch Obrony Praw Czlowieka i Obywa-*

tela), and the Confederation of Independent Poland (*KPN, Konfederacja Polski Niepodleglej*).[27] Ironically, it was the Nixon-Ford Administration's *Detente* policy, one which had been so chafing to many in the Polish American Congress, which proved also to be of unexpected significance in helping engender the changes in Poland. Of particular note were the repercussions from the Helsinki Final Act of 1975. [28] Helsinki itself had been the brainchild of Soviet leader Brezhnev, its objective the winning of Western recognition of the communist regimes in Eastern Europe which Stalin had established in 1945. Not surprisingly, Ford's decision to sign the agreement had caused great discontent among Americans of Eastern European heritage. Still, a retrospective look at the Helsinki Treaty must view its meaning differently.

One key section of the treaty underscored the signatories' recognition of the rights of the peoples of Eastern Europe to freedom of thought, religion and conscience, principles long accepted in the Western democracies and long desired but not tolerated in the satellites. Many activists, in Poland and elsewhere in Eastern Europe, took the agreement seriously and began efforts to press their views upon their rulers. While the Polish opposition was to prove the most significant and successful in its impact, the Poles were by no means unique in challenging their government to comply with an agreement its own leaders had signed. Of no less significance was Helsinki's recognition of the legitimacy of Poland's western frontiers with Germany. For thirty years, Poland, backed by the Soviet Union, had been unsuccessful in winning the United States' formal approval of its new border and try as it might, the Polish American Congress had met only with frustration on this issue. Only at Helsinki, where the United States, the two Germanies, the Soviet Union and Poland all agreed on the permanent and inviolable character of the Odra-Nysa line was Poland's position at last buttressed by an international covenant. In a few strokes of the pen, an historic objective of the PAC was seemingly realized.

Gierek's retreat before the workers of Ursus and Radom in 1976 had not only demonstrated his regime's ineptitude and failure, it placed the government on a collision course with its own subjects. Already that year, the country's foreign debt was acknowledged as having surpassed $10 billion and by 1980 it would balloon to $20 billion. (In Gomulka's last year, Poland's foreign debt obligations had stood at $700 million.) Worse, the regime found itself unable to meet its interest repayment obligations and was thus in fact bankrupt; as a consequence it could no longer contract any additional foreign loans. Unable to curtail domestic consumption either by raising prices or cutting wages, Gierek and his colleagues instead permitted shortages to build unabated: within months lines of consumers were everywhere shopping for nonexistent goods at officially constant prices. Thus meat, an important part of the average worker's diet, was soon to be found only in certain special stores charging prices much higher than those officially quoted. When even these measures failed, Gierek again approved a substantial across-the-board hike in food and consumer goods prices, in July 1980.

Predictably, the move was met again by widespread worker opposition followed by swift government capitulation to demands that wages be hiked to match the price increases. This time, however, events would take a far different course, leading to the birth of a new nationwide independent social movement, Solidarity (*Solidarnosc*), which while ostensibly a trade union was committed to bringing about nothing less than the end of communist party domination over Polish life. Solidarity's birth in the shipyards of Gdansk in August 1980 would not only lead to Gierek's ignominious fall from power only a month later but also herald the emergence of a profound new crisis that would eventually end the Party's dictatorship. That struggle would be long and painful, redirecting and draining Polish society through the entire decade of the 1980s.

Phase Three: The Struggles for Poland Renewed

For the PAC, the decline of Gierek's regime coincided with growing disenchantment with *Detente* in America; this change in public attitude helped usher the organization into a new phase of its activities under President Mazewski and freed its leaders from the need to couch their views about Eastern Europe and Communism in the terminology that had become so popular with Nixon, Ford and Kissinger. Increasingly after

1976, the Congress was focusing its attention once again upon events in Poland in a renewed and systematic effort to provide Washington with solid intelligence about developments there. This effort had two consequences, enhancing the American government's understanding of the changing Polish situation as well as its own stature in the nation's capital.

An important and totally unpredictable boost to Poland's cause occurred in October 1978 when the Archbishop of Krakow, Karol Cardinal Wojtyla, was elected to head the Roman Catholic Church as the 262nd successor to Saint Peter. As Pope John Paul II, the new "Polish Pope" brought the world's attention to his homeland's cause as had never before been possible. The Polish people in turn were understandably ecstatic in hearing the news of Wojtyla's elevation. Already in June 1979, the Pontiff made his first visit to Poland; there before millions of his countrymen he articulated his vision of Poland's future, one rooted in its thousand year old tradition of Christian fidelity to the rights of the individual. In this context, he could only show scorn for the pretensions of the Leninist regime which only temporarily, it seemed, held sway. The Pope's homilies in 1979, furthermore, were credited later with greatly bolstering the nation's confidence in the continued validity of its heritage, one which had survived more than a century of foreign partition, two disastrous World Wars fought on Polish soil, and nearly four decades of communist totalitarianism. It was this heritage with which Solidarity would fervently identify a year later in proclaiming its vision of Poland's future. Later visits by John Paul II in 1983 and 1987 would generate still broader understanding, both in the Polish population and in the Polonia communities abroad, of the Holy Father's devotion to his countrymen's aspirations.[29]

As already noted, Edward Gierek's decision to raise consumer prices in 1980 provoked widespread resistance and yet another speedy retreat on the part of his regime in rescinding the hikes. This time, however, the workers' response was not to take their grievances into the streets where the security forces could intervene in the guise of restoring order, as they had done in 1956, 1970 and 1976. Instead, laborers in several localities organized sitdown strikes with the aim of wringing salary increases large enough to neutralize the effects of the price hikes.

Faced with this novel form of resistance, Warsaw's representatives rushed to the strike sites and quickly conceded to the laborers' demands, assuming that conditions might then return to a semblance of normality.

Instead, news of the concessions spread throughout the country over the next two months, sparking waves of new strikes against the hated increases. One action begun in mid-August in the Gdansk shipyards was historic in its leaders' inclusion of political demands to accompany their wage and workplace grievances. These included the regime's guarantee to empower the workers to form their own independent trade union with the right to strike and the authority to publish its own uncensored newspaper, access to the mass media for the Roman Catholic Church, and the immediate release of political prisoners. On August 31, 1980, after two weeks of steadily mounting tension, the regime's representatives acceded to all 21 of the strike committee's demands.

The Gdansk shipyards agreement set the stage for regime acceptance of similar workers' demands throughout the country. It also heralded the formation of a nationwide trade union movement called "Solidarity." Within less than one month, Solidarity, under the leadership of Lech Walesa, a heretofore obscure 37 year old unemployed electrician and veteran union activist of peasant background, already counted as many as 10 million members in a country of 36 million. (Some three million other workers opted to form independent unions not affiliated with Solidarity; the regime's own trade union organization disappeared.)[30]

Solidarity soon won over Cardinal Stefan Wyszynski to its cause through its leaders' outspoken commitment to social justice and the non-violent resolution of the workers' differences with the regime, along with their pledge to work with the Church in the defense of human rights. Not long afterwards, independent farmers in several regions of the country initiated their own demands for a regime-approved "rural solidarity" movement aimed at defending peasants' rights to the state. They too eventually carried the day.

With the sudden gathering together of this enormous and extraordinarily diverse grass roots coalition, the ruling Polish United Workers Party was wracked by indecision in dealing with what was clearly an unprecedented and revolutionary set of developments. Gierek himself was removed as First Secretary just a week after the signing of the Gdansk agreement and later expelled from the Party. Replacing him was Stanislaw Kania, the government's chief of internal security. But Kania had no plan to deal with either Solidarity or the country's ever worsening economic problems. Even more troubling, during the months from September 1980 until July 1981, when the PUWP held an extraordinary party congress to try, futilely, to chart a new course for the nation, Kania failed to build a basis for productive cooperation between his regime and Solidarity.

Indeed, through those ten months, Solidarity found itself repeatedly forced to threaten the calling of general strikes in order to remind the regime of its obligations under the Gdansk agreements, in particular its pledges to grant the union true freedom of action and to carry out the promise of a five day work week. The latter had been accepted in principle in the August 31 agreement. In fact, both issues became critical tests of will between the two sides. The resulting tensions undermined whatever hopes existed for the evolution of a political consensus as to how the nation might effectively cope with its deepening crisis.

Every indicator, moreover, pointed to the country's economic collapse. Thus, overall production figures for 1980 showed a 4 percent decline from the previous year and were bad enough by any standards. Yet in 1981, production was even more dismal and showed a decline of 15 percent from 1980. Everywhere there were shortages of the most basic consumer needs at the very same time that wages were rising almost unchecked.

Yet Kania and his colleagues in the PUWP and the state administration could arrive at no strategy aimed at reestablishing even a modest measure of confidence in their leadership. Worse, some Party officials, by hinting their support of a Soviet military intervention to quash Solidarity, caused many union activists to conclude that the regime was not at all serious in adhering to its pledges of cooperation.

Too, within the ranks of the Party, there occurred a profound crisis which paralleled the country's economic tailspin. In short order more than two hundred thousand party members simply withdrew from the PUWP; of the 2.9 million persons who remained, approximately one-third became active in Solidarity, most apparently out of a commitment to its goals. Calls were heard everywhere for the democratization of the Party's internal structure and these were eventually implemented before the PUWP's extraordinary congress in July 1981. There, the nearly two thousand delegates, chosen for the first time in secret and competitive balloting, cleaned house by removing nearly every Party leader associated with the discredited Gierek regime. Thus, of the two hundred individuals who were elected to the PUWP's powerful Central Committee, only 16 were holdovers. In the ruling Political Bureau, only four of the fifteen persons elected at the congress had served previously in that traditionally most significant of decision-making bodies.[31]

The extraordinary Party congress, while seemingly endorsing First Secretary Kania's suggestive but vague idea of "renewal" to meet the country's mounting crisis, in fact resolved nothing. Kania himself proved to be an ineffective leader and already by the Summer of 1981 had lost Moscow's trust. With the new Political Bureau hopelessly divided between moderates and vociferous opponents of Solidarity, real leadership was forfeited to General Wojciech Jaruzelski, the long time Minister of Defense and Poland's Prime Minister from February 1981. In mid-October, Jaruzelski replaced Kania at the helm of the PUWP, thus concentrating into his hands an unprecedented measure of power over the Polish system.

Within Solidarity, tensions mounted too in reaction to the Party's failure to make good on its pledges of cooperation. At the trade union's first national conference, which was held in Gdansk in September and October of 1981, Walesa was elected to continue on as head of the movement but only after defeating a number of critics of both the style and substance of his past leadership. Symptomatic of the conclave's atmosphere was its adoption of a resolution which called upon workers throughout the communist world to emulate Solidarity in organizing their own independent trade union movements. This rhetoric brought an immediate condemnation from both the Soviet and Polish communist parties.

One still-born idea hatched in the Fall of 1981 involved the forming of a "front of national accord" to deal with the ever

worsening crisis. This new leadership body was ostensibly to be
headed by Jaruzelski, Walesa and Archbishop Jozef Glemp of
Warsaw and Gniezno, Primate of the Roman Catholic Church
following the death of Cardinal Stefan Wyszynski the previous
May. But the November 4 meeting of the three men was unproductive, due to Jaruzelski's insistence that the Church and
Solidarity recognize the PUWP's leading role over the country
by joining the regime-dominated national front.

Filled with frustration over the Party's failure to keep its
commitments, Solidarity's leaders began to discuss the merits of
mounting a direct challenge to the PUWP's control over the
country. On December 11, they approved a resolution calling
for a general strike for the purpose of dissuading the Parliament
from approving a bill to outlaw future work stoppages. A second resolution called for a referendum on the regime's leadership and a third proposed that free elections be held in the
coming Spring to elect a new Parliament accountable to the
people. At this point, Jaruzelski, acting as head of an emergency committee supreme even over the PUWP's Political
Bureau, imposed Martial Law throughout the country on the
evening of December 12, 1981. Within a few hours, several
thousand Solidarity leaders, including nearly every member of
its top echelon, had been arrested and communication and
physical movement paralyzed throughout the country. The regime later announced that some 5,906 Solidarity activists, including Walesa, had been interned although this figure was
immediately dismissed as far too low. It would be several
months before a new underground Solidarity organization
could be set in place, headed by the few leaders who had
somehow escaped the dragnet.

The crushing of Solidarity, carried out by special military
units, occurred with extraordinary speed and effectiveness. The
action caught practically everyone by surprise, although neither
Solidarity nor the U.S. Government were unaware of its possibility due to information supplied by a Polish security officer
who left the country on the eve of Martial Law.[32]

In Polonia, the events in Poland occurring between August
1980 up through Martial Law (expressively called "a state of
war" or *stan wojenny* by Jaruzelski) had been the source of both
soaring hopes and deep anxieties. Polish Americans, already

heartened by John Paul II's election, joined with their fellow citizens throughout the United States in responding with enthusiasm to the appearance of Solidarity and its commitment to Polish society's eventual democratization. To members of the Polish American Congress, the events culminating in the Gdansk accords vindicated their long-held belief in the Polish people's continued commitment to Western democratic principles and their rejection of the Leninist dictatorship forced upon the country following World War II. Through more than thirty-five years that regime had failed utterly in sprouting roots of support in Polish soil under a succession of leaders, from the Stalinists through Gomulka and Gierek, Kania and Jaruzelski.

Already in August 1980, with the outcome of the Gdansk strike still in doubt, the PAC had issued its first formal pronouncement on the crisis. That memorandum called upon the United States government to reassert its official position on human rights as most recently stated at the signing of the Helsinki accords in 1975 and to influence the Soviet Union from intervening militarily into Poland's affairs. At the same time, the PAC leadership urged Washington to offer increased economic aid to enable Poland to begin to come to grips with its problems. Noting that Poland's current crisis had been "brought about mainly by the inefficient, wasteful and corrupt communist system of centralized planning and management," the PAC cautioned that any future U.S. offers of assistance be conditional upon the regime's prompt introduction of structural reforms, the prerequisites of a genuine recovery.

The PAC called upon Radio Free Europe and Radio Liberty, the American government-sponsored stations beamed to the Soviet Union and East Central Europe, to continue their extensive coverage of Polish events. Speaking on behalf of American Polonia, the PAC declared "its full support and solidarity for the efforts of Polish workers as they seek a greater measure of human rights and freedom. The demands formulated by the strike committee," the PAC stated flatly," are just."[33]

In the weeks following the signing of the Gdansk agreement, the United States, partly acting under steady PAC prodding, took an increasingly bold, two-pronged stance toward Warsaw. Thus, the Carter administration grew insistent in declaring that Poland's problems be resolved by the Poles themselves and without Moscow's interference, a position especially helpful to Solidarity in November and December 1980, when the Soviets stepped up their propaganda campaign against the trade union movement and hinted ominously of military action. Simultaneously, the U.S. acted to provide Poland with some $670 million in agricultural and technical credits to demonstrate its good will, despite Warsaw's failure to repay $800 million in credits extended by Washington during the previous three years. While American assistance to Poland diminished considerably, to $120 million under Ronald Reagan, who followed Carter into the White House in January 1981, a new credit package totalling $1.2 billion was being prepared with strong PAC support just as the Jaruzelski regime declared Martial Law.[34]

Following that action, the PAC backed the U.S. decision to impose economic and diplomatic sanctions against the Soviet Union and Poland, to underscore America's dissatisfaction with the General's move and to apply what pressure was available to help bring about Solidarity's restoration. On December 20, 1981 President Mazewski was accompanied to the White House by PAC Vice President Helen Zielinski (President of the Polish Women's Alliance), Treasurer Joseph Drobot (President of the Polish Roman Catholic Union of America), and John Cardinal Krol of Philadelphia, the ranking Roman Catholic Churchman of Polish heritage in the country. There this delegation delivered a memorandum to President Reagan and Vice President George Bush calling for an immediate end to Martial Law, the release of all political prisoners detained through Jaruzelski's action, and the reinstatement of Solidarity together with a new reaffirmation by the Polish regime of the gains made by the democratic trade union over the past sixteen months. These ideas were largely incorporated into the President's message of December 23 to the American public in which he outlined the United States' response to the Polish events.

Identifying the Soviet Union as primarily responsible for Martial Law, the President then enumerated the actions the United States had decided to take in response to Jaruzelski's move. Significantly, however, Reagan concluded his remarks by offering new and substantial economic assistance to Poland if it acted decisively to reverse its stance toward Solidarity:

> If the Polish government will honor the commitments it has made to basic human rights in documents like the Gdansk agreement, we in America will gladly do our share to help the shattered Polish economy, just as we helped the countries of Europe after both World Wars.[35]

More than symbolic were the sanctions, which largely terminated U.S. economic relations with Poland. Lost was Poland's prized "most favored nation" status which had been hard won in 1960 and with the support of the PAC.* Also ended were U.S.-sponsored food shipments and credits, along with economic assistance through the Export-Import Bank. In addition, Washington declared itself opposed to Poland's future applications for new loans and credits from the International Monetary Fund, an action which blocked its eligibility for foreign assistance.[36]

But while the sanctions announcement signalled an end to U.S. government food subsidies, a door was left open for private agencies to help meet the Polish population's needs in this area. Here, the Polish American Congress was quick to expand its efforts on Poland's behalf by mobilizing Polonia as best it could. Through the PAC's Charitable Foundation, a wide assortment of goods, from foodstuffs to clothing and medical supplies, were soon finding their way to the ancestral homeland.

The Polish American Congress Charitable Foundation dated back to 1971 and had been established as the *de facto* successor of the *Rada Polonii Amerykanskiej* charitable federation of the Second World War era. Heading the Foundation was Eugene Rosypal of Chicago, who served as its executive secretary. From 1981, when the Foundation's efforts began in earnest, through 1990, goods valued at nearly $170 million would be shipped to Poland, distributed to the truly needy through a charitable commission directed by the Roman Catholic Church.

Substantial assistance was also rendered from 1981 onward by a number of other agencies, most notably Catholic Relief Services, the charitable arm of the Catholic Church in America,

---

* On the complex story of Polish-U.S. trade after World War II, see Wandycz, *The United States and Poland,* pp. 366 ff.

and CARE. In addition, individual giving by Polish Americans to relatives and friends in Poland also increased markedly. Thus, by the mid 1980s, such private help in the form of clothing, food and donations was estimated at $600 million annually.

The adverse impact of the sanctions upon Poland's economy led to sharp complaints from the Jaruzelski regime which named the United States as responsible for the country's plight. For its part, the PAC initially backed the policy as the only available means of persuading Warsaw to restore Solidarity and to resurrect the processes of political and economic reform which had been aborted by Martial Law. Thus, at its leaders' meetings with U.S. policy-makers in June 1982 and January 1983, the Congress reiterated its support for sanctions despite Mazewski's appreciation of the policy's effects upon Poland's population.

In June 1983 Pope John Paul II made his second visit to Poland following Jaruzelski's first effort to begin normalizing conditions by lifting Martial Law on New Year's eve, 1982. The Holy Father's visit, of extraordinary significance in showing his solidarity with the Polish nation, also had its impact upon Polonia and PAC thinking over the continuing utility of sanctions. Clearly, Warsaw's response to U.S. pressure during the previous eighteen months had been equivocal at best. Martial Law had been lifted and with it had come the release of most of the political prisoners jailed in December 1981 and an announced commitment to economic reform. Yet, the regime remained adamant in its refusal to restore Solidarity to legal status; indeed, in October 1982 the union was formally dissolved by the Polish Parliament. (In Solidarity's place Jaruzelski approved the formation of a new federation of regime-sponsored workers' organizations; these failed, however, to attract substantial grass-roots support.)

Given the situation in Poland, pressure mounted within the PAC to call for an end to U.S. sanctions, a view endorsed in December 1983 in Gdansk by the recently released Walesa. On May 5, 1984 the Polish American Congress observed its fortieth anniversary at a dinner in Chicago attended by more than 1,000 activists from around the country. The assembly sat uncomfortably through a speech by a deputy secretary of state in which the Reagan Administration's policy was once again defended.

Significantly, however, the speaker's emphasis was to underscore Washington's commitment to normalizing relations with Poland in response to "positive steps" by Warsaw, namely its resumption of a dialog with genuine representatives of the nation from the ranks of the Catholic hierarchy and the outlawed Solidarity movement. Furthermore, the State Department representative was careful to list the various humanitarian initiatives, either already undertaken or contemplated by the Reagan Administration, a clear indication of Washington's sensitivity to growing criticism in Polonia over the damaging effects of its sanctions.[38]

Also announced at the anniversary gathering was Reagan's support for the construction of a new wing to the children's hospital in Krakow built with U.S. funds back in 1965. This addition was eventually completed at the cost of $10 million.[39]

Ten million dollars were also earmarked by the Administration in support of a Polish Church initiative to create an internationally-sponsored private foundation to assist farmers in raising their yields and modernizing their agricultural methods. Though the U.S. Congress approved this appropriation, the proposal was rejected by the Jaruzelski regime, which claimed that its real purpose was to spread negative propaganda into the countryside.

In July 1984 Warsaw announced its amnesty of nearly all of the 700 political prisoners still incarcerated following the imposition of Martial Law; this action prompted both the U.S. government and the PAC to seriously review their commitment to sanctions. As a result, the PAC decided to somewhat alter its position and began an effort to persuade Washington to withdraw its veto of Poland's entry into the International Monetary Fund, a move that was necessary for Warsaw to become eligible for the foreign credits it so desperately required.[40]

In the August 2, 1984 issue of the *Christian Science Monitor*, President Mazewski was characterized as strongly favoring IMF membership for Poland. As he put the matter, "the IMF issue will really put to the test whether the amnesty is real or just a sham. The burden will be on the Polish government." At the same time, he went out of his way to reaffirm Polonia's support for President Reagan in his upcoming reelection campaign. The President merited such backing given his past and continued espousal of tough policies toward the Soviet Union, asserted Mazewski.

Real progress in bringing about a normalizing of relations between Washington and Warsaw proceeded, however, at a tortuously slow pace, with the entire process greatly complicated by worsening tensions inside the Polish regime. Two incidents in particular threatened to derail things, the murder of the outspoken pro-Solidarity priest, Jerzy Popieluszko by members of Poland's own security police in October 1984 and a new wave of arrests of recently released Solidarity activists.* Both developments were highly provocative in character and seemed aimed at bringing down the Jaruzelski regime in favor of one far more hostile to the West.[41]

PAC reactions to these developments involved the creation, in June 1985, of a national assistance committee for the Democratic opposition in Poland under the leadership of Polonia activists Jan Jurewicz and Bonaventure Migala.[42] The committee had as its aim the raising of money for the Solidarity cause in America and the transfer of funds surreptitiously into Poland. The Congress was also active in protesting General Jaruzelski's policies during his visit to New York in September 1985 on the occasion of the fortieth anniversary of the founding of the United Nations. To further dramatize its position, the PAC took what was, for it, the unusual step of purchasing a one-half page of space in the *New York Times* to state its concerns directly to the world.[43]

As already noted, the PAC's continued support of the Reagan Administration's sanctions policy was not without its critics in Polonia, particularly in light of Washington's reluctance to extend comparable penalties to the Soviet Union and Warsaw's own stubborn refusal to alter its own position.[44] On July 9, 1986 Mazewski at last broke openly with the Administration. Speaking for the Polish American Congress he declared:

---

* Four low ranking officers of the security police were eventually tried and sentenced for Popieluszko's murder. In October 1990 two generals in the agency were arrested and charged with directing the plot to kill the troublesome priest.

What bothers us is an apparent lack of any clear concept of U.S. policy in relation to Poland. Instead there are conflicting signals. First there was an official visit of the former U.S. ambassador in Warsaw in March and his four hour talk with Jaruzelski, which looked like a beginning of dialog aimed at obtaining some concessions in human rights. Only a month later, the United States was the only country which abstained from supporting Poland's application for membership in the IMF. Abstention could not have changed the outcome but was received in Warsaw as a manifestation of hostility which brought about an outburst of anti-American propaganda and an escalation of repression...

Our message is simple. The situation changed when the U.S. removed all sanctions against the Soviet Union after the Afghanistan invasion and after the crackdown on Solidarity... Poland remains under the political and military control of Russia. In the absence of any pressure on Moscow we should redefine and reconsider our policy towards Poland. Above all, the Administration should know what it wants to achieve and what can be achieved under the present circumstances.

The President of the PAC then made plain his organization's growing concern for Poland by declaring:

Ten million Americans of Polish extraction continue to oppose and fight the totalitarian government imposed upon the Polish nation by the U.S.S.R. At the same time we want to avoid anything which would hurt the people more than their rulers and we ask for a policy which would help support most effectively non-violent resistance as an important force promoting peaceful change within the Soviet bloc. Further deterioration in living and health conditions of the Polish people is not conducive to strong resistance. In this respect, the U.S. government should not place its judgment above the views of leading Polish moral authorities, such as the Polish Church and Lech Walesa.[45]

This judgment was shared by many, notably by such experts on Soviet affairs as former National Security Advisor Zbigniew Brzezinski. In a talk presented in May 1986 on the occasion of Polonia's annual observance of the 1791 Polish Constitution, Brzezinski took the Administration to task in holding to what

he termed a sanctions policy which had become "purely negative" in character. Arguing that the policy's impact was causing
Poland increased economic troubles while providing its rulers
with no incentive to modify their repressive stance toward their
subjects, Brzezinski concluded:

> Were the United States to combine a policy of very
> limited contact with Poland so long as repression continued
> while at the same time indicating our willingness to greatly
> facilitate the modernization of the Polish economy by back-
> ing the flow of capital to Poland through the IMF, we would
> have some leverage.
>
> We would be in a position to influence choices in Po-
> land.
>
> We ought not to underestimate the degree to which
> Polish society itself can begin to exercise pressure upon its
> own rulers in its making of more intelligent policy choices.
> At the same time, we also should not forget that the govern-
> ment's choices can also be shaped from the outside. The
> Polish government ought to know that if there is to be some
> American help, it must be connected with political relaxa-
> tion in Poland...[46]

The sought after changes in U.S. policy were at last announced by President Reagan on February 19, 1987, at a White
House meeting attended by PAC leaders. This action came on
the heals of the Polish regime's release of nearly all of its
remaining political prisoners. In fact, however, Warsaw had yet
to address Washington's call that it initiate genuine dialogs with
Church leaders and representatives of the still outlawed Solidarity movement. For the time being, therefore, the regime's
intransigent line appeared to have prevailed, although the triumph had come at an extraordinary cost--more than five years
of political repression and economic deterioration. As events
during the next two and one half years would show, the communists' victory would prove to be pyrhic.

For the Polish American Congress, growing frustration in
Polonia over Poland's worsening plight had led Mazewski to
press for an end to economic sanctions. But in Washington,
another development served to influence the Administration to
review its approach toward Poland, the appearance onto the

international scene of a new and reform-minded leadership in Moscow headed by Mikhail Gorbachev. Clearly, in softening the U.S.'s position toward Warsaw, Reagan was signalling an intention to establish better relations with a Soviet leader with whom it might finally deal.

For its part, the PAC's posture toward Poland remained consistent. As its Vice President, Kazimierz Lukomski, put matters in early 1988:

> Poles do want economic reforms, which have a chance to lead the country out of the doldrums of its current stagnation. They are in favor of democratic freedoms for which they have been striving courageously over the past four decades to replace the authoritarian one-party state that rules them. They want a voice in the development of economic and socio-political reform programs and they want to be able to control their implementation through a genuine, democratic representative system. Poland's future depends on whether the authorities will respond to these legitimate demands.[47]

This statement, expressed some forty-four years after the PAC's founding, was firmly in keeping with its founders' perspectives. Indeed, time and again, events in Poland had only served to validate them.

Thus, for the Polish American Congress, the central problem facing Poland concerned its post World War II fate as a country under Soviet military occupation, saddled with a political system whose objectives were largely unacceptable to the overwhelming majority of the population. Illegitimate from its birth, Poland's communist regime had never succeeded in winning its subjects' hearts and minds; indeed, nowhere else in East Central Europe over the years had there been as many challenges to communism's power as in Poland.

Some observers could point to the regime's chronically poor record in managing Poland's economy as a good explanation for its lack of popular approval and there is much truth to this judgment. But to PAC activists, the regime's problems were fundamentally rooted in the alien character of a Soviet form of communist dictatorship imposed against the will of the Polish population, maintained in power by the Soviet Union, and unwilling even to consider sharing its responsibilities for the nation's destiny with authentic representatives of its citizenry, much less permit the evolution of a democratic government. Thus, in 1947, the communists had broken the back of Mikolajczyk's democratic peasant movement in an election campaign disfigured by massive repression and fraud. In 1956 and 1970, it had held onto power in the face of massive popular pressures from below. With the onset, in the mid 1970s of Poland's most extended and painful economic crisis had come the most insistent challenge yet to Communist dictatorship. Out of this crisis had sprouted the sprawling Solidarity movement in 1980.

In December 1981, the Jaruzelski regime managed to outlaw Solidarity, only to learn that its repressions brought neither the movement's eradication nor any new popular acceptance of its own rule. Significantly, in the years that followed Jaruzelski would call several elections to register the public's approval of his leadership. Each, however, was boycotted by substantial numbers of voters and counted for little in building a semblance of respectability for his policies.

In November 1987, the government called a referendum on the General's long delayed economic reform program in yet another vain attempt on his part to gain a measure of approval for the regime. A legitimately based government might have succeeded in persuading its people that the sacrifices called for in its reform proposals needed to be made. Jaruzelski's regime, however, was in no position to do so. On the day of the referendum, much of the electorate simply refused to participate in what was widely perceived as a meaningless exercise. Among those who did vote, many defiantly cast their ballots against the reform package.

Incredibly, when the results of the referendum were announced, the regime itself admitted that its proposals had been rejected since fewer than half of all registered voters had supported the "reform" proposals. This admission, unprecedented anywhere in the history of Leninist rule, proved to be Jaruzelski's most telling acknowledgement yet of the communists' political bankruptcy. The announcement, true to form however, was not followed by their formal resignation from national leadership.[48]

In May 1988, workers in factories and mines around the country once more organized strikes in protest against the regime's imposition of yet another round of consumer price increases. These had gone into effect despite the electorate's vote in the referendum the previous year. At first Jaruzelski was able to restore order by employing a strategy combining repression, the implementation of new anti-strike laws and the granting of salary increases whose effect was to nullify the impact of the price hikes. Still, the regime for the time being remained firm in rejecting demands for the reinstatement of Solidarity.

In the United States, the Reagan Administration's response to the May strikes was decidedly mixed. While sympathetic to Poland's plight, Washington was anxious that disturbances there not lead to a Soviet intervention, an action which would torpedo the President's long-planned Summit with Gorbachev in Moscow. The events in Poland did not, however, constrain the PAC from siding strongly with the strikers. Already on May 6, the Congress' top leadership declared:

> Through the past forty-odd years the rulers of the Polish People's Republic have not learned the clear lesson of history, that they cannot govern Poland without the support and the cooperation of the society, that they cannot continue to violate the proper demands of the people for social justice. It is not the striking workers, as the spokesmen for the regime would have it, but the authorities themselves who have committed acts of terror. It is they who have ignored the moderate and just demands of the workers and the efforts of the Polish hierarchy to create the conditions necessary to bring about reforms, social understanding and cooperation to deal with the reconstruction of an economy ruined by that regime and the creation of a system of legitimate government based upon the trust of its citizens.[49]

The PAC pronouncement was soon shown to be correct in its analysis of Poland's seemingly unending political crisis. In mid August, the country was hit by a new wave of strikes and everywhere the workers' demand was the same: relegalization of Solidarity. At last, on August 31, 1988, the eighth anniversary of the Gdansk agreement, Lech Walesa met with General Czeslaw Kiszczak, Minister of the Interior of the Polish People's Republic, for the purpose of ending the strikes and initiating the process of bringing about Solidarity's full reinstatement. This meeting would be historic; by the beginning of 1989 "Round Table" talks would be underway in Warsaw between leaders of the democratic opposition, the Roman Catholic Church and the regime which would eventually bring about not only Solidarity's full restoration but the collapse of communist domination over the country's political system.

Within the leadership of the Polish regime, division continued to prevail over the course to be taken. Thus in September 1988 the cabinet headed by Prime Minister Zbigniew Messner resigned in response to growing criticisms of its management of the steadily worsening economy. Significantly, Messner had come to power in 1985 as Jaruzelski's hand-picked successor and had been heralded as the man best able to carry out the General's reform plan. Now the task fell to Mieczyslaw Rakowski, Poland's sixth head of government since 1980.

The issue of Poland did not prove to be a salient question during the 1988 U.S. Presidential campaign as had been the case on more than one occasion since World War II. Indeed a general consensus about Poland and the causes of its troubles had clearly emerged in the 1980s, one shared by both of the major party candidates and shaped to some degree by the PAC's own concerted efforts over the years. Late in the campaign, both George Bush, the Republicans' nominee, and Michael Dukakis, the candidate for the Democratic Party, were asked by the PAC to express their views on Poland. Their replies were interesting in several respects. Thus Vice President Bush declared:

> Present day Poland, more significantly than ever, brings into focus the tragedy of the forced division of Europe (following the great power summits at Teheran in 1943 and Yalta in 1945)...(This division) does violence to history and to the substance of post World War II international agreements...Through the 'peace through strength' policies of the Reagan/Bush Administration, careful negotiation has replaced confrontation in U.S.--Soviet relations. However, meaningful change must be measured by concrete evidence of what the U.S.S.R. does in areas crucial to the United States and to world peace. East Central Europe is such an

area... Solidarity is a beacon for all peoples in Poland and the rest of the world who are fighting for individual freedom and basic human rights... I look forward to the legalization of Solidarity, the legalization of true freedom of individual and political association in Poland. I applaud the continuing attempts by Polish workers and all Polish citizens to achieve greater freedom... I am committed to direct and effective support for the Polish nation in its striving for freedom, prosperity and peace, for its rightful place in the family of Europe...

Continued U.S. economic assistance to Poland...requires concrete progress by the Polish government in recognizing the need for democratic representation for the people of Poland. I hope that current discussions between the leadership of Solidarity and the government will prove fruitful in establishing a national dialogue, pluralism, and the right of association. Polish economic recovery is contingent on the government's acceptance of economic, political and social reform...

For his part the Democratic candidate, Massachusetts Governor Michael Dukakis, expressed very similar ideas in outlining his views on Poland's situation:

The people of Poland want what we want, what all people want--the right to express their views openly, to choose their leaders freely, to worship their God without fear... In a Dukakis administration, the cause and courage of Polish miners and shipyard workers will be part of any summit with the Soviet General Secretary... With dramatic indications of a potential shift in the nature of U.S.--Soviet relations, Poland's significance has greatly increased. Nevertheless, until word becomes deed...we must be cautious. Decentralization of economic decision-making authority, political pluralism and the reduction of Soviet troop levels in Eastern Europe must take place before we can mark a fundamental shift in U.S.--Soviet relations. There is no better place to see such steps taken than in Poland... The return of Poland, indeed of all Eastern Europe, to the dignity of self-determination will be a vital step toward improved relations between the United States and the Soviet Union... On Poland's economy: for the United States to contribute meaningfully to the economic recovery of Poland, structural changes in its economic system must first take place... Without extensive reforms, U.S. assistance can not ensure long-term recovery in Poland. To secure U.S. economic assistance and assure the implementation of reforms, the Polish government must come to some agreement with its workers through an independent trade union movement...[50]

If Bush and Dukakis' comments permitted the PAC to applaud the emergence of a genuine national consensus over Poland and Eastern Europe, the tendency of both Presidential candidates to couch their words on Poland within the framework of Soviet-American relations demonstrated once again the constraints under which the Polish American Congress has been forced to operate ever since its founding. The efforts of Polonia's representatives on Poland's behalf have succeeded only when they have been in accord with the perceived best interests of the U.S. in its dealings with Russia.

If George Bush's election to the Presidency in November 1988 was widely predicted, the events which would follow one upon another in Eastern Europe throughout 1989 would be anything but the expected. Still for activists in the Polish American Congress, which in 1989 observed its forty-fifth anniversary, it was possible to be optimistic about the future and proud of decades of dedicated labor to the cause of Poland's restoration to freedom and independence. Indeed, while there had been many frustrations over the years, organized Polonia had succeeded in significantly enhancing recognition for Poland's aspirations among Americans of all ethnic backgrounds. Even more important, the PAC and its spokesmen had persuaded many of their fellow Americans that a free and independent Poland was not simply a nice thought, but an objective to be pursued because it was indeed in this country's national interest.

They could also take pride in the fact that so many hundreds of thousands of Americans of Polish origins continued to maintain contact with relatives and friends who remained in Poland. This human tie has not only helped revitalize the life of Polonia again and again, it has also brought material and spiritual benefits to the citizens of Poland in reminding them that their isolation within the Soviet imperium was neither complete nor permanent.

VI. Humanitarian Efforts for Poland in the 1980s: The Work of the Polish American Congress Charitable Foundation

From its formation in 1944 through the next three decades, the Polish American Congress carried on a number of humanitarian activities in addition to its primary political work of lobbying for Poland. Thus, from 1948 into the late 1950s, the PAC sponsored the American Committee for the Resettlement of Polish Displaced Persons under the chairmanship of Judge Blair Gunther of Pittsburgh. This body, which was formally created as a subcommittee of the PAC, assisted more than 35,000 newcomers in establishing themselves in the United States in the late 1940s and early 1950s after enduring years of wartime hardship.

The Congress was also helpful in supporting two other relief committees created after the War in their activities on behalf of the new immigrants. These were the Polish American Immigration Committee in New York headed by the Reverend Felix Burant and the Committee on Polish Immigration Matters, directed by the veteran Polonia activist and New York industrialist, Ignace Nurkiewicz. Notable too was the PAC's continued financial support of the *Rada Polonii Amerykanskiej* or "American Relief for Poland," as the organization was popularly known after the War. The *Rada Polonii* not only received help from the Congress, however; it also benefited from the support rendered by the many fraternal societies belonging to the PAC which frequently directed their generosity to a select number of hospitals, orphanages and schools whose plight had been brought to their attention by the *RPA*. Aid of this sort often continued on for many years, even into the 1960s.

Following Gomulka's return to power in 1956, the improved relations between Warsaw and Washington also had its effects upon the Polish American Congress, leading it to support a program of U.S. economic assistance to the Polish people. In doing this, the PAC was taking its first steps in reevaluating it policies of the previous decade, which had been opposed to any direct humanitarian assistance to Poland. In the years that followed, that position would be reversed, especially with the creation of the Congress' own Charitable Foundation.

Indeed, with the *de facto* demise of the *Rada Polonii* in 1969 following the United States' termination of its program of shipping surplus food to Poland (a program with which the *RPA* had been heavily involved), the stage was set for the PAC to set up its very own effort in the humanitarian realm for the first time. This in fact occurred in 1971 with the decision to establish a Polish American Congress Charitable Foundation (PACCF) as a separate tax exempt agency of the Congress with the power to raise moneys for humanitarian and educational purposes of benefit to Poland and Polonia.

In the first decade of its operation, the PACCF, whose executive officers were simultaneously the heads of the Polish American Congress, focused upon the publication of books and pamphlets aimed at enlightening the public about Poland's heritage. Groundwork was also laid to set up a scholarship program on behalf of meritorious college students of Polish origin and to raise funds to support research of a scholarly nature dealing with issues of concern to the Polish American community. However, between 1971 and 1981, these activities remained very modest, due to the Foundation's inability to increase its financial base.[1]

The PACCF's work on Poland's behalf began at the end of 1980 with its officers' decision to provide whatever material assistance they could in response to the country's deepening crisis. It was at this time that Lech Walesa, as head of the newly legalized Solidarity trade union federation, issued an appeal to Polonia throughout the world to gather medical supplies that were in short supply in Poland for shipment to the homeland. The country's situation by then had grown serious; unable to meet its mounting foreign debt obligations, the Polish government lacked the hard currency funds it needed to purchase sufficient supplies of medical goods and drugs that were available solely from Western providers. In these conditions, thousands of Poles who required major medical care were

increasingly finding themselves at risk. In response to this new
and looming health care crisis, Walesa's first appeal enlisted
Polonia's help in generating $5.5 million so that some 58 differ-
ent medications and surgical materials could be shipped speedily to Poland.

The Polish American Congress, in concert with Polonia
organizations in sixteen other countries in the free world,
promptly established a Medical Commission (*bank lekkow*) under the auspices of the PAC Charitable Foundation. Leading
the Commission were several Chicago area physicians and PAC
activists including Dr. Walter Cebulski, Dr. Antoni Mianowski,
Drs. Mitchell Kaminski senior and junior, Dr. Arthur Wolski,
Professor Stanislas Smolenski, Jerzy Przyluski, and Maria
Czyzewska. Working with them was a British-based agency, the
Medical Aid for Poland Fund, headed by Dr. Bozena
Laskiewicz.

In March 1981, the Medical Commission's activities were
advanced by the visit of Walesa's emissary, an attorney named
Zbigniew Gryszkiewicz, who came from Gdansk, the "capital"
of the Solidarity movement. Gryszkiewicz's appearance in the
United States proved to be productive on several counts. For
one, he was effective in providing Americans with their first
direct contact with a well-placed representative of the Solidarity movement and appeared frequently on American television
and radio. (On one occasion Gryszkiewicz spoke to a national
audience on the McNeil-Lehrer news program with PAC President Mazewski serving as his translator.) Second, he was helpful in strengthening ties between the Polish American Congress
and Solidarity's own medical commission. That agency had initially been given responsibility for distributing the medical
supplies that were beginning to arrive into the country from the
West.

For its part, the Polonia Medical Commission was quite
successful in generating both financial support and gifts of
needed medical supplies for its cause. Especially noteworthy
was the generosity of the J. Seward Johnson and Barbara Piasecki Johnson Foundation, which contributed $1 million to the
Commission in the Fall of 1981. Given the urgency of Poland's
needs, some of the early supply efforts directed by the PACCF
and the Medical Commission proved to be rather dramatic.

One memorable action involved the Flying Tiger Airlines, which loaned its planes to transport goods that were in especially short supply to the homeland and in literally airmail delivery fashion.

In June 1981, President Mazewski travelled to Warsaw as a member of the official United States delegation attending the funeral of Cardinal Stefan Wyszynski. While there he met with many leading Church authorities, Walesa, and other Solidarity representatives, and was able to make his own first hand analysis of the situation in the country. His visit thus impressed the Polish American leader with the seriousness of Poland's mounting needs and the ancestral homeland's appreciation of Polonia's potential significance as a constructive force in its time of troubles.

Mazewski's brief stay in Warsaw and Gdansk marked the first time the head of the Polish American Congress had ever travelled to Poland and in that sense it was historic. (Up till then the PAC had staunchly resisted any contact with Polish officialdom since it regarded the Communist regime as one having no legitimate right to govern the Polish nation. Even Mazewski's presence in Poland was characterized as one based upon an invitation from the President of the United States in honor of Cardinal Wyszynski and was not to be seen as a change in the Congress' policy of non-recognition of the Polish regime.)

But the trip was more significant in its reaffirming of the ties that had in the past linked the immigration and its descendants with Poland. Even more pertinent perhaps, Mazewski, by his presence in Poland was establishing new and direct contacts between Polonia, the Polish Church and Solidarity, which were widely recognized in America as the authentic representatives of the Polish nation in its continuing struggle for freedom from Communist rule.

Concurrently with the inauguration of the Polonia Medical Bank, the PACCF set to work to mobilize the Polish American community in support of broader needs in the ancestral homeland. These included the providing of food and clothing to those whose difficulties were especially pressing, namely the poor, the elderly, expectant mothers and parents of the very young. To generate funds for this "Relief for Poland" project, telethons were organized in Buffalo and Chicago by PAC activists. The first Buffalo effort, in March 1981, raised more than $200,000; the Chicago telethon, featuring the popular Polish American entertainer, Bobby Vinton, took place in August 1981 and generated approximately $1 million. Both cities repeated the efforts with similar good results, in Buffalo in 1982 and Chicago in 1985. Leading the efforts in Chicago was City Alderman and former U.S. Congressman Roman Pucinski, acting in his capacity as President of the Illinois state division of the Polish American Congress. Responsible for the telethons in Buffalo were Brian Rusk, Richard Solecki, Alice Posluszny and Bogdan Durewicz. Significantly, Chicago's telethons, carried by "superstation" WGN-TV, entered not only into the homes of local residents of the city's vast Polonia but also reached thousands of people across the country with their messages of concern for Poland. Participation in the Buffalo fund raisers was also extensive and stretched into Canada, western New York, Pennsylvania and Eastern Michigan.

Fund raising efforts directed by individual state divisions of the Polish American Congress also constituted an essential element of the relief effort. Such assistance enabled the PAC to purchase medical supplies, surplus United States food products and goods available in Western Europe and to cover the costs of the shipment of all donated materials to the homeland. Particularly helpful in the early fund raising work were the Congress' Illinois, Michigan and three New York state divisions, those in Delaware, Ohio, Indiana, Eastern Pennsylvania, and its two California divisions. Each of these units sent in over $100,000. Through a variety of activities from television and radio appeals to carnivals and parish solicitations, the state divisions came forth with approximately $4 million in financial aid. Without their assistance, much of the work of the PAC Charitable Foundation in the years that followed would not have been possible.

To dramatize Polonia's concern for Poland, especially after the communist authorities imposed martial law throughout the country in December 1981, the PAC organized two massive shipments of food, clothing and medical materials under the direction of its Washington, D.C. representative, Myra Lenard. The first shipment was nicknamed the "Solidarity Express" and consisted of a coordinated gathering of goods from all parts of the country, with materials sent by rail to Baltimore, Maryland. This project was aided considerably by the management of the Norfolk and Western and the Southern railway companies, which donated the use of their cars to make the "Solidarity Express" a success.

In all, volunteers stationed at delivery points around the country, including Chicago, Detroit, Cleveland, Columbus, Cincinnati, Baltimore and Washington, D.C. filled some twenty-two railway cars with materials. From Baltimore, Polish vessels then shipped the goods across the Atlantic to their destination. There they were distributed by the Polish Episcopate's Charitable Commission. The Commission, headed by the Auxiliary Bishop of Katowice, Czeslaw Domin, operated directly with parishes and hospitals throughout the country to ensure that Polonia's assistance went to individuals having the greatest need.

In all some 854,000 pounds or 427 tons of goods were transferred to Poland by means of the "Solidarity Express." Of this total, 530,000 pounds of food, 216,000 pounds of medical supplies and 106,900 pounds of clothing were gathered for delivery to the homeland. The total estimated value of this shipment was estimated at $6,174,000.

Lenard also played a key role in a second supply-gathering shipment to Poland organized for December 1982. This was the "Solidarity Convoy," the product of a cooperative action realized through efforts of the Sun Truck carrier company of Philadelphia. For this project, some thirty freight trucks travelled from coast to coast bringing medical items, food and clothing valued at more than $10 million. The convoy arrived in Washington, D.C. on December 13, 1982, passing the nation's capitol on the first anniversary of Solidarity's repression. Shortly afterward, these goods too were in Poland for distribution under the auspices of the Church's Charitable Commission.

As early as September 1981, PAC deliveries of foodstuffs were already being shipped to the ancestral homeland in other, less dramatic ways, in cooperation with CARE and Catholic Relief Services. The first such shipment was substantial, involving the delivery of food packages having a combined weight of 2.2 million pounds. The effort, like others of its kind that would follow over the years, underscored the PAC's interest in making

certain that the packages' recipients were aware of their donors' identity. Thus, all were labelled "*Dar Polonii Amerykanskiej,*" or "Gift from the Polish American community."

In August 1982, the first major combined shipment of goods
purchased or donated in Western Europe headed by truck to
Poland in an arrangement made with the London-based "Food
for Poland" organization headed by Albin Tybulewicz. The first
convoy provided some 122,726 pounds (61 tons) of food for the
homeland; shipments of the same type continued for several
years afterward. Indeed, between September 1982 and March
1983 alone, another 140 tons of food reached Poland through
this agency.

One estimate of overall assistance to Poland from the
United States from 1981 through 1983 showed that it amounted
to 140 ship containers of food, clothing and medical supplies
which together weighed several thousand tons. During that
period, the PACCF, working with Catholic Relief Services and
CARE, launched a special monthly delivery of food parcels to
families of Solidarity leaders who had been imprisoned for their
involvement in the outlawed union. At its height, approximately 2,000 such parcels, each weighing about twenty pounds,
were being shipped every month to Poland.

Yet another effort undertaken by the tireless Lenard, in
concert with PACCF activists Przyluski and Eugene Rosypal in
Chicago, was a shoe drive directed to meeting the needs of
Poland's children. Initiated in 1983, this nationwide program
produced donations of some 1.25 million pairs of shoes.

To gain a sense of the size of the "Relief for Poland" assistance rendered by the PACCF, a look at the figures themselves
might be warranted. Thus, and according to data culled from
the issues of the Charitable Foundation's newsletter which
appeared two to four times annually after 1980, together with
the Foundation's semi-annual reports presented to the Polish
American Congress National Council of Directors, one finds
that the total dollar value of all such assistance amounted to
nearly $169 million between 1981 and the end of October 1990.

Table 1. Total Value of Goods Transferred to Poland by the Polish American Congress Charitable Foundation

Through Its "Relief For Poland" Campaign: January 1, 1981 Through October 31, 1990

Category of Goods	Dollar Value	Percentage of Total
Medical Materials	$106,494,861	63.0
Foodstuffs	17,362,508	10.3
Clothing, especially shoes	17,594,000	10.4
Miscellaneous goods, including books, farm tools	27,482,477	16.3
Total	**$168,933,846**	**100.0**

Table 2. Total Value of Goods Transferred to
Poland by the PACCF
Through Varying Time Periods, 1981-1990

Period of Time	Total Amount	Average per Month
From January 1, 1981 through March 31, 1983 (27 months)	$33,975,719	$1,258,370
From April 1, 1983 through October 31, 1984 (19 months)	$19,171,281	$1,009,015
From November 1, 1984 through June 30, 1986 (20 months)	$26,853,000	$1,342,650
From July 1, 1986 through May 31, 1987 (11 months)	$14,043,990	$1,276,263
From June 1, 1987 through May 31, 1988 (12 months)	$21,525,624	$1,793,802
From June 1, 1988 through November 1, 1989 (17 months)	$24,536,437	$1,443,320
From November 1, 1989 through October 31, 1990 (12 months)	$28,827,795	$2,402,316
Total (118 months)	**$168,933,846**	**$1,431,643**

Various year by year summaries of the estimated value of goods gathered and sent abroad in the "Relief for Poland" campaign have been provided by Rosypal since the mid 1980s. These are helpful in providing additional understanding of the character of the PACCF's efforts. Significantly, such data show that by the end of 1990 the total value of all assistance rendered by the Charitable Foundation had surpassed even that of the World War II era *Rada Polonii Amerykanskiej.*

Table 3. Annual Assistance to Poland
Through the Polish American Congress
Charitable Foundation, 1981-1990

Year	Donations Received	No. of Shipments to Poland	Value of Goods	Average Amount of Aid per month
1981	$1,655,261	34	$5,591,054	$465,921
1982	1,929,455	42	21,657,700	1,804,808
1983	185,785	64	13,871,884	1,155,990
1984	172,791	27	10,907,241	908,937
1985	698,480	71	18,742,768	1,561,897
1986	275,988	96	14,474,997	1,206,205
1987	68,270	90	19,092,110	1,591,009
1988	61,213	118	20,468,297	1,705,691
1989	255,287	103	20,161,940	1,680,162
1990	293,038+	166+	23,965,855	2,396,586
Total	$5,595,568*	809	$168,933,846	$1,431,643

+Figures are for the first ten months of 1990. Included in the total number of containers for 1990 were six special air shipments of medical supplies.

* PACCF records show total revenues during the 118 month period as $7,836,714, of which all but $25,118 had already been spent for the relief cause. The difference between this total and the sum listed above as donations is accounted for by two U.S. Government A.I.D. grants, a smaller grant from the National Endowment for Democracy, income from its deposits collected by the PACCF over the years, and a set of donations having a restricted character.

Aside from the magnitude of the Foundation's assistance activities, one should also note its particular character, that of providing help to the homeland largely in the form of medical supplies and equipment that were in short supply there. Thus the aid rendered by the PACCF differed markedly from the Polonia relief efforts conducted during the First and Second World War years, since those had been involved with the delivery of food and clothing. Though such goods continued to be part of what the Charitable Foundation sent to Poland, the "Relief for Poland" drive of the 1980s focused mainly upon helping to meet Poland's medical and health needs.

Of note too was the constancy of the assistance extended over the last ten years' time. Under the direction of Myra Lenard and Eugene Rosypal, an average of more than $1.4 million in goods was transferred to Poland each month with aid actually on the increase by the end of the decade and into 1990. This, despite the fact that the American media's attention to Poland's perilous economic situation diminished considerably after the imposition of Martial Law in 1981.

Commenting on the relief effort, Bishop Domin, who visited a number of Polonia communities in the United States in 1986 made the following assessment:

> In 1981, the Polish Episcopate's Charity Commission received from the Polish American Congress about 63 tons of relief goods. In 1982, this aid reached about 701 tons, in 1983 about 1,439 tons, in 1984 about 706 tons and in 1985 about 842 tons. A major portion of the contents of PAC relief shipments consist of medical items, such as drugs, dressing materials, needles, syringes, medical instruments and hospital equipment. Other forms of help include not only food products, clothing or shoes, but also vegetable seeds,small farm and garden tools and books.[3]

Domin reported that goods weighing in excess of 3,751 tons had already been delivered to Poland. Since 1985 one should add that the total amount of aid amounting to more than $98 million in value has translated into another 6,600 tons of goods on behalf of people in need. Thus, by 1990 goods weighing more than 10,000 tons in all had reached Poland.

Writing again in November 1988, Domin described Polonia's aid effort as nothing less than "immense." He went on to observe that while assistance from other organizations in the European countries had gradually diminished, the PACCF's support activities were on the upswing.

President Mazewski, in his June 1988 report to the PAC National Council of Directors, drew a different kind of picture to characterize the scope of the Relief for Poland effort. Through the past seven and one-half years, he declared, the Charitable Foundation had shipped some 490 marine containers to Poland. Each of these containers was forty-two feet long and could carry a cargo of up to 42,000 pounds. If laid end to end, they would have made a train load extending some four miles. (By the end of 1990, that same train would be more than 6.4 miles long and include 809 containers.)[4]

Aside from the character and scale of the Foundation's efforts, there were several other features about the Relief for Poland drive that merit some note. Given the drive's focus upon the delivery of medical materials to Poland, the PACCF's leadership concentrated its work into persuading a number of American foundations, hospital and pharmaceutical supply companies, and private concerns to make donations of goods from their inventories on Poland's behalf. For its part, the fund raising work undertaken by the Charitable Foundation was directed into generating money to cover the shipping costs of donated materials to American seaports on the East Coast, from which they were transported by Polish ships headed across the ocean. Only in certain special cases was the Charitable Foundation thus involved in purchasing supplies from its own funds.

Enlisted into the effort to help Poland were a wide variety of American organizations, some national in scope, some local, some secular, some religious. Many were most generous in their donations and became committed to the cause for lengthy periods of time. Among the most helpful of these agencies were the World Medical Relief organization of Detroit, the Walgreen's Company, Pfizer Pharmaceuticals, Colonial Sentry Hospital Supply Company of Chicago, the Salvatorian Brothers' Mission in Burlington, Wisconsin, the MAP International Relief Agency of Atlanta, the Mead Johnson Pharmaceutical

Company, Direct Relief International of Santa Barbara, California, the Brother's Brother Foundation of Pittsburgh, the Larry Jones Evangelical Association of Oklahoma City, the Franciscan Missionary Union of Cincinnati, Church World Services, the Deborah Hospital Foundation of Newark, New Jersey, the Church of Jesus Christ of the Latter Day Saints (the Mormons) in Utah, the Holy Spirit Mission in Techny, Illinois, Project Hope, CARE, the Catholic Relief Services, and the J. Seward Johnson and Barbara Piasecki Johnson Foundation.

Through Mazewski'a leadership and the work of Lenard and Rosypal, a network of donor organizations was already delivering goods to Poland by 1982 and at a very modest cost. And, while the moneys raised by the Charitable Foundation declined markedly after 1982 (except for 1985 thanks to the funds received from the second Chicago telethon), the PACCF's level of giving continued at a fairly constant rate through the decade.Indeed by the last months of 1988 and in the years after, the Charitable Foundation's main problem was no longer that of collecting goods for overseas distribution, but that of simply generating enough new money to underwrite the cost of transporting the material it had collected from its Chicago warehouse to U.S. ports on the Atlantic coast. This "cash crisis" was one that the PAC's new President, Edward Moskal, would tackle aggressively following his election to head the Congress in November 1988 following Mazewski's death. A first initiative was to organize a "radiothon" over Chicago's Polish language radio stations in December 1988 and January 1989, an effort subsequently imitated in Detroit, Buffalo and Milwaukee. This effort succeeded in generating nearly $200,000 to meet the Foundation's immediate financial needs.

In the months after, Moskal reviewed a number of other possible avenues for meeting the financial needs of both the PAC and its Charitable Foundation. One approach involved his announcement of a direct appeal to the members of his own fraternal, the Polish National Alliance, the first such action in the Polish American Congress' history. This effort took the form of a Christmas 1989 letter addressed to all PNA families and eventually yielded more than $170,000 on behalf of the Foundation. A similar action directed toward the members of the Polish Roman Catholic Union by PRCUA President Edward Dykla (himself the PAC's Treasurer) came soon afterward and brought in $34,000 by May 1990. By that time comparable letters had gone out to the members of the Polish Women's Alliance from PAC Vice President Helen Wojcik and to the Polish Falcons of America from PAC Secretary Lawrence Wujcikowski. (Also significant were plans announced at the PAC National Council of Directors meeting in June 1990 in Dearborn, Michigan to carry out a professional fund raising campaign in Polonia in the near future, its aim that of at last placing both organizations on a firm financial footing.)

Of special concern throughout the Charitable Foundation's Relief for Poland campaign has been its interest in making sure the goods it had collected reached people who were truly in need. This was a consideration of no small significance given the fact that the country's worsening economic crisis was so tightly intertwined with the Communist regime's failing attempts to maintain its political power. (In this connection, one Polish official had darkly acknowledged that given the conditions that prevailed in the country, food had become a weapon.)[5]

Given such circumstances, the Charitable Foundation from the start coordinated its every activity with people it considered to be the authentic representatives of the Polish nation, so as to insure that the drive would truly reach its mark. Thus, until December 1981 the PACCF worked with leaders of the Solidarity movement; when that became impossible it collaborated closely with high ranking dignitaries of the Polish Roman Catholic Church.

The Charitable Foundation's tie with Polish Church authorities distinguished its activities from that of the U.S. charitable agency, CARE, which out of necessity performed its work in concert with the Polish government's Ministry of Health and Social Welfare. (Catholic Relief Services also cooperated with the Polish Episcopate.)

This decision in the long term proved to be wise. By maintaining an arms length distance from the regime, the PACCF found its efforts gaining enhanced credibility in the Polish American community.

A last consideration concerns the Foundation's success in carrying out its work in an extraordinarily efficient and nearly cost-free manner. To this end, practically every effort to gather goods and money donations was performed by volunteers; only the small PAC staff in Washington, D.C. and in Chicago was salaried and even these individuals' modest stipends were covered out of the regular dues contributed to the national PAC office by its affiliated state divisions and member fraternals and not out of donations. Consequently, nearly every penny raised by the Charitable Foundation was used to purchase and ship goods needed in Poland. This achievement, itself modelled upon the World War II era *Rada Polonii* effort, was probably unique in the annals of American charity. Mazewski and Moskal frequently drew attention to this point, if only to encourage Polish Americans to be more generous in their support of the drive. As Mazewski described the situation in 1988, "we really stretch every donated dollar." Indeed, for every one of those dollars collected by the Charitable Foundation on Poland's behalf, $28 in materials were being shipped overseas.[6]

In its humanitarian activities from 1981 on, the PACCF was never alone in serving the needs of the beleaguered Polish people. Other agencies which contributed their resources to the cause were many and included Project Hope, CARE, and Catholic Relief Services. Their combined efforts were substantial and brought several hundred million dollars in aid to Poland. Still, without the prompting of PAC leaders and their friends, such help might not have materialized, at least not in the amounts that were eventually realized. Thus, within the American Catholic hierarchy, several ecclesiastical leaders of Polish heritage played important roles in enlightening their colleagues about Poland's needs and thus gaining their support for fund raising efforts for Catholic Relief Services throughout the United States in 1982 and 1983. Here, mention should be made of such worthy activists as John Cardinal Krol, Archbishop of Philadelphia, Archbishop Edmund Szoka of Detroit, Bishop Aloysius Wycislo of Green Bay, Wisconsin and Auxiliary Bishop Alfred Abramowicz of Chicago. Understandably, questions were sometimes raised in the Church over the propriety of singling out Poland for help when the peoples of many other countries were also facing great misfortune. In these circumstances, local PAC members often played constructive roles in persuading Church officials to back the collections for Poland, actions that enjoyed great success thanks to the generosity of American Catholics of many different ethnic and racial origins. For example, in the Archdiocese of Milwaukee, Wisconsin, the idea of a Spring 1982 collection for Poland was promoted aggressively by the Wisconsin PAC division and yielded more than $117,000 in support of the work of Catholic Relief Services.

Polish spokesmen repeatedly expressed their recognition of the scope and significance of Polonia's efforts in letters and statements addressed to the PACCF. Thus, on the occasion of the fortieth anniversary observances of the PAC's founding, Bishop Domin praised the Foundation by noting:

> A commendable tradition of the Congress is its coming to the aid of the homeland...And now, when a new and deep crisis has again touched the Motherland and its inhabitants, you the members of the Polish American Congress have quickly erected a pontoon bridge bringing aid to the Motherland--something you are continuing to maintain to this day...

For the same anniversary occasion, Joseph Cardinal Glemp, Archbishop of Warsaw and Gniezno and Wyszynski's successor as Primate of Poland wrote:

> On the occasion of the celebration of the fortieth anniversary of your service to Polonia and your countrymen living in Poland I extend my words of appreciation, gratitude and wishes for continued, fruitful and generous work in the service of God and mankind. In particular we thank the Congress for its generous moral and material aid. We are very grateful for your defending our rights to a religious, national and economically healthy life in accordance with our more than one thousand year old culture and Catholic tradition...With brotherly affection and best wishes, may God bless you.

From Pope John Paul II came yet more heartfelt recognition:

> I express my appreciation to my brothers and sisters in the United States of America, who directed by their concern

for the fate and spiritual heritage of the Polish nation, have
offered it bountiful aid over the past years. To all the members of the Polish American Congress and their families, I
bless you all from my heart and hope you will continue to
fruitfully serve this great cause in a spirit of solidarity with
the people and the country of your forefathers.[7]

Very similar expressions of recognition and appreciation
were addressed to President Moskal by Poland's newly elected
democratic leaders and by dignitaries of the Roman Catholic
Church during his visits there in October, November and December, 1989. What is more, both Solidarity leader Lech
Walesa and Prime Minister Tadeusz Mazowiecki were full of
praise for Polonia during their visits to the United States in
November 1989 and March 1990, respectively. Significantly,
Walesa's trip in particular helped spur new public interest in
assisting Poland on the humanitarian level with a number of
donors coming onto the scene for the first time on the country's
behalf. Substantial contributors to Poland's neediest thus included the Pillsbury Company, General Mills, Procter and
Gamble, Abbot Laboratories, the ADM Milling Company,
ConAgra Specialty Grain Company, Illinois Cereal Mills, Inc.,
the Tillotson Corporation of Boston and the Baxter Healthcare
Corporation. These firms' involvement amply demonstrated
that interest in the work of the PAC Charitable Foundation had
by no means been dissipated.

PACCF assistance to Poland was complemented by still
other humanitarian activities rendered by the Polish American
Congress during the 1980s. One involved the PAC's lobbying
work to provide fair treatment for Polish nationals in the
United States who were threatened with deportation. Their
problems varied but all were rooted in legal objections raised
against their continued residence in this country.

Thousands of Poles had entered the United States during
the 1970s, prompted mainly by the steadily deteriorating condition of Poland's economy. On their behalf, the PAC voiced its
strong support for passage of the Simpson-Mazzoli Bill in the
U.S. Congress; this measure was eventually signed into law as
the Immigration Reform and Control Act of 1986. It provided
all illegal aliens in the U.S. prior to January 1, 1982 with a

general "amnesty" enabling them to remain permanently, based on their ability to document their claims of having actually resided in this country before that cut-off date.

A different but related problem confronted another group of Poles who had entered the United States in the weeks immediately following the imposition of Martial Law in December 1981. Most of these individuals feared to return home in the tense and uncertain months which followed. Some 7,000 to 10,000 individuals found themselves in this predicament, one which became particularly precarious because the U.S. government would provide no assurance as to their right to remain in this country. Eventually, the U.S. Department of State established a temporary policy to deal with the plight of the Poles, together with a larger number of people who had entered the country from Haiti and Central America. This policy was named "Extended Voluntary Departure" (EVD). Accordingly, individuals finding themselves classified as EVD cases were permitted to remain in the United States for periods of six months to one year, during which time the State Department would review their requests for permanent residency status.

The Poles affected by the EVD ruling had not entered the United States illegally and seldom made any effort to hide from the authorities. Hence, they were vulnerable to official actions ordering their deportation, sometimes on rather short notice. Moreover, their status placed them outside the normal quota allotments available to Polish immigrants and in fact prohibited them from requesting political asylum.

Ironically, while the Reagan administration had vigorously denounced the Jaruzelski regime's crushing of Solidarity as a violation of the Polish people's human and political rights, the U.S. government's representatives in the State Department and the Immigration and Naturalization Service persisted in following a quite different policy, one of ordering deportation of Poles covered by EVD rules on the grounds that their motives for remaining in this country had little or nothing to do with Poland's political situation. President Mazewski, in his report to the PAC National Council of Directors meeting in November 1985 in Buffalo, New York noted this apparent contradiction and complained that a number of Poles had already been deported, following rejection of their requests for asylum. Still more faced the same fate, although they had not yet been given their deportation orders.[8]

Between 1982 and 1987, the PAC did succeed in wringing a series of extensions of the EVD deadlines from the State Department. At last, however, and through the considerable efforts of Senator Barbara Mikulski of Maryland and Congressman William Lipinski of Illinois, a large coalition of supportive legislators representing a variety of constituencies was formed to support the granting of permanent residence status to Poles affected by the EVD policy. Legislation to realize this aim came in the form of an amendment to the Federal Appropriations bill which Congress approved and President Reagan signed into law in December 1987.

As a result, all Polish nationals residing in the United States before July 21, 1984 and who had been permitted to stay in the country under the Extended Voluntary Departure privilege since 1981 were allowed to remain permanently in the United States. As Senator Mikulski declared, "these Polish refugees knew fear and hardship in their native country. Since coming here, they have become productive members of American society. They are committed to building better lives for themselves and their children...Their only future is here."[9]

Efforts by the PAC and its Charitable Foundation on Poland's behalf extended into still other directions during the 1980s. Thus, in April 1987, a serious accident at the Soviet nuclear energy facility at Chernobyl near the Ukrainian capital of Kiev caused a radioactive discharge into the atmosphere that drifted into eastern Poland and a number of other countries. The real danger the disaster posed together with the mass anxieties caused by Chernobyl once again led to an immediate PAC response. Declaring its first concern to be the protection of children from contaminated food and milk and their inoculation with iodine solutions to head off the danger of thyroid cancer, the PAC arranged to ship some 25,000 doses of iodine to Poland in cooperation with several generous U.S. firms and foundations only five days after receiving news of the disaster. Soon afterward, and through the help of a coalition of private organizations, medical supplies valued at more than $560,000 were transported to Poland, along with some three million vitamin tablets. There, goods were promptly distributed throughout the eastern Polish district of Suwalki, whose residents were particularly vulnerable to the nuclear discharge. In addition to such shipments of medical goods, the PAC funded the transfer of some 430 tons of food supplies to Poland, goods that were targeted primarily for infants and children.[10]

Among the chief contributors to the emergency efforts were the London-based Medical Aid for Poland Fund, the Deborah Hospital Foundation, Catholic Relief Services, World Medical Relief, The "Feed the Children" division of the Larry Jones International Ministries, the H. J. Heinz Corporation, the Beech-Nut Corporation, and the Johnson and Johnson Foundation. The PAC also secured the prompt support of Senators Paul Simon and Alan Dixon of Illinois to introduce resolutions in Congress authorizing an emergency food shipment to Poland through the U.S. Department of Agriculture.

Yet another effort undertaken by the PAC Charitable Foundation focused upon its providing assistance to a number of hospitals and medical centers throughout Poland. One major recipient has been the Center for Cardiac Surgery near Katowice, with the Foundation committing itself to purchasing an array of medical equipment for the hospital and assisting in the training of surgeons and nurses to staff the Center. The hospital's primary work involved the performing of cardiac surgery on the approximately 25,000 Polish infants born annually with congenital heart defects. Prior to its establishment, such operations could not be performed in Poland; indeed the first response of the PAC Charitable Foundation in learning of the problem had been to fund the training of Polish surgeons in the United States, an effort undertaken in 1981 but superseded by the creation of the Cardiac Center.[11] In addition to the PACCF's assistance, which ran into the hundreds of thousands of dollars, the United States government provided a separate grant of $5 million through legislation introduced by Senator Edward M. Kennedy of Massachusetts. More modest but still considerable assistance activities directed at other Polish hospitals were also part of the Foundation's work, most notably institutions located in Gdansk, Warsaw, and Lublin.

Not to be ignored in this review are the PAC's continuing lobbying efforts to win United States government support for a number of other humanitarian programs on Poland's behalf, among them the organization's success, as noted earlier, in winning some $1.5 million from the U.S. Agency for International Development for the purchase of medical supplies for use in Poland under the direction of the PAC Charitable Foundation. (These funds were expended between October 1988 and June 1990 and further assistance was being sought for the coming year.) Perhaps the PAC's most satisfying success came with U.S. Congressional funding of an additional wing to the Children's Hospital in Krakow, an institution whose creation it had backed in the mid 1960s. Another accomplishment involved gaining Washington's support for an internationally financed foundation for the development of Poland's agriculture, a project that had been proposed initially by the Roman Catholic Episcopate. Some $10 million was eventually allocated by the U.S. Government in support of the plan, although the proposed project was later rejected by the Polish government. Committed, but not spent, in 1984, the funds remained in the United States foreign aid package in the years that followed, however.

In sum, the charitable and humanitarian efforts of the Polish American Congress Charitable Foundation along with the PAC's lobbying efforts for Poland in Washington, D.C. reached historic heights in the 1980s. The political and economic crises that plagued Poland were met effectively by Polonia's chief representatives, whether this meant articulating Polonia's concerns for Poland's freedom, working for the betterment of the Polish people in their own land, or defending those who had decided to come to the United States to pursue new lives in this country.

At a time when the efforts of organizations like the Polish American Congress might have been expected to have become diminished due to assimilation's affects upon the ethnic life in the United States, in point of fact the PAC's activities throughout the 1980s were both substantial and productive. That this was the case was due in no small measure to the presence of a number of talented activists throughout the country who gave considerable time and energy to implementing the Congress' agendas with respect to Poland.[12]

On the political level, they helped the PAC continue to work for its historic goal of an independent and democratic

Poland, an unalterable commitment through more than four decades. And through the creation of the PAC Charitable Foundation, the organization's leaders had established a second, humanitarian, arm with real muscle to work in the interest of Poland's inhabitants. And while the Charitable Foundation's great achievements after 1980 were on behalf of Poland, it might also be noted that the very same organization retained the potential to play a real role in promoting the cultural revival of American Polonia, whenever its officers choose to take up that important and too-long neglected task.

Sadly, given Poland's continuing economic and societal crisis, the priorities of the PAC Charitable Foundation are likely to focus upon the needs of the ancestral homeland for some time to come. In such circumstances, both Poland's new democratic political leadership and that of the Polish American Congress much benefited from the visit to Poland in October 1989 by a twelve member PAC delegation headed by President Moskal. The group's week-long stay, the first ever in the forty-five year history of the Congress, served to both underscore Polonia's commitment to the new Solidarity-led government and to afford the delegation a first-hand perspective of Poland's actual situation. As a result, everyone in the group would return home with a renewed commitment to continuing the Foundation's efforts on behalf of Poland.

At the same time, Poland's leaders, in the government, the Church and the restored Solidarity movement, were made mindful as perhaps never before of Polonia's dedication to the well-being of the homeland. Indeed, through the Charitable Foundation's considerable labors to aid the needy of Poland, the historic ties between the motherland and its emigration had once again been renewed--not only in words but in actions. In the process, the Polish American Congress Charitable Foundation has proven itself to be a genuine and worthy successor to the World War I era Polish Central Relief Committee and the World War II *Rada Polonii,* which in their time had done what they could in extending helping hands across the ocean.

Conclusions:
Into the Future

On August 2, 1988 Aloysius Mazewski left Chicago with several friends and drove to his summer cottage near Portage, Wisconsin for a few days of relaxation and golf. The next morning he suffered a massive and fatal heart attack. He and his family had observed his 72nd birthday seven months before.

Mazewski had been an active President of both the Polish American Congress and the Polish National Alliance fraternal and had served as head of the Alliance from 1967 and the PAC from 1968. He had been responsible for the creation of the PAC's Charitable Foundation in 1971; that organization had gone on to play an important role in assisting the American relief efforts for Poland after 1980. For many of his friends and co-workers it was hard to imagine how anyone could succeed him as Polonia's principal spokesman. Nonetheless, both the PNA and the PAC carried on their work.

Helen Szymanowicz, since 1971 the First Vice President of the PNA, took over temporarily at the helm of the Alliance. She was succeeded in November 1988 by Edward J. Moskal of Chicago, who was elected to complete Mazewski's term at a special October 12 meeting of PNA leaders in Pittsburgh. The 64 year old Moskal had served from 1963 on the Board of Directors of the PNA and since 1967 as its Treasurer; in addition to his extensive knowledge of the fraternal's inner workings he brought a distinctive vigor to his new responsibilities.[1]

Kazimierz Lukomski of Chicago succeeded Mazewski as *interim* chief of the Polish American Congress. One of the PAC's national vice presidents and the veteran chairman of its influential Polish Affairs Commission, Lukomski, like Szymanowicz, immediately made known his decision not to seek the PAC presidency. Instead, he called a meeting of the Congress' National Council of Directors to fill the position.

On November 11, 1988, the 70th anniversary of Poland's independence, the National Council met in Chicago with some one hundred directors from 32 state divisions and 23 Polonia organizations present.[2] The next day, five men were nominated for the presidency--Hilary Czaplicki of Philadelphia, Censor of the Polish National Alliance and a veteran of the Congress' Eastern Pennsylvania division; Edward Dykla of Chicago, President of the Polish Roman Catholic Union of America fraternal and Treasurer of the PAC; Moskal; Paul Odrobina of Hamtramck, Michigan, President of his state's PAC division and a member of the PNA Board of Directors; and Chicago Alderman and former U.S. Congressman Roman Pucinski, President of the Congress' Illinois Division.[3]

Just prior to the election, Czaplicki, Dykla and Odrobina withdrew from further consideration and subsequently Moskal won over Pucinski by a margin of 53 votes to 34. Following the contest he pledged to continue the Congress' work in its traditional areas.

Moskal's election was not entirely unexpected and upheld a tradition dating back to the Congress' founding in 1944. In that year Charles Rozmarek, President of the Polish National Alliance, had been elected to head the PAC and had continued to hold both officers until 1967, when he was defeated for reelection at the Alliance's convention by Mazewski. The next year Mazewski had also taken over the Presidency of the PAC and went on to hold both posts through the next twenty years.

Given this situation, there had been some discussion in the weeks preceding the election on the merits of electing the President of the PNA as head of the Congress. But when Moskal expressed his willingness to lead, his wish was served, largely out of a general recognition of the Alliance's central role as Polonia's largest and most influential unit.[4] Nevertheless, upon his election Moskal made clear his view that for the Congress to remain viable, cooperation among all member organizations and state divisions was essential. And, in rejecting the notion of the Congress as a "one man organization," he expressed the hope that in the future everyone would pull together to help realize the PAC's various objectives.

Elected with Moskal to new two year terms on the PAC's national executive committee were Lukomski, Helen Wojcik, Dykla, and Bernard Rogalski. Lukomski continued on as one of the Congress' two national vice presidents, with special responsibility for helping to formulate its perspectives toward Poland. Wojcik, who had only recently succeeded Helen Zielinski as President of the Polish Women's Alliance fraternal centered in Chicago, now replaced her as the PAC's Lady Vice President.* Dykla remained the organization's Treasurer, while Rogalski, the just retired President of the Polish Falcons of America fraternal headquartered in Pittsburgh, continued for the time being as PAC National Secretary. (In 1989 he would step down in favor of Lawrence Wujcikowski, his successor as President of the Falcons.)

The year following Moskal's election proved to be an extraordinary one for the PAC and the most significant for Poland since World War II. On the home front, the PAC Charitable Foundation suddenly found itself faced with a serious shortfall in contributions, which temporarily threatened its ability to continue its regular shipments of medical and food supplies to Poland. To meet the crisis Moskal announced a year long fund drive to raise $500,000 so as to place the Foundation on a more solid financial footing. For the moment he initiated an emergency appeal through the Polish language radio programs in Polonia. Inaugurated in December 1988, the appeal yielded more than $150,000 in Chicago alone over the next month, with an added $20,000 coming in similar campaigns from Detroit, $16,000 from Buffalo and $12,000 from Milwaukee.

In the Fall of 1989 the PAC launched a second major appeal on behalf of its Foundation, this one in the form of a mail solicitation directed to the members of the Polish fraternals belonging to the Congress. Responses to this "first ever" effort to seek financial support from individual members of the fraternals (as opposed to help originating from the organizations

---

* Wojcik's duties have included her chairing of a special committee to gather funds in support of the Ellis Island Immigration Museum in New York harbor. The Congress' drive on behalf of this project was very successful and more than $560,000 was raised to assure that the Polish immigrants' story would be presented. The Museum opened in September 1990. Earlier, her predecessor, Helen Zielinski, had enjoyed similar success in heading the PAC's fund drive to help in the restoration of the statue of "Liberty Enlightening the World," completed in 1985.

themselves) were quite encouraging. From the PNA more than $170,000 was collected with another $34,000 coming from donors belonging to the PRCUA. Similar appeals to members of the Polish Women's Alliance and the Falcons were also organized.[5]

At the same time, the PAC continued in its efforts to generate revenues to meet the regular operating expenses of its Chicago and Washington, D.C. offices. One project was directed by Pucinski after 1987--a national raffle. Unfortunately, funds derived from this effort were never great and continued to decline each year, from a high of approximately $60,000 in 1987 to 40,000 in 1990. This has left the Congress with a chronic deficit in managing its monthly operations.

Abroad, Poland's seemingly unending crisis entered what proved to be a new and climactic stage. In February 1989, formal talks began in Warsaw between officials of the communist government and the democratic opposition headed by the leadership of the still unrecognized Solidarity movement and the Roman Catholic Church. This "round table" negotiation was historic in its significance, both for Poland and the entire communist world. Back in 1981, the Polish regime had seemingly crushed Solidarity forever by imposing martial law throughout the country and then acting to permanently outlaw the movement.

But the stratagem had failed to stabilize Poland's political situation, a necessary precondition for any attempt on the government's part to even begin to deal with the country's economic woes.

In May 1988, shaken once again by a new wave of strikes in protest against its hopeless policies, the Jaruzelski regime had done the unthinkable and called upon the long-belittled Walesa to use his skills in bringing a semblance of order to the country's mines, steel works and shipyards. In return, Walesa had exacted from Warsaw its grudging pledge to hold serious discussions over Solidarity's eventual restoration.

By the time the talks actually began, however, the Solidarity-led opposition's agenda had broadened considerably to include its intention to play a genuine role in a future government moving resolutely toward democracy. For its part the regime's spokesmen seemed unwilling to go beyond the "relegalization" of Solidarity. Even this they sought to make conditional upon the trade union's agreement to a two-year no-strike pledge that would somehow be made binding upon the nation's increasingly alienated and unruly workers.*

Meeting in Chicago in mid-February soon after the start of the round table talks, the leadership of the PAC's Polish Affairs Commission and President Moskal gathered to chart the Congress' future course and to determine how it might most effectively present its positions to the new Bush Administration. Not surprisingly, there was general accord in support of Solidarity in the round table negotiations; a consensus also emerged quickly in favor of pressing the United States government and its allies to offer emergency economic assistance to Poland, conditional upon Warsaw's readiness to move toward democratization and economic reform. The participants were similarly agreed in calling for continued American pressure upon the U.S.S.R. to expand political freedom in Eastern Europe and to repudiate its past espousal of the so-called "Brezhnev Doctrine," which justified Soviet military intervention to preserve communist power in the region.

Two specific actions were also taken in Chicago. One involved pushing ahead with arrangements for a meeting between Moskal and the President's National Security Adviser, General Brent Scowcroft, in order to outline the PAC's concerns and recommendations to the new Administration. A second move authorized the dispatching of a quasi-official PAC representative to Warsaw to observe the progress of the round

---

* Walesa's opening remarks at the first session of the talks were characteristically forthright and sent a clear signal to the regime as to Solidarity and the democratic opposition's views and objectives. He declared that "Poland has been ruined by a system of government that deprived citizens of their rights and wasted the fruits of their labor..." He went on to call for "changes that would transform Poland from a one-party state to a state belonging to the entire nation" and demanded "the reinstatement of Solidarity--the main and perhaps the only guarantee for (Poland's) future." *From Radio Free Europe Research, Weekly Record of Events in East Europe,* February 2-8, 1989. See also "Przemowienie Lecha Walesy" (Speech of Lech Walesa) in *Dziennik Zwiazkowy,* February 7, 1989.

table talks and to offer Polonia's support to Solidarity. Significantly, Boleslaw Wierzbianski, Editor and Publisher of the New York-based Polish language daily, *Nowy Dziennik*, was soon in Poland. His trip was precedent-setting in a sense for it ended a forty-five year period of strict PAC ostracism of everything connected with the communist regime and its policies.

In its statement prepared for the Scowcroft meeting, the PAC urged the United States to take full advantage of its emerging new relationship with the reform-minded regime of Mikhail Gorbachev in Soviet Russia to assist the Eastern European nations in their struggle for democracy. High among the Congress' priorities was a call to end the Yalta legacy of a Europe divided. Also included was a proposal for a U.S. initiative to further reduce the Soviet military presence in Eastern Europe, a response to Gorbachev's U.N. announcement of December 1988 wherein some reductions in Soviet forces in the Warsaw Pact had been promised. At the same time, the statement included concerns that Gorbachev's programs, while welcome, might still be reversed and with unpredictable consequences for America's security interests.

With regard to Poland and Eastern Europe, the PAC statement asserted:

> The Cold War began in Europe with the imposition by the Soviet Union of communist regimes in the countries of Eastern Europe and the threat of further expansion of Soviet aggressiveness against Western Europe. It will not end until this threat is removed by the reduction, and eventual elimination, of Soviet domination over Eastern Europe, the key arena of continuing East-West confrontation, and a principal concern in relation to U.S. and N.A.T.O. security interests. We submit, therefore, that the problem of Soviet domination of Eastern Europe be placed high on the agenda of the forthcoming summit meeting between President George Bush and General Secretary Mikhail Gorbachev, with the Soviets' renunciation of the Brezhnev Doctrine made a litmus test of their intentions.[6]

In strongly endorsing Lech Walesa's leadership of Solidarity in the round table talks, the PAC also tied democratization with economic reform and urged the U.S. government to play a major role in the process of change:

> Developments in Poland...portend the emergence of a new alignment between Solidarity and the government...and the introduction of social, political and economic pluralism leading to concerted efforts to regenerate the country's devastated economy. Successful U.S. "sticks and carrots" policies as well as determined internal pressures share in influencing these unprecedented developments.
>
> To provide the Polish regime with an added impetus to act constructively, the U.S. should reiterate its firm commitment to support Poland's application for assistance from the International Monetary Fund and World Bank, contingent only on the progress and successful conclusion of the "round table" negotiations. Further, in cooperation with other industrial democracies, serious consideration should be given to other measures designed to ease Poland's plight, such as renegotiation of its foreign debt servicing and assistance to clean its polluted and health endangering environment.[7]

The participants at the Chicago meeting also agreed that President Moskal carry a proposal to the White House arguing for a U.S. economic aid package for Poland amounting to $2-3 billion. This idea was in fact presented and (based upon an article in the April 12, 1989 issue of the *Washington Post*) given some favorable attention; for the time being, however, the Administration opted against making any such commitments.

However, on April 17, 1989 President Bush journeyed to the largely Polish American city of Hamtramck, Michigan to announce his interest in working with the Polish government in bringing about real economic reforms. This in recognition of the just announced agreements originating from the round table talks which had concluded a few days earlier. Clearly, the speech's timing dramatically linked America's offers of help to good faith on the part of the Polish regime in agreeing to an unprecedented democratization of the country's political life.

Indeed, on the very day of Bush's address, Solidarity was officially "relegalized." What is more, it was also announced in Warsaw that genuinely free and competitive elections would be held in June to establish a new legislative chamber, the 100 member Senate. At the same time, elections were also called for the 460 member parliament, or *Sejm*. There, the political opposition would be permitted to contest 161 seats, with the ruling Polish United Workers Party and its junior partners, the United Peasants Party and the Democratic Party, guaranteed the others.

The agreement also contained a compromise with respect to the election of Poland's president. While the post was to be filled by a majority vote of the two legislative bodies gathered in joint session, General Jaruzelski was assured that his candidacy would not be opposed, regardless of the outcome of the parliamentary elections.

Looking ahead to the June elections, President Bush put in a ringing, if diplomatically worded endorsement of the democratic opposition forces:

> Under the auspices of the round table agreements, the free trade union *Solidarnosc* was today--this very day...formally restored. And the agreements also provide that a free opposition press will be legalized, independent political and other free associations will be permitted, and elections for a new Polish Senate will be held. These agreements...are inspiring testimony to the spiritual guidance of the Catholic Church, the indomitable spirit of the Polish people and the strength and wisdom of Lech Walesa.

The President's remarks in Hamtramck included words of praise for the Polish American Congress and a friendly welcome to Moskal, who was on hand for the event. Most significant was the speech's inclusion of practically every theme the PAC leadership had discussed in February.[8]

On June 4, 1989 the Poles were at last permitted to exercise their right to vote in a fairly contested, if limited, free election. Their voice, after forty-five years of communist rule, was deafening in calling for the PUWP's complete repudiation.[9] Thus, of the 261 Solidarity candidates nominated to seats in the Senate and the *Sejm*, all but one were elected. In contrast, not a single officially endorsed PUWP candidate received the needed majority to gain office and therefore they were required to seek their constituents' acceptance in a run-off election held later the same month. Even a select group of top party and state officials, including Prime Minister Rakowski, all running unopposed on a national list was rejected when more than one-half of the voters heeded Solidarity's appeal and crossed out their names from the ballots.*

The party's rout was complete, almost "too bad to be true" in the opinion of some observers who worried that regime hardliners might try to negate the elections' results and with them the round table agreements, perhaps even by reimposing martial law. So pessimistic a view ignored several considerations, however. One involved the manifest bankruptcy of military repression in dealing with Poland's mounting crises. Indeed Jaruzelski's suppression of Solidarity seven years before had not brought the country a single step closer to resolving any of its problems.

Second and even more telling for Poland's future was the impact of Gorbachev's momentous reforms upon the Soviet Union and Eastern Europe. Into the winter of 1990, Gorbachev's priorities remained those of bringing about *Perestroika* and *Glasnost'* at home and persuading the West of the seriousness of his calls for a new *Detente* abroad. In this context, Soviet relations with its Eastern European satellites were changing rapidly. Where for years, Moscow's ever present threat of military intervention had been a key factor in stifling popular opposition to the communist regimes in the region, conditions had suddenly and fundamentally been altered in the wake of Gorbachev's efforts to pressure his allies into adopting internal reforms of their own and in his renunciation of the Brezhnev Doctrine. Consequently, by the end of 1989 communist rule in Eastern Europe was everywhere under siege, in Hungary, East Germany, Bulgaria, Romania and Czechoslovakia as well. Even in the Soviet Union itself, the Party of Lenin was facing unprecedented challenges to its seven decades long domination over a society that was itself in growing internal turmoil.

---

* More than sixty percent of the electorate had voted in the first balloting; only 20 percent bothered to make a choice in the run-offs -- yet another rejection of the communists.

Not to be minimized in analyzing the collapse of Polish communism (the party itself officially dissolved in January 1990) was the character of the democratic opposition itself. After all, Solidarity's electoral landslide was not only due to general alienation from the regime and its policies but to popular identification with an opposition which had heroically espoused the cause of democracy and economic reform for many years. Indeed, Solidarity's best known figures had been opponents of the regime even before the creation of the Solidarity trade union in 1980. Perhaps as significant, their years of struggle, sacrifice and suffering had not led them to choose violence as a strategy against their foes. Rather, Solidarity's perspective had continued to be moderate in its commitment to peaceful change, yet principled and patriotic in its vision for a Poland reunited with the West.

Within Solidarity's ranks genuine differences indeed existed which would lead to splits in the movement after the collapse of its communist opponents. Still, uniting Solidarity in 1989 was its leaders' appreciation of the country's tragic past, its commitment to democracy and its recognition of the scale of the economic hardship that still had to be endured in the wake of more than four decades of communist misrule.

Given Solidarity's character and the crushing effects of the regime's defeat in the June 1989 elections, pressures quickly mounted in the weeks that followed to go beyond the round table agreements and to achieve the unthinkable--the end of communist rule. Thus, by July Walesa was calling publicly for a new and Solidarity-led government, one of necessity backed by the PUWP's erstwhile minor party allies who, after reviewing the election results, were more than willing to part company with their former big brother. Amazingly, President Jaruzelski (who was barely elected in July in yet another show of popular disgust with continued communist rule) accepted this idea "in principle." One day later, Tadeusz Mazowiecki, a 61 year old attorney, Catholic intellectual and veteran Solidarity activist who had just been named editor of the movement's independent daily newspaper, was called upon to head Poland's first democratically-based government since World War II. On September 12, his Solidarity-led cabinet was installed by a 402-0 vote of the *Sejm*. This was an auspicious beginning for a new government facing enormous economic problems, yet willing to meet them in a forthright and courageous fashion.

In any event, for the first time since the Great Powers had determined Poland's postwar fate at Teheran and Yalta, the path seemed open for the Poles to once more become masters of their own house. While the country's future could hardly be predicted with any certainty, one could expect that the U.S. and its European allies would assist Poland in its economic reconstruction. Back home, a new mission awaited the Polish American Congress, that of helping persuade the government of the United States that its help was essential to the success of Poland's democratic rebirth. This objective, moreover, was not only in Poland's but in America's best interests.

And while the conditions of Polish economic life after 1989 remained bleak, the situation could hardly be compared unfavorably to what the nation had faced in 1945. Then, the survivors of six devastating years of war and occupation had indeed pulled together to rebuild their country. They achieved much too, in spite of the heavy burden they had to bear in the form of a communist dictatorship imposed by Moscow, one which had to obey Stalin's order rejecting Marshall Plan aid America offered to all of war-torn Europe. Looking both back and into the future, one might well hope that a new generation of Poles, this time aided by the West and capable of managing its own affairs, could achieve as much if not more in restoring its country to a healthy state.

In 1988 Polonia had observed the 70th anniversary of Poland's independence. In 1989 Polish Americans commemorated yet two more events of historic significance. Especially momentous was the recalling of the fiftieth anniversary of the outbreak of the Second World War on September 1, 1939. Throughout Polonia, tribute was paid to all who had fought in Poland's defense and to the millions who had suffered the consequences of a conflict whose impact continues to be felt to the present time.

Of special meaning to the Polish American Congress was its own 45th anniversary. This occasion too was an appropriate time in which to look back upon the work done by two generations of activists in service to Poland's concerns.

In 1991, the Congress' members could also look forward to yet another momentous anniversary, the bi-centennial of the promulgation of Poland's Constitution of May 3, 1791. This event, coming at a time when Poland was at last free and independent, is not only of historic note but in at least two respects possesses profound contemporary significance. For one, the "Third of May Constitution" is a link between the Poles of today, wherever they reside, and their centuries' old heritage of constitutionalism, respect for human rights and representative government. As important, Poland's 1791 Constitution is an undeniable affirmation of its ancient identification with the preeminent principles of societal life that have characterized the development of Western Europe and America for the past two hundred years. This is a truth, that Poland has been *of* the West even though it has not been *in* the West, that has been too seldom recognized by statesmen and citizens alike. It deserves to be underscored, particularly in the wake of the revolution of 1989.

Today, the work of the Polish American Congress continues under the leadership of its third President, Edward Moskal. Already noted have been his efforts to mobilize Polonia anew in financing the activities of the PAC's Charitable Foundation. Similarly, Moskal has aggressively presented the Congress' positions on Poland's concerns to the leaders of the U.S. government. Indeed, between March 1989 and June 1990 alone, Moskal met on at least five separate occasions with President Bush and at least seven times with high ranking members of the White House staff. Even more frequent were his talks with Congressional leaders and representatives in the Department of State and the Immigration and Naturalization Service.

Particularly noteworthy has been Moskal's renewal of the historic ties between Polonia and Poland's legitimate representatives in the Solidarity-led government and the Church. An historic initiative here came in October 1989 when he headed a twelve member PAC delegation to Poland for a week of substantive discussions with the country's highest leaders, among them Lech Walesa, Prime Minister Tadeusz Mazowiecki, and Cardinal Glemp. A few weeks later the Congress would host Walesa in Chicago during his week-long visit in the United States, a spectacular trip highlighted by his address to a joint session of the Congress of the United States.* In March 1990, Moskal would again play the host, this time to Mazowiecki, who too was making his first visit to the United States on Bush's invitation.

The PAC visit to Poland marked, as Moskal acknowledged, "a departure from the political line pursued by the Congress during the past forty-five years" and was not without controversy. The trip was justified out of his conviction that it was "imperative that an official PAC delegation...announce to the people of Poland its support for the new government led by Tadeusz Mazowiecki...(and) Polonia's deep interest in helping the country deal with its economic problems."[10]

The PAC delegation's October visit would mark but the first of three Moskal would make to Poland over the next three months.** At the end of November he was again in Warsaw, this time as a member of a U.S. delegation that included the Secretaries of Agriculture, Commerce and Labor. This twenty

---

* Climaxing Walesa's visit was the U.S. Congress' approval of legislation providing Poland with $852 million in economic assistance over the next three years. As overwhelmingly supported in both houses, the "Support for Eastern European Democracy Act of 1989" pledged $125 million in emergency food shipments, $240 million in grants to Polish businesses to encourage their growth, $200 million in funds to strengthen and stabilize Poland's currency, $200 million in federally-guaranteed loans to Polish firms importing U.S. products and the remainder to a variety of projects dealing with the country's environmental problems and its people's need for training in the practice of market economics and grassroots representative democracy. Congress also directed President Bush to initiate a generous and early rescheduling of Poland's foreign debt and to cooperate with Warsaw in organizing job retraining and unemployment compensation programs for its citizens. The so-called SEED Act, which included an additional $86 million in assistance to Hungary in its efforts toward political and economic reform, in fact represented a major step forward from President Bush's earlier pledge of $100 million to Poland which he had made during his visit to the country following its June 1989 elections. That promise had been widely criticized and Congress' far more substantial action was a clear indication that America's elected leaders were listening to the public, and to organizations such as the PAC. *New York Times*, November 19, 1989.
**In August 1990 Moskal was again in Poland, this time to represent Polonia at the Solidarity movement's tenth anniversary.

member group was given responsibility for collecting information on Poland's most pressing needs so that the Administration could better fashion a practical program to help in its economic recovery. At the end of December Moskal was once more in Poland, this time to participate in the forming of an international charitable campaign, the Polish National Fund (*Fundusz daru narodowego*). Heading the effort was Cardinal Glemp.

Moskal supported the objectives of the Fund appeal and upon his return to the United States proposed that the PAC raise at least one million dollars for the cause. This idea was approved by the Congress in June 1990 at the semi-annual meeting of the PAC National Council of Directors in Dearborn, Michigan. There, the directors resolved to turn over what they collected during the coming year to Glemp in time for the bi-centennial observances of the Third of May Constitution. They also approved a proposal to publicize the sale of a special commemorative silver coin throughout the United States. The coin was valued at 100,000 Polish *zloty* and had the status of legal tender in Poland; part of the proceeds of the sale were earmarked for the Polish National Fund.

Moskal had benefited a good deal from his Polish visits and his conversations with the country's leaders. As he wrote to President Bush following his return in December 1989:

> I was once again overwhelmed by the magnitude of the economic problems that Poland is facing. Despite their awareness of the difficult road ahead, the Polish people have made an irrevocable commitment to democratic change. They have reconfirmed their faith in the Catholic Church and in their own ability to govern themselves. Their support for the Mazowiecki government seems to be solid. It is important that our efforts produce positive results within as short a time as possible. Such successes are vital if we are to be able to enlist the Polish people in a joint effort for them to help themselves.[11]

Also remarkable was Moskal's experience during his third visit, which coincided with the Polish parliament's decisions making the crowned eagle the nation's symbol once again, the renaming of the country the "Republic of Poland" instead of the "Polish People's Republic," and the removal of all references to the construction of socialism from the constitution. None of these acts added a penny to Poland's economy. Each in its own fashion underscored the Polish people's aspirations to bury the memory of communism once and for all. Perhaps as meaningful were the words he heard from Cardinal Glemp at the founding of the Polish National Fund on December 31, 1989. As Glemp put matters in his remarks to the leadership of the world's Polonia who were together for the occasion, "the history of Poland is not complete without including the history of its Polonia."

The sudden collapse of the East German communist state in the last months of 1989 and beginning of 1990 presented yet another challenge to the Polish American Congress in its efforts on Poland's behalf. With East Germany's unification with the West German Federal Republic an ever more certain reality, the future borders of the reunited country became a subject of increasing concern to the new Polish government and its friends in the United States. The issue became particularly troubling due to the ambivalent statements of West Germany's Chancellor, Helmut Kohl, who for domestic political reasons refused to come out explicitly and unequivocally in favor of the inviolability of the Polish-German borders established at the end of the Second World War. Indeed he continued to hold fast to his position in the face of growing criticism both at home and from abroad.[12]

In February 1990, the foreign ministers of the United Kingdom, France and the Soviet Union met with the Secretary of State of the U.S. in Ottawa where an arrangement was approved to carry forth the process of Germany's unification with due regard to the border concerns of its neighbors. Poland's response to the announcement of the so-called "Four plus Two Talks" was to demand that its representatives be included in any discussions pertaining to its western borders. For its part, the PAC vigorously backed Warsaw in its own communications to the White House and Congress. Thus in a letter of February 15, 1990 to President Bush, Moskal wrote:

> We ask you, Mr. President, to reiterate publicly the long-standing American position concerning the safeguarding of the territorial integrity of Poland. A statement by

you...reaffirming unequivocally U.S. support for the present Polish-German border will go a long way in alleviating some of the present fears about a possible strong, reunited Germany... The subject of the inviolability of the present Polish-German border is of utmost interest to my organization, the more than 10,000,000 Americans of Polish heritage, and most importantly, to the brave people of Poland...[13]

The PAC's lobbying effort in Washington, together with the thousands of letters, telephone calls and telegrams from ordinary Polish Americans from around the country, all helped greatly in persuading the Administration of the depth of Polonia's concerns. Thus on February 25, in his press conference with Chancellor Kohl following their weekend meeting in Camp David, President Bush categorically stated that "the United States respects the provisions of the Helsinki Final Act regarding the inviolability of the current borders in Europe. And the United States formally recognizes the current German-Polish border."*

With respect to Poland's participation in the "Four plus Two Talks" Moskal and the PAC were equally vigorous in making America's leaders aware of Polonia's solidarity with Warsaw. Here there were great obstacles to be overcome, since as late as February 20, the U.S. Department of State had put forward the view that there was no way for Poland to participate in the talks.

---

* One might say that the U.S. had backed the permanence of the Odra-Nysa border for the past twenty years, when Washington acquiesced to West German Chancellor Willy Brandt's *Ostpolitik* initiatives that culminated in the signing of a Polish-West German Treaty in December 1970. This posture was further strengthened in August 1975 by American participation in the signing of the Helsinki Final Act. Still, President Bush's manner as much as his words at the press conference with Chancellor Kohl, and the fact that he interrupted the Chancellor to make his point about the settled character of the Polish-German border matter testified to the increasingly explicit character of the United States' position and its commitment to Poland's security. Interview with PAC National Executive Director John Kordek, August 10, 1990.

Nevertheless, Moskal together with the Polish American Congress' newly appointed Executive Director, former Ambassador John F. Kordek, PAC Washington Office Director Myra Lenard, and PAC Director Jan Nowak, again went to work to vigorously lobby the White House and the members of the U.S. Congress to support their position. Thus, to U.S. Senator Barbara Mikulski Moskal wrote on February 21:

> Madame Senator, we note that a meeting of the four victorious powers of World War II and the two Germanies has now been approved. We welcome this decision which could ensure that the future, reunited Germany would present no danger to the territorial integrity and sovereignty of its neighbors, especially Poland. The conference of the six should not, however, become another Potsdam, where smaller nations were deprived of their voice in decisions concerning their vital interests. We believe that Poland should be included especially when the security and borders of a reunified Germany and the security of its neighbors are discussed.[14]

These efforts too had great effect. For one thing, Senator Mikulski, joined by many of her colleagues in both Houses of Congress responded forcefully to the PAC's urgings to call upon the President to alter the Administration's position on Poland's involvement in the Four plus Two Talks. Thus, as one letter from Mikulski and eleven of her fellow Senators concluded, it should be the "duty of the United States and all of our European allies to guarantee that (Germany's reunification) does not threaten our friends in Poland, Czechoslovakia or anywhere in Europe."[15]

Most telling, however, was the impact of a telegram from thirty-four U.S. Senators to Chancellor Kohl in early March calling upon his government to reverse its position on Polish involvement in the Four plus Two Talks. This move, inspired by the PAC, caused Kohl to call an extraordinary meeting of his Cabinet which resulted in West Germany's decision to accept Polish participation in the Talks.[16]

On March 14, Moskal was again in the White House, this time to argue for a change in the United States' position with respect to Poland's participation in the Talks. Again, his statements and the PAC's position papers presented to President Bush on the issue had their effect. Within a week's time the Administration had announced that it had reversed its stance on the matter and was now prepared to support Poland's involvement. This major shift for all practical purposes ended the controversy.[17]

At the same meeting, President Bush also took action on yet another significant issue confronting Poland and of concern to the PAC. This involved his naming of the Board of Directors of the Polish American Enterprise Fund established the previous year through Congress' passage of the Support for Eastern European Democracy Act. Under the terms of the SEED Act, some $240 million had been set aside for the Fund whose purpose was to implement the development of joint ventures between U.S. and Polish businesses. However, until March 1990 the Administration had not taken any concrete measures to activate and direct the work of the Enterprise Fund.

President Bush's action was soon followed by Congress' authorization of some $34 million for expenditure in the current fiscal year by the Polish American Enterprise Fund. In June 1990 the Congress approved an additional $105 million in appropriations for the Fund's use for the 1991 fiscal year, to begin on October 1, 1990. These actions at last enabled the United States to begin systematic efforts to assist Poland's economic recovery in the spirit of the SEED Act. Moreover, the Fund's Board of Directors benefited from the advice offered by the Polish American Congress' representatives in making its own investment decisions, thanks to the PAC's continuing contacts with its members and through a series of written presentations addressed to its attention.[18]*

---

* Named Chairman of the Polish American Enterprise Fund was John Birkeland, Chairman of Dillon Read and Company in New York, the investment firm formerly headed by U.S. Secretary of the Treasury Nicholas Brady. The members of its Executive Board included Lane Kirkland, President of the AFL-CIO, John Harper, Chief Executive Officer of ConAgra Corporation, Nicholas Rey, Managing Director of Bear Stearns, Inc. of New York, and Dr. Brzezinski of Georgetown University's Center for Strategic and International Studies. (The latter

Both of President Bush's March announcements were in fact timed to coincide with Prime Minister Mazowiecki's visit to the United States and they helped make his trip highly beneficial to Poland's economic and political prospects. For his part Mazowiecki was emphatic in expressing the Polish nation's appreciation to the PAC for its very effective work on his country's behalf. Thus, in remarks in Chicago to more than 1,200 Polonia leaders Mazowiecki had this to say about the Polish American Congress' activities on the border issue:

> Quick, decisive and shrewd diplomatic action by the Polish government as well as the action of the Polish American Congress succeeded in convincing the participants of the (Four plus Two) Conference in the matter of German reunification that, in the issues pertaining to Poland, Poland's participation must be acknowledged.[19]

* * * * * * *

The accomplishments of the Polish American Congress Charitable Foundation since 1980 and the efforts of the PAC as a political lobby have already been described. A sense of the organization's current agenda in the nation's capital from a reading of comments made by PAC Washington, D.C. Executive Director Myra Lenard:

> Our lobbying efforts primarily concentrate on foreign affairs policies as they affect Poland and the United States as well as immigration and refugee issues. The PAC office monitors daily the issues that are important to Polonia and the people of Poland. Traditionally, the PAC has maintained contact with legislators of Polish heritage so that we might have their strong backing of bills we support. I am happy to report that we have three Senators, eleven Congressmen and one Congresswoman of Polish heritage. We now also keep contact with some 105 legislators who are dependent on the

two are both of Polish heritage.) Robert Faris was later chosen to serve as the President of the Polish American Enterprise Fund with two Polish representatives to be named in the near future by the Polish government.)

votes of Polish American constituents to win election to office. They are informed on every position and statement made by the President of the PAC.

We can take pride that the PAC has been instrumental over the years in initiating and helping win passage of many bills for the benefit of our own people of Polish heritage, for our fellow Americans of Eastern European origin and for the American people as well... Since 1981, the PAC has lobbied strongly for the recognition of Solidarity and for the appropriation of funds to assist the people of Poland through Solidarity and the Church in Poland. In 1988 we have probably seen the most Congressional support of our labors over any of the past seven years. Thus, for Fiscal Year 1989, the U.S. Congress appropriated and authorized the following: one million dollars for the independent trade union Solidarity, one million dollars for Solidarity social and medical programs, one million for the purchase of medical supplies and hospital equipment to be directed through the Polish Church, one million to implement the U.S. science and technology agreement with Poland, ten million dollars for private agriculture to be managed by the Polish Church to aid 9,000 private farms in increasing their productivity, authorization for the shipment of 8,000 metric tons of eligible agricultural commodities for each year from 1988 to 1992.

The PAC lobbied for the Voice of America, Radio Free Europe and Radio Liberty, and the modernization and expansion of their systems to strengthen the uninterrupted flow of information, something of great value to a free world and meriting our strong support.

Equally important was PAC support for the appropriation for the National Endowment for Democracy, which plays a crucial role in supporting world-wide non-violent freedom movements like Solidarity. Through the Endowment the PAC Charitable Foundation received a grant of $300,000 in each of the past two years to provide a variety of educational and humanitarian benefits to the people of Poland.[20]*

---

* In 1989 and 1990 the PACCF received additional grants for medical assistance projects in Poland totalling $1.5 million. These funds originated out of the U.S. Agency for International Development with

This record is one to be proud of; it is even more impressive when one recognizes that the various efforts of the Polish American Congress have been conducted thanks mainly through voluntary labor and a budget that is minuscule when compared to other lobbies seeking to influence policy in Washington.[21]

The Future

For more than forty-five years, hundreds, if not thousands of dedicated men and women have contributed their energies to the work of the Polish American Congress. But what of the future--who is to be found among younger Polish Americans who can infuse new vigor into the organization so that it can continue as a significant force in American society?

Fortunately, there are able and potentially productive individuals of Polish birth and ancestral heritage who might contribute significantly to the PAC, if recruited effectively to enter its ranks. Some are the descendants of immigrants to America from long ago, during the years preceding World War I. By the late 1980s many of these representatives of the "old Polonia" immigrations had in every respect become part of America's mainstream, especially in terms of their educational and professional attainments in a host of fields, business, the Church, law, medicine, and education. A few are university professors who teach and perform research on the history and cultural dynamics of the Polish experience. This last *cadre* of knowledgeable and articulate specialists constitutes a particularly important yet seldom recognized resource. As the ethnic community's "keepers of the flame" in preserving Polonia's memory of its members' roots, accomplishments and aspirations, the academic people of Polish heritage have an important place in the PAC's future.

---

the supplies to be distributed by the Foundation in cooperation with the Polish Episcopate's Charitable Commission headed by Bishop Czeslaw Domin. In addition the PAC continued to receive funds from the National Endowment for Democracy, primarily to assist in training Poles in developing their skills in parliamentary politics.

Others who might help in reenergizing the Congress are the offspring of the post World War II political emigration, individuals whose parents played a crucial role in PAC activities in the past. Still others include representatives from the more recent migrations from Poland over the last fifteen to twenty years, whether they or their families came to America out of political or mainly economic motives. While many among these "newcomers" are presently and necessarily occupied with the tasks of establishing themselves in their new homeland, in time they too can be expected to contribute substantially to Polonia. Clearly, they have much to offer, including their more recent and vivid memories of life in Poland, their fluency in the Polish language and their familiarity with Polish history and culture-- experiences that can be shared with the broad Polish American population, whose roots go back much earlier.

Thus, to remain vital the Polish American Congress must draw into its ranks talented and informed members from all three of these "groups" in the ethnic community. Just as important, the PAC must more effectively address itself than it has in the past to the "domestic" concerns of Polish Americans, concerns which have usually been overshadowed by the organization's understandable emphasis upon Polish affairs. These domestic concerns need to be clearly defined and ordered, so that realistic efforts can begin to preserve a sense of knowledge and pride in the Polish ethnic heritage among larger numbers of Polish Americans, a set of attitudes and values that they in turn will transmit to the next generation.

Clearly, this is a daunting task, given the impact of pressures of assimilation in America. Yet if the problem of finding ways to preserve ethnic consciousness is not confronted, Polonia will inevitably find itself increasingly composed only of the foreign born and some of its offspring, and thus separated from the great mass of Americans of Polish origin due to the latter's lack of knowledge of, and contact with, its heritage.[22]*

---

* For a recent statement of concern about the PAC's need to give serious attention to formulating, and carrying out, its "domestic agenda," see the Appendix to this work and PAC Vice President Lukomski's comments

Poland's Place in Polonia's Prospects

There is a last question to cover in discussing Polonia's future, that of Poland's role in the ethnic community's continued vitality.

Historically, that is, before the First World War and the homeland's restoration to independence in 1918, an especially rich relationship evolved between the emigration and the old country, one originally based upon the maintenance of familial ties and obligations across the ocean. Economically the homeland was the beneficiary of this relationship, of course. But the emigration also gained much from the steady stream of newcomers to America, whose presence served to constantly reinvigorate its communal life.

With the rise of an organized Polonia, individual and familial assistance to the homeland was complemented by group efforts to unite the ever-growing immigration behind the cause of Poland's independence. Indeed, by the time of World War I, the American Poles could proudly call their community the "fourth partition"--so significant and multi-faceted was their record of service to the homeland.

During the years from 1918 up to the outbreak of World War II in 1939, when Poland's independence was again lost,

---

on the subject. In his own remarks to the PAC leadership in Dearborn, Michigan John Kordek, the Congress' newly appointed National Executive Director added yet another task to the organization's agenda. This involved its broadened obligations toward other ethnic organizations. "This is a high priority because it is in the interest not only of Poland but of all Americans of Polish heritage for the PAC to work with other nationalities and ethnic lobbies, and most importantly, to get their support for our legislative agenda... We must continue to build broader and stronger ties and coalitions with other ethnic groups on the political, cultural and religious levels... We cannot do it alone. We need political allies to support our domestic and international agenda if we hope to be successful. No ethnic community nor any single lobbying organization can, by itself, get legislation through the U.S. Congress. Everyone needs allies. This is a simple fact of life in Washington. Therefore, building coalitions in support of our agenda should be one of our major objectives." *Report of the PAC National Director for the Period from January 1 through June 25, 1990.*

relations between Polonia and the old homeland underwent a substantial change. After World War I, the overwhelming majority of the four million member Polish community in America had chosen to remain in this country rather than to return "home." Nonetheless, most continued to maintain a style of life that was at least partly outside the American "mainstream." Indeed, while younger and American born Poles did master the English language, they together with their immigrant parents tended to reside in heavily Polish neighborhoods, worship in nationality-based parishes, marry within their ethnic heritage, work and play with people of similar cultural origins.

This second generation of "Americans of Polish extraction" possessed its own distinctive culture, one readily differentiated from those of both the Polish and American societies of the time. By the 1930s, it was said of Polish Americans that their culture was "suspended halfway between the sky and the ground" since they were viewed as hyphenates by their fellow Americans but as "Americans" when they visited the old country.

It was no less vexing for Polish Americans to adequately define the relationship between the government of interwar Poland and the Polonia. Thus, Warsaw mistakenly tended to look upon the large and fairly affluent Polish community in America as a kind of colony possessing resources of great potential benefit if only properly harnessed. For their part Polish Americans found their options, whether these involved subordination to the Polish state, immersion in their own domestic ethnic affairs, or separation from the life of Polonia, all unsatisfying in some respect. Still, at least on a psychological level, most could hardly help but feel pride in the fact of Poland's restoration to independence after five generations of foreign rule and some pleasure in their knowledge that the organized ethnic community had played a part in that achievement.

In the five decades since the outbreak of World War II, Poland--Polonia relations have largely reverted to their pre 1914 forms, with the ethnic community's energies once more focused upon the providing of political and humanitarian assistance to a homeland neither free nor sovereign.

After the War, Polonia, now led by the Polish American Congress, also united to reject the communist regime Stalin imposed upon the Poles; instead it looked to the Roman Catholic Church in Poland and to the organizations of political emigres that formed in the West for guidance in defining its agenda.[23] On the mass level, the ties that continued to bind remained those of a family nature; as in the past these were again expressed largely through material assistance. To a much lesser extent, travel to, and study in, Poland have also played a role in helping enliven interest in the homeland.

Polonia's ideological alienation from the postwar Polish regime was most profound between 1945 and 1956, the early years of Stalinist communism and the most intense period of Cold War animosity. Conditions eased somewhat during the first decade of Wladyslaw Gomulka's rule after 1956 and again in the early 1970s, when Edward Gierek took over amid hopes that his regime would be more responsive to his subjects' aspirations. But the failures of both Gomulka and Gierek, the dramatic decline of Poland's economy beginning in the mid 1970s, the suppression of Solidarity in 1981, and the subsequent emigration of several hundred thousand Poles who despaired of ever witnessing their country's recovery may have convinced many Americans of Polish heritage that Poland's problems were simply insoluble.

Yet conditions in the old homeland had also been a profound source of pessimism before World War I. What then differentiated the post World War II period from the years before 1914 (and at the same time made it reminiscent of the interwar era) was the general isolation of an increasingly assimilated Polish American population from healthy and extensive contact with Poland's people and its culture, a condition that was aggravated by popular distrust of practically every Polish communist initiative taken toward organized Polonia. Given these factors and together with the impact of assimilation upon the increasingly Americanized Polish ethnic population, interest in Poland and the Polish heritage could only gradually diminish.

Thus, in the circumstances of the past 150 years or so, one can well appreciate why Poland has only occasionally been of much help to Polonia in its efforts to preserve ethnic community life in the United States. Lacking such help and operating in an American environment where general knowledge and interest about Poland was minimal, it is not surprising that Polonia's organizations have found it increasingly difficult to find the resources they needed to preserve a high degree of mass involvement in their work.

Looking to the future, what can be said of Polonia's capacity to remain a significant force in American society? As has already been noted, Polonia faces the task of better exploiting the existing intellectual resources which are to be found in the Polish American population. Not only must more individuals possessing good educations and professional training in their respective fields of work be enlisted into Polonia's service, greater effort must be directed into enlightening more Polish Americans, both those belonging to Polonia's organizations and those outside this network, about their heritage. Ethnic pride, after all, must be rooted in knowledge of the Polish experience in Poland and America, and not only in slogans.

Yet for Polonia to remain a force in American society, Poland itself must begin to play a greater role in the work of educating Polish Americans about the worth of their ethnic identity. In the past, especially after 1945, this did not occur -- to Polonia's detriment. Of course, conditions have changed radically since 1989 and with the appearance of a democratic and pro Western government in Poland, the ancestral homeland may at last be in the position to assist Polonia more systematically in the monumental work of renewing the ethnic community.

Indeed, this objective can be realized and on two distinct levels. One involves actions on the part of the Polish authorities to promote interest in their country in a variety of legitimate, non-manipulative ways--by fostering scholarly and student exchanges, through sponsoring film, artistic and cultural exhibitions in the U.S., and by developing tourism and business cooperation between citizens of the two countries. All these sorts of programmatic activities can have a positive effect in building greater interest in Poland among Americans, Polish and non-Polish alike.

Of potentially even greater significance to the revitalization of Polonia is something having little to do with any specific set of Polish initiatives aimed at the Polish American population, however. Here one thinks of the possibilities that flow from Poland's eventual and successful integration into the European community, its development of a healthy economy and a polity founded upon democratic precepts. Clearly, such a Poland will win esteem in this country, just as other successful nation states such as Germany, the Scandinavian countries and Italy have, by their advances, strengthened the prestige and self confidence of millions of Americans of German, Scandinavian and Italian ancestry. Similarly, a healthy and dynamic Poland can be a subject of increased interest on the part of Polish Americans and thus a source of Polonia's own renewal in its efforts to achieve its historic mission--the preservation of the Polish tradition in the United States.

This is no inconsiderable objective. Indeed, for more than 150 years Poles have come to America in large numbers in search of a better life while remaining mindful of the families and culture they left behind. For nearly 130 years Poles in this country have organized on behalf of the homeland's independence and its people's material well-being. Their efforts and achievements during the past five generations have been substantial, as this work, it is hoped, has shown. Americans, whether Polish or not, should be aware of this story, which in fact is also a great testimony to the validity of the core principles of freedom upon which the American nation itself was founded. At the same time, the people of Poland should also better know what their fellow countrymen across the ocean have sought to do on their behalf and that they have never been truly alone even in their times of greatest hardship.

But just as Poland's history cannot be understood without recognizing the place of its diaspora, so also should the ties that link Polonia to Poland include more than a collective memory of Kosciuszko, Pulaski and Paderewski and the two countries' commitment to freedom and constitutionalism, significant as these happen to be. Most important of all, perhaps, have been the human bonds forged by countless Polish immigrants to America, bonds that have produced much of worth to both societies in the past and which possess real potential value to both nations in the years to come.

Table 1.
THE POLISH AMERICAN CONGRESS;
AFFILIATED ORGANIZATIONS, 1990

Name of Organization and Year Established	Headquarters	Recent Membership
I. Fraternal Insurance Societies:		
Polish Roman Catholic Union (1873)	Chicago	95,000
Polish National Alliance (1880)	Chicago	270,000
Polish Falcons of America (1887)	Pittsburgh	28,200
Polish Union of America (1890)	Buffalo	9,100
Alliance of Poles of America (1895)	Cleveland	16,000
Polish Women's Alliance (1898)	Chicago	68,100
Union of Poles of America (1898)	Cleveland	10,000
Polish Beneficial Association (1900)	Philadelphia	13,200
Polish National Alliance of Brooklyn (1903)	Brooklyn	8,700
Polish National Union (1908)	Scranton	27,500
Union of Polish Women (1920)	Philadelphia	7,000
II. Veterans, Associations:		
Polish Army Veterans Association (1921)	New York	7,000
Polish Legion of American Veterans (1921)	Detroit	8,000
Polish Veterans of World War II (1952)	New York	5,000
Polish Home Army Association (1947)	Chicago	*

| Polish Air Force Veterans Association (1950) | Lake Bluff, IL | * |

III. Cultural Societies:

American Council for Polish Culture (1948)	Philadelphia	*
North American Studies Center for Polish Affairs (1976)	Ann Arbor, MI	*
Polish American Historical Association (1943)	Chicago	*
Polish Scouting Association (1910)	Detroit	*
Polish Singers Alliance (1889)	New York	*
Polish Supplementary School Association (1954)	New York	*
Polish Western Association	Chicago	*

IV. Other Groups:

Polish Highlanders Alliance (1929)	Chicago	*
Polish American Immigration and Relief Committee (1947)	New York	*
Polish Association of Former Political Prisoners (1950)	Westfield, NJ	*

State Divisions of the PAC (N=31):

Arizona, Northern California, Southern California, Connecticut, Delaware, Florida, Western Florida, Illinois, Indiana, Maryland, Eastern Massachusetts, Western Massachusetts, Michigan, Nebraska, Southern New Jersey, Northern New Jersey, Central New York, Downstate New York, Western New York, Ohio, Oklahoma, Eastern Pennsylania, Northeastern Pennsylvania, Pennsylvania--Scranton, Western Pennsylvania, Rhode Island, Texas, Washington, D.C., Washington State, Central Wisconsin (Oshkosh), Wisconsin State (Milwaukee).

**Organizations Previously
But No Longer Affiliated:**
Polish Alma Mater (a Chicago based fraternal merged into the PNA), Sea League of America (Headquartered in Chicago), Alliance of Polish Clubs (Chicago), National Advocates Society (Chicago), Polish National Relief Fund Committee (Chicago), Dmowski Institute (New York).

Presently Inactive State Divisions:
Missouri, Oregon, West Virginia, Minnesota.

**Polish American Organizations
Not Affiliated With the PAC:**
Educational Organizations: Kosciuszko Foundation (New York), Polish Institute of Arts and Sciences of America (New York), Pilsudski Institute (New York).

Fraternals: Federation Life Insurance of America (Milwaukee, affiliated with the Wisconsin State PAC), Association of the Sons of Poland (Jersey City), Polish Union of the United States (Wilkes Barre, Pennsylvania), Northern Fraternal Life (Milwaukee).

Others: National Medical and Dental Association (Chicago), Polish American Guardian Society (Chicago).

Dues paid to the national organization by affiliated member organizations in 1988 amounted to $19,065; state divisions provided $39,815. In addition $23,406 was contributed by the state divisions to help defray home office expenses that year. The PAC's national raffle generated another $55,000.

Sources: 1989 Membership and Financial Report distributed to Directors of the PAC; Pienkos, *PNA*, pp. 295-297; and 1989 *Statistics of Fraternal Benefit Societies* (Naperville, Illinois: National Fraternal Congress, 1990), and Barbara Chalko of the PAC national office in Chicago.

* membership below 5,000.

Documents on Polish American Relations and Concerns

This section includes a selection of historically significant pronouncements on issues pertaining to the freedom and well-being of the Polish people, in Europe and America, by leaders of the government of the United States, Poland and Polonia.

LIST OF DOCUMENTS

1. Proclamation of the Poles in America concerning Poland, May 1, 1899; Excerpts.
2. Resolutions adopted by the Delegates to the First Polish National Congress, in Washington, D.C., May 11-14, 1910.
3. Aims and Tasks of the National Department, August 17, 1916.
4. Telegram from President Franklin D. Roosevelt to the Delegates to the founding meeting of the Polish American Congress, May 27, 1944.
5. Memorial of the Polish American Congress to President Roosevelt, May 30, 1944.
6. Resolution of the Polish American Congress, May 30, 1944.
7. Congratulatory letter to President Roosevelt on his reelection from President Charles Rozmarek of the Polish American Congress, November 14, 1944.
8. Excerpts from President Roosevelt's Address to the Congress of the United States on the Results of the Yalta Conference, March 1, 1945.
9. Excerpts from the Polish American Congress' Memorandum to President Roosevelt in Connection with the Yalta Conference, March 15, 1945.
10. President Harry Truman's Special Message to the Congress on U.S. Participation in the United Nations Relief and Rehabilitation Administration (UNRRA), November 13, 1945.

11. President Rozmarek's Statement to the Press in Paris, France, September 12, 1946.

12. Telegram to United States Secretary of State George C. Marshall from President Rozmarek on the Polish Election of January 20, 1947.

13. President Truman's Special Message to Congress on the Admission of Displaced Persons, July 7, 1947.

14. President Truman's Statement upon signing the bill amending the Displaced Persons Act, June 16, 1950.

15. President Truman's campaign speech in Hamtramck, Michigan of October 30, 1952.

16. Excerpts from the Final Report of the Select Committee of the U.S. House of Representatives investigating the Katyn Massacre, December 22, 1952.

17. President Dwight D. Eisenhower's letter to the Congress of the United States on a proposed resolution on Subjugated Peoples, February 20, 1953.

18. President Eisenhower's views on U.S. Policy toward Eastern Europe; Excerpt from his Press Conference of November 14, 1956.

19. President Eisenhower on the purposes of U.S. economic assistance to the Eastern European satellites; Excerpt from his Press Conference of June 18, 1958.

20. President Eisenhower on the Congressional Resolution establishing "Captive Nations Week" observances; Excerpt from his Press Conference of July 22, 1959.

21. President Eisenhower's remarks at the quadrennial national convention of the Polish American Congress, September 30, 1960.

22. President John F. Kennedy on the purposes of U.S. economic assistance to Eastern Europe; Excerpt from his Press Conference of June 7, 1962.

23. President Kennedy's remarks at the annual Pulaski Day Parade in Buffalo, October 14, 1962.

24. President Kennedy on the problem of overturning communist dictatorships; Excerpt from his Press Conference of February 7, 1963.

25. President Lyndon B. Johnson's remarks on the occasion of the Twentieth Anniversary of the Warsaw Uprising, July 31, 1964.

26. President Johnson's remarks at a ceremony commemorating Poland's Millennium, May 3, 1966.

27. President Johnson's remarks at the dedication of the Shrine of Our Lady of Czestochowa in Doylestown, Pennsylvania, October 16, 1966.

28. Statement by President Aloysius Mazewski of the Polish American Congress in support of Radio Free Europe, September 15, 1971.

29. President Richard M. Nixon's message to the Congress of the United States on U.S. Foreign Policy, Excerpts, May 3, 1973.

30. President Gerald R. Ford's remarks to representatives of Americans of Eastern European background prior to his departure to attend the European Security Conference at Helsinki, Finland, July 25, 1975.

31. President Ford's remarks at the quadrennial national convention of the Polish American Congress, September 24, 1976.

32. Excerpt from the second Presidential debate of 1976 between President Ford and James Carter of Georgia, October 6, 1976.

33. President Ford's remarks at a meeting with Americans of Eastern European Ancestry, October 12, 1976.

34. President James Carter's remarks to Polish Americans in the White House following his trip to Poland, February 6, 1978.

35. Polish American Congress Memorandum to President Carter on Current Conditions in Poland, August 25, 1980.

36. President Carter's remarks announcing U.S. agricultural credit guarantees to Poland, September 12, 1980.

37. President Carter on the growing crisis in Poland, December 3, 1980.

38. Polish American Congress Memorandum to President Ronald W. Reagan, December 20, 1981.

39. President Reagan's address to the nation on the situation in Poland, December 23, 1981.

40. President Reagan's statement on U.S. measures taken against the Soviet Union concerning its involvement in Poland, December 29, 1981.

41. President Reagan's Proclamation on the Fortieth Anniversary of the Warsaw Uprising, August 17, 1984.

42. President Reagan's remarks on the Fortieth Anniversary of the Warsaw Uprising, August 17, 1984.

43. Polish Americans Protest Jaruzelski's visit to the United Nations, a statement published in the *New York Times*, September 25, 1985.

44. President Reagan's statement on the lifting of U.S. sanctions against Poland, February 19, 1987.

45. Polish American Congress statement of May 5, 1988 on the crisis in Poland.

46. Polish American Congress statement in support of Solidarity on its eighth anniversary, August 29, 1988.

47. Polish American Congress statement on the eve of the "Round Table" Negotiations in Poland, October 3, 1988.

48. Polish American Congress statement on the Agreement of April 5, 1989 concluding the Round Table Talks.

49. President George H. Bush's remarks in Hamtramck, Michigan on the occasion of the Polish government's formal relegalization of Solidarity, April 17, 1989.

50. Polish American Congress statement of June 8, 1989 following Poland's elections.

51. Polish American Congress statement of August 23, 1989 following Tadeusz Mazowiecki's appointment as Poland's Prime Minister.

52. Lech Walesa's address to a joint meeting of the Congress of the United States of America, November 15, 1989.

53. Statements of Polish American Congress Edward Moskal to President Bush on matters concerning Poland, November 1989 to March 1990.

54. Text of a Cable from thirty-four U.S. Senators to West German Chancellor Helmut Kohl and East German Prime Minister Hans Modrow, March 2, 1990.

55. Remarks of Polish American Congress Vice President Kazimierz Lukomski on Polonia's "Domestic Agenda," October, 1990.

1. PROCLAMATION OF THE POLES IN AMERICA CONCERNING POLAND, MAY 1, 1899

With reference to the peace conference in the Hague, to the American people and to other civilized nations:

Section I.

WE HAVE THE RIGHT AND THE DUTY TO SPEAK ABOUT THE POLISH QUESTION ON THE EVE OF THE CONFERENCE.

The Russian emperor, Nicholas II, has convened a conference, purportedly international, with a noble goal -- claims his minister, Count Muraviev -- *to put an end to the growth of militarism*, to reduce the burden of the people paying excessive taxes for *supporting a too large a number of unproductive military forces*, and to find ways to *avoid future wars*, the blemish of civilized societies.

Words of sincere appreciation are due to a man whose goal is to secure the blissful results of a stable peace for the civilized peoples of the world, regardless of who this man is and *what other motives prompt him*. His project would undoubtedly meet with recognition in the government spheres of all nations, if the governments of a considerable number of the states had the right to speak at the forthcoming "international" conference on behalf of the ruled and *if the interests of the rulers were not so often in such drastic conflict with the interests of the ruled*.

Such a conflict of interests was the cause of restrictions by the project initiator of the peace conference, who gives the right to speak exclusively to representatives of governments, and *denies the right to speak to representatives of those nations which do not like the existing state of affairs in individual countries and which strive openly for a change in these existing conditions*. Such a restriction can contribute little to a favorable solution of the question of international peace. Thus we have an agreement of the governments to the planned exclusion at the coming conference of all discussions concerning current matters of international politics *which constitute a bone of contention* among the governments of individual peoples and an obstacle to general disarmament for a period as long as they are not solved according to the will of the peoples, regardless of the will of the rulers.

One of the reefs on which must crash the project of ending the further strengthening of the military forces of individual great powers and the wish to secure for Europe the fruits of a stable peace, is *the question of compensating the wrong inflicted by the crime of dismembering Poland,* committed one hundred years ago by three major European states, which keep their conquest to this day in uninterrupted possession. The Poles in the Russian, German and Austrian partitions can not demand compensation for this wrong, as they do not want to be liable in the light of the binding laws in those countries to the accusation of high treason. But we, the Poles in America, free citizens of the American republic, citizens of the United States, which does not have an excessive number in the standing army, but in spite of this is strong enough to win freedom for the subjugated nations, as the last war against Spain on behalf of the Cubans showed, demand compensation before the American people and other civilized peoples on the entire globe. We believe that we have not only the right but also the duty to raise our voice in the matter of the restoration to Poland of her natural and political rights and this is for the following reasons:

We belong in our ancestry to a nation which in spite of over one hundred years of bondage *did not renounce its unexpired rights,* which forms a separate whole not only in its own understanding but also is recognized as such by the very same oppressors. *This is evidenced by constant persecutions* aimed directly against us and a *whole range of statutes limiting our national development.* This nation possesses to this day its distinct features, its own splendid historical past, its own ideals, and has not abandoned its mission of creating a strong link in one, great chain of peoples, striving to achieve the highest level of moral and intellectual excellence. *This nation points with pride to its past great historical significance, to its past and present rich literature, to its large host of men of science and art.* This nation should not be missing from the peace conference, which is so important for all nations, *at which the history of the world, and the literature and science of individual tribes and peoples should be taken into consideration.*

It is difficult to prevent this absence in view of the fact that the Polish lands, partitioned by three rapacious powers, *in contravention of all international laws* and against a sense of simple justice, do not have their own, visible, joint representation. This does not prevent, however, *the Polish nation from being seized with a feeling of tribal unity of all its component parts forever* and a part of this nation, according to its power, from raising its voice on behalf of the whole, whenever the opportunity presents itself. Such a voice always finds a response in the whole Polish nation, in the hearts of the people, in whose *eyes the treaties, concluded under the pressure of force, do not have any moral value.*

If we think that what we quoted above give us the RIGHT to take the floor before the peace conference, we also believe that it is our DUTY to raise this voice. *There is no branch of science, art or knowledge, in which the Poles would not give to the whole world for common usage their own achievements.* Therefore in a matter so important as the peace conference, the voice of the Poles should not be absent. Unable to speak before the government delegates, we have the right and the duty to raise this voice before the peoples of the civilized world, who are sincerely interested in the matter of universal peace and the cessation of wars, no less vividly than the *diplomats* in the service of the crowned heads.

In our opinion, therefore, *to eradicate the evil one should examine the cause of this evil;* to prevent the intolerable existing state of *armed peace* and the deplorable results of war, with the perfected means of the military craft, it is necessary to consider the fact that the cause of this armed peace is *not only the fear of governments of military aggression by the neighbors into the territories of the given nations,* but also an urgent *need to maintain with an iron hand the existing order, or rather the existing disorder,* which rouses the indignation of nearly all of mankind, even those most loyal to their own governments. The first condition for at least partial disarmament and the securing of universal peace is, in our opinion, *the repairing of the wrong* committed by some governments, *because as long as these wrongs exist in their blatant manifestation, the danger that either the neighboring governments will stand up for the wronged or the wronged them-*

selves will attempt to shake off the yoke imposed by force will not be removed.

Section V

....(In conclusion) We, the undersigned representatives of the Polish organizations and publications in the United States, upon hearing the news of the conference at the Hague called by the emperor of Russia, have decided to present this Memorial addressed to the civilized peoples of the world, in the name of the Polish citizens of the United States, as a reminder of the wrongs done to the Polish people, without whose righting no conference calling itself a conference of peace can be either an act of peace or justice aimed at bringing about an end to bloody and fratricidal conflicts throughout the world.

Chicago, Illinois
May 1, 1899

Dr. Casimir W. Midowicz, Francis P. Danisch, Szczesny Zahajkiewicz, Casimir Neumann, Stefan Barszczewski, Leon Szopinski (Members of the Executive Committee)

Theodore M. Helinski, Frank H. Jablonski, M.J. Sadowski: Polish National Alliance

Casimir Zychlinski, Marian Steczynski: Polish Falcons Alliance

Max Kucera, Ignace Sawicki: Polish Singers Alliance in America

Adalbert Kabat, Michael Skowronski: Polish Roman Catholic Union in Bay City, Michigan

T. Olsztynski, T. Rutkowski: Alliance of Poles in the State of Ohio

Rev. Eugene Sedlaczek, Theodore Ostrowski, Jan Manna: Polish Roman Catholic Union in America

Stanislas K. Sass, John M. Sienkiewicz, F.T. Wolowski: Polish Young People's Alliance in America

Rev. Dominic Majer, M. Tondrowski, M. Zagorski: Polish Union in America

C. Duzewski, W. Perlowski: Polish Singers Alliance in the United States

Stanislas Szwajkart, Editor: *Dziennik Chicagoski*

Michael Kruszka, Editor: *Kuryer Polski* (Milwaukee)

Dr. Ignace Machnikowski, Editor: *Dziennik Milwaucki*
Stefan Barszczewski, Editor of *Zgoda* and of *Sokol,* both of Chicago
Leon Szopinski, Editor: *Gazeta Katolicka* (Chicago)
Wladyslaw Dyniewicz, Editor: *Gazeta Polska* (Chicago)
Szczesny Zahajkiewicz, Editor: *Narod Polski* (Chicago)
Z. Chrzanowski, Editor: *Gazeta Pittsburska*
J.J. Chrzanowski, Editor: *Harmonia* (Chicago)
George Mirski, Editor: *Slonce* (New York)
J. Janusz, Editor: *Kuryer Nowojorski*
A.A. Pardo, Editor: *Tygodnik Polski* (St. Louis)
G.W.J. Kalczynski, Editor and Publisher, *Goniec Polski* (South Bend, Indiana)
T.J. Strozynski, Editor: *Gornik* (Wilkes-Barre, Pennsylvania)
C. Petkoske, Editor and Publisher: *Telegraf*
Francis P. Danisch, Editor: *Sztandar* (Chicago)
Anthony Mallek, Editor: *Ziarno* (Chicago)

2. RESOLUTIONS ADOPTED BY THE DELEGATES TO THE FIRST POLISH NATIONAL CONGRESS, IN WASHINGTON, D.C., MAY 11-14, 1910.

The following motions were approved for later consideration at the meeting of the Political Section of the Polish National Congress:

- The first Polish National Congress resolves that Polish National Congresses should become a permanent national institution and convene regularly at certain intervals of time...
- The Political Section of the First Polish National Congress declares, requests, and recommends that all Polish emigrants in America join for the good of the national cause in one political body under the banner of the Polish National Alliance.
- We, the Poles, have a right to an independent national existence and consider it our sacred duty to strive towards political independence for Poland, our Fatherland.

The resolutions of the Economic-Emigration Section:
- The Polish National Congress in Washington calls upon all Polish people, both in the native land and in emigration, to support as firmly and as eagerly as possible the action of caring for the emigrants, carried out in order to protect our national interests and to defend the emigrants against exploitation and harm resulting from ignorance of the new conditions. The Congress expresses the hope that the official institutions which lead the activity towards this goal will experience greater support from the public and from the Polish press, because without the support of all involved, they could not be expected to achieve their aims. At the same time, the Congress expresses the hope that these institutions, which are appointed to care for the emigrants and returning emigrants, will develop lasting bonds among themselves to be more effective and will remain in constant contact. Particularly indispensable is a systematic and planned activity of protecting Polish girls who emigrate from the danger threatening them from merchants of the white-slave traffic. In connection with this matter, attempts should be

made to obtain from the government state protection for girls travelling in order to earn a living.

- The Congress resolves that the Polish representatives in the United States request that the Federal government of the United States open an American Consulate in Krakow.

- The Congress requests of its Polish deputies in the state legislatures that they use their full influence in the respective governments in order to establish immigration offices in the communities which are the major centers of immigration activity.

- The Congress requests that the *Sejm* of the Kingdom of Galicia and Lodomeria together with the Grand Duchy of Krakow establish in the United States as soon as possible a branch of the National Bank of Lwow, so that it is easier for Polish emigrants in America to send money to their native land and conversely from Galicia to emigrants in America -- or to authorize the National Bank in Lwow to entrust its representation in these matters to the Polish banks in America.

- The Polish National Congress in Washington turns to all countrymen residing in the provinces which constituted the former Polish Republic with the charge that they not sell land that is still kept in Polish hands to people of other nationalities, and in this way prevent the transfer of Polish land into foreign hands.

- The Polish National Congress in Washington considers it necessary and ardently recommends that in all three partitions the Polish people organize in such a fashion that with the help of proper institutions they can maintain the present level of Polish land ownership.

- The Congress expresses the fear that the continued accumulation of the Polish population in the cities and large industrial centers of the eastern United States may cause decreases in workers' wages and, with constantly rising prices in the cities, will make the economic development of immigrants more difficult.

- In the interest not so much of economics, but in the national interest of our emigration, we should direct the Poles who have already settled in the United States and the new arrivals who come to the United States with the intention of permanent residence, to work in agriculture in the states in which the Poles already own sizable amounts of land and where in time, with the further steady and consciously set goal of colonization, their influence will, of necessity, grow, until they obtain the desired self-government.

The Educational Section accepted the resolutions of the Polish Medical Society in America:

1. To influence Polish papers to cease advertising all patented medicines harmful to health, also the announcements of fraudulent medical institutions, which with their misleading advertisements cause much harm to the health and economy of the Polish people.

2. To influence all institutions and associations which promulgate the health and welfare of the nation to use all possible means to stop drunkenness.

3. The Polish Medical Society in America resolved that all members (physicians) conscientiously investigate hygiene and all improvement in factories, workshops, mines, etc., which are not applied in spite of the law of the given state.

The Educational Section, discussing the question of education from a perspective general to all three partitions and America, approved the following resolution:

- Acknowledging that Polish people in separate provinces find themselves in different conditions to which they have to accommodate their institutions, we believe that:

The general goal of the Polish school is: the moral, intellectual and physical education of the young generation in the national spirit, excluding all party and clerical tendencies. (Motion by deputy J. Moszczenski.)

On this basis, the Educational Section addresses the education of the Polish Nation in America and recommends:

- To create an organization of an educational council or body whose goal would be to implement the following points:

a) To implement a uniform educational system in the Polish schools. (Motion by delegate S.K. Sass.)

b) To obtain educational textbooks for Polish schools.

c) To obtain suitable, competent teachers.

d) To propagate knowledge in the broadest meaning of the word among adult Polish emigrants, so that those who return to the native land could propagate there the commendable results of popular education. (Motion b, c, d, by delegate J.J. Hertmanowicz.)

e) To attempt to introduce into American elementary schools classes in the Polish language, and into high schools Polish history and literature. (Motion by delegate Stefania Chmielinska.)

f) To make an effort to open in the public libraries Polish sections under Polish supervision. (Motion by J. Kudlicka.)

g) To establish relations with European academic associations in order to be able to import the best and newest works and academic textbooks. (Motion by Dr. Lewandowski.)

+ + + + + + +

The motion regarding the independence of Poland caused a long and animated discussion -- not because any of the delegates denied us, the Poles, the right and the duty to strive towards achieving the political independence of our Fatherland, Poland, but a contentious point of the discussion was the question whether it is needed and necessary to vote on such a motion.

Many delegates discussed this motion, analyzing in detail the arguments for -- among them Mr. A. Debski, S. Reizacher and others spoke eloquently and convincingly in its favor -- and against passing it. Finally Dr. A. Doboszynski spoke in favor of passing it, on the assumption that since this motion was presented to the Chamber, it would have been out of place to reject it and somehow deny the just rights and endeavors to achieve the independence of Poland.

Out of the organizations represented at the Congress, all supported the motion, namely the Polish National Alliance, whose president proposed and authored the motion, and the Polish Women's Alliance, the Alliance of Polish Armies, the Singers, and the Young People's Alliance, as well as other organizations and associations -- with the single exception of the delegate J.B. Wleklinski, who protested on behalf of the Polish Falcons Alliance in the United States of America and Canada, as its president, against this resolution*.

After passing this motion, Professor Majerski, who was in principle against discussing this motion at the Congress, in a moment of excitement put the chairman's gavel in the hands of the second president, Mr. Sypniewski, and went to an adjacent room for a short period of time. The debate of the plenary session continued until 11 p.m. At the end the Chamber expressed heartfelt thanks to the Polish National Alliance for convening the Congress. After the singing of the hymn *Boze cos Polske,* the First Polish National Congress concluded.

* Mr. J.B. Wleklinski was forced to resign from his position of President at the next meeting of the Falcons on May 20, 1910.

Note:

The Polish National Congress was the first of its kind in the history of Polonia and took place in the capital of the United States following the dedication of the monuments to Pulaski and Kosciuszko by President William Howard Taft.

Sponsorship of the Congress was in the hands of the Polish National Alliance and representatives from the clergy and the Catholic fraternals declined to participate in its deliberations. Attending the four day long gathering were leaders of the Alliance and representatives of like-minded Polonia groups such as the Falcons, the Polish Women's Alliance, the Singers and numerous smaller associations. A number of individuals from partitioned Poland were also in attendance.

Chairman of the Congress was Thomas Siemiradzki, Editor in Chief of the newspapers of the Polish National Alliance. Romuald Piatkowski, another Alliance activist, served as the secretary of the Congress; his 1911 volume summarizing the events in Washington richly memorializes what took place.

Alexander Debski of the Polish Socialist Alliance served as the Secretary of the Program committee. Siemiradzki chaired the controversial political section of the Congress, while John Smulski of Chicago chaired the Economic-Emigration section. Dr. John Czaki chaired the Educational section.

Author of the controversial resolution in favor of Poland's independence was Marian Steczynski, President of the Polish National Alliance. At the time of the Congress, there were two separate Polish Falcons organizations, the larger of which was connected to the PNA. Following Wleklinski's removal as head of Falcons' group allied to the PNA he was replaced by another Chicagoan, John Kikulski. The two Falcons organizations reunited in 1912 as an independent movement.

3. AIMS AND TASKS OF THE NATIONAL DEPARTMENT AUGUST 17, 1916

(a) To cooperate with the Polish organizations in Europe which are working for the restoration of all the Polish lands to independence;

(b) To support all efforts to achieve Poland's independence;

(c) To broaden opinion in America in favor of Poland's restoration to sovereignty within borders guaranteeing its viability and strength as an essential postulate of justice, humanity and lasting international peace;

(d) To watch over all news and information about Poland so as to correct any false or unfounded charges and attacks upon the Polish nation that appear in the press;

(e) To organize support in favor of all efforts to aid in recovery of Polish economic life;

(f) To work on behalf of the organization of Polish national life in America;

(g) To maintain its own permanent representative both in Europe and in Washington, D.C. with the aim of defending and caring for Poland's interests and in keeping informed on all issues pertaining to Poland.

These are aims with which everyone in the Polish emigration can solidarize.

Therefore, called by the will of our organized Polonia to take responsibility for our emigration's political work in America, we stand before you filled with confidence that you will lend a fraternal hand to our cause for the political and economic rebirth of our Fatherland.

We will not close the door on anyone who as a fellow Pole feels himself in agreement with our patriotic plan and who wishes to work with us. There is work enough for everyone. What we do not recognize are any artificial passions caused by partisan differences or any regional divisions linked to pro-Russian, Prussian or Austrian leanings. We do strongly believe all Poles, whether in Poland or in the emigration should hold but one common objective -- a free, united and independent Poland!

Differences over the means to achieve this objective do not entitle anyone to make foolish criticisms of others or to engage in name calling. Let us not waste our energies in belittling ourselves in the eyes of others by such fruitless in-fighting -- instead let us concentrate all our efforts, spiritual and material, into making this organization a powerful center of productive activity that will lead to the achievement of our common aim.

Let us also not allow ourselves to become partisans identified with the position of the various partitioning powers. This will only divide and weaken our cause. One thing is certain -- none of the partitioners will willingly give Poland its independence and therefore we must not allow ourselves to blindly accept the promises they might make.

Fellow countrymen! We have much work before us. We must use all our resources even to accomplish part of our task. The people of our Fatherland are counting on us -- will we fail to meet their expectations? Never! Let us thus draw our ranks together without regard for camps or parties. Let us create one powerful movement whose solidarity can enormously influence the future fate of Poland. So help us God!

Officers of the National Department of the Polish Central Relief Committee

C.W.Sypniewski, President

Dr. Francis Fronczak, Secretary

J.F. Smulski, Chairman of the Executive Committee

Casimir Zychlinski, Deputy Chairman

Henry Setmajer, Secretary

Peter Rostenkowski, Treasurer

Directors: Rev. Bronislas Celichowski, Rev. W. Zapala, Anna Neumann, Stanislas Szwajkart, Francis Rezmerowski

4. TELEGRAM FROM PRESIDENT FRANKLIN D. ROOSEVELT TO THE DELEGATES TO THE FOUNDING MEETING OF THE POLISH AMERICAN CONGRESS IN BUFFALO, NEW YORK, MAY 27, 1944.

I take pleasure in sending greetings to the Polish American Congress. All of us are proud of the contributions made by Americans of Polish ancestry to the development of our country, and particularly of the unsparing efforts of this group of Americans in our war effort, at the front, in our factories, and in our farms. It is the unity of purpose and spirit of cooperation, which all the citizens of our country have shown in meeting the supreme test of war that will assure victory and a just and equitable peace.

Franklin D. Roosevelt

5. MEMORIAL OF THE POLISH AMERICAN CONGRESS TO FRANKLIN DELANO ROOSEVELT PRESIDENT OF THE UNITED STATES OF AMERICA, MAY 30, 1944.

Mr. President:

This historic assembly of twenty five hundred duly authorized delegates representing over six million citizens of Polish ancestry assembled, in the city of Buffalo, N.Y. the 28, 29 and 30th day of May 1944, constituting the Polish American Congress, to devise means for intensifying service to our Country, deem it our duty to report to you, our President and Commander-in-Chief, and to place before you our heart-felt appeal for aid to one of our Allies, Poland.

We raise our voices today to bespeak the cause of Poland because we are deeply conscious of an old and noble friendship, of a prideworthy heritage bequeathed to us from the days when our forefathers fought and died for the glory and freedom of this country to this day when our beloved sons are giving their lives in the same spirit and for the same cause. We invoke the noblest ideals and principles of the United States, following in the footsteps of the many great Americans, both before and after Woodrow Wilson, who have defended Poland's cause.

We fully endorse the position adopted by you in recognizing the Polish government in London as the only legal, constitutional and representative government of Poland and trust that this recognition based on fair premises of law and fact, will undergo no changes until the whole of the Polish people, entirely free of outside pressure, shall independently and of its own free will, chose its own government.

We are gratefully aware of the fact that the government of the United States still firmly refuses to recognize any territorial changes which have been brought by use of force in Europe, especially in Poland since September 1939, and that it continues to sustain the assurances made to that effect.

We have been heartened by the publication of the noble tenets embodied in the Four Freedoms and the declarations of our aims contained in the Atlantic Charter.

The democratic world considers the Atlantic Charter as an expression of the true and just principles for the settlement of the problems of all the oppressed nations. We submit that these principles should in no way be amended, modified or abridged.

Every nation is now looking up to the United States as the country which has the moral and material power to lead the United Nations. Their hopes are pinned on the United States, their faith is built on trust that we shall not let them down when the end of their misery is approaching and the last opportunity to rise in crucial battle is near.

We are in favor of a United Nations council to coordinate post war planning and through it lay the foundations for collective security and collective responsibility.

Our victory must mean not only the destruction of the military might of Germany and Japan, not only the triumph of our superior armies or military genius, but the ultimate vindication of our ideals as expressed in the Atlantic Charter and the Four Freedoms.

America need not surrender her ideals and principles or appease any of her Allies by accepting exigencies which violate our honor or sense of justice. We hold that the comradeship in arms imposes upon the United States full moral responsibility not only for our own deeds but also for the deeds and aims of our Allies.

The Polish cause is clearly of great concern to the United States and the rest of the world. The permanency of the peace will depend upon the successful and just solution of the problem of Poland. It engages the sympathy of our Country and challenges its sincerity and determination. In expressing the hope that you will as hitherto pursue the only true American course, we especially plead with you, Mr. President, not to permit the United States to be involved in designs against Poland and its future, whether in the East or in the West.

Poland has not broken faith, nor has the Polish nation laid down arms or provided a Quisling. Faithful from the beginning, loyal to her ideals, the first to fight, unwilling to yield her liberty, her soil or the souls of her citizens, Poland was the first to put an end to the era of appeasement. Poland was the only nation willing to sacrifice herself so that the rest of the world might become aware of the imminent danger and prepare to meet it. She was almost simultaneously invaded by her two neighbors, inhumanly treated by both, tortured and destroyed - not broken in spirit or faith.

Poland carried on! Her gallant fliers destroyed one out of every eight enemy planes in the battle of Britain; her soldiers fought in France, in Africa, in Norway and now, at a great sacrifice, in Italy. Polish sailors have given their lives, transporting our arms to England, Iceland, Iran, Africa and Russia; the Polish underground has carried on a relentless war paying with hundreds of innocent lives for every German criminal killed - all for the common cause.

Poland has the right to liberty, and full sovereignty, a right so dearly purchased and so well earned.

The occupation and retention of Polish soil by invading Russian Armies would establish an accomplished fact that would be in total disregard of international morality and justice. It is a challenge to the United Nations very similar to that caused by the occupation of the Rhineland by Nazi Germany, and no less pregnant with disastrous consequences of moral defeat than was Germany's act and brutal use of military force.

Russia's rejection of our Country's offer of mediation causes serious apprehension in our minds and grave fears that the peace is endangered and our mission in Europe jeopardized. Let us not risk the danger of winning the war and losing the peace.

Deeply concerned and dedicated to the ideal of the United States and its leading role in the destiny of the world, we appeal to you, Mr. President, to accept no compromise incompatible with the honor and tradition of this Country, nor to accept facts accomplished by injustice and violence. Every drop of American blood shed on the battlefields should be redeemed by liberty and justice for those in whose behalf we are making the supreme sacrifice.

The subjugation of half of Poland would be a great injustice. Poland deserves well of the United States. Poland has the right to be free, independent and to have her territorial integrity maintained. She has earned the right to claim the assistance of the United States in securing these rights and the privilege of participating in the making of the future world as an equal among nations which have fought by our side.

We are confident that you will take full cognizance of the justice of Poland's cause. With expressions of the deepest faith and esteem we are

Yours respectfully,

POLISH AMERICAN CONGRESS
Charles Rozmarek
John J. Olejniczak
Dr. Bronislaw L. Smykowski
Helen L. Sambor
Zygmunt Grabowski
John F. Mikuta
Thaddeus M. Machrowicz
Wladyslaw S. Pytko
Msgr. Joseph C. Dworzak, D.D.
Thaddeus V. Adesko

6. RESOLUTION OF THE POLISH AMERICAN CONGRESS, MAY 30, 1944.

Three thousand one hundred and seventy four delegates gathered in council at the call of the Polish Congress in Buffalo on May 28, 29 and 30th, authorized by mandates given to them by societies, organizations, churches and clubs in their communities to speak in behalf and in the name of 6,000,000 Americans have unanimously voted to address the following appeal to the civilized world now engaged in total war against the enemies of democracy.

We are mindful that this appeal is being written on Memorial Day, when our Nation pays tribute to those who have given their lives for the United States. Many thousands of old graves of Americans of Polish ancestry, many monuments of Polish heroes, will be decorated today with the American flag. Thousands of mothers will weep today, their hearts will bleed not knowing where the graves of their beloved sons are.

There is in this sacrifice a holy unity between them and all the mothers in America, Poland and other lands.

We are also mindful that the thoughts and sentiments of this appeal are being written on the eve of the invasion of Europe. We all live in grave anticipation of news that will announce victory - and the deaths of many.

We can, therefore, speak only in solemn seriousness in the name of our beloved ones who are there with our consent and with our blessing.

To all of us there shall be only one consolation that will redeem this great sacrifice - the knowledge that they have not died in vain. The principles for which they fought are accepted by all the Nations who signed the Atlantic Charter.

Poland signed the Atlantic Charter accepting these principles as rights as well as obligations.

We wish to remind the world that on September 1st, 1939, when the German barbarians invaded Poland there was only ONE boundary question. Poland's boundaries were violated by the Germans. The whole world stood up in arms BECAUSE the boundaries of one Nation were violated by force and brutality of another Nation.

England and France declared war because this violation of a principle challenged international morality, the principle that the boundaries of every country are a sacred responsibility of the whole world. One could enumerate many sins of diplomacy that have brought upon us this global war. All started with violations of boundaries, as in China, Ethiopia, Austria and Czechoslovakia. A fourth partition of Poland by any Nation would be dangerous to peace and tend to destroy the moral influence and responsibility of the United States. Our soldiers undertook the perilous trip to the battlefronts of the world and will march on carrying the flag of the United States as a symbol that America not only lends and leases money, food and arms, but also lends and leases the lives of millions of Americans who are carrying with them the American tenets of a new world embodied in the Four Freedoms and the Atlantic Charter. This specifically applies to Russia, to whom Poland as one of the United Nations will be the best guarantee against Germany. Poland had repeatedly rejected German attempts to win her into an alliance against Russia, always faithful to her pledges and pacts.

Unjustified propaganda claims that Poland may become a fascist country. There need be so such fear. Poland had been partitioned three times before - because she was a democracy and she now, sacrificed herself for the cause of democracy rejecting fascism and religious oppression.

Russia need not fear Poland - unless she fears democracy.

The Atlantic Charter pledges that "no territorial or other aggrandizement should be tolerated."

- That the United Nations "desire to see no territorial changes that do not accord with the freely expressed wishes of the people concerned."

The Polish people will never give accord to Russia claims or grabs by force. They will continue to repeat this pledge of the Charter and we Americans shall join them because the Atlantic Charter is America's moral responsibility to humanity.

The Atlantic Charter plainly states that:

"The United Nations believe that all nations of the world - for realistic as well as spiritual reasons, must come to the abandonment of use of force."

It is for this reason - that we resolve to unite our material and spiritual forces to defend the Atlantic Charter, which is a passport for every American soldier on his way to victory, and any attempted act repudiating the Atlantic Charter is a thrust at the unity of nations.

We solemnly appeal to our fellow Americans and to the citizens of all civilized countries to stand by and adhere to collective responsibility for Poland. This is a test of international morality.

To the Polish government in London, the only legitimate and constitutional representative government of Poland, to the Poles whose country is again a battlefield in the common cause of civilization and Christianity, to the gallant soldier in the American Armed Forces, to our sons in the Polish Armed Forces, and to the armies of all United Nations we send this message that we dedicate ourselves to the end that they will not have suffered, fought and died in vain.

RESOLUTIONS COMMITTEE
B.F. Gunther
Manfield G. Amlicke
Peter P. Yolles
Rev. F. J. Kachnowski
Honorata B. Wolowska

7. CONGRATULATORY LETTER TO PRESIDENT ROOSEVELT ON HIS REELECTION FROM PRESIDENT CHARLES ROZMAREK OF THE POLISH AMERICAN CONGRESS NOVEMBER 14, 1944.

Dear Mr. President:

In conveying to you, Mr. President, sincere and cordial congratulations on your victory of November 7 I am certain that millions of Americans of Polish ancestry join me in these felicitations. As the election returns from the localities in which they reside conclusively prove, they cast their ballots overwhelmingly for your re-election.

Americans of Polish descent voted for you, Mr. President, because in this crucial period of history, they regard you not only as the preeminent pilot of the American ship of state, a distinguished and experienced statesman in the field of foreign relations, but likewise as a sincere friend and champion in behalf of the righteous cause of Poland and other subjugated nations.

They firmly believe that in keeping with the noble ideals of the Atlantic Charter initiated by you, in keeping with the American principles of "fair play" of which you are an ardent adherent and follower, and in keeping with the century and a half old friendship between Poland and America, dating from the birth of the American nation--from the times of Washington, Kosciuszko and Pulaski--you will not allow our trusted ally, Poland, to be deprived of one half of her ancient lands. Nor do these Americans of Polish stock believe that you will allow a foreign-sponsored puppet government to be forced upon Poland against the will of her people. Freedom is a God-given right and the thirteen million inhabitants of the century-old Polish lands to the east, which are now being coveted by a powerful neighbor, never renounced their right to be free.

At the conference which took place at the White House on October 11th, as spokesman for the Polish American Congress delegation, I presented to you, Mr. President, a plea of justice for martyred Poland. Seeking no personal or political benefits of any nature, and being motivated solely by the sacred obligation as an American and a Christian to champion the rights of the oppressed, I again reiterated that plea at the conference you so graciously accorded me, during your last visit to Chicago. From the assurances given, we have every reason to believe that the Atlantic Charter will not be abandoned.

To permit Poland, fighting our common enemy the longest, to be torn apart and other freedom-loving nations to be obliterated, would not only be a violation of our war aims, a travesty of justice but a major blow to freedom. America, faithful to the best traditions of her noble history, cried out against the ruthless annexation of Poland and the Baltic Countries in 1939. What was wrong then can never be right today.

The six million loyal Americans united in the Polish American Congress, desire to assure you, Mr. President, that in all your efforts to achieve an early and complete victory of freedom for all the United Nations, big and small, and a just and permanent peace to follow, you shall find in us your sincere, zealous and faithful supporters.

May Divine Providence grant you, Mr. President, moral courage, strength and health for the all-important tasks before you for the good of the United States and all humanity.

> Sincerely yours,
> (-) CHARLES ROZMAREK
> President of the Polish American Congress

8. EXCERPTS FROM PRESIDENT FRANKLIN D. ROOSEVELT'S ADDRESS TO THE CONGRESS OF THE UNITED STATES ON THE RESULTS OF THE YALTA CONFERENCE, MARCH 1, 1945.

... But I am sure that under the agreements reached at Yalta, there will be a more stable political Europe than ever before.

Of course, once there has been a free expression of the people's will in any country, our immediate responsibility ends--with the exception only of such action as may be agreed on in the International Security Organization that we hope to set up.

The United Nations must also soon begin to help these liberated areas adequately to reconstruct their economy so that they are ready to resume their places in the world. The Nazi war machine has stripped them of raw materials and machine tools and trucks and locomotives. The have left the industry of these places stagnant and much of the agricultural areas are unproductive. The Nazis have left a ruin in their wake.

To start the wheels running again is not a mere matter of relief. It is to the national interest that all of us see to it that these liberated areas are again made self-supporting and productive so that they do not need continuous relief from us. I should say that was an argument based on plain common sense.

One outstanding example of joint action by the three major Allied powers in the liberated areas was the solution reached on Poland. The whole Polish question was a potential source of trouble in postwar Europe--as it has been sometimes before--and we came to the Conference determined to find a common ground for its solution. And we did--even though everybody does not agree with us, obviously.

Our objective was to help to create a strong, independent, and prosperous Nation. That is the thing we must always remember, those words, agreed to by Russia, by Britain, and by the United States; the objective of making Poland a strong, independent, and prosperous Nation, with a government ultimately to be selected by the Polish people themselves.

To achieve that objective, it was necessary to provide for the formation of a new government much more representative than had been possible while Poland was enslaved. There were, as you know, two governments--one in London, one in Lublin--practically in Russia. Accordingly, steps were taken at Yalta to reorganize the existing Provisional Government in Poland on a broader democratic basis, so as to include democratic leaders now in Poland and those abroad. This new, reorganized government will be recognized by all of us as the temporary government of Poland. Poland needs a temporary government in the worst way--an *ad interim* government, I think is another way of putting it.

However, the new Polish Provisional Government of National Unity will be pledged to holding a free election as soon as possible on the basis of universal suffrage and a secret ballot.

Throughout history, Poland has been the corridor through which attacks on Russia have been made. Twice in this generation, Germany has struck at Russia through this corridor. To insure European security and world peace, a strong and independent Poland is necessary to prevent that from happening again.

The decision with respect to the boundaries of Poland was, frankly, a compromise. I did not agree with all of it, by any means, but we did not go as far as Britain wanted, in certain areas; we did not go so far as Russia wanted, in certain areas; and we did not go so far as I wanted, in certain areas. It was a compromise. The decision is one, however, under which the Poles will receive compensation in territory in the North and West in exchange for what they lose by the Curzon Line in the East. The limits of the western border will be permanently fixed in the final Peace Conference. We know, roughly, that it will include--in the new, strong Poland-- quite a large slice of what now is called Germany. And it was agreed, also, that the new Poland will have a large and long coast line, and many new harbors. Also, that most of East Prussia will go to Poland. A corner of it will go to Russia. Also, that the anomaly of the Free State of Danzig will come to an end; I think Danzig would be a lot better if it were Polish.

It is well known that the people east of the Curzon Line--just for example, here is why I compromised--are predominantly white Russian and Ukrainian--they are not Polish; and a very great majority of the people west of the line are predominantly Polish, except in that part of East Prussia and eastern

Germany, which will go to the new Poland. As far back as 1919, representatives of the Allies agreed that the Curzon Line represented a fair boundary between the two peoples. And you must remember, also, that there had not been any Polish government before 1919 for a great many generations.

I am convinced that the agreement on Poland, under the circumstances, is the most hopeful agreement possible for a free, independent, and prosperous Polish state.

The Crimea Conference was a meeting of the three major military powers on whose shoulders rested chief responsibility and burden of the war...

The Conference in the Crimea was a turning point--I hope in our history and therefore in the history of the world. There will soon be presented to the Senate of the United States and to the American people a great decision that will determine the fate of the United States--and of the world--for generations to come.

There can be no middle ground here. We shall have to take the responsibility for world collaboration, or we shall have to bear the responsibility for another world conflict.

I know that the word "planning" is not looked upon with favor in some circles. In domestic affairs tragic mistakes have been made by reason of lack of planning; and, on the other hand, many great improvements in living, and many benefits to the human race, have been accomplished as a result of adequate, intelligent planning--reclamation of desert areas, developments of whole river valleys, and provision for adequate housing.

The same will be true in relations between Nations. For the second time in the lives of most of us this generation is face to face with the objective of preventing wars. To meet that objective, the Nations of the world will either have a plan or they will not. The groundwork of a plan has now been furnished, and has been submitted to humanity for discussion and decision.

No plan is perfect. Whatever is adopted at San Francisco will doubtless have to be amended time and again over the years, just as our own Constitution has been.

No one can say exactly how long any plan will last. Peace can endure only so long as humanity really insists upon it, and is willing to work for it--and sacrifice for it.

Twenty-five years ago, American fighting men looked to the statesmen of the world to finish the work of peace for which they fought and suffered. We failed them then. We cannot fail them again, and expect the world again to survive.

The Crimea Conference was a successful effort by the three leading Nations to find a common ground for peace. It ought to spell the end of the system of unilateral action, the exclusive alliances, the spheres of influence, the balances of power, and all the other expedients that have been tried for centuries--and have always failed.

We propose to substitute for all these, a universal organization in which all peace-loving Nations will finally have a chance to join.

I am confident that the Congress and the American people will accept the results of this Conference as the beginnings of a permanent structure of peace upon which we can begin to build, under God, that better world in which our children and grandchildren--yours and mine, the children and grandchildren of the whole world--must live, and can live...

9. EXCERPTS FROM THE POLISH AMERICAN CONGRESS MEMORANDUM TO PRESIDENT ROOSEVELT IN CONNECTION WITH THE YALTA CONFERENCE, MARCH 15, 1945.

...We address you, Mr. President, not as Poles but as Americans....An injustice was committed against Poland at the Yalta Conference. But an injustice was also perpetrated against the United States, since American principles adopted by our government with respect to the Four Freedoms and the Atlantic Charter were brutally trampled there. American wartime aid, whose objective had involved the making of a just peace with freedom and independence to all nations--the basis for our struggle against Nazism--was betrayed...

Poland has been the victim of unspeakable cruelties unparalleled in history. Its occupiers, German and Soviet alike, have subjected the nation to great oppression. Even here in America Poland has been victimized in an unheard of campaign of slander at the hands of communists, both self-proclaimed and covert. The Polish government-in-exile, comprised of individuals who were the first to fight Nazi Germany, has also been continually labelled "fascist" and "reactionary"...

We further protest the unjust decisions that were made at Yalta ...the windfall transfer of Polish territories to Russia ...and the shameful determination of a new Polish government without any consultation with any of its true representatives. Our Polish ally indeed has been deprived of even the rights that criminals are afforded in defending themselves...

All of this runs entirely counter to the traditional character of American conduct in its dedication to justice, honor and fair play. (At Yalta our government behaved more in the manner) of Poland's historic European partitioners. It is surely a profane tragedy that in our President's first decisions as they related to Europe's future he would ratify the fifth partition of Poland and cooperate in the fashioning of a Polish puppet regime manufactured in Moscow...

For the Polish American Congress: Charles Rozmarek, President; Teofil A. Starzynski, Vice President; Frank Januszewski, Vice President; Ignace Nurkiewicz, Director; U.S. Congressmen John Lesinski, Martin Gorski, William Link.

10. PRESIDENT HARRY TRUMAN'S SPECIAL MESSAGE TO THE CONGRESS ON U.S. PARTICIPATION IN THE UNITED NATIONS RELIEF AND REHABILITATION ADMINISTRATION, NOVEMBER 13, 1945.

To the Congress of the United States of America:
This country has pledged itself to do all that is reasonably possible to alleviate the suffering of our war-torn allies and to help them begin the task of restoring their economic productivity. The United Nations Relief and Rehabilitation Administration is one of the most important instrumentalities for accomplishing this great task.

As I stated in my message to the Congress on September 6, 1945, the forty-seven nations of the Council of United Nations Relief and Rehabilitation Administration determined at their Third Meeting in London last August that contributions beyond those originally made would be necessary if we expect to complete the minimum tasks assigned to UNRRA. The Council recommended, on the motion of the United States Delegate, that each member country, whose territory had not been invaded by the enemy, should contribute an additional amount equal to one percent of its national income for the fiscal year 1943.

In accordance with this recommendation, the United States' share would be $1,350,000,000, matching our original contribution authorized by the Act of Congress of March 28, 1944.

The original contributions of all the member nations have been applied principally to the activities of UNRRA in providing relief and rehabilitation assistance to the countries of eastern and southeastern Europe, and to the care of United Nations displaced persons stranded in enemy territory. UNRRA, of course, does not undertake relief or rehabilitation responsibilities in either Germany or Japan.

The invaded countries of northwest Europe, comprising France, Belgium, Holland, Denmark and Norway, by and large, possess sufficient resources in foreign currency and credit to acquire their own essential imports from abroad. Direct assistance to northwest Europe is, therefore, not being furnished by UNRRA.

Poland, Czechoslovakia, Yugoslavia, Greece and Albania, on the other hand, not only have suffered greatly at the hands of the enemy in the course of the war but they are almost entirely without foreign exchange or credit resources. Consequently to date they have been the chief objects of UNRRA's activity.

UNRRA has undertaken a limited program of $50,000,000 in Italy to provide for the health and care of children, and expectant or nursing mothers.

Italy, since her participation in the war as a co-belligerent with the United Nations, has contributed substantially in both manpower and facilities to the Allied victory, becoming, at the same time, one of the most severely contested battlefields of the war. The destruction and needs there are appalling. Italy has virtually no foreign exchange resources and without the aid of UNRRA the country might well lapse into starvation.

UNRRA has also assisted in the care and repatriation of millions of allied victims of Axis aggression who were deported to and enslaved in Germany. It has initiated a preliminary program of assistance to China.

By the end of this year UNRRA anticipates that all the funds which will be made available to it from all sources in accordance with the original contributions will have been spent or encumbered. The flow of supplies purchased with these funds cannot last beyond the early spring.

The end of the war with Japan has made it possible to estimate the magnitude of the relief requirements of China and other Far Eastern areas. Reports on the European harvest of 1945 reveal a serious shortage of all types of foodstuffs.

China presents the largest of all the relief responsibilities which UNRRA now faces. With inadequate supplies and resources it has struggled bravely for eight years to combat the enemy as well as the ravages of famine, disease and inflation. Other programs are required for Korea and Formosa, two areas of the Far East which are now being restored to the peaceful ranks of the United Nations after decades of Japanese oppression and extortion.

UNRRA proposes the extension of aid to Austria. This proposal is in accordance with the Moscow and Potsdam Declarations by the major powers to the effect that Austria should be treated independently of Germany and encouraged to resume the free and peaceful role which it played before being invaded by Hitler's legions.

A limited program of aid is also intended for the Soviet Republics of White Russia and the Ukraine. These areas constituted the principal battlefields in the struggle between Russia and Germany. They were the scene of some of the worst German atrocities, devastation and pillage.

The recommended additional contributions will hardly suffice to permit UNRRA to meet the most urgent and immediate needs for relief and rehabilitation for which it is responsible. We hope to fulfill a substantial part of this contribution through the use of military and lend-lease supplies which have become surplus since the surrender of our enemies.

I know that America will not remain indifferent to the call of human suffering. This is particularly true when it is suffering on the part of those who by sacrifice and courage kept the enemy from realizing the fruits of his early victories and from bringing his military might to bear upon our own shores.

UNRRA is the chosen instrument of forty-seven United Nations to meet the immediate relief and rehabilitation needs of the invaded countries.

UNRRA is the first of the international organizations to operate in the post-war period, one which the United States originally sponsored and in which it has played a leading part. Apart from purely humanitarian consideration its success will do much to prove the possibility of establishing order and cooperation in a world finally at peace.

I, therefore, request the Congress to authorize a new appropriation of $1,350,000,000 for participation in the activities of UNRRA.*

HARRY S. TRUMAN

* On December 18, 1945 the President approved legislation enabling the United States to continue its participation in UNRRA.

11. PRESIDENT CHARLES ROZMAREK'S STATEMENT TO THE PRESS IN PARIS, FRANCE, SEPTEMBER 12, 1946.

Our delegation has come to Paris in order to submit to Secretary Byrnes the views of 6,000,000 Americans of Polish descent concerning recent developments in the international forum. Peace and the future course of international relations depend on the way in which difficulties now outstanding will be tackled. As Americans of Polish descent, we take a particularly keen interest in the fate of Poland. We want to ascertain that international decisions which affect Poland are wholly consistent with the principles of justice, liberty and respect for law, principles embodied in our American democracy. We represent the Polish emigration in the U.S.A., an emigration of workers -- its founders were Polish peasants who came to the New World in quest of work and bread. As such no one can accuse us of acting from motives of material gain. We only demand that Poland should have her full independence restored and that she should be allowed to decide for herself in matters concerning her fate. It is, however, not only the interests of the country of our forefathers, for which we have a deep sentimental attachment, that we have come to defend. As American citizens we have also at heart the security of the U.S.A. We believe that peace and security can only be attained if all nations are given equal rights and relations between them are based on respect for law and not deference to power and material wealth...

We are of the opinion that thus far all the decisions of the Big Three over the Polish issue, have been in evident contradiction to the obligations of America and Great Britain towards that most faithful ally and are besides manifestly inconsistent with the principles of the Atlantic Charter by which all the United Nations have pledged themselves to abide. We demand, therefore, that the Polish question be either brought up for full review at the Peace Conference, or be raised at a UN meeting. We demand that Poland be freed from the foreign occupation under which it now finds itself, that she be freed from the government of foreign agents which was forced upon her by the Big Three and is now kept in power by Soviet military support. We demand moreover that the Polish Nation which is being treated worse than Hitler's satellites be allowed to determine her own fate and that the territories of which it was unlawfully deprived on the strength of the arbitrary Yalta decisions be now returned. We affirm, that if elections were to take place in the now existing conditions and throughout the territories administered at present from Warsaw, they would merely be a fraud designed to legalize the existence of a Soviet regime in Poland and to endorse Poland's partition effected by the Big Three at Yalta.

In the course of our visit to Paris two major issues have come to the forefront of international discussion, issues which affect directly not only the fate of Poland, but also that of the political structure of Europe and more generally of peace. First among them is the question of Poland's western frontiers. Second, is the plan to base the future of peace on the division of the world into two spheres of influence, the American and the Soviet.

Secretary Byrnes' statement which he made in his already somewhat notorious Stuttgart speech to the effect that Poland "ceded" her eastern provinces in exchange for territories which she is to be given in the West and that Poland's present western frontier which runs along the line of the rivers Oder and Niesse is not definite and can still be rectified in favour of Germany, has met with violent disfavour among wide masses of Americans of Polish descent. Our delegation received by cable from the U.S.A. a number of strongly worded messages of protest. We have never considered and we can never consider the recovery by Poland of her western provinces up to the Oder-Niesse line as compensation for the loss of her eastern territories. Poland had never "ceded" the eastern half of her territory to Russia. She was deprived of it by a unilateral decision of the Big Three at Yalta, a decision in which the Polish Nation has never acquiesced. The acceptance of the Yalta terms by the Warsaw administration is of no significance, since it is a government which was installed in Poland by the Big Three for that very purpose and can on no account be considered as the mouthpiece of the Polish Nation. It should be remembered that the legal Polish Government, which was then still recognized by London and Washington, issued a formal protest against the Yalte decisions and unhesitatingly rejected them.

In so far as Poland's western frontiers are concerned, we believe that the present Oder-Niesse line should at once be recognized as definite and final, and no longer open to future revision. Besides only such a solution would be consistent with the provisions of the Potsdam agreement on the strength of which the present western frontier of Poland was outlined. Though it was agreed at Potsdam that Poland's western frontier would be given full formal recognition at the Peace Conference, the territories up to the Oder-Niesse line handed over to Poland were described as "former" German territories. Moreover all the three Big Powers recognized the necessity of providing for a gradual transfer from those territories of all German population. What better proof could there be that all the Three Big Powers represented at Potsdam already then considered the Oder-Niesse line as Poland's permanent western frontier? Any change of policy in this matter would constitute an additional injustice towards Poland and would meet with determined disapproval and opposition from the Polish Nation and from its many friends throughout the world.

The plan to split the world into two spheres of influence, outlined in Mr. Wallace's latest speech, is to our mind not only thoroughly condemnable, but also fictitious in conception. To effect such a division there would have to exist two opposing imperialisms. We readily acknowledge the existence of an aggressive Soviet imperialism. Its impact is felt by all the nations of Central and Eastern Europe which have found themselves under Soviet domination. But are there any signs of American imperialism? Are there any American soldiers who want to remain in a foreign country after their presence there is no longer essential? Where are the puppet governments brought to power by the armed hand of Washington? Do there exist any exclusive and prohibitive economic agreements forced upon foreign states by the U.S.A. in order to subordinate them to American policy? No one would be more indignant than the American public, if it were told that the U.S.A. entered the Second World War for the sake of winning for herself a sphere of influence. Both in the First and Second World War the American Nation fought not for spheres of influence, but for the reinstatement in international relations of law, justice and liberty. It fought against tyranny and subjugation by power. The

American Nation will feel secure only when it ascertains that the democratic principles of the Atlantic Charter are honestly applied to all the nations without exception.

The first step to prevent Central and Eastern Europe from remaining a constant source of danger to world peace, is to free it from Soviet domination and restore it to liberty. All the nations situated in that area must be allowed to organize their life and cooperation according to their own principles. There are good reasons to believe that after the experience of the Second World War and the Soviet occupation that followed, the nations of Central Europe have grasped the necessity of a far-reaching economic and political integration. The idea of a Central-European Federation which would extend from the shores of the Baltic to the Black Sea, the Aegean and the Adriatic and which would number some 150 million people, has won great popularity. Even back at home in the U.S.A., Americans representing the various nations of Central and Eastern Europe, have found in the slogan "united we stand, divided we fall" common ground on which to base their constructive co-operation.

How grave the conditions in Poland and in other Central and Eastern European countries are is best borne out by the ceaseless flow of refugees to the West as well as by the presence in Germany of over a million DPs who are either unable or unwilling to return to their native countries. To understand fully what is here implied it is enough to recall that here is no one who seeks refuge in the Soviet zone and that among the DPs there are no citizens of states liberated by Great Britain and America.

Our delegation takes especial interest in the fate of the 400,000 Polish DPs dispersed in camps situated in the American, the British and the French zones of occupation. Apart from civilians who were deported by the Germans for forced labour or placed in concentration camps there are also some 100,000 former prisoners of war. These men, though they are entitled to treatment on an equal footing with all other allied soldiers, have been denied these basic rights. Moreover, they are unable to return to their country which finds itself now under Soviet occupation. In those circumstances they should receive at the hands of the American, British and French authorities all the possible care and help. Our delegation is leaving for Germany to make a tour of the camps of Polish DPs, and former Polish prisoners of war.

12. TELEGRAM TO UNITED STATES SECRETARY OF STATE GEORGE C. MARSHALL FROM PRESIDENT ROZMAREK ON THE POLISH ELECTION OF JANUARY 20, 1947.

Hon. George C. Marshall
Secretary of State
Washington, D.C.

The Moscow-engineered Polish elections, held under complete Communist control and characterized by arrests, intimidations, deportations and murder, mark a turn for the worse in international affairs.

The fraudulent Polish elections are a warning of destiny that annexation of all Europe, Asia and eventually of America will take place by similar methods as in Poland, unless stern and effective measures are adopted by the United States, the only country capable of stopping Russia's ruthless drive for world domination.

The flagrant violation of even the meager obligation of holding free elections in Poland, as guaranteed by Yalta, should definitely shatter any illusions that the United States may have concerning the sanctity of Russian pledges. Mikolajczyk's forlorn effort, under pressure of the United States and England, to cooperate with Russia should now thoroughly convince our statesmen that it is impossible to do any legitimate business with Soviet Russia.

The Polish American Congress, the authentic voice of six million Americans of Polish descent, vigorously protests against the crime of dishonest elections aimed at the complete enslavement of the Polish nation. At the same time it calls on the United State Government to repudiate the fake elections, to withhold recognition of the counterfeit government imposed upon the Polish nation by a foreign power and to demand, above all, an immediate United Nations investigation concerning the elections in Poland and the presence of Russian troops in that country.

However, it is done, Soviet domination in Europe must be curbed and Soviet troops and agents must be sent home where they belong if world democracy is to survive.

Stalin has willfully broken his pledges. His Polish puppets have deliberately ignored all American notes of protest with reference to the elections. The next move is now up to our government. What does the U.S., a signatory to the Yalta pact propose to do about the intolerable situation?

The time has come for America, the leading military and economic power on earth to speak courageously and act fearlessly.

Charles Rozmarek
President, Polish American
Congress

13. PRESIDENT TRUMAN'S SPECIAL MESSAGE TO CONGRESS ON THE ADMISSION OF DISPLACED PERSONS, JULY 7, 1947.

To the Congress of the United States:
On several occasions I have advocated legislation to enable a substantial number of displaced persons to enter the United States as immigrants. I stated this view in opening the Second Session of the General Assembly of the United Nations. In the Message on the State of the Union on January 6, 1947, I said:

"...The fact is that the executive agencies are now doing all that is reasonably possible under the limitation of existing law and established quotas. Congressional assistance in the form of new legislation is needed. I urge the Congress to turn its attention to this world problem, in an effort to find ways whereby we can fulfill our responsibilities to these thousands of homeless and suffering refugees of all faiths."

I express appreciation to the Congress for the attention already being given to this problem, an appreciation which appears to be generously shared by the public with increasing understanding of the facts and of our responsibilities.

Because of the urgency of this subject I should like again to call attention to some of its fundamental aspects. We are dealing here solely with an emergency problem growing out of the war--the disposition of a specific group of individuals, victims of war, who have come into the hands of our own and the other Western Allied Armies of Occupation in Europe.

We should not forget how their destiny came into our hands. The Nazi armies, as they swept over Europe, uprooted many millions of men, women, and children from their homes and forced them to work for the German war economy. The Nazis annihilated millions by hardship and persecution. Survivors were taken under the care of the Western Allied Armies, as these Armies liberated them during the conquest of the enemy. Since the end of hostilities, the armies of Occupation have been able to return to their homes some 7,000,000 of these people. But there still remain, in the western zones of Germany and Austria and in Italy, close to a million survivors who are unwilling by reason of political opinion and fear of persecution to return to the areas where they once had homes. The great majority come from the northern Baltic areas, Poland, the Russian Ukraine and Yugoslavia.

The new International Refugee Organization, supported by the contributions of this and other countries, will aid in the care and resettlement of these displaced persons. But, as I have pointed out before, the International Refugee Organization is only a service organization. It cannot impose its will on member countries. Continuance of this Organization and our financial support of its work will be required as long as the problem of these homeless people remains unsolved.

It is unthinkable that they should be left indefinitely in camps in Europe. We cannot turn them out in Germany into the community of the very people who persecuted them. Moreover, the German economy, so devastated by war and so badly overcrowded with the return of people of German origin from neighboring countries, is approaching an economic suffocation which in itself is one of our major problems. Turning these displaced persons into such chaos would be disastrous for them and would seriously aggravate our problems there.

This government has been firm in resisting any proposal to send these people back to their former homes by force, where it is evident that their unwillingness to return is based upon political considerations or fear of persecution. In this policy I am confident I have your support.

These victims of war and oppression look hopefully to the democratic countries to help them rebuild their lives and provide for the future of their children. We must not destroy their hope. The only civilized course is to enable these people to take new roots in friendly soil. Already certain countries of Western Europe and Latin America have opened their doors to substantial numbers of these displaced persons. Plans for making homes for more of them in other countries are under consideration. But our plain duty requires that we join with other nations in solving this tragic problem.

We ourselves should admit a substantial number as immigrants. We have not yet been able to do this because our present statutory quotas applicable to the Eastern European areas from which most of these people come are wholly inadequate for this purpose. Special legislation limited to this particular emergency will therefore be necessary if we are to share with other nations in this enterprise of offering an opportunity for a new life to these people.

I wish to emphasize that there is no proposal for a general revision of our immigration policy as now enunciated in our immigration statues. There is no proposal to waive or lower our present prescribed standards for testing the fitness for admission of every immigrant, including these displaced persons. Those permitted to enter would still have to meet the admission requirements of our existing immigration laws. These laws provide adequate guarantees against the entry of those who are criminals or subversives, those likely to become public charges, and those who are otherwise undesirable.

These displaced persons are hardy and resourceful or they would not have survived. A survey of the occupational backgrounds of those in our Assembly Centers shows a wide variety of professions, crafts, and skills. These are people who oppose totalitarian rule, and who because of their burning faith in the principles of freedom and democracy have suffered untold privation and hardship. Because they are not communists and are opposed to communism, they have staunchly resisted all efforts to induce them to return to communist-controlled areas. In addition, they were our individual allies in the war.

In the light of the vast numbers of people of all countries that we have usefully assimilated into our national life, it is clear that we could readily absorb the relatively small number of these displaced persons who would be admitted. We should not forget that our Nation was founded by immigrants, many of whom fled oppression and persecution. We have thrived on the energy and diversity of many peoples. It is a source of our strength that we number among our people all the major religions, races and national origins.

Most of the individuals in the displaced persons centers already have strong roots in this country--by kinship, religion or national origin. Their occupational background clearly indicates that they can quickly become useful members of our American communities. Their kinsmen, already in the United States, have been vital factors in farm and workshop for generations. They have made lasting contributions to our arts and sciences and political life. They have been numbered among our honored dead on every battlefield of war.

We are dealing with a human problem, a world tragedy. Let us remember that these are fellow human beings now living under conditions which frustrate hope; which make it impossible for them to take any steps, unaided, to build for themselves or their children the foundations of a new life. They live in corroding uncertainty of their future. Their fate is in our hands and must now be decided. Let us join in giving them a chance at decent and self-supporting lives.

I urge the Congress to press forward with its consideration of this subject and to pass suitable legislation as speedily as possible.*

HARRY S. TRUMAN

* On June 25, 1948 the President signed the Displaced Persons Act of 1948 which made possible the admission of approximately 200,000 European Displaced Persons into the United States over a limited period of time.

14. PRESIDENT TRUMAN'S STATEMENT UPON SIGNING A BILL AMENDING THE DISPLACED PERSONS ACT, JUNE 16, 1950.

It is with very great pleasure that I have today signed H.R. 4567, which amends the Displaced Persons Act of 1948.

The improvements embodied in H.R. 4567 now bring the American principles of fair play and generosity to our displaced persons program.

When I reluctantly signed the Displaced Persons Act of 1948, I did so in spite of certain of its provisions which imposed unworkable restrictions and resulted in unfair discriminations. Nevertheless, I felt it was necessary to make a start toward a resettlement program for these victims of totalitarianism who yearned to live as useful citizens in a free country.

I had no doubt then, and I have been confident ever since, that when the will of the American people was truly expressed, these defects in the program would be corrected. This confidence has been fully justified.

H.R. 4567 corrects the discriminations inherent in the previous act. Now, the postwar victims of totalitarianism will be on an equal footing with earlier victims of Nazi aggression.

I am also glad that the new act wisely and generously extends opportunity for immigration to the United States to additional groups of deserving persons who should make fine citizens. Special provisions are made for 10,000 war orphans from the free countries of Europe and for 4,000 European refugees who fled to the Far East to escape one form of totalitarianism and must now flee before a new tyranny. Eighteen thousand honorably discharged veterans of the exiled Polish Army, who were given temporary homes in England after the war, will now have an opportunity to settle permanently in the United States. Ten thousand Greek refugees and 2,000 displaced persons now in Trieste and Italy will also have an opportunity to immigrate to the United States. Provision has been made for the admission into this country of 54,744 refugees and expellees of German origin. In all the amended law authorizes a total of 400,744 visas, including the 172,230 which have been issued up to May 31, 1950.

It is especially gratifying to me that this expression of American fairness and generosity has been brought about by the combined efforts of both political parties, supported by groups and organizations broadly representative of all parts of our country. H.R. 4567 is a splendid example of the way in which joint action can strengthen and unify our country.

The countrymen of these displaced persons have brought to us in the past the best of their labor, their hatred of tyranny, and their love of freedom. They have helped our country grow in strength and moral leadership. I have every confidence that the new Americans who will come to our country under the provisions of the present bill will also make a substantial contribution to our national well-being.

I have today also signed the Executive order required by law, designating the Displaced Persons Commission to carry out the investigations and make the reports required by the statute, regarding the character, history, and eligibility of displaced persons and persons of German ethnic origin seeking admission into the United States. In the discharge of this statutory duty, I am directing the Commission to continue its vigorous and effective protection of the security of the United States.

15. PRESIDENT TRUMAN'S CAMPAIGN SPEECH
IN HAMTRAMCK, MICHIGAN ON OCTOBER 22, 1952.

I appreciate most highly this cordial reception... This is the best Democratic town in our country, and I am always glad to be here for that reason.

I remember how well you treated me when I came here in 1948. And I remember also how you voted for me that year, too--and I appreciate that most highly, and always will--for I needed it then.

Now I am out here for another purpose this time. I hope that you will do even better for Adlai Stevenson. Governor Stevenson is a great American, and he will make you a great President--I haven't any doubt of that at all. If you will elect him and a good Democratic Congress, then you will continue to have a government that works for the welfare of the plain people--the everyday people in this country. That is what the Democratic Party believes in. It believes in the people. Its first consideration is the welfare of the people.

The Republican Party has no heart. I have always said that they use a calculating machine for a heart, for they are thinking about the big wealth all the time.

The Democrats think of the people that make up the country--the vast majority of them. We believe that the Government ought to help provide jobs for people, and help make it possible for workingmen to raise their families in decency and health.

We believe that people ought to have decent homes in which to live, and a chance to send their children to good schools. We believe that people are entitled to some security in their old age.

Now that is the kind of government you have had for 20 years under the New Deal of Franklin Roosevelt, and the Fair Deal of Harry Truman. That is the kind of government you will get from Adlai Stevenson. But I will tell you right now, it is not the kind of government you would get from the Republicans and their five-star general. Oh no, my friends, they don't believe in that kind of thing. They are coming around now, at election time, making you a lot of promises, giving you a log of false propaganda. But I hope you won't believe them. You have been through that kind of propaganda five times before, and you weren't fooled, and I don't want you to be fooled this time.

Ask your good Democratic Congressman about them--ask Thad Machrowicz. He can tell you what the Republicans really stand for and what they have been doing down there in the Congress. Thad has done a fine job for you in the Congress. He has fought for the St. Lawrence Seaway. He has done good work for the committee that investigated the Katyn Forest massacre. I was glad to cooperate with that committee, because they were doing a job that needed to be done. The facts about that terrible crime ought to be fully exposed.

Thad Machrowicz helped me fight that terrible immigration law that Congress passed over my veto. That law discriminates against the Poles and other people in eastern Europe. It gives a second-class status to naturalized citizens. That is un-American, and the Democratic Party platform promises to get it changed. The platform also pledges further aid to refugees from communism, and we ought to change our laws so we can take into this country more of the people who escape from behind the Iron Curtain.

I have been working for that for 7 long years. Blair Moody has been in this fight, too. Send him back to the Senate to work with Thad Machrowicz--and Adlai Stevenson. I am sure you will do that. And if the rest of the country will send us enough good Democrats like yours, we will get those terrible immigration laws corrected.

We don't believe in the Republican theory that the Poles and other people from eastern Europe are not desirable immigrants. On the contrary, we welcome them with open arms--and we always will.

Now the Republicans have been coming around telling you all the things they would do about Poland. But they don't tell you what they have been doing down in Washington to cripple our fight against Communist aggression. You know and I know that for the peoples behind the Iron Curtain to achieve their freedom, the free nations of the world must first have strong defenses against Communist aggression. That is what we have been working for, and we have made a lot of progress. We have built up the strength of our own Armed Forces, and we have helped our allies build up theirs.

But we haven't had much help from the Republicans. They have been voting to cut the funds for our national defense and for help to our friends abroad. That is still what they want to do. And if you were to elect a Republican President and a Republican Congress, they would wreck our programs against Communist aggression, just as sure as I am standing here. And we would be that much closer to a third world war.

But I know you are not going to do that. I know you are not going to turn this country over to the Republican isolationists and reactionaries. Instead, you are going to vote for this fine bunch of Democratic candidates you have here in the great State of Michigan. You are going to send Thad Machrowicz to Congress, Blair Moody to the United States Senate, Mennen Williams you will make your Governor again, because he has made you a good Governor--and because a man has been tried and true you ought to give him another chance.

I have been going up and down this country from one end to the other--I have been between 17,000 and 18,000 miles, and I have made over 180 talks on the subject of government and the issues that are before the people. The only way you can find out what the issues really are and get the truth on them is to have the President of the United States tell you about them. That is what the President of the United States has been doing. That is one of his duties, to let the people know and to report to them just exactly what the situation is.

You will not find out what the issues are from the Republican press. The Republicans won't tell you anything about the issues. They want to get you off on a side street and keep you from looking at the issues.

I want you to do a little thinking. I want you to study the record, and that is the only way you can find out--because what people will do is what they have done in the past. Study the record of the Republicans in the Congress. Study the record of the Democrats in the Congress, and find out which of those records is for the people, and which of those records is for the special interests. When you do that, I won't have to argue with you. You will vote your own interests. You will vote the Democratic ticket on November the 4th, and you will send Adlai Stevenson to the White House for the next 4 years, and we will have 4 more years of good government. Now vote in your own interest on election day.

16. EXCERPTS FROM THE FINAL REPORT OF THE SELECT COMMITTEE OF THE U.S. HOUSE OF REPRESENTATIVES INVESTIGATING THE KATYN MASSACRE, DECEMBER 22, 1952.

On September 18, 1951, the House of Representatives unanimously adopted House Resolution 390. This resolution provided for the establishment of a select committee to conduct a full and complete investigation concerning the Katyn massacre, an international crime committed against soldiers and citizens of Poland at the beginning of World War II.

The Katyn massacre involved some 4,243 of the 15,400 Polish Army officers and intellectual leaders who were captured by the Soviets when Russia invaded Poland in September 1939. These officers were interned in three Soviet prison camps in the territory of the U.S.S.R. They were permitted to correspond with their families in Poland until May 10, 1940. Then all trace of these men was lost after that date. Nothing further of their whereabouts was known until several mass graves containing remains of Polish bodies were discovered in the Katyn Forest near Smolensk, U.S.S.R., by the German troops in April of 1943.

The Katyn massacre was one of the most barbarous international crimes in world history. Since the discovery of the graves, and until this committee completed its investigation, the massacre remained an international mystery. The Soviets blamed the Germans for the crime. They charged the Poles fell into Nazi hands when Germany invaded Russia in the summer of 1941. The Germans organized a medical commission investigation consisting of leading doctors from 12 European nations including the neutral country of Switzerland. This medical commission met at Katyn on April 29 and 30, 1943, and unanimously determined that the Poles were massacred in the spring of 1940. At that time the Katyn area was under the complete domination of the Soviets...

PROCEDURE

The committee's investigation was divided into two phases; First, to establish which nation actually was guilty of the massacre; and, second, to establish whether any American officials were responsible for suppressing the fact of the massacre with all of its ramifications from the American people.

INTERIM REPORT

On July 2, 1952, this committee filed with the House of Representatives an interim report (H. Rept. 2430) in which it fixed the guilt for the Katyn massacre on the Soviet NKVD (Peoples' Commissariat of Internal Affairs). On the basis of voluminous testimony, including that of recognized medical expert witnesses, and other data assembled by our staff, this committee concluded there does not exist a scintilla of proof, or even any remote circumstantial evidence, that this mass murder took place any later than the spring of 1940. The Poles were then prisoners of the Soviets and the Katyn Forest area was still under Soviet occupation.

In the interim report this committee recommended the Soviets be tried before the International World Court of Justice for committing a crime at Katyn which was in *violation of the general principles of law recognized by civilized nations.* The United Nations Charter presently carries provisions for the legal action recommended by this committee...

The evidence, testimony, records, and exhibits recorded by this committee through its investigations and hearings...overwhelmingly will show the people of the world that Russia is directly responsible for the Katyn massacre. Throughout our entire proceedings, there has not been a scintilla of proof or even any remote circumstantial evidence presented that could indict any other nation in this international crime.

It is an established fact that approximately 15,000 Polish prisoners were interned in three Soviet camps: Kozielsk, Starobielsk, and Ostashkov in the winter of 1939-40. With the exception of 400 prisoners, these men have not been heard from, seen, or found since the spring of 1940. Following the discovery of the graves in 1943, when the Germans occupied this territory, they claimed there were 11,000 Poles buried in Katyn. The Russians recovered the territory from the Germans in September 1943 and likewise they stated that 11,000 Poles were buried in those mass graves.

Evidence heard by this committee repeatedly points to the certainty that only those prisoners interned at Kozielsk were massacred in the Katyn Forest. Testimony of the Polish Red Cross officials definitely established that 4,143 bodies were actually exhumed from the seven mass graves. On the basis of further evidence, we are equally certain that the rest of the 15,000 Polish officers--those interned at Starobielsk and Ostashkov--were executed in a similar brutal manner. Those from Starobielsk were disposed of near Kharkov, and those from Ostashkov met a similar fate. Testimony was presented by several witnesses that the Ostashkov prisoners were placed on barges and drowned in the White Sea. Thus the committee believes that there are at least two other "Katyns" in Russia.

No one could entertain any doubt of Russia guilt for the Katyn massacre when the following evidence is considered:

1. The Russians refused to allow the International Committee of the Red Cross to make a neutral investigation of the German charges in 1943.

2. The Russians failed to invite any neutral observers to participate in their own investigation in 1944, except a group of newspaper correspondents taken to Katyn who agreed "the whole show was staged" by the Soviets.

3. The Russians failed to produce sufficient evidence of Nazi guilt for Katyn before the International Military Tribunal in Nuremberg.

4. This committee issued formal and public invitations to the Government of the U.S.S.R. to present any evidence pertaining to the Katyn massacre. The Soviets refused to participate in any phase of this committee's investigation.

5. The overwhelming testimony of prisoners formerly interned at the three camps, of medical experts who performed autopsies of the massacred bodies, and of observers taken to the scene of the crime conclusively confirms this committee's findings.

6. Polish Government leaders and military men who conferred with Stalin, Molotov, and NKVD chief Beria for a year and a half attempted without success to locate the Polish prisoners before the Germans discovered Katyn. This renders further proof that the Soviets purposely misled the Poles in denying any knowledge of the whereabouts of their officers when, in fact, the Poles already were buried in the mass graves at Katyn.

7. The Soviets have demonstrated through their highly organized propaganda machinery that they fear to have the people behind the iron curtain know the the truth about Katyn. This is proven by their reaction to our committee's efforts and the amount of newspaper space and radio time devoted to denouncing the work of our committee. They also republished in all newspapers behind the iron curtain the allegedly "neutral" Russian report of 1944. The world-wide campaign of slander by the Soviets against our committee is also construed as another effort to block this investigation.

8. This committee believes that one of the reasons for the staging of the recent Soviet "germ warfare" propaganda campaign was to divert attention of the people behind the iron curtain from the hearings of the committee.

9. Our committee has been petitioned to investigate mass executions and crimes against humanity committed in other countries behind the iron curtain. The committee has heard testimony which indicates there are other "Katyns." We wish to impress with all the means at our command that the investigation of the Katyn massacre barely scratches the surface of numerous crimes against humanity perpetrated by totalitarian powers. This committee believes that an international tribunal should be established to investigate willful and mass executions wherever they have been committed. The United Nations will fail in their obligation until they expose to the world that "Katynism" is a definite and diabolical totalitarian plan for world conquest.

SECOND PHASE

The Congress requested that our committee determine why certain reports and files concerning the Katyn massacre disappeared or were suppressed by departments of our Government.

Records and documents assembled from the State Department and War Department files provided a clear-cut picture of the tremendously important part the Katyn massacre played in shaping the future of postwar Europe.

From these hitherto secret documents this committee learned that as early as the summer of 1942 American authorities considered a Polish Army extremely vital to the Allied war effort against Hitler and Mussolini. Documents introduced in our hearings describe conclusively the efforts made to create such an army on Russian soil as quickly as possible. We learned further that American authorities knew as early as 1942 of Poland's desperate efforts to locate her missing officers who could lead the Polish Army being formed on Russian soil.

These same documents show that when high-level Polish officials failed to obtain an adequate reply from the Soviets regarding the whereabouts of their missing officers, American emissaries intervened. In every instance, American officials were given the same reply: The Soviets had no knowledge of their whereabouts.

United States Ambassador to Moscow, Admiral William H. Standley, advised the State Department of September 10, 1942 that Soviet officials were opposed to United States intervention in Russo-Polish problems. This attitude was stated to Admiral Standley by Molotov when Standley inquired about the missing Polish officers.

Throughout 1942-43--or until the mass graves were discovered at Katyn--this committee's record recites a long series of efforts being made by the United States to aid the Poles. But it also shows the total lack of cooperation the United States received from the Soviets.

When Russia finally broke diplomatic relations with Poland (April 26, 1943) following the Polish request for an International Red Cross investigation of the Katyn massacre, Ambassador Standley warned the State Department that Russia had been seeking a pretext to break with Poland for some time. He emphasized that the Soviets were plotting to create a pro-Communist satellite Polish government which would take over Poland after the war. He warned that Russia was planning to create an entire belt of pro-Soviet governments in eastern Europe, which would jeopardize the peace of Europe.

It is apparent that American authorities knew of the growing tension between the Soviets and the Poles during 1942-43--and they likewise knew about the hopeless search for the Polish officers--but at the time, all of these factors were brushed aside, on the theory that pressing the search would irritate Soviet Russia and thus hinder the prosecution of the war to a successful conclusion.

TOP UNITED STATES OFFICIAL TESTIFY

The Katyn investigation revealed that many individuals throughout the State Department, Army Intelligence (G-2), Office of War Information and Federal Communications Commission, and other Government agencies, failed to properly evaluate the material being received from our sources overseas. In many instances, this information was deliberately withheld from public attention and knowledge. There was a definite lack of coordination on intelligence matters between Army Intelligence (G-2) and the State Department, at least as far as the missing Polish officers and the Katyn massacre was concerned.

The possibility exists that many second-echelon personnel, who were overly sympathetic to the Russian cause or pro-Communist-minded, attempted to cover up derogatory reports which were received concerning the Soviets.

Former American Ambassador Averell Harriman--now Mutual Security Director--and former Under Secretary of State, Summer Welles, explained why the United States acquiesced so frequently to outrageous Soviet demands.

Both said the underlying consideration throughout the war was military necessity. They agreed that American foreign policy called for a free postwar Poland to assure stability in Europe. Both concurred in the fact that the United States wanted a Polish Army very urgently in the near east campaign. They insisted, however, that these considerations had to give way to military necessity and to the maintenance of our alliance with Russia. These witnesses further maintained the Allies feared Russia might make a separate peace with the Germans.

American emissaries who reported the status of conditions concerning the Soviets were either bypassed or disregarded if their views were critical of the Soviets. When some of the emissaries expressed anti-Soviet observations, President Roosevelt sent his personal representative to confer directly with Marshal Stalin.

This was borne out by testimony of Ambassador Standley, who said that when he warned against Russia's postwar plans for forming a pro-Soviet bloc of nations around the U.S.S.R., President Roosevelt sent Wendell Willkie to confer with Stalin. Mr. Standley said he was not given the details of Mr. Willkie's mission.

In retrospect, we now realize the prophetic truth of Admiral Standley's warning about the Soviets which he made in 1943, when the Katyn massacre was announced to the world for the first time. (See vol. VII of the published hearings.)

Both Mr. Harriman and Mr. Welles, in testifying before our committee, conceded in effect that the United States officials had taken a gamble on Russia's pledge to work harmoniously with the western democracies after the war--and lost.

However, they presented arguments to justify their actions. Mr. Harriman insisted that agreements made at Teheran and Yalta would have assured a lasting peace if only the Soviets had kept their promises.

Mr. Harriman insisted that territorial concessions made to the Soviets at the Big Three conferences were predicated on the military reality that the Soviets were actually in physical control of these lands. To have resisted their demands, or to have tried to drive the Soviets out by force, would have meant prolonging the war, Mr. Harriman maintained.

He further testified that concessions made to the Soviets at Yalta were made at a time when the American Joint Chiefs of Staff insisted on getting the Soviets into the Japanese war at all costs.

Mr. Harriman said he personally "was full of distrust of the Soviets at the time." He declared the Yalta agreements were breached by the Soviets. He stated that the present government in Poland is not representative of its people. He added, "It is a puppet government of the Soviet Union."

Mr. Harriman testified:

The fact that they [the Soviets] broke these agreements has been one of the reasons why the Free World has become more and more united. (See vol. VII. of the published hearings.)

This committee believes the tragic concessions at Yalta might not have taken place if the Polish officer corps had not been annihilated by the Soviets at Katyn. With proper leadership, the Polish Army could have relieved a great deal of the early reverses suffered by the Allies. The Kremlin's hand could not have been as strong at the Yalta Conference, and many of the concessions made because of "military necessity," as maintained by Mr. Harriman, would have been obviated.

This contention is borne out by a portion of a telegram sent to the State Department on June 2, 1942, by A.J. Drexel Biddle, Jr., American Ambassador assigned to the Polish Government in Exile in London. (See exhibit 21, pt. VII of the published hearings.)

"The absence of these officers is the principal reason for the shortage of officers in the Polish forces in Russia, wither officers from Scotland had to be sent lately. The possible death of these men, most of whom have superior education, would be a severe blow to the Polish national life."

PRESIDENT ROOSEVELT INTERCEDES

This committee heard testimony and studied documents which clearly show President Roosevelt himself appeared concerned about Polish-Soviet relations. When Marshal Stalin informed the President of his decision to break off diplomatic relations with the Poles following their demand for an International Red Cross investigation of Katyn, Mr. Roosevelt sent a personal message urging Stalin to reconsider his action.

The tone of Mr. Roosevelt's message clearly demonstrated his desire, above all, to retain cordial relations with the Soviets. (See exhibit 17, pt. VII of the published hearings.)

When again, in 1944, former Ambassador George Howard Earle, who served as a special emissary for President Roosevelt in the Balkans, tried to convince Mr. Roosevelt that the Soviets were guilty of the Katyn massacre, the President dismissed the suggestion.

Testifying before this committee that he based his statement to the President on secret documents and photographs of Katyn clearly establishing Soviet guilt, Mr. Earle quoted the President as replying:

"George, this is entirely German propaganda and a German plot. I am absolutely convinced that the Russians did not do this."

It becomes apparent to this committee that the President and the State Department ignored numerous documents from Ambassador Standley, Ambassador Biddle, and Ambassador Winant, American emissary to London, who reported information which strongly pointed to Soviet perfidy.

It becomes obvious Mr. Roosevelt's dealings with the Soviets throughout the war were based on a strong desire for mutual cooperation with Russia in the war effort. This desire was based on a belief in Soviet Russia's sincerity. It is equally obvious that this desire completely overshadowed the dictates of justice and equity to our loyal but weaker ally, Poland...

> Ray Madden, Chairman
> Daniel Flood
> Foster Furcolo
> Thaddeus Machrowicz
> George Dondero
> Alvin O'Konski
> Timothy Sheehan
> Members of the U.S. House of
>   Representatives
> Roman Pucinski, Chief Investigator

17. PRESIDENT DWIGHT D. EISENHOWER'S LETTER TO THE CONGRESS OF THE UNITED STATES ON A PROPOSED RESOLUTION ON SUBJUGATED PEOPLES, FEBRUARY 20, 1953.

In my message to Congress of February 2, 1953, I stated that I would ask the Congress at a later date to join in an appropriate resolution, making clear that we would never acquiesce in the enslavement of any people in order to purchase fancied gain for ourselves, and that we would not feel that any past agreements committed us to any such enslavement.

In pursuance of that portion of the message to Congress, I now have the honor to inform you that I am concurrently informing the President of the Senate (the Speaker of the House) that I invite the concurrence of the two branches of the Congress in a declaration, in which I would join as President which would:

(1) Refer to World War II international agreements or understandings concerning other peoples;

(2) Point out that the leaders of the Soviet Communist Party who now control Russia, in violation of the clear intent of these agreements or understandings, subjected whole nations concerned to the domination of a totalitarian imperialism;

(3) Point out that such forceful absorption of free peoples into an aggressive despotism increases the threat against the security of all remaining free peoples, including our own;

(4) State that the people of the United States, true to their tradition and heritage of freedom, have never acquiesced in such enslavement of any peoples;

(5) Point out that it is appropriate that the Congress should join with the President to give expression to the desires and hopes of the American people;

(6) Conclude with a declaration that the Senate and the House join with the President in declaring that the United States rejects any interpretations or applications of any international agreements or understandings, made during the course of World War II, which have been perverted to bring about the subjugation of free peoples, and further join in proclaiming the hope that the peoples, who have been subjected to the captivity of Soviet despotism, shall again enjoy the right of self-determi-

nation within a framework which will sustain the peace; that they shall again have the right to choose the form of government under which they will live, and that sovereign rights of self-government shall be restored to them all in accordance with the pledge of the Atlantic Charter.

I am enclosing a form of draft resolution, which, in my opinion carries out the purposes outlined above, and in which I am prepared to concur.*

Sincerely,
DWIGHT D. EISENHOWER

* Soon after entering office, President Eisenhower declared his opposition to the forceful "liberation" of the Eastern European peoples under Soviet Communist rule, although this idea had been included to the 1952 Republican Party platform.

18. PRESIDENT EISENHOWER'S VIEWS ON U.S. POLICY TOWARD EASTERN EUROPE; EXCERPT FROM HIS PRESS CONFERENCE OF NOVEMBER 14, 1956.

Q. John Herling, Editors Syndicate: Mr. President, when the uprising in Poland and Hungary occurred, Vice President Nixon told an Occidental College audience on October 29 in California, that this proved the rightness of the "liberation position" of the Eisenhower administration. Now, in view of the latest developments, could you explain, sir, what the liberation position of the administration is?

THE PRESIDENT. I think it's been perfectly clear from way back in 1950, as far as I am concerned, and I happened to have had the administration when I was then in NATO.

I believe it would be the most terrible mistake for the free world ever to accept the enslavement of the Eastern European tier of nations as a part of a future world of which we approve. Now, we have said this in every possible way, and because of this we try to hold out to all the world the conviction that freedom will live, human freedom will live.

We have never asked, as I pointed out before, for a people to rise up against a ruthless military force; of course we think, on the other hand, that the employment of such force is the negation of all justice and right in the world.

What I do say is the policy is correct in that we simply insist upon the right of all people to be free to live under governments of their own choosing.

19. PRESIDENT EISENHOWER ON THE PURPOSES OF U.S. ECONOMIC ASSISTANCE TO THE EASTERN EUROPEAN SATELLITES; EXCERPT FROM HIS PRESS CONFERENCE OF JUNE 18, 1958.

Q. Mrs. May Craig, Portland (Maine) *Press Herald:* In view of the execution of Nagy and his colleagues by the Soviet overlords of Hungary, will you still seek authority from Congress to give foreign aid to the Soviet satellites?

THE PRESIDENT. I will help. I would give aid to anything that I would think would help to weaken the solidarity of the Communist bloc.

If we can set up centrifugal as opposed to centripetal forces, we are, in my mind, doing a great service for the free world. And, through trade, through possibilities for these people--I suppose, the ones we are talking about now are Poland and Yugoslavia--if they can make stronger their independent action, *vis-a-vis* the Soviets, that is all to the good.

It has often been said, you know, that trade follows a flag; it's entirely possible, too, that the flag tends to follow trade; and there could be some trading in this way that would awaken new interest in these countries to pull away from Moscow. I think to that extent we would be advantaged...

20. PRESIDENT EISENHOWER ON THE CONGRESSIONAL RESOLUTION ESTABLISHING "CAPTIVE NATIONS WEEK" OBSERVANCES; EXCERPT FROM HIS PRESS CONFERENCE OF JULY 22, 1959.

THE PRESIDENT. Please sit down.

Good morning. Ready for the questions.

Q. Marvin L. Arrowsmith, Associated Press: In Warsaw yesterday Premier Khrushchev professed to be puzzled about why Vice President Nixon is going to Russia and he apparently linked this puzzlement with criticism of your proclamation on the captive nations. Do you see this attitude as a sort of strike against the Nixon visit even before it starts?

THE PRESIDENT. Well, no. I wouldn't think of it in that way. The Nixon visit was of course proposed quite awhile back, and it's really an exchange of visits between Mr. Kozlov and Mr. Nixon. It's a good will gesture and we wanted to have a prominent American to officiate at the opening of our exhibit.

Now, as far as the resolution about the captive nations, this was a resolution by the Congress, asked me to issue a proclamation, which I did; and asked the United States to conduct ceremonies in memory of the plight of such peoples.

But I don't think there is any specific relationship between the two things.

Q. Merriman Smith, United Press International: In the same connection, sir, what do you think, quite aside from the Nixon visit, of the proposition of the Russians through *Pravda,* in a three-column article this morning, and through statements by Khrushchev, literally criticizing the proclamation by you of a week of prayer for the captive people?

What do you think of their basic criticism of you for proclaiming a week of prayer?

THE PRESIDENT. Well, of course they don't admit there are any captive nations. They have their own propaganda. They present a picture to their own peoples, including the world, so far as they can, that we know is distorted and is untrue.

This, to our way of thinking, is quite important not only because it is a matter of simple justice and human concern for all these people, but when you come down to it this country is made up of a great many of those people. We have relatives and people of the ethnic derivation of all those captive nations, and it becomes sort of a personal thing with us and would be almost unusual for us to be silent all the time and just acquiesce, presumably in their right to express themselves on the form of their government....

21. PRESIDENT EISENHOWER'S REMARKS AT THE QUADRENNIAL NATIONAL CONVENTION OF THE POLISH AMERICAN CONGRESS, CHICAGO, SEPTEMBER 30, 1960.*

Mr. Rozmarek, distinguished guests, and my fellow Americans:

First of all, I must thank you personally, Mr. Rozmarek, for the very generous terms in which you have introduced me.

I want to say, first, that I am especially delighted to have a chance to meet briefly with the Polish American Congress. This is not a mere formality, because from time immemorial, the people of Poland have shown such a fierce dedication to the conception of liberty and personal freedom, that they have been an example for all the world.

We must remember that spirit is, after all, the major force that animates all human action. Material strength we have, and we are fortunate in having it; we have economic strength and intellectual strength--but what is in the heart of the human is, after all, the thing we must seek when we say he is our friend or our ally, or our brother in the convictions and beliefs that we hold.

So, from the days of Kosciuszko (and here I must pause for a moment, because once in Poland they used that name quite often, and it was a whole day before I knew what they were saying, but my pronunciation is Kosciuszko) from the day he came to help in our struggle for independence in this country, there has never been a time when the Polish people and Polish fortunes have been absent from the hearts and minds of the American people.

Only in the time of Woodrow Wilson, one of his Fourteen Points that he laid out as his formula for peace with Germany after World War I, was the permanent independence and the territorial integrity of Poland.

That the people of our country and the people of Poland have been akin in spirit, I think was again demonstrated very definitely when Vice President Nixon went to that country only a year or so ago, and had a quarter of a million people cheering him, voluntarily bringing in arms of flowers to throw in his path, trying to let him know that through him they hoped to send a message to America, "We still, with you, believe in freedom."

In 1952, I promised the American people that whatever I could do by peaceful means would be done, in order that those people who are held in bondage by a tyrannical dictatorship might finally have the right to determine their own fates by their own free votes.

This is still a tenet in the faith of every right-thinking American. It is as yet unachieved, but this does not mean that anyone must give up hope. We must continue, by our unity and freedom throughout the world, to oppose the bloc that by making the State a deity and the individual just a plodding animal do the bidding of that State.

So, just as we keep faithful to our religious teachings, and the religious background on which this Nation was formed, we keep faithful to that ideal of freedom, well realizing that freedom and peace are in the long run indivisible.

There must be peace for the world, or no nation can truly enjoy it.

People of your blood have come to this country. You are citizens of the United States. Your loyalty to the United States is exactly as that of your forefathers, of yourselves, to your mother country. But citizenship is not a merely a matter of expressing our pride in our traditions, in our historical figures. Citizenship is the carrying forward of the ideals on which nations based on freedom are maintained and sustained. It is a matter of discharging our responsibilities.

The individual's way of discharging his responsibilities is found in many channels. It is in obedience to the law; it is performing with others the cooperative works of communities and sects and organizations that have to do with the alleviation of suffering.

But there is one thing that right now is uppermost in our minds: it is discharging your responsibility of expressing your view about the political future of our country.

This you do by registering and by placing your vote in the ballot box. It makes no difference, so far as I am concerned--but I don't mean to say I am disinterested--but it makes no difference for what individual or party you vote, as long as you are voting your own honest convictions. And if you do not do that, you are not discharging your responsibilities either to this great country, or to the traditions that you have brought with you from the culture from which you came.

I cannot tell you what great importance I attach to this business of making certain that our government is surely a representative one. It is not representative of us at all if anyone fails to perform this duty. You know, after I go, but before you people leave this room, I would like each person here to turn to his two neighbors or her two neighbors and say, "Have you registered? Are you going to vote?" If you can get a hundred percent "yes," this will be one of the most magnificent meetings that I have ever attended--and it will be an example for all the United States. And then, as you go out, and you meet two other people--in your home, at your work, wherever you are living-- and say "Have you registered and are you going to vote?" This is truly what we must do, if self-government, representative government, is going to exist permanently and healthily.

Because, if you are doing this, you are also thinking of what are the issues, who are the leaders you want to follow. You are going to do it thoughtfully, you are not going to let a brand name, or anything else, influence you. And I cannot tell you how earnestly I pray that every person here will do just that.

Now there's one other phase of this relationship among free countries that I should like to mention, before I close these brief and very informal remarks.

I was told the other day that there are 213 nationalities recognized by our Immigration Service--213 nationalities that have in some way or other contributed to the development of our civilization in this country. There is one point I want to make. Our country has found it necessary to establish quotas, quotas on immigration. Whether or not you and I happen to think that quotas are correct at this time, and used properly, or we may think they are not generous enough, the fact is we have had quotas.

Has any Communist country had to establish quotas to keep people from immigrating to their nation?

So when we talk about this prestige between free countries and Communist countries, I would like to make that simple test: how many of you here want to apply for passports and visas to go to Russia?

In other words, we are not only proud of our citizenship, we are proud of every nation that, with us, gives the opportunity to the individual to realize the most out of his talents and his opportunities. In other words, it is the human spirit that must be free. And this is the thing that brings 213 nationalities finally into one single nation.

I think that each of these nations should be proud of its heritage. It should be proud of the traditions and the faiths that it brings, because with that kind of pride in traditions it helps to build our country. Our country is a great amalgamation, and we each live with the other in friendship, with mutual self-respect, and because we find that in this great mixture of cultures and thinking, and traditions and history, each of us is enriched.

Now among the free nations of the world, we have got to have something of that kind of spirit. We must not, as I see it, appear superior to any other country that is, like ourselves, working for the same kind of civilization which respects the dignity of men. We must not be either patronizing, resentful, or either because of race or religion or color or background or some other inconsequential factor treat them as a stranger or enemy.

Just as we seek peace and order and progress and greater unification among our own people, we must seek it through all those people who like ourselves believe in God and base their whole ideals concerning humanity on that faith.

Now, my friends, I was told I was to come over here and just greet you, and wish you well, but I guess possibly I have been so long in political life that I can't help, when I've got an opportunity, to just start talking.

But I might tell you one little story about that. We had one State that had in its laws a provision that anyone convicted for murder and was to be executed, was to be given 5 minutes to say anything he wanted to, before the final act.

And there was in this State a man who was so convicted and was just about on the brink. And the sheriff, in front of the assembled crowd--and they had come from everywhere to see this thing--offered this man very solemnly and officially his 5 minutes.

Well, the man promptly refused it. But another man in the gathering jumped up quickly and says he's running for Congress, "Can I have the 5 minutes?"

I didn't mean to take the time that somebody else should have had--although not in those circumstances, of course. But I cannot tell you how much I wish you well, how proud I am of the record of your country, its convictions, of the great contributions the people of Polish extraction have brought to this New World.

And again to say, don't forget to make sure that you have registered and your two neighbors have. And vote for somebody!

Thank you very much indeed.

* Also addressing the delegates was Senator John F. Kennedy of Massachusetts, the Democratic Party Presidential nominee.

22. PRESIDENT JOHN F. KENNEDY ON THE PURPOSE OF U.S. ECONOMIC ASSISTANCE TO EASTERN EUROPE; EXCERPT FROM HIS PRESS CONFERENCE OF JUNE 7, 1962.

Q. Mr. President, why do you think the Senate voted so sharply yesterday to tie your hands on sending aid to Communist countries, especially in defiance of pleas from the White House on the point? And do you think anything can be done to rectify the situation beyond the amendment put in today on food?

THE PRESIDENT. Well, the amendment that was put in today on food will be very helpful, because the primary assistance that we have been giving, for example, to Poland, has been through food. In addition, it permits the private organizations to continue to function.

In Yugoslavia we have been giving aid in food; there was some limited development assistance which would not be possible under the Senate amendment. There has been a good deal, of course, of frustration about these programs. They have been under attack for many years and we've carried this aid program since the Marshall plan days, and I suppose people do get tired. The desire of people to remain independent-- the Polish people want to be independent, they are not Communist by choice but by hard circumstances forced upon them, and I think that we should continue to hold out some hope for them. We are not prepared to take military action to free them, quite obviously, and we did not undertake anything like that during the Hungary revolt, but I do think that we should not slam the door in their face. So that I am glad that the Senate went as far as it went today.

Yugoslavia has been more complicated, and I know that the programs of assistance have been under attack, but the primary assistance now is foodstuffs and it has been quite limited. But Yugoslavia is not a member of the Warsaw bloc. The break between Yugoslavia and the Soviet Union in the late forties probably did more to maintain the independence of Greece, when that border was closed, than any other single action. And those who were associated with that effort know how close it was in Greece, and I think there is an advantage in encouraging national independence. We may not approve of the government of Yugoslavia, or they may not approve of our government, but at least they have maintained an independent status in regard to joining the Warsaw bloc, or in regard to their dependence upon Moscow. Now, that might change. But I do think that flexibility is necessary. No one has any idea what the circumstances will be in the next 12 months. We might find it necessary or desirable to give some assistance to a country which was following an independent policy; we might find the language of yesterday denying us that flexibility. I am glad the Senate went back as far as it did. I do think that they should give us the right to give assistance when we deem it in the national interest. I remember this fight was made under President Eisenhower and I supported his efforts at that time to maintain this flexibility--on two occasions--and I am glad at least we have been given some flexibility by the action of the Senate today.

23. PRESIDENT KENNEDY'S REMARKS AT THE ANNUAL PULASKI DAY PARADE IN BUFFALO, NEW YORK, OCTOBER 14, 1962.

I want to express my thanks to all of you for being generous enough to invite me to come to an occasion which has significance to this city and this country, and the free world, because today, in remembering Pulaski, we remember all those millions from Poland and America and all around the globe who have fought and died, who fight now and live, in the cause of freedom. And that's what brings us here to this city today.

Some years ago I visited Poland. I walked through the Cathedral of Czestochowa. I saw the Matka Boska. I saw the sword of John Sobieski, who saved Christianity at the gates of Vienna. I saw a small scale, centuries-old model of a cathedral made by the hand of Thaddeus Kosciusko, who translated Polish commitment to liberty to assistance to our colonies. And I saw a small cross--the Cross of Pulaski.

One hundred and eighty-three years ago this month General Pulaski died. He was only 32. He was not an American. He had been on these shores for less than 2 years. He represented a different culture, a different language, a different way of life. But he had the same love of liberty as the people of this country, and, therefore, he was an American as much as he was a Pole.

This is the common theme that runs throughout our history--the millions of people who come to these shores to find freedom and who, as Americans, fight for freedom around the globe. Just a year ago I called attention to this commitment of freedom in a speech before the United Nations. Colonialism, then as now, was the key issue before that Assembly, and I said:

"There is no ignoring the fact that the tide of self-determination has not reached the Communist empire where a population far larger than that officially called 'dependent' lives under governments installed by foreign troops instead of free institutions--under a system which knows only one party and one belief--which suppresses free debate, and free elections, and free newspapers, and free books, and free trade unions-- and which builds a wall to keep the truth a stranger, and its own citizens prisoners. Let us debate colonialism in full--and apply the principle of free choice and a plebiscite to every corner of the globe, Eastern Europe as well as Africa."

We pay tribute to Pulaski today because the truths for which he fought in 1779 are just as strong today. My own belief and observation shows me, and all of us, that there is no stronger reservoir of freedom in the world today than imprisoned Poland. They know the meaning of freedom as no one else can.

What policies can we pursue to permit what Thomas Jefferson called the disease of liberty to be catching behind the Iron Curtain? It's not enough to make speeches about liberation. Our Government must pursue those policies which hold out eventual promise of freedom for the people who live behind the Iron Curtain.

First, we need economic flexibility. Too often our hands are tied by rigid statutory perspectives of the Communist world. Everything is seen in terms of black and white. Either nations are for us or against us; either completely under Soviet domination or completely free. But this is not the case. There are varying shades even within the Communist world. We must be able to seize the initiative when the opportunity arises, in Poland in particular, and in other countries as time goes on, behind the Iron Curtain. We must be ready to gradually, carefully, and peacefully work for closer relations by nourishing the seeds of liberty.

It is for this reason that I was disappointed by the amendment to the trade bill which specifically discriminates against Polish goods. The Polish people press their government for independence. Our policy should be to hold out a helping hand to them and not to shut the door.

Secondly, we must recognize that Soviet domination of these areas is temporary. We must never, in statement, treaty, declaration, or any other manner, recognize Soviet domination of Eastern Europe as permanent. We must never. Twice--in 1961 and '62--I have issued proclamations endorsed by this Congress to that effect.

Third, we must strengthen the economic and cultural ties that bind Poland to the West. The Polish language population, all of you, can be most effective in the ties that you maintain with the people of Poland. I am gratified by the number of students, officials, technicians, going from the United States to Poland and coming from Poland here to the United States. More than three times as many Americans on more than twice as many projects are going to Poland than ever before. Twice as many Poles, on twice as many projects, come here to the United States. This gives us a chance to show that we still remember Poland, that we have not forgotten them. "I was in prison and you visited me," is the best advice for the United States in 1962 in regard to the people of Poland.

Fourth, all of the ties which make Poland so much a part of the Western World, a part of the European World, must be strengthened. There is no easy solution to any of the problems which face us in Poland, in Asia, in Latin America, or around the world. But the people who count, the people who've been able to maintain their freedom, are the ones who have persevered, who have not gotten tired, who have not become fatigued, who have not given up. Poland, in its history, has been overrun, cut apart, occupied, partitioned, but it has remained free in the hearts of the Polish people, and as the old song says, "As long as you live, Poland lives"--"*Jeszcze Polska nie zginela.*" That is still true, as it was in the history of Poland.

Some years ago I visited the Polish cemetery near Cassino, where thousands of Polish soldiers died far from their country in World War II for the independence of their country, and on that cemetery are written these words: "These Polish soldiers, for your freedom and theirs, have given their bodies to the soil of Italy, their hearts to Poland, and their souls to God."

We give our hearts and our bodies to the cause of freedom here in the United States, in Poland, and all around the globe.

Thank you.

24. PRESIDENT KENNEDY ON THE PROBLEM OF OVERTURNING COMMUNIST DICTATORSHIP; EXCERPT FROM HIS PRESS CONFERENCE OF FEBRUARY 7, 1963.

Q. Mr. President, what chances do you think or do you believe there are of eliminating communism in Cuba within your term?

THE PRESIDENT. I couldn't make any prediction about the elimination. I am quite obviously hopeful that it can be eliminated, but we have to wait and see what happens. There are a lot of unpleasant situations in the world today. China is one. It's unfortunate that communism was permitted to come into Cuba. It has been a problem in the last 5 years. We don't know what's going to happen internally. There's no obviously easy solution as to how the Communist movement will be removed. One way, of course, would be by the Cubans themselves, though that's very difficult, given the police setup. The other way would be by external action. But that's war and we should not regard that as a cheap or easy way to accomplish what we wish.

We live with a lot of dangerous situations all over the world. Berlin is one. There are many others. And we live with a good deal of hazard all around the world and have for 15 years. I cannot set down any time in which I can clearly see the end to the Castro regime. I believe it's going to come, but I couldn't possibly give a time limit. I think that those who do, sometimes mislead. I remember a good deal of talk in the early fifties about liberation, how Eastern Europe was going to be liberated. And then we had Hungary, and Poland, and East Germany, and no action was taken.

The reason the action wasn't taken was because they felt strongly that if they did take action it would bring on another war. So it's quite easy to discuss these things and say one thing or another ought to be done. But when they start talking about how, and when, they start talking about Americans invading Cuba and killing thousands of Cubans and Americans. With all the hazards around the world, that's a very serious decision, and I notice that that's not approached directly by a good many who have discussed the problem.

25. PRESIDENT LYNDON B. JOHNSON'S REMARKS ON THE OCCASION OF THE TWENTIETH ANNIVERSARY OF THE WARSAW UPRISING, JULY 31, 1964.*

...I want to thank you for coming. I want to review with you some of my thoughts, very briefly.

Twenty years ago tomorrow, in the city of Warsaw, there occurred a demonstration of human courage that the world will never forget. The courageous people of a captive city challenged the chains of their captors. Three hours after the start of what is known as "Operation Tempest," the flag of the Polish Republic was flying in the heart of Warsaw, for the first time in 5 years. For 63 days proud Poles fought to liberate their beloved capital from the occupying army.

On October 2, 1944, a decision to cease the valiant fight was dictated and required by lack of food, a lack of water, a lack of ammunition, and a desire to save the remaining civilian population from systematic destruction. Eighty percent of Warsaw had been destroyed. Twenty thousand Polish soldiers had been killed, or seriously wounded. The toll among civilians was too high to even count.

But as the Polish forces marched past on that final day, the citizens in the streets sang to them, "Poland is not yet lost, while we still live." We, in America, know that kind of spirit well. It attended us at the birth of our Nation. We have seen it shine from the Polish character time and time again. We see it, again, now in Warsaw rebuilt from the ashes and the rubble.

We see it in the steadfast faith of the Polish people. We see it gratefully in our fellow citizens of Polish ancestry and I visited only a few months ago in Chicago with hundreds of thousands of them. They live among us now as patriots of the cause of freedom for all mankind. The congressional district from which I come is inhabited by hundreds and thousands of people of Polish ancestry.

So, we know the Polish spirit well. We know the unswerving dedication of the Polish people to the goals of liberty and equality and independence. That is why our policy is designed to help the Polish people so they may increasingly help themselves. We have done much toward this goal in many fields.

Today all Americans are proud to join with the Poles of Poland, the Poles abroad, and the Polish Americans to commemorate the 20th anniversary of the Warsaw Uprising. We repeat with them now the motto of the Polish struggle for independence: For Your Freedom and Ours.

I want to acknowledge the presence in our audience this morning of the former Commander in Chief of the Underground, General Tadeusz Bor-Komorowski, from Warsaw.

And now it is my pleasure to present the President of the Polish American Congress, Mr. Charles Rozmarek.

* The President spoke at noon in the Rose Garden at the White House. Following Mr. Rozmarek's remarks the President read and signed a proclamation which proclaimed August 1, 1964, as Warsaw Uprising Day.

Included in the group were representatives of Polish American organizations and presidents of Polish American fraternal societies. Other Americans of Polish ancestry attending the reception included Government officials, Congressmen, veterans of military units who served during World War II, editors of Polish American newspapers, and representatives of State legislatures.

26. PRESIDENT JOHNSON'S REMARKS AT A CEREMONY COMMEMORATING POLAND'S MILLENNIUM, MAY 3, 1966.

Senator Muskie, Members of the Cabinet, Members of the Congress, distinguished guests and friends:

Senator Muskie, I enjoyed hearing so much what you had to say, and I am deeply honored by this gesture of the Polish American community.

I am well aware of the historical significance of this beautiful work of art. For hundreds of years the Black Madonna has brought strength to the brave citizens of Poland. It has been a symbol both of greatness and of hope.

As much as I treasure the gift, I feel that others will treasure it with me. So I am asking Archbishop Krol to put it on permanent display at the Catholic Church in Panna Maria, Texas, the first Polish church in the United States.

I accept it with great gratitude and with much pleasure because--I might add incidentally, and it hasn't always been incidentally--those who attend that church and I have always had something in common every election year.

So I accept it with this pledge: that as long as I am allowed to serve as your President I will never cease to work for closer ties, for closer friendship, and for closer cooperation between the United States of America and Poland.

Today as we meet here at the 1,000th anniversary of Polish Christianity and nationhood, it is also the 175th anniversary of a document that holds a place of honor among the noble statements of human rights, the Polish Constitution of 1791.

All men who revere liberty acknowledge their indebtedness to those landmarks in the struggle for individual freedom.

And that is why I have asked you to come here to the Rose Garden today.

Life has never been easy for the people of Poland. Time and again she has endured the unwelcome intrusion of her larger and her more powerful neighbors.

Time and again she has endured suffering and sacrifice, only to recover and to rebuild.

In all of this, her proud and resourceful people left an indelible mark on Western civilization.

We, in America, owe a very special debt to Poland. For almost two centuries ago her sons joined our own Revolution and Polish patriots fought under the American flag.

Nor can we forget the millions of Polish immigrants whose personal faith and whose tenacious labor helped to tame this continent. Our national heritage is rich with the gifts of Polish people.

Our debt and our long ties with the people of Poland give us a very special interest in their problems and in their future.

Twice in this century Poland has been devastated by war, yet her people have remained loyal to the ancient faith and to the human values that it represents. Even as we meet here today, they are meeting by the hundreds of thousands at the historic monastery of Jasna Gora. Led by a great Polish cardinal, they are offering prayers of hope and thanksgiving which reflect their enduring belief in God and in their national destiny.

In Poland, and in other countries in Eastern Europe, new ideas are winning friends. Windows are opening to the world-- only slightly in many places, but they are opening.

And despite the severe limitations on its national freedom, limitations that prevent many Polish Americans from celebrating this day on Polish soil, the ancient spirit of Poland is not dead. Her people still yearn for a lively future in Europe and among the community of nations.

We see this, for one thing, in economic policy.

Poland, and some of her neighbors in Eastern Europe, are sensing the vigor of individual enterprise. Men are coming to understand that decentralized decision-making is proving more efficient than highly centralized state control.

Profits are coming to be understood as a better measure of productivity and personal incentive as a better spur to effective action on behalf of the national economy.

How hopeful these signs are, we cannot yet say.

I will be meeting with our distinguished Ambassador very shortly and we will be reviewing all the problems and concerns in that part of the world. There is no greater American today, no one performing a more valuable service than our own distinguished Ambassador John Gronouski, who is returning home.

We can only trust that they foreshadow a new reliance upon, if not a new understanding of, the individual as the most important element of society.

If they reflect a willingness to respond to reality, if they signal a readiness to sift ideas for their own worth rather than to dismiss them as politically impure, if they reflect a gradual rebirth of reason and open discourse among men, then seeds exist for genuine confidence that things, indeed, may yet change.

For this reason, it is not vain, on this day of great memories, for us to also think of great dreams and to speak of great hopes.

Chief among them is the future of Europe.

So vast are the resources of that continent, so important its policies to the rest of the world, so vital its prosperity to the entire world economy that Americans ignore the future of Europe only at the expense of peace and progress on both continents.

Men and nations must labor long to bring to reality a Europe free of artificial political barriers that block the free movement of people, of ideas, and of commerce; a Europe that is secured by international inspected arms control arrangements that remove the age-old fears of East and West alike; a Europe of interdependent friends in which the strength of each adds to the strength of all; a Europe in which the people of every nation know again the responsibilities and the rewards of free political choices.

Not because we have treasure to gain or territory that we desire to acquire, but because we have common roots and common interests, the United States of America today seeks to help build that kind of Europe.

It was in that spirit that the Marshall plan was offered 19 years ago and it is still the spirit of American policy.

Our guiding principles are these:

First, our alliance with Western Europe, we believe, is in the common interest of all who seek peace. It is a charter for changing needs and not a relic of past requirements.

It was and it continues to be a basis for security, solidarity, and advance in Europe. It remains our conviction that an integrated Atlantic defense is the first necessity and not the last result of the building of unity in Western Europe, for expanding partnership across the Atlantic, and for reconciling differences with the East.

As we revise the structure of NATO to meet today's realities, we must make sure that these forward-looking purposes are served and are served well.

Second, we believe that the drive for unity in Western Europe is not only desirable but we believe it is necessary. Every lesson of the past and every prospect for the future argue that the nations of Western Europe can only fulfill their proper role in the world community if increasingly they act together. From this base of collaboration, fruitful ties to the East can best be built.

Third, we will encourage every constructive enrichment of the human, cultural, and commercial ties between Eastern Europe and the West.

Fourth, we will continue to seek ways to improve relations between the people of Germany and their fellow Europeans to the east, and to move towards a peaceful settlement of the division of Germany on the principle of self-determination.

Fifth, we welcome growing participation by the nations of Eastern Europe in common efforts to accelerate economic growth in the developing areas of the world and to share in the worldwide war on poverty, hunger, and disease among the peoples of the world.

It was almost 2 years ago at the George Marshall Memorial Library in nearby Lexington, Virginia, when I said that we must continue to build bridges across the gulf which has separated us from Eastern Europe. Since that time, we have taken limited steps forward along what will no doubt be a very long road.

In Poland alone, we have dedicated an American-financed children's research hospital in Krakow, increased support for CARE, Church World Services, and American Relief for Poland in their food and medical programs for hospitals and needy individuals. We have reached an understanding between our National Academy of Science and the Polish Academy of Science on an important exchange program, similar to the one that we have reached with Rumania, Yugoslavia, and the Soviet Union.

We have invited Poland to cooperate in our satellite program.

We have increased by 44 percent in the second half of 1965 the number of Polish visitors who come to the United States for academic, scientific, and technical purposes. We have increased by more than $200,000 the sale in Poland of American books, newspapers, plays, motion pictures, and television programs. Our International Media Guarantee program with Poland is the largest in the world.

These have all been taken under the direction of one of our greatest Americans, as I mentioned a few moments ago, who will report back to the President and the Cabinet in the next few days--John Gronouski.

These are small steps. But, as Cicero once said, "The beginnings of all things are small." From these, we will take other steps to help revive the intellectual, the commercial, and the cultural currents which once crisscrossed Europe, from London to Budapest, from Warsaw to Paris, from Frankfurt to Krakow, from Prague to Brussels.

As one additional step, and as I pledged in my State of the Union Message, I am today instructing the Secretary of State, Mr. Dean Rusk, to send to the Congress legislation making it possible to expand trade between the United States of America and Eastern Europe. The intimate engagement of peaceful trade, over a period of time, can influence Eastern European societies to develop along paths that are favorable to world peace.*

After years of careful study, the time has now come, I think, for us to act, and act we should and act we must.

With these steps, we can help gradually to create a community of interest, a community of trust, and a community of effort. Thus will the tide of human hope rise again.

It is a good occasion that has brought us together here today.

In issuing this proclamation, I am asking all of the American people to join in the observance of historic events which have inspired man's long walk on this earth.

May we draw new resolve, even now, from the Polish Millennium and Constitution Day.

Thank you, my friends, for coming here.

* The legislation making it possible to expand trade between the United States and Eastern Europe, to which the President referred near the close of his remarks, was not adopted by the 89th Congress.

27. PRESIDENT JOHNSON'S REMARKS AT THE DEDICATION OF THE SHRINE OF OUR LADY OF CZESTOCHOWA IN DOYLESTOWN, PENNSYLVANIA, OCTOBER 16, 1966.

...This is a very proud day for all Americans of Polish descent.

For what we are dedicating this afternoon is much more than a beautiful structure of stone and glass.

It is a symbol of 1,000 years of Polish civilization and Polish Christianity. And to me, it is also a symbol of millions of men and women who have come to our shores as immigrants--come here in search of a better way of live in America.

They were poor, most of them, and had to take what they could get.

And life was hard at its best.

Many of them were illiterate, and the language barriers seemed almost impossible for most of them to surmount.

They were no strangers, of course, to discrimination. Their names were hard to pronounce, they spoke with a strange accent. They did not come from the "right" part of Europe.

But they did have faith, and having that, they overcame every barrier that confronted them. And looking back now, we, all of us, realize how much--how very much they contributed to the richness and the diversity of the United States of America.

They brought their culture--and that has enriched us. But they brought much more. They brought brawn to our industrial might.They brought scholarship to our universities. They brought music to our concert halls. And they brought art to decorate our walls.

And most of all, they brought a love of freedom and a respect for human dignity that is unsurpassed by any group in America.

I expect that it is a little known fact of history, but it was a group of Polish Americans who conducted America's first recorded labor strike. And they did it for the right to vote.

The first Polish immigrants landed at Jamestown, Virginia, in 1608. They followed their usual practice of paying for their passage by working for the company after their arrival. But in the process, they discovered that the company authorities had disenfranchised them because they were "foreigners." And so, in 1619, they simply stopped working. And in a very short time thereafter, they won their rights as free citizens.

This is the spirit of Polish Americans.

You just really don't know how glad I am that you won that first strike.

This is not an isolated example. The freedom that we have enjoyed for nearly 200 years was bought not only with American blood, but it was bought--our freedom--with Polish blood as well. Casimir Pulaski once pledged himself before the high altar of a church to defend faith and freedom to the last drop of his blood. And he redeemed that pledge at Savannah, so that a young nation could choose its own destiny.

This is the spirit of Polish Americans.

Another great man, Thaddeus Kosciusko, like Pulaski, came here to help us win our freedom. And when the war ended, a grateful Congress gave him American citizenship, a pension with landed estates in Ohio, and the rank of brigadier general.

But he was much more than a professional soldier. He was a great and outstanding humanitarian. And before he returned to Europe in 1798, he drew up his will that placed him at the forefront of the movement to abolish slavery and discrimination--some 60-odd years before the Emancipation Proclamation.

Here is what Thaddeus Kosciusko wrote in his will:

"I, Thaddeus Kosciusko, hereby authorize my friend Thomas Jefferson to employ the whole of my property in the United States in purchasing Negroes from among his own or any other and giving them liberty in my name...."

And this, too, is the spirit of Polish Americans.

We need that spirit in America today--perhaps more than we have ever needed it before. We need the spirit that says that another man's dignity is more precious than life itself.

We need the spirit that says a man's skin shall not be a bar to his opportunities--any more than a man's name or a man's religion or a man's nationality.

And finally, we need the spirit that says, as Pulaski said it nearly two centuries ago, "Wherever on the globe men are fighting for freedom, it is as if it were our own affair."

Well, today, when we pray here on this peaceful Sabbath day, this Sunday afternoon, in this beautiful green valley, there are millions of our fellow citizens who are fighting for freedom--millions in this country and hundreds of thousands across the water.

Millions of our fellow citizens here are fighting for freedom:

-Freedom from want.

-Freedom from ignorance.

-Freedom from fear.

-And most of all, freedom from discrimination.

And I hope that each of you will understand that their struggle is your affair, too. So let us make it our cause as well.

As we dedicate this magnificent shrine here this afternoon, let us not be ashamed to say that we are generous or that we care about human beings. When we reach out to help those who are less fortunate than ourselves, let us remember the words of Christ: "Inasmuch as ye have done it unto one of the least of these my brethren, ye have done it unto me."

And now as we are striving to expand the horizons of 20 million Americans, we have not forgotten the urgent pleas of the millions of others throughout the world. They, too, are our brothers--all of them, in all directions. "Love thy neighbor as thyself."

In the morning, we will leave to visit six countries in Asia. We will go to an area of the world where more than half of the people live. We will go to an area of the world where in some parts of it the life expectancy is only 35 years of age, where the per capita income per year is $65.

They are fighting their battle for freedom:

-Freedom to determine who shall govern them.

-Freedom from want.

-Freedom from hunger.

-Freedom from disease.

-Freedom from ignorance.

They are now carrying on their battle against all the ancient enemies of mankind. They need your blessings, they need your prayers, and they need your help.

And I am going to carry all of them with me on your behalf.

We must not forget your friends and your relatives in Poland. We have not forgotten the traditional bonds that have united our peoples since our earliest days as a nation.

We intend to strengthen those bonds. As I said at the Virginia Military Institute in an address in 1964, we intend to build bridges to Poland--bridges of friendship, bridges of trade, and bridges of aid. And following through, last year, it was my privilege to appoint one of the outstanding living Polish Americans as our Ambassador to Poland to help start building those bridges--John A. Gronouski. He is writing a great record for himself and for his Nation.

We have not been idle here at home.

Our postwar contribution to the United Nations Relief and Rehabilitation Administration in Poland has now exceeded $360 million.

Many Poles have had a better diet, thanks to what you in America have done for them through America's food for peace program.

We have donated $37 million in food through CARE and other private organizations. And through these organizations, we have been able to provide hot meals to hundreds of thousands of children in our schools and our summer camps and to the sick and to the aged in our hospitals and our institutions.

Last December, a great children's hospital, a gift from the American people, was dedicated at Krakow.

Last week, in New York, I announced further steps that the American Government plans to take.

We will press for legislative authority to negotiate trade agreements which could extend most-favored-nation tariff treatment to Eastern European states, including Poland.

We have reduced export controls on East-West trade in the last few days with respect to hundreds of nonstrategic items that they would like to have from America.

On behalf of your Government, we have extended to Poland an invitation to cooperate with America in our satellite program.

We have taken steps to allow the Export-Import Bank to guarantee commercial credits to four additional Eastern European countries--including Poland.

We are now carefully looking at ways in which we may use some portion of our Polish currency balance for the benefit of both countries--ways which will symbolize America's continuing friendship for Poland.

We are trying to determine ways and means to liberalize our rules on travel in our two countries in order to promote much better understanding and increased exchanges between our people.

And, finally, I am quite hopeful that I will be able to arrange to send to Poland a mission of leading American businessmen and others to explore ways to widen and to enrich the ties between Poland and the United States of America.

My fellow Americans, we are living in times of ferment and unrest--both at home and abroad. But I genuinely believe--I truly know--that there is more in America that unites us than there is to divide us. And I believe that our generation now has the opportunity to establish a new era of friendship and cooperation with the peoples of the world. I believe we have the power to eradicate ancient injustices and to ease traditional tensions.

When I leave tomorrow, I shall say that my purpose will be not to accomplish any miracles, but to tell the people of the countries that I visit that the best way to judge America's foreign policy is to look at our domestic policy.

Our domestic policy here at home is to find jobs for our men at good wages, an education for our children, a roof over their heads, and a church that they can worship in according to the dictates of their own conscience, adequate food for their bodies, and health for their families. Because with food, and with income, and with education, and with health, and with a strong defense that will protect our liberty, if we can do that here at home, we can set an example that all the people of the world will want to emulate.

We would like to see all of the 3 billion people have the blessings, advantages, freedom, and prosperity that we have here in America in Pennsylvania this afternoon.

And while we cannot wave any wand and we do not expect to achieve any miracles, we do expect to tell them what interests our people, what we want, and what we would also want for them. And we want to assure them that we do not look at self alone. We "love thy neighbor as thyself."

Yes, our ultimate task is reconciliation--to bring us all to perceive, at home and abroad, regardless of our faith or where we worship, regardless of our sex or our religion, regardless of our color, whether it is white or brown or black or green, to bring to all of us at home and abroad, that men are children of God and brothers.

Yes, we are living in an exciting age. Much is at stake. The fabric of our whole society is at stake. The future of all civilization is at stake. But remembering the words, "Thou shalt love thy neighbor as thyself," I have great hopes for the future. And I believe you do, too.

Thank you very much.

28. STATEMENT BY ALOYSIUS MAZEWSKI, PRESIDENT OF THE POLISH AMERICAN CONGRESS TO THE FOREIGN AFFAIRS COMMITTEE OF THE U.S HOUSE OF REPRESENTATIVES IN SUPPORT OF RADIO FREE EUROPE, SEPTEMBER 15, 1971.*

I sincerely appreciate this opportunity to appear before this Congressional Committee and testify in a matter which is of deep and abiding interest to the Polish American Congress.

At first I would like to emphasize the importance Radio Free Europe broadcasts have in Poland. I am well acquainted with this phase of the RFE operations and I have reasons to believe that similar, beneficial results of its activities can be observed in other countries of East Central Europe.

The Polish American Congress and the entire community of Americans of Polish ancestry do not recognize the Communist regime in Warsaw as the true representative of the Polish people, and our contacts with its representatives are limited to strictly legal matters.

At the same time, Americans of Polish ancestry are, by and large, in intimate contacts with Polish people. Tens of thousands of Polish Americans journey to Poland each year to visit their relatives or to obtain better knowledge of the culture and history of the land of their ancestry.

The contacts between Polish Americans and Poles have already created an atmosphere of sincerity and confidence. I mention this to underscore the fact that I am well acquainted with the opinions, needs and aspirations of the people of Poland apart from their Soviet-dominated government.

Thus we are well aware of the importance that Radio Free Europe has for the Polish people. Its broadcasts provide the people of Poland and other countries of East Central Europe with objective news and commentaries denied them by Communist governments. Without these broadcasts, the nations of East Central Europe would be deprived of true facts and fed with Communist propaganda in the communications media, which serve the aims of Communist dictatorships. Radio Free Europe is the only, and the best, substitute for a free press and radio these people could enjoy.

For this very reason, Radio Free Europe exerts considerable influence on the peoples it serves, by giving them factual information and keeping the hope of a better future alive in their hearts.

We do not have precise figures as to how many people listen to Radio Free Europe in Poland. We do know, however, that there are very few persons in Poland not cognizant of the most important news broadcast by Radio Free Europe, regarding Polish as well as world events.

The best example of this was evidenced during the December riots in Polish cities on the Baltic. Radio Free Europe kept informing not only the Polish people, but the rest of Europe of these events, and by the very factuality of its reporting, prevented the Communist regime in Warsaw from blacking out or distorting the reports of this bloody struggle.

What is even more important, through the Radio Free Europe broadcasts, Polish people knew the reasons for these riots, which stemmed from the workers' protests against the high cost of living and low wages. With these facts, known to practically every Pole, the Communist regime could not put the blame for the riots on "hooligans" and other irresponsible elements. It had to admit, after long delay, that the workers had legitimate reasons for protests against the tyrannical and doctrinaire treatment of their basic economic needs.

The important role Radio Free Europe played in informing the people of Poland and the Western World of these events, was duly noted by the West European press. For instance, the London *Daily Telegram* stated in its December 1970, issue: "With the outbreak of angry rioting in Poland, part of the world's attention focuses once again on Radio Free Europe.... Without the station, few Poles outside the immediately affected area would have known until yesterday what was going on, for it was only then that Radio Warsaw and the official Polish news agency broke their silence on the street battles in the north."

Radio Free Europe is not the only radio facility broadcasting news and commentaries to the Communist-dominated part of Europe. There are programs of the Voice of America, of the British Broadcasting Corporation, of the German unit, and others. These, however, are government-sponsored programs and must toe the diplomatic line of their governments. They are very careful not to provoke an accusation that they are interfering in the internal affairs of the communist-dominated states. It is for this reason, these government-sponsored broadcasting facilities keep avoiding news and commentaries pertaining to the internal affairs or events of East Central European countries. The very fact that they are officially controlled agencies minimizes their effectiveness as far as listeners behind the Iron Curtain are concerned.

It is no secret that the communist regimes concentrate their almost entire efforts on jamming Radio Free Europe broadcasts, while paying a scant attention to programs, for instance of Voice of America, BBC, or German stations.

The Communist governments of the states to which Radio Free Europe broadcasts are beamed, spend considerable sums of money and efforts to jam these programs. In addition they are exerting increasing diplomatic and even economic pressure on the Government of the Federal Republic of Germany to cancel the broadcasting license of Radio Free Europe. The Soviet Union, for instance, threatened to boycott the 1972 Olympics in Munich if Radio Liberty is not liquidated soon. Parenthetically, Radio Liberty has an organization similar to that of Radio Free Europe, only it specializes in broadcasts to the Soviet Union.

The Polish regime, in a note sent to West Germany's chancellor William Brandt, stated that Radio Free Europe and Radio Liberty are the remnants of the Cold War and must be liquidated before the Polish-German and Soviet-German treaties, initialed last year become effective.

It is for these reasons extremely important that Radio Free Europe keeps its independent status. Therefore we wholly support the plan to form a public corporation for Radio Free Europe, which would not be subject to control, or any influence by such governmental agencies as the United States Information Agency or Voice of America.

Only this way can Radio Free Europe continue its very important, vital and crucial mission of freedom, and keep the hope of deliverance alive in the hearts of the people, who, under communist tyranny, long for freedom and self-expression.

I would be happy, as, of course, you gentlemen of the Committee would be happy to state that Radio Free Europe is no longer necessary. A statement like that, however, could be only made in the improbable event when the communist regime would grant freedom of the press and expression to its oppressed people.

But this will not be as long as the Communist totalitarianism is in power.

In the case of Poland, Radio Free Europe is vitally important for one additional reason. Namely no free Polish press from the West, and specifically, no Polish American newspapers and periodicals are allowed in Poland. They cannot reach the Polish people through the mail or other means of circulation.

The only way a free flow of information reaches Poland is by Radio Free Europe.

Therefore I am firmly convinced that this radio broadcasting facility should and must be kept in an independent operation.

The people behind the Iron Curtain know that Radio Free Europe is, in a larger sense, a gift of freedom from the American people. And by creating this good will and a sense of friendship, Radio Free Europe lies in the sphere of America's best, enlightened interest.

* Radio Free Europe, formally established in 1949 as a private agency broadcasting to the Communist satellites in Eastern Europe, was staunchly supported by the Polish American Congress from the outset. In 1970, it was learned that the radio station was being subsidized by the U.S. Central Intelligence Agency. In the face of calls for terminating further American sponsorship of RFE's various activities, legislation was introduced in Congress to set up a Government-supported Corporation for International Communications, an agency under the auspices of the State Department with a mission distinguishable from that of the Voice of America--the broadcasting of news and commentary about Eastern European developments free of Communist censorship.

29. PRESIDENT RICHARD M. NIXON'S MESSAGE TO CONGRESS ON U.S. POLICY; EXCERPTS, MAY 3, 1973.

...The improvement in our relations with the Soviet Union during 1972 has created a better atmosphere for our relations with the countries of Eastern Europe. But we do not regard our relations with the East European countries as a function of our relations with Moscow. We reject the idea of special rights or advantages for outside powers in the region. We welcomed and responded to opportunities to develop our relations with the East European countries long before the Moscow Summit. And we shall continue to seek ways to expand our economic, scientific, technological, and cultural contacts with them. Mutual benefit and reciprocity are governing principles.

As the postwar rigidity between Eastern and Western Europe eases, peoples in both areas expect to see the benefits of relaxation in their daily lives. These aspirations are fully justified. An era of cooperation in Europe should produce a variety of new relationships not just between governments but between organizations, institutions, business firms, and people in all walks of life. If peace in Europe is to be durable, its foundation must be broad.

My visits to Romania in 1969, Yugoslavia in 1970, and Poland in 1972 were designed to help open the door to these broader relationships.

During my visit to Warsaw last June, I agreed with the Polish leaders to increased U.S.-Polish trade and exchanges in science, technology, culture, tourism, and transportation. A joint American-Polish trade commission has been established. After our governments had reciprocally agreed to export financing arrangements, I determined that Export-Import Bank credits should be made available for transactions with Poland. Other agreements to facilitate trade, increase exchanges in science and technology, and improve consular facilities also have been signed.

Secretary of State Rogers' visit in July to Yugoslavia reaffirmed our long-standing and cordial relationship with that important nonaligned country. Its independence, political stability, and economic well-being are key factors for continuing peace in Europe.

Romania's desire for close and mutually beneficial relations has led during the past three years to practical cooperation and to helpful consultations, including my visit to Bucharest and President Ceausescu's trip to Washington. Last year we approved the extending of guarantees to private investment in Romania, and I continue to hope that the Congress will provide authority to extend Most Favored Nation tariff treatment to that country. In December we signed the most comprehensive cultural and scientific exchange agreement in the history of our relations with Romania.

Last summer Secretary Rogers signed consular conventions with both Romania and Hungary. His visit to Budapest and the subsequent settlement of the longstanding United States claims against Hungary have improved prospects for more normal relations.

We remain ready to establish constructive relationships on a reciprocal basis with all countries in Eastern Europe. Differences in social, economic, and political systems exist, and must be acknowledged frankly. But they will not bar our cooperation with any country that seeks it...*

* This message is included in a report that was subsequently published as a 234 page book, *United States Foreign Policy for the 1970s: Shaping a Durable Peace.* Earlier, upon his return from his summit meeting in Moscow and visit to Poland in June 1972, the President hosted 55 Polish American community leaders at the White House.

30. PRESIDENT GERALD R. FORD'S REMARKS TO REPRESENTATIVES OF AMERICANS OF EASTERN EUROPEAN BACKGROUND PRIOR TO HIS DEPARTURE TO ATTEND THE EUROPEAN SECURITY CONFERENCE AT HELSINKI, FINLAND, JULY 25, 1975.*

I am glad to have this opportunity, before taking off for Europe tomorrow, to discuss with you frankly how I feel about the forthcoming European Security Conference in Helsinki.

I know there are some honest doubts and disagreements among good Americans about this meeting with the leaders of Eastern and Western European countries and Canada--35 nations altogether.

There are those who fear the Conference will put a seal of approval on the political division of Europe that has existed since the Soviet Union incorporated the Baltic nations and set new boundaries elsewhere in Europe by military action in World War II. These critics contend that participation by the United States in the Helsinki understandings amounts to tacit recognition of a status quo which favors the Soviet Union and perpetuates its control over countries allied with it.

On the other extreme, there are critics who say the meeting is a meaningless exercise because the Helsinki declarations are merely statements of principles and good intentions which are neither legally binding nor enforceable and cannot be depended upon. They express concern, however, that the result will be to make the free governments of Western Europe and North America less wary and lead to a letting down of NATO's political guard and military defenses.

If I seriously shared these reservations, I would not be going, but I certainly understand the historical reasons for them and, especially, the anxiety of Americans whose ancestral homelands, families, and friends have been and still are profoundly affected by East-West political developments in Europe.

I would emphasize that the document I will sign is neither a treaty nor is it legally binding on any participating State. The Helsinki documents involve political and moral commitments aimed at lessening tensions and opening further the lines of communication between the peoples of East and West.

It is the policy of the United States, and it has been my policy ever since I entered public life, to support the aspirations for freedom and national independence of the peoples of Eastern Europe--with whom we have close ties of culture and blood--by every proper and peaceful means. I believe the outcome of this European Security Conference will be a step--how long a step remains to be tested--in that direction. I hope my visits to Poland, Romania, and Yugoslavia will again demonstrate our continuing friendship and interest in the welfare and progress of the fine people of Eastern Europe.

To keep the Helsinki Conference in perspective, we must remember that it is not simply another summit between the super powers. On the contrary, it is primarily a political dialog among the Europeans--East, West, and neutral--with primary emphasis on European relationships rather than global differences. The United States has taken part, along with Canada, to maintain the solidarity of the Atlantic Alliance and because our absence would have caused a serious imbalance for the West.

We have acted in concert with our free and democratic partners to preserve our interests in Berlin and Germany and have obtained the public commitment of the Warsaw Pact governments to the possibility of peaceful adjustment of frontiers--a major concession which runs quite contrary to the allegation that present borders are being permanently frozen.

The Warsaw Pact nations met important Western preconditions--the Berlin Agreement of 1971, the force reduction talks now underway in Vienna--before our agreement to go to Helsinki.

Specifically addressing the understandable concern about the effect of the Helsinki declarations on the Baltic nations, I can assure you as one who has long been interested in this question that the United States has never recognized the Soviet incorporation of Lithuania, Latvia, and Estonia and is not doing so now. Our official policy of nonrecognition is not affected by the results of the European Security Conference.

There is included in the declaration of principles on territorial integrity the provision that no occupation or acquisition of territory in violation of international law will be recognized as legal. This is not to raise the hope that there will be any immediate change in the map of Europe, but the United States has not abandoned and will not compromise this longstanding principle.

The question has been asked: What have we given up in these negotiations and what have we obtained in return from the other side? I have studied the negotiations and declarations carefully and will discuss them even more intensely with other leaders in Helsinki. In my judgment, the United States and the open countries of the West already practice what the Helsinki accords preach and have no intention of doing what they prohibit--such as using force or restricting freedoms. We are not committing ourselves to anything beyond what we are already committed to by our own moral and legal standards and by more formal treaty agreements such as the United Nations Charter and Declaration of Human Rights.

We are getting a public commitment by the leaders of the more closed and controlled countries to a greater measure of freedom and movement for individuals, information, and ideas than has existed there in the past, and establishing a yardstick by which the world can measure how well they live up to these stated intentions. It is a step in the direction of a greater degree of European community, of expanding East-West contacts, of more normal and healthier relations in an area where we have the closest historic ties. Surely this is the best interest of the United States and of peace in the world.

I think we are all agreed that our world cannot be changed for the better by war, that in the thermonuclear age our primary task is to reduce the danger of unprecedented destruction. This we are doing through continuing strategic arms limitation talks with the Soviet Union and the talks on mutual and balanced force reductions in Europe. This European Security Conference in Helsinki, while it contains some military understandings such as advance notice of maneuvers, should not be confused with either the SALT of MFBR negotiations. The Helsinki summit is linked with our overall policy of working to reduce East-West tensions and pursuing peace, but it is a much more general and modest undertaking.

Its success or failure depends not alone on the United States and the Soviet Union but primarily upon its 33 European signatories--East, West, and neutral. The fact that each of them, large and small, can have their voices heard is itself a good sign. The fact that these very different governments can agree, even on paper, to such principles as greater human contacts and exchanges, improved conditions for journalists, reunification of families and international marriages, a freer flow of information and publications, and increased tourism and travel, seems to me a development well worthy of positive and public encouragement by the United States. If it all fails, Europe will be no worse off than it is now. If even a part of it succeeds, the lot of the people in Eastern Europe will be that much better and the cause of freedom will advance at least that far.

I saw an editorial the other day entitled: "Jerry, Don't Go." But I would rather read that than headlines all over Europe saying: "United States Boycotts Peace Hopes."

So I am going, and I hope your support goes with me.

* PAC President Mazewski was largely responsible for organizing the meeting at the White House.

31. PRESIDENT FORD'S REMARKS AT THE QUADRENNIAL NATIONAL CONVENTION OF THE POLISH AMERICAN CONGRESS, PHILADELPHIA, SEPTEMBER 24, 1976.*

I feel great. How do you feel this morning?

I am greatly honored by your invitation to address the convention of the Polish American Congress, and I am mighty proud to be here, not just as President but as a friend of American Polonia.

It has been the policy of mine--and the policy of my administration--to listen carefully to the voice of Polish America. When it comes to sacrifice and achievement, you have given more, far more than your share in making this the greatest country in the history of mankind.

Fifty-eight years ago another Polish American conference was addressed by the great patriot, Jan Paderewski. His feats as an orator were no less stunning than his genius as a musician and as the leader of the Polish American people. His address to his audience, in Polish, for over 2 1/2 hours-I will not try to emulate that performance--however, let me repeat a few of Paderewski's comments and observations. He said, and I quote, "The Poles in America do not need any Americanization. It is superfluous to explain to them what are the ideals of America. They know very well, for they have been theirs for 1,000 years."

Another Polish American leader put the same thought this way. "I feel I am 200 percent American because I am 100 percent Pole."

Much of what America celebrates in its Bicentennial Year we owe to Polish Americans. Before the Pilgrims even landed at Plymouth, Poles had already first built the first factory in America in the colony at Jamestown. Poles had already pioneered American civil liberties, demanding and receiving from the Virginia colony a voice in their own government.

For more than three and a half centuries, Polish Americans have been working hard to build a better life for themselves and for their children. You have been soldiers and settlers, teachers and clergymen, scientists, craftsmen and artists, You have earned a distinguished place in the New World as your ancestors did in the old.

Yet today, you are troubled. You look abroad and see friends and relatives who do not fully share your freedom in America. You look at home and see too many of your neighborhoods deteriorating. I share your deep concern, and I am also troubled.

But there is much we can do, as much as we have been doing, both at home and abroad. In the first 2 years of this administration, I have worked hard to build a positive and expanding relationship with the people and the Government of Poland. A powerful motivation for that policy has been the knowledge that for many, many Americans, Poland is the home of their ancestors and their relatives.

I have sought to tie our countries closer together economically and culturally. In the last 2 years, trade between our countries has almost doubled. For America, that means more jobs and more production. For Poland, that means a higher standard of living and greater exposure to the American way of life.

A valuable worker in this important task has been the head of the Small Business Administration, Mitch Kobelinski. Last week in Washington, I met with Mitch. He told me personally how badly he wanted to be here this weekend, but this week he is in Poland discussing how and by what means we can expand trade between our two peoples.

My own meetings with Polish officials in Washington, in 1974, and in Warsaw and Krakow, in 1975, have led to a better understanding between our two countries. In 1974, we signed a Joint Statement of Principles of Polish-American Relations. In that statement, I reaffirmed for the United States the importance we attach to a sovereign and independent Poland. That statement was a part of a broader policy I have advocated throughout my entire life.

The United States must continue to support by every peaceful and proper means the aspirations for freedom and national independence of peoples of Eastern Europe. As I have said many times before, as I told a group of Polish American leaders at the White House just 2 weeks ago, the so-called Sonnenfeldt doctrine** never did exist and does not exist. The United States is totally opposed to spheres of influence belonging to any power. That policy is fundamental to our relationship with Poland, and that policy will continue as long as I am President of the United States.

In my several meetings with Polish leaders, I also stressed the importance that all Americans attach to humanitarian issues. People everywhere should have the right to express themselves freely. People everywhere should have the right to emigrate and travel freely. People everywhere should have the right to be united with their families. I will continue to see that humanitarian matters are treated with the highest priority not only in our relationships with Poland but with the rest of the world.

If we are to keep the respect throughout the world that the United States has today and must maintain, we must keep America strong. We must make sure that America not only has strong defenses but a strong heart. Polish Americans know what it means to be strong. Many of your families came here without material wealth. In the countryside you cleared the land and made productive farms. In the cities you built neighborhoods you could be proud of. You built and paid for your own churches. Your built your own schools and financial institutions. You built orphanages for the young and hospitals for the aged. You built your own institutions, the great fraternal organizations represented here today.

We must ensure that what you have done, what you have earned, what you have built, will be here for your children to enjoy--these wonderful young people here on this podium and in this hall. We must ensure that your families will have the neighborhoods they need to build a decent life of their own.

A family needs a neighborhood that is safe. A family needs a neighborhood that is stable. A family needs a neighborhood with local churches, local shops, and local schools.

Some of the healthiest neighborhoods in our cities are Polish American neighborhoods, but today too many neighborhoods are threatened by urban decay. You are paying a terrible price in lost property values--property you worked hard to buy and maintain and that you love.

In cities like Philadelphia, Detroit, Chicago, too many young men and women are finding it impossible to remain in the neighborhoods where they were raised. Too many parents are forced to watch helplessly as all they have worked and saved to build up is eaten away. This does not have to happen. I will continue to do everything in my power to see to it that it does not happen.

On the first day of this year, I signed into law the Mortgage Disclosure Act to prevent redlining and neighborhood decline. Last month, I met with the ethnic leaders to see what more we could do. As a result of that meeting, I created the President's Committee on Urban Development and Neighborhood Revitalization. I charged that Committee with developing a sound Federal policy to help preserve our neighborhoods. That policy will be based on local initiative and local control.

Revitalizing our neighborhoods will help preserve your investments in your homes, your churches, and your community facilities. It will help keep families together; it will help keep America together. America itself is a wonderful family. We must keep that family close--closer in the future than it has been in the past.

As a young boy in Grand Rapids, Michigan, I was very fortunate to have as close friends Americans from many backgrounds. In high school I was lucky. I worked as a part-time waiter and a dishwasher in a restaurant owned by a man named Bill Skouges, who was of Greek descent. That was in 1929 and 1930, when jobs and money were not easy to come by. I earned $2 a week and my lunches, and Bill Skouges earned my admiration and affection and respect.

As a young Congressman, my first administrative assistant was my long and dear friend John Milonowski, who is, incidentally, running for probate judge out there, and let's get him elected. John and I worked together for many, many years, and on my recommendation he became our United States District Attorney in the Western District of Michigan. I was proud of the job he did, and it earns him the opportunity to be one of our three probate judges in the city of Grand Rapids.

But, as President of all of the people, I am determined that every voice in the American family must be heard. The voice of American Polonia will be listened to because all of us are proud of the red, white, and blue. We should be proud of the great heritage of the red and white.

Thank you very, very much.

* Also addressing the delegates was former Governor James Carter of Georgia, the Democratic Party Presidential nominee.

** Helmut Sonnenfeldt, Counselor for the State Department.

32. EXCERPT FROM THE SECOND PRESIDENTIAL DEBATE OF 1976 BETWEEN PRESIDENT FORD AND JAMES CARTER OF GEORGIA, OCTOBER 6, 1976.

...THE MODERATOR. Mr. Frankel, a question for President Ford.

MR. FRANKEL. Mr. President, I'd like to explore a little more deeply our relationship with the Russians. They used to brag, back in Khrushchev's day, that because of their greater patience and because of our greed for business deals, that they would sooner or later get the better of us. Is it possible that, despite some setbacks in the Middle East, they've proved their point? Our allies in France and Italy are now flirting with communism; we've recognized a permanent Communist regime in East Germany; we virtually signed, in Helsinki, an agreement that the Russians have dominance in Eastern Europe; we bailed out Soviet agriculture with our huge grain sales, we've given them large loans, access to our best technology, and if the Senate hadn't interfered with the Jackson Amendment, maybe you would have given them even larger loans. Is that what you call a two-way street of traffic in Europe?

THE PRESIDENT. I believe that we have negotiated with the Soviet Union since I've been President from a position of strength. And let me cite several examples.

Shortly after I became President, in December of 1974, I met with General Secretary Brezhnev in Vladivostok. And we agreed to a mutual cap on the ballistic missile launchers at a ceiling of 2,400, which means that the Soviet Union, if that becomes a permanent agreement, will have to make a reduction in their launchers that they now have or plan to have. I negotiated at Vladivostok with Mr. Breshnev a limitation on the MIRVing of their ballistic missiles at a figure of 1,320, which is the first time that any President has achieved a cap either on launchers or on MIRVs.

It seems to me that we can go from there to the grain sales. The grain sales have been a benefit to American agriculture. We have achieved a 5 3/4-year sale of a minimum of 6 million metric tons, which means that they have already bought about 4 million metric tons this year and are bound to buy another 2 million metric tons, to take the grain and corn and wheat that the American farmers have produced in order to have full production. And these grain sales to the Soviet Union have helped us tremendously in meeting the cost of the additional oil that we have bought from overseas.

If we turn to Helsinki--I am glad you raised it, Mr. Frankel-in the case of Helsinki, 35 nations signed an agreement, including the Secretary of State for the Vatican. I can't under any circumstances believe that His Holiness the Pope would agree, by signing that agreement, that the 35 nations have turned over to the Warsaw Pact nations the domination of Eastern Europe. It just isn't true. And if Mr. Carter alleges that His Holiness, by signing that, has done it, he is totally inaccurate.

Now, what has been accomplished by the Helsinki agreement? Number one, we have an agreement where they notify us and we notify them of any military maneuvers that are to be undertaken. They have done it in both cases where they've done so. There is no Soviet domination of Eastern Europe, and there never will be under a Ford administration.

MR. FRANKEL. I'm sorry, could I just follow--did I understand you to say, sir, that the Russians are not using Eastern Europe as their own sphere of influence and occupying most of the countries there and making sure with their troops that it's a Communist zone, whereas on our side of the line the Italians and the French are still flirting with the possibility of communism?

THE PRESIDENT. I don't believe, Mr. Frankel, that the Yugoslavians consider themselves dominated by the Soviet Union. I don't believe that the Romanians consider themselves dominated by the Soviet Union. I don't believe that the Poles consider themselves dominated by the Soviet Union. Each of those countries is independent, autonomous; it has its own territorial integrity. And the United States does not concede that those countries are under the domination of the Soviet Union. As a matter of fact, I visited Poland, Yugoslavia, and Romania, to make certain that the people of those countries understood that the President of the United States and the people of the United States are dedicated to their independence, their autonomy, and their freedom.

THE MODERATOR. Governor Carter, have you a response?

MR. CARTER. Well, in the first place, I am not criticizing His Holiness the Pope. I was talking about Mr. Ford.

The fact is that secrecy has surrounded the decisions made by the Ford administration. In the case of the Helsinki agreement, it may have been a good agreement at the beginning, but we have failed to enforce the so-called Basket 3 part, which ensures the right of people to migrate, to join their families, to be free to speak out. The Soviet Union is still jamming Radio Free Europe. Radio Free Europe is being jammed.

We've also seen a very serious problem with the so-called Sonnenfeldt document which, apparently, Mr. Ford has just endorsed, which said that there is an organic linkage between the Eastern European countries and the Soviet Union. And I would like to see Mr. Ford convince the Polish Americans and the Czech Americans and the Hungarian Americans in this country that those countries don't live under the domination and supervision of the Soviet Union behind the Iron Curtain...

33. PRESIDENT FORD'S REMARKS AT A MEETING WITH AMERICANS OF EASTERN EUROPEAN ANCESTRY, OCTOBER 12, 1976.

I appreciate this opportunity to meet with you today because I want to set the record straight on an issue that has received prominent attention in the past week--the question of the Soviet domination of Eastern Europe.

Let me be blunt: I did not express myself clearly when this question came up in the debate last Wednesday night. So that there can be no doubt about where I stand, let me spell out precisely what I believe:

-First, the countries of Eastern Europe are, of course, dominated by the Soviet Union. Were it not for the presence of more than 30 Russian divisions there now, the countries of Eastern Europe would long since have achieved their freedom.

-Second, the United States never has, does not now, and never will recognize, accept, or acquiesce in this Soviet domination of Eastern Europe.

-Third, the peoples of Eastern Europe yearn for freedom--while their countries may be physically dominated, their spirit is not. Their spirit has never been broken and never will be. And some day they will be free.

That, ladies and gentlemen, is the essence of my position. It is what my commitment to the dignity of man and his inalienable right to freedom compels me to believe. It is what my whole record of public service has demonstrated I believe. And any man who seeks to persuade you that I think otherwise is engaging in deceit and distortion.

The original mistake was mine. I did not express myself clearly; I admit it. But in the last analysis, my record of 30 years of service in the Congress, as Vice President, and as President must speak for itself. More than a year ago, in July of 1975, I said that, "It has always been my policy ever since I entered public life, to support the aspirations for freedom and national independence of the peoples of Eastern Europe--with whom we have close ties of culture and blood--by every proper and peaceful means." I stand by that record today, and I am proud of it. I welcome making it an issue in this campaign.

But another critical issue--one which you, with particularly close ties to Eastern Europe, as well as the American people as a whole, should consider--is whether a man who shows so little appreciation of America's strength, America's respect, and America's needs-as my opponent has done in this campaign--should be allowed to guide the fortunes of the most powerful nation on earth.

The American people have a right to ask whether a political candidate, who has variously called for a $15 billion cut, or a $7 or 8 billion cut, or a $5 to 7 billion cut in the defense budget, and who then complains that we are "not strong anymore"--as Governor Carter has done--is truly the man to govern the only country in the world that can assure the defense of freedom and give hope to the millions of oppressed in Eastern Europe and throughout the world.

Finally, let me address the critical question of leadership, which Governor Carter has rightly raised. Do we want to entrust the leadership of this great Nation to a man who seeks to lift himself up to the White House by running down the reputation of the United States? Is the leadership we want that which claims that America "is not respected anymore" when it is the United States--and the United States alone--that is trusted by all sides in the Middle East and by both black and white in southern Africa?

America is the leader of the free world, and the American people are proud of it. But the kind of leadership America seeks for itself, the kind of leadership America offers the world, the kind of leadership we need for the future, is the leadership of example, compassion, and common sense. And if that is what we are, if that is what we want to be, then phrases such as "a disgrace to our country"--phrases that demonstrate moral conceit rather than example, compassion, or common sense--have no place.

I want the American people to understand the profound differences between us in areas of policy as well as philosophy. Therefore, I intend to fight Mr. Carter on the issues with all the ability I can command.

The challenges before us are immense if we are to successfully defend the principles of freedom and independence we celebrate this Bicentennial Year. The free world looks to us as the last best hope for preserving this heritage. To be successful we must be strong. The fact is we are, and I intend to assure that in this critical hour America remains the strong, steady defender of freedom for all humanity.

34. PRESIDENT JAMES CARTER'S REMARKS TO POLISH AMERICANS IN THE WHITE HOUSE FOLLOWING TRIP TO POLAND, FEBRUARY 6, 1978.*

First of all, let me say that Rosalynn and I are very delighted to have all of you come. In our desire to make you feel at home and arrange some Warsaw weather, I'm afraid we cut the size of the crowd down too much--[laughter]--but it is beautiful outside, and it's just as pleasant and pure and friendly as it was when we left the wonderful country of Poland.

As you noticed from the photographs outside, we had a delightful and, I think, a very fruitful visit. Rosalynn and Dr. Brzezinski had a long meeting with Cardinal Wyszynski. It was a very inspiring report that I got back from my wife. I don't think any First Family members had had a chance to meet with him from the Western nations. And it was very important to us as Christians to recognize the overwhelming influence of the Christian faith in Poland.

Later, when I talked to First Secretary Gierek, I told him that I congratulated him on going to visit Cardinal Wyszynski just recently. I told him to visit him often and we had not given up yet on converting him to Christianity. I told him it was never too late for him to have the same faith as we. [Laughter]

He and I got along well. And I thought that the Polish Government, who could have done otherwise, made it easy for us to reach literally millions of people in Poland through the fully broadcast news conference, which was unprecedented, and almost all of the news reporters were permitted to come. I commented publicly on the ones that weren't permitted to come, and I answered their written questions later for them.

It was truly an inspiring thing for me. And with a few variations in the interpretation that went out to the Polish people--[laughter]--the written transcript of the interview, which was a freewheeling, open press conference, went verbatim in the major Polish news media throughout the land. So, I thought it was an excellent opportunity for us to communicate freely with them.

I was overwhelmed with the response of the Polish people when we discussed the historic ties that have long bound our countries together. As a southerner from Georgia, my own earliest studies of both Georgia and United States history have included in a major way the reports of the great heroism and dedication of Kosciuszko and Pulaski. My own son Chip's wife is from Pulaski County in Georgia, named in honor of the Polish patriot who helped us win our independence. And we discussed quite freely, both with people whom we met on the streets and those who were servants in the beautiful mansion we stayed and those in the government, the common effort that we had made in the world wars, when Poland was so nearly destroyed.

I have heard from a child about the devastation of the War Between the States that afflicted my own grandparents and some of yours. But I have never seen a nation which had been so terribly damaged by war as Poland.

We learned about the history of Warsaw and the heroism of the people there and the courage in rebuilding that beautiful city. And we saw the small portion of the visual treasures of ancient Poland that had been preserved, and we were thankful to have a chance to see that beautiful display of Polish art.

We had also an opportunity to learn at first hand about the relative freedom that the Polish people have to worship, and I commented on it publicly because I think it's a precious thing. We have many very fine Polish Americans in our Nation who have occupied positions of great importance. And you have honored us by coming here this evening.

I have decided to ask Danny Rostenkowski and Senator Muskie and Senator Robert Byrd, all of whom have contacted me about it, to introduce a special bill to authorize Mrs. Eddie Slovik to receive her insurance payments from the last war.

I had a letter earlier from the Polish American Guardian Society asking me to do this. And I have inquired with the Attorney General and with the Secretary of Defense--it's not legal for me to authorize these payments. So, there will be a special bill introduced in Congress which I will support. And Senator Byrd, the majority leader in the Senate, Congressman Rostenkowski, Congressman Rangel have already expressed their eagerness to see this introduced in the House, and I hope it will pass without delay.

I would like to say in closing that this is an opportunity for us to reassert the appreciation in our country for those historic ties between Poland and our Nation. We are tied together militarily through a long series of wars which we hope will never come again. We are tied together politically in generations past, and we still have strong friendships of trade and hope for the future in Poland now. And we are tied together culturally, and I think perhaps most importantly of all, we are tied together through blood kinship.

There are millions of Polish Americans here. I have gotten varying reports on how many millions. [*Laughter*] I was cautioned before I went there to be conservative in my estimates so that I wouldn't claim too much. When I was with First Secretary Gierek, the first thing I said was there are 8 million Americans of Polish descent. He said, "No, that's not right. There are at least 12 or 14 million." So I didn't argue with him. [*Laughter*]

But I think you know that this is a very important thing to cherish. And during the campaign, I was permitted to visit many communities in our Nation which have a heavy concentration of Americans of Polish descent. Dr. Brzezinski, who was in the receiving line, is very close to me, and the man who's had the most effect on my life, other than my own father, Admiral Hyman Rickover, as you know, is also from Poland...

* President Carter visited Poland in December, 1977 as part of an international trip that also took him to Romania, Iran and India. The meeting arranged upon his return was distinctive in that guests included not only the leaders of the Polish American Congress but also Americans of Polish origin from the professions and the arts, some of whom were not active in the Polonia organizations.

During the 1976 Presidential elections, Aloysius Mazewski and the PAC had been closely associated with the candidacy of Gerald Ford; his defeat caused a temporary chill in relations between the White House and the Polish American Congress. In August 1979, however, President Carter hosted the leadership of the Polish National Alliance, of which Mazewski was also President, at a special reception in the White House at the time of the PNA national convention in Washington, D.C. On September 20, 1980 Carter delivered a speech in Chicago to the members of the Alliance on the occasion of its centennial anniversary, the first time in history that an American Chief

Executive had so honored a Polish fraternal. (The address is reprinted in full in Donald Pienkos, *PNA*, pp. 415-419.) Furthermore, Carter soon afterward delivered several significant messages to Poland and the Soviet Union concerning the United States' response to the rise of the Solidarity movement. These are reprinted below and demonstrate Carter's interest in Polish affairs and Polonia's concerns, and the influence upon the President exerted by National Security Adviser Zbigniew Brzezinski and to a lesser degree Secretary of State Edmund Muskie, who was also of Polish ancestral origin.

35. POLISH AMERICAN CONGRESS MEMORANDUM TO PRESIDENT CARTER ON CURRENT CONDITIONS IN POLAND, AUGUST 25, 1980.

Developments in Poland--culminating in the current confrontation between the striking workers and the country's Communist dictatorship pose a challenge and a test of the consistency of the United States policy of support for human rights.

The Polish American community expresses its full support and solidarity for the efforts of the Polish workers and people as they seek a greater measure of human rights and freedoms.

The initial reaction of the Department of State in order to avoid or minimize the risk of Soviet intervention was to state that these developments are exclusively an internal matter of Poland. This was interpreted by the mass media and many others, especially Poles and Polish Americans, as a lack of understanding and concern, and an abandonment of the United States' commitments under the Helsinki accords.

Soviet Union does not need a pretext to intervene militarily. It will--pretext or no pretext--if and when it concludes that the monopoly of Communist power and the cohesiveness of the Warsaw Pact bloc is being challenged. Polish strikers, as well as opposition groups in Poland, are fully aware of this reality.

Accordingly, no such direct challenge is contained in the demands advanced by striking workers, even though they include abolition of censorship, freedom of speech and establishment of free trade unions, which are all within the parameters of the Helsinki Act, the International Covenant on Civil and Political Rights, and more so the Constitution of Poland.

Demands formulated by the strike committee are just. Resolution of the economic and political crisis which paralyses Poland requires establishment of conditions leading to full participation of its citizens, especially workers and farmers, in the vital decisions affecting their lives. Such participation and cooperation must be based on free representation and uninhibited debate of problems and their solutions.

We are cognizant of the fact, that the implementation of these just demands, can be achieved through an evolutionary process.

We believe that consistent with our professed policy of support for human rights, within the framework of the Helsinki Declaration, the United States government should urgently:

-Express its moral support for the strikers' demands for respect of their human rights and dignity;

-Denounce possible recurrence of repression and intimidation;

-Emphasize that in the interests of current and future international relations and cooperation, peace and stability, the conflict must be resolved by the Polish people and Polish authorities, without any outside physical interference;

-Call upon both sides to act with a sense of realism and judicious restraint.

The underlying cause of strikes is the deepening economic crisis, brought about mainly by the inefficient, wasteful and corrupt Communist system of centralized planning and management of the country's economy. To help restore Poland's economic viability we recommend the United States government offer to Poland an extended program of economic assistance. It should be predicated on the Polish government's introduction of remedial, structural reforms, which are prerequisites to its future economic progress.

Accordingly we also urge the United States Government to immediately establish a strong economic assistance program to Poland which would focus upon:

1) The rescheduling of the repayment of Poland's foreign debt.

2) The extension of additional grain credits of at least 675 million dollars for 1980.

3) An emergency food program.

4) Doubling Poland's fishing quotas in Alaskan waters for 1980.

Such an economic assistance program is simply a reflection of the moral commitment that is a necessary part of any effective human rights program.

Events in Poland demonstrate the crucial importance of the free flow of information provided by the Radio Free Europe/Radio Liberty and the Voice of America.

In summary, we are confident, that this two-pronged approach by the United States Government: efforts to promote negotiated settlement of Polish workers' demands and a parallel offer to aid Poland to enable it to overcome the pervasive economic stagnation, will significantly strengthen Poland internally. We firmly believe that this would enhance United States national interests and security, since Poland, traditionally a friend and ally of western democracies, and of the United States particularly, will thus provide a strong element of European stability and peace.

The Polish American community trusts that our requests will be urgently considered and that it will be informed and consulted concerning their implementation.

Aloysius A. Mazewski
President

36. PRESIDENT CARTER'S REMARKS ANNOUNCING AGRICULTURAL COMMODITY CREDIT GUARANTEES TO POLAND, A FIRST U.S. RESPONSE TO EVENTS THERE, SEPTEMBER 12, 1980.

The Government and the people of the United States have watched with concern and with hope as events have unfolded in Poland in recent days. Our response has been careful, constructive, and prudent. All of us have sympathized with the aspirations of the Polish people. All of us are glad that a crisis in Poland's evolution appears to be on its way to a peaceful and constructive resolution.

These events touched the emotions of all who care about the rights and dignity of people. There was progress. There's also continued economic dislocation. Now there's a need, the most basic kind of need--the need for food. On behalf of the American people I'm acting on an urgent basis to help meet that need for food.

I've directed today the U.S. Department of Agriculture to extend $670 million in new credit guarantees to Poland for the purchase of agricultural commodities. In plain language this means that the American people and American farmers will guarantee loans to sell some 4 million tons of grain and other farm products to the people of Poland.

I'd like to say just a word about why we are doing this. In taking this action the Government of the United States is responding quickly and completely to a request from the Government and the people of Poland. But in a deeper sense we are responding to the moral obligation that's rooted in the fundamental beliefs of the people of the United States and the people of Poland.

This action is a significant proof of the solidarity between the American people and the Polish people. It's an expression of our admiration for the dignity with which the entire Polish nation--the workers, the Government, and the church--is conducting itself during this difficult time of evolution and change. It's a demonstration of our willingness to use our greatest material asset, the bounty of the American earth, for humanitarian and constructive reasons.

Finally, it's a manifestation of the undiminished belief that a central human reality, the yearning for basic human rights, that yearning is one of the most powerful and constructive forces in the world, and our support for it is more than just a matter of words.

Thank you very much...

37. PRESIDENT CARTER ON THE GROWING CRISIS IN POLAND, DECEMBER 3, 1980.*

The United States is watching with growing concern the unprecedented building of Soviet forces along the Polish border and the closing of certain frontier regions along the border. The United States has also taken note of Soviet references to alleged "anti-Socialist" forces within Poland. We know from postwar history that such allegations have sometimes preceded military intervention.

The United States continues to believe that the Polish people and authorities should be free to work out their internal difficulties without outside interference. The United States, as well as some Western governments, and also the Soviet Union, have pledged economic assistance to Poland in order to alleviate internal Polish difficulties. The United States has no interest in exploiting in any fashion the Polish difficulties for its political ends.

Foreign military intervention in Poland would have most negative consequences for East-West relations in general and U.S.-Soviet relations in particular. The Charter of the United Nations establishes the right of all states, both large and small, to exist free of foreign interference, regardless of ideology, alliances, or geographic location. I want all countries to know that the attitude and future policies of the United States toward the Soviet Union would be directly and very adversely affected by any Soviet use of force in Poland.

* The statement was reiterated on December 7, 1980.

38. POLISH AMERICAN CONGRESS MEMORANDUM TO PRESIDENT RONALD W. REAGAN, DECEMBER 20, 1981.

We appreciate the opportunity to discuss the current crisis in Poland. We offer our support and concur that Solidarity's right to exercise those civil and political rights enshrined in many international documents to which Poland is a party, should not be impeded.

We concur with you that the Soviets are deeply involved and should bear the responsibility.

In fact the Soviets have invaded by proxy, with their General Kulikov's presence and the plans for the Martial Law prepared and orchestrated by the Soviets. *Now* is the time to reinstitute the grain embargo.

The Declaration of Martial Law in Poland has created a state of repression and in violation of the Helsinki Act--as:

1. Arrest of Lech Walesa and his Solidarity staff.

2. Arrests of numerous thousands of persons placed in jails and camps, whose facilities are totally inadequate, and inhuman treatment.

3. Violence, repression, and force causing hundreds to be injured and many dead.

4. Extreme shortages of food.

5. Influx of many refugees in Vienna, Frankfort, seeking asylum.

What do we demand of Poland, through our government:

1. Immediate removal of Martial Law and a resumption of negotiations with Solidarity to arrive at an amicable solution.

2. Immediate release of Lech Walesa and members of Solidarity and giving him an opportunity to address his countrymen.

3. Immediate release of all political prisoners be they in jails or internment camps.

4. Restoration of the gains made by Solidarity.

We are strongly suggesting that the United States take the following action:

1. Develop means of communications informing the Polish Government of the above demands.

2. Institute an immediate embargo on shipment of Soviet grain for their part in the Polish crisis.

3. Request the International Red Cross and the Commission in the United Nations for an immediate investigation of the inhumane conditions in jails and camps and the violation of human rights under the Helsinki Act.

4. Reconsideration of stopping shipment of foods to Poland. The Polish people are not to be blamed, since the real perpetrators are the Soviets. We are making the innocent suffer.

5. Support of private charitable organizations in the food distribution by supplying of surplus foods.

6. Lack of news and information requires pooling of transmitters of Radio Free Europe and Voice of America. It is the only source of information for the Poles.

7. Requesting a meeting of the Security Council of the United Nations on the crisis in Poland.

8. The U.S. should request various international forums as the League of International Red Cross Societies, to raise legitimate questions, of cruel and inhuman treatment of persons, violations of human rights and processing for admissions to Poland of neutral observers to look after the interest of the world in the observance of the laws of war. These actions are not abandonment of neutrality or intervening in Polish internal affairs.

9. Plans of action of the U.S. and the Atlantic Allies in the event of a possible Soviet invasion, should be made public, as to the consequences that the Soviets will suffer. This should be a joint statement from the Atlantic Allies as to imposition of total economic and diplomatic sanctions against the Soviets. It should be made now, so that the Soviets would know of the price they would have to pay.

10. In view of the great number of Polish refugees in Vienna and Frankfurt due to the critical conditions in Poland, we urge you to order the following:

a. Declare the existence of an emergency refugee situation under Section 207(s) of the Refugee Act of 1980 as to Polish Refugees.

b. Order that Polish immigrants be granted political asylum and *num pro tunc* employment authorization thereby allowing Polish immigrants to adjust their status in the U.S.

c. Reappraise the attitude of the State Department and Immigration and Naturalization Service in the handling of Polish refugees and asylum requests. This should apply to all who have requested political asylum be they in U.S. or elsewhere.

Our experience during the Hungarian and Czechoslovak crises should certainly warn us, that what we have done in the past was fruitless and that a more firm positive action is necessary.

These amongst many other remedies should be instituted to alleviate the crisis in Poland, that could have great disastrous results on the entire world. We just cannot sit by but we must take necessary action which will give aid and comfort to Poland and all freedom loving people, having in mind the best interests of the U.S.

Respectfully,
Aloysius A. Mazewski, President Polish
   American Congress
Helen Zielinski, Vice President
Kazimierz Lukomski, Vice President
Harriet Bielanski, Secretary General
Joseph A. Drobot, Treasurer

39. PRESIDENT REAGAN'S ADDRESS TO THE NATION ON THE SITUATION IN POLAND, DECEMBER 23, 1981.

...As I speak to you tonight, the fate of a proud and ancient nation hangs in the balance. For a thousand years, Christmas has been celebrated in Poland, a land of deep religious faith, but this Christmas brings little joy to the courageous Polish people. They have been betrayed by their own government.

The men who rule them and their totalitarian allies fear the very freedom that the Polish people cherish. They have answered the stirrings of liberty with brute force, killings, mass arrests, and the setting up of concentration camps. Lech Walesa and other Solidarity leaders are imprisoned, their fate unknown. Factories, mines, universities, and homes have been assaulted.

The Polish Government has trampled underfoot solemn commitments to the U.N. Charter and the Helsinki accords. It has even broken the Gdansk agreement of August 1980, by which the Polish Government recognized the basic right of its people to form free trade unions and to strike.

The tragic events now occurring in Poland, almost 2 years to the day after the Soviet invasion of Afghanistan, have been precipitated by public and secret pressure from the Soviet Union. It is no coincidence that Soviet Marshal Kulikov, chief of the Warsaw Pact forces, and other senior Red Army officers were in Poland while these outrages were being initiated. And it is no coincidence that the martial law proclamations imposed in December by the Polish Government were being printed in the Soviet Union in September.

The target of this repression is the Solidarity movement, but in attacking Solidarity its enemies attack an entire people. Ten million of Poland's 36 million citizens are members of Solidarity. Taken together with their families, they account for the overwhelming majority of the Polish nation. By persecuting Solidarity the Polish Government wages war against its own people.

I urge the Polish Government and its allies to consider the consequences of their actions. How can they possibly justify using naked force to crush a people who ask for nothing more than the right to lead their own lives in freedom and dignity?

Brute force may intimidate, but it cannot form the basis of an enduring society, and the ailing Polish economy cannot be rebuilt with terror tactics.

Poland needs cooperation between its government and its people, not military oppression. If the Polish Government will honor the commitments it has made to human rights in documents like the Gdansk agreement, we in America will gladly do our share to help the shattered Polish economy, just as we helped the countries of Europe after both World Wars.

It's ironic that we offered, and Poland expressed interest in accepting, our help after World War II. The Soviet Union intervened then and refused to allow such help to Poland. But if the forces of tyranny in Poland, and those who incite them from without, do not relent, they should prepare themselves for serious consequences. Already, throughout the Free World, citizens have publicly demonstrated their support for the Polish people. Our government, and those of our allies, have expressed moral revulsion at the police state tactics of Poland's oppressors. The Church has also spoken out, in spite of threats and intimidation. But our reaction cannot stop there.

I want emphatically to state tonight that if the outrages in Poland do not cease, we cannot and will not conduct "business as usual" with the perpetrators and those who aid and abet them. Make no mistake, their crime will cost them dearly in their future dealings with America and free peoples everywhere. I do not make this statement lightly or without serious reflection.

We have been measured and deliberate in our reaction to the tragic events in Poland. We have not acted in haste, and the steps I will outline tonight and others we may take in the days ahead are firm, just, and reasonable.

In order to aid the suffering Polish people during this critical period, we will continue the shipment of food through private humanitarian channels, but only so long as we know that the Polish people themselves receive the food. The neighboring country of Austria has opened her doors to refugees from Poland. I have therefore directed that American assistance, including supplies of basic foodstuffs, be offered to aid the Austrians in providing for these refugees.

But to underscore our fundamental opposition to the repressive actions taken by the Polish Government against its own people, the administration has suspended all government-sponsored shipments of agricultural and dairy products to the Polish Government. This suspension will remain in force until absolute assurances are received that distribution of these products is monitored and guaranteed by independent agencies. We must be sure that every bit of food provided by America goes to the Polish people, not to their oppressors.

The United States is taking immediate action to suspend major elements of our economic relationships with the Polish Government. We have halted the renewal of the Export-Import Bank's line of export credit insurance to the Polish Government. We will suspend Polish civil aviation privileges in the United States. We are suspending the right of Poland's fishing fleet to operate in American waters. And we're proposing to our allies the further restriction of high technology exports to Poland.

These actions are not directed against the Polish people. They are a warning to the Government of Poland that free men cannot and will not stand idly by in the face of brutal repression. To underscore this point, I've written a letter to General Jaruzelski, head of the Polish Government. In it, I outlined the steps we're taking and warned of the serious consequences if the Polish Government continues to use violence against its populace. I've urged him to free those in arbitrary detention, to lift martial law, and to restore the internationally recognized rights of the Polish people to free speech and association.

The Soviet Union, through its threats and pressures, deserves a major share of blame for the developments in Poland. So, I have also sent a letter to President Brezhnev urging him to permit the restoration of basic human rights in Poland provided for in the Helsinki Final Act. In it, I informed him that if this repression continues, the United States will have no choice but to take further concrete political and economic measures affecting our relationship.

When 19th century Polish patriots rose against foreign oppressors, their rallying cry was, "For our freedom and yours." Well, that motto still rings true in our time. There is a spirit of solidarity abroad in the world tonight that no physical force can crush. It crosses national boundaries and enters into the hearts of men and women everywhere. In factories, farms, and schools, in cities and towns around the globe, we the people of the Free World stand as one with our Polish brothers and sisters. Their cause is ours, and our prayers and hopes go out to them this Christmas.

Yesterday, I met in this very room with Romuald Spasowski, the distinguished former Polish Ambassador who has sought asylum in our country in protest of the suppression of his native land. He told me that one of the ways the Polish people have demonstrated their solidarity in the face of martial law is by placing lighted candles in their windows to show that the light of liberty still glows in their hearts.

Ambassador Spasowski requested that on Christmas Eve a lighted candle will burn in the White House window as a small but certain beacon of our solidarity with the Polish people. I urge all of you to do the same tomorrow night, on Christmas Eve, as a personal statement of your commitment to the steps we're taking to support the brave people of Poland in their time of troubles.

Once, earlier in this century, an evil influence threatened that the lights were going out all over the world. Let the light of millions of candles in American homes give notice that the light of freedom is not going to be extinguished....

40. PRESIDENT REAGAN'S STATEMENT ON U.S. MEASURES TAKEN AGAINST THE SOVIET UNION CONCERNING ITS INVOLVEMENT IN POLAND, DECEMBER 29, 1981.

The Soviet Union bears a heavy and direct responsibility for the repression in Poland. For many months the Soviets publicly and privately demanded such a crackdown. They brought major pressures to bear through now public letters to the Polish leadership, military maneuvers, and other forms of intimidation. They now openly endorse the suppression which has ensued.

Last week I announced that I had sent a letter to President Brezhnev urging him to permit the restoration of basic human rights in Poland as provided for in the Helsinki Final Act. I also informed him that, if the repression continued, the United States would have no choice but to take further concrete political and economic measures affecting our relationship.

The repression in Poland continues, and President Brezhnev has responded in a manner which makes it clear the Soviet Union does not understand the seriousness of our concern, and its obligations under both the Helsinki Final Act and the U.N. Charter. I have, therefore, decided to take the following immediate measures with regard to the Soviet Union:

-All Aeroflot service to the United States will be suspended.

-The Soviet Purchasing Commission is being closed.

-The issuance or renewal of licenses for the export to the U.S.S.R. of electronic equipment, computers and other high-technology materials is being suspended.

-Negotiations on a new long-term grains agreement are being postponed.

-Negotiations on a new U.S.-Soviet Maritime Agreement are being suspended, and a new regime of port-access controls will be put into effect for all Soviet ships when the current agreement expires on December 31.

-Licenses will be required for export to the Soviet Union for an expanded list of oil and gas equipment. Issuance of such licenses will be suspended. This includes pipelayers.

- U.S.-Soviet exchange agreements coming up for renewal in the near future, including the agreements on energy and science and technology, will not be renewed. There will be a complete review of all other U.S.-Soviet exchange agreements.

The United States wants a constructive and mutually beneficial relationship with the Soviet Union. We intend to maintain a high-level dialog. But we are prepared to proceed in whatever direction the Soviet Union decides upon--towards greater mutual restraint and cooperation, or further down a harsh and less rewarding path. We will watch events in Poland closely in coming days and weeks. Further steps may be necessary, and I will be prepared to take them. American decisions will be determined by Soviet actions.

Secretary Haig has been in communication with our friends and allies about the measures we are taking and explained why we believe such steps are essential at this time.

Once again I call upon the Soviet Union to recognize the clear desire of the overwhelming majority of the Polish people for a process of national reconciliation, renewal, and reform.

41. PRESIDENT REAGAN'S PROCLAMATION ON THE FORTIETH ANNIVERSARY OF THE WARSAW UPRISING, AUGUST 17, 1984.*

Forty years ago, one of the most heroic battles of World War II, the Warsaw Uprising, occurred. Polish resistance to aggression throughout World War II had been courageous and uncompromising. As the Nazi forces retreated before advancing Soviet armies, the Polish Home Army that led the resistance seized its chance to throw off the Nazi yoke. For sixty-three days, the people of Warsaw fought against insurmountable odds, endured unimaginable suffering, and made countless sacrifices to regain their independence. Nevertheless, the lightly-armed resistance fighters were overwhelmed by the full weight of Hitler's war machine. The Nazis mercilessly crushed the uprising while Soviet forces passively looked on from across the Vistula River. Warsaw lay in rubble. Two hundred-fifty thousand Poles were killed, wounded, or missing. Yet the victims of the Warsaw Uprising did not die in vain.

The example of those who fought for freedom during the Warsaw Uprising is a stirring chapter in history, as vivid today as it was then. The ongoing struggle of the faithful, the shipyard workers of Gdansk, the miners of Silesia, and farmers throughout the countryside is but a continuation of the proud history of the Polish quest of freedom.

It is right that we pay tribute to those who sacrificed all for independence and freedom. All of us who share their passion for freedom owe the heroic people of Warsaw and all of the valiant people of Poland a profound debt.

The Congress, by Senate Joint Resolution 272, has resolved that the United States should join in recognizing the Anniversary of the Warsaw Uprising.

Now, Therefore, I, Ronald Reagan, President of the United States of America, hereby proclaim August 1, 1984, as the Fortieth Anniversary of the Warsaw Uprising.

In Witness Whereof, I have hereunto set my hand this seventeenth day of August, in the year of our Lord nineteen hundred and eighty-four, and of the Independence of the United States of America the two hundred and ninth.

* On the same day, the President also issued a proclamation declaring August as Polish American Heritage month across the country.

42. PRESIDENT REAGAN'S REMARKS AT A WHITE HOUSE LUNCHEON MARKING THE FORTIETH ANNIVERSARY OF THE WARSAW UPRISING, AUGUST 17, 1984.

...It's always an honor for me to be with individuals like yourselves who understand the value of freedom. I'm reminded of a story about a conversation between one of our citizens and a Soviet citizen. The American described the freedom of speech that we have here in the United States, and the citizen of the Soviet Union said, "Well, we're free to speak in the Soviet Union just like you are in the United States." He said, "The only difference is you're free after you speak." [*Laughter*]

But today we pay tribute to a nation which for two centuries has struggled for freedom and independence. From the uprisings in 1794, the November uprising in 1830, and then again in 1863, the people of Poland demonstrated courage and a commitment to human liberty that inspired free men and women everywhere.

And this 200-year record of perseverance and bravery coincided with the development of our own precious liberty here in the United States, and that is no mere coincidence. Our two peoples drank from the same well of freedom, held dear the same Judeo-Christian values, respected the simple virtues of honesty and hard work. And even today, it's often noted that unlike many others, our two peoples take their religious convictions seriously. These heartfelt convictions have kept the spirit of freedom burning in our hearts, especially during times of great adversity.

Pope John Paul II has said, "Freedom is given to man by God as a measure of his dignity...." And "as children of God," he said, "we cannot be slaves." Well, I know that you feel as I do; we're truly blessed in this time of great need, to have a spiritual leader like Pope John Paul II.

The continuing suppression of the Polish national identity brought wave after wave of Polish immigrants to the United States. And for that, we can be grateful. We all know the list of contributions and the names of those who rose to great prominence. But just as important are the millions who came here and, with their hard work and with their moral strength, helped shape the American character.

During this century, Americans and Poles have stood side by side in those two conflagrations that swept the world. The First World War, unfortunately, did not end all wars, but it did result in the reestablishment of the Polish state.

This month, we commemorate a desperate battle of the Second World War, an heroic attempt by free Poles to liberate their country from the heel of Nazi occupation, and to protect it from postwar, foreign domination. For years they covertly resisted the occupation forces. And then in 1944, for 63 brutal and agonizing days, ill-equipped and overwhelmingly outnumbered, they--and I could say, many of you--held off the Nazi war machine. And it's fitting that we and all free people take special care to remember this occasion.

Of those who fought for freedom, and those who put their lives on the line for human liberty, I can think of none who should be prouder than those who can say, "I fought in the Polish Home Army."

And today we honor three individuals, heroes of the Polish Home Army, never given their due after the allied victory. And it's my great honor to now present the Legion of Merit to the families or representatives of these men.

(The President then presented awards in tribute of Stefan Rowecki, leader of the resistance until he was captured and executed by the Gestapo; Tadeusz Bor-Komorowski, leader of the Warsaw Uprising; and Leopold Okulicki, Bor's successor as Commander of the Polish Home Army, who died under suspicious circumstances in Moscow.)

These brave men and the courageous individuals who fought under their command represent the best of the human spirit. They risked all for their ideals, for their God and country, at a time when the odds were so much against them. They're now part of the inspiring legacy of the Polish people.

If there's a lesson to be learned from the history books, it is that Poland may be beaten down, but it is never defeated. It may be forced into submission, but it will never give up. It may be pressured to acquiesce, but it will never accept foreign domination and the suppression of God-given freedom. After four decades of brutal foreign domination, we witnessed, just a short time ago, a resurrection of the indomitable spirit of the Polish people. And I assure you we have not forgotten and will never forget Solidarity and the freedom of the Polish people.

There are some, of course, who seem all too willing to turn a blind eye to Soviet transgressions, ostensibly to improve the dialog between East and West. But those who condemn firm support for freedom and democracy--who, in order to prove their sincerity, would project weakness--are no friends of peace, human liberty, or meaningful dialog.

Our policies toward Poland and other captive nations are based upon a set of well-established principles.

First. let me state emphatically that we reject any interpretation of the Yalta agreement that suggests American consent for the division of Europe into spheres of influence. On the contrary, we see that agreement as a pledge by the three great powers to restore full independence and to allow free and democratic elections in all countries liberated from the Nazis after World War II, and there is no reason to absolve the Soviet Union or ourselves from this commitment. We shall continue to press for full compliance with it and with the Charter of the United Nations, the Helsinki Final Act, and other international agreements guaranteeing fundamental human rights.

Passively accepting the permanent subjugation of the people of Eastern Europe is not an acceptable alternative. In 1981, when it appeared that Poland would suffer a similar fate to that of Hungary in 1956 or Czechoslovakia in 1968, we raised our voices in support of the Polish people. And we did not remain passive when, under intense Soviet pressure, martial law was imposed on them.

Many credit, trade, and fishing privileges extended to Poland, due to its somewhat broader degree of freedom than other Eastern European countries, were suspended. At the same time, we have assisted voluntary organizations to provide humanitarian aid through the Polish church to avoid hurting the very people we want to help.

I would especially like to commend the work of Al Mazewski and the Polish American Congress. In cooperation with the church, they've provided over $40 million worth of food, clothing, and medical supplies to the people of Poland. And I know that I speak for Nancy--my wife is thrilled to have been selected honorary chairman for the Polish American Congress' Infant Charity Drive. We both wish you the best on this worthwhile project.

I've pledged that our sanctions can be lifted, one by one, in response to meaningful improvement of the human rights situation in Poland. For example, a complete and reasonable implementation of the Polish Government's amnesty decree would create a positive atmosphere that would allow reactivation of Poland's application for membership in the International Monetary Fund.

In the meantime, we've agreed, along with our allies and private organizations, to help fund a Polish church program to assist individual farmers. I am pleased to announce today that I am seeking support for a $10 million American contribution to the pilot phase of the church's program. And we will follow the progress of this program carefully to determine whether additional support should be forthcoming.

Perhaps the most significant thing that we can do is let the Polish people and all the people of Eastern Europe know that they're not forgotten. And that's why we're modernizing Radio Free Europe, Radio Liberty, and the Voice of America. Our radio programming is becoming the mighty force for good that it was intended to be. As the Scriptures say, "Know the truth and the truth will make you free." Well, our broadcast will carry the truth to captive people throughout the world.

The free peoples of the world are in ideological competition with the followers of a doctrine that rejects the basic tenets of freedom and declares the worship of God to be a social evil. As important as this competition is, until recently the democracies, including the United States, seemed paralyzed by uncertainty and lacking the will to compete.

In the last 3 1/2 years, we've quit apologizing, and at long last we're standing up and being counted. As our United Nations Ambassador, Jeane Kirkpatrick, said, we've taken off our "Kick Me" sign. We're proud of our way of life; we're confident that freedom will prevail, because it works and because it is right. We believe the free peoples of the world should support all those who share our democratic values.

The National Endowment for Democracy, which I first proposed in a speech before the Parliament in London 2 years ago, has been established to encourage the democratic forces and the development of free institutions throughout the world. Its concerns include nonviolent, democratic movements like that of Solidarity in Poland.

And the rise of Solidarity is a matter of historic significance. It continues to be an inspiration of all free people that the Marxist-Leninist myth of inevitability is crumbling. Communism has brought with it only deprivation and tyranny. What happened in Poland is one sign that the tide is turning. The Polish people, with their courage and perseverance, will lead the way to freedom and independence, not only for themselves but for all those who yearn to breathe free.

The battle cry of the Polish Home Army still rings true: "Poland is fighting. Poland will live. Poland will overcome."

Thank you all for being here today, and God bless you.

Mr. Korbonski. * Mr. President, on behalf of former underground Home Army soldiers, who celebrate this month the 40th anniversary of the Warsaw uprising, in my native Poland and throughout the world, and who are presently here, I thank you very much for what you said about our history, about the Warsaw uprising, about your understanding of the Yalta agreement, and about Solidarity, which, in my opinion, is also underground, but which fights for freedom and independence of Poland by other means than arms.

Your words broadcast to Poland by Voice of America and Radio Free Europe will bring a new inspiration, new hope, to our people in Poland. To what you said about the Warsaw uprising, I want only to add a few words.

First of all, that you, our American allies, contributed to this heroic struggle. On the 18th of September, the American Air Force armada welcomed enthusiastically by the embattled population of Warsaw, parachuted very badly needed supplies.

Mr. President, 1984 is not a year for mourning. It is true that we suffered tremendous human and material losses during the uprising. But they were well balanced by the immaterial, spiritual, moral gains. In these defeats, there were seeds of victory. The Warsaw uprising demonstrated to the whole world the indomitable Polish spirit--our unshakable will to live free and independent.

From then, 36 years later, Solidarity was born. There would be no Solidarity in 1980 if there were no Warsaw uprising in 1944. Mr. President, such spirit, such will are not alien to you. You practice them daily in the pursuit of your foreign policy.

Mr. President, I, as the last chief of the Polish wartime underground State, thank you very much for bestowing these high American military decorations on our dead national heroes--Generals Rowecki, Komorowski, and Okulicki, who were my close friends. And in order to express our gratitude for your unshakable support for the Polish cause, I have the great honor to decorate you with the Home Army Cross.

The President. Thank you very much.

* Stefan Korbonski (1901-1989), political activist in pre-War Poland, during the War and in exile in the United States.

43. POLISH AMERICANS PROTEST
JARUZELSKI'S VISIT

(The full text of a statement of the Polish American Congress published in the *New York Times* of September 25, 1985 on the day of Polish leader Wojciech Jaruzelski's visit to the United Nations to mark its fortieth anniversary.)

Gen. Wojciech Jaruzelski, an obedient servant of Soviet leader Mikhail Gorbachev, heads a Communist dictatorship determined to break down the Polish people's resolute resistance to Communist enslavement.

Jaruzelski's appearance at the Opening Session of the United Nations General Assembly on September 27, 1985, follows a dramatic escalation of repression in Poland as evidenced by over 300 political prisoners being held in jails and several thousand victims of acts of administrative repression of people standing up for their rights; summary dismissals from jobs and black-listing from other employment, denial of food ration cards and state controlled medical services, imposition of exorbitant fines, etc.

In Jaruzelski's Poland, the recently enacted amendments to the penal code have turned the law into an instrument of repression. A single judge can summarily sentence a citizen to a prison term, or impose a heavy monetary fine solely on the strength of a police agent's report, without a public prosecutor, defense lawyer, or the defendant himself being present in court. Simultaneously, efforts are being made to subordinate the legal community, i.e. all defense lawyers, to the regime's control.

The recent trial of "Solidarity" leaders Wladyslaw Frasyniuk, Bogdan Lis and Adam Michnik was conducted with total disregard for the law and public opinion. The defendants were sentenced to terms of 2 1/2 to 3 1/2 years for alleged support of a fifteen minute demonstration strike.

In Jaruzelski's Poland, the Independent, Self-Governing Trade Union "Solidarnosc," the nonviolent, mass movement representing the true aspirations and interests of the Polish people has been suppressed by brutal force since December 1981.

Solidarity's continued existence, despite drastic measures undertaken to suppress it, represents a serious challenge to the seemingly omnipotent police regime--a challenge unprecedented in the history of Communist dictatorships. In the long run, successful Polish resistance will have far-reaching repercussions throughout the Soviet orbit.

In Jaruzelski's Poland, the Church and the Catholic clergy have been subjected to increased attacks. The murder of Father Jerzy Popieluszko by henchmen of the political police marked the beginning of escalating harassment, threats and blackmail directed at priests standing up for people's rights and dignity in the spirit of the Gospel.

In Jaruzelski's Poland, the newly enacted law on higher education has removed the last vestige of academic freedom and established full government control over educational and scientific institutions. Any scholar can be arbitrarily removed from his post is he does not servilely toe the Party line.

In Jaruzelski's Poland, abolition of professional associations of writers, journalists, actors and artists, while pervasive censorship is being tightened even more, reflects an undeniable attempt to deny the people of Poland their right to know and to muzzle any independent expression of thoughts and opinion.

Over the past 40 years, demonstrating unprecedented fortitude, the Polish nation has victoriously resisted Communist efforts to break its will, enslave its mind and destroy its national consciousness. We are confident that the people of Poland will overcome the renewed onslaught of Communist forces led by the Gorbachev-Jaruzelski alliance.

As in the past, *Polish Americans stand shoulder to shoulder with the people of Poland,* representing in the free world Poland's critical needs, real interests and aspirations, as well as its strategic importance in the context of the global confrontation of the democratic West with the oppressive dictatorship of Soviet Communism.

Polish Americans condemn violations of human rights whether they occur in Poland, South Africa, Latin America, or in any other part of the world. We must use the same moral yardstick everywhere. Secure peace is indivisible from the universal respect of human rights.

We appeal to all free and democratic nations to support the Polish people's non-violent struggle and to demand that the Polish regime adhere fully to the provisions of the United Nations Declaration on Human Rights, the Helsinki Final Act and the U.N. Convention on Economic, Social and Cultural Rights, all of which bear the signature of the government of the Polish People's Republic.

To resolve the continuing socio-economic crisis and avert deepening confrontation and alienation between the people and the authorities, it is essential that the government revert to a policy of moderation and restraint.

Specifically the Government must:

- Initiate a real dialog with the genuine representatives of the Polish people leading to a measure of reconciliation;

- Free all political prisoners and desist from other acts of repression, intimidation and harassment;

- Institute sweeping reforms of the centralized, command-structure economic system, which are essential to restore Poland's economic viability.

A FREE AND INDEPENDENT POLAND IS OUR GOAL.

For the Polish American Congress:

ALOYSIUS A. MAZEWSKI, PRESIDENT, POLISH AMERICAN CONGRESS, INC., President, Polish National Alliance; HELEN ZIELINSKI, VICE PRESIDENT, President, Polish Women's Alliance; KAZIMIERZ LUKOMSKI, VICE PRESIDENT; DR. EDWARD ROZANSKI, SECRETARY GENERAL; JOSEPH A. DROBOT, TREASURER, President, Polish Roman Catholic Union--National Vice Presidents: MICHAEL BLICHASZ--Philadelphia, PA, President, PAC Eastern Pennsylvania Division; EDWARD DYKLA--CHICAGO, IL, Treasurer, Polish Roman Catholic Union; ZBIGNIEW KONIKOWSKI--New York, NY, *SWAP*--Polish Army Veterans Association of America, Inc.; JANUSZ KRZYZANOWSKI--New York, NY, President, *SPK*--Polish Veterans of World War II; VERONICA MACZKA--Chicago, IL, Polish National Union of America; GEORGE MIGALA--Chicago, IL; KAZIMIERZ OLEJARCZYK--Detroit, MI; ALFREDA PLOCHA--Philadelphia, PA, President, Union of

Polish Women in America; MICHAEL PREISLER--New York, NY, President, PAC Downstate New York Division; JOSEPH PTAK--Cleveland, OH, President, PAC Ohio Division; ROMAN PUCINSKI--Chicago, IL, President, PAC Illinois Division, Alderman, City of Chicago; BERNARD ROGALSKI--Pittsburgh, PA, President, Polish Falcons of America; REV. FERDINAND E. SLEJZER--Lynn, MA, President, PAC Eastern Massachusetts Division; REINHOLD SMYCZEK--Perth Amboy, NJ, President, PAC New Jersey Division; RICHARD SOLECKI--Buffalo, NY; STEVE TOKARSKI--Schererville, IN, President, PAC Indiana Division;

Division Presidents: Arizona Division, VICTOR ZIELKA; California Northern Division, ANTONI ZUKOWSKI; California Southern Division, KRZYSZTOF CIESIOLKIEWICZ; Connecticut Division, DR. STANISLAUS A. BLEJWAS; Delaware Division, JESSE W. SAMLUK; Florida Division, MARIA DAMBSKA; Florida Western Division, OLGIERD SZCZENIOWSKI; Illinois Division, ROMAN PUCINSKI; Indiana Division, STEVE TOKARSKI; Indiana-South Bend Division, MIECZYSLAW BARAN; Maryland Division, MELVIN LASZCZYNSKI; Eastern Massachusetts Division, REV. FERDINAND SLEJZER; Western Massachusetts Division, CHARLES TOMASZEWSKI; Michigan Division, PAUL ODROBINA; Nebraska Division, JOHN S. TYRCHA; New Jersey Division, REINHOLD SMYCZEK; New Jersey Southern Division, CHESTER PRZYWARA; New York Central Division, EDMUND SULKOWSKI; New York Downstate Division, MICHAEL PREISLER; New York Western Division, BRONISLAW DUREWICZ; Ohio Division, JOSEPH PTAK; Oklahoma Division, EMILY BRIGGS; Pennsylvania Eastern Division, MICHAEL BLICHASZ; Pennsylvania Northeastern Division, JOSEPH R. MROS; Pennsylvania Northern Division, IRENE SIDEROWICZ; Pennsylvania Western Division, JOSEPH DOLEGOWSKI; Rhode Island Division, REV. ANTHONY D. IWUC; Texas Division, COL. FRANCIS C. KAJENCKI; Washington, D.C. Metro Division, COL. CASIMIR LENARD; West Virginia Division, JULIA G. BURDA; Wisconsin State Division, EDWARD WOJTKOWSKI; Wisconsin Central Division, LESZEK ZIELINSKI.

44. PRESIDENT REAGAN'S STATEMENT ON THE LIFTING OF U.S. SANCTIONS AGAINST POLAND, FEBRUARY 19, 1987.

Five years ago, I asked all Americans to light a candle in support of freedom in Poland. During that Christmas season of 1981, candles were lit in millions of American homes. We had confidence that the spirit of freedom would continue to shine in the darkness that martial law had brought to that brave country. As Americans, we were showing solidarity with Solidarity.

Symbolic gestures were not enough. Economic and other sanctions were imposed on Poland in response to the repression that descended on the Polish people as a result of martial law. Our message was that America would not passively stand by while a grand experiment in freedom was brutally smashed in Poland. If the Polish government wanted a decent relationship with the United States, we made it clear they would have to lift martial law, release the political prisoners and enter into a real political dialogue with Polish society.

Today, more than five years later, the light of freedom continues to shine in Poland. The commitment and sacrifice of hundreds of thousands of Polish men and women have kept the flame alive, even amid the gloom.

In 1983, martial law was lifted and thousands of political prisoners have been freed in a series of amnesties. Since the final amnesty last September, no one has been arrested on political charges in Poland.

Yet, there is still far to go. The threat of arrest still hangs over those who seek their freedom. The right to genuinely independent trade unions is still stifled. Independent political activity continues to be repressed by various governmental measures. National reconciliation remains a dream, a goal for the future, rather than a reality of today.

I continue to believe, as do the Polish people, that it is a possible dream. The Church in Poland has greeted the major amnesty of political prisoners last September as a "significant step" by the Polish government. In response to that amnesty, we started a step-by-step process of expanding our dialogue with the government of Poland. In our dealings with Polish authorities, we have made one point clear: the continuation of better relations between our countries, and their further improvement, will be possible only if we see maintained the spirit and principle of the amnesty and a reliance on dialogue and respect for human rights. Only through genuine and meaningful reconciliation can the plight of the Polish people be alleviated. We will be watching to see that further steps are taken toward national reconciliation in Poland, and that the progress made is not reversed.

Significantly, the leaders of Solidarity and of the Catholic Church in Poland agree that this is the right course for us to take. They have now urged us to lift our remaining economic sanctions in order to encourage further movement in the right direction.

In considering this question, I have drawn on a broad cross-section of views. We have been in touch at the highest levels with the Polish government, with the Church and with Solidarity. We have also consulted with our allies.

After careful review, I have decided that the economic sanctions imposed in December 1981 and October 1982 should be rescinded, and I am accordingly restoring "most-favored-nation" tariff treatment for Poland and lifting the ban on Poland's eligibility for official U.S. credits and credit guarantees.

We have always worked closely with our allies on issues concerning Poland, and they have sent messages of support for this step forward.

I am honored by the expression of concern from distinguished members of Congress, leaders of the Polish American community in this country, and Solidarity. Together, we underscore the heartfelt concern of our citizens about Poland. Let no one doubt our brothers and sisters who struggle to build a freer and more humane Poland, or our resolve to stand by them.

As it was in 1981 freedom is precious to us. The slogan of the Polish independence struggle of the last century was "For Your Freedom And Ours." That is our slogan, too, and it is more than a slogan. It is a program of action.

Today is a first step, a big step. Our relations with Poland can only develop in ways that encourage genuine progress toward national reconciliation in that country. We will be steady. We will be committed. The flame that burns in the hearts of the Polish people, a flame represented by the candles we lit in 1981, that flame of justice and liberty will never be extinguished.

45. POLISH AMERICAN CONGRESS STATEMENT OF MAY 5, 1988 ON THE CRISIS IN POLAND.

Police terror and arrogance of power remain the only arguments in the arsenal of the communist dictatorship in Poland. The Polish American Congress expresses its outrage and denunciation of the use of brutal force to break the strikes of Polish workers.

Throughout the past 40 years, the communist regime has failed to learn the seemingly obvious lesson of history, that it is impossible to govern without the support and cooperation of the Polish people, violating instead their just demands for social justice.

It is not the striking workers, as alleged by the regime, but the authorities themselves who instituted terror, ignoring the moderate and just demands of Polish workers and the efforts of the Polish episcopate to create conditions conducive to the institution of reforms, establishment of a social contract and undertaking of a joint effort to rebuild the country's economy, devastated by the communist regime, and the establishment of a system of government based on the principles of law and the trust of its citizens.

At this dramatic juncture, the Polish American Congress reiterates its uncompromising solidarity and the support of American Polonia for the courageous and responsible stand of Polish workers and their leaders headed by Lech Walesa.

The Polish American Congress will continue to pursue determinedly its efforts to secure the rights of the Polish people and to support their resistance against communist enslavement.

EXECUTIVE COMMITTEE OF THE
POLISH AMERICAN CONGRESS;
Aloysius A. Mazewski, President
Helen Zielinski, Vice President
Kazimierz Lukomski, Vice President
Bernard Rogalski, Secretary General
Edward G. Dykla, Treasurer

46. POLISH AMERICAN CONGRESS STATEMENT IN SUPPORT OF SOLIDARITY ON ITS EIGHTH ANNIVERSARY, AUGUST 29, 1988.

The Independent, Self-governing Trade Union "Solidarity", born in the aftermath of the widespread strikes of Polish workers during the unforgettable days of August and September 1980, became the epitome of the collective will of the people of Poland to break the shackles of communist enslavement and to take up the struggle for national renewal.

"Solidarity" effected a breakthrough in people's consciousness, restoring their sense of purpose, unity and faith. Eight years later, despite the trauma of martial law and the continuous, brutal repressions, "Solidarity," led by Lech Walesa, remains the inspirational and political force leading the people of Poland in their determined struggle for national sovereignty and democratic freedoms.

It is with the utmost concern that we watch the deepening economic and socio-political disintegration of Poland, a direct result of the totalitarian system ruling the country by a self-perpetuating communist elite and the colonial exploitation of its economy by the Soviet Union.

Recurring strikes indicate the workers' determination to pursue their demands for improved working and living conditions and for the restoration of the legal status of "Solidarity" as the national representation of the people's interests and aspirations.

"Poland's recovery requires that the authorities initiate *bona fide* negotiations with "Solidarity", led by its chairman Lech Walesa, and other leaders of the democratic opposition movements, leading to a social contract, which would provide for the recognition of the people's right to participate in planning and management of the country's economy, determining the choices of ways and means designed to increase productivity and streamline its economic structure, and acceptance by the authorities of the principle of pluralism in Poland's national life," urged the Polish American Congress National Council of Directors in a statement issued on June 24, 1988.

Talks with leaders of "Solidarity" and other democratic opposition movements, currently proposed by the government, may constitute a significant opening leading towards national understanding, which is essential for the recovery of the country's economy, and reform of its socio-political structure. Further stresses resulting from the authorities' intransigence may lead to dangerous confrontations.

On the anniversary of the birth of "Solidarity", the Polish American Congress reiterates its support for the people of Poland in their resistance to Communist domination and their determined struggle for freedom and independence.

> POLISH AMERICAN CONGRESS
> Helen Zielinski, Vice President
> Kazimierz Lukomski, Vice President
> Bernard Rogalski, Secretary General
> Edward Dykla, Treasurer

47. POLISH AMERICAN CONGRESS STATEMENT ON THE EVE OF THE "ROUND TABLE" NEGOTIATIONS IN POLAND, OCTOBER 3, 1988.*

The next round of negotiations between the representatives of the government of the Polish People's Republic and Lech Walesa, chairman of NSZZ "Solidarnosc" and his associates, scheduled in mid-October, portend an effort to conclude a social contract, which would have a chance to start a process leading to the reversal of the deepening stagnation of Poland's economic and sociopolitical life.

The until now pursued policy of the authorities, negating the just demands of the people, is a road to nowhere. Thus, it is essential that the authorities forego the narrow interests of the party monopoly of power and urgently open talks aimed at national reconciliation. It should be obvious to anyone that it is impossible to govern Poland without the cooperation of the broad spectrum of its society which, represented by the Independent, Self-Governing Trade Union "Solidarity," constituted and authenticated by the nation, must be assured a voice in determining the country's affairs.

Polish Americans have full confidence that "Solidarity's" chairman Lech Walesa, mindful of Poland's realities, will realize to the fullest extent possible the just aspirations and welfare of the people of Poland.

From the standpoint of the broad spectrum of Poland's independent society, the road to national reconciliation is wide open. It is up to the government whether it will be pursued. The alternative is the continuing, threatening in its consequences, disintegration of the country's national existence.

The Polish American Congress anxiously awaits further developments. We expect, however, that this time reasonableness and moderation will guide the government's position in the forthcoming negotiations. The future of the nation is at stake.

POLISH AMERICAN CONGRESS
Helen Zielinski, Vice President
Kazimierz Lukomski, Vice President
Bernard B. Rogalski, Secretary General
Edward G. Dykla, Treasurer

* After many delays, the negotiations began on February 6, 1989.

48. POLISH AMERICAN CONGRESS STATEMENT ON THE AGREEMENT OF APRIL 5, 1989 CONCLUDING THE ROUND TABLE TALKS.

The agreement between SOLIDARITY and the representatives of the Polish government signed in Warsaw today is without a doubt a triumph for SOLIDARITY and its leader Lech Walesa. His consistently firm position forced the authorities to make concessions which establish new sociopolitical conditions guaranteeing the Polish people, represented by their acknowledged leaders, participation in decisions which will affect essential aspects of their daily lives. This creates an opportunity to rebuild the country's economy, thus improving the living conditions of the harassed population. In this sense, we expect that the agreement will be gaining popular support.

Further development of the situation will depend on future application of the terms of the agreement in such a way that they will become a reality in the lives of the Polish people. We are all aware of the difficulties remaining to be overcome. In spite of the sad experiences of the past, however, we are hopeful that those difficulties will be worked out successfully. The future of the Polish nation depends on this.

This agreement does not fulfill all the aspirations of the Polish people, who have for many years been demanding freedom, democracy, and independence. It is, however, a significant step in the right direction towards the realization of these hopes. The Polish American community has always been on the side of the people of Poland in this struggle. Our efforts on behalf of the interests of the Polish nation continue to be our main objective.

FOR THE POLISH AMERICAN CONGRESS:
Edward J. Moskal, President
Helen V. Wojcik, Vice President
Kazimierz Lukomski, Vice President
Bernard B. Rogalski, Secretary General
Edward G. Dykla, Treasurer

49. PRESIDENT GEORGE H. BUSH'S REMARKS IN HAMTRAMCK, MICHIGAN ON THE OCCASION OF THE POLISH GOVERNMENT'S FORMAL RELEGALIZATION OF SOLIDARITY, APRIL 17, 1989.

Thank you all very, very much. Cardinal Szoka, Your Eminence. Bob, thank you for the warm greeting to your wonderful community. Governor Blanchard--it's an honor to have the Governor of the great state here. And I want to pay my respects to the members of the Michigan congressional delegation that came out here with me--Senator Riegle, and several distinguished members of the House of Representatives sitting over here--and also to Senator John Engler, who is the Majority Leader of the Michigan State Senate, and to other leaders-- elected leaders not only from your community, but in other parts of this state.

I'm delighted to be here. Bread and salt are both of the earth, and ancient symbols of a life leavened by health and prosperity. And in this same spirit, I wish you all the same. And now, if I may, I want to address at this important gathering the health and prosperity of a whole nation--the proud people of Poland.

You know, we Americans are not mildly sympathetic spectators of events in Poland. We are bound to Poland by a very special bond--a bond of blood, of culture and shared values. And so it is only natural that as dramatic change comes to Poland we share the aspirations and excitement of the Polish people.

In my Inaugural Address, I spoke of the new breeze of freedom gaining strength around the world. "In man's heart," I said, "if not in fact, the day of the dictator is over. The totalitarian era is passing, its old ideas blown away like leaves from an ancient lifeless tree." I spoke of the new potency of democratic ideals--of free speech, free elections and the exercise of free will.

And we should not be surprised that the ideas of democracy are returning with renewed force in Europe--the homeland of philosophers of freedom whose ideals have been so fully realized in our great United States of America. As Victor Hugo said, "An invasion of armies can be resisted, but not an idea whose time has come." My friends, liberty is an idea whose time has come in Eastern Europe. And make no mistake about it.

For almost half a century, the suppression of freedom in Eastern Europe, sustained by the military power of the Soviet Union, has kept nation from nation, neighbor from neighbor. And as East and West now seek to reduce arms, it must not be forgotten that arms are a symptom, not a source, of tension. The true source of tension is the imposed and unnatural division of Europe.

How can there be stability and security in Europe and the world as long as nations and peoples are denied the right to determine their own future--a right explicitly promised by agreements among the victorious powers at the end of World War II? How can there be stability and security in Europe as long as nations, which once stood proudly at the front rank of industrial powers, are impoverished by a discredited ideology and stifling authoritarianism? The United States--and let's be clear on this--has never accepted the legitimacy of Europe's division. We accept no spheres of influence that deny the sovereign rights of nations.

And yet the winds of change are shaping a new European destiny. Western Europe is resurgent and Eastern Europe is awakening to yearnings for democracy, independence and prosperity. In the Soviet Union itself we are encouraged by the sound of voices long silent and the sight of the rulers consulting the ruled. We see new thinking in some aspects of Soviet foreign policy. We are hopeful that these stirrings presage meaningful, lasting and more far-reaching change.

So let no one doubt the sincerity of the American people and their government in our desire to see reform succeed inside the Soviet Union. We welcome the changes that have taken place and we will encourage--continue to encourage greater recognition of human rights, market incentives and free elections.

East and West are now negotiating on a broad range of issues, from arms reductions to the environment. But the Cold War began in Eastern Europe, and if it is to end, it will end in this crucible of world conflict--and it must end. The American people want to see East and Central Europe free, prosperous and at peace. With prudence, realism and patience, we seek to promote the evolution of freedom--the opportunities sparked by the Helsinki Accords and the deepening East-West contact.

In recent years, we have improved relations with countries in the region, and in each case, we looked for progress in international posture and internal practices--in human rights, cultural openness, emigration issues, opposition to international terror.

While we want relations to improve, there are certain acts we will not condone or accept--behavior that can shift relations in the wrong direction--human rights abuses, technology theft and hostile intelligence or foreign policy actions against us.

Some regimes are now seeking to win popular legitimacy through reforms. In Hungary, a new leadership is experimenting with reforms that may permit a political pluralism that only a few years ago would have been absolutely unthinkable. And in Poland, on April 5, Solidarity leader Lech Walesa and Interior Minister Kiszczak signed agreements that, if faithfully implemented, will be a watershed in the postwar history of Eastern Europe.

Under the auspices of the Roundtable Agreements, the free trade union Solidarnosc was today--this very day, under those agreements--formally restored. And the agreements also provide that a free opposition press will be legalized, independent political and other free associations will be permitted, and elections for a new Polish Senate will be held. These agreements testify to the realism of General Jaruzelski and his colleagues, and they are inspiring testimony to the spiritual guidance of the Catholic Church, the indomitable spirit of the Polish people, and the strength and wisdom of Lech Walesa.

Poland faces, and will continue to face for some time, severe economic problems. A modern French writer observed that communism is not another form of economics. It is the death of economics. In Poland, an economic system crippled by the inefficiencies of central planning almost proved the death of initiative and enterprise. Almost. But economic reforms can still give free rein to the enterprising impulse and creative spirit of the great Polish people.

The Polish people understand the magnitude of this challenge. Democratic forces in Poland have asked for the moral, political and economic support of the West. And the West will respond. My administration is completing now a thorough review of our policies toward Poland and all of Eastern Europe. And I've carefully considered ways that the United States can help Poland. And we will not act unconditionally--we're not going to offer unsound credits. We're not going to offer aid without requiring sound economic practices in return. And we must remember that Poland still is a member of the Warsaw Pact. And I will take no steps that compromise the security of the West.

The Congress, the Polish American community--and I support, I endorse strongly Ed Moskal and what he is doing in the Polish American Congress, I might say, and I'm delighted he's here. A good Chicago boy right here in Hamtramck. That the Congress, the Polish American community, the American labor movement, our allies and international financial institutions--our allies all must work in concert if Polish democracy is to take root anew and sustain itself. And we can and must answer this call to freedom. And it is particularly appropriate here in Hamtramck for me to salute the members and leaders of the American labor movement for hanging tough with Solidarity through its darkest days. Labor deserves great credit for that.

Now, the Poles are now taking steps that deserve our active support. And I have decided as your President on specific steps to be taken by the United States, carefully chosen to recognize the reforms underway and to encourage reforms yet to come now that Solidarnosc is legal:

I will ask Congress to join me in providing Poland access to our Generalized System of Preferences, which offers selective tariff relief to beneficiary countries.

We will work with our allies and friends in the Paris Club to develop sustainable new schedules for Poland to repay its debt, easing a heavy burden so that a free market can grow.

I will ask Congress to join me in authorizing the Overseas Private Investment Corporation to operate in Poland, to the benefit of both Polish and U.S. investors.

We will propose negotiations for a private business agreement with Poland to encourage cooperation between U.S. firms and Poland's private businesses. Both sides can benefit.

The United States will continue to consider supporting, on their merits, viable loans to the private sector by the International Finance Corporation.

We believe that the Roundtable agreements clear the way for Poland to be able to work with the International Monetary Fund on programs that support sound, market-oriented economic policies.

We will encourage business and private nonprofit groups to develop innovative programs to swap Polish debt for equity in Polish enterprises; and for charitable, humanitarian and environmental projects.

We will support imaginative educational, cultural and training programs to help liberate the creative energies of the Polish people.

You know when I visited Poland in September of 1987, I was then Vice President, and I told Chairman Jaruzelski and Lech Walesa that the American people and government would respond quickly and imaginatively to significant internal reform of the kind that we now see. Both of them valued that assurance. So it is especially gratifying for me today to witness the changes now taking place in Poland, and to announce these important changes in U.S. policy. The United States of America keeps its promises.

If Poland's experiment succeeds, other countries may follow. And while we must still differentiate among the nations of Eastern Europe, Poland offers two lessons for all. First, there can be no progress without significant political and economic liberalization. Our friends and European allies share this philosophy.

The West can now be bold in proposing a vision of the European future: We dream of the day when there will be no barriers to the free movement of peoples, goods and idea. We dream of the day when Eastern European peoples will be free to choose their system of government and to vote for the party of their choice in regular, free, contested elections. And we dream of the day when Eastern European countries will be free to choose their own peaceful course in the world, including closer ties with Western Europe. And we envision an Eastern Europe in which the Soviet Union has renounced military intervention as an instrument of its policy--on any pretext. We share an unwavering conviction that one day, all the peoples of Europe will live in freedom. And make no mistake about that.

Next month at a summit of the North Atlantic Alliance, I will meet with the leaders of the Western democracies. The leaders of the Western democracies will discuss these concerns. And these are not bilateral issues just between the United States and the Soviet Union. They are, rather, the concern of all the Western allies, calling for common approaches. The Soviet Union should understand, in turn, that a free democratic Eastern Europe as we envision it would threaten no one and no country. Such an evolution would imply and reinforce the further improvement of East-West relations in all dimensions-- arms reductions, political relations, trade--in all ways that enhance the safety and well-being of all of Europe. There is no other way.

What has brought us to this opening? The unity and strength of the democracies, yes. And something else--the bold, new thinking in the Soviet Union, the innate desire--the innate desire for freedom in the hearts of all men. We will not waver in our dedication to freedom now. And if we're wise, united and ready to seize the moment, we will be remembered as the generation that made all Europe free.

Two centuries ago, a Polish patriot, Thaddeus Kosciuszko, came to these American shores to stand for freedom. Let us honor and remember this hero of our own struggle for freedom by extending our hand to those who work the shipyards of Gdansk and walk the cobbled streets of Warsaw. Let us recall the words of the Poles who struggled for independence: "For your freedom and ours." Let us support the peaceful evolution of democracy in Poland. The cause of liberty knows no limits; the friends of freedom, no borders.

God bless Poland. God bless the United States of America. Thank you all very much. "Niech Zyje Polska." Let Poland Live! Thank you very much.

50. POLISH AMERICAN CONGRESS STATEMENT OF JUNE 8, 1989 FOLLOWING POLAND'S ELECTIONS.

The elections to the "Sejm" and the Senate which took place in Poland on June 4, were undoubtedly a success well-deserved by "Solidarity." They demonstrated the universal support of the Polish people for the Citizens Committee's election platform which advocated the introduction of political pluralism and reforms of the economic system, essential to avert the severe economic crisis and consequently improve the standard of living of the Polish people.

The election success of "Solidarity" cannot hide, however, the immense difficulties which remain to be solved before these goals can be realized. It is definitely a first significant step in the right direction.

The Polish American community is well aware that the Polish people will now be faced with a period of intense work, psychological endurance, and social discipline. We believe that these efforts will be undertaken with a firm conviction that they are absolutely necessary and of purpose and that they will lead to a renewal of all aspects of life in Poland.

At this critical moment, the Polish American Congress is committed to continue its past policies of full support and assistance to the Polish people in their struggle for a brighter tomorrow.

POLISH AMERICAN CONGRESS
Edward J. Moskal, President
Helen V. Wojcik, Vice President
Kazimierz Lukomski, Vice President
Bernard B. Rogalski, Secretary General
Edward G. Dykla, Treasurer

51. POLISH AMERICAN CONGRESS STATEMENT OF August 23, 1989 FOLLOWING TADEUSZ MAZOWIECKI'S APPOINTMENT AS POLAND'S PRIME MINISTER.

Establishment of the Solidarity-led coalition government represents an unprecedented event in the post-World War II history of Poland. It is, in fact, Poland's first government elected by the people, rather than an imposed communist regime.

Led by Tadeusz Mazowiecki, a respected Catholic lay leader, close associate and adviser of Lech Walesa, it commands the support and trust of the Polish electorate. Polish Americans are confident that it will succeed in leading Poland out of the morass of economic stagnation and political confrontation.

Tadeusz Mazowiecki's government faces tremendous problems. It must induce Poles to accept necessary, further austerity measures, and insure increased productivity of Poland's frustrated work force. It must move the country out of the doldrums of the bankrupt system of centrally-planned economy, towards a free market economy.

The Polish people cannot do it all alone. The recovery of their economy, devastated by the over 40 years of communist mismanagement, waste and corruption, requires a substantial, carefully considered program of economic assistance by the industrial democracies led by the United States.

The stakes are high. Poland's success could have a profound and long-lasting impact on further developments in all of the Soviet bloc countries. Its failure would lead to escalating confrontations which would reverse the course of reforms in Poland, Hungary and in the Soviet Union itself.

We must not fail the people of Poland in their determined struggle for freedom and democracy.

POLISH AMERICAN CONGRESS
Edward J. Moskal, President
Helen V. Wojcik, Vice President
Kazimierz Lukomski, Vice President
Bernard B. Rogalski, Secretary
Edward G. Dykla, Treasurer

52. LECH WALESA'S ADDRESS TO A JOINT MEETING OF THE CONGRESS OF THE UNITED STATES OF AMERICA, NOVEMBER 15, 1989.

Mr. Speaker, Mr. President, members of the Cabinet, distinguished members of the House and Senate,
Ladies, and Gentleman,

"We the people...."
With these words I wish to begin my address. I do not need to remind anyone here where these words come from. And I do not need to explain that I, an electrician from Gdansk, am also entitled to invoke them.

"We the people...."
I stand before you as the third foreign non-head of state invited to address the joint Houses of Congress of the United States. The Congress, which for many people in the world, oppressed and stripped of their rights, is a beacon of freedom and a bulwark of human rights. And here I stand before you, to speak to America in the name of my nation. To speak to citizens of the country and the continent whose threshold is guarded by the famous Statue of Liberty. It is for me an honor so great, a moment so solemn, that I can find nothing to compare it with.

The people in Poland link the name of the United States with freedom and democracy, with generosity and high-mindedness, with human friendship and friendly humanity. I realize that not everywhere is America so perceived. I speak of her image in Poland. This image was strengthened by numerous favorable historical experiences, and it is a well known thing that Poles repay warm-heartedness in kind.

The world remembers the wonderful principle of the American democracy: "government of the people, by the people, for the people."

I too remember these words; I, a shipyard worker from Gdansk, who has devoted his entire life--alongside other members of the Solidarity movement-- to the service of this idea: "government of the people, by the people, for the people." Against privilege and monopoly, against violations of the law, against the trampling of human dignity, against contempt and injustice.

Such in fact are the principles and values--reminiscent of Abraham Lincoln and the Founding Fathers of the American republic, and also of the principles and ideas of the American Declaration of Independence and the American Constitution-- that are pursued by the great movement of Polish Solidarity; a movement that is effective. I wish to stress this point with particular strength. I know that Americans are idealistic but at the same time practical people endowed with common sense and capable of logical action. They combine these features with a belief in the ultimate victory of right over wrong. But they prefer effective work to making speeches. And I understand them very well. I too am not fond of speeches. I prefer facts and work. I prefer effectiveness.

Ladies and Gentlemen,

Here is the fundamental, most important fact I want to tell you about. The social movement bearing the beautiful name of Solidarity, born of the Polish nation, is an effective movement. After many long years of struggle it bore fruit which is there for all to see. It pointed to a direction and a way of action which are today affecting the lives of millions. It speeded the march to- wards freedom and democracy, a march that is now being joined by swelling throngs of people speaking various languages. It has swayed monopolies, overturning some altogether. It has opened up entirely new horizons.

And this struggle was conducted without resorting to vio- lence of any kind--a point that cannot be stressed too much. We were being locked up in prison, deprived of our jobs, beaten and sometimes killed. And we did not so much as strike a single person. We did not destroy anything, did not smash a single windowpane. But we were stubborn, very stubborn, ready to suffer, to make sacrifices. We knew what we wanted. And our power prevailed in the end.

The movement named Solidarity received massive support and scored victories because at all times and in all matters it opted for the better, more human and more dignified solution, standing against brutality and hate. It was a consistent move- ment, stubborn, never giving up. And that is why after all these hard years, marked by so many tragic moments, Solidarity is today succeeding and showing the way to millions of people in Poland and other countries.

Ladies and Gentlemen,

It was nine years ago, in August 1980, that there began in the Gdansk shipyard the famous strike which led to the emergence of the first independent trade union in communist countries, which soon became a vast social movement supported by the Polish nation. I was nine years younger then, unknown to anybody but my friends in the shipyard, and somewhat slimmer. This last circumstance was quite important, and here's why. An unemployed man at that time, fired from my job for earlier attempts to organize workers in the fight for their rights, I jumped over the shipyard wall and rejoined my colleagues who promptly appointed me the leader of the strike. That's how it all began.

When I recall the road we have travelled I often think of that jump over the fence. Now others jump fences and tear down walls. They do it because freedom is a human right.

But there is also another reflection that comes to my mind when I think of the road behind us. In those days, at the beginning, many warnings, admonitions and even condemnations reached us from many parts of the world. What are those Poles up to? - we heard. They are mad, they are jeopardizing world peace and European stability. They ought to stay quiet and not get on anybody's nerves.

We gathered from these voices that the other nations have the right to live in comfort and well-being, they have the right to democracy and freedom, and it is only the Poles who should give up these rights so as not to disturb the peace of others.

In the days before the Second World War there were many people who asked: Why should we die for Gdansk? Isn't it better to stay at home? But war soon paid them a visit, and they had to start dying for Paris, for London, for Hawaii. This time too there were many who complained: There is that Gdansk again disturbing our peace.

But the recent developments in Gdansk carried a different meaning. This was not the beginning but the true end of that war. This was the beginning of a new, better, democratic and safe era in the history of our world. There is no longer a question of dying for Gdansk but of living for it.

Looking at what is happening around us today we may state positively that the Polish road of struggle for human rights, struggle without violence, the Polish stubbornness and firmness in the quest for pluralism and democracy show many people today, and even nations, how to avoid the greatest dangers. If there is something threatening European stability, it certainly is not Poland. Poland's drive towards profound transformations, transformations achieved through peaceful means, through evolution, negotiated with all the parties concerned, makes it possible to avoid the worst pitfalls, and may be held up as a model for many other regions. And as we know, changes elsewhere are not so peaceful.

Peacefully and prudently, with their eyes open to dangers, but not giving up what is right and necessary, the Poles gradually pave the way for historic transformations. We are joined along this way, albeit to various extents, by others: Hungarians and Russians, the Ukrainians and people of the Baltic Republics, Armenians and Georgians, and, in recent days, the East Germans. We wish them luck and rejoice at each success they achieve. We are certain that others will also take our road, since there is no other choice.

I ask now: Is there any sensible man understanding the world around him who could now say that it would be better if the Poles kept quiet because what they are doing is jeopardizing world peace? Couldn't we rather say that Poles are doing more to preserve and consolidate peace than many of their frightened advisers? Could we not say that stability and peace face greater threats from countries which have not yet brought themselves to carry out long-ranging and comprehensive reforms, which do their utmost to preserve the old and disgraced ways of government, contrary to the wishes of their societies?

Things are different in Poland. And I must say that our task is viewed with understanding by our eastern neighbors and their leader Mikhail Gorbachev. This understanding lays foundations for new relations between Poland and the USSR, much better than before. These improved mutual relations will also contribute to stabilization and peace in Europe, removing useless tensions. Poles have had a long and difficult history, and no one wants peaceful coexistence and friendship with all nations and countries--and particularly with the Soviet Union--more than we do. We believe that it is only now that the right and favorable conditions for such coexistence and friendship are emerging.

Poland is making an important contribution to a better future for Europe, to a European reconciliation--also to the vastly important Polish-German reconciliation--to overcoming of old divisions and to strengthening of human rights on our continent. But it does not come easily for Poland.

In the Second World War Poland was the first country to fall victim of aggression. Her losses in terms of human life and national property were the heaviest. Her fight was the longest; she was always a dedicated member of the victorious alliance; and her soldiers fought in all the war's theaters. In 1945 she was, theoretically speaking, one of the victors. Theory, however, had little in common with practice. In practice, as her allies looked on in tacit consent, there was imposed on Poland an alien system of government, without precedent in Polish tradition, unaccepted by the nation, together with an alien economy, an alien law, an alien philosophy of social relations. The legal Polish government, recognized by the nation and leading the struggle of all Poles throughout the war was condemned, and those who remained faithful to it were subjected to the most ruthless persecution. Many were murdered, thousands vanished somewhere in Russia's east and north. Similar repression befell soldiers of the underground army fighting the Nazis. It is only now that we are discovering their bones in unmarked graves scattered among forests.

These atrocities were followed by persecutions of all those who dared think independently. All the solemn pledges about free elections in Poland that were made in Yalta were broken.

This was the second great national catastrophe, following the one of 1939. When other nations were joyously celebrating victory, Poland was again sinking into mourning. The awareness of this tragedy was doubly bitter, as the Poles realized they had been abandoned by their allies. The memory of this is still strong in many minds.

Nonetheless, the Poles took to rebuilding their devastated country and in the first years following the war they were highly successful. But soon a new economic system was introduced, in which individual entrepreneurship ceased to exist and the entire economy ended up in the hands of a state run by people who were not elected by the nation. Stalin forbade Poland to use aid provided by the Marshall Plan, the aid that was used by everyone in Western Europe, including countries which lost the war. It is worth recalling this great American plan which helped Western Europe to protect its freedom and peaceful order. And now it is the moment when Eastern Europe awaits an investment of this kind--an investment in freedom, democracy and peace--an investment adequate to the greatness of the American nation.

The Poles have travelled a long way. It would be worthwhile for all those commenting on Poland, often criticizing Poland--not always rightly--to bear in mind that whatever Poland has achieved she achieved through her own effort, through her own stubbornness, her own relentlessness. Everything was achieved thanks to the unflinching faith of our nation in human dignity and in what is described as the values of Western culture and civilization.

Our nation knows well the price of all this.

Ladies and Gentlemen,

For the past fifty years the Polish nation has been engaged in a difficult and exhausting battle. First to preserve its very biological existence, later to save its national identity. In both instances Polish determination won the day. Today Poland is rejoining the family of democratic and pluralistic countries, returning to the tradition of religious and European values.

For the first time in half a century Poland has a non-communist and independent government, supported by the nation.

But on our path there looms a serious obstacle, a grave danger. Our long subjection to a political system incompatible with national traditions, to a system of economy incompatible with rationality and common sense, coupled with the stifling of independent thought and disregard for national interests. All this has led the Polish economy to ruin, to the verge of utter catastrophe. The first government in fifty years elected by the people and serving the people has inherited from the previous rulers of the country a burden of tremendous debts they incurred and subsequently wasted, of an economy organized in a manner preventing it from satisfying even the basic needs of the people.

The economy we inherited after almost five decades of communist rule is in need of thorough overhaul. This will require patience and great sacrifice. This will require time and means. The present condition of the Polish economy is not due to chance, and is not a specifically Polish predicament. Today all the countries of the Eastern Bloc are bankrupt. The communist economy has failed in every part of the world. One result of this is the exodus of the citizens of those countries, by land and by sea, by boat and by plane, swimming and walking across borders. This is a mass-scale phenomenon, well known in Europe, Asia and Central America.

And Poland entered this new road and will never be turned back. The sense of our work and struggle in Poland lies in our creating situations and prospects that would hold Poles back from seeking a place for themselves abroad, that would encourage them to seek meaning in their work and a hope for a better future in their own country, their own home.

One hears sometimes that people in Poland do not care to work well. But even those who say this, know that Poles work well and effectively if only they see the sense and usefulness of their toil. The working people know their arithmetic too. They are working much harder and in worse conditions than their opposite numbers abroad, and on top of that are paid much lower wages. The economic system around them is absurd. To make matters worse, every several or dozen years the country has suffered a new crisis, a new crunch, and time and time again it ruled out that past efforts went to waste. How many of these wasted efforts, how many disappointed hopes and broken promises we have lived to witness! Show me people who would have worked well, stuck for decades under such a system! Wouldn't they too have succumbed to pessimism? But I wish no one experiences such as these. What matters is that we too be spared them in the future.

This system had to be changed. And the Poles took it upon themselves to change it.

We know that America has her own problems and difficulties, some of them very serious. We are not asking for charity, or expecting philanthropy. But we would like to see our country treated as a partner and a friend. We would like cooperation under decent and favorable conditions. We would like Americans to come to us with proposals of cooperation bringing benefits to both sides. Americans are known to be energetic and practical businessmen. And since we want to introduce a free market and free competition to our country, Americans should show an interest, for it is on this that their prosperity is based. And this is precisely what we are counting on.

We believe that assistance extended to democracy and freedom in Poland and all of Eastern Europe is the best investment in the future and in peace, better than tanks, warships and war planes, an investment leading to greater security.

Poland has already done much to patch up the divisions existing in Europe, to create better and more optimistic prospects. Poland's efforts are viewed with sympathetic interest by the West - and for this thanks are in order. We believe that the West's contribution to this process will grow now. We have heard many beautiful words of encouragement. These are appreciated, but, being a worker and a man of concrete work, I must tell you that the supply of words on the world market is plentiful, but the demand is falling. Let deeds follow words now.

The decision by the Congress of the United States about granting economic aid to Poland opens a new road. For this wonderful decision, I thank you warmly. I promise you that this aid will not be wasted, and will never be forgotten.

Ladies and Gentlemen,

From this podium I'm expressing words of gratitude to the American people. It is they who supported us in the difficult days of martial law and persecution. It is they who sent us aid, who protested against violence. Today, when I am able to freely address the whole world from this elevated spot, I would like to thank them with special warmth.

It is thanks to them that the word "Solidarity" soared across borders and reached every corner of the world. Thanks to them the people of Solidarity were never alone. In this chain of people linked in solidarity there were many, very many Americans. I wish to mention here with warm gratitude our friends from the U.S. Congress, the AFL-CIO trade unions, from the institutions and foundations supporting freedom and democracy, and all those who lent us support in our most difficult moments. They live in all states, in small and large localities of your vast country. I thank all those who through the airwaves or printed word spread the truth. I also wish to say thank you and to greet all Polish Americans who maintain warm contacts with their old fatherland. Their support was always priceless for us.

I wholeheartedly thank the President of the United States and his Administration for involvement in my country's affairs. I will never forget the then Vice-President George Bush speaking in Warsaw over the tomb of the Rev. Jerzy Popieluszko, the martyr for Poland. I will not forget President George Bush speaking in Gdansk in front of the monument of the Fallen Shipyard Workers: It's from there that the President of the United States was sending a message of freedom to Poland, to Europe, to the world.

Pope John Paul II once said: "Freedom is not just something to have and to use, it is something to be fought for. One must use freedom to build with it personal life as well as the life of the nation."

I think this weighty thought can equally well be applied to Poland and to America.

I wish all of you to know and to keep in mind that the ideals which underlie this glorious American republic and which are still alive here, are also living in faraway Poland. And although for many long years efforts were made to cut her off from these ideals, Poland held her ground and is now reaching for the freedom to which she is justly entitled. Together with Poland, other nations of Eastern Europe are following this path. The wall that was separating people from freedom has collapsed. The nations of the world will never let it be rebuilt.

Thank you.

53. STATEMENTS OF POLISH AMERICAN CONGRESS PRESIDENT EDWARD MOSKAL TO PRESIDENT BUSH ON MATTERS CONCERNING POLAND, NOVEMBER 1989 TO MARCH 1990.*

Excerpts from Moskal's report to the President following his participation in a Presidential Fact-finding Commission to Poland, November 29 - December 2, 1989:

...Although I have been to Poland on several occasions, I was once again overwhelmed by the magnitude of the economic problems that Poland is facing.

Despite their awareness of the difficult road ahead, the Polish people have made an irrevocable commitment to democratic change. They have reconfirmed their faith in the Catholic Church and in their own ability to govern themselves. Their support for the Mazowiecki government seems to be solid.

It is important that our efforts produce positive results within as short a time as possible. Such successes are vital if we are to be able to enlist the Polish people in a joint effort to help themselves. Forty-five years marked by scarcity, poor quality, and absence of any choice in what they buy have helped to create a high level of expectation as they await our assistance.

The Polish American Congress has been providing assistance to Poland over the past four decades... It is clearly not a question of where we can help because the needs are everywhere. Rather, we must prepare a priority list and then determine what should be done which will have an immediate impact.

The most important thing we can do right now is to assure the Polish people that they will be able to feed themselves, not only this winter but in the years to come. To accomplish this, I propose that our initial focus be in making the agricultural sector self-sufficient and flourish...

The United States should also give particular attention to ecological issues facing Poland...

Of course there are other sectors of the economy besides agriculture that desperately need help. At some point these areas should also be addressed. (These include a gradual program of industrial privatization and job retraining to assist Poles to function in a society more heavily shaped by the dynamics of the market place.)

...We must move quickly. If there is anything that the PAC or any of our companion organizations can do, please let me know...

Letter of February 15, 1990 to the President on German reunification, the Polish-German border and Eastern Europe's economy recovery:

...Now, as the two Germanies move rapidly toward re-unification, we ask you, Mr. President...to reiterate publicly the long-standing American position concerning the safeguarding of the territorial integrity of Poland.

A statement by you...during Prime Minister Mazowiecki's March visit to the United States, reaffirming unequivocally U.S. support for the present Polish-German border will go a long way in alleviating some of the present fears about a possible strong, re-united Germany. A re-united Germany, we believe, could play a very positive role in establishing economic and political stability in East Central Europe. Such a Germany and a democratic, economically sound Poland with inviolable and definitive borders would help strengthen democracy in the area as well...

The dismantling of the communist system continues in much of Eastern Europe. The emerging democracies remain, however, very frail. A failure of the economic reforms in Poland and other countries could lead to chaos and eventually to another form of dictatorship. If this were to occur, East Central Europe could become a hotbed for territorial and ethnic conflicts dangerous to peace and stability in Europe.

In order to avert such dangerous scenarios we see an urgent need for an American long-range plan to consolidate democracy and to reintegrate the eastern part of Europe into the family of European nations rooted in their common values and based on mutual respect for their sovereignty and territorial integrity. Such a plan would call for participation and cooperation of Western democracies under the leadership of the United States. I would call for political as well as economic measures...

(We support) Poland's participation in the scheduled meeting of the four victorious powers of World War II and the two Germanies... Such a meeting should be followed by Helsinki II, a conference of thirty-five European countries with the participation of the U.S. and the Soviet Union which would establish the framework for the reintegration of Europe...and include provisions for the inviolability of the post World War II European borders...

Points made in Moskal's meeting with the President, March 14, 1990:

We are encouraged by your February 25th statements that "the United States respects the provisions of the Helsinki Final Act regarding the inviolability of the current borders in Europe. And the United States formally recognizes the current German-Polish border."

We request that you reiterate this long-standing policy in the strongest possible terms during the visit next week of Prime Minister Mazowiecki (leaving) no doubt in Chancellor Kohl's or in anyone else's mind where the United States stands on this crucial issue... Such a statement would be much appreciated by the more than ten million Americans of Polish heritage and the brave people of Poland.

We also believe, Mr. President, that it is absolutely essential that the border question be resolved at the earliest by a legally binding treaty. We are not willing to wait until the people of the two Germanies elect a parliament to decide the issue... Let us not wait for the Germans to decide for us. It is the (World War II) Allies' responsibility to do so...

Secretary of State (James) Baker rejected the Polish demand that Poland should participate in the Four-Plus-Two mechanism on the grounds that negotiations will concern only the remaining rights of the former occupying powers. We strongly feel that another...forum be set up to allow Poland to participate in any decisions concerning its territorial integrity and security. You were the first, Mr. President, who rejected and condemned the procedure excluding Poland from the Yalta conference... We trust you will not allow a repetition of this historic injustice.

We and the Polish people remember all too clearly the lessons of Yalta when Poland was left out of the discussions and decisions were then taken which adversely affected them. They are still paying for these mistakes today. This cannot and should not happen again. LET THERE BE NO YALTA II!...

We are deeply disappointed that the Polish-American Enterprise Fund (established in the SEED Act of 1989 by the Congress of the United States) is not yet a working reality. We simply cannot understand the reasons for the delay in setting up this important vehicle to aid Poland... Our effort to consult with the Administration on the establishment of this program have met with little or no response from the Administration... The Polish American community feels strongly that it should have a voice and play a major role in implementing an aid program. We, the PAC, know the country, the people, the culture, the mores, and most importantly, the needs of Poland... (We have made specific recommendations on the management and direction of the Enterprise Fund and) trust that our proposal will be given the serious consideration it deserves... (Note: President Bush appointed as Chairman of the Polish-American Enterprise Fund, John Birkeland of Dillon Read and Company in response to Moskal's request.)

* Excerpts from the Report of the President of the Polish American Congress from November 18, 1989 to June 27, 1990.

54. THE TEXT OF THE CABLE DISPATCHED TO WEST GERMAN CHANCELLOR HELMUT KOHL AND EAST GERMAN PRIME MINISTER HANS MODROW BY THIRTY-FOUR MEMBERS OF THE UNITED STATES SENATE, MARCH 2, 1990.

Dear Chancellor Kohl and Prime Minister Modrow:

We believe, as you do, that inviolability of the postwar European borders is a cornerstone for world peace and stability and the stability of Europe. Any remaining ambiguity about German intentions concerning the present German borders with Poland should be eliminated as soon as possible. Both the Federal Republic of Germany and the German Democratic Republic have separate treaties with Poland that recognize present borders as final and are satisfactory to all parties concerned. Both German states are also signatories of the Helsinki Final Act and its territorial clauses (Basket I, section 1 (a), paragraphs III-IV). We recommend that both German states and Poland should engage without delay in negotiating the consolidation of these two treaties into one legal instrument. The new treaty would be initialed now and ratified by the future parliament of a united Germany. This process could run parallel to the Two-Plus-Four negotiations.

We believe that such a mechanism would put to rest legitimate concerns of Poland and would facilitate the process leading to German unification. It would also respond to Chancellor Kohl's concern that the present treaty between Poland and the Federal Republic of Germany could not be legally binding on a united Germany.

Sincerely, United States Senators Barbara Mikulski, Paul Simon, Dale Bumpers, Dennis DeConcini, Alfonse M. D'Amato, Alan J. Dixon, Alan Cranston, Claiborne Pell, John F. Kerry, Herb Kohl, Daniel Patrick Moynihan, Kent Conrad, Carl Levin, Harry Reid, Al Gore, Tom Harkin, Donald W. Riegle, Spark M. Matsunaga, Joe Lieberman, Quentin N. Burdick, Frank Murkowski, Edward M. Kennedy, Brock Adams, Charles S. Robb, John Breaux, James F. Jeffords, Joe Biden, Bob Graham, David Pryor, Richard C. Shelby, Jeff Bingaman, Robert Kasten, John Glenn, and Lloyd Bentsen.

55. ON THE DEVELOPMENT OF POLONIA'S "DOMESTIC AGENDA." EXCERPTS FROM A STATEMENT BY POLISH AMERICAN CONGRESS VICE PRESIDENT KAZIMIERZ LUKOMSKI PUBLISHED IN THE OCTOBER 1990 ISSUE OF THE *POLISH AMERICAN JOURNAL.*

In a recent editorial in the Buffalo-based *Am-Pol Eagle*, Stan Franczyk, posed a timely question: "Will American Agenda Finally Prevail at the PAC?" Indeed it's a question that for too long has never been properly addressed. Not because, as Franczyk wrote, "a bloc of aging activists, most heroes of events five decades ago, has been running and dominating the PAC agenda dealing almost totally with Polish affairs," but rather, I submit, because the American "domestic" agenda has never been effectively formulated, publicly debated, and accepted as one of the principal objectives of the Polish American Congress.

A panel on the domestic agenda was given prominence at the June 1990 meeting of the PAC National Council. No recommendations of specific activities and programs were submitted, and consequently the issue remains on the back-burner, lacking resolve and direction.

Polonia and the PAC did play an important role in the Polish people's successful struggle for freedom and democracy. Speaking to Polish Americans during his recent visit, Poland's Prime Minister Tadeusz Mazowiecki addressed "special words of gratitude to the leadership of the Polish American Congress for its efforts on behalf of, and in defense of matters which are especially important to Poland... The rebuilding of democracy in Poland is due--in no small measure--to the achievement and efforts of Americans of Polish heritage." While we take pride in his acknowledgement of our past support, Polonia's role in relation to Poland is by no means ended. "Poland needs a strong and organized Polonia, and Polonia needs a strong and sovereign Poland," the Prime Minister said.

And let us note here that our involvement in Polish affairs and in Polonia's domestic problems are not exclusionary but, indeed, complement each other.

To be strong, to effectively serve its needs Polonia must develop its internal strength through a well conceived and determinedly pursued "domestic" agenda. Its principal objective is to assure recognition and acceptance of Polish Americans as worthy, second-to-no-one members of the American society, sharing in full measure, as in the past decades, in this country's economic, cultural and political development.

The key to the American agenda are efforts that must be undertaken to expand the existing--and establish new centers of--Polish and Polish American studies at American universities. Located preferably where there are large Polish American communities they would serve a triple purpose: disseminate the at-present woefully inadequate knowledge of Polish and Polish American history and cultural values, which would also help to fight defamation and stereotyping of Poles and Polish Americans; simultaneously promote Polish American students' recognition of the attractiveness of their heritage, and thus interest them in becoming active members of the community; and lastly help establish cultural, educational and social programs designed to develop internal vitality of the Polish American communities.

It is only through such an ambitious program that we can accomplish our main objective: respect and recognition of past and present contributions to the development of the American society by Polish Americans, and opening opportunities for their continued involvement in government, politics and public service positions.

It is a tall order that requires long term planning and, let's face it, considerable investment of financial resources. Instead of factionalism and generational divisiveness, it requires consolidation and cooperation of all Polish American organizations, such as the PAC, the fraternal benefit societies like the PNA, PRCU, PWA, Polish Falcons, etc., the Kosciuszko Foundation, PAHA, the Polish Institute of Arts and Sciences, ACPC, and others, including the most recent immigrants who are searching for opportunities to employ their talents, energy and fresh insights on Polonia's problems, in service of our community.

Primarily it requires strong and forward-looking leadership, conscious of its responsibility for Polonia's future. The past is just a prologue.

A Chronology of Major Dates in Polish American History*

1608   Arrival of first Polish settlers in America (to the Jamestown colony founded in 1607).

1776-81   American Revolution; Kazimierz Pulaski (killed in 1779) and Tadeusz Kosciuszko play noteworthy roles in the War of Independence.

1795   Third Partition of Poland by Russia, Prussia and Austria means the end of an independent Polish state, in existence since the tenth century. Earlier partitions occurred in 1772 and 1793, the latter in reaction to Poland's adoption, in 1791, of a constitution aimed at reforming the country's political system.

1818   Arrival in America of Polish emigres following the abolition of the Duchy of Warsaw created by Napoleon.

1834   Emigres from the failed "November" insurrection of 1830-31 arrive in America; forming of the first Polish patriotic organization in the United States, the Polish National Committee.

1854-58   First, largely peasant, settlements of Polish immigrants, in Texas, Michigan and Wisconsin.

1863   Formation, in March, of the Polish Committee, in New York, to work to mobilize American and Polonia support for the cause of Polish insurrectionists against Russian rule. The Committee, the first of its kind, is headed by Henry Kalussowski, an emigre from the November insurrection.

1880   Founding of the Polish National Alliance of the
              United States of North America, the first viable
              Polonia federation committed to Polish inde-
              pendence; in 1886 the Alliance adds a program of
              insurance to its political agenda, thus making possi-
              ble its later development into a mass membership
              movement.

1886   Appearance of the book, *On Active Resistance and
              the National Fund* by the political emigre Zygmunt
              Milkowski. Milkowski was a veteran of the 1863
              uprising and a founder in 1887 of *Liga Polska* (the
              Polish League), a Swiss-based group working for
              independence. The Polish National Alliance sub-
              scribes to Milkowski's ideas and to raising funds in
              America for *Liga Polska*.

1891   Commemorations throughout Polonia celebrate
              the centennial anniversary of the 1791 Constitu-
              tion, an action stimulating patriotic feeling in the
              immigrant community.

1892   Founding, in Paris, of the Polish Socialist Party,
              which soon adopts a political agenda asserting Po-
              land's independence as a precondition for social
              reform; Jozef Pilsudski is a major figure in the
              movement.

1893   Founding, in Poland, of the National League under
              the leadership of Roman Dmowski. The League
              supercedes the Swiss-based *Liga Polska* as the chief
              independence movement based upon national soli-
              darity against the partitioners. In Chicago, the Co-
              lumbian Exposition is held and serves as an
              occasion for Polish immigrant solidarity on Poland's
              behalf.

1894   Creation, in Chicago, of the Polish League under
              the leadership of the philanthropist Erasmus Jerz-
              manowski and the Reverend Vincent Barzynski, a

founder of the Polish Roman Catholic Union fraternal. The League focuses upon Polonia concerns, although it also establishes its own Polish National Fund. The Polish National Alliance declines to join, leaving the League stillborn.

1899   An all-Polonia statement on behalf of Poland's independence is issued for presentation at an international peace conference called by the Russian tsar for the Hague, Netherlands, the first of its kind. The statement is presented to the President of the United States in hope that the American delegation will bring up their concerns at the Conference. Polish independence is ruled out of order, however, and ignored at the meeting.

1905   In response to unrest throughout partitioned Poland following a revolution against the tsar, a Polish National Committee is established in Chicago to organize fund raising activities in Polonia.

1910   A first Polish National Congress is held in Washington, D.C. in May following the dedication of monuments to Kosciuszko and Pulaski. At the Congress delegates from Polonia and partitioned Poland call for the homeland's independence. In July Polish Americans travel to Krakow where they join thousands of Poles to dedicate a monument recalling the 500th anniversary of the victory over the Teutonic Knights at Grunwald (Tannenberg); there they assert Poland's right of independence.

1912   Reunification, in December, of the Polish Falcons movement in Pittsburgh; founded in 1887 the Falcons rededicate themselves to Poland's independence, including volunteering for military service on the homeland's behalf. Following the Falcons convention, delegates from other Polonia organizations gather in Pittsburgh to form the Polish National Defense Committee *(Komitet Obrony*

Narodowej, KON) in cooperation with inde-
pendence-minded political groups in the homeland.

1913   Withdrawal, in June, of the clergy and the Catholic
fraternals from *KON* at its first plenary meeting in
Chicago; the conservatives form their own federation aligned with Dmowski's forces in Poland which
they name the Polish National Council *(Rada
Narodowa)*.

1914   Outbreak of the First World War (August); Pilsudski forms his Polish legion in the Austrian partition.
    Formation, in October, of the Polish Central
Relief Committee *(Polski Centralny Komitet Ratunkowy, PCKR)* with headquarters in Chicago.
This federation includes nearly all of Polonia in
gathering aid for the homeland, the battleground
upon which the partitioners struggle.

1915   Novelist Henryk Sienkiewicz's *Appeal to the Civilized Nations* appears (February); pianist Ignacy
Paderewski arrives in the United States to mobilize
support for Poland's cause (April).

1916   Establishment of the Polish National Department
(Wydzial Narodowy) in August under the leadership of the Chicago Polonia leader and banker,
John Smulski. The National Department is originally a subcommittee of the *PCKR* but soon super-
sedes it as the cause of Poland's restoration comes
to the forefront. The National Department works
closely with Dmowski and Paderewski. The Two
Emperors' Manifesto (November) proclaims German and Austrian support for an autonomous postwar Poland; the proclamation is denounced by the
National Department and most of Polonia but is
backed by *KON*.

1917   Collapse of the Russian imperial government
(March).

At an extraordinary Falcons' convention in Pittsburgh Paderewski calls for creation of a 100,000 man "Kosciuszko Army" of Polish Americans fighting on the Allied side under Poland's colors (April 3). U.S. entry into the war (April 6).

Formation of a Polish National Committee under Dmowski's leadership in Switzerland, an erstwhile government-in-exile aligned with the Western powers (August).

Establishment of the Polish Military Commission in the United States (September). Eventually more than 20,000 men serve in the Polish Army from America, helping to comprise a force including more than 90,000 men on the Western Front. Bolshevik Revolution in Russia (November).

1918   President Wilson's Fourteen Points Speech includes Polish independence as one of America's War Aims (January).

First Congress of the Polish Emigration meets in Detroit, in August, under the leadership of the National Department and there welcomes Dmowski and Paderewski. Later Congresses are held in 1919 (in Buffalo), 1921 (Pittsburgh), 1923 (Cleveland), and 1925 (Detroit) before the National Department itself is dissolved. In its place arises the Polish Welfare Council in America *(Polska Rada Opieki Spolecznej w Ameryce, PROSA)*, whose focus is on Polonia rather than Polish issues.

Armistice on the Western front ends the War; in Warsaw Pilsudski declares Poland independent (November 11).

National Department and *KON* leaders join together to rally Polonia against Zionist charges criticizing the new Polish state (November 28).

1919   Treaty of Versailles; recognition of an independent Poland.

1919-21   Polish American soldiers see action in Polish-So-
            viet War culminating in Pilsudski's victory at War-
            saw (August 15, 1920) and Treaty of Riga (March
            1921).

1926   Pilsudski's *coup d'etat* (May).

1934   Second Congress of the World Union of Poles from
            Abroad is held in Warsaw in August (a first meeting
            had been held there in 1929). There, the chairman
            of the American delegation, Francis X. Swietlik,
            Censor of the Polish National Alliance, expresses
            opposition to membership in the Union. He de-
            clares that Polish Americans comprise "a compo-
            nent part of the great American nation" with their
            first love and loyalty toward the United States.
            Nonetheless, Swietlik remains firm in promoting
            interest in the Polish heritage and support for
            causes serving the people of Poland.

1936   Founding of the Polonia Interorganizational Coun-
            cil, an agency uniting the Polish fraternals head-
            quartered in Chicago for benevolent causes within
            the Polish ethnic community and on Poland's be-
            half. At its third convention in 1938, the organiza-
            tion is renamed the Polish American Council *(Rada
            Polonii Amerykanskiej, RPA)*. Under Censor
            Swietlik's leadership during World War II, it plays a
            significant humanitarian role on behalf of the Pol-
            ish people.

1939   Molotov-Ribbentrop Pact between the U.S.S.R.
            and Nazi Germany (August 23). German invasion
            of Poland and the beginning of the Second World
            War (September 1). Soviet invasion of eastern Po-
            land (September 17) brings about the fourth parti-
            tion of Poland. General Wladyslaw Sikorski
            becomes Prime Minister and Commander-in-Chief
            of the Polish Armed Forces in the West on Septem-
            ber 30. Beginnings of underground resistance.

1940   Murder of Polish officers at Katyn.

1941   Sikorski's first visit to the United States (April); German invasion of Soviet Russia (June). Death of Ignacy Paderewski at age 81 in New York (June 29); he is buried in Arlington Cemetery until the day of Poland's restoration as a free and independent nation. In 1986 Paderewski's heart is placed in the Shrine of the American Czestochowa in Doylestown, Pennsylvania in ceremonies arranged by the Polish American Congress. Polish-Soviet Pact (July); United States entry into the war (December 8).

1942   Formation of the National Committee of Americans of Polish Descent *(Komitet Narodowy Amerykanow Polskiego Pochodzenia, KNAPP)* in New York. Critical of the *Rada Polonii*'s apolitical stance, KNAPP is staunchly committed to Poland's postwar restoration with its prewar borders intact. It is hostile to the Soviet Union and to Sikorski's policies.

1943   Katyn discovered; Soviet Union breaks off diplomatic relations with Sikorski's government (March). Warsaw Ghetto Uprising (April). Sikorski killed in plane crash; he is replaced as Prime Minister by   Stanislaw Mikolajczyk (July). Roosevelt-Stalin-Churchill   meeting   at   Teheran (November-December);   there FDR secretly agrees with Stalin on postwar Poland's eastern borders.

1944   Creation, in May, of the Polish American Congress *(Kongres Polonii Amerykanskiej, KPA)* at a mass gathering in Buffalo. Elected to head the PAC is Charles Rozmarek, President of the Polish National Alliance. The Congress strongly supports the American war effort but is at the same time influenced by *KNAPP* in its suspicions toward the Soviet Union. Warsaw Uprising (August-October).

Rozmarek endorses Roosevelt's candidacy for a fourth term, unaware of his actual position on Poland (November).

1945   Yalta Conference (February); Provisional Polish government dominated by the Communists is recognized by the United States, Soviet Russia and Britain (July). World War II ends (August). In Poland, a Soviet satellite state is established through Red Army occupation of the country, a massive campaign of terror against democratic opponents of the Communist regime, and Western reluctance to take any action critical of Stalin's conduct. The results of a 1946 referendum and of parliamentary elections in January 1947 are falsified and the Communists declare themselves the rulers of the country. President Rozmarek and a PAC delegation attempt to represent Poland's interests at the first meeting of the United Nations (May 1945), at the Paris Foreign Ministers' Conference (September 1946) and by constant appeals to U.S. leaders and the American public.

1946   Secretary of State Byrnes' speech at Stuttgart, Germany (September).

1948   With strong PAC support, the United States government approves legislation permitting thousands of displaced persons to enter the country, including large numbers of Polish war victims. Eventually, more than 140,000 Poles settle permanently in the U.S. thanks to this legislation. To assist Polish refugees the PAC organizes a special "American Committee for the Resettlement of Polish Displaced Persons."

Creation of the Polish United Workers Party by a merger of the Polish Workers (communist) Party and the Socialist Party (December); ouster of Communist Party chief Wladyslaw Gomulka and his replacement by Stalin's choice, Boleslaw Bierut.

1949   Founding of the National Committee for a Free Europe, followed by the creation of the Assembly of Captive European Nations (1950) and Radio Free Europe.
NATO Alliance established (April).

1952   Report of a select committee of the United States House of Representatives on the Katyn Massacre. The committee fixes guilt upon the Soviet Union; its work is in response to extensive lobbying by the Polish American Congress and other organizations.

1953   Stalin's death begins the process of internal change in the Soviet Union and its East European satellites (March).

1956   20th Congress of the Soviet Communist Party; Khrushchev's "secret speech" attacks Stalin's leadership and undermines East European Stalinists (February).
At least fifty-three individuals are killed and three hundred others injured in the Polish regime's repression of workers' demonstrations for "bread and freedom" in Poznan (June); the event deepens the crisis within the Communist party leadership and leads in October to Wladyslaw Gomulka's return to power in place of the discredited Stalinists.

1957   The Polish American Congress backs U.S. economic assistance to Poland amounting to nearly $600 million over the next seven years, along with "Most Favored Nation" status.

1960   Outgoing President Dwight D. Eisenhower speaks to PAC delegates at their fifth quadrennial convention in Chicago; his appearance is a first by an

American chief executive. Also addressing the conclave is the Democratic Party's Presidential nominee, Massachusetts Senator John F. Kennedy.

1963   Inauguration of a surplus food delivery program by the United States to Poland using the services of the *Rada Polonii Amerykanskiej* organization; during its seven years in operation, more than 7,000 tons in food are shipped to the needy in Poland.

1964   President Lyndon B. Johnson addresses an assemblage of PAC leaders at the White House on the twentieth anniversary of the Warsaw Uprising.

1966   President Johnson speaks to Polonia leaders on the occasion of Poland's Millennium as a Christian nation and independent state; "Building Bridges" policy toward Eastern Europe promoted.

1968   March crisis in Poland; "Anti-Zionist" campaign fails to unseat Gomulka. Soviet forces joined by Warsaw Pact troops intervene militarily in Czechoslovakia (August).
        Aloysius A. Mazewski succeeds Rozmarek as President of the Polish American Congress; in 1967 Mazewski defeated Rozmarek for reelection as President of the Polish National Alliance. Rozmarek headed the PAC for 24 years.

1970   Polish--West German Treaty; workers' rising on the Polish seacoast in opposition to food price increases topples Gomulka after as many as three hundred persons are killed. Edward Gierek takes over as Communist Party leader and rescinds the price increases (December).

1972   President Richard M. Nixon visits Poland following his historic May meeting in Moscow with Soviet Communist Party leader Leonid Brezhnev. There several major agreements on nuclear arms control are signed, signalling the formal beginning of *Detente*. Nixon's visit to Warsaw is the first by a sitting American chief executive.

1974   Gierek visits the United States in October, and meets with President Gerald Ford in the White House; Polonia largely ignores his visit.

1975   President Ford travels to Poland for a state visit in July *en route* to sign the international treaty on Security and Cooperation in Europe in Helsinki, Finland. This agreement both formally recognizes the permanence of the borders of all European states and   provides support for the rights of dissidents in the Communist countries.

1976   Polish Constitution amended; workers riots follow announced increases in food prices, which are rescinded (June). Formation of the Workers Defense Committee *(Komitet Obrony Robotnikow, KOR)* in September.

1977   In December, Jimmy Carter becomes the third United States President in five years to visit Poland. There he expresses support for the regime's progress in broadening human rights. Carter's National Security Adviser is Soviet and East European politics expert Zbigniew Brzezinski.

1978   World meeting of Polonia representatives in Toronto (May). Archbishop Karol Wojtyla of Krakow is elected Pope John Paul II (October); he makes his first Papal visit to Poland in June 1979.

1980   Nationwide strikes greet Polish government price increases (July-August); regime approves right of workers to organize independent trade unions, in Gdansk (August 31). Stanislaw Kania replaces Gierek as Communist Party chief. Founding of Solidarity (September 17). Outgoing President Carter warns the Soviet Union against military intervention in Poland against Solidarity (December). The threat soon subsides.

1981   Amid continuing tension between the regime and Solidarity, General Wojciech Jaruzelski takes over as Prime Minister (March). Death of Cardinal Stefan Wyszynski, Primate of Poland (May). Extraordinary Congress of the Polish United Workers Party (July). Congress of Solidarity Trade Union (September and October). Jaruzelski replaces Kania as Party First Secretary (October). Unsuccessful meeting between Jaruzelski, Solidarity leader Lech Walesa and the new Primate, Archbishop Jozef Glemp to deal with the crisis (November 4). "State of War" imposed by Jaruzelski, December 12-13.

Following his meeting with PAC head Aloysius Mazewski and other Polonia representatives, President Ronald Reagan announces sanctions against the Polish government in response to its imposition of martial law. The President calls upon the regime to lift the martial law and to permit Solidarity to operate freely in accordance with its own pledge of August 31, 1980.

Through the Polish American Congress Charitable Foundation, substantial efforts begin to ship medical goods, food and clothing to Poland; through 1990 nearly $170 million in assistance is sent to the people of Poland in cooperation with the episcopate of the Polish Roman Catholic Church.

1982   Major demonstrations against the regime are organized by the Solidarity underground on May 1 and August 31; Polish Parliament dissolves Solidarity (October).

1983   Pope's second visit to Poland (June); Martial Law is "lifted" (July); Walesa awarded the Nobel Prize for Peace (December).

1984   Fortieth anniversary of the Polish American Congress (May); amnesty of most political prisoners in Poland (July). President Reagan presides at the fortieth anniversary commemoration of the Warsaw Uprising in the White House, in August. Murder of Father Jerzy Popieluszko (October).

1985   PAC protests General Jaruzelski's visit to New York and the United Nations, in September. Polish Parliament elections (October); low voter turnout is credited to Solidarity opposition. Jaruzelski resigns as Prime Minister and becomes Chairman of the Council of State (November).

1986   Amnesty of nearly all political prisoners (July-September).

1987   United States sanctions against Poland are lifted, in February, although the Polish government continues to refuse to recognize Solidarity, one of the American conditions for resumption of normalized relations. Pope John Paul II's third visit to Poland (June); idea of an Agricultural Fund under Church auspices is revived.

    Vice President George Bush visits Poland and praises Solidarity cause (September). With Poland's foreign debt announced at $35 billion, the regime calls for public approval of its economic reform plan through a national referendum, in November. The program is rejected.

1988   Workers strikes at Nowa Huta and Gdansk (April-May) and in the coal mines (August) greet new regime-sponsored price increases. Walesa is called upon in September to urge the miners to go back to work in return for negotiations leading to Solidarity's relegalization.

    Soviet Party Leader Mikhail Gorbachev visits Poland (July). Mieczyslaw Rakowski becomes

Prime Minister (September); Walesa wins a nationally televised debate over the head of the government trade unions (November 30). Jaruzelski consolidates his power in a major Party leadership shakeup (December).

Death of President Mazewski, in August. He had served as PAC chief for nearly twenty years and is succeeded in November by Edward J. Moskal. Moskal had been elected President of the Polish National Alliance a month earlier.

1989   "Round Table" talks in Warsaw begin in February between government officials and leaders of Solidarity and the Roman Catholic Church. They herald the start of a revolutionary year in the history of world communism. In April the Round Table talks end with the restoration of Solidarity to full legal status. Free elections are called for early June to choose a new legislative body, the Senate, and to permit the democratic opposition to contest 35 percent of the seats in the parliament, or *Sejm*. On April 17, President Bush promises economic aid to Poland in recognition of its positive steps toward political pluralism. His ideas are strongly backed by the Polish American Congress. In the June elections, Solidarity's candidates win an astounding victory and capture 99 of the 100 seats in the Senate and all 161 seats it is permitted to contest in the Parliament. Nearly every Communist Party candidate is defeated in his/her quest for office, even those who ran unopposed, including Rakowski. Following the Communists' debacle, the way is paved for Solidarity's entry into power and in August, one of its leaders, Tadeusz Mazowiecki is nominated to be Prime Minister, the first democratic leader in Eastern Europe in more than forty years. Mazowiecki's coalition cabinet is approved by the parliament in September and begins the great tasks of reforming the country's shattered economy and organizing a democratically based political system. In October, PAC President Moskal heads a delegation of Polonia leaders to Poland to underscore its strong support for the Mazowiecki government and its aims. In November, Solidarity leader Lech Walesa travels to the United States where he becomes only the third private citizen of a foreign country to address a joint session of the Congress; he and the Solidarity cause are acclaimed everywhere. At the same time an economic aid package from the U.S. to Poland amounting to more than $850 million is approved. Throughout the Communist world, the events in Poland generate enormous popular upheavals in favor of political democratization and an end to Leninist dictatorship. By year's end, the communist regimes in Hungary, East Germany, Bulgaria and Czechoslovakia will make serious moves towards reform and the tyrannical system of Nicolae Ceausescu of Romania will be overthrown in a violent revolution. Reforms undertaken in the Soviet Union by Mikhail S. Gorbachev lead to growing criticism of Communist Party domination and the spectre of secession by the country's dissatisfied ethnic republics. A similar crisis is shaping up inside multi-ethnic Yugoslavia. Only in China is the democratic surge brutally repressed, while in Albania local autocrats do their best to isolate their subjects from any contact with the Polish contagion. Throughout Europe and the United States there is considerable talk about the end of the Cold War and even the reunification of the two Germanies.

1990   In January, the Polish United workers party holds its last Congress and formally disbands. In its place are two parties, a "reform-minded" Social Democracy of the Polish Republic which represents the old PUWP and a smaller, more liberal group calling itself the Social Democratic Union of the Polish Republic. Together the two parties claim fewer than 70,000 members, in contrast to the old PUWP which included more than 2.3 million members into the mid 1980s. In local elections in April, the communists' candidates win only one-third of one percent of the nearly 52,000 contested offices throughout the country and in June the Party's remaining members in Mazowiecki's cabinet are removed. In February, President Bush strongly backs the permanence of Poland's western border with East Germany in his talks with West German Chancellor Helmut Kohl. His support is the strongest ever by an American president and is followed in March by his backing of Poland's participation in the so-called "Four Plus Two Talks" determining Germany's future and its borders. Both of these actions are vigorously argued for by the Polish American Congress. In March Prime Minister Mazowiecki visits Chicago in connection with his state visit to America; he is the second Polish Prime Minister (General Sikorski was the first) to be welcomed officially in Washington and by Polonia. While in the Windy City Mazowiecki addresses an assembly of more the 1,100 Polonia leaders and extols the PAC for its "efforts on behalf and defense of matters which are especially important to Poland" -- the inviolability of the Polish-German border, humanitarian aid to Poland, and the promotion of investment in the new and democratic Poland. On April 13, the Soviet government at long last publicly acknowledges Stalin's responsibility for the Katyn Massacre. Between March and June, free and contested elections are held in the East European nations. In East Germany, the communists win but 16 percent of the vote as pro-unification parties gain a sweeping victory. In Hungary and Czechoslovakia the democratic parties win convincing victories and both countries gain Soviet approval of their request that its troops depart from their territories. In Romania and Bulgaria, "reform" communists parties operating under new names do continue in power in elections with embryonic political oppositions. In the Soviet Union, the ruling CPSU makes massive concessions to critics demanding that it relinquish its leading and unchallenged leadership role over the country. By the Summer, the secession of the Baltic republics from the U.S.S.R. appears to be an inevitability with the remaining ethnic republics moving toward a dramatic reconstruction of their relationships with Moscow in favor of much greater internal autonomy and democratization.

In September, the Ellis Island Immigration Museum opens to the public. This cause was supported by the Polish American Congress and its member organizations which together contributed more than $560,000 to insure that the Polish immigrants' story would be told to all who frequent the Museum in the years to come.

In November the national council of PAC directors convenes in Washington, D.C. and elects Edward Moskal to a second two year term as President. Illinois PAC President Roman Pucinski is elected a national vice president and joins Moskal, Helen Wojcik, Kazimierz Lukomski, Edward Dykla, and Lawrence Wujcikowski on the organization's expanded executive committee.

In recognition of Poland's progress in building democracy at home, the PAC leadership agrees to give greater attention to Polonia's needs, a position shared by Poland's new Ambassador to the United States, Kazimierz Dziewanowski, who addresses the assembly.

On November 14, heads of the governments of Poland and the unified Germany sign a treaty guaranteeing the permanence of the borders between the two countries.

On December 9, Lech Walesa is elected President of the Polish Republic.

1991   President and Mrs. Walesa visit the United States
            (March); in Washington, D.C. President Bush an-
            nounces a substantial reduction in Poland's debt to
            the U.S. in support of its economic reform efforts.
                In May, the 200th anniversary of Poland's 1791
            Constitution is celebrated. In June, Pope John Paul
            II travels to Poland a fourth time.
                Warsaw Pact military alliance is dissolved (July).
                PAC Vice President Lukomski resigns and is
            replaced by Jan Nowak.
                Coup d'etat by hard-line opponents of Soviet
            reforms fails, leading to the apparent collapse of
            Communist Party rule, repudiation of KGB repres-
            sion, and enhanced autonomy for the ethnic repub-
            lics at the expense of Moscow. Lithuania, Latvia
            and Estonia win universal recognition of their de-
            mands for full independence (August 19 - Septem-
            ber 5). Polish Parliamentary elections are set for
            October.

    * Other useful chronological summaries of Polish and Pol-
ish American developments can be found in Frank Renkiewicz,
editor, *The Poles in America* (1973); Piotr Wandycz, *The United
States and Poland* (1980); Andrzej Brozek, *Polish Americans:
1854-1939* (1985); Donald Pienkos, *PNA* (1984); and Pienkos,
One Hundred Years Young (1987).

Biographies

Julius Andrzejkowicz (1821 - 1898). Founder and First Censor of the Polish National Alliance. Born in Lithuania, Andrzejkowicz was involved in patriotic activities in the homeland as a young person. When his group, which had planned a revolt against Russian rule in 1848 was exposed, Andrzejkowicz left the country, emigrating first to France then to America, where he took part in the California gold rush.

Invited to Philadelphia by distant relatives, he worked as a chemist in a paint-making company in which he later purchased a partnership. The firm, "Andrejkovicz and Dunk," was successful and set up offices in various cities around the country. Andrzejkowicz himself published a book on chemical dye processes which went into several editions and he introduced the use of aniline colors in the United States.

In 1880, Andrzejkowicz played a leading role in founding the Polish National Alliance, which grew to be the first fraternal federation of local Polish societies based upon work for the homeland's independence and the material needs of its people, both in Poland and in America. Open to all emigrants from the ancient Polish lands regardless of their religious affiliation, the Alliance was a response to appeals coming from political exiles from the failed 1863 uprising that the growing immigrant community in America unite on behalf of the Polish cause. In 1881, the Alliance established its own weekly newspaper, *Zgoda,* to promote its aims and in 1886 it set up the first successful program in Polonia to provide insurance benefits to its members and their families. In time the Alliance became Polonia's largest and most influential fraternal.

Elected the Alliance's Censor, or Chief Judge, at its founding convention, or *sejm,* in September 1880, Andrzejkowicz declined reelection to that office in 1883 because of ill health. However, he remained an influential voice in the movement. For example, in 1886 he visited the headquarters of the exiles in Raperswil, Switzerland and following his return to America persuaded the Alliance to support the idea of raising money in

Polonia for the Polish National Fund, or *Skarb Narodowy*. The idea for such a fund was a product of the thinking of the veteran patriotic activist, Zygmunt Milkowski (T. T. Jez). The Alliance not only made the fund raising project part of its official by-laws, it also established enduring contacts with Milkowski's *Liga Polska*, the forerunner of the National Democratic movement headed after 1893 by Roman Dmowski inside partitioned Poland.

Aleksander Debski (1857-1935). Leader of the Polish socialists in America, Polonia activist and head of the Polish National Defense Committee *(Komitet Obrony Narodowej* or *KON)* during the First World War years. Born in the Russian-ruled zone of partitioned Poland and an engineer by training, Debski took part in the founding of the Polish Socialist Party in Paris in 1892. Coming to America in 1899, he sought to unite Poles inclined to socialism to support the cause of Poland's independence.

Debski recognized the importance of the Polish National Alliance as the largest Polonia movement and worked, with some success, in bringing it closer to the aims of the Polish socialists, thereby weakening its historic ties with the National Democratic party and its program. Events inside Poland, particularly the unrest throughout the Russian-ruled provinces during the 1905 Revolution encouraged support for his perspective within the Alliance and throughout Polonia. Later, Debski and his colleagues were leading participants at the historic Polish National Congress held in Washington, D.C. in 1910, at which Polonia's commitment to Polish independence was underscored.

In December 1912, Debski and his colleagues won a last major victory at a meeting of Polish organization leaders in Pittsburgh. There they founded the Polish National Defense Committee in direct support of the homeland's freedom. This all-Polonia federation was the first of its kind within the emigrant community and included not only the socialists and their sympathizers but also the clergy and every major fraternal. *KON*'s achievement was short-lived; in June 1913 the clergy and conservative fraternals withdrew to form their own federation in support of the homeland, the Polish National Council *(Rada*

Narodowa). The following year witnessed the departure of the Committee's remaining allies among the progressive fraternals, the Polish National Alliance, the Falcons and the Polish Women's Alliance. These organizations soon joined with the conservatives to form the Polish Central Relief Committee to generate humanitarian aid for the homeland upon the outbreak of the World War in 1914. Later they also organized the Polish National Department *(Wydzial Narodowy)* to better express the emigration's political concerns. Debski's *KON* group was left with only the socialists and the members of the Polish National Catholic Church and was reduced to playing a minor role in Polonia during the war years.

In 1919, Debski left the United States for Poland and was an active supporter of Jozef Pilsudski throughout the rest of his career. In 1930, he was elected to a seat in the Polish Senate.

Edward Dykla (born in 1933). President of the Polish Roman Catholic Union of America and Polonia leader. Born in Chicago, Dykla taught for nineteen years at Weber High School before becoming a national officer in the PRCUA. The fraternal's Secretary General from 1974 to 1982, he was its Treasurer between 1982 and 1986. Dykla was first elected President of the PRCUA in 1986, succeeding Acting President Frank Rutkowski of Cleveland, who had taken over for Joseph Drobot when he retired due to illness in 1985. Treasurer of the Polish American Congress, he also serves on the Boards of Chicago's Felician College, the St. Joseph's Home for Senior Citizens, St. Mary of Nazareth Hospital and the Polish Ministry of the Archdiocese of Chicago.

Francis Fronczak (1874-1955). Public official and Polonia activist. A native of Buffalo (his father had come to America after having taken part in the 1863 insurrection), Fronczak was one of the first well-educated American-born leaders in Polonia. From Canisius College he earned both his Bachelor's and Master's degrees and later from the University of Buffalo he was awarded a Law degree and a Doctorate in Medicine. After the First World War he was granted honorary degrees in Medicine from both the University of Warsaw and the Jagiellonian University in Krakow.

In 1896 Fronczak was the first Polish American elected to the New York state legislature and in 1910 he became Buffalo City Health Commissioner, a post he held for 36 years. He was long recognized as one of the country's foremost public health authorities. During his career Fronczak authored some twenty-seven publications in the field of public medicine and regularly represented the United States at international health conferences. Fronczak was long an activist in the Polish Roman Catholic Union of America.

A lieutenant colonel in the Medical Corps in World War I Fronczak played a significant role linking the concerns of Polonia with those of the American war effort. President of the Polish Central Relief Committee, he was also American Polonia's delegate to the Polish National Committee in Paris representing Poland to the Allied powers. In France in 1918, he supervised the creation of adequate living and medical conditions for the Polish Army organized to take part in the war effort on the side of the Allies. Fronczak was also involved in developing humane conditions for Polish prisoners of war and refugees in France. He was part of the three-man Council of War of the Polish forces in France and a member of the first American Red Cross Commission to Poland.

After World War II Fronczak was a medical adviser, observer and coordinator of the Polish Mission of the United Nations Relief and Rehabilitation Administration (UNRRA).

Blair F. Gunther (1903-1966). Polonia activist and leader in the Polish American Congress. A native of western Pennsylvania, Gunther was a graduate of Saint John Kanty College in 1922 and earned a Law degree from Duquesne University in 1928. Active in local and state politics, he became a county judge in 1942 and later was elected to the Supreme Court of the Commonwealth of Pennsylvania. In 1947, Gunther was chosen Censor of the Polish National Alliance fraternal and held that office until 1959.

At the second national convention of the Polish American Congress in 1948, Gunther was selected to chair its Committee for the Resettlement of Polish Displaced Persons. Created in anticipation of Congressional passage of special legislation permitting thousands of European war refugees to enter the

United States, the Committee succeeded in assisting in the resettlement of more than 30,000 Polish displaced persons.

In 1957, there was speculation that Gunther would be nominated to the United States Supreme Court, thus making him the first Polish American to gain entry into that august body. President Eisenhower, however, chose William J. Brennan for the post.

In 1959 Gunther was defeated for reelection as PNA Censor. By this time he had become a major political opponent of the President of the Alliance and the Polish American Congress, Charles Rozmarek.

Frank Januszewski (1886-1953). Newspaper publisher and an organizer of Polonia's World War II political efforts for Poland. Born in Lomza, Poland, Januszewski took part in the 1905 uprising against the tsar under Jozef Pilsudski's leadership and following its suppression had to leave the country for America in 1907. He first settled in Cleveland, where he became active in the Polish Falcons Alliance.

Soon active in the militant wing of the Falcons -- its aim that of organizing fighting units to help liberate the partitioned country -- Januszewski became a leader in the "Free Falcons" movement which seceded from the national organization in 1909.

Moving to Detroit in 1912 where he gained employment with the local Polish language newspaper, *Dziennik Polski* (the Polish Daily), Januszewski became a supporter of the Polish National Defense Committee *(KON)* in World War I.

Over the years Januszewski rose to various responsible positions with the *Dziennik Polski* and in 1930 succeeded in purchasing the publication. He became a leading force in the Polish language press of the time and held high office in the Polish Publishers and Editors Guild of the United States.

With the outbreak of World War II in 1939 Januszewski became an outspoken backer of a strong Polonia political stance on Poland's behalf. In 1942 he and his friend Max Wegrzynek, publisher of the New York *Nowy Swiat,* took the lead in founding a new political action organization to promote Poland's objectives in the U.S. This group was the National Committee of Americans of Polish Descent, *KNAPP.* In 1944 the two men played critical roles in helping organize the Polish American Congress together with Charles Rozmarek, President of the Polish National Alliance. At the PAC's founding meeting Januszewski and Wegrzynek were elected national vice presidents. Following Wegrzynek's death later that same year Januszewski succeeded him as President of *KNAPP*, an office he held until his own death.

A sharp critic of the policies and methods of Rozmarek from 1946 onward, Januszewski took *KNAPP* out of the PAC in 1948. He remained a powerful voice for Poland's rights and a strong ally of U.S. Senator Arthur Vandenberg of Michigan, one of the earliest national leaders to call for American diplomatic and military opposition to Soviet postwar expansionism.

Always a powerful exponent of the Pilsudski vision of Polish independence, Januszewski was a crucial force shaping the ideological perspective of the PAC and Polonia for years after his own passing. He was succeeded as President of *KNAPP* by Walter Cytacki of Detroit (1884-1954), himself a past national leader in the PNA.

Erasmus Jerzmanowski (1844-1909). Polonia leader and Philanthropist. Born of an aristocratic family near Kalisz in the Russian zone of partitioned Poland, Jerzmanowski took part in the 1863 insurrection. Following its defeat he became an exile in France. Taking up studies in Chemistry at the Polytechnical Institute of the University of Paris, he became interested in work dealing with natural gas, a new fuel with great potential if it could be burned safely. Later, Jerzmanowski was awarded the Legion of Honor for his service in the Franco-Prussian War of 1870-1871.

In the United States in 1875, Jerzmanowski invented and patented the modern gas lamp and organized the Equitable Gas Company, which won the rights to produce and sell street lamps for the city of New York. Overnight Jerzmanowski's success made him Polonia's first millionaire. Turning his attentions to philanthropic matters, Jezmanowski joined the newly established Polish National Alliance and organized the Central Welfare Committee to support the Alliance in New York, its aim to help immigrants upon their arrival in the new land. He also established an immigration bureau, a reading room and a library, all of which remained in operation for many years under the Alliance's sponsorship.

Active in organizing a number of PNA local lodges on the East coast, Jerzmanowski nonetheless was unsuccessful in his efforts to win a leadership post in the Alliance. In 1894, he became a strong supporter of the Polish League, a new Polonia-wide federation committed to working on behalf of the immigration and the Polish homeland. Centered in Chicago and led by the Rev. Vincent Barzynski, the League failed to win the support of the Alliance and soon disappeared. Jerzmanowski then served for a short time as the American representative of the Polish National Treasury headquartered in Raperswil, Switzerland, with the responsibility of raising funds for Poland's independence. In 1896, he retired from further involvement in Polish American matters and returned to Poland, where he spent his remaining years on his estate near Krakow. Upon his death, his fortune was given to the Jagiellonian University, helping to make possible the creation of what today is known as the Polish Academy of Sciences.

Henry Kalussowski (1806-1894). Early Polonia leader and founder of the first immigrant patriotic organizations committed to Poland's independence. Born in Poland, Kalussowski participated in the 1830 insurrection and left the country after its defeat. In 1842, he played a leading role in organizing one of the earliest patriotic groups in the United States, the Society of Poles in America. Involved in 1848 in another unsuccessful Polish revolt, he returned, permanently, to this country and organized another emigre group, the Democratic Society of Polish Refugees in America. During the 1863 insurrection, Kalussowski formed the Polish Central Committee headquartered in New York to raise funds for the rebels and to publicize their cause. He was also helpful to Polish emigrants seeking military commissions in the Union forces during the American Civil War.

In 1878, Kalussowski wrote for advice to the Polish exile leader Agaton Giller, then in Raperswil, Switzerland, in successfully organizing the American Poles in support of patriotic activities on behalf of Poland's independence. Giller's response is credited with leading in 1880 to the formation of the Polish

National Alliance, the first viable effort to unite the immigrants in support of Poland's restoration.

A long time backer of the Alliance in his advanced years, Kalussowski donated his extensive library and collection of personal papers to the PNA in return for its pledge to sponsor a library and reading room open to all in Polonia. This collection became the basis for the Alliance's library in Chicago; following the establishment of the PNA's school in Cambridge Springs, Pennsylvania in 1912, Kalussowski's donation was transferred there.

Employed in the U.S. Treasury Department in Washington, D.C. beginning in 1850, Kalussowski lectured frequently on the Polish question; in 1867 he translated the Russian documents for the U.S. purchase of Alaska. He was a personal friend of the Hungarian freedom fighter, Louis Kossuth.

Joseph Kania (1897-1953). President of the Polish Roman Catholic Union of America and Polonia leader. Born in Tarnowiec near Jaslo in Southeastern Poland, Kania came to the United States with his parents who settled first in Philadelphia before moving permanently to Detroit. Following his studies in business administration at the Hamilton Institute in Detroit, Kania found employment in a local bank and established a career in this field. He was also active in Detroit civic affairs and was appointed to several municipal and county commissions.

Kania's involvement in Polonia affairs stretched back to his participation in the Polish National Department *(Wydzial Narodowy)* during the 1920s. Active early on in the Polish Roman Catholic Union in America, Kania served from 1928 to 1934 as its Vice President, and from 1934 to 1941 as President, stepping down from that office as required by the fraternal's two term limit. Returned to the Presidency in 1946 he served until his death in 1953 at age 56.

As PRCUA President Kania was responsible for establishing the Polish Museum of America in the fraternal's home office building in Chicago. The Museum remains one of the centers of Polish art, culture and ethnic memorabilia in the United States. Kania was active in the work of the *Rada Polonii Amerykanskiej* humanitarian organization throughout his years in Chicago and in 1942 was one of the founders of the National

Committee of Americans of Polish Descent, *KNAPP,* a forerunner of the Polish American Congress.

Kazimierz Kozakiewicz (1900-1968). President of the Polish Roman Catholic Union of America and Polonia leader. Born in Plock, Poland, Kozakiewicz was brought to America at age 2 and grew up in Lowell, Massachusetts. He earned a doctorate in the field of Oculism from Boston University.

Active in the PRCUA from his teens, Kozakiewicz was elected its Vice President in 1950 and succeeded to the Presidency upon the death of Joseph Kania in 1953. He served an additional term in his own right from 1954 to 1958. A leader in the *Rada Polonii,* it was Kozakiewicz who returned the PRCUA to the Polish American Congress in 1954. Under President Kania the PRCUA had withdrawn from the Congress out of opposition to Charles Rozmarek's leadership practices. Kozakiewicz in contrast worked smoothly with Rozmarek, and served as Treasurer of the PAC.

Adele Lagodzinska (1896-1990). Polonia leader and President of the Polish Women's Alliance. Born in Chicago and the daughter of respected local Polish community activists, Lagodzinska was already a veteran in the Polish Women's Alliance when she was elected its fifth President, succeeding Honorata Wolowska in 1947. She went on to serve in that office until her retirement in 1971 whereupon she was named the PWA's Honorary President.

Throughout her years as a leader in the Polish Women's Alliance, Lagodzinska was also active in the highest councils of both the Polish American Council and the Polish American Congress. Thus she served for more than twenty years as the Secretary General of the Polish American Council under the leadership of Francis X. Swietlik. At the same time, Lagodzinska was a national Vice President of the PAC and worked effectively with both Charles Rozmarek and Aloysius Mazewski, Presidents of the Congress during those years.

Beginning with her trip in August 1956, Lagodzinska made a number of visits to Poland for the purpose of viewing for herself the character of the country's needs and the manner in which Polonia's assistance was used following the resumption of contacts between the Polish American Council and the Polish regime headed by Wladyslaw Gomulka. Through her efforts, the Polish Women's Alliance and the organizations of Polonia extended considerable assistance to a number of hospitals, orphanages and schools in Poland, including the Catholic University in Lublin and the School for the Blind in Laski. For many years she was also a strong supporter of the Polish American Historical Association, whose members study the Poles' immigration and settlement experiences in this country.

Upon her retirement, Lagodzinska received the medal of *Polonia Restituta* from the Polish Government in Exile headquartered in London, in recognition for her many humanitarian activities on behalf of the homeland. A third generation American of Polish heritage and a person who only mastered the Polish language as an adult, Lagodzinska nonetheless was a dedicated activist in Polonia on behalf of her ancestral homeland.

Kazimierz Lukomski. National Vice President, Polish American Congress. Born in 1920 near Siauliai, in Lithuania, Lukomski's family emigrated to Poland from Lithuania where he finished high school just a year before the outbreak of the Second World War. A member of the Army reserves in September 1939, Lukomski served in the Polish armed forces in the West in a Polish paratroop brigade headquartered in Great Britain during the war. Following the conflict, he remained in England until 1955 when he and his family came to the United States, settling permanently in Chicago. An accountant by profession, he served as the head of that department in a Chicago-based firm. Lukomski became active in the Polish Army Veterans Association in the 1950s and in the Polish American Congress in the 1960s; in 1968 he was elected the PAC's Vice President. Chairman of the Congress' Polish Affairs Commission since then, Lukomski has played a major role in formulating the organization's policy toward Poland and in expressing its views, both through the *Polish American Congress Newsletter,* and through the many brochures, pamphlets and occasional statements of the Congress that have appeared over the years. Between August and November, 1988 he served as the chief of the Polish American Congress from the time of the sudden death of President Mazewski to the election of his successor, Edward Moskal.

Aloysius Mazewski (1916-1988). President of the Polish American Congress and the Polish National Alliance. Born in North Chicago, Illinois of immigrant parents, Mazewski earned a law degree from DePaul University on the eve of World War II and was a highly successful attorney into the late 1960s. A volunteer for military duty, he served as an intelligence officer and later became a military hospital chief administrator. Mazewski completed his military duties in 1946 holding the rank of major.

Active in the Polish National Alliance since his teen age years, Mazewski was elected to the Board of Directors of the fraternal in 1947 and reelected to a second four year term in 1951. Ambitious to one day lead the Alliance, he was instead "dumped" from the Board at the 1955 PNA convention by President Charles Rozmarek. In 1959, Mazewski backed the unsuccessful candidacy of Adam Tomaszkiewicz for the presidency and in 1963 he waged his own failed campaign for the office against Rozmarek. In 1967, however, Mazewski bested Rozmarek at the 35th quadrennial convention in a bitter contest, winning the votes of 221 delegates to 189 for his adversary. Thereafter, he was reelected to five additional terms with little difficulty and in 1987 ran unopposed for the office.

Interestingly, during his 1967 campaign Mazewski had criticized Rozmarek for holding the top office in the Polish American Congress in addition to heading the Alliance. Following his victory, however, he changed his position on the issue and was elected to succeed Rozmarek at the PAC's 1968 convention. Thereafter, he continued in that office as well until his sudden death in August 1988.

As PAC President Mazewski worked to improve the Congress' visibility in the nation's capital and gradually built a productive relationship between Polonia and each successive U.S. President, from Richard Nixon through Ronald Reagan. He was on excellent terms with Vice President George Bush as well and was a frequent visitor to the White House and Congress in representing the concerns of the Polish American community.

A great believer in the importance of Polish Americans' involvement in the democratic political process, Mazewski was a skilled Polonia politician himself. Thus, he was adept in forging a deeper sense of unity within organized Polonia and the many groups belonging to the Polish American Congress, most significant among them the various fraternal societies and veterans' associations operating throughout the country. Perhaps his greatest achievement was in creating the Polish American Congress Charitable Foundation. This agency complemented the political lobbying activities of the PAC and generated more than $130 million in relief assistance to Poland between 1980 and 1988.

As head of the chief political organization speaking for the largest Polish ethnic community in the emigration, Mazewski represented the PAC at countless American government meetings and ceremonies and on those occasions when the representatives of the worldwide Polonia gathered. He also hosted many visits to America by dignitaries of the Polish Church, including that of Karol Cardinal Wojtyla of Krakow in 1976. Mazewski attended Wojtyla's investiture as Pope John Paul II in 1978 as a member of the official United States delegation which travelled to Rome. In 1981 he became the first PAC President to visit Poland when he flew to Warsaw as part of the American delegation present for the funeral of Stefan Cardinal Wyszynski. While in Poland Mazewski met with Solidarity's leader, Lech Walesa and remained a powerful voice in support of Solidarity's aims throughout the 1980s.

Throughout his tenure as PAC President, Mazewski remained a strong supporter of Radio Free Europe and Radio Liberty and actively backed the creation of the National Endowment for Democracy. He was particularly significant in helping shape United States policy toward Poland following the creation of Solidarity in 1980 and was an outspoken advocate of just treatment of the thousands of individuals who sought U.S. residency status following the invoking of martial law in December 1981.

Edward J. Moskal. President of the Polish American Congress. Born in Chicago in 1924, Moskal joined the Polish National Alliance fraternal in the 1940s and was elected to its

Board of Directors in 1963. In 1967 he was elected the PNA's Treasurer and served in that office for the next twenty-one years. In October 1988, he was chosen President of the Alliance following the death of Aloysius Mazewski. The next month found Moskal also succeeding Mazewski as the third President of the Polish American Congress and thus continuing the tradition that has placed the President of the PNA at the head of the Congress from the time of its founding in 1944.

Dramatic and historically significant events beginning in Poland and extending throughout the Communist world combined to make Moskal's first years in office extraordinarily active. Polish Solidarity's victory over the then ruling communist party in the free elections of June 1989 was so complete that within months its leaders succeeded in taking over the government, thereby ending more than four decades of communist domination in the country and paving the way in the months to come for the end of Soviet-sponsored rule throughout East Central Europe.

In the face of these turbulent and unforeseen developments, Moskal acted decisively to underscore American Polonia's support for Solidarity and its aims of democratization and economic reform. In October 1989 he headed a Polish American Congress delegation to Poland for this purpose and during this visit met with Poland's Prime Minister, Tadeusz Mazowiecki, Solidarity's Chairman Lech Walesa, Cardinal Jozef Glemp and many in the country's newly elected and democratic parliamentary leadership. Over the next two months alone Moskal would travel twice more to Poland, first as a member of a high level United States government fact-finding delegation, and then as a representative of American Polonia at the founding of a new international humanitarian effort for Poland headed by Glemp, *Fundusz Daru Narodowego.* Significantly, both Walesa and Mazowiecki would soon travel to America and meet with Moskal and the PAC leadership in Chicago to dramatize their appreciation of Polonia's support for their cause.

At home, Moskal's and the PAC's efforts on the ancestral homeland's behalf included an effective lobbying campaign to persuade Congress to provide Poland with substantial economic aid. In November 1989, these activities helped bring about passage of the Support for East European Democracy

Act, which set aside more than $850 million to assist Poland's new government in rebuilding the country's economy.

In early 1990 Moskal aggressively championed Poland's concerns over the security and permanence of its western borders following the collapse of the East German communist regime and its imminent incorporation into the West German Federal Republic. Moreover, the position taken by Moskal and the PAC won wide backing throughout the country and in February 1990 was publicly endorsed by President Bush and America's N.A.T.O. allies.

Throughout his tenure, Moskal also acted vigorously to stimulate increased giving in Polonia to the Polish American Congress Charitable Foundation. Thus, for the first time, direct appeals to the memberships of the Polish fraternals were launched and these yielded nearly one million dollars in support of the Foundation's important work. An additional $560,000 was also generated by the PAC and its member organizations to realize the Ellis Island Immigration Museum in New York, a project where the Polish contribution to America will be amply displayed thanks to Polonia's generosity. Moskal was reelected to a second term as PAC President in November 1990.

Anna Neumann (1860-1947). President of the Polish Women's Alliance and World War I Polonia leader. Born near Warsaw, Neumann came to America as a child and settled with her parents in Chicago. Employed as a seamstress, Neumann joined the Polish Women's Alliance, the first independent Polish women's "fraternal" organization in the United States, in 1900, just two years after its conception. In 1902 she was elected the organization's second President, succeeding Stefania Chmielinska (1866-1939), herself a dedicated believer in women's rights, the educational and cultural advancement of the Polish immigrants, and the cause of Poland's freedom. Neumann served as President between 1902 and 1906 and again from 1909 to 1918 and was particularly visible within the leadership of the Polish American community as the PWA's representative on behalf of the Polish independence cause during the First World War.

Already in 1914, Neumann volunteered the then sizable sum of $3,000 to Ignacy Paderewski during his visit to the

United States in quest of funds for a Polish propaganda center headquartered in Switzerland. Under her leadership, the Women's Alliance also raised thousands of dollars for the independence cause through its *Fundusz Bojowy* (War Fund). Neumann was the Polish Women's Alliance representative in both the Polish Central Relief Committee and the Polish National Department *(Wydzial Narodowy)*, the immigrant community's chief humanitarian and political action federations throughout World War I. Following her retirement as head of the PWA, Neumann continued to work for her organization as its Honorary President. She was also the PWA's librarian and helped found its museum. She was also awarded the Gold Cross of Achievement by the Government of independent Poland for her services to the homeland. Neumann was succeeded as President by Emilia Napieralska (1882-1943), herself a great champion of the Polish independence cause in the World War I years and a worthy continuer of Chmielinska and Neumann's work in the Polish Women's Alliance.

John Olejniczak (1886-1963). President of the Polish Roman Catholic Union of America and Polonia leader. Born in Chicago, as a child he moved with his parents to South Bend, Indiana where he eventually became active in business and local politics. In the latter capacity he was an alderman and later chairman in South Bend's city council. Olejniczak was an active fraternalist, rising to leadership in the Polish Falcons of America in the South Bend district and later winning a series of elections to national office in the PRCUA. He served as PRCUA President between 1928 and 1934 and again from 1941 to 1946. National Treasurer of the *Rada Polonii Amerykanskiej* relief organization, Olejniczak was one of the founders of the Polish American Congress in 1944.

Joseph Osajda (1909-1979). President of the Polish Roman Catholic Union of America and Polonia leader. Born in Poland, Osajda came to America in 1925 and settled in Chicago where he graduated from Holy Trinity High School. Initially employed in the business office of the Sherman Hotel, he eventually rose to the rank of general manager and vice president of the great facility. He also earned a law degree and Master of Business Administration along the way.

Active in the PRCUA from 1929 onward, Osajda became one of the fraternal's most successful insurance salesmen. After having served as the PRCUA's Counsel, he was elected its President in 1970 and served until 1978. During his term, the fraternal celebrated its centennial in 1973-1974 and the activities of the Polish Museum of America were revitalized. In addition to his fraternal duties Osaja served as Treasurer of the Polish American Congress under the leadership of Aloysius Mazewski.

In 1977 Osajda was incapacitated by a stroke. In 1978 he retired, to be succeeded as President by Joseph Drobot of Detroit. Osajda's predecessor as head of the PRCUA was Joseph Pranica of Chicago.

Roman C. Pucinski (born in 1919). Political official and Polonia leader. A graduate of Chicago's John Marshall Law School, Pucinski served in the U.S. Air Force in the Pacific theater during World War II. His active service during the war earned him the Distinguished Flying Cross and promotion to the rank of Captain.

For some twenty years into the late 1950s Pucinski worked as a staff reporter and investigative writer for the Chicago Sun-Times; a particularly significant service during those years was his work as the Chief Investigator for the Select Committee of the U.S. House of Representatives which reviewed the facts of the 1940 Katyn Massacre in 1951-52.

In 1958 Pucinski won a seat in the House of Representatives on his second try for that office; he went on to serve 14 years in Congress and served as a member of its Committees on Education and Labor as well as Veterans Affairs. In 1972 Pucinski was defeated in his bid to unseat Republican Charles Percy for the office of U.S. Senator of Illinois; the following year he won election as Alderman of Chicago's 41st Ward, an office he held until April 1991. In 1977 he campaigned unsuccessfully for the Democratic Party nomination for the office of Mayor of Chicago in a special election to fill the vacancy created by the death of Richard J. Daley.

Pucinski has served for many years as a leader in the Polish American Congress in the Chicago area and worked closely with both Charles Rozmarek and Aloysius Mazewski during their tenures as President of the PAC. He is presently the President of the Illinois Division of the Congress and for several years has served as the national chairman of its annual fund raising drive. In November 1988, Pucinski was a candidate for the Presidency of the PAC following Mazewski's death but lost out to Edward J. Moskal. In November 1990, he was elected a national PAC Vice President along with Helen Wojcik and Kazimierz Lukomski.

Pucinski is the owner of a Chicago-based radio station, WEDC, where his mother Lydia was a well-known personality throughout Polonia for some fifty years. Pucinski's daughter, Aurelia, is active in local politics and in 1988 was elected Clerk of the Circuit Court of Cook County. Pucinski himself has been much involved in leading the Illinois PAC Division in assisting the newest migrations of Poles to successfully resettle as citizens and to help them learn the English language and find jobs throughout the metropolitan Chicago area.

Paul Peter Rhode (1871-1945). Clergyman and Polonia leader. Born in Wejherowo in Poland, Rhode came to America at the age of nine with his mother, with the family settling in Chicago. Rhode later studied Philosophy and Theology at St. Francis Seminary near Milwaukee and was ordained a Priest in 1894.

In 1908, Rhode was consecrated an auxiliary bishop for the Archdiocese of Chicago after having served some twelve years as a parish pastor on the city's far south side. His elevation made Rhode the first Polish bishop in the United States; his selection followed a strenuous campaign led by the Rev. Waclaw Kruszka of Milwaukee to persuade the Roman Catholic Church hierarchy to give the burgeoning Polonia its own representative. Rhode remained auxiliary Bishop in Chicago until 1915 when he was appointed Bishop of the diocese of Green Bay, Wisconsin, an office he held until his death.

Rhode was active in the life of the Polish community and was a founder of the Polish Priests' Association in the United States and the honorary chaplain of the Polish Roman Catholic

Union of America fraternal. During the First World War era he played a major leadership role in the Polish National Council *(Rada Narodowa),* the Polish Central Relief Committee, and the Polish National Department.

Bernard Rogalski (born in 1918). Polonia and fraternal activist. A native of Jackson, Michigan and employed as a tool and die designer, Rogalski became active in the Polish Falcons of America in the 1950s. Recognized for his record setting efforts in recruiting new members to the Falcons at the fraternal's 1960 convention, Rogalski was elected for the first time to national office at that conclave. Following terms as a Falcons' vice president, national field manager and national secretary, he was elected PFA President in 1980, succeeding Walter Laska, who had held the post for 28 years.

During Rogalski's eight years as President, the Polish Falcons of America experienced dramatic growth in membership, insurance in force and total assets, making it one of Polonia's great success stories of the decade. In 1986, Rogalski was elected national secretary of the Polish American Congress and was reelected in November 1988. Following his retirement from the Falcons' presidency (he was succeeded by Lawrence Wujcikowski of Buffalo), Rogalski was named President Emeritus of the PFA. Wujcikowski also succeeded him as Secretary of the PAC.

Peter Rostenkowski (1868-1936). Polonia activist and President of the Polish Roman Catholic Union of America. Born in Poland, Rostenkowski settled in Chicago in 1886 and eventually became a widely recognized figure in the city's burgeoning Polish immigrant community.

Active early on in the Polish Roman Catholic Union fraternal, he rose to become its President and later its Treasurer. Rostenkowski also served as Treasurer of the Polish National Council *(Rada Narodowa)* in the First World War years and in that capacity played a major role in its many humanitarian activities on behalf of Polish war victims. He was also involved in the leadership of the Polish Central Relief Committee and the Polish National Department. For his many efforts Rostenkowski was decorated with the Order of *Polonia Restituta* by the Polish government.

Rostenkowski was the founder of a prominent Polish American political family. A son, Joseph, was an influential Chicago Alderman and an activist for Poland in World War II. A grandson, Daniel, has served as a member of the U.S. House of Representatives since 1959 and is presently Chairman of its Ways and Means Committee.

Charles Rozmarek (1897-1973). President of the Polish American Congress and the Polish National Alliance. Born in Wilkes-Barre, Pennsylvania and the son of an immigrant coal miner, Rozmarek earned a law degree from Harvard University and was a practicing attorney in his home town for a number of years before becoming active in the Polish National Alliance. Appointed to the school board of the PNA's college in Cambridge Springs, Pennsylvania Rozmarek was an unsuccessful candidate for the Presidency of the Alliance in 1935, narrowly losing to the incumbent, John Romaszkiewicz.

Elected over Romaszkiewicz in 1939 Rozmarek went on to hold the Alliance's highest office for twenty-eight years, the longest tenure in the history of the largest of Polish fraternals. During his term the PNA membership surpassed 300,000 for the first time and its net worth increased from $30 million to $133 million.

Rozmarek's election coincided with the outbreak of the Second World War and in 1944 he played a critical role in organizing the Polish American Congress to unite Polonia politically behind the postwar restoration of a free and independent Poland. Elected President of the PAC at its founding convention in Buffalo, he continued in this office until 1968.

As PAC head, Rozmarek's achievements were many. From the start he courageously condemned the Great Powers' agreements at Yalta even though his actions brought him into sharp opposition to the enormously popular leadership of President Franklin D. Roosevelt. In the years immediately following the war Rozmarek aggressively championed Poland's cause, most notably at the founding meeting of the United Nations in San Francisco in 1945 and the 1946 Foreign Ministers' conference in Paris. He mobilized public support for special Federal legislation to permit hundreds of thousands of displaced persons to enter the United States and as a result more than 140,000 refugees, ex-soldiers and orphans from Poland were able to come to America outside the existing immigration restrictions.

Rozmarek's complaints made the Katyn massacre a salient issue in the halls of Congress. Partially through his efforts, a select committee of the U.S. House of Representatives was established in 1951 and it found the Soviet Union responsible for the murder of some 15,000 Polish military officers and soldiers in 1940, a conclusion officially acknowledged only in 1989 in Poland and the U.S.S.R.

Throughout his long leadership of the Polish American Congress, Rozmarek remained an eloquent advocate of Poland's right to secure, internationally recognized borders. He was at the same time a bitter critic of Soviet domination over Eastern Europe and a dedicated proponent of the region's "liberation" from Communist rule. Nonetheless he appreciated the meaning of the political changes occurring inside Poland in 1956 with the return of Wladyslaw Gomulka to power and his defeat of the Stalinist faction. Thus he gave strong support to the Eisenhower Administration's decision to provide substantial economic assistance to the reform-minded Gomulka regime, aid which continued into the 1960s.

An aggressive, powerfully built man whose leadership style was both autocratic and charismatic, Rozmarek often found himself in conflict with other Polonia activists. One whom he defeated was Francis X. Swietlik, Censor of the Polish National Alliance and Chairman of the Polish American Council. Ironically it had been Swietlik who had strongly supported his early campaigns for the PNA presidency.

In contrast, Rozmarek was eventually himself beaten by a younger rival, Aloysius Mazewski, who replaced him at the helm of the Alliance in 1967 after twelve years of continued struggle and in 1968 took over the Presidency of the PAC as well. Nonetheless even in defeat Rozmarek left a substantial legacy of commitment to Poland and Polonia and many noteworthy accomplishments.

John Smulski (1867-1928). Polonia leader and civic leader. Born and educated in the German-ruled partition of

Poland, Smulski came to America with his family as a young man. Due partly to his father's success as a publisher in Chicago, Smulski was able to attend Northwestern University where he earned a Law Degree in 1890.

Already a recognized activist in Chicago's growing Polonia by the 1890s, Smulski was elected a Director of the Polish National Alliance in 1893 before turning his attentions to career and civic activity. He eventually was elected Treasurer of the State of Illinois and Controller for the City of Chicago, although his bid to become Mayor of Chicago in 1911 was unsuccessful. In 1906 Smulski organized the Northwestern Trust and Savings Bank of Chicago, popularly known as the "Smulski Bank." The institution became the largest Polish-owned commercial lending operation in America.

In World War I, Smulski worked with Ignacy Paderewski to lead the Polish National Department *(Wydzial Narodowy)* in its lobbying efforts for an independent Polish state. Under the National Department, millions of dollars for Polish relief were raised in Polonia and an army of more than twenty thousand men was dispatched from the United States to fight on the Allied side in France and later for Poland as well. For his enormous contributions to Polish independence and the Allied cause Smulski was honored on many occasions.

Teofil Starzynski (1979-1952). Long-time leader of the Polish Falcons movement in America and Polonia activist. Born near Gniezno in the Prussian zone of partitioned Poland, Starzynski's father worked as a manager of an estate owned by a patriotic Polish family. There he was educated with the children of the landowner and filled with a love of learning and feeling for Poland's independence aspirations.

In 1887, Starzynski's widowed mother and her children came to America and settled in Pittsburgh. Starzynski eventually completed his studies in Pharmacy and later entered medical studies at the University of Pittsburgh, where he earned his M.D. in 1904.

Already active by then for some time in the Polish Falcons Alliance, itself established in 1894, Starzynski became a widely respected regional leader in the organization and a supporter of its "Free Falcons" faction, which seceded from the national movement in 1909. At the Falcons' reunification convention in December 1912, he was elected President and the headquarters of the Alliance transferred from Chicago to Pittsburgh. Starzynski would remain President of the Falcons from then until his death in 1952, except for the years between 1918 and 1924. Then he resigned to volunteer for the Polish Army in America which fought in France and later in Poland following the First World War.

Starzynski played a significant role in Polonia's efforts to assist Poland on all fronts during the war. His greatest contribution was in helping organize the Polish American army to fight for Poland's independence, an historic dream of the Falcons movement from its inception.

Appointed a member of the three-man Polish Military Commission to establish this force following the United States' entry into the war in April 1917, Starzynski worked hard to put into the field an army of more than 20,000 men. In 1919 Starzynski went to Poland as a Major in the Army and was later decorated for his many services to the Allied war effort by the Governments of France and Poland. Upon his return to the United States in 1920 Starzynski was active in organizing the Polish Army Veterans Association, of which he was later President.

Reelected President of the Polish Falcons in 1924, Starzynski was responsible for maintaining the Alliance's commitment to its historic principles of pride in the Polish heritage and work to develop its physical fitness and sports program. Under his leadership, the Polish Falcons established a fraternal insurance program by 1928.

Active in the Polish National Department *(Wydzial Narodowy)* in the First World War era, Starzynski was a leader in the World War II organizations of Polonia, both the *Rada Polonii* charitable federation and the Polish American Congress. His successor, Walter Laska, continued Starzynski's policies during his 28 year long presidency, thus insuring that the memory of Starzynski's work would be preserved within the membership of the Polish Falcons of America.

Zygmunt Stefanowicz (1886-1978). Editor and Polonia activist. Born in Lida, Poland he came to America as a teenager.

His education included studies in Wilno and at Valparaiso University in Indiana.

Finding work as a journalist Stefanowicz was employed as an associate editor and editor in a number of Polish Catholic newspapers, becoming editor-in-chief of the *Dziennik Zjedno-czenia,* the daily newspaper of the Chicago-based Polish Roman Catholic Union of America fraternal, in 1938. At the same time he also held the same responsibilities with the PRCUA's fraternal publication, *Narod Polski* (the Polish Nation). Stefanowicz remained in charge of *Narod Polski* practically through the remainder of his life.

Active in patriotic Polonia affairs from the time of World War I onward, Stefanowicz was involved in the *Wydzial Narodowy,* the Polish Welfare Council in America *(PROSA),* and the Polish American Council *(Rada Polonii).* In 1944 he was a founder of the Polish American Congress. For many years he was the national secretary of the PAC and also worked as the national secretary of the Polish Museum of America. He passed away in Poland, where he retired to spend his last years.

Together with such activists as Stefan Barszczewski, Stanislas Osada, Karol Piatkiewicz, and Arthur Waldo, Stefanowicz was one of the leading publicists in Polonia of the era between the First World War and the 1960s.

Francis X. Swietlik (1890-1983). Polonia leader and Censor of the Polish National Alliance. Born in Milwaukee of Polish immigrants, Swietlik earned his Law degree from Marquette University in 1914 and shortly afterward became involved in Polonia affairs. During World War I he was delegated by the Polish National Alliance to travel to Canada in order to evaluate the conditions of Polish refugees there; later on he served in the American armed forces in Europe where he rose to the rank of captain. Following the war he practiced law until 1934 when he was appointed Dean of Marquette University's Law School. He held this position until 1952 when he was appointed to a judgeship in the Circuit Court of Milwaukee County. He was elected to this post, retiring due to age requirements in 1959. He remained active in his profession and in local and state civic affairs into the mid 1970s.

In the 1920s Swietlik became a recognized leader in the Polish National Alliance, which was then split ideologically into two powerful factions. Elected to the high office of Censor of the PNA in 1931, a post he would hold until 1947, his victory signalled the gradual end of internal conflict within the Alliance; during his years as Censor Swietlik also worked to insure that the assets of the Alliance would be more soundly invested, a major achievement during the Great Depression of the 1930s.

In 1936 Swietlik took the lead in organizing a new all-Polonia federation to work for the betterment of needy Poles in America and the homeland. This organization, the Polish American Council *(Rada Polonii Amerykanskiej, RPA)*, made its greatest contribution to Poland's people in World War II and the years immediately afterward; in this period it provided more than $20 million in assistance to Polish war victims around the world. For his many efforts on Poland's behalf, Swietlik became a target of particular Nazi hatred during the war.

Already in 1945 Swietlik visited the refugee camps in Europe to determine how the *Rada Polonii* might assist them; soon afterward the *RPA* was also established inside Poland where it cooperated with Catholic Church authorities to provide food, clothing and medical goods to those in need in the devastated country. For these efforts he was knighted into the Order of Saint Gregory.

Swietlik had strongly backed the successful candidacy of Charles Rozmarek for the Presidency of the Polish National Alliance in 1939. However, by 1945 relations between the two men had cooled. In 1947 Swietlik decided to retire from the PNA leadership, leaving the field to Rozmarek, by then President of both the PNA and the Polish American Congress political action federation. He nonetheless continued to devote his energy to the *RPA,* which remained an active charitable society into the late 1960s.

Aside from his many services to Polonia as a leader in ethnic organizational life, Swietlik also made a notable intellectual contribution to the community. This was in 1934 when he headed the Polish American delegation to the meeting, in Warsaw, of the World Union of Poles from Abroad. There he declared American Polonia's "independence" from Poland, emphasizing that the ethnic community should no longer be thought of as a Polish "colony" but rather as an integral part of American society, with its primary loyalties to the United States. At the same time Swietlik underscored the value of maintaining knowledge of, and pride in, the Polish heritage in America and his later efforts as head of the *RPA* amply demonstrated the depth of his commitment to the ancestral homeland.

Edward J. Tomasik (Born in 1921).Polonia and Polish American Congress Activist. A native of Chicago and an optometrist by profession, Tomasik became involved in the PAC in the mid 1960s following his development of what he called the "Wisconsin Plan," an effort to organize and mobilize Polish Americans around the country to communicate actively with their elected representatives in Washington, D.C. on matters pertaining to Poland and Polonia. Rebuffed in his efforts by President Rozmarek, Tomasik backed Aloysius Mazewski for the leadership of the Congress in the expectation that he would be responsive to his ideas. From 1976 to 1982 Tomasik served as a national Vice President of the PAC and was also President of its Wisconsin Division for one term. Among his other activities he chaired the committee which organized commemorative observances and cultural programs throughout Wisconsin in 1973 in honor of the 500th anniversary of the birth of the astronomer Nicolaus Copernicus (Mikolaj Kopernik).

An advocate of activating Polish Americans toward greater organized efforts to promote their ethnic concerns to their elected leaders, Tomasik remained an important voice of the "loyal opposition" for more than twenty years, not so much over the policies of the Rozmarek and Mazewski regimes but their respective methods of operation.

Stanley Turkiewicz (1898-1983). President of the Polish Roman Catholic Union of America and Polonia leader. Born in Buffalo, New York, Turkiewicz spent most of his career engaged in journalism. He was City Editor of Buffalo's Polish newspaper, *Dziennik dla Wszystkich* (Everybody's Daily) until it closed in 1957. He later was managing editor of Buffalo's weekly *Am-Pol Eagle* during the 1970s. Long active in the PRCUA Turkiewicz served one term as its President from 1958 to 1962. Earlier, he had worked extensively on behalf of the

Rada Polonii Amerykanskiej and in the years immediately after World War II had been responsible, with his wife, for aiding hundreds of displaced Poles in their resettlement in America. Turkiewicz also served as Treasurer of the Polish American Congress during his term as PRCUA President.

Turkiewicz and his wife spent three years in Warsaw between 1962 and 1965 directing the *RPA*'s relief work in Poland and thus helping to insure that food and medicines collected in Polonia were properly distributed. A civic activist in Buffalo, Turkiewicz served on the city's Public Library Board of Trustees and was an amateur actor.

Max Wegrzynek (1892-1944). Newspaper publisher and an organizer of Polonia political efforts in World War II for Poland. Born in Poland, Wegrzynek came to America in 1914 and graduated from the City College of New York in 1917. From 1922 he was the publisher of New York's Polish language daily, *Nowy Swiat* (the Polish Morning World) and between 1928 and 1938 he also published an Hungarian language daily in the city, *Amerikai Magyar Nepszava*.

With the outbreak of World War II Wegrzynek became a Director of the Polish American Council and in 1942 he, along with Frank Januszewski of Detroit, helped organize the National Committee of Americans of Polish Descent, *KNAPP,* its aim to defend occupied Poland's national interests in this country. Working with Wegrzynek, who was elected *KNAPP*'s first President, were Joseph Kania, past President of the Polish Roman Catholic Union fraternal, Walter Cytacki, a former leader of the Polish National Alliance from Detroit, New Yorkers Ignacy Nurkiewicz and Ignacy Morawski, Alex Hinkelman of Chicago, and several recent emigres from Poland including Ignacy Matuszewski and Waclaw Jedrzejewicz.

Led by Wegrzynek, *KNAPP* forthrightly argued Poland's position to the public in the face of withering left wing and communist criticisms branding his group "fascist" and anti-American. Though already seriously ill in May 1944 and unable to attend the founding of the Polish American Congress, he was elected one of its national vice presidents. Wegrzynek's death on November 8, 1944 deprived Polonia of a fiery activist. Like Januszewski, who succeeded him as President of *KNAPP,* he was a militant nationalist and an uncompromising Pilsudski loyalist. Honored twice by the Polish government for his services, Wegrzynek also served as a vice president of the New York-based Kosciuszko Foundation.

Helen Wojcik. Vice President of the Polish American Congress, President of the Polish Women's Alliance and Polonia Activist. Born in Chicago, Wojcik was already involved in the Polish Women's Alliance as a child; her mother, Veronica Siwek, was a Director of the PWA for 28 years. In 1971, Wojcik was elected Vice President of the Polish Women's Alliance and after sixteen years in that office succeeded Helen Zielinski to the fraternal's Presidency in 1987. In 1988 she also succeeded Zielinski as a Vice President of the Polish American Congress and in that capacity chaired its committee to raise funds for the Ellis Island Museum project in New York. By early 1990, the Committee far exceeded its aim of gathering $250,000 from the Polish American community in support of the Museum; indeed more than $560,000 was raised.

Throughout her life, Helen Wojcik has been involved deeply in the affairs of her neighborhood community as well as Polonia. Active in local school matters while her four children were being educated, she and her husband also owned their own business, a food store, and later she was employed by the International Telephone and Telegraph Corporation during its work on several U.S. sponsored missile projects.

A staunch supporter of Polish Women's Alliance involvement in all facets of Polonia work for Poland, Helen Wojcik carried on in the tradition established by her predecessors, including Mrs. Zielinski, who guided the PWA between 1971 and 1987. Zielinski's many services to Poland and Polonia included her successful leadership efforts to preserve the American Shrine to the Blessed Virgin of Czestochowa in Doylestown, Pennsylvania during its time of financial distress in the 1970s, and her chairmanship of the national Polonia campaigns to restore the Statue of Liberty in the mid 1980s and to fund the construction of the Polish pilgrims' hostel in Rome which honors Pope John Paul II.

Honorata Wolowska (1875-1967). President of the Polish Women's Alliance and World War II era Polonia leader. Born in Torun, Poland, Wolowska came to the United States in 1890, first settling in Chicago and then in 1896 in Pennsylvania. Trained as a teacher and as a social worker, she served as a teacher in night school classes for coal miners for many years. Wolowska was initially active in the Polish Falcons Alliance movement and worked hard to win equal membership rights for women in that youth-oriented patriotic organization. Joining the Polish Women's Alliance in 1900, she was the leader of its Western Pennsylvania district for many years.

A visitor to Poland in 1910 at the time of the five-hundredth anniversary commemoration of the victory over the Teutonic Knights at Grunwald, Wolowska was active on all fronts in mobilizing Polonia on Poland's behalf during World War I, as a recruiter for the Polish American army established in 1917, as a leader in fund raising activities for Polish relief and in helping to organize the Polish Grey Samaritans nursing corps which travelled to Poland following the war to work with the poor and orphaned victims of the conflict. For her many services to Poland, Wolowska was awarded the "Cross of Warriors" *(Krzyz walecznych)* from Marshal Pilsudski. Elected President of the Polish Women's Alliance to succeed Emilia Napieralska in 1935, Wolowska served twelve momentous years in that office, years which coincided with the Second World War. Already active in the Polish American Council before the outbreak of the conflict, Wolowska was also elected a Vice President of the Polish American Congress at its founding convention in 1944 and served with great distinction in both Polonia federations. As PWA President, Wolowska issued a dramatic appeal in 1939 to "all women and mothers of the world" and to the press of the United States, Britain and France to bring an immediate end to the brutal devastation of the Polish nation by the Nazis. Under her leadership, the Women's Alliance organized drives to "Save the Infants" and to provide "Shoes for Polish Children." A PWA fund to raise $100,000 for the benefit of Polish children wherever they lived was also established, this in honor of General Sikorski's wife following her husband's tragic death in a 1943 airplane accident at Gibraltar.

Wolowska also worked to win PWA support of the American war effort, especially in the purchase of U.S. War Bonds, both by individual members and by the Alliance itself. From the proceeds of these purchases, the U.S. government procured two B-15 bombers which carried the name of the Polish Women's Alliance.

Following her retirement in 1947, Wolowska remained an active leader in both the Polish American Council and the Polish American Congress and travelled to Poland to review conditions there to better determine how Polonia could continue to be of help. She was also named an Honorary President of the Polish Women's Alliance and continued to support its work in her later years.

Casimir Zychlinski (1859-1927). President of the Polish Falcons Alliance and the Polish National Alliance and World War I era Polonia leader. Born and educated in Poland, Zychlinski came to America in 1876 where he settled initially in New York. Already a member of the Polish National Alliance in 1881, he moved to Chicago in 1883 where he became an active figure in the life of the Polish immigrant community centered on the city's near South Side. In 1888, he became active in the newly created Polish Falcons society in Chicago, an organization committed to promoting physical fitness among the young people in the community's rapidly growing Polonia while at the same time maintaining patriotic feeling for Poland's heritage among the immigrants.

In 1894, Zychlinski was elected President of the newly formed Alliance of Polish Falcons by delegates from four Chicago societies, or "nests." This federation eventually grew into a movement embracing some 25,000 members at the outbreak of the First World War; by then the Falcons Alliance had come to embrace the idea of organizing an army to help liberate Poland in addition to maintaining its traditional physical fitness and education activities. Zychlinski, who remained President of the Falcons for six years before resigning to take on new work responsibilities outside of Chicago, nevertheless was always a supporter of the movement and its programs, holding office for some years, for example, as the President of District Two of the Falcons Alliance.

Continuing his long time involvement in the Polish National Alliance, Zychlinski was a close friend and associate of Marian Steczynski, President of the Alliance from 1903 to 1912. Together with Steczynski, he travelled to Poland in 1910 to participate in the five hundredth anniversary commemoration of the Victory at Grunwald over the Teutonic Knights, a major event within Poland and throughout Polonia which deepened patriotic feeling and support for national independence.

In 1912 Steczynski resigned as President of the Alliance to take over the responsibilities of organizing the newly purchased Alliance school in Cambridge Springs, Pennsylvania. Soon afterwards, Zychlinski was elected to succeed him as head of the PNA and went on to continue in this office until 1927, when he passed away on the eve of the Alliance's twenty-fifth national convention.

Zychlinski's leadership of the Polish National Alliance coincided with the onset of the First World War and the restoration of an independent Polish state in 1918. Throughout the war years, Zychlinski personally played a major leadership role in every Polonia effort on Poland's behalf, serving in the Polish National Defense Committee *(KON)* from 1912 to 1914, in the Polish Central Relief Committee, the Polish National Department and in the Polish Military Commission. As the head of the PNA, Zychlinski also saw to it that the Alliance continued to play a major role in the efforts on Poland's behalf, not only through its involvement in fund raising work but also through propagandizing the Polish independence cause in its newspapers.

After the war, the PNA participated actively in the meetings of the Congress of the Polish emigration under the sponsorship of the Polish National Department. Following the demise of the National Department in 1925, Zychlinski was a moving force behind the creation of the Polish Welfare Association in America, which among its various aims, sought to maintain productive relationships with the independent Polish state.

During Zychlinski's fifteen year presidency of the Alliance, his organization grew from 90,000 to 250,000 members. For his many services to Poland's independence, Zychlinski was honored by the Polish government in special ceremonies in 1921 presided over by Ignacy Paderewski.

Footnotes

FOOTNOTES to the Introduction

1. Several comprehensive histories of the Polish American experience can be noted here. These include Andrzej Brozek, *Polish Americans 1854-1939* (Warsaw: Interpress Publishers, 1985); Helena Z. Lopata, *Polish Americans: Status Competition in an Ethnic Community* (Englewood Cliffs, New Jersey: Prentice-Hall, 1976); and W.S. Kuniczak, *My Name is Million: An Illustrated History of the Polish Americans* (New York: MacMillan, 1978). Other useful works are those of Eugene Kleban and Thaddeus Gromada, editors, "The Polish Americans," a special issue of the *Polish Review,* 23, number 3 (1976); John Bukowczyk, *And My Children Did Not Know Me: A History of the Polish Americans* (Bloomington, Indiana: Indiana University Press, 1987); and Joseph Wytrwal, *America's Polish Heritage* (Detroit, Endurance Press, 1961).

2. For accounts of Polish American efforts for Poland in World War I, one might cite a number of articles appearing in *Polish American Studies,* the journal of the Polish American Historical Association. Of special interest is its Autumn 1981 issue, volume 38, number 2, in which articles appear by M.B. Biskupski, Louis Zake and Joseph Hapak. A valuable collection of research in the Polish language is the volume edited by H. Florkowska-Francic, M. Francic and H. Kubiak, *Polonia wobec niepodleglosci Polski w czasie I wojny swiatowej* (American Polonia and Poland's independence in the First World War. Wroclaw:Ossolineum Press, 1979).

Two excellent works on Polonia's role in Polish affairs in the World War II era are the following studies by Richard Lukas: *The Strange Allies: The United States and Poland, 1941-1945* (Knoxville, Tennessee: University of Tennessee Press, 1978) and *Bitter Legacy: Polish-American Relations in the Wake of World War II* (Lexington, Kentucky: University of Kentucky Press, 1982).

A broad overview of the history of U.S.-Polish relations which includes information on the Polish American contribution is by Piotr Wandycz, *The United States and Poland* (Cambridge, Massachusetts: Harvard University Press, 1980).

3. Of all those who left Poland before World War I, approximately 2.6 million or 70 percent of the total came to the United States. About 500,000 others went to Western Europe (mainly Germany), while 300,000 wound up in Russia. Still another 200,000 travelled to Canada or Latin America. Aleksander Gieysztor, *et. al., A History of Poland* (Warsaw: Polish Scientific Publishers, 1968), pp. 585-586. See also Stefan Kieniewicz, *The Emancipation of the Polish Peasantry* (Chicago: University of Chicago Press, 1969).

4. According to Brozek, pp. 39-42, the number of Polish Americans is estimated as follows: 30,000 (1860), 50,000 (1870), 500,000 (1880), 1,000,000 (1890), 2,000,000 (1900), 3,000,000 (1910).

5. Donald E. Pienkos, *PNA: A Centennial History of the Polish National Alliance of the United States of North America* (New York: Columbia University Press, 1984), pp. 35-66.

6. Frank Renkiewicz, "An Economy of Self-Help: Fraternal Capitalism and the Evolution of Polish America," in Charles Ward, Philip Shashko and Donald Pienkos, editors, *Studies in Ethnicity: The East European Experience in America* (Boulder, Colorado: East European Monographs, 1980), pp. 71-92.

7. Donald E. Pienkos, *One Hundred Years Young: A History of the Polish Falcons of America, 1887-1987* (Boulder, Colorado: East European Monographs, 1987), pp. 91-112.

8. In its decennial enumerations of the American population over the years the U.S. Bureau of the Census has compiled a substantial amount of data on inhabitants who were themselves born in another country (the "foreign born") and those individuals having at least one parent who was born abroad ("foreign stock"). Occasionally, the Bureau has also looked at

foreign nationality in terms of the extent of foreign language competence in the population. These efforts, however, have been criticized since the 1960s as leading to a substantial undercount of the "ethnic population" since they excluded from consideration those persons who were more distantly removed from the immigration experience but who continued to identify in some fashion with their heritage.In 1980 the Census Bureau responded to this complaint by performing a survey of the ethnic nationality identification of approximately one-sixth of the American population. Out of that study, the Bureau estimated the total number of Polish Americans to be 8,228,037, with 3,805,740 identifying themselves to be fully Polish in ancestry and another 4,442,297 stating that they were partly Polish in origin.

According to the 1980 Census, the size of the Polish American population was indeed shown to be larger than had been previously indicated. But the survey also had its limitations. One involved the Bureau's decision to no longer ask respondents about their foreign-born or foreign-stock status, an action which made it next to impossible to determine the effects of time upon ethnic identification. And, since only a portion of the entire population was surveyed, the Bureau's findings were faulted for continuing to undercount the actual number of ethnic Americans.

Still, the 1980 enumeration showed Polish Americans to be by far the largest ethnic population having East European origins, far surpassing Czechs and Czechoslovaks (who came in second with a total of 1,892,456 identifiers in all), Hungarians (1,776,902), Slovaks (776,806), Lithuanians (742,776), and Ukrainians (730,056), the next five largest "groups." Of all groups identified in the Census survey, Polish Americans ranked among the largest after Americans with origins in Great Britain, Ireland, Germany, Italy and the Hispanic countries. For an encyclopedic review of the 1980 census, see James Paul Allen and Eugene J. Turner, *We the People: An Atlas of American Ethnic Diversity* (New York: MacMillan, 1988).

Given the Polish Americans' natural rate of increase since 1980, the possibility of undercounting, and the subsequent entry of at least two hundred thousand Poles into the country during the past decade, one might estimate that the total number of Polish Americans in 1990 was around 12 million, or nearly 5 percent of the entire population.

9. Waclaw Soroka, *Polish Immigration in the United States* (Stevens Point, Wisconsin: University of Wisconsin--Stevens Point, 1976), pp. 151ff; Wandycz, pp. 182ff; Lukas, *Bitter Legacy;* Pienkos,*PNA,* chapters 4, 6, 12; Tyler Marshall, "Powerful Political Force,"*Los Angeles Times,* reprinted in the *Polish American Journal* (Buffalo), 74, number 3 (March 1985), pp. 1-2.

On Polonia investment activities in Poland after the First World War see Adam Walaszek, *Reemigracja ze Stanow Zjednoczonych do Polski po I wojny swiatowej, 1919-1924* (Reemigration from the United States to Poland after World War I, 1919-1924. Warsaw: Panstwowe Wydawnictwo naukowe, 1983).

10. Gieysztor, pp. 584-586; Adam Zamoyski, *The Polish Way: A Thousand Year History of the Poles and Their Culture* (London: John Murray Publishers, Ltd., 1987), pp. 304, 306.

11. Norman Davies, *Heart of Europe: A Short History of Poland* (Oxford, United Kingdom: Oxford University Press, 1986), pp. 258-259.

12. Wandycz; and Dziewanowski, *Poland in the Twentieth Century* (Cambridge, Massachusetts: Harvard University Press, 1977), pp. 141, 223-225 and *passim.*

13. Benjamin Murdzek, *Emigration in Polish Social and Political Thought, 1870-1914* (Boulder, Colorado: East European Monographs, 1977). Gloomy assessments of the emigrants' fate typified the writings of Henryk Sienkiewicz, the celebrated novelist and later Nobel Laureate. Sienkiewicz visited the United States as a young man and wrote occasionally on the subject.

Another example is from the writings of the influential interwar sociologist, Ludwik Krzywicki. The following passage is from his introduction to his massive study of the life experiences of the Polish peasants, which appeared in 1935:

In the majority of cases, the emigrants...returned home with some savings. Unfortunately, this money was often wasted... These emigrants' memories are filled with the bitterness of their misfortune.

After their return...they took up farming once again...but what was good in America brought other results in Poland.

"American" initiative and methods did not work well on the tiny Polish plot. After exhausting their savings, the plots of the "Americans"...very frequently declined to a greater degree than their neighbors' and with this decline came an erosion of the emigrants' moral influence as well.

Ludwik Krzywicki, *Pamietniki chlopow* (Peasants' Memories. Warsaw: Instytut gospodarstwa spolecznego, 1935), volume I, p. xxxix.

14. The failure to refer to Polonia's role in Polish affairs continues, what is more, to this time. Thus, in his otherwise excellent study of the Solidarity movement, Timothy Garton Ash makes no mention of the emigration's efforts on behalf of Solidarity. Timothy Garton Ash, *The Polish Revolution: Solidarity* (New York: Random House, 1983).

In a different vein one can cite James Michener's panoramic novel, *Poland* (New York: Random House, 1985) wherein the author missed the opportunity to weave the emigrants' experiences into his otherwise epic story. Similarly, the nine-hour long television documentary series, *The Struggles for Poland*, shown in the United States on the Public Broadcasting System in 1988, ignored the emigration in spite of its relevance to the homeland throughout the twentieth century.

15. Mark Kulikowski, "A Bibliography on Polish Americans, 1975-1980," *Polish American Studies*, 39, number 2 (Autumn, 1982), 24-85; and Kulikowski, "A Bibliography on Polish Americans, 1980-1985," *Polish American Studies*, 43, number 2 (Autumn, 1986), 40-110.

16. The literature on the "new ethnicity" dates back to the work of Nathan Glazer and Daniel P. Moynihan, *Beyond the Melting Pot: The Negroes, Puerto Ricans, Jews, Italians and Irish of New York City* (Cambridge, Massachusetts: M.I.T. Press, 1963); and Milton M. Gordon, *Assimilation in American Life* (New York: Oxford University Press, 1964). Andrew Greeley and Michael Novak have also written extensively on the subject.

17. See in particular the works cited earlier by Lopata, Gromada and Kleban; and articles appearing in *Polish American Studies* and the journal, *Ethnicity.*

18. Note, for example, Stanislaus Blejwas, "Old and New Polonias: Tensions within an Ethnic Community," *Polish American Studies,* 38, number 2 (Autumn, 1981), 55-83; and Thaddeus Radzilowski, "The Second Generation: The Unknown Polonia," *Polish American Studies,* 43, number 1 (Spring, 1986), 5-12.

For an interesting recent analysis of white ethnic advancement in the U.S. see Harriet O. Duleep, *et al., The Economic Status of Americans of Southern and Eastern European Ancestry* (Washington, D.C.: U.S. Commission on Civil Rights, Publication 89, 1986).

19. Most of the information in this table is from Helena Z. Lopata, "Polish Immigration to the United States: Problems of Estimation and Parameters," *Polish Review,* 21, number 4 (1976), 85-107.

FOOTNOTES to Chapter I

1. Pulaski (1747-1779), a wealthy landowner in Southeastern Poland, took part in the unsuccessful Confederation of Bar rebellion between 1768 and 1772 to reverse the growing Russian imperial domination of his country. The rebellion's defeat led to the first partition of the Polish-Lithuanian Commonwealth in 1772 and Pulaski's escape into foreign exile. In the American colonies in 1777, Pulaski participated in a number of campaigns against the British, rose to the rank of Brigadier General and organized the first cavalry regiments in the revolutionary army. He lost his life at the battle of Savannah on October 11, 1779. Pulaski was recognized throughout the colonies for his services to the independence cause and the Continental Congress approved a resolution soon after his death to fund a monument in his honor.

Kosciuszko (1746-1817) had arrived in America in 1776 to offer his services to the independence cause. Trained in engineering, he played an important role in organizing the fortifications in a number of battles, most notably the great victory at Saratoga in 1777. Kosciuszko also oversaw the defense of New York on the Hudson River at West Point, later the site of the United States Military Academy. Following America's independence he returned to Poland to lead the unsuccessful national uprising of 1794 to preserve the homeland's independence.

Both Pulaski and Kosciuszko were highly respected patriots to Americans grateful for their contributions to the independence cause, and in time their names were memorialized in towns, counties, and school buildings across the land. For later waves of Polish immigrants entering the United States in the nineteenth and twentieth centuries, the respect showed to Pulaski and Kosciuszko was a great source of national pride and was frequently recognized as symbolic of a shared American and Polish commitment to freedom, something enjoyed in the new homeland and desired for the "old country." Beginning in the first years of the twentieth century, organized Polish American efforts to erect statues in their memory led to a number of monuments to the heroes in cities with large Polish populations throughout the country. The old Congressional promise to fund a Pulaski monument in the nation's capital was recalled and in 1910 memorials to both Pulaski and to Kosciuszko (the latter paid for by the Polish National Alliance) were dedicated by the President of the United States in Washington, D.C. before a large gathering which included representatives from partitioned Poland. In 1913, a Kosciuszko monument was also erected at West Point by the Polish American community and in 1929 a Pulaski monument built in the 1850s was rededicated in Savannah, Georgia on the 150th anniversary of the General's death. For some excellent background on the lives of the heroes of two lands, see M. K. Dziewanowski, "Tadeusz Kosciuszko, Kazimierz Pulaski and the American War of Independence: A Study in National Symbolism and Mythology," in Jaroslaw Pelenski, editor, *The American and European Revolutions, 1776-1848* (Ames, Iowa: University of Iowa Press, 1980), pp. 125-148; and Angela T. Pienkos, "A Bicentennial Look at Casimir Pulaski: Polish, American and Ethnic Folk Hero," *Polish American Studies*, 33, number 1 (Spring, 1976), 5-17.

For the interesting story behind the creation and dedication of the heroes' monuments in 1910, see Romuald Piatkowski, *Pamietnik wzniesienia i odsloniecia pomnikow Tadeusza Kosciuszki i Kazimierza Pulaskiego tudziez polaczonego z ta uroczystoscia pierwszego kongresu narodowego polskiego w Washingtonie, D.C.* (The memorial commemorating the unveiling of the Kosciuszko and Pulaski monuments along with the celebration of the first Polish national congress in Washington, D.C. Chicago: Alliance Printers and Publishers, 1911).

2. The pre-history of the Poles in America in fact goes back even further with its origins dating to the arrival of an undetermined number of "Polanders" or "Polonians" aboard the ship "Margaret and Mary" to the Jamestown colony in Virginia on October 1, 1608. This was less than a year after the founding of the very first permanent settlement established in the new world under English auspices. In 1619, the Poles and the Hollanders in the colony protested the local government's decision to deny them the right to take part in the political affairs of the Jamestown settlement, this despite their contributions to its development. Their "strike" was successful and the decision was rescinded, an early victory for civil rights in America. (Other

early names in the era before large scale Polish immigration to America were such seventeenth century figures as Daniel Litscho, a leader in Dutch-ruled New Amsterdam, later New York; Alexander Curtius, that colony's first school teacher; and Albert Zaborowski, commonly called Zabriskie, a prominent member of the New Jersey colony. In the eighteenth century, Anthony Sadowski became a well-known pioneer of the wilderness and a compatriot of Daniel Boone; the city of Sandusky, Ohio may have been named for him.)

The Polonia historian of the earliest Polish migrations to America, Mieczyslaw Haiman (1885-1949) estimated that approximately five hundred people were living in the United States between 1790 and 1812, meaning that individuals like Kosciuszko and Pulaski were hardly the only Poles in America during this earliest period of American independence. For more information on this subject see Haiman, *Polish Past in America, 1608-1865* (Chicago: Polish Museum of America, second edition, 1974), translated by J. P. Wachowski.

For two useful overviews of the early emigrations from Poland see Brozek, *Polish Americans,* Chapter I; and Wandycz, *The United States and Poland,* pp. 32-84. A recent, if propagandistic, summary of the Jamestown experience is by Joseph Wiewiora, editor, *Jamestown Pioneers From Poland* (Chicago: Polish American Congress Charitable Foundation, 1976, second revised edition).

3. Joseph Wieczerzak, "Pre- and Proto-Ethnics: Poles in the United States before the Immigration 'After Bread,'" *Polish Review,* 21, number 3 (Fall, 1976), 12.

4. Excellent accounts are those by Jerzy J. Lerski, *A Polish Chapter In Jacksonian America: The United States and the Polish Exiles of 1831* (Madison: University of Wisconsin Press, 1958); Wierczerzak, "Pre- and Proto-Ethnics," 7-38; and Maria J.E. Copson-Niecko, "The Poles in America from the 1830s to 1870s: Some Reflections on the Possibilities of Research," in Frank Mocha, ed., *Poles in America: Bicentennial Essays* (Stevens Point, Wisconsin: Worzalla Publishers, 1978), pp. 45-302. Of interest too is a brief biographical account of the life of Count Vincent Dziewanowski (1804-1883), who settled in Wis-

consin following his arrival in America in 1834. See Mrs. William F. Allen, "A Polish Pioneer's Story," *Wisconsin Magazine of History,* 6 (June, 1923).

5. For the American groups' connections with emigre politics centered in France after 1831, see Gieysztor, pp. 473-480. Kalussowski's biography is in Donald Pienkos, *PNA,* pp. 378-379 and *passim.*

6. Zygmunt Wardzinski, "The Oldest Slavic Magazine in the United States: 'Poland, Historical, Literary, Monumental, Picturesque' and its Article on Copernicus (1842)," *Polish Review,* 19, numbers 3-4 (1974), 83-98.

7. For a full-scale biography of Krzyzanowski (1824-1887) see James S. Pula, *For Liberty and Justice: The Life and Times of Wladimir Krzyzanowski* (Chicago: Polish American Congress Charitable Foundation, 1978). On October 11, 1937 Krzyzanowski's remains were reinterred to Arlington National Cemetery through the efforts of Polish American leaders. President Franklin D. Roosevelt delivered a radio address to the nation that morning in his memory.

8. Wieczerzak, 38-39; Wandycz, pp. 78-88.

9. Waclaw Kruszka, *Historja Polska w Ameryce* (The History of the Poles in America, volume I, second revised edition. Milwaukee: *Kuryer Polski* Publishers, 1937), pp. 346-349. Many of these early settlements, inhabited by only a small number of individuals, disappeared, often without a trace. See also Brozek, pp. 44-45; and Waclaw Soroka, *Polish Immigration to the United States: Authorized Notes from the Lectures of Professor Waclaw W. Soroka* (Stevens Point, Wisconsin: The University of Wisconsin-Stevens Point, 1976), pp. 46-51. For a recent biography of Moczygemba (1824-1891) see T. Lindsay Baker, "The Reverend Leopold Moczygemba, Patriarch of Polonia," *Polish American Studies,* 41, number 1 (Spring, 1984), 66-109.

10. Brozek, p. 45.

11. The phrase "za chlebem" is from Henryk Sienkiewicz (1846-1916), the celebrated novelist and Nobel Laureate. It is the title of a novelette which appears in a collection of stories, *Sielanka: A Forest Picture and Other Stories,* published in 1893 and translated by Jeremiah Curtin. In fact, Sienkiewicz characterized this emigration in largely negative terms and reflected the prevailing view of Polish intellectuals of the time as to the futility of the peasant's search for a better life in America. See also Pienkos, *PNA,* pp. 40-41; Soroka, pp. 27-28, 37ff; Brozek, pp. 18-21; and Kieniewicz, *The Emancipation of the Polish Peasantry,* pp. 190-235.

12. The condition of the peasants by the end of the nineteenth century in terms of land ownership shows dramatically how important emigration was as a factor in both alleviating the numbers of people in the countryside and providing needed sources of money by work abroad for those who remained in the countryside. Yet despite this process, in 1900, in Austrian-ruled Galicia, four-fifths of all peasant farms were less than 10 acres in size; in the German-ruled provinces, 312 thousand of 575 thousand Polish-owned farms were under 3 acres in size in 1907; in Russian-ruled Poland, the number of landless peasant households grew from 226 thousand in 1870 to 849 thousand in 1891. Kieniewicz, *ibid.*

13. A salient point is made by William I. Thomas and Florian Znaniecki in their classic sociological study, *The Polish Peasant in Europe and America,* two volumes (New York: Dover Press, 1958, originally published between 1918-1920). It is their contention that peasants came *en masse* out of ambition to improve their conditions by finding work in America and saving sufficient money to return home to buy farmland for their families. In their view, while opportunities to earn money existed in both Poland and by seasonal migration in Western Europe, these were not sufficiently attractive to satisfy the most ambitious peasants. Not surprisingly, large numbers of the immigrants to the U.S. were young men, many of whom were either landless or nearly so. Thomas and Znaniecki, volume II, pp. 1489-1511. See also Victor Greene, "Pre World War I Polish

Immigration to the United States of America: Motives and Statistics," *Polish Review,* 6, number 3 (Autumn, 1961) 45-68.

14. Brozek, pp. 36-39. Several excellent studies of the size and character of the Polish migrations to America "za chlebem" exist, including Lopata, "Polish Immigration to the United States of America: Problems of Estimation and Parameters," and Greene, "Pre World War I Polish Emigration."

15. Pienkos, *PNA,* p. 332.

16. M. Szawleski, *Wychodztwo Polskie w Stanach Zjednoczonych Ameryki* (The Polish Emigration in the United States of America. Krakow: Ossolineum, 1924), p. 193.

17. Solid scholarly research on the extent of German repression of the Poles under its control has been provided by John Kulczycki, *School Strikes in Prussian Poland, 1901-1907* (Boulder and New York: East European Monographs, 1981).

18. For a recent discussion of this process, see Victor Greene, *For God and Country: The Rise of Polish and Lithuanian Ethnic Consciousness in America* (Madison: State Historical Society of Wisconsin, 1975), pp. 1-13.

19. Quoted in Brozek, p. 47. See also Joseph Wytrwal, *America's Polish Heritage,* pp. 59, 67. The idea of the Polish parish as helping, at least in the beginning, to recreate the traditional community life the peasant immigrants had left behind is brought out in detail in Thomas and Znaniecki, volume II, pp. 1524 ff.

20. In 1908, the Reverend Paul Rhode of Chicago was consecrated an auxiliary bishop in its Roman Catholic archdiocese, his selection the product of a lengthy campaign by Poles in America to gain such recognition. In 1915 he became Bishop of the Diocese of Green Bay, Wisconsin, the first Pole to administer the Church's affairs at that level. See Greene, *For God and Country,* pp. 122-142; and Anthony Kuzniewski, *Faith and Fatherland: The Polish Church War in Wisconsin, 1896-*

1918 (Notre Dame, Indiana: The University of Notre Dame Press, 1980).

21. For a lucid analysis of the subject, see Adam Bromke, *Poland's Politics: Idealism Versus Realism* (Cambridge, Massachusetts: Harvard University Press, 1967).

22. For a discussion of this conflict and its implications, see Greene, *For God and Country,* chapters 4 and 5.

23. The authoritative history of the Polish Roman Catholic Union is that of Mieczyslaw Haiman, *Zjednoczenie Polskie Rzymsko-Katolickie w Ameryce, 1873-1948* (Chicago: PRCUA Publishers, 1948), written for the diamond jubilee of the fraternal. For the founding of the Union, see especially pp. 30-35. Also, Kruszka, *Historja Polska w Ameryce,* second edition, published in 1978 by the Polish Falcons of America, Pittsburgh), pp. 158-171, volume II. Other accounts of the early years of the PRCUA are found in Arthur Waldo, *Sokolstwo Przednia Straz Narodu* (The Falcons Movement, Advance Guard of the Polish Nation. Pittsburgh: Polish Falcons of America, 1953), volume I, pp. 293-299; and Stanislas Osada, *Historia Zwiazku Narodowego Polskiego i rozwoj ruchu narodowego w Ameryce* (The History of the Polish National Alliance and the Development of the Polish National Movement in America, 1905, 1957). For the history of the Polish Seminary of Saints Cyril and Methodious, see Rev. Joseph Swastek, *The Formative Years of the Polish Seminary in the United States* (Orchard Lake Michigan: Center for Polish Studies, 1985, first published 1959), and Frank Renkiewicz, *For God, Country and Polonia: One Hundred Years of the Orchard Lake Schools* (Orchard Lake, Michigan: Center for Polish Studies, 1985). See also Baker, "The Reverend Leopold Moczygemba." Moczygemba presided over the Polish Roman Catholic Union as its president from 1875-1880. One measure of the inactivity of the PRCUA after Gieryk's withdrawal indicates that in 1880, the only groups in the entire organization were the five parish societies belonging to Saint Stanislas Kostka Parish in Chicago (Osada, p. 65). Haiman admits that in 1885, twelve years after its formation, the Union included about 400-500 members. Haiman, *Zjednoczenie,* p. 71.

24. For the origins of the Polish National Alliance see Osada, *Historia ZNP* and Pienkos, *PNA,* pp. 51-56.

25. *Ibid.,* pp. 52-53. For the full text in the Polish language, see Osada, *Historia ZNP,* pp. 97-108. Frank Renkiewicz provides an English translation of salient sections of Giller's essay in his work, *The Poles in America 1608-1972* (Dobbs Ferry, New York, 1972), pp. 64-65.

26. A fifth aim is included in the first official history of the Alliance, by Stefan Barszczewski, and appearing in 1894: "to promote moderation in the consumption of alcohol." Osada's official history published on the occasion of the Alliance's twenty-fifth anniversary in 1905 identifies a different fifth aim: "to provide a fraternal burial insurance program to members," a goal realized in 1886.

27. A good description of the conflict between the two fraternals is provided by Kruszka, volume II, pp. 781-87. A contemporary account is that of Greene, *For God and Country,* pp. 66-99. See also, Pienkos, *PNA,* pp. 70-72.

28. Quoted in Peter Brock, "Polish Nationalism," in Peter Sugar, ed., *Nationalism in Eastern Europe* (Seattle: University of Washington Press, 1969), pp. 347-348. In some respects the party was orthodox in asserting its commitment to the "gradual socialization of the means of production and distribution." Yet the Polish socialists also adopted the *Liga Polska* idea of working for a restored multi-ethnic Polish state that would embrace Lithuania, Byelorussia and the Ukraine, a position hardly in accord with Marxist views on the matter.

29. Witos has received little attention in English language studies of twentieth century Poland, in spite of his significant place in the nation's interwar politics. Andrzej Korbonski in his *Politics of Socialist Agriculture in Poland, 1945-1960* (New York: Columbia University Press, 1965) touches upon him while Olga Narkiewicz presents an uneven account of his career in her *The Green Flag: Polish Populist Politics, 1867-1970* (London: Croom

Helm, 1976). Witos' life is presented in Polish in his own interesting autobiographical and semi-autobiographical accounts, *Moje wspomnienia,* 3 volumes (Paris: Instytut Literacki, 1964-1965) and *Moja tulaczka* (Warsaw: Ludowa spoldzielnia wydawnicza, 1967).

30. Published in *Zgoda,* the organ of the Polish National Alliance, January 23, 1887 and cited by Osada, p. 248.

31. Several of the leading figures in the Alliance were active in directing the *Skarb Narodowy* and thus were involved regularly in meetings with Polish activists in Switzerland. See Brozek, *Polish Americans,* pp. 62-63.

32. Earlier, in 1886, Jerzmanowski, who had made his fortune in the natural gas business, had sought and failed in his attempt to gain high office within the Polish National Alliance, thus making his comments prior to the founding of the Polish League sound like sour grapes. In 1896, Jerzmanowski, disappointed by his failures to lead Polonia, retired permanently to Poland. Upon his death in 1909 he bequeathed much of his estate to the Jagiellonian University in Krakow for the purpose of developing what later became known as the Polish Academy of Sciences. Pienkos, *PNA,* pp. 377-378 and *passim.*

The Catholic camp's effort to create the Polish League was by no means its last attempt to unite Polonia under its banner. Indeed, these continued into the 1930s and one might even count the creation of the Polish American Council (*Rada Polonii Amerykanskiej*) as perhaps its greatest accomplishment. For more information on these efforts see Haiman, *Zjednoczenie,* and Brozek, *Polish Americans.*

33. For a recent overview of the history of the Falcons organization, which continues to this day as a fraternal benefit society providing physical education and sports activities for its members, see Donald E. Pienkos, *One Hundred Years Young: A History Of The Polish Falcons Of America, 1887-1987* (New York and Boulder, Colorado: East European Monographs, 1987).

34. The history of the Polish Women's Alliance has been written in the Polish language in chronological fashion by two authors. Jadwiga Karlowiczowa's work (published in 1938) covered the years through the 1930s and Maria Lorys brought the story up to 1959 in a second volume that appeared in 1980. Both works are entitled *Historia Zwiazku Polek w Ameryce* and have appeared under the PWA's auspices.

FOOTNOTES to Chapter II

1. Kulczycki, *School Strikes in Prussian Poland, 1901-1907.* See also Kieniewicz, *The Emancipation of the Polish Peasantry,* pp. 190-202, for a summary of German agriculture policy.

2. Ivo Pogonowski, *Poland, A Historical Atlas* (New York: Hippocrene Books, 1987), pp. 170-171. See also Waclaw Jedrzejewicz, *Pilsudski: A Life For Poland* (New York: Hippocrene Books, 1990), for additional discussion about events after 1904, pp. 34-40.

3. Brozek, *Polish Americans,* p. 133.

4. The significance of symbols in the history of Poland's relations with its neighbors is something deserving mention here. In 1914, the first great battle between Germany and Russia in World War I took place in the general vicinity of Grunwald, called Tannenberg by the Germans. There, they decisively crushed the Russian forces and then announced that the historic defeat of the Teutonic Knights at the hands of the Slavs five centuries earlier had at last been avenged. The Jagiello monument, paid for by the pianist-patriot Ignacy Paderewski, was demolished on Hitler's orders at the beginning of World War II. It was restored in the 1970s.

5. For a discussion of the ideological basis for the merger concept in Polonia see Waldo, *Sokolstwo,* volume III, pp. 1-34.

6. Pienkos, *One Hundred Years Young,* pp. 51-73, 227. In 1905 there were approximately 70 local Falcons' groups, or "nests," in existence; at the time of the merger of the movement seven years later no fewer than 352 such groups were active.

7. For the story of the monument projects and the Polish National Congress of 1910, see Pienkos, *PNA,* pp. 88-91, 398; and Piatkowski, *Pamietnik.*

8. The statement produced some disagreement because a minority of the delegates (including several of those from Poland who were planning to return home after the Congress) believed it was inflammatory and undiplomatic.

9. A brief biography of Kulakowski (1862-1924) can be found in Francis Bolek, editor, *Who's Who in Polish America* (New York: Harbinger House, 1943), third edition, p. 247. Similar biographies of Debski and Siemiradzki (1850-1939) are in Bolek, pp. 93, 407 and in Pienkos, *PNA*. Debski's career is also summarized in this work's biographical section.

10. Making the trip to Poland on the Alliance's behalf were Anthony Karabasz, the Censor, or chief judicial officer of the fraternal, and Vice Censor Adolf Rakoczy. For details on their mission, see A. Garlicki, "Misja A. Karabasza i A. Rakoczego" (Karabasz and Rakoczy's Mission), *Przeglad Historyczny*, 10, number 2 (1961), 232-246. For the story of Falcons President Starzynski's stay in Poland, see Pienkos, *One Hundred Years Young*, pp. 81-82.

11. For background on *KON* and its activities during the war see several useful articles in H. Florkowska-Francic, M. Francic and H. Kubiak, eds., *Polonia wobec niepodleglosci Polski w czasie I Wojny Swiatowej* (Polonia and Polish Independence in the Time of the First World War. Wroclaw: Ossolineum Publishers, 1979), particularly those by M. Drozdowski (on organized Polonia's efforts on behalf of Polish independence) and M. Francic (on the various problems facing *KON*).

12. M. Drozdowski, ""Dzialalnosc Polonii Amerykanskiej w walce o niepodleglosc Polski w latach 1914-1918" (Polonia efforts in the struggle for Polish independence between 1914 and 1918) in Francic, et al., *Polonia wobec niepodleglosci;* and Brozek, *Polish Americans*, pp. 68, 74-81 and *passim*.

13. Already on September 22, 1914 Paderewski had publicly called for the creation of a Polish army to serve alongside Britain and France.

The PNA made available the building and grounds of its newly established school in Cambridge Springs, Pennsylvania for the training of officers, whose program the Falcons agreed to supervise. In all, 167 men applied for acceptance in the first session, with 60 eventually taking part - at their own expense. But the effort was curtailed because of America's neutrality and did not resume until the United States' entry into the war in April 1917. Pienkos, *PNA,* p. 106.

14. Paderewski had several contacts and communications with Wilson's most trusted confidante, Colonel Edward M. House after 1914; moreover Wilson met on several occasions with Polonia representatives who urged him to support their cause. On February 10, 1915, for example, the President received a group of Polish Americans led by Starzynski, and there accepted a memorial on behalf of the Polish independence cause. In his informal remarks, Wilson is reported to have said, "Your concerns are just and I assure you today that at some point we will decisively and categorically demand freedom for Poland. This you can be sure of and on this you have my word." Pienkos, *One Hundred Years Young,* p. 88. In May 1916, Wilson repeated his public support of the rights of all nations to self-government, without, however, expressly mentioning Poland.

A controversial argument interpreting Wilson's statement as his response to the solid support he received in the 1916 election from the Polish community has been made by Louis Gerson, *Woodrow Wilson and the Rebirth of Poland, 1914-1920* (New Haven, Connecticut: Yale University Press, 1953, 1972). A look at the vote shows that the President either lost the states with the largest Polish populations or carried them comfortably even without Polonia's backing. Not to discount his probable appreciation of Polish support, one must look to Wilson's philosophical commitment to the principle of national self-determination as the key to his thinking on the subject. For a rebuttal to Gerson's view see Kay Lundgreen-Nielsen, "Woodrow Wilson and the Rebirth of Poland," in Arthur Link, ed., *Woodrow Wilson and a Revolutionary World, 1913-1921* (Chapel Hill: University of North Carolina Press, 1982), pp. 105-126.

15. Pienkos, *One Hundred Years Young,* pp. 95-96; the text of Paderewski's speech is to be found in this work on pages 300-304.

16. *Ibid.,* pp. 97-98. A detailed discussion of the forming of the Polish Army in America is by Joseph Hapak, "Recruiting a Polish Army in the United States, 1917-1919," Diss. University of Kansas, 1985; and Hapak, "The Polish Military Commission, *Polish American Studies,* 38, number 2 (1981), 26-38.

17. Pienkos, *One Hundred Years Young,* pp. 101ff.

18. *Ibid.,* p. 101.

19. *Ibid.,* pp. 197-108. Data on the casualties suffered by the Polish Americans in France and Poland between 1918 and 1920 are to be found in Jerzy Walter, compiler, *Czyn zbrojny wychodztwa Polskiego w Ameryce* (The Military Service Contribution of the Polish Emigration in America, New York: Polish Army Veterans Association, 1957); and in *Dziennik Zwiazkowy,* December 20, 1947. Andrzej Brozek has this to say of the significance of Polonia's military contribution to Polish independence:

> If we remember that recruitment into Pilsudski's legions in Poland itself took in about 23,000 men, then the 24,000-25,000 American Poles who travelled willingly across the ocean to serve in France to achieve the ideal of an independent Poland must cause us to pay homage to their patriotic dedication, a commitment that characterized American Polonia throughout the First World War period (*Polish Americans, p. 144*).

20. Pienkos, *ibid.,* p. 107; Jedrzejewicz, *Pilsudski,* pp. 85-6, 98.

21. J. Orlowski, *Helena Paderewska w pracy narodowej i spolecznej* (Helena Paderewska in Patriotic and Social Work, Chicago, 1929); Robert Szymczak, "An Act of Devotion: The Polish Grey Samaritans and the American Relief Effort in

Poland, 1919-1921," *Polish American Studies,* 43, number 1 (Spring, 1986), 13-36.

22. Between November 1919 and December 1920, the drive collected but $670,400 and the following year contributions fell another fifty percent before its termination in 1923.
Solid studies of the National Department are those by Rev. Louis J. Zake, "The Development of the National Department *(Wydzial Narodowy)* as Representative of the Polish American Community in the United States, 1916-1923," Diss. University of Chicago, 1979; and "The National Department and the Polish American Community, 1916-1923," *Polish American Studies,* 38, number 2 (1981), 16-25; and William Galush, "American Poles and the New Poland: An Example of Change," *Ethnicity,* 1, number 3 (1974), 209-221. According to one Polish scholar, the drive yielded $4,954,000 between October 30, 1918 and February 1, 1921, with nearly all donations in by the end of 1919. Tadeusz Radzik, *Spoleczno-ekonomiczne aspekty stosunku Polonii Amerykanskiej do Polski po I Wojny Swiatowej* (Socio-economic Aspects of the Relationship of Polonia to Poland after World War I. Wroclaw: Polish Academy of Sciences, 1989), pp. 27-32.
This author notes that popular response to the campaign was uneven, depending on the commitment of local committees to the cause. Thus, strong backers of the drive like the Rev. Lucjan Bojnowski of New Britain, Connecticut, produced results far greater than expected: his committee brought in more than $44,000, nearly $10,000 more than had been called for. Elsewhere donations were disappointing, despite appeals by leaders like Bishop Rhode who asserted that "a person can't call himself a worthy Pole if he doesn't significantly help his brother across the ocean."
The drive had been predicated on a calculation of $6 yearly for every Pole earning less than $1200 annually and one percent from those who were better off. The fraternals were called upon to also give, and led by the PNA and the Falcons, they did their part -- nearly $120,000 from the Alliance and some $44,000 from the Falcons. Radzik, p. 30 and *passim.*

23. Emile J. Dillon, *The Peace Conference* (London: Hutchinson and Company, 1919), pp. 67-68, 215, 219, 227-230; Jan Karski, *The Great Powers and Poland, 1919-1945* (Lanham, Maryland: University Press of America, Inc., 1985), pp. 31-41 and *passim*.

24. Adam Olszewski, *Historia Zwiazku Narodowego Polskiego* (History of the Polish National Alliance. Chicago: Alliance Printers and Publishers, 1957). volume III, p. 354; and Pienkos, *PNA* pp. 115-116.

25. Radzik, pp. 44-52.

26. The story of the American Relief Administration and the significant role played by Herbert Hoover on Poland's behalf in both the First and Second World Wars is told by George J. Lerski, compiler, *Herbert Hoover and Poland: A Documentary History of a Friendship* (Stanford, California: Hoover Institution, 1977).

27. Lerski, pp. 15-17; Wandycz, *Poland and the United States,* pp. 158-169. For Polonia's defense of Poland on the Jewish atrocity issue, see Olszewski, volume III, pp. 275ff.

28. Anna Cienciala and Titus Komarnicki, From *Versailles to Locarno: Keys to Polish Foreign Policy,* 1919-1925 (Lawrence: University of Kansas, 1984). The PNA alone raised more than $250,000 for this effort. Pienkos, *PNA,* pp. 116.

29. For a list of such firms along with the names of their organizers, see Adam Walaszek, *Reemigracja ze Stanow Zjednoczonych do Polski po I wojny swiatowej, 1919-1924* (Reemigration from the United States to Poland after World War I, Warsaw: *Panstwowe Wydawnictwo Naukowe,* 1983), pp. 155-164; Radzik, pp. 97-154, *passim.*

FOOTNOTES to Chapter III

1. Pienkos, *PNA*, pp. 144ff. In 1929, a number of Polonia activists, many of them from the Polish National Alliance, had played an active role in the first congress of *Swiatpol*. By 1934, however, they had been largely defeated for reelection and succeeded in office by individuals like Swietlik, who favored a more distant and less politically engaged relationship with Poland. This position, one which asserted Polonia's "independence" from Poland and its members' American loyalties was even more fervently held within the Polish Roman Catholic Union fraternal. Indeed, the PRCUA had boycotted the 1929 proceedings.

For more on American Polonia's position toward Poland at the 1934 Congress, see Brozek, *Polish Americans*, pp. 188-192, and Haiman, *Zjednoczenie*, pp. 427ff.

2. Wojciech Bialasiewicz, *Pomiedzy loyalnoscia a serc porywem: Polonia Amerykanska we wrzesniu 1939 roku* (Between loyalty and Heartfelt Enthusiasm: American Polonia in September 1939. Chicago: Privately printed, 1989), pp. 10, 41. Approximately one million dollars may have been collected through the efforts of the Polish National Defense Fund's efforts up to 1939.

3. On the Depression's impact, see John J. Bukowczyk, *And My Children Did Not Know Me: A History of the Polish Americans* (Bloomington and Indianapolis: Indiana University Press, 1987), pp. 75-84; and Ewa Morawska, *For Bread with Butter: Life-Worlds of East Central Europeans in Johnstown, Pennsylvania, 1890-1940* (New York: Cambridge University Press, 1985).

4. Pienkos, *One Hundred Years Young*, pp. 137-140, and Bialasiewicz, pp. 118ff. on the failure to recruit Polish Americans into a Polish legion. Bialasiewicz in particular cites an estimate of manpower available for such a force that was made by the Polish consulate in New York in 1939. Accordingly, only 60,000 Polish-born males between the ages of 20 and 50 were seen as eligible for military service throughout the entire country; of these only 5,000 were viewed as likely to join such a

legion if actively recruited. If these figures are accurate, the "pool" of eligible volunteers in 1939 was but a small fraction of what it had been in 1917.

5. For a contrary evaluation see Andrzej Brozek, "Polonia w Stanach Zjednoczonych wobec inicjatyw Paderewskiego oraz Sikorskiego w czasie I i II wojny swiatowej" (American Polonia's response to Paderewski and Sikorski's initiatives in the First and Second World Wars), *Przeglad Polonijny,* volume 7, number 2 (1981), 41-67.

Six Polish Americans, all Democrats, were in Congress at the outbreak of the war: Leonard Schuetz and Anthony Maciejewski of Illinois, John Dingell, Sr., John Lesinski and Rudolph Tenerowicz of Michigan, and Boleslas Monkiewicz of Connecticut. In November 1940, Schuetz, Maciejewski, Lesinski, Tenerowicz and Dingell were reelected and joined by Democrats Thaddeus Wasielewski of Wisconsin and Lucien Maciora of Connecticut, thus increasing the size of the "Polish delegation" to seven members. In the 1942 elections, nine Polish Americans were elected, with Republicans Alvin O'Konski of Wisconsin and Joseph Mruk of New York, Illinois Democrats Thomas Gordon and Martin Gorski joining Wasielewski, Monkiewicz, Schuetz, Lesinski and Dingell in office. In 1944, Polish American representation was reduced to seven members with Wasielewski, O'Konski, Gorski, Gordon, Lesinski, and Dingell reelected to their posts and Joseph Ryter replacing Monkiewicz in Connecticut. On the limits of Polonia's political influence, see Peter H. Irons, "The Test is Poland: Polish Americans and the Origins of the Cold War," *Polish American Studies,* 30, number 2 (Autumn, 1973), 5-65.

6. A recent estimate of the strength of the resistance in 1944 places the pro-London Home Army *(Armia Krajowa)* at 250-350,000, with the pro-Communist "People's Army" at 20-60,000. Antoni Polonsky and Boleslaw Drukier, *The Beginnings of Communist Rule in Poland* (London and Boston: Routledge and Kegan Paul, 1980), pp. 140-141. In March, 1943 the Poles' estimate of the Home Army's size was 300,200. John Coutouvidis and Jaime Reynolds, *Poland, 1939-1947* (Leicester, U.K.: Leicester University Press, 1986), p. 84.

7. Stalin and Hitler agreed, in a secret protocol to the treaty, that "in the event of a territorial and political rearrangement of the areas belonging to the Polish state the spheres of influence of Germany and the U.S.S.R. shall be bounded approximately by the line of the rivers Narew, Vistula and San. The question of whether the interests of both parties make desirable the maintenance of an independent Polish state and how such a state should be bounded can only be definitely determined in the course of further political developments. In any event both governments will resolve this question by means of a friendly agreement." The secret protocol also determined the fate of the Baltic states, with Finland, Esthonia and Latvia together with the eastern provinces of Romania going to the Soviets while Lithuania was ceded to the Nazis. On September 28, the two aggressors agreed to rearrange their division of the spoils with Stalin trading central Poland to Hitler in return for Lithuania. General Sikorski Historical Institute, *Documents on Polish-Soviet Relations 1939-1945* (London: Heinemann, 1961), volume I, pp. 40-54.

The literature on Poland's wartime diplomatic fortunes is rich and instructive. Among the best works are those of Edward Rozek, *Allied Wartime Diplomacy: A Pattern in Poland* (New York: John Wiley and Sons, 1958); Adam B. Ulam, *Expansion and Coexistence: The History of Soviet Foreign Policy, 1917-1967* (New York: Praeger, 1968); and Jan Karski, *The Great Powers and Poland, 1919-1945* (New York and London: University Press of America, 1985).

8. Bialasiewicz, pp. 18ff. This author cites public opinion data compiled in September, 1939 which indicate that while 81 percent of those questioned viewed Germany to be responsible for starting the war, 88 percent were opposed to America's intervention into the European conflict with only 9 percent in favor of this proposition. Presumably, opinion among Polish Americans did not differ sharply from the views of their fellow citizens. Bialasiewicz, pp. 37-38.

9. *Ibid.*, pp. 73ff.

10. During this period, the funds accumulated in the *Rada Polonii* treasury were as small as its disbursements. For example, in July 1938 the *Rada Polonii* reported holdings of only $2,704. Expenditures at that time went out in support of a few commemorative events and several youth and veterans' activities. Meetings of the Executive Committee frequently centered around the issue of *Swiatpol,* with Swietlik in continuing disagreement with Romaszkiewicz as to the advisability of cooperation. The growing crisis in Europe ultimately caused a resolution of the debate, with the *RPA* agreeing in June 1939 to send three delegates to an extraordinary gathering of *Swiatpol's* executive committee in Warsaw in early August. *Minutes of the Meetings of the Directorate of Rada Polonii Amerykanskiej,* May 1938--September 1939, in the Polish Museum of America, Chicago. The Museum's holdings on *RPA* activities are voluminous. They include minutes of the meetings of the Board of Directors and Executive Committee of the *Rada Polonii* from 1938 through 1974, reports of the local and state districts, affiliated national fraternals, and conventions.

11. According to one commentator, the *Rada Polonii's* decision to focus solely on charitable work was a serious mistake since there then existed no political federation in the Polish American community to represent its concerns. "When the *(Rada)* was founded, it was assumed that this organization would also undertake the political representation of the vast masses of Americans of Polish descent and the Polish-American communities. There was hope that the Polish Council would formulate a program of action as the representative of six million Americans of Polish descent, and thus act in the defense of the independence of the Polish state. These hopes were futile. The Council restricted itself to only one phase of aid to Poland: relief..." Joseph Wytrwal, *Behold! The Polish Americans* (Detroit: Endurance Press, 1977), p. 355.

12. Pienkos, *PNA,* pp. 151-152.

13. Bialasiewicz, p. 41.

14. *Ibid.,* pp. 60ff.

15. The *RPA's* proclamation of its drive for Poland's relief reads as follows: "Due to the United States' declaration of neutrality and the further impossibility of fund raising for any foreign army engaged in military action, the Polish American Council calls for an end to collections on behalf of the Polish National Defense Fund. At the same time the Council calls upon Polonia organizations and our entire community to at once initiate collections on a far wider basis on behalf of our Relief Fund, whose purpose is to aid war victims in Poland and which in no way contradicts the Neutrality Act." Bialasiewicz, p. 76. For biographical information on Szymczak (1894-1978), see Edward Kantowicz, "The Limitations of Ethnic Politics: Polish Americans in Chicago," in Angela T. Pienkos, editor, *Ethnic Politics in Urban America: The Polish Experience in Four Cities* (Chicago: Polish American Historical Association, 1978), pp. 98-99.

16. *Minutes of the Meeting of the Directorate of the RPA,* October 21, 1939. A significant independent drive was already underway in New York City area by the end of September, *Polska Rada Narodowa* (The Polish National Council), under the leadership of the veteran Polonia activists Frank X. Wazeter and Felix Poplawski. This group made its first shipments of goods to Polish refugees in Romania, Lithuania and Hungary in December. (Letter to the Business Manager of the Milwaukee *Kuryer Polski* newspaper from Dr. Stefan Mizwa along with an undated news story. In the *Kuryer Polski* collection of the Milwaukee Public Library.)

Uniting groups like the *Polska Rada Narodowa* into the *RPA* effort remained a challenge for Swietlik's organization throughout the war. Even in March 1944, of 181 local committees then in operation, 91 groups in 19 states were still not officially registered with the *RPA*. Ultimately, the drive to unite all Polonia under the *RPA's* wings did succeed, however. Thus in 1948 Swietlik could report that it had received donations of goods from no fewer than 609 state, district and local organizations. *Minutes of the Meeting of the Directorate of RPA,* March 18, 1944; *Reports on Gifts in Kind Received by American Relief for Poland from Polish Committees, Organizations and Parishes,*

July 1943--September 1948 inclusive. Mimeographed report in the *RPA* archives in Chicago. See also Bialasiewicz, pp. 77-78.

17. Estimates of the number of Poles who perished in Soviet exile vary from 300,000 to 750,000. Jan T. Gross, *Revolution from Abroad: The Soviet Conquest of Western Ukraine and Western Belorussia* (Princeton, New Jersey: Princeton University Press, 1988), p. 229 and *passim.* For the Poles' experience under Nazi rule see Gross' earlier work, *Polish Society under German Occupation: The General Government, 1939-1944* (Princeton, New Jersey: Princeton University Press, 1979), and Richard Lukas, *The Forgotten Holocaust: The Poles under German Occupation, 1939-1944* (Knoxville: University of Tennessee Press, 1986). On the total number of Polish refugees in World War II, one recent study places the total at 4.5 million, of whom 2.1 million were forced to work in Germany. Barbara Stern Burstin, *After the Holocaust: The Migration of Polish Jews and Christians to Pittsburgh* (Pittsburgh: University of Pittsburgh Press, 1989), p. 42 and *passim.*

18. *New York Times,* February 11, 1940.

19. *Dziennik Zwiazkowy,* April 21, 22, 1941.

20. Sikorski Memorial Committee, *General Sikorski w dziesiata rocznice smierci* (General Sikorski on the Tenth Anniversary of his Death. London: General Sikorski Historical Institute, 1954), pp. 17-18, 60-61, *passim.*

21. *Minutes of the Meeting of the Directorate of RPA,* May 17, 1940. The 1940 convention in Pittsburgh brought together 34 delegates representing 20 Polonia organizations. Five representatives from the Union of Polish Priests were in attendance along with 22 delegates from twelve Polish American fraternals. The others represented a variety of professional, business, youth and veterans' associations.

In October 1942, the *RPA's* convention in Buffalo attracted 167 delegates, including a large number of representatives from the 29 district units of the federation by then in operation.

Minutes of the Meeting of the Directorate of RPA, March 30, 1940 and November 28, 1942.

22. F. X. Swietlik, *Rada Polonii Amerykanskiej od 1939 do 1948* (The Polish American Council and its work from 1939 to 1948, Chicago, 1948), pp. 11-14. This is the published account of Swietlik's review of his previous nine years as Chairman of the *RPA* and was presented to its national convention in Buffalo, December 4-5, 1948.

23. *Minutes of the Meeting of the Directorate of RPA,* April 24, 1942; Pienkos, *PNA,* pp. 151-2.

24. Swietlik, *Rada Polonii,* pp. 84-85. Clearly, the charitable drives launched by the National War Fund helped the *RPA* considerably. The efforts were far better publicized than *Rada Polonii* appeals and reached out to all Americans, Polish and non-Polish alike.

25. Swietlik, *Rada Polonii,* pp. 18ff.

26. *Reports of Gifts in Kind Received by American Relief for Poland from Polish Committees, Organizations and Parishes between July, 1943 and September, 1948.* Mimeographed report in the Polish Museum of America. See also the report of the director of district 16 of the *Rada Polonii,* John Tyrka, presented at the plenary meeting of the directors of the organization, February 21 and 22, 1948. In addition to donations made through the *RPA* to Poland immediately after the war, the organization also served as an intermediary funneling assistance into the country for many private charitable organizations concerned about conditions in that country. According to the mimeographed report on gifts in kind as of the end of 1948, twenty different American agencies, most of them not directed by Polish Americans, had already contributed 2,325,086 pounds in relief materials to Poland including the Church World Service headquartered in New York, the Unitarian Service Committee, the American Federation for Polish Jews, the Polish Red Cross in New York, the Watchtower Society, the Salvation

Army, the YWCA, the Polish Army Veterans Association in New York and the Kosciuszko Foundation.

27. Swietlik, *Rada Polonii,* pp. 4-9. Regarding the "real" value of goods collected and distributed Swietlik further noted that the one dollar figure in no way adequately reflected the worth of the goods but merely followed U.S. government regulations in accounting for such donations. Indeed, he concluded that if the dollar value of aid to the Polish people was truly accurate, the total estimate of goods shipped would have been $20-25 million.

28. *Ibid.* pp. 30-35; see also Lucjan Krolikowski, O.F.M., Conv. *Stolen Childhood: A Saga of Polish War Children* (Buffalo: Father Justin Rosary Hour and Franciscan Fathers Minor Conventuals, 1983). The story of the orphans is especially poignant. Gathered together from various parts of Soviet Central Asia and Siberia after having endured conditions of near starvation, the children were permitted to leave the U.S.S.R. at the time General Anders' forces exited through Iran. Under the care of the Polish Government in London, the *RPA,* the Polish National Alliance, the Resurrectionist order of Sisters, the Felician Sisters, and the National Catholic Welfare Council, they eventually made their way to the town of Santa Rosa, Mexico. There, most remained for more than three years together with children who had parents elsewhere around the world, along with a number of other refugees from the Soviet Union. The children, educated by the Polish Felicians, gradually regained their health. In time families were reunited and the orphans resettled, for the most part in the United States. Many were initially brought to the PNA's College in Cambridge Springs, Pennsylvania where they were able to continue their studies and learn useful trades. All adjusted successfully to their new lives in America and a number achieved great success in their adopted homeland. Based upon conversations with Chester Sawko, John Stanclik, Lucy Rozwadowska, Blanche Malinowicz and Mary Jankowska.

29. Francis Swietlik, *The Polish Displaced Persons* (Chicago: American Relief for Poland, no date but probably printed in 1946), p. 2.

30. Richard Lukas, *Bitter Legacy: Polish American Relations In the Wake Of World War II* (Lexington, Kentucky: University of Kentucky Press, 1982), chapters 6 and 7.

31. *Minutes of the Meeting of the Directorate of RPA*, August 19, 1949.

32. In the opinion of several participants at the convention, Swietlik could have won reelection had he campaigned actively against Rozmarek's candidate for Censor. Four years later, in 1951, he did run again but was beaten decisively. Pienkos, *PNA*, pp. 169-170, 346. An interesting discussion of the conflict that developed between Rozmarek and Swietlik which reached its climax at the 1947 convention is to be found in the official history of the PNA by Adam Olszewski, *Historia ZNP,* volume VI, pp. 211-216.
See also the minutes of the convention which are in the archives of the Polish National Alliance in Chicago. Olszewski's view is that Swietlik's popularity had considerably diminished by the time of the convention.

33. Walter Zahariaszewicz, "Polish American Organizations," in Frank Mocha, ed., *The Poles in America: Bicentennial Essays* (Stevens Point, Wisconsin: Worzalla Printers, 1977). See Burstin, *After the Holocaust,* chapter 4, for a recent review of the Committee's activities and achievements.

34. Swietlik, *Rada Polonii,* pp. 57-60; Adam Olszewski, *Historia ZNP,* volume VI, p. 357.

35. Florian Piskorski had served as the chief postwar representative of the *Rada Polonii* in Poland until the organization was shut down. In 1958 Antoni Mioduski took over following the resumption of *RPA* activity and was followed by Stanley Turkiewicz, a Buffalo, New York activist in the organization who remained in Poland until his retirement in 1965. He was

succeeded by M. M. Royek until his death and then by Z. Henry Wajda, who became the last *RPA* representative in the country, serving there until 1973.

36. Between 1939 and 1974, more than one hundred Polish American activists from around the nation served as members of the Board of Directors of *RPA*. Most prominent in terms of their involvement in the work of the organization over long periods of time were Swietlik, Midowicz, an attorney with the Polish National Alliance who served as an *RPA* Vice President, Wolowska and Lagodzinska, each in her time President of the Polish Women's Alliance and an officer in *RPA*, Soska, President of the Polish *Alma Mater* fraternal and the *RPA's* Secretary General during the war years, Joseph Kania, John Olejniczak, and Turkiewicz, each a President of the Polish Roman Catholic Union fraternal and at various times Treasurer of the *Rada Polonii,* and Board members Zygmunt Stefanowicz, Armella Mix, Antoinette Czerniak, Bronislas Smykowski, Aniela Wojcik, Bishop Stefan Woznicki, Eugenia Bar, and Teofil Starzynski, President of the Polish Falcons of America.

FOOTNOTES to Chapter IV

1. The earlier partitions, in 1772, 1793 and 1795, had had as their consequence the abolition of Polish independence and statehood, not to be restored until 1918. Dziewanowski, *Poland in the Twentieth Century,* pp. 25-29.

2. An excellent history is by Jozef Garlinski, *Poland in the Second World War* (London: MacMillan, 1985). Figures on the Polish forces in the West are provided by Garlinski, and Dziewanowski, p. 143. For the activities of the Home Army see Stefan Korbonski, *The Polish Underground State, 1939-1945* (New York: Minerva Press, 1978), and Lukas, *Forgotten Holocaust,* pp. 40-94.

3. Thomas Bailey, *A Diplomatic History of the American People* (New York: Appleton-Century-Crofts, 1958), sixth edition, pp. 718-729. Already America's neutrality was somewhat fictitious. "Lend-lease" aid had already been approved in Congress, enabling Roosevelt to provide Britain with some fifty overage destroyers in its fight against Nazi encirclement.

4. Criticism of the *Rada Polonii's* "failure" to lobby for Poland on occasion alleged that there had been expectations along these lines within the Polish American community. See for example the remarks of Charles Rozmarek, President of the Polish National Alliance and the Polish American Congress at the 1947 PNA convention, in Olszewski, *Historia ZNP,* volume VI, pp. 215-216.

One historian writes: "The outbreak of World War II found the Polish American community unprepared for any political activity on behalf of Poland. The tragedy and destruction of Poland by Germany, the treacherous stab in the back of September 17 (by the Soviet Union), the heroic battles of the Polish army--whose culminating exploits were the defense of Westerplatte (a fort on the Baltic Sea) and of Warsaw, the transfer of the Polish government to Romania, the formation of a new government in Paris--all these historical events had failed to produce a political response from the Polish American community. Not a single Polish word (sic) was heard in the U.S.

Congress during the months of Poland's struggle. No declaration had been made in the name of the Polish American community condemning the fourth partition of Poland. The major Polish fraternals had expressed in fervent words their sympathy in the tragedy of the Polish nation and had passed corresponding resolutions. However, there is a vast distance between resolutions and political action." Joseph Wytrwal, *Behold! The Polish Americans* (Detroit: Endurance Press, 1977), p. 355.

Given Poland's plight, it is easy to appreciate the frustration within Polonia at the time. But due to the United States' neutrality in 1939, it is difficult to imagine just what even the most well supported Polonia political organization could have then achieved.

5. Their activities are documented by Waclaw Jedrzejewicz, *Polonia Amerykanska w Polityce Polskiej: Historia Komitetu Narodowego Amerykanow Polskiego Pochodzenia* (American Polonia's Involvement in Polish Politics: A History of the National Committee of Americans of Polish Descent, New York: *KNAPP,* 1954). An English language summary of *KNAPP's* activities based upon Jedrzejewicz's work is that of Richard Lukas, *The Strange Allies: The United States and Poland, 1941-1945* (Knoxville: University of Tennessee Press, 1978), Chapter 6.

6. Jedrzejewicz, pp. 16-18.

7. *Ibid.*, p. 19.

8. *Ibid.,* p. 53. The statement was quickly picked up by English language newspapers, and used regularly thereafter against *KNAPP,* especially in the left-wing press.

9. *Ibid.,* pp. 58-59.

10. The definitive study of the Katyn Massacre is by Janusz Zawodny, *Death in the Forest* (Notre Dame, Indiana: Notre Dame University Press, 1962). The author concludes that the Soviets were responsible for the atrocity, although they persisted into 1989 to deny this.

In Poland, an official silence about the subject of Katyn through the 1970s made it a matter creating a sense of deep alienation between the citizenry and the regime. Following Solidarity's birth in 1980, however, a monument in Warsaw with the inscription, "Katyn," was erected in memory of the victims. Significantly, individuals repeatedly found ways to add the date "1940" to the memorial, only to cause officials to order their efforts erased.

Upon Mikhail Gorbachev's accession to power in the U.S.S.R., the regimes began at last to look at the Katyn Massacre as one of several "blank spots" in post 1939 Polish-Soviet relations requiring an honest review. Discussions among historians from the two countries led in February 1989 to an official Polish press statement declaring the Soviets responsible, a pronouncement *Pravda* indirectly acknowledged several days later in the spirit of Gorbachev's anti-Stalin *Glasnost'* campaign. In 1990, the Soviet government finally gave its public acknowledgement of its criminal action against the Polish nation at Katyn. For the PAC's part in spurring on the U.S. House of Representatives' own investigation of Katyn in the early 1950s, see below.

11. The Communist Party of Poland had been an ineffectual and eventually negligible factor in interwar Polish politics. In 1938 Stalin ordered it dissolved and many of the party's activists then in the U.S.S.R. were summarily executed. Beginning in December 1941, however, the Soviets reconstituted the party. In Russia, work got underway to conceive a "Union of Polish Patriots," a group which Stalin recognized in 1943 following his break with Sikorski over Katyn. In January 1942 a "Polish Workers Party" was established in Nazi-occupied Poland. By July 1944 the two groups had been merged and would form the core leadership of the future communist state. M. K. Dziewanowski, *The Communist Party of Poland* (Cambridge: Harvard University Press, 1976), second edition.

12. For the positions of Roosevelt and Churchill regarding Poland, see Jan Karski, *The Great Powers and Poland, 1919-1945: From Versailles To Yalta* (New York and London: University Press of America, 1985), especially pp. 473-481; Charles E.

Bohlen, *Witness to History, 1929-1969* (New York: Norton, 1973); and Edward J. Rozek, *Allied Wartime Diplomacy* (New York: Wiley, 1958). Following his private talk with Stalin, Roosevelt disingenuously informed the American press that he had made "no secret treaties" with the Soviet leader. Whether of not Churchill and Roosevelt would have spoken as they did about Poland's interests had Sikorski and not Mikolajczyk been Prime Minister is an interesting question; what seems clear is that Sikorski's death made decision-making about Poland somewhat smoother. One reason for their willingness to grant Stalin what he wanted was the Allies' inordinate fear that the Soviets might make a separate peace with Germany as they had done under Lenin in March 1918, thus leaving the United States and Britain to fight on alone. For his part, the Soviet leader questioned why his Western partners had failed to mount a second front to take some of the pressure off his embattled forces, a complaint met by the decision to launch the Normandy invasion the following year. Stalin also won from Churchill and Roosevelt an agreement demanding Germany's "unconditional surrender" and denazification as the price of ending the conflict.

Exemplifying *KNAPP* press criticisms of Roosevelt, see the New York *Nowy Swiat* editorial of March 21, 1942. In it America's allies were warned that the Allied victory over Hitler might only mean that the Poles, French, Lithuanians and Serbs would ultimately be delivered over to Stalin. Note also the Detroit *Dziennik Polski* editorial of January 20, 1944 which pointed out that 6-7 million Polish voters would cross over to the Republicans if Roosevelt refused to help Poland. Faulting the President's failure to issue a clear statement about Poland, the editorial asserted "Soviet Russia is morally and deeply responsible to the people of the entire world for the spread of this war" (because of the Molotov-Ribbentrop Pact).

13. Membership in the Polish Workers Party was only 8,000 in 1943 and 20,000 a year later, at a time when participation in the Home Army and its pro-London allies was between 300-350,000 men and women. As late as January 1946, after having been in command of the country for more than a year, the Communists could claim only 235,000 members to the 600,000

in the democratic Polish Peasants Party *(PSL)*. Andrzej Korbonski, *The Politics of Socialist Agriculture* in Poland 1945-1960 (New York and London: Columbia University Press, 1965), p. 53; Jan B. DeWeydenthal, *The Communists of Poland: An Historical Outline* (Stanford, California: Hoover Institution, 1978), pp. 43-44, 177.

14. Louis Gerson, *The Hyphenate in Recent American Politics and Diplomacy* (Lawrence: University of Kansas, 1964), pp. 168-176 discusses the genesis and activities of the American Slav Congress.

15. For instance, publicist Matuszewski, the author of more than five hundred articles expounding *KNAPP's* views, was continually criticized for his activities and required to register as an agent of a foreign state, something not required of the pro-Soviet Polish Americans. They in turn continued to wield a certain influence in Washington. A comment by Roosevelt to Churchill at the Yalta summit conference in February 1945 was revealing. Polish Americans, he observed, had a "distant view on the Polish question... Most...favored the Curzon line compensated by Germany." This was the official position on Poland's eastern border held by the American Slav Congress and the American Polish Labor Council, a view denounced repeatedly by *KNAPP* representatives and after 1944 by the Polish American Congress.

Another pro-Soviet group was the Kosciuszko League, led by a parish priest in Springfield, Massachusetts, the Rev. Stanislas Orlemanski. In April 1944 Orlemanski, together with the Polish-born Oskar Lange, a Professor of Economics at the University of Chicago, secured permission from Washington to travel to the Soviet Union where they met with Stalin. Upon their return each praised the Soviet leader's intentions toward Poland and castigated those in Polonia who backed the "anti-Soviet" London government of Sikorski's successor, Mikolajczyk. In turn both were severely criticized by the newly formed Polish American Congress. Orlemanski was subsequently silenced by his bishop and the Kosciuszko League soon disappeared. Lange, who had tried to play a diplomatic role of sorts in Moscow, eventually renounced his U.S. citizenship, only to return as Communist Poland's first ambassador in Washington. Charles Sadler, "'Pro-Soviet Polish Americans': Oskar Lange and Russia's Friends in the Polonia, 1941-1945," *Polish Review*, 22, number 4 (1977), 25-39.

16. Garlinski, pp. 217ff.

17. Remarks of Charles Rozmarek, in Romuald Bilek, *Jak powstal Kongres Polonii Amerykanskiej* (How the Polish American Congress Arose, Chicago: Privately printed booklet appearing on the 40th anniversary of the forming of the Polish American Congress in memory of Rozmarek, 1984), pp. 16-18. Censor Swietlik took part in the same event and spoke extensively as Chairman of the *Rada Polonii Amerykanskiej.* The speeches of the two men are interesting, revealing their differences as much as their areas of agreement. Rozmarek stoutly defended the Polish government in exile as representative of the Polish nation; he termed the Soviet demand that Polish eastern territories be given to Russia as amounting to nothing less than a fifth partition of the country. This view reflected the thinking of *KNAPP.* Swietlik, still faithful to the official position of the London government, declared that "Americans are not so interested in the question of where the borders between Poland and Soviet Russia will be drawn, but rather whether mutual trust, faith in cooperation among the nations, and whether the rights of all nations, large and small, will be respected and protected... We are convinced that our Government will never agree to the idea that in a disagreement between Poland and Soviet Russia over borders that one Ally would gain at the expense of a second Ally..." Bilek, pp. 23, 25. See also, Jedrzejewicz, pp. 94-98.

18. Among those present were Rozmarek and four other national officers of the Polish National Alliance; President John Olejniczak and three of his associates from the Polish Roman Catholic Union; President Honorata Wolowska and two colleagues from the Polish Women's Alliance; President Teofil Starzynski of the Polish Falcons of America; and leaders of nine smaller fraternals from around the country. In addition, a number of individuals of the Polish language press took part

in the meeting along with several representatives from the clergy and the Polish veterans' organization. Bilek, pp. 30-31.

19. Bilek, pp. 34, 37. Swietlik attended the meeting but did not sign the resolution. However, in his remarks to the assembly he praised the decision to organize politically. And while he did not become involved in the PAC, he shared its orientation and publicly supported its positions as well. For example, on a radio discussion program beamed out of Chicago in the Spring of 1945, Swietlik sharply criticized the agreements on Poland arrived at by the Great Power leaders at Yalta. He went so far as to assert that if the Soviet Union were permitted to have its way in stripping Poland of its eastern territories, the West would in effect have lost the war, since the Allied principles of the Atlantic Charter would have been violated. Francis X. Swietlik, Ernest von Martz, Mulford Q. Sibley, and James McBurney, "The Yalta Declarations and the San Francisco Conference," *Northwestern University Reviewing Stand*, 4, number 20 (April 1, 1945).

Incidentally, the original name approved for the new Polonia political organization was that of the Congress of United Polish Organizations in America, *Kongres Polaczonych Organizacji Polskich w Ameryce.*

20. Jedrzejewicz, *ibid.;* Lukas.

21. Bilek, pp. 44-45.

22. Cited by Richard Lukas, "The Polish American Congress and the Polish Question, 1944-1947," *Polish American Studies*, 38, number 2 (Autumn, 1981), 40.

23. The President's statement was general in tone and could as easily have been addressed to a meeting of the American Polish Labor Council: "I take pleasure in sending greetings to the Polish American Congress. All of us are proud of the contributions made by Americans of Polish ancestry to the development of our country, and particularly of the unsparing efforts of this group of Americans in our war effort, at the front, in our factories, and in our farms. It is this unity of purpose and

spirit of cooperation, which all the citizens of our country have shown in meeting the supreme test of war that will assure victory and a just and equitable peace." Bilek, p. 63.

24. Left-wing reaction to the Buffalo conclave was bitterly hostile, with the PAC questioned as treasonable and fascist in the weeks before and after its founding. A Brooklynite named Kaminski declared that the new organization would have been more properly called a "Polish Fascist Congress." An "Emergency Conference on American Unity" called for Detroit to coincide with the PAC meeting and co-chaired by the veteran left-wing labor activist Stanley Nowak took the same line. Its resolution, approved at the meeting and signed by some eighty well-known Americans, including author Thomas Mann, film actors Edward G. Robinson and Bela Lugosi, concert master Serge Kousevitski, and Leo Krzycki, asserted, "We need unity in the war effort and we oppose fascism at home and abroad." Polish American Congress files in the Immigration History Research Center, University of Minnesota.

25. Janusz Zawodny, *Nothing But Honor: The Story of the Uprising of Warsaw, 1944* (Stanford, California: Hoover Institution, 1978), *passim.*

26. Pienkos, *PNA,* pp. 162-163; Lukas, "The Polish American Congress," 42-43.

27. Averill Harriman and Elie Abel, *Special Envoy to Churchill and Stalin, 1941-1946* (New York: Random House, 1975), pp. 359-360; Karski, *The Great Powers and Poland,* pp. 559-562.

28. Rozmarek had earlier assured Dewey of his support; his last minute change of heart infuriated the Republican candidate. Edward Rozek, *Allied Wartime Diplomacy: A Pattern in Poland* (New York: Wiley, 1958), p. 324.

29. Lukas, *The Strange Allies,* pp. 126-127; John L. Moore, ed., *Congressional Quarterly's Guide to U.S. Elections,* second edition (Washington, D.C.: Congressional Quarterly, Inc., 1985), pp. 303, 356. Moderate voter defections could well have

revised the outcomes in a number of states. In Michigan, FDR's margin of victory was only 22,000 votes out of more than 2.2 million that were cast; the President won in New Jersey by 26,000 votes out of nearly 2 million. In Illinois and Pennsylvania, where the largest Polish American populations were to be found, FDR won by 140,000 and 105,000 vote margins, respectively; in Illinois more than 4 million voters had taken part in the election while in Pennsylvania the total was nearly 3.8 million.

30. Gross, *Revolution from Abroad, Ibid.* The new postwar Poland, with approximately 120,000 square miles of territory was thus only 80 percent the size of the prewar state. The problem of compensation was a particularly sensitive issue for many Poles, especially since Poland was the first victim of Nazi and Soviet aggression in 1939. How later Soviet demands that its prewar legal borders could be redrawn against the will of the Poles, who were at the same time allies of Britain, the United States *and* the Soviet Union throughout World War II remains difficult to understand, even after more than four decades. At the same time, physically moving Poland westward, while justified for many reasons, was not formally approved by either the United States or Britain until the signing of the Helsinki Final Act in 1975. In the meantime, Polish claims to those lands would be backed only by the Soviets and consequently served for nearly thirty years as a major justification for continued communist rule. Only a firm Soviet-Polish alliance, it was alleged, provided Poland with a secure western border against German aggression. The term "recovered territories" was used by Warsaw to make the point that most of the lands acquired after 1945 had at some time in history been part of the Polish state. All in all, the border issue could only be a source of continued uneasiness in Poland.

31. Following Mikolajczyk's resignation, Tomasz Arciszewski (1877-1955), a veteran Socialist Party leader was elected Prime Minister in London. While dedicated to the Polish cause, he did not enjoy the renown of his predecessors. Both the American and British governments thus found it relatively easy to end diplomatic relations with his government in June 1945.

32. A Gallop Poll released on March 10, 1945 found, for example, that 61 percent of the respondents had favorable opinions about the Yalta conference, with only 9 percent holding unfavorable views on the Summit; 30 percent were undecided. *Public Opinion Quarterly,* volume 9 (Spring 1945), 95.

33. Quoted in the *Chicago Sun,* February 14, 1945. During its first decade the Polish American Congress reprinted collections of newspaper articles culled from the American press which publicized and defined its aims. These volumes did not include articles and news stories appearing in the Polish language newspapers and periodicals of the time. *The Story of the Polish American Congress in Press Clippings* (Chicago: Alliance Printers and Publishers), volume I (covering "a partial collection of the thousands of press clippings in our files") reported on stories appearing between 1944 and 1948; volume II covered the years 1948 to 1952; and volume III included articles published between 1952 and 1954. In all, the three volumes amount to nearly 500 pages and include more than 1,500 articles from around the country.

A similar fourth volume of clippings covered the period from 1955 to 1958. However, it was titled *The Polish National Alliance in the Press of America: A Partial Collection of Clippings from Leading United States Newspapers covering (the) Period from 1955 to 1958* (Chicago: Alliance Printers and Publishers, 1958).

34. *Press Clippings, 1944-1948,* pp. 58-63.

35. Lukas, "The Polish American Congress," 44-45. In April 1945 Rozmarek was received by Truman at the White House and there made another appeal on Poland's behalf. The President for his part did act to send Roosevelt's old close advisor, Harry Hopkins, to Moscow to take up the issue once again with Stalin. But Hopkins' mission failed entirely largely thanks to his dismal presentation of Poland's cause.

Wandycz concludes flatly: Hopkins' mission...effectively destroyed the hope that Stalin might relax his grip in Poland." *The United States and Poland,* pp. 301-302.

36. *Polish American Congress Bulletin,* 3, number 6 (February 1947), 3-12.

37. *Ibid.;* Olszewski, *Historia ZNP,* volume VI, p. 73 for Rozmarek's meeting with Byrnes on September 11, 1946.

The United States government defended Byrnes' statement at Stuttgart; indeed its policy for nearly three decades after was to reject the permanency of Poland's western borders until they could be affirmed at a Great Power peace conference. Only on August 1, 1975 at a summit-level gathering of thirty-three European states, the United States and Canada in Helsinki, Finland was this achieved. There, the Final Act of the Conference on Security and Cooperation in Europe was signed.

This international agreement would be criticized by many Americans because of the Soviet Union's subsequent failure to pay serious attention to its pledge to respect the human rights and fundamental freedoms of its subjects. At the same time, however, the "Helsinki accords" provided that the borders of all signatory states, including Poland, be regarded as "inviolable." All participants in the conference further promised to "refrain from assaulting those frontiers."

Thus through its participation at the Helsinki conference, the United States agreed for the first time to recognize the permanent character of Poland's western borders with East Germany. In point of fact, the West German Government had already formally done so in 1970 in treaties it had signed with both the U.S.S.R. and Poland. In his visit to Poland that year, the West German Chancellor, Willy Brandt, formally apologized for the crimes committed by the Nazis against the Polish nation.

38. Discussions with veteran PAC activist Jerzy Przyluski and former U.S. Congressman Roman Pucinski, June 28, 1987.

39. *Polish American Congress Newsletter,* November 1960 and June 1964 issues; interview with Przyluski.

40. Olszewski, *Historia ZNP,* volume V, pp. 397-8, volume VI, pp. 24-26.

41. According to one authority, at least 20,000 of the Polish gentiles who came to America had been insurgents in the Warsaw Uprising of 1944, another 20,000 had been participants in the Polish armed forces in the West, 25,000 others were family members of the ex-servicemen, with the rest coming from the DP camps. Barbara Stern Burstin, *After the Holocaust* (Pittsburgh: University of Pittsburgh, 1989), pp. 55, 116 and *passim.* The following data are provided in the official U.S. publication on immigration under the Displaced Persons Acts and are somewhat different. Accordingly, some 143,848 individuals of Polish origin were refugees who had been occupants of camps in Western Germany, Austria and Italy. Another 10,472 were former Polish soldiers living in Great Britain who were admitted along with their spouses and children. Of the remaining immigrants, most were war orphans. *Memo to America: The DP Story. Final Report of the United States Displaced Persons Commission* (Washington, D.C.: U.S. Government Printing Office, 1952), pp. 366, 376 and *passim.* See also Stanislaus Blejwas, "Old and New Polonias: Tensions within an Ethnic Community," *Polish American Studies,* 38, number 2 (Autumn, 1981), 73; and Anna D. Jaroszynska," The American Committee for Resettlement of Polish Displaced persons (1948-1968) in the Manuscript Collection of the Immigration History Research Center," *Polish American Studies,* 44, number 1 (Spring, 1987), 68. On the conditions of the Displaced Persons, see Olszewski, *Historia ZNP,* volume VI, pp. 114-120, 160-174, 345. It might here be noted that Swietlik had estimated the number of Polish refugees to be as high as 500,000 following his visit to the camps in the Fall of 1945. During his 1946 travels through Germany, Rozmarek revised the figures downward to some 195,000, although during the Congressional debate over the refugee act, the figure of 233,000 Poles was given in discussions of a total European DP population of 1,214,500 persons.

Total refugee estimates made between 1945 and 1948 reflect a similar downward pattern.

Thus in 1945, it was believed that there were about 7 million refugees in Europe. In 1947 the United States Nations-sponsored International Refugee Organization counted about 1,250,000 persons in this category. In 1948 the number had been further reduced to 835,000, largely due to their decisions to leave the camps and reside permanently in the countries where they had found themselves. Some had returned to their original homelands, although Poles making that decision were relatively few in number.

For a sharply worded critique of the original Displaced Persons legislation, which Truman himself attacked even as he signed the bill into law, see Burstin, chapter 3.

42. From the *By Laws of the American Committee for the Resettlement of Polish Displaced Persons,* as revised, June 24, 1949, in the Files of the Displaced Persons Committee, (ACR-PDP), in the Immigration History Research Center, University of Minnesota. I am indebted to the staff of the IHRC and in particular to Anna Jaroszynska , for assisting me in my work at the Center. The visit was itself facilitated by a travel grant from the IHRC in August 1987.

43. For Gunther's report, see Ignacy Morawski, *Sprawozdania zarzadu wykonawczego poszczegolnych komisji i komitetow oraz biur Chicago i Washingtonie na trzecie krajowe konwencje Kongresu Polonii Amerykanskiej, 30-31 Maja i 1 Czerwca, 1952* (Reports of the Executive Board and particular commissions and committees and the Chicago and Washington, D.C. bureaus of the Polish American Congress from May 30 through June 1, 1952. Chicago: Alliance Printers and Publishers, 1952).

From the records of the Displaced Persons Committee in the IHRC files it is clear that the Committee had a difficult time in explaining and promoting the purposes of its fund appeal within Polonia. For instance, one Pennsylvania PAC activist wrote several times to assert that 20 percent of the funds raised by his group should be returned, in accord with the procedure the Polish American Congress leadership had followed earlier to induce state divisions to work hard at fund raising in its "One

Million Dollar" campaign. This strategy had not, however, been adopted by the Displaced Persons Committee. Another leader in Massachusetts could not understand why there was any need for a fund appeal at all, since money lent to the new arrivals was to be repaid to the Committee. Still, there were activists such as Frank Wazeter, President of the New York state division who possessed a better understanding of the Committee's aims; he continually urged that cooperation among all Polonia organizations, the PAC, its Displaced Persons Committee and the *Rada Polonii* be promoted in order to assist the refugees in their resettlement.

44. Interview with Mrs. Wanda Rozmarek, April 12, 1980. Rozmarek was much beloved by former Displaced Persons for his efforts on their behalf. Following his death on August 5, 1973 many paused to express their feelings to his family, including one Anatol Rychalski who wrote these words of condolence to Rozmarek's widow: "Thousands of ex-refugees walk with you, hearts filled with gratitude, memories and prayers. Those of us who were fortunate to be touched by his fatherly goodness and compassion are orphans no more; he is with us and we are with him forever."

45. On the experiences of the Displaced Persons and prevailing atmosphere in America following the war, see the materials in the IHRC collection dealing with the work of Committee. Aside from interviews I conducted with several former DPs, comments about their original experiences can also be found in Burstin's generally excellent work, *After the Holocaust,* pp. 126-127. In this study based upon the author's interviews with some sixty Polish Christian and sixty Polish Jewish immigrants living in Pittsburgh, one can find one of the very few extended discussions of the refugees' fate in America. One significant piece of fiction dealing with the Polish refugee in America remains well worth reading, Flannery O'Connor's "The Displaced Person." First published in 1952, it can be found in Flannery O'Connor, *The Complete Stories* (New York: Farrar, Straus and Giroux, 1971), pp. 194-235.

46. Anna Jaroszynska, letter to the author, September 4, 1987: "Though the Committee was one of the most active and influential Polish American organizations during its existence, it is difficult to find any records of its activity in published materials. Publications dealing with the problems of displaced persons...often only mention the existence of the Committee...(yet) it is impossible to overestimate the importance of the work (it) carried out..."

47. Writing some three decades after the appearance of the "nowa emigracja" on America's shores and in the wake of succeeding waves of newcomers to this country, Historian Piotr Wandycz noted "it is quite evident that the Polonia or its most articulate and active members constitute an important although thus far not a decisive factor in American-Polish relations." Wandycz, *The United States and Poland,* pp. 412-413. See also Blejwas, "Old and New Polonias," 81-83.

48. *Kongres Polonii Amerykanskiej: Alfabetyczny spis czlonkostwa od Maja 1944 do 31 Marca 1948* (Alphabetical list of PAC Membership from 1944 through March 31, 1948. Chicago: Polish American Congress, 1948), 204 pages. See also Morawski, *Sprawozdania,* for details on membership for 1952.
   In that year membership stood at 4,704 local Polish American organizations and 3,832 individuals. Not counted then were *KNAPP* and the Polish Roman Catholic Union fraternal, which had withdrawn due to dissatisfaction with Rozmarek's leadership.

49. Stefan Korbonski, "Polish Election, 1947," letter published in the *Washington Post,* February 16, 1985.

50. According to an official history, "The unmasking and rout of the *PSL* and those reactionary underground forces grouped about it was a triumph of the working class, the toiling peasantry and the intelligentsia, a victory of all democratic and progressive forces of the nation over capitalist-landlord reaction, and which dreamed of reversing Poland's course down the old road dependent upon the imperialist states and political and economic backwardness." Wladyslaw Gora, *Historia Polskiego*

ruchu robotniczego 1864-1964 (The History of the Polish Workers' Movement, 1864-1964, Warsaw: Ksiazka i Wiedza, 1967), volume II, p. 328. For a top communist's admission of the Party's conduct in the 1947 campaign and its falsification of the election results, see Teresa Toranska, *'Them': Stalin's Polish Puppets* (New York: Harper and Row, 1987), interview with Jakub Berman, pp. 275-281. A recent and comprehensive overview of the Communists' triumph is provided by Coutouvidis and Reynolds, *Poland 1939-1947,* pp. 137-316. See also M. K. Dziewanowski, *The Communist Party of Poland* (Cambridge, Massachusetts: Harvard University Press, 1959), pp. 201-205; and *Elections in Poland* (Edinburgh: Scottish League for European Freedom, 1947), which details the Communists' pre-election campaign of terror.

51. Stanislaw Mikolajczyk, *The Rape of Poland: Pattern Of Soviet Aggression* (New York: Mc-Graw-Hill, 1948); Arthur Bliss Lane, *I Saw Poland Betrayed* (Indianapolis: Bobbs-Merrill, 1948); Stefan Korbonski, *Warsaw In Exile* (New York: Praeger, 1966).

52. The PRCUA action was based as much on its unhappiness with Rozmarek's autocratic style as its criticisms of his controversial alliance with Mikolajczyk. This point was reasserted once more in 1954, when Polonia's second largest fraternal rejoined the Congress. Pienkos, *PNA,* p. 170. For one evaluation of Rozmarek's leadership style see Jedrzejewicz, pp. 209-216.

53. At the second PAC convention in 1948, Rozmarek made this same point, although he exaggerated the change in opinion, declaring that in 1944, 90 percent of the public was in favor of close Soviet-American relations while four years later the figures had been reversed. Olszewski, *Historia ZNP,* volume VI, p. 300-301. Evaluations of Lane can be found in John N. Cable, "Arthur Bliss Lane: Cold Warrior in Warsaw, 1945-1947," *Polish American Studies,* 30, number 2 (Autumn, 1973), 66-82; Stefan Korbonski, Letter to the Editor commenting upon Professor Cable's article, *Polish American Studies,* 31, number 1 (Spring, 1974), along with Cable's response, 60-64; Robert Szymczak,

"Hopes and Promises: Arthur Bliss Lane, the Republican Party and the Slavic-American Vote, 1952," *Polish American Studies,* 45, number 1 (Spring, 1988), 12-28.

54. For an overview of American foreign policy during this period see Bennett Kovrig, *The Myth of Liberation: East Central Europe in U.S. Diplomacy and Politics since 1941* (Baltimore: The Johns Hopkins Press, 1973).

On American political party efforts in 1948 and 1952 to win over the Polish American vote see Samuel Lubell, *The Future of American Politics* (Garden City, New York: Doubleday, 1955 revised edition); and Gerson, *The Hyphenate In Recent American Politics and Diplomacy.*

55. See for example, Zdzislaw M. Rurarz, "Soviets Murder the Truth in Memorial to Katyn Massacre," *Wall Street Journal,* January 6, 1989. It is known that there were three mass graves but only the Katyn site had been discovered as of the Summer of 1990. Prior to their executions in early 1940 the officers were interrogated and a small number were spared since they possessed possibly pro-Soviet feelings. They later headed the First Polish Army, which accompanied the invading Soviet forces into Poland and Germany in 1944 and 1945.

56. For a discussion of PAC efforts in support of the Congressional investigation, see Robert Szymczak, "A Matter of Honor: Polonia and the Congressional Investigation of the Katyn Forest Massacre," *Polish American Studies,* 41, number 1 (Spring, 1984), 25-65; and Ray J. Madden, Chairman, *The Katyn Forest Massacre: Final Report of the Select Committee to Conduct an Investigation and Study the Facts, Evidence, and Circumstances on the Katyn Forest Massacre* (Washington, D.C.: U.S. Government Printing Office, 1952. Reprinted 1987).

57. See Pienkos, *PNA,* pp. 151-185, for an overview of Rozmarek's career.

58. Peter Irons, "The Test is Poland: Polish Americans and the Origins of the Cold War," *Polish American Studies,* 30, number 2 (Autumn, 1973), 61.

59. *Ibid.,* 63.

60. The Captive Nations Assembly was especially active in the 1950s. A major figure in its work was Stefan Korbonski, one of the leaders in emigration of the Polish Peasants Party. Early in its operation, the Assembly had been addressed by Secretary of State John Foster Dulles, a clear indication of its significance to the Eisenhower administration and its outlook toward Eastern Europe. For information on its activities, see its bi-monthly magazine, *ACEN News,* and Stephen Garrett, *From Potsdam to Poland: American Foreign Policy Toward Eastern Europe* (New York: Praeger, 1986).

61. Radio Free Europe operated as a "privately funded " station until 1971 when it was revealed that the Central Intelligence Agency had subsidized the effort from the start; in 1973 management of RFE was reorganized with the station funded directly by the U.S. Congress under the direction of an independent Board for International Broadcasting. *Polish American Congress Newsletter,* September, 1972, p. 6.

62. *Protokol Piatej Krajowej Konwencji KPA* (Minutes of the Fifth National Convention of the PAC, Chicago, 1960), pp. 65-67. The Captive Nations Proclamation in time became an annual action on the part of the U.S. Government, although its aims ran counter to later statements of American policy, most notably the Helsinki agreement of 1975, which placed this country on record as recognizing the legitimacy of the Eastern European states. In contrast, the Captive Nations resolution declared the U.S. as sharing with these nations "their aspirations for the recovery of their freedom and independence..." Ukrainian Congress Committee of America, *The Captive Nations: Continuing Exploitable Weakness of the Soviet Russian Empire* (New York, 1979), 12 pages.

Among Polish Americans, the "Captive Nations" idea was most strongly endorsed by political emigres identified with the Assembly of Captive European Nations headquartered in New York. Thus, at the dinner held to recognize Captive Nations Week on July 20, 1961 at New York's Statler Hilton Hotel, seven representatives from the Polish Section of ACEN were present, including Korbonski. The only PAC leader in attendance was the organization's Washington, D.C. representative, Karol Burke. This particular dinner, with 112 guests in all, was well attended by elected officials from Capitol Hill. Three U.S. Senators and sixteen Congressmen, among them four Polish Americans, were present. *Polish American Congress files of Karol Burke,* IHRC holdings.

63. *Chicago Daily News,* July 2, 1956, in *The Polish National Alliance in the Press of America: A Partial Collection of Clippings from leading U.S. Newspapers covering the period between 1955 and 1958* (Chicago, 1958).

64. *Los Angeles Times,* October 22, 1956, in *The Polish National Alliance in the Press of America.*

65. By this time, opinion within Polonia critical of the liberation idea had surfaced. For example, in April 1957 a long time friend of the PAC, U.S. Congressman Thaddeus Machrowicz of Michigan, declared in a speech to 1,000 people in Chicago that events in Hungary in October and November 1956 had shown the policy to be "folly." *Chicago Sun-Times,* April 1, 1957, in *The Polish National Alliance in the Press of America.*

There were other indications of the growing realism of the PAC after 1956. One symbolic but significant change was in Rozmarek's choice of speakers at the annual Polish Constitution Day observances in Chicago. In 1956, Republican Senator William Knowland of California, one of the harshest hardline critics of the Eisenhower administration's foreign policy had delivered the speech to an audience numbering some 100,000 people. In 1957, Congressman Alvin O'Konski of Wisconsin, another advocate of liberation addressed the assemblage. But in 1958, it was U.S. Secretary of Labor James Mitchell who provided the major address, a clear sign of the Polish American Congress' identification with the Eisenhower Administration's policies toward Poland. See also Garrett, *From Potsdam to Poland,* especially Chapter 2.

66. A critical view of the wisdom of American assistance is that of Stephen Kaplan, "U.S. Aid to Poland, 1957-1964: Concerns, Objectives and Obstacles," *Western Political Quarterly,* 28, number 1 (March, 1975), 147-166. Though supportive of the aid idea, one observer questions whether it might not have been used more effectively, for example, in constructing hospitals or in rebuilding the Royal Castle in Warsaw which had been destroyed during the war by the Nazis. Such actions would have provided more visible evidence of America's friendship and solidarity with the Polish people. Piotr Wandycz, *The United States and Poland,* pp. 365-366, 373.

67. Eisenhower's remarks are found in the Appendix of this work.

68. Of the ten states having the largest concentrations of Polish Americans, Kennedy took seven (New York, Illinois, Pennsylvania, Michigan, New Jersey, Massachusetts and Connecticut) and thus won a total of 164 of the 268 electoral votes he needed to become President. Nixon won three states having heavy concentrations of Polish Americans, Ohio, Indiana and Wisconsin, with 50 electoral votes among them. Kennedy won the Electoral College by a 303-219 margin but his popular vote margin was less than 120,000 out of 68.8 million cast. The Polish vote was particularly critical for Kennedy in Illinois, New Jersey and Michigan, which together provided him with 63 electoral votes, just enough to give him the election victory. In Illinois, Kennedy's margin in the two party vote was 6,397 votes out of 4,744,093 and in New Jersey he received 22,454 more votes than Nixon out of 2,747,614. In Michigan Kennedy's triumph was by 65,134 votes out of 3,299,448. Donald Pienkos, "Polish American Ethnicity in the Political Life of the United States," in Joseph S. Roucek and Bernard Eisenberg, eds., *America's Ethnic Politics* (Westport, Connecticut: Greenwood Press, 1982), pp. 286-290; Nelson W. Polsby and Aaron B. Wildavsky, *Presidential Elections* (New York: Scribner's, 1964), pp. 19, 168-169.

69. Zbigniew Brzezinski and William Griffiths, "Peaceful Engagement in Eastern Europe," *Foreign Affairs,* (July, 1961).

See also Brzezinski's *Alternative to Partition: For A Broader Conception of America's Role in Europe* (New York: Praeger, 1965). Another, then far more highly visible Polish American figure in the Kennedy-Johnson Administrations was John A. Gronouski of Wisconsin. Gronouski served from 1961 to 1965 as Postmaster-General of the United States, a post which at the time was a Cabinet-level appointment. From 1965 to 1968 he was U.S. Ambassador to Poland. In the late 1970s he headed the government corporation directing Radio Free Europe.

70. Marshall, "Powerful Political Force," reprinted from the *Los Angeles Times,* in *Polish American Journal,* volume 74, number 3 (March, 1985), p. 1. Roman Pucinski, President of the Illinois State Division of the Polish American Congress has argued that such private assistance amounted to as much as $1 billion annually by 1988. Pucinski, remarks at a special meeting of PAC policy advisers, Chicago, February 17, 1989.

71. *Centrum ambulatoryjnego leczenia dzieci im. Clementa J. Zablockiego* (Clement J. Zablocki Children's Ambulatory Care Center. Krakow: Institute of Pediatrics Medical Academy, 1985). Zablocki's successor in the House of Representatives, Congressman Gerald R. Kleczka, attended the ceremonies and sent this publication to the author.

72. Registered letter from Edward Tomasik of Cudahy, Wisconsin to Charles Rozmarek, February 16, 1965, returned unopened to sender.

73. Indeed, the sum and substance of PAC activities on the domestic front up till then consisted largely of its ceremonial participation on the 350th anniversary, in 1958, of the arrival of the first Poles to America (at the Jamestown colony in Virginia), and its involvement in Polonia's celebration of Poland's thousandth anniversary (or Millennium) as a European state and Christian nation. Even its backing of Federal legislation to liberalize immigration into this country came only in response to a proposal originating in the White House, although the PAC did what it could to promote the bill, which became law in 1965.

74. For the story of Mazewski's 1967 bruising victory and Rozmarek's own bitter comments upon his loss, see Pienkos, *PNA,* pp. 178-185. The following year's Polish American Congress convention in Cleveland was anti-climactic in that Mazewski was the delegates' near-consensus choice to assume command. Rozmarek refused to bow out gracefully and a long debate centered on whether he would be permitted to deliver his report to the delegates summarizing his activities over the previous four years. Instead, a motion was approved to provide everyone with a printed text of his speech. *Protokol Siodmej Krajowej Konwencyi KPA,* 1968, pp. 19-20, 114-140. In September 1969, when the PAC held its twenty-fifth anniversary banquet in Washington, D.C. an affair attended by more than seven hundred guests, Rozmarek declined to attend.

75. Summary of speech by A. A. Mazewski in the *Polish American Congress Newsletter,* volume 10, number 3 (September 15, 1969).

76. For this outline of Rozmarek's achievements as President of the Polish American Congress I am indebted to Przyluski and Pucinski, who spoke about Rozmarek at ceremonies in Chicago on June 28, 1987 on the ninetieth anniversary of his birth.

For a more extensive summation see also *Prace Kongresu Polonii Amerykanskiej w okresie 24-ch lat istnienia: Krotki zarys dzialalnosci* (The work of the PAC during the period of its past 24 years of activity. Chicago: Polish American Congress, 1968), pp. 25. Information on Rozmarek's leadership is in the Chicago office of the Polish American Congress.

77. *Sprawozdanie Prezesa Kongresu Polonii Amerykanskiej na szosta krajowa konwencje* (Report of the President of the Polish American Congress at its sixth national convention in Chicago, September 18-20, 1964. Chicago, 1964, pp. 49-50. Regarding the *Der Speigel* incident, see Alex Dragnich and Jorgen Rasmussen, *Major European Governments* (Homewood, Ill.: Dorsey, 1978), pp. 321-322.

78. *Ibid., Polish American Congress Newsletter,* April 1, 1970, p. 3.

79. *Sprawozdanie Prezesa Karola Rozmarka na Siodmy Zjazd Rady Naczelnej Kongresu Polonii Amerykanskiej, 29 lipca, 1966 w Washington, D.C.* (President Charles Rozmarek's report to the seventh meeting of the PAC Supreme Council in Washington, July 29, 1966); Rozmarek letter to President Johnson, December 13, 1965 and reply of January 11, 1966 from Assistant Secretary of State James Greenfield, pp. 5-8.

80. For a recent analysis of the Plan, see David Stefancic, "The Rapacki Plan: A Case Study of European Diplomacy," *East European Quarterly,* 21, number 4 (Winter, 1987), 401-412. U.S. opposition to the plan was based primarily on Washington's heavy reliance upon West Germany as its chief N.A.T.O. partner on the European continent and its concerns that a "nuclear-free" West Germany would seriously undermine the viability of the Atlantic Alliance.

81. On December 7, 1970, the German-Polish Treaty was signed after having been approved by the U.S., Britain and France. The document affirmed that the Odra-Nysa boundary "shall constitute the western state frontier of the People's Republic of Poland" and further asserted the "inviolability of the existing frontiers." (A German-Soviet treaty had already been signed in August). For the October 13, 1970 PAC Memorandum see *Sprawozdanie prezesa Kongresu Polonii Amerykanskiej na dziewiata krajowa konwencje* (Report of the President of the Polish American Congress at its ninth national convention in Detroit, October 6-8, 1972. Chicago, 1972, pp. 7-8. Moskal's letter is in the *Report of the President of the Polish American Congress from November 18, 1989 to June 27, 1990,* mimeographed.

FOOTNOTES to Chapter V

1. For information on the commissions, see Donald Pienkos, "The Polish American Congress--An Appraisal," *Polish American Studies*, 36, number 2 (Autumn, 1979), 27; *Polish American Congress Newsletter* (Chicago, Illinois), issues of May 1, 1969 and April, 1977.

2. The literature on the subject is voluminous. Significant publications include Nathan Glazer and Daniel Patrick Moynihan, *Beyond the Melting Pot* (Cambridge, Massachusetts: M.I.T. Press, 1963); Andrew M. Greeley, *Why Can't They Be Like Us? America's White Ethnics* (New York: Dutton, 1971); and Michael Novak, *The Rise of the Unmeltable Ethnics: Politics and Culture in the Seventies* (New York: MacMillan, 1971). For a provocative analysis of the ethnic revival in reaction to the social and political upheavals of the 1960s, see the introductory chapter of A.A. Said, ed., *Ethnicity and U.S. Foreign Policy* (New York: Praeger, 1977). Useful discussions focusing upon Polish Americans include John Bukowczyk, *And My Children Did Not Know Me: A History of the Polish Americans*, pp. 105-146; Piotr Taras, Angela T. Pienkos, Thaddeus Radzialowski, "Paul Wrobel's *Our Way* -- Three Views," *Polish American Studies*, 37, number 1 (Spring, 1980), 32-51 and Alfred F. Bochenek, ed., *American Polonia: The Cultural Issues* (Detroit: American Council of Polish Cultural Clubs, 1981).

3. Pienkos, "The Polish American Congress," 20.

4. Aloysius A. Mazewski, Speech on the thirtieth anniversary of the founding of the Polish American Congress, Buffalo, New York, November 2, 1974.

5. For the most part their demise was associated with their voluntary character, which presented many difficulties in realizing their aims in an American environment where distance made travel and communication both difficult and expensive. Financial support for their activities was always an obstacle but so also was the shortage of able workers who could help put the commissions' agendas into effect. Another explanation for the

decline of the domestic commissions involved the upsurge in PAC attention to Poland after 1976 and its subsequent commitment of nearly all its resources to that cause throughout the 1980s. Pienkos, "Polish American Congress," *ibid.*

One other domestic commission, focusing upon the promotion of schools training children in the Polish language and culture, has experienced a rebirth in its activities in the 1980s and early 1990s. A third convention of Polish school teachers was held in May 1991 in Washington, D.C. and was very well attended.

6. Among them were Mitchell Kobelinski of Chicago, Leonard Walentynowicz of Buffalo, Mitchell Kafarski of Detroit, Blair Kolasa, Floyd Placzek, General Edward Rowny, former Postmaster General John A. Gronouski, former U.S. Congressman Edward Derwinski of Illinois, and Stanley Glod of Washington, D.C. Pienkos, *PNA,* pp. 292-293.

The issue of greater Polish American representation through U.S. government appointments was a Mazewski concern from the start. Thus, in his speech in Washington, D.C. on the 25th anniversary of the founding of the Polish American Congress, Mazewski asserted:

> I would be lacking in candor if I did not touch upon the current political realities... We have men and women eminently successful in all walks of life, people experienced in serving the public who occupy positions of trust and responsibility. However, we have not received proper recognition in politics on all levels... The time has come to remind... White House functionaries that ours is a pluralist society, deriving its strength and unity from the...mosaic of ethnic backgrounds that contributed so much to the richness, stamina and beauty of the American way of life... Neglecting them...could in time result in the corrosion of the political cohesiveness of our land... *Polish American Congress Newsletter,* September 15, 1969.

7. See Aloysius Mazewski, Recommendations of the Polish American Congress to the Democratic Party Platform Committee, *Polish American Congress Newsletter,* July 1976. Several

other 1970s PAC efforts in the area of discrimination might be noted. One involved PAC Illinois Division co-sponsorship (with the Joint Civic Committee of Italian Americans of Chicago) of research work on the presence of ethnics in the executive leaderships of major Chicago-based corporations. The study, undertaken by Dr. Russell Barta of Mundelein College, found that only one percent of all top officers in 106 major corporations appeared to be Polish, while 6.9 percent of the metropolitan area population was of Polish birth or parentage. Even this research did not take into account the large population of third and fourth generation Polish Americans, which would have shown the problem of "underrepresentation" to be even greater. A similar study conducted in Detroit yielded the same results. See *Polish American Congress Newsletter,* December 1973 and July 1976.

A major PAC success in winning recognition for Polonia's concerns was achieved in league with other ethnic organizations. It involved persuading the U.S. Census Bureau to perform a more comprehensive enumeration of the total number of ethnic Americans in the 1980 Census. Historically, only the foreign born and their offspring were counted as members of particular nationality groups in the U.S., a practice that ignored individuals of ethnic ancestry who continued to identify with their forefathers' heritage. With U.S. Congressional support, changes in the Census were made to survey large numbers of individuals for the first time about their ethnic identification. The results showed some 8.2 million Polish Americans, still an undercount in the opinion of PAC activists but a much higher figure than earlier 1970s estimates of 4.1 to 5.1 million. Lopata, *Polish Americans,* pp. 88-90; "Barbara Mikulski and Dan Rostenkowski urge Better Census," *Polish American Congress Newsletter,* August 1978.

For an enlightening study based upon the 1980 Census data which investigated the actual economic, occupational and educational attainments of Polish Americans and other white ethnics in a comprehensive fashion, see the Report of the United States Commission on Civil Rights, *The Economic Status of Americans of Southern and Eastern European Ancestry* (Washington, D.C.: Clearinghouse Publication 89, 1986).

8. Leonard F. Walentynowicz, *Reports to the President and National Council of Directors of the Polish American Congress, 1977-1981; Brief of the Polish American Congress, the National Advocates Society and The National Medical and Dental Association as Amici Curiae in the Supreme Court of the United States in The Regents of The University of California v. Allen Bakke,* June 7, 1977; and *Brief of the Polish American Congress and the National Advocates Society as Amici Curiae in the Supreme Court of the United States in the United Steelworkers of America, AFL-CIO-CLC v. Brian F. Weber, et. al.,* February 24, 1979.

9. That ethnic defamation was a concern through the 1970s is clear from the frequent appearance of articles on the subject in the *Polish American Congress Newsletter* and other Polonia newspapers. Thus pieces published in the July 20, 1970, December 1972, December 1973, July 1976, and February 1979 issues of the PAC periodical carried titles such as "Anti-Defamation Off to a Good Start," "A Call to Action: A Word from the National Anti-Defamation Commission Chairman" (then Chicago attorney Thaddeus Kowalski), "Anti-Defamation Commission Appeals FCC Decision" (in ruling against the PAC contention that Polish jokes on television were slanderous), "Buffalo Polonia Fights 'Polish Jokes'" and "Ethnic Defamation High on List of Michigan PAC Priorities."

10. Significant recent attempts to tell this story include Richard C. Lukas, *Forgotten Holocaust: The Poles under German Occupation, 1939-1944* (Lexington: University of Kentucky Press, 1986) and Lukas, editor, *Out of the Inferno: Poles Remember the Holocaust* (Lexington: University of Kentucky Press, 1989); and Bohdan Wytwycky, *The Other Holocaust: Many Circles of Hell* (Washington, D.C.: Novak Report Research project, 1980). The standard study of the tragedy is by Raul Hilberg, *The Destruction of the European Jews* (Chicago: Quadrangle Books, 1961).

11. Wiktor Weintrob, "Tolerance and Intolerance in Old Poland," *Canadian Slavic Papers,* 13 (Spring, 1971); J. Tazbir, *A State Without Stakes* (New York: Kosciuszko Foundation,

1974); Bernard Weinryb, *The Jews of Poland: A Social and Economic History of the Jewish Community in Poland from 1100 to 1800* (Philadelphia: Jewish Publication Society of America, 1973); Norman Davies, *God's Playground: A History of Poland,* 2 volumes (New York: Columbia University Press, 1982).

12. The first of these programs, which had the character of "docudramas"--fictional stories based upon historic events but purporting to present those events in an accurate manner--was "QB Seven," shown for the first time in 1972. In 1979 a ten part film entitled "The Holocaust" was released, followed in the 1980s by several other films made especially for television and reaching enormous audiences. Perhaps the most widely discussed program was "Shoah," made originally as a nine hour long theatrical film but shown repeatedly in shorter segments over the Public Broadcasting System beginning in 1987. Over the same period of time, not a single dramatization of the Polish gentile experience in World War II was produced in the West.

It may well be that given these programs' character, the public's understanding of Poland's actual fate in the Second World War has been distorted. Clearly, the programs in question have presented the perspective that Jews were the sole victims of Nazi genocide, a view that ignores the tragedy that befell millions of non-Jews under German occupation.

A thoughtful PAC response to questions raised in the airing of "Shoah" was its 24 page publication, *Polish Americans Reflect on 'Shoah'* (Chicago: Polish American Congress, 1986). On the silence of Jewish scholars on the Poles' fate in World War II see the letter from representatives of the Polish-Jewish Forum of Milwaukee, Wisconsin to the Editors of the American Jewish Committee magazine, *Commentary,* April 1988.

Earlier PAC reactions published in its *Newsletter* include "'Traditional Polish AntiSemitism'--QB Seven, ABC-TV" (September 1972) and "'Holocaust'--Misrepresentations of Historical Facts" (August 1978). An early and serious effort to analyze the problem is that of Kazimierz Lukomski. "Polish-Jewish Relations--One Sided Recriminations perpetuate Prejudice," *Polish American Congress Newsletter,* February 1979.

13. For the rationale and aims of the Ethnic Heritage Studies Act, see the articles by Schweiker and Pucinski in Michael Wenk, S.M. Tomasi and Geno Baroni, editors, *Pieces of a Dream: The Ethnic Worker's Crisis with America* (New York: Center for Migration Studies, 1972), pp. 63-68.

14. These include: Kazimierz Iranek-Osmecki, *He Who Saves One Life, Polish Efforts on Behalf of Jews in World War II* (1970); Joseph Wiewiora's edited work, *Jamestown: Pioneers from Poland* (1976); James Pula's biographical study, *For Liberty and Justice: The Life and Times of Wladimir Krzyzanowski* (1978); Donald Pienkos, *The Polish American Congress: An Appraisal* (1979); and Daniel Buczek, *et. al., Saint Stanislaw Bishop of Krakow* (1979).

More recent efforts in the same vein have been the Congress' support of the present volume and its decision, in 1988, to promote the sale of some 5,000 copies of the new translation of Henryk Sienkiewicz's "Trilogy" performed by W.S. Kuniczak and published by the Copernicus Society of America in cooperation with Hippocrene Books of New York. The first volume in the trilogy, *With Fire and Sword*, was scheduled to appear in early 1991. *Zgoda*, September 1 and November 15, 1990.

An early benefactor of the PAC Charitable Foundation was Stanley O'Brakta of Florida, who contributed $25,000 in 1975 to help underwrite its activities.

Another initiative of the PAC and many of its state divisions occurred in 1973 to commemorate the five hundredth anniversary of the birth of the astronomer Nicholas Copernicus (Mikolaj Kopernik, 1473-1543). Stressing Copernicus' Polishness, the celebrations also underscored his scientific achievements as the theorist of the heliocentric universe and "father of the space age." (A major force in the Copernican year commemoration was Edward Piszek, then the owner of Mrs. Paul's Kitchens, Inc. and earlier the chief sponsor of the "Project Pole" ethnic pride campaign centered at Saint Mary's College in Orchard Lake, Michigan in the early 1970s, Piszek was later a prime mover in the above-noted Sienkiewicz "Trilogy" project.)

In 1984 the Polish American Congress won the White House's approval to have August identified as "Polish American Heritage Month" throughout the country. Under the chairmanship of Michael Blichasz of Philadelphia, President of the PAC's Eastern Pennsylvania division, Polish American Heritage Month (since moved to October) has become an annual opportunity for Polonia organizations to promote educational and cultural programs designed primarily for school children and aimed at enlightening them about the Poles' contributions to the world.

In recent years, the PAC has also played a major role in mobilizing Polish Americans in support of numerous other worthy projects, including the fund raising activities to establish a Pilgrims' hostel in Rome to honor Pope John Paul II, a drive to help renovate the Statue of Liberty in 1986, and yet another effort to establish an immigration museum at Ellis Island in New York harbor. The hostel was dedicated for the benefit of visitors from East Central Europe in 1981 with American Polonia contributing more than $300,000 for the project under the chairmanship of Helen Zielinski, President of the Polish Women's Alliance and a Vice President of the PAC. Zielinski also headed the Statue of Liberty campaign to a successful conclusion. In 1989, her successor, Helen Wojcik, chaired the Ellis Island museum drive and with excellent results once again. Thus at the time of the museum's opening in September 1990, nearly $600,000 in donations had come from the Polish American Congress and its member organizations.

15. *Minutes of the Conference of Intellectuals of Polish Ancestry held under the auspices of the Polish American Congress at the Alliance College, Cambridge Springs, Pennsylvania, June 27-28, 1969.* Following the conference a nine-member "Advisory Council to the President of the PAC on Educational and Cultural Matters" was created and chaired by the Very Rev. Walter Ziemba, Rector of Saint Mary's College and the Polish Seminary in Orchard Lake, Michigan. The Council did hold a couple of meetings but soon became inactive. Perhaps the most important question raised by Mazewski at the conference dealt with the issue of reversing what he described as "the incipient signs of disassociation of Americans of Polish ancestry from participation in the activities of Polonia organizations," a concern that remains central to the present time. Participants at the June 8, 1986 meeting took up the same general question, and agreed

"that the effective dissemination of knowledge about the Polish heritage--the history and contemporary condition of Poland, its language and literature, and the Polish American experience-- is essential for Polonia's continuing vitality." *Zgoda*, August 1, 1986. That far more needs to be done in building practical and significant linkages between Polonia and the scholars specializing in Polish studies goes without saying. For two recent expressions of such concern, note the "Report of the Pre-Convention Alliance College Committee" in *The official Minutes of Fortieth Convention of the Polish National Alliance, September 13-17, 1987 in Chicago, Illinois* (Chicago: Alliance Printers and Publishers, 1987), pp. 166-181, especially pp. 173-178; and the remarks of Donald Pienkos at the panel discussion on the Polish American Congress held at the special conference of Polish National Alliance officers and leaders, January 12, 1989, Anaheim, California. See also: Polish American Congress Charitable Foundation, *A Proposal to Establish the United Polish American Community Endowment for the Humanities. A Proposal Narrative* (Chicago, 1988).

16. Polish American Congress Charitable Foundation, *A Culture at the Crossroads: Humanities Perspectives on the Polish and the Polish American Heritage. An Application Narrative to the National Endowment for the Humanities for the Period between October 1, 1988 and September 30, 1991.* Plonski served as Project Director in this proposal as he had in earlier grants funded by NEH, beginning in 1982.

17. PAC interest in promoting knowledge of Poland's history and culture extended to its financial support of a nine part documentary television series produced by a coalition of British, West German and American networks. The series, "The Struggles for Poland," was shown throughout the U.S. by Public Broadcasting System stations in the Summer of 1988 and met with modestly favorable reviews. Another PAC effort involved its support of a short film on the life of Casimir Pulaski aimed at school children, in response to the establishment of commemorative days honoring his birth on March 4 in several states, including Illinois, Wisconsin, and New York. That effort in the state legislatures was itself spearheaded by PAC activists.

For reactions in Polonia to "The Struggles for Poland," see the Polish National Alliance bi-weekly newspaper, *Zgoda,* for the months of September and October, 1988.

18. Pienkos, *PNA,* pp. 282-283. An early effort to analyze the problems facing Jews and Poles in America was that of Joseph Lichten, a participant in the first dialogs. His views were later published under the title "Polish Americans and American Jews: Some Issues which Unite and Divide," *Polish Review,* 18, number 4 (1973), 52-62.

The first PAC committee to take up Polish-Jewish relations was chaired by Joseph Bialasiewicz, then the Editor of the *Dziennik Chicagoski* (Polish Daily News of Chicago). Early participants in this effort included Jan Krawiec, Editor of the *Dziennik Zwiazkowy* newspaper of Chicago, Stanley Krajewski, Editor of Detroit's *Dziennik Polski* newspaper, Professor Stanislaw Piwowarski of Chicago's Loyola University and Dr. Eugene Kusielewicz of Saint John's University in New York and then Vice President of the Kosciuszko Foundation.

For a description of the activities of the Polish American/Jewish American Task Force, see Nancy Knop, "Dialog Enters 10th Year," *New Horizon* magazine (New York), July 1987.

Unfortunately, the rather tentative attempts on the part of Poles and Jews and their organizations to build understanding have often been overshadowed by the persistence of a powerful strain of militant nationalism within the American Jewish community. Central to this nationalism is an over-riding concern for the security of the state of Israel, coupled with a tendency to view the Holocaust as an exclusively Jewish tragedy. Among individuals holding such views, the notion of entering into dialogs with groups like the Poles has held little or no appeal and indeed may have served to undermine interest in such activities among more moderate, coalition-oriented, members of the community. Over the years Poles have come in for quite a bit of criticism due to their supposed anti-semitic outlook and their alleged failures to have made greater sacrifices on behalf of Jews in Poland during the World War II Nazi occupation of the country. Most recently, in the Summer of 1989, this bitterness exploded into vitriolic condemnations of "Polish anti-semitism" in connection with a widely reported controversy over the establishment of a convent of cloistered Polish Carmelite sisters outside the Auschwitz death camp. Indeed, when the Primate of the Polish Church, Jozef Cardinal Glemp, chose to express himself in support of the sisters' purpose of devoting their lives to praying for the victims of Auschwitz, he was widely accused of making several anti-semitic statements in the U.S. press (which failed, however, to print his offending speech in full). The resulting uproar compelled him to cancel a long awaited pastoral visit to the Polonia of the United States. Allegations about anti-semitic propaganda in the 1990 Polish presidential election campaign also received considerable coverage in the American press, as if this was one of the overriding issues before the voters, when it clearly was not.

A separate but related matter has involved the minimal involvement of Polish Americans in the establishment of the U.S. Holocaust Memorial Museum in Washington, D.C. Approved in 1980, the work on this project has been spearheaded by a U.S. Holocaust Memorial Council of 61 prominent individuals. However, into 1990, only two Polish Americans had been invited to serve in its ranks, Mazewski and the Rev. John Pawlikowski, a member of the faculty of the Catholic Theological Union in Chicago. Responsible for raising funds to help build and design the Museum and to encourage the planning of Holocaust observances around the country, the Council has not, unfortunately, shown a particular concern for commemorating the non-Jewish victims of Nazism. During his years on the Council Mazewski was an isolated critic of this policy; following his death his place on the Council was not filled by another Polish American. Under Mazewski's successor, Edward Moskal, the PAC renewed its commitment to the Polish-Jewish dialog, and an editorial appearing in the Polish language daily newspaper of the Polish National Alliance underscores this. See "Laczy nas bardzo wiele" (Very Many Things Draw Us Together), *Dziennik Zwiazkowy* (Chicago), January 27-28, 1989.

19. Mazewski was not without his critics, none of whom proved especially successful, however, in their opposition to him or his policies. Particularly sharp in their printed comments

were Anthony Czelen of Pennsylvania, who edited a modest magazine of opinion in the 1970s and early 1980s, the *Polish American Patriot,* and Chester Grabowski, a New Jersey-based publisher of an English language Polonia newspaper, the *Post Eagle.* Other perennial critics included Edward Tomasik of Wisconsin and Eugene Kusielewicz, who served as President of the Kosciusko Foundation from 1970 to 1981.

Mazewski's most severe opponents within the Polish emigration were the members of an organization called *Pomost* (the Bridge), which came into existence after 1980. Most of the leaders of this quite active group were rather young and had settled in the United States in the 1970s and early 1980s; they sharply criticized Mazewski's lobbying activities in Washington for failing to adopt a militant enough stance against the Jaruzelski regime. For several years *Pomost* published its own newsletter and also held editorial control of *Gwiazda Polarna,* a Polonia weekly published in Stevens Point, Wisconsin, but having a nationwide readership.

20. Raymond L. Garthoff, *Detente and Confrontation: American-Soviet Relations from Nixon to Reagan* (Washington, D.C.: Brookings Institution, 1985), *passim.*

21. Wandycz, *The United States and Poland,* pp. 405-406; and William G. Hyland, *Mortal Rivals: Superpower Relations From Nixon to Reagan* (New York: Random House, 1987), pp. 174-182. Ford's comments concerning American support of the Helsinki Treaty, his speech to the PAC and his remarks in the Presidential debate are in the Appendix.

22. Gomulka (1905-1982) had initially served as the First Secretary of the Polish Workers, later Polish United Workers Party between 1943 and 1948 and was a key figure in the establishment of the Communists' dictatorship at the close of World War II. His removal from his post at Stalin's orders followed by imprisonment had been due to the views Gomulka tenaciously clung to, which made him a "deviationist" in the judgment of the Soviet despot.

Following Stalin's death in 1953, his successor Nikita Khrushchev shocked the world by denouncing many of his policies at the Soviet Communist Party's 20th Congress in February 1956. Khrushchev's attack caused tremors throughout Soviet-dominated Eastern Europe and had particularly unsettling consequences in Hungary and Poland. In Hungary, Communist rule nearly ended in the wake of a popular revolution and was saved only by Soviet military intervention. In Poland, serious economic problems and growing resentment against the repressive policies of the regime led to a massive workers demonstration in Poznan for "bread and freedom." Not long afterward, the Stalinist regime was replaced and Gomulka returned to power as Party First Secretary in October.

After winning Moscow's grudging acceptance of his new regime, Gomulka moved quickly to put into place the very program which had landed him in prison, his "Polish road to socialism." Arguing that Polish societal conditions were different in many respects from those found in Soviet Russia, he permitted the collapse of the unpopular collectivization campaign in the countryside in favor of greater government support of private land ownership and individual family farms. Gomulka also called a halt to the fruitless war against the Roman Catholic Church in return for its general endorsement of his regime.

Nevertheless, Gomulka on other matters was an orthodox communist, deeply loyal to the Soviet Union and committed to maintaining his party's firm control over every aspect of Poland's national life. In most economic matters he was a traditionalist, a believer in centralized state planning and continued austerity in consumer spending. By the mid 1960s these policies were beginning to meet with widespread discontent. Poland's rate of economic growth was slowing down instead of continuing to rise as Gomulka's advisers had forecast; many Poles loudly questioned how long they would have to wait to experience the good life promised for so long under socialism but enjoyed, not in Poland, but in the capitalist societies of Western Europe.

Characterizations of Gomulka are found in Zbigniew K. Brzezinski, *The Soviet Bloc: Unity and Conflict,* revised and enlarged edition (Cambridge, Mass.: Harvard University Press, 1971), chapters 2, 3, 11, and 14; M. K. Dziewanowski, "The Communist Party of Poland," in Stephen Fischer-Galati, ed., *The Communist Parties of Eastern Europe* (New York: Colum-

bia University Press, 1979), pp. 245-280; Nicholas Bethell, *Gomulka, His Poland and His Communism* (New York: Holt, Rinehart and Winston, 1969); and Jan T. Gross, "Poland: Society and the State," in M. M. Drachkovitch, ed., *East Central Europe: Yesterday, Today, Tomorrow* (Stanford, California: Hoover Institution Press, 1982), pp. 303-307.

23. Dziewanowski gives a generally favorable review of Gierek's program in his *Poland in the Twentieth Century* and in the revised edition of his *Communist Party of Poland* (1976). A discussion of the reasons for its failure is in J. F. Browne, *Eastern Europe and Communist Rule* (Durham, North Carolina and London: Duke University Press, 1988), pp. 158-182. See also Timothy Garton Ash, *The Polish Revolution: Solidarity* (New York: Vintage Press, 1985), pp. 12-34; Adam Bromke, *Poland: The Last Decade* (Oakville, Canada: Mosaic Press, 1981), pp. 63-112, and *passim;* and Gross, "Poland," pp. 307-325.

24. Gomulka's father had lived unhappily for a time in Detroit as an emigrant "after bread" before returning to the Krosno oil fields prior to World War I. Gomulka, who was attracted to Communism early in life, rarely had anything good to say about America. For him, an almost monastic membership in the Party was more attractive. In contrast, Gierek had spent many years before World War II in Belgium working as a coal miner. His orientation to the Polish emigration was more positive, as was his commitment to a more generous policy regarding economic consumption.

25. In this period, powerful tensions became visible within the PAC over its continued capacity to define its aims on Poland's behalf in the face of U.S. *Detente* with Soviet Russia. Mazewski complained of the problem in his thirtieth anniversary speech in 1974, when he took some pains to restate the historic purposes of the Congress.

In these remarks, Mazewski singled out two "small groups" in the Polish American community for criticism, the "lunatic fringe" on the right wing of the political spectrum and the "extremists" of the left. The former Mazewski condemned for their frequently vociferous attacks upon fellow Polish Americans who favored improved cultural and economic exchanges with Poland, travelled to Poland for personal, family or professional reasons, and were interested in building business ties in the old country. Such activities, Mazewski asserted, were justifiable and did not necessarily merit criticism. As for the "extremists of the left," such unnamed individuals were criticized for their denial of the Congress' right to make judgments about individual contacts with the old homeland and the PAC's continued opposition to the Polish regime. Seeking to steer the PAC on a middle course, Mazewski argued for a policy expressing support of the Poles' aspirations and the legitimacy of engaging in businesslike contacts with Polish authorities which might improve conditions in the ancestral homeland.

The problem of PAC orientations toward contact with Poland had long troubled the organization. Thus, fears that the Congress along with other Polish organizations might be infiltrated by communist sympathizers of the Stalinist regime in Warsaw led the PAC to require as early as its 1952 convention that all delegates to the conclave be American citizens. That year the delegates approved new language defining the aims of the PAC to include "wholehearted support (of) the Government of the United States in its efforts to realize a just peace on the basis of the Atlantic Charter."

In 1960, and faced with the entry of thousands of new immigrants from Poland following the coming to power of the Gomulka regime, the PAC at its fifth quadrennial convention approved additional language defining as its aims "to fight the infiltration of communism, nazism and other subversive ideologies and organizations."

Such attitudes, so reflective of "cold war" fears of Soviet communism and the extremist ideas of "McCarthyism" during the 1950s possessed a degree of plausibility. Clearly, the Polish government's interests in bettering its image in America were hardly served by the existence of a PAC in shrill opposition to its very existence.

On the other hand, fear of communist subversion in America sometimes produced hostility toward some newcomers from Poland, thus making their adaptation to life in the United States all the more difficult. By discouraging individual Polish Americans from reestablishing family ties with loved ones in Poland, the PAC may have cost itself some credibility within Polonia, especially among the thousands of apolitical members of the ethnic community who ignored its injunctions and travelled to Poland, in the process providing their relatives with much financial assistance and moral comfort.

Indicative of the Congress' continuing concerns on the issue even into the late 1980s was its publication of a widely distributed pamphlet, "Relations of Polish Americans with the Communist Regime in Poland" (1988).

Among the "domestic" issues on the organization's agenda, one that was satisfactorally resolved concerned American medical aid to Polish veterans of the two World Wars who had fought for the Allied cause and were residing in the United States. Federal legislation initiated by Representative Frank Annunzio of Illinois was approved to provide such benefits and in October 1976 President Ford signed the Polish Veterans Assistance Act into law. Mazewski was a prominent guest at the White House signing ceremonies.

26. On the Constitution debate see Jacques Rupnik, "Dissent in Poland, 1968--1978: The End of Revisionism and the Rebirth of Civil Society," in Rudolf L. Tokes, editor, *Opposition in Eastern Europe* (Baltimore and London: The Johns Hopkins Press, 1979), pp. 78-80; and the *Polish Review,* 21, number 1-2 (1976), 41-58.

27. For a review of the rise of *KOR* and other Polish opposition groups see Rupnik, *ibid.,* pp. 60-112; Alexander J. Matejko, "The Structural Roots of Polish Opposition," *Polish Review,* 27, number 1-2 (1982), 111-140; and Ash, *The Polish Revolution.*

A significant political statement is the publication by Leszek Moczulski, founder of *KPN,* of *Rewolucja bez rewolucji* (Revolution without a Revolution. Warsaw: Polish Publishers, 1979, reprinted in the United States in 1986 by the Polish American Congress). The Confederation of Independent Poland was consciously organized as a political opposition party. Moczulski travelled throughout the United States to promote its aims in 1987 following his release from prison for his activities. During his tour, which was sponsored by the PAC, he repeatedly expressed Poland's recognition of Polonia's assistance to the ancestral homeland and his own belief in the Polish nation's eventual victory over its oppressors. "I see independence" was his message to America.

Information about the intellectual and political opposition is also a major contribution of the quarterly publication, *Studium Papers*. This magazine was established in 1976 by Dr. Andrzej Ehrenkreutz; its present editor is Marian J. Krzyzowski (who wrote under the pseudonym of Marek Nowak until 1990). *Studium Papers* is published by the North American Study Center for Polish Affairs, an affiliate of the PAC.

28. Ulam, *Dangerous Relations,* pp. 141-144 and *passim;* and Tokes, *Opposition in Eastern Europe, passim.* Ash goes so far as to conclude, "It is arguable that without *Detente* there would have been no Solidarity." *The Polish Revolution,* p. 322.

29. See the articles in the special issue of the *Polish Review,* 24, number 2 (1979), particularly that of Andrej Biernacki, and John Paul's Apostolic Letter on the occasion of the nine hundredth anniversary of the death of Saint Stanislas Bishop and Martyr and patron of Poland. See also *The Pope In Poland* (Munich: Radio Free Europe Research, 1979), for extensive quotations from the Pope's addresses during his nine day visit.

30. For detailed and dispassionate descriptions of Solidarity's story, see Ash, *The Polish Revolution;* Nicholas G. Andrews, *Poland 1980-1981: Solidarity Versus The Party* (Washington, D.C.: National Defense University Press, 1985); and Neal Ascherson, *The Polish August: The Self-Limiting Revolution* (London: Allen Lane, 1981). Ascherson's work includes Solidarity's 21 points agreed to on August 31. Lech Walesa's own account appears in his *A Way of Hope* (New York: Holt, 1987). These are only a very few of the extraordinary number of studies of Solidarity's rise and fall to appear in the English language. One piece of social science scholarship using Polish public opinion data to analyze the period is by David Mason, *Public Opinion and Political Change in Poland, 1980-*

1982 (Cambridge and London: Cambridge University Press, 1985).

31. Andrews, pp. 179-188.

32. For the disturbing story of the Kuklinski affair, one should read the interview in the Polish emigre journal published in Paris, *Kultura*, which appeared in April 1987. (The same interview was excerpted and reprinted in English in the American foreign affairs magazine, *Orbis*, in January 1988 under the title, "Special Report: Poland in Crisis, 1980-1981," 7-31). Colonel Ryszard Kuklinski was a veteran member of the Polish security apparatus who had provided the U.S. Central Intelligence Agency with secret information on Warsaw Pact activities from the early 1970s. During the Polish crisis, Kuklinski was present at high level meetings where discussions about the imposition of martial law occurred as early as mid August 1980, some two weeks before the historic settlement of the Gdansk and Baltic seacoast strikes. He reported that a draft of the martial law plan was already in Jaruzelski's hands on October 22, 1980. Plans to implement martial law were further developed in February 1981, at the same time that Jaruzelski, by then the newly chosen Prime Minister, had called publicly for a ninety day moratorium on strikes to help stabilize Poland's worsening economic situation. Kuklinski also stated that Jaruzelski seriously considered adopting the martial law solution in June 1981 and that the Polish authorities made a fairly final decision to dissolve the Solidarity trade union in mid September 1981, in response to the union's call for Solidarity-like organizations in other Communist ruled East European countries and the Soviet Union. This decision was well underway in early November when Kuklinski, by then in fear of exposure for his actions fled the country.

Still, when martial law was imposed on December 12-13, it came as a general surprise, since concern in the United States had focused upon the possibility of a Soviet invasion, not a Polish military crackdown on its own people. Thus, Kuklinski's revelations caused some understandable tensions between the Polish American Congress and the Reagan administration, which had not informed Solidarity of the impending move. This left the trade union unprepared and its leaders ready targets for capture and imprisonment. This failure was itself later played up by the Polish government when Kuklinski's revelations were made public.

While questions exist regarding the Reagan administration's failure to inform the Solidarity leadership of Jaruzelski's plans, a few points can be made about Kuklinski's information and its impact. First, the main thrust of Kuklinski's own testimony concerned the threat of an imminent Soviet invasion of Poland, an action comparable to the U.S.S.R.'s occupation of Czechoslovakia in August 1968 for which the West had been totally unprepared. In this regard, Kuklinski's communications as to Soviet actions planned against Poland in both early December 1980 and April 1981 apparently achieved their purpose: in both cases the United States, first under the outgoing Carter and later under the new Reagan administration, pressured the Soviets to reconsider their plans and to let the Poles settle their own problems.

In Kuklinski's judgment, both Jaruzelski and then Party leader Kania failed to use the opportunities available to them in 1980 and 1981 to unite the country behind a program of genuine reform which might have bridged the chasm between the PUWP and Solidarity. Instead, Jaruzelski opted to destroy Solidarity to satisfy Moscow. The Polish regime's perspective in serving the Soviet Union rather than defending Polish interests is well illustrated by the comment addressed to Jaruzelski by a colleague on the eve of martial law, "History will never forgive us if they (the Soviets) do the job for us."

Second and notwithstanding the Polish regime's denunciations of Washington for its alleged failure to alert Solidarity of martial law, Kuklinski's revelations provide distressing evidence of Warsaw's real, but secretly held, position toward the new independent trade union federation--even as its own representatives were signing their names to the Gdansk agreement guaranteeing its right to operate. The decision to impose martial law in December 1981 thus had little to do with official claims at the time that it was acting to prevent an impending civil war for which Solidarity "hotheads" were responsible. In fact, frustrated leaders of the union simply provided the provocative language used by Jaruzelski to justify his move.

33. Pienkos, *PNA,* pp. 287-288. Developments inside Poland also generated growing interest within the Polish American Congress in building linkages between American Polonia and the Polish emigrant communities elsewhere throughout the free world. Thus, in 1975 the first international gathering of Polonia representatives was held in Washington, D.C. to be followed in 1978 by a larger international congress, "Polonia Tomorrow" which was held in Toronto, Canada. For detailed information on the Toronto meeting, see *Polish American Congress Newsletter,* especially its March and August 1978 issues.

In the mid-1980s annual meetings of world Polonia became the rule, with the first such conference of the "Coordinating Council of the Free World Polonia" taking place in September, 1986 in Washington, D.C. This meeting brought together delegates from Great Britain, Canada, France, Australia and the United States in an event hosted by Mazewski and the Polish American Congress. In October 1987, a similar meeting was held in Paris, France at which eleven Polonia communities were represented--those of Great Britain, France, Austria, West Germany, Switzerland, Belgium, Italy, Denmark, Canada, Australia and the United States. Representing the U.S. delegation was President Mazewski, accompanied by PAC Vice Presidents Helen Zielinski and Casimir Lukomski, PAC Treasurer Edward Dykla and Kazimierz Rasiej, Deputy Commander of the Polish Army Veterans Association. At these meetings, serious discussions focused upon ways in which international Polonia might better aid Poland both politically and on a charitable basis, and how it might better enlighten the democracies on the plight of the more than 400,000 Polish refugees who had left their homeland due to the trying conditions prevailing there.

Yet another concern, frequently discussed within the PAC, was the condition of the approximately two to three million people of Polish origin living in the Soviet Union, members of a seemingly lost branch of Polonia and the Polish nation who needed support for the preservation of their ethnic identity despite their difficult isolation from both Poland and the West. See for example the *Polish American Congress Newsletter,* June 1975 and the excellent overview of the Polish national minority in the Soviet Union by Stanislaw Kadziewicz, "The Lost Tribe:

Poles in the U.S.S.R." *Stadium Papers,* 13, number 1 (January, 1989), 13-15.

A recent meeting of the Coordinating Council of the Free World Polonia took place in Toronto on February 26-27, 1990 with representatives from the PAC, the Polish Canadian Congress, the Congress of French Polonia, the Union of Poles in Great Britain and the Australian Executive Committee of Polish organizations in attendance. (Heading the PAC delegation for a second time was President Moskal; his first appearance at a session of the Council had taken place the previous September, in London.) The meeting was highlighted by the presence of Aleksander Hall, a member of the Polish Council of Ministers with responsibility for maintaining cooperative relations between the Solidarity-led government and its political allies in the ruling coalition. Significantly, Hall's duties included the development of constructive working relations with Polonia organizations abroad, a sign of the importance attached by the Mazowiecki government to the emigration, particularly its politically active representatives.

While cooperation has been the rule in the relations between the PAC and other Polonia organizations active in the Coordinating Council, in one area the Congress chose not to lend its support, the Polish Institute of Christian Culture established in Rome in 1981 under the direction of the Reverend Stefan Wylenzek. Among its activities is an annual Summer institute in the Eternal City aimed at educating members of Polonia from around the world about their common Polish and Christian heritage. The institute's participants are housed in the Pope John Paul II House and the program enjoys the strong support of the Holy Father.

34. Jerry Hough, *The Polish Crisis: American Policy Options* (Washington, D.C.: The Brookings Institution, 1982), pp. 11-14, 61. In Hyland's judgment, "Carter left behind one last accomplishment: his handling of the Polish crisis (of 1980). As the tensions grew over the emergence of the first genuine workers' movement, the trade union Solidarity, it became more and more likely that the Soviets would move, perhaps invading Poland and provoking a major bloodbath. As the crisis mounted Brzezinski, with Carter's support, orchestrated a campaign of

public and political pressure. This may have given the Soviets pause..." *Mortal Rivals,* p. 226.

Hough suggests that the Carter and Reagan policies were both well reasoned attempts to use economic aid to influence the course of events in Poland. Once Carter had made his point in opposing Soviet intervention, Reagan enjoyed greater latitude in withholding credits to Poland so long as the regime refused to cooperate with Solidarity during the tense and confrontational period beginning in January 1981. Significantly, in Mazewski's first meeting with Reagan in July of that year, he stressed the importance of American economic assistance to Poland together with help for the thousands of refugees streaming to the West. Hough, pp. 61-62.

35. *New York Times,* December 24, 1981, cited in Hough, p. 62. Initially, the Administration, while decrying the Soviet's hand in the crisis, did not propose economic penalties against the U.S.S.R. Thus, the U.S. grain embargo of December 1979, following the Soviet intervention into Afghanistan and lifted after Reagan had entered office, was not reimposed. This stance on the part of Washington shifted on June 18, 1982, when the U.S. came out publicly in opposition to the finalization of a natural gas pipeline agreement between Moscow and the West European states; the American position may have changed out of frustration with Poland's failure to respond to the December 1981 sanctions. Interestingly, the Polish government on July 21, 1982, announced the release of all but 637 political prisoners. For its part, the Polish American Congress called for sanctions from the start against the U.S.S.R., "the chief perpetrators of Poland's tragedy" in Mazewski's words, and it strongly approved the pipeline decision.

36. There were also some less damaging and hence more symbolic actions taken at the time, including prohibitions on the Polish airlines landing in the U.S. and an end to Polish fishing activity in American waters. Neither diplomatic relations nor cultural exchanges between the two states were severed, however. See Garrett, *From Potsdam to Poland,* Chapter 7.

37. *Polish American Congress Newsletter,* August 1987 and April 1988; CARE and Catholic Relief Services' assistance was also considerable; in 1984, President Reagan stated that these amounted to shipments valued at more than $100 million. *Polish American Congress Newsletter,* August 1984.

38. Remarks of Deputy Secretary of State Kenneth Dam, summarized in the *Polish American Newsletter,* August 1984, pp. 6-7. The memorial publication distributed at the 40th anniversary observances included a rather remarkable comment by Mazewski which implied the existence of extensive Polonia dissatisfaction with President Reagan's sanctions policy: "The Polish American Congress is the voice of organized Polonia. True it does not speak for everyone, neither does it profess to do so, but it speaks for the majority of concerned Polish Americans." Aloysius A. Mazewski, "Fortieth Anniversary of the Polish American Congress," in *Welcome to the Fortieth Anniversary of the Polish American Congress* (Chicago, 1984), p. 7.

39. See Chapter IV, footnote 71.

40. *Polish American Congress Newsletter,* December 1984, pp. 1-2.

41. Several Solidarity leaders were sentenced to prison terms for "advocating" strikes which did not even occur; significant new restrictions on the activities of university professors were also approved by the communist party-run parliament in a move to impose further controls on Polish society.

42. The National Assistance Committee for the Democratic Opposition in Poland dated its origins back to June 1976 when it had formed under Migala and Jan Jurewicz, who served as its treasurer. At that time, the Committee, operating under a slightly different name, called upon members of Polonia to support the cause of workers who had been imprisoned and then dismissed from their jobs following their protests against the food price increases decreed (and then rescinded) by the Gierek regime. In Poland, public criticism of the workers' treatment had led to the founding of *KOR* and other groups which

demanded justice on their behalf and an end to regime tactics to intimidate the population. In America, the Committee was established first as an autonomous unit within the Illinois division of the PAC. In 1985 it was formally incorporated into the activities of the national office of the Congress. Between 1976 through 1988, the Committee gathered more than $900,000 in support of the Polish democratic opposition and established effective methods to insure that these funds were sent into Poland. Funds collected in America were used to purchase medical supplies, food and clothing for the families of political prisoners and those who were incarcerated. The Committee also supported the activities of the underground press. Interview with Bonaventure Migala, November 11, 1988.

43. "Polish Americans Protest Jaruzelski's Visit," *New York Times,* September 25, 1985. After castigating the Jaruzelski regime for its repression of Solidarity and police state tactics toward the population, the PAC called upon the government to initiate genuine dialog with the representatives of the nation and to institute "sweeping reforms of the centralized...economic system...essential to restore Poland's viability." The full statement appears in the Appendix.

44. Their criticisms are alluded to by both Hough and Garrett, who observed that many Polish Americans objected to making Poland a "pawn" in Superpower relations and were concerned about the well-being of relatives in the old country. At this point, the *Polish American Congress Newsletter* also published an interview with State Department representative Mark Palmer who stressed the Administration's concern for the Polish people and its willingness to restore most favored nation status and U.S. credits if Poland's leadership made greater efforts to begin to reconcile itself with the country's authentic representatives. *Newsletter,* February 1986 issue.

45. Aloysius Mazewski,"U.S. Lacks Clear Policy on Poland," *Polish American Congress Newsletter,* September 1986, p. 1.

46. *Ibid.,* pp. 3, 6-7. At the same May 3rd gathering, which took place only a few days after the nuclear accident at Cher-

nobyl in the Soviet Ukraine, Illinois Senators Paul Simon and Allen Dixon both declared their support of an emergency shipment of powered milk to assist Poland. This action was approved by the U.S. Congress the following week.

47. *Polish American Congress Newsletter,* April 1988.

48. Note for example, Alina Perth-Grabowska, "The Polish Political Season: Autumn 1987," *Stadium Papers,* 12, number 1 (January, 1988), 3-5 as well as articles in the journal, *Poland Watch* (Washington, D.C.).

49. "Oswiadczenie Kongresu Polonii Amerykanskiej," (Declaration of the Polish American Congress), *Dziennik Zwiazkowy,* May 6, 1988, p. 1; in his own telegram to President Reagan, PAC President Mazewski thanked Reagan for his expressions of support for the Poles. At the same time, the PAC leader went further and urged the United States to call upon the U.S.S.R. to withdraw its military presence from Poland and East Europe and enable the peoples of the region to determine their own destiny.

For another view of the Polish situation, see Anthony Lewis, "Solidarity Presents Poland with a Hobson's Choice," *New York Times,* May 2, 1988.

50. From *Polish American Congress Newsletter,* October 1988, "Special Report: Vice President George Bush and Governor Michael Dukakis on Issues of Special Concern to Polish Americans."

51. A number of individuals have worked diligently as staff personnel to advance the aims of the Polish American Congress over the years, both in its Chicago home office and in Washington, D.C.

During the presidency of Charles Rozmarek, the key persons were Karol Burke (Bienkowski), Frank Dziob and Jerzy Przyluski. Burke, a journalist who had once served as Editor of the fraternal publication of the Polish Falcons of America, *Sokol Polski,* later joined the staff of the PNA daily in Chicago, *Dziennik Zwiazkowy.* He served as the chief publicist of the

Polish American Congress from 1944 until his retirement in 1969, working mainly in Washington, D.C. Dziob, another Falcons activist in his youth, was Rozmarek's personal secretary from 1939 until his retirement in 1963. During much of this period he also publicized the activities of the PAC and wrote statements of policy for the organization out of the Chicago office of the Polish National Alliance. Przyluski became involved in the Congress in the late 1950s and continued on to manage the PAC Chicago office until 1980, when he retired. Nonetheless, he remained active in the organization's affairs.

With Aloysius Mazewski's assumption of the PAC presidency, Casimir Lenard, a retired U.S. Army Colonel took over as Chief of the Congress' Washington, D.C. office in 1970 and served in that capacity until his resignation in 1974. Succeeding Lenard between 1974 and 1982 were Magda Ratajska, Dana de Fredberg, Leonard Walentynowicz, and Zdzislaw Dziekonski. Walentynowicz, a Buffalo, New York attorney, also served in the State Department in the Carter Administration.

In the Fall of 1982, Myra Lenard, the wife of Casimir Lenard, was appointed Washington, D.C. Director of the PAC and has ably represented the Congress in the capital ever since. During her tenure, the PAC Charitable Foundation has organized a series of well publicized efforts to gather medical supplies, food and clothing for Poland, including a massive "Solidarity Convoy" of freight trucks which arrived in Washington, D.C. on December 13, 1982, the first anniversary of martial law in Poland. Following this demonstration of commitment to the Solidarity cause, the convoy's goods were shipped to the needy in Poland.

In Chicago, Eugene Rosypal, a youthful Polish-born activist from Pennsylvania, took over for Przyluski to manage the PAC office there. It was during Rosypal's tenure that Chicago became a major center for the delivery of supplies gathered from all parts of the country for shipment to Poland.

Rosypal has been a propagandist in promoting the appeals of the Polish American Congress Charitable Foundation to its state divisions throughout the country, to the many organizations of Polonia and to the general media. One of his activities was to continue the regular publication of the *Polish American Congress Newsletter,* an English language periodical which had been initiated in 1954 by Burke in a tabloid form. By the late 1960s, that version of the *Newsletter* was defunct, and a new *PAC Newsletter,* edited by Przyluski and PAC Vice President Kazimierz Lukomski was inaugurated in 1969. In 1981, Rosypal took over as editor, emphasizing the activities of the PAC Charitable Foundation along with the traditional political features of the publication.

Particularly prominent as advisers to Mazewski through the 1980s were several veteran PAC activists with broad expertise on Polish affairs, among them Vice President Lukomski, Jan Nowak, formerly Director of the Polish section of Radio Free Europe, Boleslaw Wierzbianski, Editor and Publisher of the New York Polish language daily, *Nowy Dziennik* (and previously a leader in the *Swiatpol* organization), and the former editor of the Polish National Alliance's own daily newspaper in Chicago, Jan Krawiec.

Following Edward Moskal's accession in 1988 as PAC President, John F. Kordek, a retired U.S. Foreign Service Officer and former Ambassador to Botswana, was appointed to a new post in the Congress, that of National Executive Director. He officially began work in January 1990 but relinquished his position in mid 1991 in favor of new administrative duties at Chicago's De Paul University. Other influential figures in Moskal's regime have been the Legal Counsel of the Polish National Alliance, Leszek Kuczynski, the Alliance's Controller, Alex Przypkowski, and its Treasurer, Kazimierz Musielak.

FOOTNOTES to Chapter VI

1. For a list of PACCF sponsored works, see footnote 14 in the preceding chapter. One particularly promising activity was the PAC's sponsorship of twenty high school students of Polish heritage in participating in a week-long study program in Washington, D.C. The program, underwritten in cooperation with the Wasie Foundation of Minneapolis, Minnesota, was aimed at generating greater knowledge and awareness of the American political and governmental process among future Polish American adults by enabling them to meet U.S. elected and appointed governmental officials in the capital. Student responses to the program were enthusiastic; unfortunately, the program was later discontinued. *Polish American Congress Newsletter,* August 1984, p. 12.

Information for statements in this chapter, when not otherwise documented, is based upon individual issues of the *Polish American Congress Newsletter,* the minutes of the semi-annual meetings of the PAC National Council of Directors, and the author's interviews and conversations with PAC Presidents Aloysius Mazewski and Edward Moskal, Vice President Kazimierz Lukomski, Myra Lenard, Eugene Rosypal and other PAC members.

2. "Polish American Congress Makes Appeal for Charitable Foundation," *Sokol Polski* (The Polish Falcon, official newspaper of the Polish Falcons of America fraternal, Pittsburgh), December 15, 1988, p. 13. See also the PACCF's Report of activities of November 1989 and June and November 1990.

3. "Special Report: Bishop Domin Visits the United States," *Polish American Congress Newsletter,* September 1986, pp. 7-9. Domin's appearances in New York, Buffalo, Philadelphia, Doylestown, Pennsylvania, Washington, D.C., Boston, Detroit, Orchard Lake, Michigan, Chicago, Milwaukee and Perth Amboy, New Jersey were greeted enthusiastically.

4. President Aloysius A. Mazewski, "PAC Charitable Foundation Supplemental Reports," to the PAC National Council of Directors meeting in Chicago, June 24, 1988. At this meeting of

the PAC, special recognition was given to a number of activists in and outside of Polonia for their efforts on Poland's behalf. Singled out for praise were Sister Marie Therese, S.Sp.S., of the Holy Spirit Missions of Techny, Illinois, Mr. James Franks, Sr. and Mr. James Franks, Jr. of International Aid, Inc., and Mr. Stanley Stawski, President of Stawski Distributing Company of Chicago. *Polish American Congress Newsletter,* August 1988.

Singled out for special praise were the members of the Michigan division of the PAC. Through their efforts, Michigan's Polonia has continually led the way in collecting goods needed in Poland ever since the PACCF's drive began in 1981.

5. Ash, *The Polish Revolution,* p. 196.

6. Mazewski, "PAC Charitable Foundation Supplemental Reports," *ibid.*

7. *Polish American Congress Newsletter,* August, 1984, p. 15. In Bishop Domin's letter to the PAC of November 3, 1988 he once again drew attention to the significance of the Foundation's effort: "The Polish Episcopate Charity Commission, on its part and on behalf of the Polish people sincerely hopes that the Polish American Congress will...continue sending charitable aid to Poland. This type of relief on the part of American Polonia is visible evidence of the close ties and cooperation between Polish Americans and their countrymen in Poland." Letter of Bishop Czeslaw Domin to PAC Vice President Lukomski, in *Sokol Polski,* December 15, 1988.

8. *Report of the President of the Polish American Congress from June 1, 1985 to November 1, 1985;* letter to Senators Paul Simon and Frank Murkowski of November 1, 1985; in Polish American Congress National Council Meeting, November 8, 1985 (Buffalo, New York, bound copy).

9. "PAC Lobby Effective," *Polish American Congress Newsletter,* April, 1988, p. 16. The enormity of Poland's crisis of the 1980s can be appreciated by simply looking at the figures of legal and extra-legal emigration during the decade. Thus, one Polish official acknowledged that no fewer than 113,000 per-

sons had left the country legally after 1981 while another 153,000 had failed to return home following trips they made abroad. Not surprisingly, the use of temporary permits to travel abroad with no intention of returning was cited as a growing problem facing the country. This migration to secure better living conditions and opportunities abroad was particularly evident among better educated Poles, according to the same official source. Thus, in an unusually frank admission, it was reported that between 1983 and 1987, some 21,500 individuals with advanced academic training, including approximately 8,000 engineers had left permanently during the five year period. Some 38,000 holders of university diplomas had also prolonged their stays abroad in this period, with a considerable number not expected to come home. "Brain Drain from Poland," *Krajowa Agencja Informacyjna* (National Information Agency, February 23-29, 1989), pp. 1-2; and *Wall Street Journal,* July 26, 1988, p. 23.

In 1989 the PACCF again became involved in assisting in the resettlement of Polish refugees from Europe to the United States. This time the effort, headed by PAC Treasurer Edward Dykla, focused on raising moneys to help the American Bishops' Conference in bringing between 300-400 persons into the country.

10. "PAC Charitable Foundation Report: PAC First to Offer Emergency Disaster Aid," *Polish American Congress Newsletter,* September 1986, p. 4, and the PACCF brochure, "Relief for Poland" printed in June 1986, which appealed for contributions for the cause.

11. At the semi-annual meeting of the PAC National Council of Directors in Chicago on November 17, 1989 Rosypal also noted that over the years the Charitable Foundation had helped bring more than one hundred and fifty children with life threatening heart defects to the United States for surgery performed at the Deborah Heart and Lung Center in New Jersey. This activity continues in cooperation with Stanley Fryczynski of the Deborah Hospital Foundation.

12. An interesting example of such imaginative activity was the PAC's work with the U.S. Peace Corps. This work paid its first dividends in June 1990 when President Bush honored and sent off 61 specialists to Poland where they were to teach the English language. A second contingent of some forty experts in business and economic development were scheduled to leave for Poland in October 1990. The Polish American Congress, in addition to promoting the idea of Peace Corps involvement in Poland, was also engaged in helping in the recruitment of volunteers from among interested individuals of Polish heritage. Indeed, about 20 percent of the first group bound for Poland were persons of Polish origin. *Report of the PAC National Executive Director from January 1 through June 25, 1990,* p. 4.

FOOTNOTES to Conclusions

1. Nine nominees were declared eligible for the PNA Presidency: Moskal; former PNA Treasurer Adam Tomaszkiewicz of Cicero, Illinois; PNA Director Paul Odrobina of Hamtramck, Michigan; Circuit Court Judge Marilyn Rozmarek Komosa of Chicago; Joseph Wojtowicz of Ypsilanti, Michigan; former Vice Censor Anthony Czelen of Monessen, Pennsylvania; Vice Censor Edward Sitnik of Farmington, Connecticut; Karol Nawarynski of Lawrenceville, New Jersey; and PNA Director Donald Pienkos of Whitefish Bay, Wisconsin. In the run-off election, Moskal bested Tomaszkiewicz by a vote of 24-10. He took office on November 1 and at a banquet that evening in Chicago attended by nearly six hundred well-wishers received the personal congratulations of Vice President George H. Bush. One week later, Bush was elected President of the United States, carrying the heavily Polish American states of Illinois, Michigan, Pennsylvania, New Jersey, Ohio, Connecticut and Indiana on his way to an Electoral College victory of 426 to 111 over his Democratic Party opponent, Massachusetts Governor Michael Dukakis. Dukakis won ten states and the District of Columbia, including the largely Polish states of Minnesota, Wisconsin, New York and Massachusetts.

2. Over the years, two organizational units have played dominant roles within the Polish American Congress, both at its national meetings and during the time periods between these gatherings. These are the "state divisions" of the Congress and the Polonia organizations, most notably the fraternals and the veterans associations.

Over the past thirty years or more, the national organization has recognized between twenty-seven and thirty-two organizations as "state divisions." Some of these units represent sections of a particular state; others include the entire territory of a state within their jurisdictions. Thus, states such as New York, with three divisions (one centered in the New York City area, a second in the center of the state, and a third in Buffalo), Pennsylvania, with four divisions, Massachusetts and New Jersey with two divisions each, have been recognized, while others like Illinois, Michigan, Ohio, and Delaware have included only one "state division." The existence of more than one state division in a single state is simply due to the fact that in those localities there have existed more than one sizable concentration of Polish Americans, with considerations such as physical distance between these communities making it sensible to establish separate organizations to more effectively carry out the work of the organization.

In 1960, the national organization counted a total of twenty-seven divisions operating in twenty states; in 1970, the same totals were to be found although several divisions had gone out of existence while others had been formed. In 1978 there were 31 divisions in 23 states (including Washington, D.C.); in 1988 there were 32 divisions in 22 states (counting once again Washington, D.C.).

Throughout this period, there have consistently been active divisions in Illinois, Michigan New York, Pennsylvania, New Jersey, Maryland, Delaware, Massachusetts, Connecticut, Rhode Island, Wisconsin, Indiana, Ohio, California, Arizona, West Virginia, Florida and Nebraska. State divisions have been established on a somewhat more ephemeral basis in Minnesota, Missouri, Oklahoma, Texas and Oregon, where the Polish American population was smaller and less concentrated.

The organizations of Polonia participating most actively in the Congress through the years have included the fraternals, namely the Polish National Alliance of the United States of North America, the Polish Roman Catholic Union of America and the Polish Women's Alliance, all centered in Chicago; the Polish National Alliance of Brooklyn; the Polish Falcons of America, with its home office in Pittsburgh; the Alliance of Poles of America (Cleveland); the Union of Polish Women in America (Philadelphia); the Polish National Union of America (Scranton); and the Polish Union of America (Buffalo). Among the organizations of veterans belonging to the Congress are the Polish Veterans of World War II, the Polish Army Veterans Association and the Polish Legion of American Veterans. Educational and cultural associations in the Polish American Congress have included the American Council of Polish Cultural Organizations, the Polish American Historical Association and the Western Association of Polish Schools. Many other organizations also belong to the Congress or participate in the activities of its state divisions. For detailed information as to membership in the Congress see Table 1 at the end of this chapter.

3. At the 1988 meeting, the delegates reaffirmed the membership of the executive committee (the president, two vice presidents, secretary and treasurer) of the Congress, a body responsible for representing the organization between its gatherings. Slightly modified were by-laws identifying 22 vice presidents for the organization (from 19 in 1986) charged with representing the national organization in their home communities; ten delegates were also elected on an "at large" basis to the National Council. While the organization's financial condition was the focus of considerable discussion at the conclave, the idea of restoring the quadrennial national convention won relatively little support and was dropped for the time being.

4. Also indicative of the PNA's place in the Congress have been its ideological objectives, which have been reiterated frequently since its founding in 1880 and which are so similar to those of the PAC.

A recent statement of PNA aims lists them as follows: "to form a better union of the Polish people in this country, and to transmit the same to future generations; to insure to them a proper moral, intellectual, economic and social development; to foster and cherish the best traditions of the culture of the United States and of Poland; to preserve the mother tongue, and to promote, more effectually, all legitimate means for the restoration of the independence of the Polish nation in Europe..." *By-Laws of the Polish National Alliance of the United States of North America, Revised and Reenacted at the 40th Regular Convention, September 13-18, 1987 in Chicago, Illinois* (Chicago: Alliance Printers and Publishers, 1987), p. 1.

5. *Polish American Congress Charitable Foundation Report,* November 16, 1989 through June 15, 1990, p. 6; "PNA Members Generously Responded to the President's Christmas Appeal," *Zgoda,* February 1, 1990.

6. "United States Policy in Relation to Poland in the Context of Critical Developments of the Soviet System," statement

of the Polish American Congress Executive Committee, March 2, 1989; also, Jan Nowak, "U.S. Policy and the Crisis of the Soviet System," February 12, 1989. Those attending the February 17 meeting included PAC President Moskal, Vice Presidents Lukomski and Helen Wojcik, Boleslaw Wierbianski of New York, Jan Nowak of Washington, D.C., Dr. Jerzy Lerski of San Francisco, Atty. Leszek Kuczynski of Chicago, Myra Lenard, Illinois PAC Division President Roman Pucinski, Jan Krawiec of Chicago, Eugene Rosypal, Executive Director of the PAC Charitable Foundation and Dr. Donald Pienkos.

At the meeting, Pucinski observed that recent estimates of Polonia assistance to Poland amounted to approximately $1.3 billion annually and could be divided about evenly between money gifts and goods. Such private aid, he concluded, signified that Polonia's calls for increased U.S. economic assistance were backed by an already strong commitment from its members.

The participants praised the U.S. Government for supporting human rights in Eastern Europe through its continued funding of Radio Free Europe, Voice of America, Radio Liberty, and the National Endowment for Democracy and the U.S. Congress' past appropriations for Solidarity, and called for an expansion of intellectual, scientific and student exchanges with Poland, including greater contacts with representatives of the Polish democratic opposition.

7. For Solidarity's own response to the regime's offer to meet, one might note its statement in Gdansk on January 21-22, 1989:

"The National Executive Commission of Solidarity considers the communist party Central Committee's proposal for the restoration of trade union pluralism and legalization of Solidarity to be a basic step toward social dialog. We hope that other appropriate executive decisions by the government shall follow... The opportunity has arisen for negotiations on Solidarity and other national issues. Solidarity demands that the political and administrative authorities respect the principles of trade union freedom, set by...the International Labor Organization. On our part, we intend to act democratically...for the good of Poland in accordance with the legal order and our Union's statutes... Poland's dramatic economic and ecological situation is well known. The roots of the crisis lie in the current political system. Now the opportunity arises for a broad coalition to combat the crisis. A consensus must be reached regarding reform policies, programs of action and mechanisms of social control. The costs of reform must not bring about any further pauperization of the society. Inefficiency and waste must be wiped out and the state budget revised... Solidarity welcomes the prospects for political pluralism. We stand for the restoration of political liberties and democratization of state institutions, for freedom of association, for judicial autonomy, for freedom of speech and access to the media... (We stand for) a prompt start of substantive and concrete negotiations conducted under a scrutinizing public eye." *Solidarnosc News* (Brussels, Belgium), Number 126, January 15-29, 1989, p. 1. Published by the Coordinating Office Abroad of *NSZZ Solidarnosc*, Jerzy Milewski, editor.

8. For the text of Bush's speech, see the Appendix of this work.

9. A typical PAC response to the news of the Polish election results came from its Wisconsin state division. Reprinted in the July 1, 1989 issue of *Zgoda*, the official organ of the Polish National Alliance and thus slightly modified for publication, the statement, "The Polish Elections, Polish Americans and the Future," reads as follows:

The results of the June elections in Poland are now final and have caused amazement for many observers of the Communist world. Only a few weeks ago they were cautiously predicting that the Polish regime would probably do fairly well against a seemingly divided democratic opposition engaged in its first political campaign. The Polish public was portrayed as deeply apathetic, cynical and even confused about the major issues before it and was not expected to give overwhelming support for the untried Solidarity opposition movement.

Now the returns are in. They tell a far different story, that of an unprecedented popular repudiation of the Communist dictatorship -- a dictatorship imposed against the people's will by the Soviet Union at the end of World War II following the Yalta Conference.

The Polish people, when at last permitted to speak in a free election, have condemned this dictatorship and its disastrous economic policies, incompetence and corruption, which have brought the country to ruin and ecological crisis and spurred a massive emigration of hundreds of thousands of its citizens in quest of a better life.

In the election, Solidarity won every seat out of the 161 places in the Parliament it was permitted to contest with the Communists. Not one of the Communist candidates received a majority in the 299 Parliament seats reserved for them and new elections will have to be held later to fill their places. Thirty-five national leaders of the regime running unopposed for the Parliament, including the Prime Minister, were also unable to win even half of the votes in their election and were in fact defeated. In the new 100 member Polish Senate, the Democratic opposition won 99 of 100 seats.

This election in itself will not bring the democratic opposition to power but it is a first step in the process of political democratization in the country. It is to be hoped that the Communist leadership, repudiated as it has been, will honor the agreement it made with Solidarity to hold these elections -- and live and learn from what the people have told it.

But the Polish elections are significant in two larger respects, which merit mention here.

First, they represent a profound affirmation of the Polish people's deep and continued commitment to democratic values, something which we in the West have so long enjoyed. The Poles' vote in June is like the call from a long lost brother, who has suddenly proclaimed to his family that he indeed is alive and amazingly well, despite a separation of many years. There should thus be great rejoicing among all in America and the democracies in this event, for such reunions are truly special occurrences.

Second, the elections should be a source of special pride for all Polish Americans, and particularly for members of the Polish American Congress and the PNA. Certainly, the action of the Polish electorate publicly and formally reaffirms Poland's historic solidarity of beliefs with all people of Polish heritage living abroad.

At the same time the election should serve to underscore the legitimacy of the principles held for 45 years by the Polish American Congress and its member organizations. Through all these difficult years they have kept the faith. They have never tired of telling anyone who would listen, that Poland should be free and fully sovereign, and that it was important for our Government to work hard for this cause. A free and independent Poland is what Americans should want for the Poles; it is certainly what the Poles want for themselves.

10. *Report of PAC President Edward J. Moskal, June 17, 1989 to November 16, 1989*, pp. 6-8; *Minutes of the Polish American Congress National Council of Directors Meeting*, November 17-18, 1989, pp. 8-10.

Travelling to Poland in the PAC delegation with President Moskal were Vice President Wojcik, Treasurer Dykla, Myra Lenard, Eugene Rosypal, Roman Pucinski, Paul Odrobina, Jerzy Przyluski, Kazimierz Musielak, Alex Przypkowski, Leszek Kuczynski and his wife. Arriving in Warsaw on October 22, the delegation returned to the United States on October 28 after visits to Gdansk, Czestochowa, Auschwitz and Krakow.

Meetings were held with Prime Minister Mazowiecki, Cardinal Glemp, Lech Walesa, the Speakers of the Polish Senate and *Sejm*, Foreign Minister Krzysztof Skubiszewski, the Ministers of Health and Social Welfare, Labor, and Environment, the United States Ambassador and President Jaruzelski, and representatives of the Children's Hospital in Krakow and the soon to be dissolved Polonia Society.

Objections to the trip were varied but the only formal criticism of the visit came at the semi-annual meeting of the Congress on November 17, 1989 in Chicago. There, Vice President Lukomski called for a vote of censure with respect to President Moskal's "unilateral actions" in establishing relations with Poland's new government and choosing his delegation without having first gained approval from the PAC's five member Executive Committee. This motion further called upon the President to abide by the by-laws of the Congress in the future.

Whatever the merits of the complaint, only 19 members of the Council of Directors were found to support it in a roll-call vote; 58 sided with the President on the issue with 5 others abstaining. *Minutes of the Polish American Congress National Council of Directors Meeting,* pp. 13, 13b.

11. From Edward J. Moskal, "Report to the President regarding the visit to Poland of the Presidential Commission," in *Report of PAC President Edward J. Moskal, ibid.*

12. For a review of East Germany's precipitous breakdown and the revolutionary events in Eastern Europe of 1989 and 1990, see Bernard Gwertzman and Michael T. Kaufman, editors, *The Collapse of Communism* (New York: Times Books/Random House, 1990) and the Radio Free Europe weekly magazine, *RFE Report on Eastern Europe,* from 1990.

13. In *Report of (the) President of the Polish American Congress from November 18, 1989 to June 27, 1990.*

14. *Ibid.*

15. *Ibid.*

16. This is the opinion of Ambassador Kordek based upon a conversation with the author on August 10, 1990. The full text of the Senators' telegram is in the Appendix of this work.

17. In *Report of (the) President of the Polish American Congress, ibid.* A chronological review of developments in the Polish-German border controversy from November 2, 1989 through March 14, 1990 (when Chancellor Kohl's government announced its approval of Polish participation in the Four Plus Two Talks, is in the journal, *Studium Papers,* 14, numbers 1-2 (Winter-Spring, 1990), 3-4.

On July 17, 1990 the Polish Foreign Minister took part in the ongoing Four Plus Two Talks in Paris for the first time. There, he accepted a guarantee from the United States, the Soviet Union, Britain and France that Poland's western border would be respected until a united Germany would sign a binding treaty with Poland respecting the permanent inviolability of their borders. At the same time he received assurances from West Germany's Foreign Minister that such a treaty would be approved in Germany very soon after unification and that West Germany's government was interested in providing substantial economic assistance to Poland in the coming months.

As a result, Poland dropped its demand that the border issue be resolved by treaty prior to the unification of the two Germanies. *Nowy Dziennik* (New York), July 19, 1990, p. 1. On November 14, 1990 a treaty between Poland and the newly united Germany was signed in Warsaw.

18. In *Report of (the) President of the Polish American Congress, ibid.*

19. In *Dziennik Zwiazkowy*, March 26, 1990, pp. 3-4.

20. Myra Lenard, "The Polish American Congress," remarks presented to the officers of the Polish National Alliance, Anaheim, California, January 12, 1989.

21. A review of the lobbying efforts of the PAC since 1944 indicates that each of its Presidents devoted much energy to representing Polonia's concerns to America's elected leaders in Washington, D.C. All have sought to gain audiences with the President of the United States, in recognition of his key role in formulating America's foreign policy objectives with respect to Poland, Eastern Europe and the Soviet Union.

Similarly, all have worked hard to develop favorable relations with those members of the U.S. Senate and the House of Representatives who were believed to share their perspectives, either because they themselves were of Polish or Eastern European heritage, represented states or Congressional districts with sizable populations of Polish or East Central European origins, or were simply receptive to the positions taken by the PAC on ideological grounds. Clearly there have been many such legislators on Capitol Hill, and in both political parties, over the years.

The primary analytical question to be answered with respect to the PAC's lobbying activities in Washington has to do with its impact upon U.S. policy objectives and strategies over the years. Perhaps the most useful effort to deal with this issue is by Garrett, *From Potsdam to Poland.*

From 1944 into the late 1960s the PAC also sought to influence the results of U.S. Presidential elections by appealing to Polonia to support that candidate it felt was more closely identified with its position on Poland. For various reasons that effort proved generally unsuccessful in its own time; moreover it has been discarded during the past twenty years or so out of the PAC's recognition of its diminishing impact upon a Polish American population that was becoming increasingly diverse and difficult to reach. This problem has been compounded by the near disappearance of issues pertaining to Poland which might become sources of great public discord between the two political parties. For a review of Polonia's record in Presidential elections, see Donald Pienkos, "Polish American Ethnicity in the Political Life of the United States," in Roucek and Eisenberg, editors, *America's Ethnic Politics,* pp. 273-395; Bukowczyk, pp. 85-202, and *passim.*

22. In an interview conducted in 1978, Lukomski acknowledged that the post World War II political emigration had played a role that was "out of proportion" to its size, both in terms of its concerns with the "Polish question" and in the consequent neglect of Polonia's domestic agenda within the PAC.

He went on to observe that "second generation" Americans of Polish heritage had not yet developed what he called the necessary level of "civic consciousness" and thus were not yet beginning to occupy their rightful places, either in the organizations of Polonia or in the leadership of American society. Part of the problem was due to Charles Rozmarek's lengthy and autocratic rule over the Polish National Alliance and the Polish American Congress, thanks to which many individuals were discouraged from participating in Polonia organizational activities. Lukomski also noted the chronic inability of Polonia's fraternals to cooperate in generating the funds needed by the PAC to help the ethnic community achieve its objectives.

23. Playing an important role in affecting Polonia's ideological perspectives has been the journal, *Kultura,* based in Paris since the late 1940s. For more than two decades, Polish emigres in the United States were conspicuously active in both the New York-based Assembly of Captive European Nations and in Radio Free Europe. (The *KNAPP* organization which had been so active between 1944 and 1952 went out of existence, however.)

The post World War II emigration also grew influential in the leadership of a number of organizations of veterans that had operated since the 1920s in this country as well as in a new movement founded in the 1950s, the Polish Combatants' Association. The most recent manifestation of the concerns of the political emigration is the North American Studies Center for Polish Affairs. Established in the 1970s in An Arbor, Michigan, the Center continues to publish a quarterly journal, *Studium Papers.*

Bibliography

Primary Sources

Duleep, Harriet O. *et al.: The Economic Status of Americans of Southern and Eastern European Ancestry* (Washington, D.C.: U.S. Commission on Civil Rights, Publication 89, 1986).

Foreign Relations of the United States (Washington, D.C., volumes for 1946 and 1947).

Galush, William: "Forming Polonia: A Study of Four Polish American Communities, 1890-1940," Dissertation: University of Minnesota, 1975.

Glos Polek (The Polish Women's Voice. Bi-monthly official publication of the Polish Women's Alliance headquartered in Chicago, Illinois); issues of March 17, April 7, April 21, May 5, May 19, June 2, September 1, September 15, and November 3, 1988, commemorating the history of the organization over the previous 90 years.

Kongres Polonii Amerykanskiej: Alfabetyczny spis czlonkostwa od Maja 1944 do 31 Marca 1948 (The Polish American Congress: An Alphabetical Directory of Membership from 1944 to March 31, 1948. Chicago: Polish American Congress, 1948).

Kordek, John F.: *Report of the PAC National Executive Director from January 1 through June 25, 1990* (mimeographed).

"Mazewski Lists Achievements of Polish American Congress, States Case for its Continued Viability," *Zgoda,* (December 1, 1979).

Mazewski, Aloysius A.: *President's Report to the Polish American Congress National Council of Directors,* June 1986 and June 1988. Stenographic copies.

-------, "Challenges and Perspectives of American Polonia." Keynote Address to the Eighth National Convention of the Polish American Congress, Inc. August 15, 1970 (Chicago, 1970), pp. 16.

Minutes of the Conference of Intellectuals of Polish Ancestry held under the Auspices of the Polish American Congress at the Alliance College, Cambridge Springs, Pennsylvania, June 27-28, 1969. Mimeographed report at the Chicago office of the Polish American Congress.

Minutes of the Polish American Congress National Council of Directors Meeting in Chicago, November 17-18, 1989 (mimeographed).

O'Connell, Lucille: "Public and Philanthropic Facilities for the Adjustment of Immigrants in New York City, 1900-1920, as illustrated in the Polish Experience," Dissertation: New York University, 1973.

Pienkos, Donald E.: "Our Polish-Jewish Dialog Nationally and in Milwaukee--One Participant's Observations," unpublished paper, circulated among the members of the Polish-Jewish Forum of Milwaukee, 1987.

Piskorski, Florian: *Raport Delegata na Europe Rady Polonii Amerykanskiej -- American Polish War Relief -- Okres 1 Czerwiec 1945- 31 Maj 1946* (The Report of the Polish American Council's Delegate in Europe for the period June 1, 1945, to May 31, 1946). Geneva, Switzerland, 1946.

Polish American Congress, "A Memorandum to the Senate of the United States on the Crimea Decisions Concerning Poland" (Chicago, 1945), pp. 8.

Polish American Congress, By-Laws (Chicago, 1972 as amended, and 1986 as amended).

Polish American Congress Charitable Foundation Report of Activities between November 16, 1989 and June 15, 1990 (mimeographed).

Polish American Congress Newsletter, 1954-1964, forty-three issues in the English language and found in the Chicago office of the Polish American Congress.

Polish American Congress Newsletter, 1969-1990, thirty-seven issues in the English language under the editorship of Jerzy Przyluski, Kazimierz Lukomski, and Eugene Rosypal, in the Chicago office of the PAC.

Polish American Congress: Minutes of the Meetings of the National Council of Directors of June 14, 1985 in Shiller Park, Illinois; November 8, 1985 in Buffalo, New York; and June 11, 1987 in Milwaukee, Wisconsin.

Polish American Congress, "Poland in the Post-Sanctions Era: Conditionality of a Program of National Reconciliation and Economic Recovery." Statement adopted by the PAC Executive Committee and National Vice Presidents, April 10, 1987.

Polish American Congress, "United States Foreign Policy: The Polish American Agenda" and "The Time of Opportunity: Ideological Competition," two position papers of the Polish American Congress and published in August 1987.

Polish American Enterprise Fund: Investing in Poland's Future (New York, 1990), pp. 12.

Prace Kongresu Polonii Amerykanskiej w okresie 24-ch lat istnienia: krotki zarys dzialalnosci (The Works of the Polish American Congress during the Period of its past 24 Years of Activity. Chicago: Polish American Congress, 1968).

Protokol Kongresu Polonii Amerykanskiej (Minutes of the Founding Meeting of the Polish American Congress, in Buffalo, New York as prepared by Zygmunt Stefanowicz. Chicago: Alliance Printers and Publishers, 1944).

Protokol Drugiej Krajowej Konwencji Kongresu Polonii Amerykanskiej (Minutes of the Second National Convention of the Polish American Congress, in Philadelphia, Pennsylvania as prepared by Ignacy Morawski. Chicago: Alliance Printers and Publishers, 1948).

Protokol Trzeciej Krajowej Konwencji Kongresu Polonii Amerykanskiej (Minutes of the Third National Convention of the Polish American Congress, in Atlantic City, New Jersey, as prepared by Zygmunt Dybowski. Chicago: Alliance Printers and Publishers, 1952).

Protokol Czwartej Konwencji Kongresu Polonii Amerykanskiej (Minutes of the Fourth Convention of the Polish American Congress in Philadelphia, Pennsylvania, as prepared by Zygmunt Stefanowicz. Chicago, 1956, mimeographed copy).

Protokol Piatej Krajowej Konwencji Kongresu Polonii Amerykanskiej (Minutes of the Fifth National Convention of the Polish American Congress in Chicago, Illinois, as prepared by Konstanty J. Zielecki. Chicago: Alliance Printers and Publishers, 1960).

Protokol Szostej Krajowej Konwencji Kongresu Polonii Amerykanskiej (Minutes of the Sixth National Convention of the Polish American Congress, in Chicago, Illinois, as prepared by Ignacy Morawski. Chicago: Alliance Printers and Publishers, 1964).

Protokol Siodmej Krajowej Konwencji KPA (Minutes of the Seventh National Convention of the Polish American Congress in Cleveland, Ohio, as prepared by Jozef Ptak. Chicago: Alliance Printers and Publishers, 1968).

Protokol Osmej Krajowej Konwencji Kongresu Polonii Amerykanskiej (Minutes of the Eighth Convention of the Polish American Congress in Chicago, Illinois, as prepared by Edward Rozanski. Chicago: Polish American Congress, 1970).

Protokol Dziewiatej Konwencji Kongresu Polonii Amerykanskiej (Minutes of the Ninth Convention of the Polish American Congress in Detroit, Michigan, as prepared by Wlodzimierz Zmurkiewicz. Chicago: Polish American Congress, 1972).

Protokoly Posiedzen Zarzadu Rady Polonii Amerykanskiej (Minutes of the meetings of the board of directors and executive committee of the Polish American Council. From 1938 to 1974. In the Archives of the Polish Museum of America, Chicago).

Protokoly Zjazdu Rady Naczelnej Kongresu Polonii Amerykanskiej (Minutes of the Meeting of the Supreme Council of the Polish American Congress, for the years of 1945, 1947, 1950, 1954, 1962. In the Archives of the Polish American Congress in Chicago, Illinois).

Przyluski, Jerzy: "Kongres Polonii Amerykanskiej" (The Polish American Congress), unpublished paper, 1984.

-------, "Karol Rozmarek, Przywodca Polonii i Obronca Polski" (Charles Rozmarek, Leader of Polonia and Defender of Poland), unpublished paper, 1987.

Report of a Special Subcommittee of the Committee of Foreign Affairs: *Displaced Persons and the International Refugee Organization* (Washington: Government Printing Office, 1947).

Reports of Gifts in Kind Received by American Relief for Poland from Polish Committees, Organizations and Parishes between July 1943 and September 1948. Polish Museum of America Archives, Chicago, Illinois. Part of the *Rada Polonii Amerykanskiej* collection.

Reports of the President of the Polish American Congress to the delegates attending the seventh, eighth, ninth and tenth conventions of the PAC, in 1968, 1970, 1972, and 1976; published by the Polish American Congress in Chicago in the Polish language.

Report of PAC President Edward J. Moskal, June 17, 1989 to November 16, 1989 (mimeographed).

Report of (the) President of the Polish American Congress from November 18, 1989 to June 27, 1990 (mimeographed).

Rozmarek, Charles: *Foreign Policy of the United States: Memorandum of the Polish American Congress to Cordell Hull Secretary of State* (Chicago: Polish American Congress, 1944), 16 pages.

-------, *Sprawozdanie Prezesa Karola Rozmarka na siodmy zjazd Rady Naczelnej Kongresu Polonii Amerykanskiej, 29 Lipca 1966 w Washington, D.C.* (President Rozmarek's Report at the Seventh Convening of the Polish American Congress Supreme Council in Washington, D.C., July 29, 1966. Chicago: Alliance Printers and Publishers, 1966).

Sprawozdania prezesa zarzadu wykonawczego poszczegolnych komisji i komitetow wydzialow stanowych i biur Kongresu Polonii Amerykanskiej w Chicago i w Washingtonie na druga konwencje Kongresu Polonii Amerykanskiej w 29-30-31 Maja, 1948 (Reports of the President of the Executive Committee and of Specific Commissions and Committees of the State Divisions and Offices of the Polish American Congress headquartered in Chicago and Washington, D.C. at the Second Convention of the PAC from May 29 to May 31, 1948. Chicago: Alliance Printers and Publishers, 1948 as compiled by Ignacy Morawski).

Sprawozdania zarzadu wykonawczego poszczegolnych komisji i komitetow oraz biur Chicago i Washingtonie na Trzecia Krajowe Konwencje Kongresu Polonii Amerykanskiej 30-31 Maja i 1 Czerwcu, 1952 (Reports of the Executive Board and

Specific Commissions and Committees and the Chicago and Washington, D.C. Bureaus of the Polish American Congress at its Third Convention from May 30 through June 1, 1952. Chicago: Alliance Printers and Publishers, 1952 as compiled by Ignacy Morawski).

Sprawozdania Prezesa Kongresu Polonii Amerykanskiej na zjazd Rady Naczelnej (Reports of the President of the Polish American Congress at the Meetings of the Supreme Council of the PAC for the years 1962 and 1966).

Sprawozdanie Prezesa Kongresu Polonii Amerykanskiej na Piata Konwencje w Chicago Illinois (Report of the President of the Polish American Congress at the Fifth Convention of the PAC on September 30, 1960 in Chicago. Alliance Printers and Publishers, 1960).

Sprawozdanie Prezesa Kongresu Polonii Amerykanskiej na Szoste Krajowa Konwencje w Chicago, Illinois (Report of the President of the Polish American Congress at the sixth Convention of the PAC, September 18-20, 1964, in Chicago. Alliance Printers and Publishers, 1964).

Story of the Polish American Congress in Press Clippings (Chicago: Alliance Printers and Publishers. Volume I, covering 1944-1948; Volume II, covering 1948-1952; Volume III covering 1952-1954).

Swiatowy zwiazek Polakow z zagranicy: *II-gi zjazd Polakow z zagranicy 6-9 sierpnia 1934 roku* (World Union of Poles from Abroad: summaries of plenary sessions and resolutions at the Union's second congress, August 6-9, 1934. Warsaw, 1935).

Swietlik, Francis X.: *Rada Polonii Amerykanskiej od 1939 do 1948* (The Polish American Council and its work from 1939 to 1948. Chicago: Polish American Council, 1948).

-------, *The Polish Displaced Persons* (Chicago: American Relief for Poland, undated, probably 1946).

The Captive Nations: Continuing Exploitable Weakness of the Soviet Russian Empire (New York: Ukrainian Congress Committee of America, 1979).

The Polish National Alliance in the Press of America (Chicago: Alliance Printers and Publishers, 1951), volume I, covering 1947-1951; volume II 1955-1958.

Walentynowicz, Leonard F., Reports by the Executive Director of the Polish American Congress to the President and Board of Directors of the PAC, from October 20, 1977 to October 17, 1980.

-------, *Brief of the Polish American Congress, the National Advocates Society and the National Medical and Dental Association as Amici Curiae in the Supreme Court of the United States, October Term, 1976 in The Regents of the University of California v. Allan Bakke* (Washington, D.C., 1977).

-------, *Brief of the Polish American Congress and the National Advocates Society as Amici Curiae in the Supreme Court of the United States, October Term, 1978 in The United Steelworkers of America, AFL-CIO-CLC, et. al. v. Brian F. Weber, et al.* (Washington, D.C., 1979).

Welcome To The Fortieth Anniversary Of The Polish American Congress: Special Anniversary Book issued on May 5, 1984 (Chicago: Polish American Congress, 1984).

Zake, Louis J.: "The Development of the National Department *(Wydzial Narodowy)* as Representative of the Polish American Community in the United States, 1916-1923," Dissertation: University of Chicago, 1979.

Other Resources Consulted

American Committee for the Resettlement of Polish Displaced Persons. Official papers, correspondence and publicity materials in the archives of the Immigration History Research Center, University of Minnesota, St. Paul, Minnesota.

Information on the activities of the Polish Falcons movement during the First World War, in the Archives and Museum of the Polish Falcons of America, Pittsburgh, Pennsylvania.

Minutes of the meetings of the Board of Directors of the Polish National Alliance for selected years. Archives of the Polish National Alliance, Chicago, Illinois.

Polish American Congress: official papers and correspondence of the PAC provided by Karol Burke, Director of the PAC's Washington, D.C. office. In the Immigration History Research Center, University of Minnesota, St. Paul, Minnesota.

Polish American Council *(Rada Polonii Amerykanskiej):* official minutes of the meetings of its executive committee and board of directors between 1937 and 1974 and various other papers of the officers of the *RPA* along with proceedings of its conventions and reports of its affiliates. In the Polish Museum of America in Chicago.

Selected pamphlets and brochures printed by the Polish American Congress and its State Divisions: "Polish American Congress, Incorporated: Its History and Objectives" (1948); "A Short Biography of Thaddeus Kosciuszko" (1946); "A Short Biography of Gen. Casimir Pulaski" (undated, probably around 1946); "Ostrzezenie: Penetracja Komunistow Wsrod Polonii" (Warning: The Penetration of Polonia by the Communists. Illinois Division of PAC, 1959); "The Polish Constitution of the Third of May" (no date); "Communism--Enemy of Freedom" (1973); "Why We Oppose Communist Dictatorship of Poland" (1974); "The Two Faces of Poland" (no date, probably around 1975); "Anti-Defamation Guide" (no date, probably around 1975); "Polonia in the 1970s" (1970); "Polonia's Political Voice-The Polish American Congress" (Wisconsin Division of PAC, 1984); "Polish American Congress" (Michigan Division, 1984); "Polish American Congress--Your Representative Organization Serving Polonia's Vital Interests" (1980); "Relations of Polish Americans with the Communist Regime in Poland"

(1988); and "45 Years Serving the Interests of Polish Americans and the People of Poland" (1989).

Secondary Sources: Monographs

Allen, James Paul and Eugene J. Turner: *We the People: An Atlas of American Ethnic Diversity* (New York: MacMillan, 1988).

Alski, Wiktor: *Wnioski i refleksje Komisji Wspolpracy z Poloniami w innych krajach* (Recommendations and Reflections of the Commission on Cooperation with the Polonia communities in other countries. Report to the delegates to the Fourth PAC convention in Philadelphia, 1956).

Andrews, Nicholas G.: *Poland 1980-1981: Solidarity Versus The Party* (Washington, D.C.: National Defense University Press, 1985).

Acherson, Neal: *The Polish August: The Self-Limiting Revolution* (London: Allen Lane, 1981).

Ash, Timothy Garton: *The Polish Revolution: Solidarity* (New York: Vintage Press, 1985).

Bialasiewicz, Wojciech: *Pomiedzy lojalnoscia a serc porywem: Polonia Amerykanska we wrzesniu 1939 roku* (Between loyalty and heartfelt Impulses: American Polonia in September 1939. Chicago: Wici Publishing Company, 1989).

Bilek, Romuald: *Jak Powstal Kongres Polonii Amerykanskiej* (How the Polish American Congress Arose. Chicago: Privately Published, 1984).

Bolek, Francis, editor: *Who's Who in Polish America* (New York: Harbinger House, 1943), third edition.

Brodzki, Stanislaw and Maria Brodzka, editors: *Polonia 78 - Polonia Jutro* (Conference on Polonia Today and Tomorrow. Toronto: Polish Canadian Congress, 1978).

Bromke, Adam: *Poland's Politics: Idealism Versus Realism* (Cambridge, Massachusetts: Harvard University Press, 1967).

-------, *Poland: The Last Decade* (Oakville, Canada: Mosaic Press, 1981).

Brozek, Andrzej: *Polish Americans 1854-1939* (Warsaw: Interpress, 1985), second edition, translated by Wojciech Woroszylski.

Brzezinski, Zbigniew K.: *Alternative to Partition: For a Broader Conception of America's Role in Europe* (New York: Praeger, 1965).

Buczek, Daniel, *et al.*, *Saint Stanislaw Bishop of Krakow* (Chicago: Polish American Congress Charitable Foundation, 1979).

Bukowczyk, John: *And My Children Did Not Know Me: A History of the Polish Americans* (Bloomington and Indianapolis: Indiana University Press, 1987).

Burstin, Barbara Stern: *After the Holocaust: The Migration of Polish Jews and Christians to Pittsburgh* (Pittsburgh: University of Pittsburgh Press, 1989).

Byrnes, James: *Speaking Frankly* (New York: Harper, 1947).

Churchill, Winston S.: *Triumph and Tragedy* (Boston: Houghton-Mifflin, 1953).

Coutouvidis, John and Jaime Reynolds: *Poland 1939-1947* (Leicester, U.K.: Leicester University Press, 1986).

Dallek, Robert: *Franklin D. Roosevelt and American Foreign Policy, 1932-1945* (New York: Oxford University Press, 1979).

Dawisha, Karen: *Eastern Europe, Gorbachev and Reform* (Cambridge and New York: Cambridge University Press, 1988).

Davies, Norman: *Heart Of Europe: A Short History of Poland* (Oxford and New York: Oxford University Press, 1986).

DeWeydenthal, Jan: *The Communists of Poland: An Historical Outline* (Stanford, Cal.: Hoover Institution, 1978).

Dillon, Emile J.: *The Peace Conference* (London: Hutchinson and Company, 1919).

Dziewanowski, M.K.: *Poland In the Twentieth Century* (New York: Columbia University Press, 1977).

-------, *The Communist Party of Poland* (Cambridge, Mass.: Harvard University Press, 1959).

-------, *War At Any Price: World War II In Europe,* 1939-1945 (Englewood Cliffs, New Jersey: Prentice-Hall, 1987).

Elections in Poland (Edinburgh: Scottish League for European Freedom, 1947).

Florkowska-Francic, H., *et al.,* editors: *Polonia wobec niepodleglosci Polski w czasie I wojny swiatowej* (Polonia and Polish Independence in the Time of the First World War. Wroclaw: Ossolineum Publishers, 1979).

Garlinski, Jozef: *Poland In The Second World War* (London: MacMillan, 1985).

Garrett, Stephen A.: *From Potsdam to Poland: American Foreign Policy toward Eastern Europe* (New York: Praeger, 1986).

Garthoff, Raymond L.: *Detente and Confrontation: American-Soviet Relations from Nixon to Reagan* (Washington, D.C.: Brookings Institution, 1985).

General Sikorski Historical Institute: *General Sikorski w Dziesiata Rocznice Smierci* (General Sikorski on the tenth anniversary of his death. London, 1954).

-------, *Documents on Polish-Soviet Relations, 1939-1945* (London: Heinemann, 1961), three volumes.

Gerson, Louis: *Woodrow Wilson and the Rebirth of Poland, 1914-1920* (New Haven, Connecticut: Yale University Press, 1953).

-------, *The Hyphenate in Recent American Politics And Diplomacy* (Lawrence: University of Kansas Press, 1964).

Glazer, Nathan, editor: *Ethnic Dilemmas 1964-1982* (Cambridge, Massachusetts: Harvard University Press, 1983).

Gora, Wladyslaw: *Historia Polskiego Ruchu Robotniczego, 1864-1964* (The History of the Polish Workers Movement, 1864-1964. 2 volumes. Warsaw: Ksiazka i Wiedza, 1967).

Greene, Victor: *For God And Country: The Rise of Polish and Lithuanian Ethnic Consciousness in America* (Madison: State Historical Society of Wisconsin, 1975).

Gross, Jan: *Polish Society under German Occupation: The General Government* (Princeton, New Jersey: Princeton University Press, 1979).

-------, *Revolution from Abroad: The Soviet Conquest of Poland's Western Ukraine and Western Belorussia* (Princeton, New Jersey: Princeton University Press, 1988).

Haiman, Mieczyslaw: *Zjednoczenie Polskie Rzymsko-Katolickie w Ameryce, 1873-1948* (The History of the Polish Roman Catholic Union in America Fraternal, 1873-1948. Chicago: PRCUA Printers, 1948).

Harriman, Averill and Elie Abel: *Special Envoy to Churchill and Stalin, 1941-1946* (New York: Random House, 1975).

Hough, Jerry: *The Polish Crisis: American Policy Options* (Washington, D.C.: The Brookings Institution, 1982).

Hyland, William G.: *Mortal Rivals: Superpower Relations from Nixon to Reagan* (New York: Random House, 1987).

Iranek-Osmecki, Kazimierz: *He Who Saves One Life: Polish Efforts on Behalf of Jews in World War II* (New York: Crown Publishers, 1970).

Jedrzejewicz, Waclaw: *Polonia Amerykanska w Polityce Polskiej: Historia Komitetu Narodowego Amerykanow Polskiego Pochodzenia* (American Polonia's Involvement in Polish Politics: A History of the National Committee of Americans of Polish Descent. New York: KNAPP, 1954).

-------, *Pilsudski: A Life for Poland* (New York: Hippocrene Books, 1990).

Karlowiczowa, Jadwiga: *Historia Zwiazku Polek* (A History of the Polish Women's Alliance from 1898 to 1938. Chicago: Polish Women's Alliance, 1938).

Karski, Jan: *The Great Powers and Poland, 1919-1945: From Versailles To Yalta* (New York and London: University Press of America, 1985).

Kerstein, Edward: *Red Star over Poland* (Appleton, Wisconsin: C.C. Nelson, 1947).

Kieniewicz, Stefan: *The Emancipation of the Polish Peasantry* (Chicago and London: University of Chicago Press, 1969).

Korbonski, Andrzej: *The Politics of Socialist Agriculture in Poland, 1945-1960* (New York and London: Columbia University Press, 1965).

Korbonski, Stefan: *Warsaw in Exile* (New York: Praeger, 1966).

-------, *Warsaw in Chains* (London: George Allen and Unwin, Ltd., 1959).

-------, *Fighting Warsaw* (New York: Funk and Wagnalls, 1968).

-------, *The Polish Underground State, 1939-1945* (New York: Minerva Press, 1978).

Kovrig, Bennett: *The Myth of Liberation: East Central Europe in U.S. Diplomacy and Politics Since 1941* (Baltimore: The Johns Hopkins University Press, 1973).

Kowalski, W. T., *Walka dyplomatyczna o miejsce Polski w Europie, 1939-1945* (The diplomatic conflict over Poland's place in Europe, 1939-1945. Warsaw: Ksiazka i Wiedza, 1967), second edition.

Krolikowski, Lucjan, O.F.M. Conv., *Stolen Childhood: A Saga of Polish War Children* (Buffalo: Franciscan Fathers Minor Conventuals Publishers, 1983), translated by K.J. Roziatowski.

Kruszka, Waclaw: *Historja Polska w Ameryce* (The History of the Poles in America. 2 volumes, Volume I, Milwaukee: Kuryer Publishers, 1937; Volume II, Pittsburgh: Polish Falcons of America, 1978), revised second edition.

Kulczycki, John: *School Strikes in Prussian Poland, 1901-1907* (Boulder, Colorado and New York: East European Monographs, 1981).

Kuniczak, W.S.: *My Name Is Million: An Illustrated History of the Poles in America* (Garden City, New York: Doubleday, 1978).

Kuzniewski, Anthony J.: *Faith and Fatherland: The Polish Church War in Wisconsin, 1896-1918* (Notre Dame, Indiana: University of Notre Dame Press, 1980).

Lane, Arthur Bliss: *I Saw Poland Betrayed* (Indianapolis: Bobbs-Merrill, 1948).

Lerski, Jerzy J.: *A Polish Chapter in Jacksonian America: The United States and the Polish Exiles of 1831* (Madison: University of Wisconsin Press, 1958).

Lerski, George J. (Jerzy), compiler: *Herbert Hoover and Poland: A Documentary History of a Friendship* (Stanford, California: Hoover Institution, 1977).

Lorys, Maria: *Historia Zwiazku Polek* (A History of the Polish Women's Alliance from 1939 to 1959. Chicago: Polish Women's Alliance, 1980).

Lubell, Samuel: *The Future Of American Politics* (Garden City, New York: Doubleday, 1955).

Ludwikowski, Rett: *The Crisis of Communism: Its Meaning, Origins, and Phases* (Cambridge, Mass. and Washington, D.C.: Institute for Foreign Policy Analysis, 1986).

Lukas, Richard C.: *The Strange Allies: The United States and Poland, 1941-1945* (Knoxville: The University of Tennessee Press, 1978).

-------, *Bitter Legacy: Polish-American Relations in the Wake of World War II* (Lexington: University of Kentucky Press, 1982).

-------, *The Forgotten Holocaust: The Poles Under German Occupation, 1939-1944* (Lexington: University of Kentucky Press, 1986).

-------, *Out of the Inferno: Poles Remember the Holocaust* (Lexington: University of Kentucky Press, 1989).

Madden, Ray, *et al., Final Report of the Select Committee to Conduct an Investigation and Study of the Facts, Evidence and Circumstances on the Katyn Forest Massacre* (Washington, D.C.: U.S. Government Printing Office, 1952, reprinted in 1988).

Mason, David: *Public Opinion and Political Change in Poland, 1980-1982* (London: Cambridge University Press, 1985).

Memo to America: The DP Story. Final Report of the United States Displaced Persons Commission (Washington, D.C.: U.S. Government Printing Office, 1952).

Mikolajczyk, Stanislaw: *The Rape of Poland: Pattern of Soviet Domination* (New York: McGraw-Hill, 1948).

Moczulski, Leszek: *KPN: Rewolucja bez Rewolucji* (The Confederation of the Polish Nation: Revolution without a Revolution. Warsaw: Polish Publishers, 1979; reprinted in the United States by the Polish American Congress in Chicago, 1986).

Morawska, Ewa: *For Bread with Butter: Life-Worlds of East Central Europeans in Johnstown, Pennsylvania, 1890-1940* (New York: Cambridge University press, 1985).

Nowak, Jan: *Courier from Warsaw* (Detroit: Wayne State University Press, 1982).

Olszewski, Adam: *Historia Zwiazku Narodowego Polskiego* (History of the Polish National Alliance, 5 volumes, covering the period from 1905 to 1950. Chicago: Alliance Printers and Publishers, 1961-1968).

Orlowski, J.: *Helena Paderewska w pracy narodowej i spolecznej* (Helena Paderewska in Patriotic and Social Work. Chicago, 1929).

Osada, Stanislas: *Historia Zwiazku Narodowego Polskiego* (History of the Polish National Alliance. Chicago: Alliance Printers and Publishers, 1905, reprinted 1957).

-------, *Jak sie ksztaltowala Polska dusza wychodztwa w Ameryce* (How the Polish Spirit of the Emigration was Shaped. Pittsburgh: The *Sokol Polski* Printery, 1929).

Piatkowski, Romuald: *Pamietnik wzniesienia i odsloniecia pomnikow Tadeusza Kosciuszki i Kazimierza Pulaskiego tudziez polaczonego z ta uroczystoscia pierwszego Kongresu Polskiego w Washingtonie, D.C.* (A Memorial Commemorating the Unveiling of the Kosciuszko and Pulaski Monuments along with the Holding of the First Polish National Congress in Washington, D.C. Chicago: Alliance Printers and Publishers, 1911).

Pienkos, Angela T., editor: *Ethnic Politics in Urban America: The Polish Experience in Four Cities* (Chicago: Polish American Historical Association, 1978).

Pienkos, Donald E.: *PNA: A Centennial History of the Polish National Alliance of the United States of North America* (New York: Columbia University Press, 1984).

-------, *One Hundred Years Young: A History of the Polish Falcons of America*, 1887-1987 (Boulder, Colorado: East European Monographs, 1987).

Ploss, Sidney: *Moscow and the Polish Crisis: An Interpretation of Soviet Policies and Intentions* (Boulder, Colorado: Westview Press, 1986).

Pogonowski, Ivo: *Poland, A Historical Atlas* (New York: Hippocrene Books, 1987).

Polish Americans Reflect on "Shoah" (Chicago: Polish American Congress, 1986).

Pula, James S.: *For Liberty and Justice: The Life and Times of Wladimir Krzyzanowski* (Chicago: Polish American Congress Charitable Foundation, 1978).

Radzik, Tadeusz: *Spoleczno-ekonomiczne aspekty stosunku Polonii Amerykanskiej do Polski po I wojny swiatowej* (Socio-economic aspects of the relationship of Polonia to Poland after the First World War. Wroclaw: Polish Academy of Sciences, 1989).

Renkiewicz, Frank, editor: *The Poles in America 1608-1972* (Dobbs Ferry, New York: Oceana Publications, 1973).

Rozek, Edward J.: *Allied Wartime Diplomacy: A Pattern in Poland* (New York: Wiley, 1958).

Said, A.A., editor: *Ethnicity and U.S. Foreign Policy* (New York: Praeger, 1977, 1982).

Snell, John, editor: *The Meaning of Yalta* (Baton Rouge: Louisiana State University Press, 1956).

Soroka, Waclaw: *Polish Immigration to the United States: Authorized Notes from the Lectures of Professor Waclaw W. Soroka* (Stevens Point, Wisconsin: University of Wisconsin - Stevens Point, 1976).

Szawleski, Mieczyslaw: *Wychodztwo Polskie w Stanach Zjednoczonych Ameryki* (The Polish Emigration in the United States of America. Krakow: Ossolineum, 1924).

Tomczak, Anthony, editor: *Poles in America: Their Contribution to a Century of Progress* (Chicago: Polish Day Association, 1933).

Toranska, Teresa: *'Them': Stalin's Polish Puppets* (New York: Harper and Row, 1987).

Walaszek, Adam: *Reemigracja Ze Stanow Zjednoczonych do Polski po I wojnie swiatowej, 1919-1924* (Reemigration from the United States to Poland after World War I. Warsaw: Polish Scientific Publishers, 1983).

Waldo, Arthur: *Sokolstwo przednia straz narodu* (The Falcons Movement as the Vanguard of the Polish Nation. 5 volumes. Pittsburgh: Polish Falcons of America, 1953-1984).

Walesa, Lech: *A Way Of Hope* (New York: Holt, 1987).

Walter, Jerzy, compiler: *Czyn zbrojny wychodztwa Polskiego w Ameryce* (The Military Service Contribution of the Polish Emigration in America. New York: Polish Army Veterans Association, 1957).

Wandycz, Piotr: *The United States and Poland* (Cambridge: Harvard University Press, 1980).

Wenk, Michael, *et al., editors: Pieces of a Dream: The Ethnic Worker's Crisis with America* (New York: Center for Migration Studies, 1972).

Wiewiora, Joseph, editor: *Jamestown Pioneers From Poland* (Chicago: Polish American Congress Charitable Foundation, 1976), revised second edition.

Wozniak, Vladimir: *From Crisis to Crisis: Soviet-Polish Relations in the 1970s* (Ames, Iowa: Iowa State University Press, 1987).

Wytrwal, Joseph: *America's Polish Heritage* (Detroit: Endurance Press, 1961).

-------, *Behold: The Polish Americans* (Detroit: Endurance Press, 1977).

Zawodny, Janusz: *Death in the Forest* (Notre Dame, Indiana: Notre Dame University Press, 1962).

-------, *Nothing but Honor: The Story of the Uprising of Warsaw, 1944* (Stanford, California: Hover Institution, 1978).

Articles

Baker, T. Lindsay: "The Reverend Leopold Moczygemba, Patriarch of Polonia," *Polish American Studies,* 41, number 1 (Spring, 1984), 66-109.

Blejwas, Stanislaus: "Old and New Polonias: Tensions within an Ethnic Community," *Polish American Studies,* 38, number 2 (Autumn, 1981), 55-83.

Brock, Peter: "Polish Nationalism," in Peter Sugar, editor. *Nationalism in Eastern Europe* (Seattle: University of Washington Press, 1969), pp. 310-372.

Brozek, Andrzej: "Polonia w Stanach Zjednoczonych wobec inicjatyw Paderewskiego oraz Sikorskiego w czasie I i II wojny swiatowej" (American Polonia's response to Paderewski and Sikorski's initiatives in the First and Second World Wars), *Przeglad Polonijny,* 7, number 2 (1981), 41-67.

Brzezinski, Zbigniew K. and William Griffiths: "Peaceful Engagement in Eastern Europe," *Foreign Affairs,* 39, number 4 (July, 1961).

Budka, M.J.E.: "Pulaski and Kosciuszko Heroes Extremely Apropos," in Frank Mocha, editor. *Poles in America: Bicentennial Essays* (Stevens Point, Wisconsin: Worzalla Publishers, 1978), pp. 11-44.

Burks, Richard: "Eastern Europe," in Cyril Black and Thomas Thornton, editors. *Communism and Revolution: The Strategic Uses of Political Violence* (Princeton, University Press, 1964).

Dziewanowski, M.K.: "Tadeusz Kosciuszko, Kazimierz Pulaski and the American War of Independence: A Study in National Symbolism and Mythology," in Jaroslaw Pelenski, editor. *The American and European Revolutions,* 1776-1848 (Ames, Iowa: University of Iowa Press, 1980), 125-146.

-------, "Limits and Problems of Decompression: The Case of Poland," *Annals of the American Academy of Political and Social Science,* volume 317 (May, 1958).

-------, "The Communist Party of Poland," in Stephen Fischer-Galati, ed., *The Communist Parties of Eastern Europe* (New York: Columbia University Press, 1979).

Galush, William: "American Poles and the new Poland: An Example of Change," *Ethnicity,* 1, number 3 (1974), 209-221.

Garlicki, A.: "Misja A. Karabasza i A. Rakoczego" (Karabasz and Rakoczy's Mission), *Przeglad Historyczny,* 10, number 2 (1961), 232-246.

Gross, Feliks: "Notes on the Ethnic Revolution and the Polish Immigration in the U.S.A.," *Polish Review,* 21, number 3 (1976), 149-176.

Hapak Joseph: "The Polish Military Commission," *Polish American Studies,* 38, number 2 (Autumn, 1981), 26-38.

Irons, Peter: "The Test is Poland: Polish Americans and the Origins of the Cold War," *Polish American Studies,* 30, number 2 (Autumn, 1973), 5-65.

Januszewski, David G.: "The Case for the Polish Exile Government in the American Press, 1939-1945," *Polish American Studies, 43,* number 1 (Spring, 1986), 57-97.

Jaroszynska, Anna D.: "The American Committee for Resettlement of Polish Displaced Persons (1948-1968) in the Manuscript Collection of the Immigration History Research Center," *Polish American Studies,* 44, number 1 (Spring, 1987), 67-73.

Kadziewicz, Stanislaw: "The Lost Tribe: Poles in the U.S.S.R.," *Studium Papers,* 13, number 1 (January, 1989), 13-15.

Kaplan, Stephen: "U.S. Aid to Poland, 1957-1964: Concerns, Objectives and Obstacles," *Western Political Quarterly,* 28, number 1 (March, 1975), 147-166.

Korbonski, Stefan: "Polish Election, 1947," Letter to the Editor, *Washington Post,* February 16, 1985.

Kulikowski, Mark: "A Bibliography on Polish Americans, 1975-1980," *Polish American Studies,* 39, number 2 (Autumn, 1982), 24-85.

-------, "A Bibliography on Polish Americans, 1980-1985," *Polish American Studies,* 43, number 2 (Autumn, 1986), 40-110.

Kuniczak, W.S.: "The Silent Emigration" (Chicago: Polish Arts Club, 1968), pamphlet, pp. 12.

Kusielewicz, Eugene: "The Cancer in Our Side," *The Kosciuszko Foundation Newsletter,* 31, number 6 (1976-1977), 1-4.

-------, "Quo Vadis, Polish American Congress?" *Pol-Am Journal,* 69, number 9 (September, 1980), 8.

Lichten, Joseph: "Polish Americans and American Jews: Some Issues Which Unite and Divide," *Polish Review,* 18, number 4 (Winter, 1973), 52-62.

Lopata, Helena Z.: "Polish Immigration to the United States of America: Problems of Estimation and Parameters," *Polish Review,* 21, number 4 (Winter, 1976), 85-108.

Lukacs, John: "Connecting with Eastern Europe," *American Heritage* magazine, 41, number 7 (November, 1990), 47-56.

Lukas, Richard C.: "The Polish American Congress and the Polish Question, 1944-1947," *Polish American Studies,* 38, number 2 (Autumn, 1981), 39-54.

Lundgreen-Nielsen, Kay: "Woodrow Wilson and the Rebirth of Poland," in Arthur Link, editor. *Woodrow Wilson and a Revolutionary World, 1913-1921* (Chapel Hill: University of North Carolina Press, pp. 105-126.

Matejko, Alexander J.: "The Structural Roots of Polish Opposition," *Polish Review,* 27, numbers 1-2 (1982), 111-140.

Michnik, Adam: "Poland and the Jews," *New York Review of Books* (May 30, 1991), 11-12.

O'Connor, Flannery: "The Displaced Person," in Flannery O'Connor, *The Complete Stories* (New York: Farrar, Straus and Giroux, 1971), pp. 194-235.

Pienkos, Angela T.: "A Bicentennial Look at Casimir Pulaski: Polish, American and Ethnic Folk Hero," *Polish American Studies,* 33, number 1 (Spring, 1976), 5-17.

Pienkos, Donald E.: "The Polish American Congress -- An Appraisal," *Polish American Studies,* 36, number 2 (Autumn, 1979), 5-43.

-------, "Polish American Ethnicity in the Political Life of the United States," in Joseph Roucek and Bernard Eisenberg editors. *America's Ethnic Politics* (Westport, Connecticut: Greenwood Press, 1982), pp. 272-305.

Pinkowski, Edward: "The Great Influx of Polish Immigrants and the Industries They Entered," in Frank Mocha, editor. *Poles in America: Bicentennial Essays* (Stevens Point, Wisconsin: Worzalla Publishers, 1978), pp. 303-370.

Radzilowski, Thaddeus: "The Second Generation: The Unknown Polonia," *Polish American Studies,* 43, number 1 (Spring, 1986), 5-12.

Rupnik, Jacques: "Dissent in Poland, 1968-1978: End of Revisionism and the Rebirth of Civil Society," in Rudolf L.

Tokes, editor. *Opposition in Eastern Europe* (Baltimore and London: The Johns Hopkins Press, 1979), pp. 60-112.

Sachs, Jeffrey and David Lipton: "Poland's Economic Reform," *Foreign Affairs,* 69, number 3 (Summer, 1990), 47-66.

"Special Report: Poland in Crisis, 1980-1981," *Orbis* magazine (January, 1988), 7-31.

Sywak, Zofia: "Paderewski in America," in Frank Mocha, editor. *Poles in America: Bicentennial Essays* (Stevens Point, Wisconsin: Worzalla Publishers, 1978), pp. 371-186.

Szymczak, Robert: "A Matter of Honor: Polonia and the Congressional Investigation of the Katyn Massacre," *Polish American Studies,* 41, number 1 (Spring, 1984), 25-65.

-------, "An Act of Devotion: The Polish Grey Samaritans and the American Relief Effort in Poland, 1919-1921," *Polish American Studies,* 43, number 1 (Spring, 1986), 13-36.

Thackeray, Frank W.: " 'To Serve the Cause of Poland': The Polish Grey Samaritans, 1919-1922," *Polish Review,* 35, number 1 (1990), 37-50.

Wieczerzak, Joseph: "Pre- and Proto-Ethnics: Poles in the United States before the Immigration 'After Bread,'" *Polish Review,* 21, number 3 (Autumn, 1976), 7-38.

"Wojna z Narodem widziana od srodka: Rozmowa z Ryszardem J. Kuklinskim" (The War against the Polish Nation as Seen from the Inside: A Conversation with Ryszard J. Kuklinski. *Kultura* [Paris], number 475, April, 1987), 3-57. See above noted *Orbis* article.

Zahariasiewicz, Walter: "Polish American Organizations," in Frank Mocha, editor. *The Poles In America: Bicentennial Essays* (Stevens Point, Wisconsin: Worzalla Printers, 1977), pp. 627-670.

Zake, Louis J.: "The National Department and the Polish American Community, 1916-1923," *Polish American Studies,* 38, number 2 (Autumn, 1981), 16-25.

Zubek, Wojtek: "Poland's Party Self-Destructs," *Orbis* magazine (April, 1990), 179-193.

Subject Index

Name Index

Names preceded by asterisks (*) have separate biographies in this work.

610 POLISH AMERICAN EFFORTS ON POLAND'S BEHALF

Photographs

Acknowledgements for their assistance in compiling this set of photographs illustrating Polonia's identification with Poland are due the following individuals:

Marilyn Rozmarek Komosa, Florence Mazewski, Frank Swietlik, Helen Zielinski, Zofia Korbonska, Wanda Dziob, Szymon Deptula, Edward Rozanski, Casimir Lenard and Victor Modlinski.

A number of photographs also came from the libraries or archives of the Polish American Congress, Polish National Alliance, Polish Falcons of America, Polish Roman Catholic Union of America, Polish Women's Alliance and Roman B. Kwasniewski collection at the University of Wisconsin--Milwaukee Library.

To all who so graciously helped me in gathering and identifying these pictures, thank you very much.

PHOTOGRAPH SECTION

The following section contains the photographs.

Henry Kalussowski, Early Emigre Activist and Organizer of the Polish Committee
in New York in response to the 1863 Uprising against Russia. Drawing by Henry Archacki.

EARLY LEADERS OF POLONIA

Julius Andrzejkowicz

Erasmus Jerzmanowski

Anna Neumann

Rev. Vincent Barzynski

Emilia Napieralska

Honorata Wolowska

Teofil Starzynski

Members of the Supervisory Council of the Polish National Museum in Raperswil, Switzerland, Cradle of Polish and Polonia patriotism, 1910.
Seated from left: L. Tarnowski (Poland), Col. Zygmunt Milkowski (T. T. Jez, Switzerland); Eugeniusz Korytko and Jozef Galezowski (France); Zygmunt Laskowski (Switzerland); Franciszek Rawita--Gawronski (Poland); Boleslaw Rubach (France); Wladyslaw Ruzycki (Switzerland).
Standing from left: Dr. Karol Lewakowski (Switzerland); Waclaw Gasztowtt (France); Roman Abczynski (Pittsburgh, Vice Censor, Polish National Alliance);
M.B. Steczynski (Chicago, President, PNA); and Hipolit Obrzycki (France).

Leaders of the first Polish National Congress in Washington, D.C., May 1910 with representatives
from partitioned Poland, among them Stanislaw Rzepecki, a Poznan publisher (first row, second from left),
Viktor Skolyszewski, a delegate from the Polish Peasant Party (fourth from left), and Prof. Stanislaw Majerski from Lwow (center).
Among the American leaders pictured in the second row from left to right: N. K. Zlotnicki (second, an Editor with the PNA Zgoda);
Maria Sakowska (third, a PNA Director); Anthony Schreiber (fifth, Censor of PNA); Thomas Siemiradzki (sixth, Editor in chief of the PNA newspapers);
S. M. Sass (behind Siemiradzki); PNA President M. B. Steczynski (seventh); journalist Stanislaw Dangiel (ninth).

Delegates to the first Polish National Congress at the Capitol in Washington, D.C.

Delegate's badge to the first Polish National Congress. (top right)

Alexander Debski (top left), leader of the Polish National Defense Committee (KON).

Caricature by Polonia artist Arthur Szyk depicts U.S. President Woodrow Wilson and Ignacy Paderewski, Architects of Poland's independence. (bottom left)

Officers training begins in anticipation of the Polish American Army;
Cambridge Springs, Pennsylvania, 1914.

Polish Americans at Fort Niagara on the Lake, Canada (1917).

Scenes of participants at the national rally of the Polish Falcons Alliance in Buffalo, September 1914. The upper photo shows the Polish Army ready for transfer to France in 1917. The Falcons movement was a driving force behind the Polish American Army.

NIAGARA CAMP ONTARIO CANADA NOV 1ST 1917

Zlot Związku Sokołów Polskich
w Buffalo, N.Y. 1914

Msza św. Polowa

Marshal Jozef Pilsudski.

General Haller takes the oath to head the Polish Army in France (October 1918).

Leaders of the Polish National Department in Chicago (1916).
In the photo, front row from left: Chairman John Smulski (third);
Bishop Paul Rhode of Green Bay, Wisconsin (fourth);
Marian Seyda (fifth; representing the Polish National Committee in France);
second row: PRCUA Leader N. L. Piotrowski;
Casimir Sypniewski of Pittsburgh (third from left); PWA President Anna Neumann;
PRCUA President Peter Rostenkowski; Casimir Zychlinski, President PNA (far right).

Members of the Polish National Committee in Paris, August 1917. Seated from left: M. Zamoyski; Roman Dmowski, President; E. Piltz. Standing: S. Kozicki; J. Rozwadowski; K. Skirmut; Dr. Francis Fronczak of Buffalo (European Representative of the National Department); W. Sobanski; M. Seyda; M. Wielowiejski. Absent: Ignacy Paderewski, the Committee's honorary Chairman and its representative in the U.S.

Milwaukee, 1926: Paderewski honors local Polonia leaders for Wartime services on Poland's behalf. The Rev. Waclaw Kruszka, Polonia historian stands third from left.

February 1940: An early World War II fund raising event for Poland in Chicago organized by the Polish American Council (RPA). Seated from left: Chauncey McCormack; General Jozef Haller, RPA Chairman Francis X. Swietik. The youthful tenor singer Jan Kiepura seated at center.

Swietlik and the aged Paderewski meet in New York, March 25, 1941. Paderewski had come to the U.S. as Chairman of the Polish parliament in exile; he died at the age of 81 three months later and was buried with full honors at Arlington Cemetery, until Poland's freedom would be regained. Accordingly, his remains were to be reinterred in Poland in 1991. Paderewski's heart is entombed in Doylestown, Pennsylvania at the shrine of the Virgin Mother of Czestochowa, Patroness of Poland. The inscription wishes Swietlik success in work on Poland's behalf as Chairman of the Polish American Council.

Polish London Government representatives observe the relief work of
the Polish American Council in Lisbon, Portugal. Above, Florian Piskorski of the RPA
(third from left) with Minister Plenipotentiary Potworowski.

Chicago Polonia rally for U.S. National Preparedness, Summer 1941.

RPA Chairman and PNA Censor Swietlik, engages in conversation with Polish Prime Minister Wladyslaw Sikorski in Chicago, April 1941.

Sikorski addresses a massive Polonia gathering in Chicago's Soldier Field.

President Rozmarek greets General Bronislaw Duch in Chicago, April 1942 as RPA Chairman Swietlik looks on, right. Others from left: General Joseph Barzynski; Teofil Sawicki of the Polish Falcons; and PNA Atty. Casimir Midowicz, an RPA leader. Duch's mission -- to organize a new Polish American army to serve in Europe - proved to be a failure.

Polonia Leaders of the World War II Era

Max Wegrzynek
KNAPP

Frank Januszewski
KNAPP

Zygmunt Stefanowicz
"Narod Polski"

Judge Blair Gunther
PNA

Auxiliary Bishop Stefan Woznicki
of Detroit

Joseph Kania
PRCUA

Leadership meeting in Chicago to plan the Polish American Congress, March 1944.

Seated in the center is Charles Rozmarek, soon to become President of the Congress. Next to him is Polish Women's Alliance President Honorata Wolowska and PRCUA President John Olejniczak. At the far right sits Teofil Starzynski, President of the Falcons.

October 11, 1944: President Roosevelt Greets PAC delegation headed by Rozmarek, right, for Pulaski Day ceremonies while Polish uprising in Warsaw is being obliterated. Note the pre World War II Polish map, implying FDR's commitment to borders he in fact had already secretly conceded to Stalin the previous year.

May 1946: Constitution Day Dinner in Chicago. Seated from left: PAC President Rozmarek; PNA Director Caroline Spisak; Special Guest General Tadeusz Bor-Komorowski, leader of the Warsaw Uprising; Ambassador Jan Ciechanowski. Standing from third on the left: PAC Director Karol Burke; Col. Casimir Lenard; Atty. Roman Pucinski.

General Wladyslaw Anders, Commander of the Polish forces that stormed Monte Casino in 1944 is hailed in Chicago in 1947. From left: Mrs. Wanda Rozmarek; Edward Plusdrak, President of the Illinois Division of PAC; Chicago Alderman Joseph Rostenkowski; Anders and President Rozmarek.

Polish Refugee Boys on way from Santa Rosa, Mexico to Alliance College on the Chicago & Alton Train with Charles Rozmarek, Pres. P.N.A. and Jos. Kotch, Pres. of Council 65 and Lodge 128 of Bremond, Texas.

Refugee boys from the Polish colony in Santa Rosa, Mexico on the train to Alliance College meet in Chicago with President Rozmarek, 1946.

January 1948: Former Prime Minister Stanislaw Mikolajczyk at the home of President Rozmarek, standing behind his daughter Marilyn. Mikolajczyk had just escaped from Stalinist Poland following the destruction of his democratic Peasants Party. To Mikolajczyk's right--Polonia leader Frank Dziob. The young ladies--Zofia Majewska Chruscik (left) and Stefania Hrabi-Glinska were refugees who had recently come from Santa Rosa.

RPA Chief Swietlik visits a refugee camp in Germany, 1946.

Swietlik distributes gifts to children in the Polish refugee school at Maczkow, Germany.

Various seals issued by Polonia societies to raise funds for World War II relief.

Polish refugees in Switzerland receive parcels from the Polish American Council.

Polish displaced persons arrive in Chicago, 1949.

The sign reads "The Polish American Congress Welcomes You, Countrymen!"

Kurs Kongresu Polonii Amerykańskiej Dla Kierowników Zbiórki Miliona Dolarów
Chicago — Dom Związkowy — Kwiecień — 1946

Leaders of the Polish American Congress' one million dollar fund raising campaign in Chicago, 1946.
Standing tall fourth from right is Chairman Adam Tomaszkiewicz. Fourth from left is long-time activist Jean Dybal.

1951: President Harry Truman and members of the Committee investigating the Katyn Massacre. From left: U.S. Congressmen Foster Furcolo, George Dondero, Thaddeus Machrowicz, Chairman Ray Madden, Truman, Alvin O'Konski, Daniel Flood, Committee Counsel John Mitchell, Timothy Sheehan.

An editorial cartoon dated June 26, 1950 and typical of Polonia press opinion in the Cold War years. Titled "Costly Cleanup of the Stain of Yalta," K.J. Majewski of Chicago's "Dziennik Zwiazkowy" shows Uncle Sam scrubbing away to stop Stalin from further aggression.

Delegates to the third national convention of the Polish American Congress, 1952.

President Dwight Eisenhower discusses the rapidly changing situation in Eastern Europe with Rozmarek on September 28, 1956. Within weeks, Poland's Stalinist regime will be displaced by one both committed to limited change and accepted in Moscow. In Hungary, reform efforts end in tragedy due to a bloody Soviet intervention.

Delegates to the fifth PAC convention in Chicago in September 1960 press in to hear Democratic Presidential nominee John F. Kennedy.

President and Mrs. Lyndon Johnson view the unveiling of a painting of the Częstochowa Madonna in a Rose Garden commemoration of Poland's Millenium, June 17, 1966. President Rozmarek heads the Polonia delegation; Maine Senator Edmund Muskie stands fourth from left.

PAC Posters of the 1960s and 1970s.

The Polish American Congress Emblem.

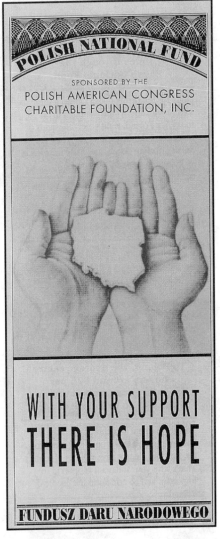

The Polish National Fund Poster of 1990-91

Polonia honors its heroes: unveiling a U.S. Postcard in 1979 recalling Pulaski on the
200th Anniversary of his death. From left: Former Postmaster
General John Gronouski, Walter Zahariaszewicz and PAC President Mazewski.

PNA Censor Hilary Czaplicki and President
Mazewski in Philadelphia making a Federal
landmark and museum of the building where
Tadeusz Kosciuszko resided.

Engraving celebrating the
300th Anniversary of King Jan Sobieski's
victory at Vienna over the Turks (1983).

Dedication of the Copernicus monument on Chicago's lakefront, October 18, 1973. (above)

Unveiling of a plaque to Copernicus at the University of Wisconsin at Milwaukee, May 1989. To the right of the plaque is Edward Tomasik, longtime Polonia and PAC activist. (lower left)

Members of the Polish American delegation in the U.S. House of Representatives at the unveiling of the Copernicus stamp in 1973. From left: Edward Derwinski and Daniel Rostenkowski of Illinois; Clement Zablocki of Wisconsin. (top left)

The Tenth Annual
Janusz Korczak Lecture

KORCZAK LECTURE SPEAKERS

M. KAMIL DZIEWANOWSKI. Visiting Professor of History, University of Wisconsin-Milwaukee. "Neglected Aspects of Polish-Jewish Relations" - April 5, 1979

LUCJAN DOBROSZYCKI, Visiting Professor of History, Columbia University and the YIVO Institute for Jewish Research. "Image Before My Eyes: A Photographic History of Jewish Life in Poland, 1864-1939" - April 9, 1980.

TADEUSZ SZAFAR, Fellow, Harvard University Russian Research Center. "Solidarity and the Historic Roots of Polish Resistance" - October 15, 1981.

JAN KARSKI, Professor of Government, Georgetown University. "The Final Solution in Poland: Polish Efforts on Behalf of the Jews, 1939-1944" - Ocotber 21, 1982.

ABRAHAM BRUMBERG, Past Editor, **Problems of Communism.** "Poland and Solidarity: Yesterday, Today and Tomorrow" - November 15, 1983.

THE REVEREND RONALD MODRAS, Associate Professor of Theology, Saint Louis University. "Polish-Jewish Relations in America: From Conflict to Coalition" - January 27, 1985.

NORMAN DAVIES, Professor of History, University of London and Visiting Professor of History, Stanford University. "The Roots of a Relationship: Poles and Jews in Pre-Twentieth Century Poland" - March 23, 1986.

NECHAMA TEC, Professor of Sociology, University of Connecticut. "When Light Pierced the Darkness - Christian Rescue of Jews in Nazi-Occupied Poland" - March 22, 1987.

ANDRZEJ BRYK, Visiting Professor of History, Amherst College. "Today's Poland and the Memory of the Holocaust" - May 4, 1988.

Program announcing the 10th annual Janusz Korczak lecture sponsored by the Wisconsin Division of the PAC and the Milwaukee Jewish Council, one of several such events established to enlighten the general public of the actual history of Polish-Jewish relations in Poland.

U.S. Senator Everett Dirksen of Illinois shares some humor with Aloysius Mazewski and Adele Lagodzinska, President of the Polish Women's Alliance and a leader in both the PAC and Polish American Council, at a banquet celebrating Poland's Millenium, 1966.

Mazewski meets with scholars of the Polish American Historical Association and the Polish Institute of Arts and Sciences of America, in Chicago, June 1986.

Honoring Arthur Rubinstein, 1970. From left: PNA officers Frank Prochot, Edward Rozanski, Rubinstein, Irene Wallace and Mazewski.

Dr. Zbigniew Brzezinski addressing Polonia on U.S.--Polish Relations, Polish Constitution Day, 1986.

Dedicated to Poland and Polonia:

Philanthropist Walter Koziol (upper left)

Jan Nowak, PAC Leader and Policy Advisor
Stefan Korbonski, Exile Leader (lower left)

PAC leaders at the U.S. State Department, June 1978. From left: Zdzislaw Dziekonski; W. Bninski; Dr. Andrzej Ehrenkreutz; unidentified; Boleslaw Wierzbianski; Aloysius Mazewski; Undersecretary of State David Newsom; Kazimierz Lukomski; Leonard Walentynowicz; Jan K. Miska; Deputy Secretary of State for Eastern European Affairs William Luers.

Mazewski and Lech Walesa in Gdansk, June 1981.

Solidarity seal issued by the PAC to raise funds for Poland's medical needs, 1981.

Demonstrations against Martial Law organized by the Illinois PAC,
December 1981 and January 1982.

Worsening conditions in Poland in the 1980s: lines outside bakeries and empty meat markets.

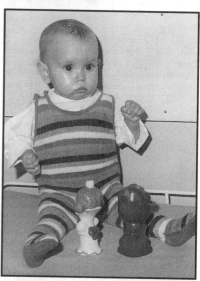

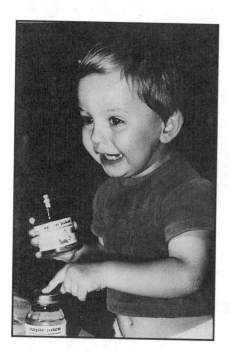

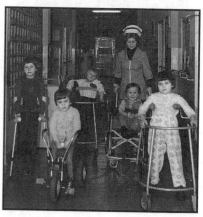

Children in need.

First Polish American Congress airlift of medical supplies to Poland (1981).

A container ready for Poland, part of the "Solidarity Express" train effort sponsored h
in August 1982. In all, 427 tons of goods are shipped to Poland in this effor'

The PAC "Solidarity Convoy" in December 1982. Truckloads loaded
with $10 million in cargo pass the Capitol.

The Relief for Poland effort in Chicago.

The 1981 Chicago Telethon for Poland: Singer Bobby Vinton kneeling with a typically stubborn Pole as Chairman Roman Pucinski (center) and Polonia industrialist and philanthropist Chester Sawko (in light suit) look on.

Buffalo Telethon, 1981: Even the volunteers taking pledges are dressed in Polish regional costumes.

PAC President Mazewski, Vice President Helen Zielinski, Treasurer Joseph Drobot and Vice President Lukomski look over the contents of a typical CARE package bound for Poland with PAC assistance.

Illinois PAC Chief Pucinski, Mazewski and Polish National Alliance Vice President Helen Szymanowicz promote the Congress' very successful Shoes for Poland's Children drive.

Buffalo: One big check for Polish Relief.

Utica, New York Polonia does its part, December 1982.

PAC Charitable Foundation Director Eugene Rosypal observes
as yet another truckload of goods is readied.

Bishop Czeslaw Domin, head of the Polish Episcopate's Charitable Distribution effort,
honors the PAC with a medal of appreciation for Polonia's generosity (1986).

Staff of the Center for Cardiac Surgery near Katowice backed by the PAC Charitable Foundation; the Center specializes in remedying heart defects among children.

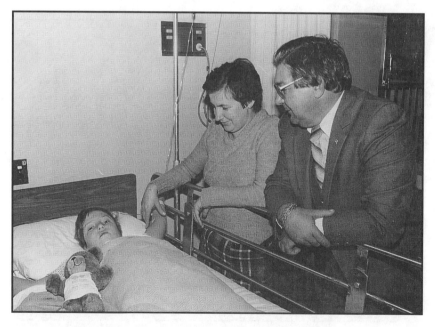

A youngster and his parents await heart surgery at the Deborah Heart and Lung Center in New Jersey, through the help of the Polish American Congress.

Relief for Poland goods arriving in Poland.